HOW TO HIDE AN EMPIRE

A HISTORY OF THE GREATER UNITED STATES

DANIEL IMMERWAHR

FARRAR, STRAUS AND GIROUX

NEW YORK

Farrar, Straus and Giroux
175 Varick Street, New York 10014

Owing to limitations of space, illustration credits can be found on pages 515–516.

Library of Congress Cataloging-in-Publication Data
Names: Immerwahr, Daniel, 1980– author.
Title: How to hide an empire : a history of the greater United States /
   Daniel Immerwahr.
Other titles: History of the greater United States
Description: First edition. | New York : Farrar, Straus and Giroux, 2019. |
   Includes bibliographical references and index.
Identifiers: LCCN 2018020388 | ISBN 9780374172145 (hardcover)
Subjects: LCSH: United States—Territories and possessions—History. |
   United States—Colonial question.
Classification: LCC F965 .I46 2019 | DDC 973—dc23
LC record available at https://lccn.loc.gov/2018020388

Designed by Jonathan D. Lippincott

Our books may be purchased in bulk for promotional, educational, or business use.
Please contact your local bookseller or the Macmillan Corporate and Premium
Sales Department at 1-800-221-7945, extension 5442, or by e-mail at
MacmillanSpecialMarkets@macmillan.com.

www.fsgbooks.com
www.twitter.com/fsgbooks • www.facebook.com/fsgbooks

1   3   5   7   9   10   8   6   4   2

ALSO BY DANIEL IMMERWAHR

*Thinking Small: The United States and
the Lure of Community Development*

HOW TO HIDE AN EMPIRE

To the uncounted

CONTENTS

HOW TO HIDE AN EMPIRE

INTRODUCTION: LOOKING BEYOND THE LOGO MAP

> The only problem is
> they don't think much
> about us
> in America.
> —Alfrredo Navarro Salanga, Manila

December 7, 1941. Japanese planes appear over a naval base on O'ahu. They drop aerial torpedoes, which dive underwater, wending their way toward their targets. Four strike the USS *Arizona,* and the massive battleship heaves in the water. Steel, timber, diesel oil, and body parts fly through the air. The flaming *Arizona* tilts into the ocean, its crew diving into the oil-covered waters. For a country at peace, this is a violent awakening. It is, for the United States, the start of the Second World War.

There aren't many historical episodes more firmly lodged in national memory than this one, the attack on Pearl Harbor. It's one of the few events that most people can put a date to (December 7, the "date which will live in infamy," as Franklin Delano Roosevelt put it). Hundreds of books have been written about it—the Library of Congress holds more than 350. And Hollywood has made movies, from the critically acclaimed *From Here to Eternity* (1953) starring Burt Lancaster to the critically derided *Pearl Harbor* (2001) starring Ben Affleck.

But what those films don't show is what happened next. Nine hours after Japan attacked the territory of Hawai'i, another set of Japanese planes came into view over another U.S. territory, the Philippines. As at Pearl Harbor, they dropped their bombs, hitting several air bases, to devastating effect.

The army's official history of the war judges the Philippine bombing to have been just as disastrous as the Hawaiian one. At Pearl Harbor, the Japanese hobbled the United States' Pacific fleet, sinking four battleships and damaging four others. In the Philippines, the attackers laid waste to the largest concentration of U.S. warplanes outside North America—the foundation of the Allies' Pacific air defense.

The United States lost more than planes. The attack on Pearl Harbor was just that, an attack. Japan's bombers struck, retreated, and never returned. Not so in the Philippines. There, the initial air raids were followed by more raids, then by invasion and conquest. Sixteen million Filipinos—U.S. nationals who saluted the Stars and Stripes and looked to FDR as their commander in chief—fell under a foreign power. They had a very different war than the inhabitants of Hawai'i did.

Nor did it stop there. The event familiarly known as "Pearl Harbor" was in fact an all-out lightning strike on U.S. and British holdings throughout the Pacific. On a single day, the Japanese attacked the U.S. territories of Hawai'i, the Philippines, Guam, Midway Island, and Wake Island. They also attacked the British colonies of Malaya, Singapore, and Hong Kong, and they invaded Thailand.

It was a phenomenal success. Japan never conquered Hawai'i, but within months Guam, the Philippines, Wake, Malaya, Singapore, and Hong Kong all fell under its flag. Japan even seized the westernmost tip of Alaska, which it held for more than a year.

Looking at the big picture, you start to wonder if "Pearl Harbor"—the name of one of the few targets Japan *didn't* invade—is really the best shorthand for the events of that fateful day.

★

"Pearl Harbor" wasn't how people referred to the bombings, at least not at first. How to describe them, in fact, was far from clear. Should the focus be on Hawai'i, the closest target to North America and the first bit of U.S. soil Japan had struck? Or should it be the Philippines, the far larger and more vulnerable territory? Or Guam, the one that surrendered nearly immediately? Or all the Pacific holdings, including the uninhabited Wake and Midway, together?

"The facts of yesterday and today speak for themselves," Roosevelt said in his address to Congress—his "Infamy" speech. But did they? JAPS BOMB MANILA, HAWAII was the headline of a New Mexico paper; JAPANESE PLANES BOMB HONOLULU, ISLAND OF GUAM was that of one in South Carolina. Sumner Welles, FDR's undersecretary of state, described the event as "an attack upon Hawaii and upon the Philippines." Eleanor Roosevelt used a similar formulation in her radio address on the night of December 7, when she spoke of Japan "bombing our citizens in Hawaii and the Philippines."

That was how the first draft of FDR's speech went, too. It presented the event as a "bombing in Hawaii and the Philippines." Yet Roosevelt toyed with that draft all day, adding things in pencil, crossing other bits out. At some point he deleted the prominent references to the Philippines

Roosevelt's December 7 draft of the "Infamy" speech. "Squadrons had commenced bombing in Hawaii and the Philippines" on the seventh line has been changed to "squadrons had commenced bombing in Oahu."

and settled on a different description. The attack was, in his revised version, a "bombing in Oahu" or, later in the speech, "on the Hawaiian Islands." He still mentioned the Philippines, but only as an item on a terse list of Japan's other targets: Malaya, Hong Kong, Guam, the Philippines, Wake Island, and Midway—presented in that order. That list mingled U.S. and British territories together, giving no hint as to which was which.

Why did Roosevelt demote the Philippines? We don't know, but it's not hard to guess. Roosevelt was trying to tell a clear story: Japan had attacked the United States. But he faced a problem. *Were* Japan's targets considered "the United States"? Legally, yes, they were indisputably U.S. territory. But would the public see them that way? What if Roosevelt's audience didn't care that Japan had attacked the Philippines or Guam? Polls taken slightly before the attack show that few in the continental United States supported a military defense of those remote territories.

Consider how similar events played out more recently. On August 7, 1998, al-Qaeda launched simultaneous attacks on U.S. embassies in Nairobi, Kenya, and Dar es Salaam, Tanzania. Hundreds died (mostly Africans), and thousands were wounded. But though those embassies were outposts of the United States, there was little public sense that the country *itself* had been harmed. It would take another set of simultaneous attacks three years later, on New York City and Washington, D.C., to provoke an all-out war.

An embassy is different from a territory, of course. Yet a similar logic held in 1941. Roosevelt no doubt noted that the Philippines and Guam, though technically part of the United States, seemed foreign to many. Hawai'i, by contrast, was more plausibly "American." Though it was a territory rather than a state, it was closer to North America and significantly whiter than the others. As a result, there was talk of eventual statehood (whereas the Philippines was provisionally on track for independence).

Yet even when it came to Hawai'i, Roosevelt felt a need to massage the point. Though the territory had a substantial white population, nearly three-quarters of its inhabitants were Asians or Pacific Islanders. Roosevelt clearly worried that his audience might regard Hawai'i as foreign. So on the morning of his speech, he made another edit. He changed it so that the Japanese squadrons had bombed not the "island of Oahu," but the "American island of Oahu." Damage there, Roosevelt continued, had been done to "American naval and military forces," and "very many American lives" had been lost.

An *American* island, where *American* lives were lost—that was the point he was trying to make. If the Philippines was being rounded down to foreign, Hawai'i was being rounded up to "American."

"Yesterday, December 7, 1941—a date which will live in infamy—the United States of America was suddenly and deliberately attacked by naval and air forces of the Empire of Japan" is how Roosevelt's speech began. Note that in this formulation Japan is an "empire," but the United States is not. Note also the emphasis on the date. It was only at Hawai'i and Midway, of all Japan's targets, that the vagaries of the international date line put the event on December 7. Everywhere else, it occurred on December 8, the date the Japanese use to refer to the attack.

Did Roosevelt underscore the date in a calculated attempt to make it all about Hawai'i? Almost certainly not. Still, his "date which will live in infamy" phrasing further encouraged a narrow understanding of the event, one that left little room for places like the Philippines.

For Filipinos, this could be exasperating. A reporter described the scene in Manila as the crowds listened to Roosevelt's speech over the radio. The president spoke of Hawai'i and the many lives lost there. Yet he only mentioned the Philippines, the reporter noted, "very much in passing." Roosevelt made the war "seem to be something close to Washington and far from Manila."

This was not how it looked from the Philippines, where air-raid sirens continued to wail. "To Manilans the war was here, now, happening to us," the reporter wrote. "And we have no air-raid shelters."

★

Hawai'i, the Philippines, Guam—it wasn't easy to know how to think about such places or even what to call them. At the turn of the twentieth century, when many were acquired (Puerto Rico, the Philippines, Guam, American Samoa, Hawai'i, Wake), their status was clear. They were, as Theodore Roosevelt and Woodrow Wilson unabashedly called them, colonies.

Yet that spirit of forthright imperialism didn't last. Within a decade or two, after passions had cooled, the c-word became taboo. "The word colony must not be used to express the relationship which exists between our government and its dependent peoples," an official admonished in 1914. Better to stick with a gentler term, used for them all: territories.

It was gentler because the United States had *had* territories before, such as Arkansas and Montana. Their place in the national firmament was a happy one. The western territories were the frontier, the leading edge of the country's growth. They might not have had all the rights that states did, but once they were "settled" (i.e., populated by whites), they were welcomed fully into the fold as states.

But if places like the Philippines and Puerto Rico were territories, they were territories of a different sort. Unlike the western territories, they weren't obviously slated for statehood. Nor were they widely understood to be integral parts of the nation.

A striking feature, in fact, of the overseas territories was how rarely they were even *discussed*. The maps of the country that most people had in their heads didn't include places like the Philippines. Those mental maps imagined the United States to be contiguous: a union of states bounded by the Atlantic, the Pacific, Mexico, and Canada.

That is how most people envision the United States today, possibly with the addition of Alaska and Hawai'i. The political scientist Benedict Anderson called it the "logo map." Meaning that if the country had a logo, this shape would be it.

The logo map

The problem with the logo map, however, is that it isn't right. Its shape doesn't match the country's legal borders. Most obviously, the logo map excludes Hawai'i and Alaska, which became states in 1959 and now appear on virtually all published maps of the country. But it's also missing Puerto Rico, which, though not a state, has been part of the country since

1899. When have you ever seen a map of the United States that had Puerto Rico on it? Or American Samoa, Guam, the U.S. Virgin Islands, the Northern Marianas, or any of the other smaller islands the United States has annexed over the years?

In 1941, the year Japan attacked, a more accurate picture would have been this:

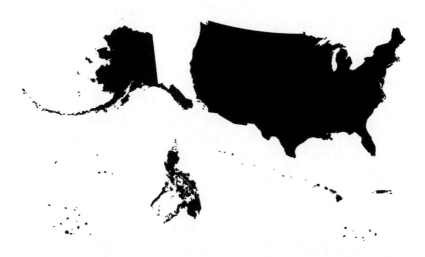

The Greater United States, 1941: (Top row, from left) Alaska, the mainland; (middle row) Guam, American Samoa, the Philippines, Hawai'i, Puerto Rico, and the U.S. Virgin Islands; (bottom row, and not to scale) the Pacific outlying islands (left) and the Caribbean outlying islands (right)

What this map shows is the country's full territorial extent: the "Greater United States," as some at the turn of the twentieth century called it. In this view, the place normally referred to as the United States—the logo map—forms only a part of the country. A large and privileged part, to be sure, yet still only a part. Residents of the territories often call it the "mainland."

I've drawn this map to show the inhabited parts of the Greater United States at the same scale and with equal-area projections. So Alaska isn't shrunken down to fit into a small inset, as it is on most maps. It's the right size—i.e., it's huge. The Philippines, too, looms large, and the Hawaiian island chain—the whole chain, not just the eight main islands shown on most maps—if superimposed on the mainland would stretch almost from Florida to California.

This map also shows territory at the other end of the size scale. In the century before 1940, the United States claimed nearly a hundred uninhabited islands in the Caribbean and the Pacific. Some claims were forgotten in time—Washington could be surprisingly lax about keeping tabs. The twenty-two islands I've included are the ones that appeared in official tallies (the census or other governmental reports) in the 1940s. I've represented them as clusters of dots in the bottom left and right corners, though they're so small that were I to draw them to scale, they'd be invisible.

Why include them at all? Was it important that the United States possessed, to take one example, Howland Island, a bare plot of land in the middle of the Pacific, only slightly larger than Central Park? Yes, it was. Howland wasn't large or populous, but in the age of aviation, it was useful. At considerable expense, the government hauled construction equipment out to Howland and built an airstrip there—it's where Amelia Earhart was heading when her plane went down. The Japanese, fearing what the United States might do with such a well-positioned airstrip, bombed Howland the day after they struck Hawai'i, Guam, Wake, Midway, and the Philippines.

When it came to strategy, those dots mattered.

The logo map excludes all that—large colonies and pinprick islands alike. And there is something else misleading about it. It suggests that the United States is a politically uniform space: a union, voluntarily entered into, of states standing on equal footing with one another. But that's not true, and it's never been true. From the day the treaty securing independence from Britain was ratified, right up to the present, it's been a collection of states *and territories*. It's been a partitioned country, divided into two sections, with different laws applying in each.

The United States of America has *contained* a union of American states, as its name suggests. But it has also contained another part: not a union, not states, and (for most of its history) not wholly in the Americas.

What is more, a lot of people have lived in that other part. Here's the census count for the inhabited territories in 1940, the year before Pearl Harbor:

Territory	Years held	1940 pop.
Philippines	1899–1946	16,356,000
Puerto Rico	1899–present	1,869,255
Hawai'i	1898–1959 (state after)	423,330
Alaska	1867–1959 (state after)	72,524
Panama Canal Zone	1904–1979	51,827
U.S. Virgin Islands	1917–present	24,889
Guam	1899–present	22,290
American Samoa	1900–present	12,908
Total in Territories		**18,833,023**
Mainland		131,669,275

These are the inhabited U.S. territories listed by the census on the eve of the Second World War. The 118,933 mainland military service members posted to territories are not listed with each territory's population, so islands with military outposts but without local residents, such as Wake, are excluded. The Panama Canal Zone was technically Panamanian land leased to the United States, but the census counted it nonetheless.

Nearly nineteen million people lived in the colonies, the great bulk of them in the Philippines. Was that a lot? Not compared with the world-girdling British Empire, which boasted at the time a population of more than four hundred million (the great bulk of whom lived in India). But the United States' empire was nonetheless sizable. Measured by population, it was, at the time of Pearl Harbor, the fifth largest in the world.

Another way to consider those nineteen million territorial inhabitants is as a fraction of the U.S. population. Again taking 1940 as our year, slightly more than one in eight (12.6 percent) of the people in the United States lived outside of the states. For perspective, consider that only about one in twelve was African American. If you lived in the United States on the eve of World War II, in other words, you were more likely to be colonized than black, by odds of three to two.

My point here is not to weigh forms of oppression against one another. In fact, the histories of African Americans and colonized peoples are tightly connected (and sometimes overlapping, as for the Afro-Caribbeans in Puerto Rico and the U.S. Virgin Islands). The racism that had pervaded the country since slavery engulfed the territories, too. Like African Americans, colonial subjects were denied the vote, deprived of the rights of full citizens, called "nigger," subjected to dangerous medical experiments, and used as sacrificial pawns in war. They, too, had to make their way in a country where some lives mattered and others did not.

What getting the Greater United States in view reveals is that race has been even *more* central to U.S. history than is usually supposed. It hasn't just been about black and white, but about Filipino, Hawaiian, Samoan, and Chamoru (from Guam), too, among other identities. Race has not only shaped lives, it's shaped the country itself—where the borders went, who has counted as "American." Once you look beyond the logo map, you see a whole new set of struggles over what it means to inhabit the United States.

★

Looking beyond the logo map, however, could be hard for mainlanders. The national maps they used rarely showed the territories. Even the world atlases were confusing. Rand McNally's wartime *Ready Reference Atlas of the World*, like many other atlases at the time, listed Hawai'i, Alaska, Puerto Rico, and the Philippines as "foreign."

A class of seventh-grade girls at the Western Michigan College Training School in Kalamazoo scratched their heads over this. They'd been trying to follow the war on their maps. How, they wondered, could the attack on Pearl Harbor have been an attack on the United States if Hawai'i was foreign? They wrote to Rand McNally to inquire.

"Although Hawaii belongs to the United States, it is not an integral part of this country," the publisher replied. "It is foreign to our continental shores, and therefore cannot logically be shown in the United States proper."

The girls were not satisfied. *Hawai'i is not an integral part of this country?* "We believe this statement is not true," they wrote. It is "an alibi instead of an explanation." Further, they continued, "we feel that the Rand McNally atlas is misleading and a good cause for the people of outlying possessions to be embarrassed and disturbed." The girls forwarded the correspondence to the Department of the Interior (in whose archives I found it) and asked for adjudication.

Of course, the seventh-graders were right. As an official clarified, Hawai'i was, indeed, part of the United States.

Yet the government could be just as misleading as Rand McNally on this score. Consider the census. According to the Constitution, census takers were required to count only the states, but they'd always counted the territories, too. Or, at least, they'd counted the continental territories. The *overseas* territories were handled differently. They weren't always counted in the same years, with the same questionnaires, or by the same agency as the mainland was. The effect was to make them incommensurable with the rest of the country, statistically segregating them.

Even when usable numbers on the overseas territories were available, they weren't used. The decennial census report duly noted the territorial populations up front, but then quietly dropped them from nearly all calculations that followed. As the 1910 report explained, those statistics covered "the United States proper" only. *The United States proper* wasn't a legal term, but census officials expected that everyone would understand. They justified this by claiming "obvious differences" between people in the overseas territories and those on the mainland.

And so, as with the logo map, the country was left with a strategically cropped family photo. Readers of the 1940 census were told that the United States' largest minority was African American, that its largest cities were nearly all in the East, and that its center of population was Sullivan County, Indiana. Had overseas territories been factored in, as western territories had previously been, census readers would have seen a different picture. They would have seen a country whose largest minority was Asian, whose principal cities included Manila (about the size of Washington, D.C., or San Francisco), and whose center of population was in New Mexico.

But that wasn't the census mainlanders saw. The country presented to them in maps, atlases, and official reports had the shape of the logo map. The result? A profound confusion. "Most people in this country, including educated people, know little or nothing about our overseas possessions," concluded a governmental report written during World War II. "As a matter of fact, a lot of people do not know that we have overseas possessions. They are convinced that only 'foreigners,' such as the British, have an 'empire.' Americans are sometimes amazed to hear that we, too, have an 'empire.'"

★

The proposition that the United States is an empire is less controversial today. The leftist author Howard Zinn, in his immensely popular *A People's History of the United States*, wrote of the "global American empire," and his graphic-novel spin-off is called *A People's History of American Empire*. On the far right, the politician Pat Buchanan has warned that the United States is "traveling the same path that was trod by the British Empire." In the vast political distance between Zinn and Buchanan, there are millions who would readily agree that the United States is, in at least some sense, imperial.

The case can be made in a number of ways. The dispossession of Native Americans and relegation of many to reservations was pretty transparently imperialist. Then, in the 1840s, the United States fought a war with Mexico and seized a third of it. Fifty years later, it fought a war with Spain and claimed the bulk of Spain's overseas territories.

Empire isn't just landgrabs, though. What do you call the subordination of African Americans? In W.E.B. Du Bois's eyes, black people in the United States looked more like colonized subjects than like citizens. Many other black thinkers, including Malcolm X and the leaders of the Black Panthers, have agreed.

Or what about the spread of U.S. economic power abroad? The United States might not have physically conquered Western Europe after World War II, but that didn't stop the French from complaining of "coca-colonization." Critics there felt swamped by U.S. commerce. Today, with the world's business denominated in dollars and McDonald's in more than a hundred countries, you can see they might have had a point.

Then there are the military interventions. The years since the Second World War have brought the U.S. military to country after country. The big wars are well-known: Korea, Vietnam, Iraq, Afghanistan. But there has also been a constant stream of smaller engagements. Since 1945, U.S. armed forces have been deployed abroad for conflicts or potential conflicts 211 times in 67 countries. Call it peacekeeping if you want, or call it imperialism. But clearly this is not a country that has kept its hands to itself.

Yet in all the talk of empire, one thing that often slips from view is actual territory. Yes, many would agree that the United States is or has been an empire, for all the reasons above. But how much can most people say about the colonies themselves? Not, I would wager, very much.

And why should they be able to? Textbooks and overviews of U.S. history invariably feature a chapter on the 1898 war with Spain that led to the acquisition of many of the territories and the Philippine War that followed it ("the worst chapter in almost any book," one reviewer griped). Yet, after that, coverage trails off. Territorial empire is treated as an episode rather than a feature. The colonies, having been acquired, vanish.

It's not as if the information isn't out there. Scholars, many working from the sites of empire themselves, have assiduously researched this topic for decades. It's just that when it comes time to zoom out and tell the story of the country as a whole, the territories tend to fall away. The confusion and shoulder-shrugging indifference that mainlanders displayed at the time of Pearl Harbor hasn't changed much at all.

Ultimately, the problem isn't a lack of knowledge. The libraries contain literally thousands of books about U.S. overseas territory. The problem is that those books have been sidelined—filed, so to speak, on the wrong shelves. They're there, but so long as we've got the logo map in our heads, they'll seem irrelevant. They'll seem like books about foreign countries.

★

I'll confess to having made this conceptual filing error myself. Though I studied U.S. foreign relations as a doctoral student and read countless books about "American empire"—the wars, the coups, the meddling in foreign affairs—nobody ever expected me to know even the most elementary facts about the territories. They just didn't feel important.

It wasn't until I traveled to Manila, researching something else entirely, that it clicked. To get to the archives, I'd travel by "jeepney," a transit system originally based on repurposed U.S. Army jeeps. I boarded in a section of Metro Manila where the streets are named after U.S. colleges (Yale, Columbia, Stanford, Notre Dame), states and cities (Chicago, Detroit, New York, Brooklyn, Denver), and presidents (Jefferson, Van Buren, Roosevelt, Eisenhower). When I'd arrive at my destination, the Ateneo de Manila University, one of the country's most prestigious schools, I'd hear students speaking what sounded to my Pennsylvanian ears to be virtually unaccented English.

Empire might be hard to make out from the mainland, but from the sites of colonial rule themselves, it's impossible to miss.

I read about the Philippines' colonial history, and I got curious about other locales: Puerto Rico, Guam, Hawai'i before it was a state. *These places are part of the United States, right?* I thought. *Why haven't I been thinking of them as part of its history?*

As I recataloged my mental library, a startlingly different version of U.S. history emerged. Events that had once seemed familiar appeared in a new light: Pearl Harbor was just the tip of the iceberg. Well-worn cultural artifacts—the musical *Oklahoma!*, the moon landing, Godzilla, the peace

Philippine Islands, U.S.A.: A ten-peso note. Throughout the territories, colonized subjects were obliged to use bills with the faces of U.S. leaders on them. Extraordinarily, this Philippine bill was the basis for the design of the familiar U.S. dollar, not the other way around.

symbol—took on new significance. Obscure historical episodes that I'd barely registered now seemed tremendously important. I found myself collaring defenseless colleagues in the halls to deliver the news. "Did you *know* that nationalists staged a seven-city revolt in Puerto Rico, culminating in an assassination attempt on Harry Truman? And that the same nationalists shot up Congress four years later?"

This book aims to show what U.S. history would look like if the "United States" meant the Greater United States, not the logo map. To write it, I've visited archives in places where U.S. historians don't usually go, from Fairbanks to Manila. Yet at the same time, I've drawn heavily on the insights and research about the territories that scholars have been producing for generations. In the end, this book's main contribution is not archival, bringing to light some never-before-seen document. It's perspectival, seeing a familiar history differently.

The history of the Greater United States, as I've come to view it, can be told in three acts. The first is westward expansion: the pushing west of national borders and the displacement of Native Americans. That isn't the main story of this book, but it's the launching point. Even this well-known history reveals unfamiliar aspects once we look at the past with territory in mind, such as the creation in the 1830s of a massive all-Indian territory—arguably the United States' first colony.

The second act takes place off the continent, and it's striking how quickly it begins. Just three years after filling out the shape of the logo map, the United States started annexing new territory overseas. First it claimed dozens of uninhabited islands in the Caribbean and the Pacific. Then Alaska in 1867. From 1898 to 1900 it absorbed the bulk of Spain's overseas empire (the Philippines, Puerto Rico, and Guam) and annexed the non-Spanish lands of Hawaiʻi, Wake Island, and American Samoa. In 1917 it bought the U.S. Virgin Islands. By the Second World War, the territories made up nearly a fifth of the land area of the Greater United States.

This sort of expansion was typical of the nineteenth and early twentieth centuries. When countries got more powerful, they generally got bigger. One might have expected, then, that the United States would keep growing. Indeed, by the end of World War II it *had* claimed a lot of territory: its Pacific empire had been reclaimed, it held thousands of military bases around the world, and it occupied parts of Korea, Germany, and Austria, and all of Japan. Adding up the land under U.S. jurisdiction—colonies and occupations alike—by the end of 1945 the Greater United States included some 135 million people living outside the mainland.

But what's remarkable is what happened next. Rather than converting its occupations to annexations (as it had after the 1898 war with Spain), it did something virtually unprecedented. It won a war and gave *up* territory. The Philippines, its largest colony, got independence. The occupations wrapped up speedily, and only one—of a set of lightly populated islands in Micronesia—led to annexation. Other territories, though they weren't granted independence, received new statuses. Puerto Rico became a "commonwealth," which ostensibly replaced a coercive relationship with a consenting one. Hawaiʻi and Alaska, after some delay, became states, overcoming decades of racist determination to keep them out of the union.

This is the third act, and it raises a question. Why did the United States, at the peak of its power, distance itself from colonial empire? I explore that question at length because it's tremendously important yet seldom asked.

One part of the answer is that colonized subjects resisted, forcing empire into retreat. This happened both within the Greater United States, leading to status changes in the four largest colonies, and outside it, where anti-imperialism impeded further colonial conquest.

Another part has to do with technology. During the Second World War, the United States honed an extraordinary suite of technologies that gave it many of the benefits of empire without having to actually hold colonies. Plastics and other synthetics allowed it to replace tropical products with man-made substitutes. Airplanes, radio, and DDT enabled it to move its goods, ideas, and people into foreign countries easily without annexing them. Similarly, the United States managed to standardize many of its objects and practices—from screw threads to road signs to the English language—across political borders, again gaining influence in places it didn't control. Collectively, these technologies weaned the United States off the familiar model of formal empire. They replaced colonization with globalization.

Globalization is a fashionable word, and it's easy to speak of it in vague terms—to talk of increasingly better technologies drawing a disparate world together. But those new technologies didn't just crop up. Many were developed by the U.S. military in a short burst of time in the 1940s, with the goal of giving the United States a new relationship to territory. Dramatically, and in just a few years, the military built a world-spanning logistical network that was startling in how little it depended on colonies. It was also startling in how much it centered the world's trade, transport, and communication on one country, the United States.

Yet even in this age of globalization, territory has not gone away. Not only does the United States continue to hold part of its colonial empire (containing millions), it also claims numerous small dots on the map. Besides Guam, American Samoa, the Northern Mariana Islands, Puerto Rico, the U.S. Virgin Islands, and a handful of minor outlying islands, the United States maintains roughly eight hundred overseas military bases around the world.

These tiny specks—Howland Island and the like—are the foundations of U.S. world power. They serve as staging grounds, launchpads, storage sites, beacons, and laboratories. They make up what I call (building on a concept from the historian and cartographer Bill Rankin) a "pointillist empire." Today, that empire extends all over the planet.

★

None of this, however—not the large colonies, small islands, or military bases—has made much of a dent on the mainland mind. One of the truly distinctive features of the United States' empire is how persistently ignored it has been. Apart from the brief moment after 1898 when the country's imperial dimensions were on proud display, much of its history has taken place offstage.

This is, it's worth emphasizing, unique. The British weren't confused as to whether there was a British Empire. They had a holiday, Empire Day, to celebrate it. France didn't forget that Algeria was French. It is only the United States that has suffered from chronic confusion about its own borders.

The reason isn't hard to guess. The country perceives itself to be a republic, not an empire. It was born in an anti-imperialist revolt and has fought empires ever since, from Hitler's Thousand-Year Reich and the Japanese Empire to the "evil empire" of the Soviet Union. It even fights empires in its dreams. *Star Wars*, a saga that started with a rebellion against the Galactic Empire, is one of the highest-grossing film franchises of all time.

This self-image of the United States as a republic is consoling, but it's also costly. Most of the cost has been paid by those living in the colonies, in the occupation zones, and around the military bases. The logo map has relegated them to the shadows, which are a dangerous place to live. At various times, the inhabitants of the U.S. Empire have been shot, shelled, starved, interned, dispossessed, tortured, and experimented on. What they haven't been, by and large, is seen.

The logo map carries a cost for mainlanders, too. It gives them a truncated view of their own history, one that excludes part of their country. It is an important part. As I seek to reveal, a lot has *happened* in the territories, occurrences highly relevant to mainlanders. The overseas parts of the United States have triggered wars, brought forth inventions, raised up presidents, and helped define what it means to be "American." Only by including them in the picture do we see a full portrait of the country—not as it appears in its fantasies, but as it actually is.

A NOTE ON LANGUAGE

The chief argument of this book is that we should think of the United States differently. Rather than conceiving of it as a contiguous blob, we should take seriously its overseas holdings, from large colonies to tiny islands. For that reason, I use *the United States* to refer to the entire polity. The contiguous portion I call *the mainland*, which is what many in the territories call it.

That usage is not universal. Puerto Rican nationalists, for example, often refer to the United States and Puerto Rico as distinct countries to signal their rejection of the legitimacy of U.S. rule. I've declined to follow their lead, because I worry that it confuses things on the other end, making the United States seem as if it were merely a union of states. Such usage can obscure the country's imperial dimensions.

Colonialism imprints foreign names on people and places. What to call the locales and populations that have come under it can thus be a politically charged question. I write *Hawai'i*, with an 'okina, a Hawaiian-language consonant pronounced as a glottal stop, rather than *Hawaii*. This follows local use and the recommendation of the Hawai'i Board on Geographic Names (but there is no 'okina in *Hawaiian*). Also in keeping with local use, I've placed accents over the vowels in Puerto Rican names (José Trías Monge) but not Filipino ones (Jose Laurel). I write *Puerto Rico* even when discussing the colony during its first three decades under U.S. rule, a period when Washington insisted on the anglicized spelling, *Porto Rico*. Activists protesting the military presence on Guam have recently begun to refer to the island by its Chamoru name, *Guåhan*, but as this practice is not yet widespread, I have stuck with *Guam*. Finally, though it is often assumed that the term *Indian* is a slur and *Native American* must be used instead, Native American communities and organizations often use both. I use the terms interchangeably here, though I use more specific names (e.g., Cherokee, Ojibwe) whenever possible.

PART I

THE COLONIAL EMPIRE

1

THE FALL AND RISE
OF DANIEL BOONE

The thirteen colonies that would make up the United States declared independence from Britain in 1776. Freedom, however, takes many forms. Just a year earlier, the hunter Daniel Boone and thirty or so followers asserted an independence of a different sort. Plagued by debt, Boone left his home on the Yadkin River in North Carolina and wandered west. His party took advantage of a convenient notch in the Appalachian mountain range, the Cumberland Gap. They traveled some two hundred miles in a month, cutting through thick brush, cane, and reed in search of better land.

Boone and his followers found what they sought in the plains of Kentucky. The Shawnees who lived there had carefully culled the area's trees, letting the grass grow high and the herbivores graze. For men used to a hardscrabble life, this was paradise. "So rich a soil we had never seen before; covered with clover in full bloom," gaped one of Boone's axmen. "The woods were abounding in wild game." They named their new settlement Boonesborough, after the man who had brought them there.

Oases in the desert often vanish upon inspection, and it didn't take long for Boone's followers to reconsider their rapture. The teeming meadows were no mirage, but those meadows were the hunting grounds of the Shawnees, whose presence made it difficult for Boone's party to venture beyond Boonesborough's defended perimeter. Confined to their few rudimentary structures and beset on all sides, many of the town's residents lost heart and returned home before the year was out.

Boonesborough's achievements were, on the face of it, modest. Yet if the *what* of Boonesborough was underwhelming, the *where* carried a larger significance. The settlement was situated on the far side of the Appalachians, which for more than a century had formed a barrier—in law and practice—to British settlement in North America. By blazing his trail through the wilderness, Boone had opened a channel through which hundreds of thousands of whites would soon pour, dragging enslaved blacks along with them. Boone wasn't exactly the "first white man of the West," as one of his biographers insisted. But he was an early drop from a faucet that was about to be turned on full blast.

For European intellectuals, the rough-hewn, frontier-dwelling Boone was catnip. Enlightenment philosophes regarded him as man in his natural state, Romantics as a refugee from civilization. An obscure biographical account of Boone, originally published as an appendix to a history of Kentucky, made the rounds in Europe, where it was republished and speedily translated into French and German.

Boone showed up in European literature, too. The British feminist Mary Wollstonecraft had an affair with one of Boone's acquaintances and, with him, published a fictionalized account of Boone's life. The French Romantic François-René de Chateaubriand lifted passages from Boone's biography for his influential epic, *Les Natchez*, about a Frenchman living among the North American Indians. Lord Byron, the leading poet of the age, devoted seven stanzas to Boone (the "happiest amongst mortals anywhere") in his poem *Don Juan*.

Yet, oddly, Boone saw almost none of this. Though celebrated abroad, he wasn't much revered at home during his lifetime. He died at the old age of eighty-five in 1820. That was the same decade Thomas Jefferson and John Adams died, both, as it happened by near-inconceivable coincidence, on the same day—the fiftieth anniversary of the signing of the Declaration of Independence. The country went understandably crazy when Jefferson and Adams died. "Had the horses and the chariot of fire descended to take up the patriarchs," a New York paper wrote, "it might have been more wonderful, but not more glorious."

But for Boone's death? Nothing of the sort. He died in the Territory of Missouri, west of St. Louis. He had no money and no land—he was living as a pensioner on his son's small estate. Territorial legislators in Missouri wore black armbands in Boone's honor, but the eastern papers took well over a month to even acknowledge his death, which they generally did with short notices. He was buried in an unmarked grave.

How could that happen? Why didn't someone *do* something? Did the leading men of the country not know about Boone? They knew. Did they not understand what he represented? They understood.

They just didn't like it.

★

The disregard in which Daniel Boone was held may come as a surprise. The United States, as the story is often told, was a buoyantly expansive nation from the start. Its founders had wrested liberty from an oppressive empire—turning subjects into citizens and colonies into states—and were eager to push their republican form of government westward across the continent, from sea to shining sea. Men like Daniel Boone, it would seem, were vital instruments of that national mission.

Yet Boone's path was strewn with obstacles. The British had set the ridge of the Appalachians as the boundary to white settlement, making Boone's journey west a crime. The end of British rule did little to improve Boone's standing. The founders viewed frontiersmen like him with open suspicion. They were the nation's "refuse" (wrote Ben Franklin), "no better than carnivorous animals" (J. Hector St. John de Crèvecoeur), or "white savages" (John Jay). George Washington warned, after the revolution, of the "settling, or rather overspreading the Western Country . . . by a parcel of banditti, who will bid defiance to all authority." To prevent this, he proposed drawing a settlement boundary, just as the British had, and prosecuting as a felon any citizen who crossed it.

Part of the objection was social; the founders were men of culture and sophistication who found rough frontier life troubling. Yet there was a deeper issue involved. As Boonesborough's settlers had discovered, the United States wasn't the only country with claim to the land west of the Appalachians. Native peoples—organized as nations, tribes, confederacies, and other durable polities—had their own cartography, their own way of mapping North America. And, in the late eighteenth century, they could back their maps with force.

This was the raw nerve Daniel Boone had touched. By hauling white settlers west, he was invading Indian lands. That meant fighting, fighting of the sort that might easily draw the United States government in. It also meant a discomfiting blurring of the lines between European and Native. Boone had killed Indians, been captured by them many times, and seen a brother and two sons die by Indian hands. But he had also, during one of his stints in captivity, been adopted into a Shawnee family, receiving the name Sheltowee (meaning "Big Turtle") and becoming "exceedingly familiar and friendly," as he put it, with his "new parents, brothers, sisters, and friends."

This was exactly the sort of business that put Washington in favor of enforcing a British-style settlement boundary. The matter wasn't merely philosophical for him; it was also personal. Much of Washington's wealth lay in large tracts of western land. That land would hold its value only if he could control its sale and settlement. "Banditti" such as Boone, who took land without consulting its eastern owners, were a threat. Boone himself was a particular threat, since his claims on Kentucky conflicted with Washington's own.

Paper claims to distant land, such as Washington's, were hard to maintain from the East. During the Revolutionary War, Washington had left his considerable estate in the unsteady hands of his distant cousin Lund Washington. Under Lund's less than entirely watchful eye, squatters took up residence on Washington's western holdings (not the Kentucky claims, but others farther north). Irate, Washington set out to put things right, crossing the Appalachians himself on a sort of landlord's vengeance mission.

The expedition did little to temper his disdain for frontiersmen. He recorded that their clashes with Indians had incited "murders, and general dissatisfaction." They "labour very little," he harrumphed, and the merest "touch of a feather" would turn their loyalties away from the United States.

Washington set his affairs in order, but he remained doubtful about westerners' political allegiances. His fears were confirmed in the 1790s, when backcountry men in Pennsylvania refused to pay a federal tax on alcohol and threatened armed secession. It was the Boston Tea Party all over again, this time with whiskey. Yet, notwithstanding his own recent leadership of a revolution against the financial machinations of a distant government, Washington's sympathy for the rebels quickly ran dry. Their opposition, he complained to Jefferson, had "become too open, violent and serious to be longer winked at."

Once again, Washington rode west across the mountains, this time to quash a rebellion. In the end, the uprising dispersed before Washington's forces arrived. But the episode remains, as the historian Joseph Ellis has observed, the "first and only time a sitting American president led troops in the field."

★

Washington's impatience with frontiersmen didn't mean that he opposed expansion. In the long term, he depended on it, both to strengthen the country and to profit from his western estates. The issue was the short term. The country was vast, but its government was weak. Squatters who rushed over the mountains were impossible to govern, and the wars they inevitably started were expensive to fight. Washington thus insisted that settlement proceed in a "compact" manner, under elite control. That way, the frontier would be not a refuge for masterless men like Boone but the forefront of the march of civilization, advancing at a stately pace.

To realize their vision, the founders created a distinct political category for the frontier: *territory*. The revolution had been fought by a union of states, but those states' borders became ill-defined and even overlapped as they reached westward. Rather than dividing the frontier among the states, the republic's leaders brokered deals by which none of the Atlantic states would extend to the Mississippi, which marked the western edge of the country. Instead, western land would go to the federal government. It would be administered not as states, but as territories.

The government accepted control of its first territory in 1784, when Virginia gave up its claims to a large swath of land north of the Ohio River. This cession came not two months before the United States formally received its independence when Britain ratified the Treaty of Paris. This meant that, from day one, the United States of America was more than just a union of states. It was an amalgam of states and territory.

By 1791, all Atlantic states except Georgia had followed Virginia and given up their far western claims. As a result, in that year only slightly more than half of the country's land (55 percent) was covered by states.

What *was* this non-state territory? The Constitution was notably close-lipped, discussing the matter only in a single sentence. It granted Congress the power "to dispose of and make all needful Rules and Regulations respecting the Territory or other Property belonging to the United States." Thus the founding document, which went into extravagant detail about amendments, elections, and the division of power, left wide open the question of how much of the land was to be governed.

Territorial policy was set, instead, by a series of laws, most famously the Jefferson-inspired Northwest Ordinance of 1787, which covered a large part of the present-day Midwest (similar laws covered other regions). The Northwest Ordinance has become part of the national mythology, celebrated in textbooks for its remarkable offer of statehood on "an equal footing with the original States in all respects whatever." The territories merely had to cross a series of population thresholds: five thousand free men, and they could have a legislature; sixty thousand free inhabitants (or sooner, if Congress allowed), and they could be states.

But the operative word was *could*. None of this was automatic, for Congress retained the power to advance or impede territories, both of which it did. Sometimes it denied, ignored, or deflected statehood petitions. That is why Lincoln, West Dakota, Deseret, Cimarron, and Montezuma—all of which sought admission to the union—did not become states.

Moreover, Congress's discretionary authority meant that until territories became states, the federal government held absolute power over them. Initially, territories were to be ruled by an appointed governor and three judges. Even after they gained legislatures, the governor retained the power to veto bills and dissolve the legislature.

"In effect," wrote James Monroe, who drafted the ordinance, it was "a colonial government similar to that which prevail'd in these States previous to the revolution." Jefferson conceded that the first stage resembled a "despotic oligarchy."

That was an apt characterization. The first governor of the Northwest Territory, Arthur St. Clair, a conservative Scotsman who'd been Washington's aide-de-camp, had little patience for the rambunctious frontier. He saw himself as a "poor devil banished to another planet." The territory, in his eyes, was a "dependent colony," inhabited not by "citizens of the United States" but by its "subjects" ("white Indians" is how one of the territorial judges described them). Feeling the territorial inhabitants too "ignorant" and "ill qualified" to govern themselves, St. Clair used his wide discretionary powers to impede the formation of states.

The same pattern held in Louisiana Territory, the land Jefferson acquired in 1803 from France. Eastern politicians fretted about the newly annexed land's inhabitants: Anglo settlers, Catholics, free blacks, Indians, and mixed-race folk. "This Constitution never was, and never can be, strained to lap over all the wilderness of the West," warned Representative Josiah Quincy, the future president of Harvard.

Jefferson understood the sentiment. The people of Louisiana were as "incapable of self-government as children," he judged, adding that the "principles of popular Government are utterly beyond their comprehension." Rather than putting Louisiana through the normal Northwest Ordinance procedures, Jefferson added a new initial phase, military government, and sent the U.S. Army to keep the peace. By 1806, the Territory of Louisiana hosted the largest contingent of the army in the country.

Jefferson's appointed governor to Louisiana Territory, like Arthur St. Clair, griped about the "mental darkness" of Louisiana's inhabitants. Allowing them to vote, he believed, "would be a dangerous experiment."

Louisianians protested their disenfranchisement. "Do political axioms on the Atlantic become problems when transferred to the shores of the Mississippi?" they asked on a trip to the capital. Jefferson shrugged his shoulders and did nothing.

★

Thomas Jefferson wasn't against expansion any more than George Washington was. It's just that, like Washington, he envisioned it as a controlled process.

In his more fanciful moments, Jefferson imagined the United States spreading to "cover the whole Northern, if not the Southern continent with a people speaking the same language, governed in similar forms, and by similar laws." Yet that vague fantasy was slated, in Jefferson's mind, for "distant times." When it came to the *pace* of expansion, his ambitions were strikingly modest. In his first inaugural address, he marveled at the "wide and fruitful land" from the Atlantic to the Mississippi and predicted that it would hold "room enough for our descendants to the thousandth and thousandth generation."

Despite his seeming satisfaction with the country's original dimensions, Jefferson came to be known as an expansionist for his acquisition of Louisiana, which extended the country far west of the Mississippi. Yet that was more of an impulse buy than a considered purchase. In sending negotiators to Paris to bargain with Napoleon, he wasn't even trying to get vast tracts of western land. Rather, he wanted valuable ports on the Gulf of Mexico. The initial response of Jefferson's emissary to Napoleon's offer of all of French North America is telling: "I told him no, that our wishes extended only to New Orleans and the Floridas."

Jefferson cared more about the ports than the land because he wasn't searching for room for settlers. Even after annexing Louisiana, he didn't see it as a home for whites. Much of the land still fell under Indian title, and "the best use we can make of the country for some time," Jefferson wrote, was to keep it that way. In his vision, all the land except an area around New Orleans would be "shut up" against whites "for a long time to come." Instead of rushing out to the edges of the new territory, whites would slowly populate the Mississippi Valley, "advancing compactly as we multiply." Jefferson imagined the West would be settled not by nomadic hunters, like Boone (and like some Indians), but by small farmers. So long as they kept to their allotted territory and didn't multiply too rapidly, they could be accommodated.

This was the founders' vision. And, with the Louisiana Purchase, it seemed easily realized. If eastern Indians could be induced by treaty to move west of the settlement border and if whites could be kept east, "advancing compactly," there'd be room for all, down to Jefferson's imagined "thousandth and thousandth generation."

★

Jefferson and Washington assumed that whites could be guided to settle the land, as they both put it, "compactly," meaning that their growing numbers wouldn't require too much room. It wasn't an unreasonable assumption, especially given how slowly European populations had grown in the past. Between A.D. 1 and A.D. 1000, Western Europe had increased by only 6 percent. Things picked up in the next seven centuries, when its population more than doubled. But that still wasn't exactly fast. By 1700, the best available statistics suggested that England was on track to double only once every 360 years.

The North American colonies weren't much different, at least not at first. Disease took so many lives in Britain's first permanent North American settlement at Jamestown, established in 1607, that it wasn't until the 1690s that births outpaced deaths there. In the first century and a half after Jamestown's establishment, the frontier of white settlement had crept west slowly, at one to two miles a year.

But by the mid-eighteenth century, something was changing. Ben Franklin was the first to notice it. In 1749 he organized a census of Philadelphia and began to collect population numbers on Boston, New Jersey, and Massachusetts. What he saw was startling. Not only was the colonial population growing, it was doubling once every twenty-five years. If that continued, Franklin predicted (with more than a little giddiness), in a century colonial North America would contain more Englishmen than Britain itself.

This was a revelation. Franklin is best remembered for his experiments with electricity and his many inventions (bifocals, the lightning rod, the circulating stove, the urinary catheter), but his demographic research was a large part of his legacy, too. His numbers quickly made the rounds in Europe, only sometimes with his name attached, and entered the thought of such philosophers as Adam Smith and David Hume. The grim prediction by the economist Thomas Malthus that food supply could never keep pace with population growth was largely based on Franklin's North American calculations (which, Malthus gasped, indicated "a rapidity of increase probably without parallel in history"). Malthus, in turn, was an important influence on Charles Darwin, both of whose grandfathers knew Franklin well. The copy of Malthus's book in Darwin's library has the Franklin passages underlined.

Not only was Franklin influential, he was right. Shockingly right. More right than he had any reason to be. Full population figures for the United States were first collected in 1790, the year of Franklin's death. A hundred years later, the 1890 census registered that the population had increased sixteenfold—i.e., a doubling every twenty-five years—Franklin had been off by *less than one-seventh of a percent*. And in 1855, exactly a hundred years after Franklin published his prediction that North American colonists would outnumber Britons in a century, the U.S. population surpassed that of Britain for the first time.

What Franklin had recognized, earlier than anyone else, was that a small population of English-speaking whites and their black slaves was going supernova. They inhabited a continent substantially cleared of its indigenous population by disease, they possessed powerful agricultural technologies, and they enjoyed close economic ties to Britain, the center of the Industrial Revolution. The combination was explosive.

The population of France at the time of U.S. independence was around thirty million. In 1900 it was slightly more than forty million. By contrast, the population of the United States at its independence was between three and four million—roughly one-tenth the size of France. And yet by 1900 it was seventy-six million, nearly twice France's size. Although the frontier had advanced by fewer than two miles a year in the 150 years following Jamestown's establishment, in the first half of the nineteenth century it shot west at nearly forty miles a year, stopping only when settlers reached the Pacific Coast.

This was growth like no one had ever seen. Part of it came from influxes from Europe and Africa, though in no decade in the nineteenth century did immigration ever account for more than a third of the increase. As Franklin pointed out, the bulk of it was handled the old-fashioned way, a fire hose of fecundity spraying settlers up and down the North American continent. With arable land stretching to the horizon, settlers spread like bacteria.

"Wave after wave has rolled on," wrote a nervous Ojibwe thinker, "till now there appears no limit to the sea of population."

You could see it in the cities the settlers built. Cincinnati, a village in 1810, had a nine-story steam-powered mill by 1815 and a fleet of 150 steamboats by 1830. Chicago grew from a settlement of fewer than a hundred people (and fourteen taxpayers) in 1830 to a towering megalopolis with the world's first dense cluster of skyscrapers and more than a million residents in 1890—despite having burned to the ground in 1871.

That phoenix-from-the-ashes routine was surprisingly common. Constructed with maximal haste and minimal regard for the principles of zoning, settler cities burst into flame with alarming frequency. But not even fire could stop the endless torrent.

★

The growth of the white population was like a flash of dynamite, and it would explode the founders' vision of the country. The great Jeffersonian system that had prevailed in the first decades, with western subjects semi-colonized, simply could not hold. There were too many Daniel Boones. The government gave up prosecuting squatters by the 1830s and instead let them buy their land. In the 1860s it began giving away parcels of public land as "homesteads" to nearly any citizen willing to live on them.

The territories with large white populations became states swiftly; California, swarming with gold-seekers, went from military government to statehood in two years. And though the inhabitants of the remaining territories still protested their lack of rights (the territorial system was "the most infamous system of colonial government that was ever seen on the face of the globe," grumbled a delegate from Montana Territory), their cause for complaint diminished. Appointed governors lost some of their discretionary powers, and, after 1848, new territories skipped the first stage of government, absolute rule by federal officials, and went straight to having bicameral legislatures.

The culture changed, too. Rather than being despised "banditti" or "white savages" on the fringes of civilization, settlers acquired a new identity: *pioneers*. No longer scofflaws, they were the proud flag-bearers of a dynamic nation.

As squatters became pioneers, Daniel Boone's reputation surged. After his death, he was retroactively claimed as an honorary founding father. A statue was placed on the steps of the Capitol in 1851: a frontiersman, bearing a conspicuous resemblance to Boone, fighting an Indian. It stood there for more than a century. In the realm of fiction, the immensely popular Leatherstocking novels of James Fenimore Cooper told, over many volumes (*The Deerslayer, The Last of the Mohicans, The Pioneers*, etc.), the tale of Natty Bumppo, also clearly based on Boone. Those novels, published from the 1820s to the 1840s, burned the character of the gruff frontier hero into the national consciousness. Natty Bumppo, Davy Crockett, Kit Carson, Wild Bill Hickok—you can trace a chain of Boone figures all the way forward to John Wayne and Han Solo.

The founders had always expected expansion of some sort, but only now, in the mid-nineteenth century, did outright and rapid continental conquest seem inevitable. In 1845 the *United States Magazine and Democratic Review* coined an indelible phrase and captured the prevailing mood when it wrote of the nation's "manifest destiny to overspread the continent allotted by Providence for the free development of our yearly multiplying millions."

A country that had started out resembling the British Empire, with centers of power in the East and subordinated territory in the West, had been turned by the population bomb into something different: a violently expansive empire of settlers, feeding on land and displacing everything in its path.

2

INDIAN COUNTRY

The detonation of the North American settler bomb was astounding. But it wasn't the only striking demographic occurrence. The growth of the settler population was tied to another event in North America: the extraordinary *de*population of the land's indigenous inhabitants.

The size of that depopulation is up for debate. It's hard to know how many Indians inhabited North America before Europeans arrived. Five million for the area now covered by the contiguous United States, calculated by the anthropologist Russell Thornton, is a medium estimate, though other researchers have suggested numbers from 720,000 to 15 million.

What is not in dispute is this: European contact triggered a profound demographic crisis. Old World diseases such as smallpox, typhus, and measles burned through the land like firestorms, moving farther and faster than the Europeans themselves. War and social dislocation followed, causing still more deaths and nonbirths. By 1800, the indigenous population was closer to half a million, having endured what may have been a 90 percent decline.

As catastrophic as depopulation was, it wasn't fatal. Indians remained a formidable presence. The British had acknowledged this in setting the ridge of the Appalachians as the limit of white settlement—partly to avoid Indian wars. That was also a reason why the founders sought "compact" white settlement rather than a Boone-style sprint to the outer frontier.

A bastion of Indian strength was the Cherokee Nation, whose land stretched across parts of Tennessee, Alabama, North Carolina, and Georgia. Cherokee numbers had fallen, perhaps by as much as half, in the seventeenth and eighteenth centuries, but the population started rebounding in the early nineteenth.

Not only were the Cherokees growing, they were carving out a place for themselves within the new republic by adopting aspects of European culture. They ran plantations, bought slaves, and built a capital ("It's like Baltimore," a leading Cherokee bragged). A silversmith named Sequoyah designed a syllabary, turning Cherokee into a written language. It caught on quickly with help from the tribe's newspaper, the *Cherokee Phoenix*, published in both English and Cherokee. In 1827 the Cherokee Nation adopted a constitution, modeled on the U.S. Constitution. Voters elected a mixed-race, wealthy, Christian president, Koo-wi-s-gu-wi, who had fought beside Andrew Jackson and went by his European name, John Ross.

The Cherokees were, Ross explained to the U.S. Senate, "like the whiteman in manners, morals and religion."

Not all Native Americans chose that path. Whether to stick to indigenous ways or take up foreign ones was a hard call, and opinions understandably varied. But by doubling down on Europeanization, the Cherokees were calling the government's bluff. They were "civilized" by every rule of white society. So shouldn't their land claims be respected?

In the early years of the republic, their claims *had* been respected, roughly speaking. The Washington administration, unable to either ignore or dislodge the Cherokees, had signed a treaty with them and had appeared to accept the prospect of "civilized" Cherokees joining the United States as citizens.

Yet such fragile achievements were hard to maintain in the face of white land hunger. Georgia's population grew by more than half during the 1820s. That, plus the Southern cotton boom and the discovery of gold in the Cherokee Nation, put the Cherokees in a precarious position. In 1828 the state of Georgia declared the Cherokee constitution invalid and demanded the Cherokees' land. President Andrew Jackson approved. An Indian nation "would not be countenanced," he declared. The Cherokees must either submit to Georgia's authority or head west, to the territories.

The Supreme Court declared Georgia's actions unconstitutional. But high-court rulings meant little in the face of the squatter onslaught.

Cherokee landowners watched with alarm as Georgia divided the Cherokee Nation into parcels and started distributing it to whites by lottery. In 1835 John Ross returned home to find a white man living in his house— Ross had to abandon his large estate for a one-room log cabin. Later that year, he was arrested on the trumped-up charge of inciting a slave rebellion. Other Cherokees faced similar harassment.

Much of this was plainly illegal, but the Cherokees had little recourse. The secretary of war advised them that the only solution was "removal beyond the Mississippi" to the lands acquired in the Louisiana Purchase. There, he assured them, they would finally enjoy "protection and peace."

Though Ross wanted to stay and fight, other Cherokees threw up their hands. "We can't be a Nation here," John Ridge announced despondently. Ridge was part of a faction that, bypassing the elected tribal government, signed a treaty with the federal government on behalf of the Cherokee Nation. Cherokees would exchange their homeland for new land west of the Mississippi.

At least that was the idea. Around two thousand left voluntarily, as per the agreement. But the rest, some sixteen thousand, refused. The government sent seven thousand militiamen and volunteers to round them up at bayonet point and imprison them. The incarcerated Cherokees were then forcibly relocated to present-day Oklahoma. The Cherokees called this journey *Nunna daul Isunyi*, the "trail where we cried." The Trail of Tears, as it is known in English, was a bitter march, undertaken by some on foot. Starvation, cold, and disease killed thousands, including Ross's wife.

The deaths continued. Disease, hunger, and violence ravaged the new Cherokee land for years. The population resurgence of the early nineteenth century was obliterated. By 1840, deaths on the march, deaths in the new territory, and accompanying nonbirths had knocked the Cherokee population down by a third or half of what it would have been had the nation remained in the East.

★

The Trail of Tears was notorious, but it wasn't anomalous. Thomas Jefferson had fantasized about dividing the entire country, with Native on one side and European on the other—hence his plan for the Louisiana Purchase. By reserving most of the new territory for Indians, he could free up land in the East for whites.

For the first few decades of the country's history, this continental-scale apartheid had remained informal and incomplete. It was the population boom—particularly the crisis surrounding the lands of the Cherokees and neighboring tribes in the Southeast in the 1830s—that gave the issue a new urgency. To handle it, Andrew Jackson sought and won new legislation to allow him to aggressively negotiate east-for-west deals.

But making those deals plausible required having western land to offer. The Jackson administration thus sought to turn the West into something resembling an Indian colony. Forty-six percent of the United States—stretching from the top of present-day Texas to the Canadian border and from Michigan to the Rockies—would be officially designated Indian Country (known also as Indian Territory). It would be walled off from white settlement and commerce. If forced removal was the stick, this promise of a permanent territory, free of whites, was the carrot.

Jackson sweetened the pot. Within Indian Country, his administration proposed to designate a smaller-but-still-really-large area, somewhere between the size of California and Texas, as Western Territory. This would be an organized territory, governed by a confederacy of Indian polities and given a delegate in Congress. The goal, as the government's representative explained, was that Western Territory would be "admitted as a state to become a member of the Union."

It was a striking proposal. The government had reserved plots of land for individual polities before, but it hadn't created any Indian political units. Now the idea was to establish a permanent territory inhabited solely by Native Americans. Like Illinois or Arkansas, but bigger.

The cost, however, was that this would formally divide the country into unequal parts, a settler part and an Indian part. It was a starker and potentially more permanent partition than the existing state/territory division, and former president John Quincy Adams fretted about what it might do to the nation's character. The idea, he warned, was "not republican at all." It was something an empire would do, an act of "despotism."

Adams's Southern colleagues in Congress raised another concern. If Congress were to "add to our Union men of blood and color alien to the people of the United States," the Virginia representative asked, "where was that right to stop? Why not introduce our brethren of Cuba and Hayti?" And then there was that business of Western Territory's congressional delegate. "I am not prepared to receive the Indians into this hall," declared Georgia's representative with a huff.

In the end, the thought of a "full-blood savage" with a desk in the

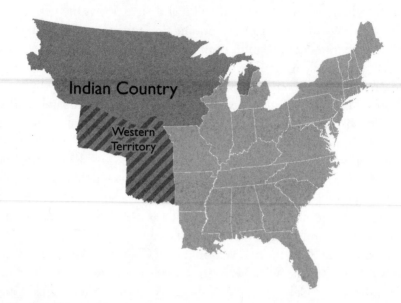

Indian Country as designated in 1834. Western Territory, rejected by Congress, forms the southern part.

Capitol proved too much for the delicate sensibilities of the members of the 23rd Congress. They tabled the Western Territory proposal. Still, Indian Country remained. The federal government provided farming equipment and livestock, distributed food, sent blacksmiths and physicians, and set aside funds for the poor, in keeping with its treaty obligations.

Such arrangements were temporary, though. The government's true focus was on policing the borders: keeping Indians in and whites out. Without the representative government that Western Territory would have provided, Indian Country was, from the perspective of Washington, less a colony than a holding pen.

★

Indian Country rarely appeared on maps as such. It had been defined in law, yet there was something indistinct about it, at least in the minds of whites. In principle, it offered "effectual and complete protection" to Native Americans, as the Jackson administration had guaranteed. But the settler boom was far from over. Could the borders of this promised land hold against further white expansion?

If Indian Country looked tenuous from its start in the 1830s, it looked even more so in the 1840s, with the annexation of Texas, the conquest of much of Mexico, and the extinction of the British claims in Oregon. Suddenly Indian Country was no longer pressed up against the nation's western border. It stood exposed in the middle, right between the bustling East and the burgeoning West.

Where gold had just been discovered.

"The Indian barrier must be removed," demanded Senator Stephen Douglas, who longed to run a transcontinental railroad through Indian Country to California. William Henry Seward noted that eighteen tribes lived on the land that Douglas wanted. "Where will they go?" Seward asked. "Back across the Mississippi? . . . To the Himalayas?"

Who cared? Eager white settlers streamed in, and Congress obliged by carving Kansas and Nebraska out of the heart of Indian Country—two new territories open to white settlement. The Kansas-Nebraska Act of 1854, which created those territories, is best known for inciting the Civil War, as the struggle over whether the territories would allow slavery led to bloody conflicts in Kansas. But that wasn't the only violence in the area. Whites fought one another on land they had wrested from Indians in a complex process involving railroad companies, federal agents, armed squatters, the military, and a haze of dubious legal claims.

Readers of Laura Ingalls Wilder's *Little House on the Prairie* will be familiar with this dynamic, as it is the hinge on which the novel turns. The titular house is three miles into Indian Country. Ma is a little shaky on the details:

> She didn't know whether this was Indian country or not. She didn't know where the Kansas line was. But whether or no, the Indians would not be here long. Pa had word from a man in Washington that the Indian Territory would be open to settlement soon.

Pa demonstrates a slightly firmer grasp on the matter:

> "When white settlers come into a country, the Indians have to move on. The government is going to move these Indians farther west, any time now. That's why we're here, Laura. White people are going

to settle all this country, and we get the best land because we get here first and take our pick. Now do you understand?"

"Yes, Pa," Laura said. "But, Pa, I thought this was Indian Territory. Won't it make the Indians mad to have to—"

"No more questions, Laura," Pa said, firmly. "Go to sleep."

At the end of the book, Pa learns that federal troops are coming to evict him from his illegal settlement. "I'll not stay here to be taken away by the soldiers like an outlaw!" he exclaims, and he packs the family up to head back to Wisconsin.

Little House was closely based on Laura Ingalls Wilder's childhood. There *was* a little house, and it *was* in Indian Country. But Wilder's family was never ousted by federal troops. In the 1990s an editor at *The Washington Post*, the Osage journalist Dennis McAuliffe Jr., researched his family history and discovered that it wasn't the whites who had been pushed off the land, but the Osages. Pa's neighbors, and perhaps Pa himself, had driven them out by stealing their food, killing their livestock, burning their houses, robbing their graves, and murdering them outright.

"The question will suggest itself," wrote an aghast federal agent who witnessed it all: "Which of these people are the savages?"

★

Pushed off their "permanent" lands, Native Americans moved yet again. Indian Country was successively whittled down until it had been reduced to its southern tip, present-day Oklahoma. The territory's population, drawn from all over the map, spoke to the wrenching dislocations of the nineteenth century. By 1879, it contained Cherokees, Choctaws, Chickasaws, Quapaws, Seminoles, Senecas, Shawnees, Modocs, Odawas, Peorias, Miamis, Wyandots, Osages, Kaws, Nez Perces, Pawnees, Poncas, Sacs and Foxes, Kickapoos, Creeks, Potawatomis, Cheyennes, Arapahos, Wichitas, Wacos, Tawakonis, Kichais, Caddos, Delawares, Comanches, Kiowas, and Apaches.

It was as if someone had depopulated most of Europe and shunted remnants from each country to an allotment in Romania.

And yet, even this compressed neutron star of Indian polities was vulnerable to incursions. There was talk of organizing it into a territory, as had been done with Kansas and Nebraska. And, as in those two territories, whites

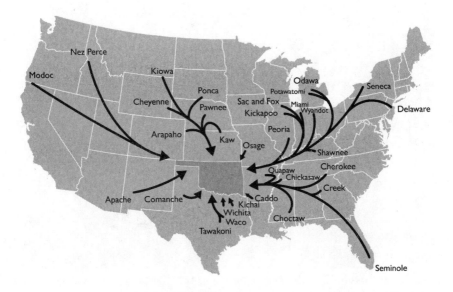

Pushing Indians off the land: Removals to a much-diminished Indian Country

started pouring in illegally. "We are here with our axes and our plows," one group announced defiantly in an 1885 petition to Congress. "Hundreds and thousands of our friends are on their way to join us from all States of the West. We are here to stay. We deny the right of any man, or mob of men, whether in uniform or plain clothes, to molest us."

Indians regarded these squatters with horror. "No matter how little is left the red man, such heartless wretches will never rest content or let the Government rest until the Indians are made landless and homeless," warned *The Cherokee Advocate*. "It is beyond the power of words to express the character of such men—dead to all human feeling and knowing no law."

Just as *The Cherokee Advocate* feared, the government acquiesced to the settlers' demands, squeezing Native American land claims over to the territory's eastern side via allotment and distributing the western side to whites. Some of that western land was parceled off by lottery. More was apportioned by race: at the firing of a federal official's gun, settlers sprinted to stake their claims. It was, the Census Bureau declared, "the most rapid settlement of a territory in the history of the United States."

A delirious land rush: At the shot of a pistol in 1893, settlers scramble to claim land that was formerly Indian Country.

In the venerable U.S. tradition of naming places for the people who have been driven from them, the newly opened territory was called Oklahoma, a Choctaw word meaning "red people."

That left the eastern part as the sole vestige of Indian Country. But squatters were streaming in there, too. Seeing which way the wind was blowing, leading tribes called a convention, open to all, Indian and non-Indian alike. They would apply for admission to the union as a state that would not be exclusively Indian, but would at least have a substantial Indian population. It would be called Sequoyah, after the silversmith who had designed the Cherokee syllabary.

Congress refused to consider the petition. Instead, it allowed the settler-dominated Territory of Oklahoma to absorb the would-be state of Sequoyah. Oklahoma was admitted as a state in 1907, with a population less than one-quarter Indian.

The final extirpation of Indian Country was a profoundly important event for Native Americans. Two decades later, the Cherokee playwright Lynn Riggs set out to tell the tale. Riggs conceived and wrote his play in Paris—he frequented the café Les Deux Magots, where Ernest Hemingway and F. Scott Fitzgerald were also scribbling away. But his mind was on his childhood home. The result, *Green Grow the Lilacs*, offered a wistful celebration of Indian Country on the cusp of change. It is a gentle, nostalgic play, though with a defiant ending. When, in the last act, a federal marshal appears on the scene, the characters refuse to cooperate with him, explaining that they are "jist plumb full of Indian blood" and that they regard the United States as a "furrin country." With that uneasy confrontation, the curtain falls.

Riggs's play was well received when it debuted in 1931. Today, however, it is remembered less on its own merits than as the basis for the musical *Oklahoma!* by Richard Rodgers and Oscar Hammerstein. "I kept most of the lines of the original play without making any changes in them, for the simple reason that they could not be improved upon—at least not by me," Hammerstein told the press.

Yet there was one noticeable change. Though the musical concludes with a confrontation with a marshal (it ends happily), the characters in *Oklahoma!* say nothing about having "Indian blood." Indeed, the word *Indian* is not uttered once in the production. *Oklahoma!* presents its characters as whites enchanted by available land and brought to spasms of ecstasy by the thought that they might soon "be livin' in a brand-new state!" "We know we belong to the land," they sing, "And the land we belong to is grand."

It is the jubilant refrain of the white settler.

3

EVERYTHING YOU ALWAYS WANTED TO KNOW ABOUT GUANO BUT WERE AFRAID TO ASK

It is a little-noted feature of world history that in the past few decades, the map hasn't changed much. Of course there have been trouble spots (Iraq/Kuwait, Russia/Ukraine, Sudan) and the dramatic dismantling of the Soviet Union. But there hasn't been anything like the wrenching cartographic tumult of previous centuries: the invasions, revolutions, conquests, and annexations that turned Poland into a cursed accordion, madly expanding and contracting, and that wiped Indian Country off the map.

The tendency of today's borders to stick in place can make the shapes of countries seem inevitable. The hexagon of France, the stilettoed boot of Italy, the impossibly thin needle of Chile ("a dagger pointed at the heart of Antarctica," quipped Henry Kissinger)—though they were obviously the result of historical fortune, it's difficult to imagine them taking forms other than the ones they did.

That's one reason why it's hard to remember the U.S. founders' hesitations about westward expansion. Surely, we think, they must have seen how stunted, how unfinished their little stub of a country was. There's something satisfying about following the story to its end, like putting together a jigsaw puzzle. The Louisiana Purchase, *click*, East and West Florida, *click click*, Texas, *click*, Oregon, *click*, the war with Mexico, *click*, and the Gadsden Purchase, a sliver of land on the Mexican border that filled out the familiar logo-map profile of the United States. *Click*. Picture complete, destiny manifested.

Except that the puzzle wasn't finished. The logo-map silhouette accurately captured the borders of the United States for only three years. Because in 1857, not long after the Gadsden Purchase was ratified (1854), the United States began annexing small islands throughout the Caribbean and the Pacific. By the end of the century, it would claim almost a hundred of them.

The islands had no indigenous populations and, at the time, no strategic value. They tended to be remote, rocky, and rainless—poor places to grow things on. But that didn't matter. They had the one thing that everyone in the nineteenth century badly wanted. They had "white gold," known in less polite circles as bird shit.

★

To understand why anyone would care about bird droppings, it helps to know a little about preindustrial agriculture.

Farming in the nineteenth-century United States was not like it is today, acres of staggeringly prolific fields bristling with high-yield crops. It was a touch-and-go business. The reason Benjamin Franklin's population numbers had alarmed Thomas Malthus was that Malthus couldn't see where the food would come from to feed those multiplying generations. New farmland and virgin soil had given North Americans a margin of ease, he acknowledged, but that could only be temporary. In the end, he wrote, "the power of population is so superior to the power in the earth to produce subsistence for man, that premature death must in some shape or other visit the human race."

As the nineteenth century progressed, agricultural scientists got a better sense of why land fertility lagged behind human fertility. Arable land contains nutrients, without which plants will not grow. The most important by far is nitrogen, one of the four building blocks of life (CHON: carbon, hydrogen, oxygen, nitrogen). Soil short of it yields underdeveloped plants with pale leaves and protein-poor seeds.

Luckily, nitrogen makes up nearly four-fifths of the earth's atmosphere by volume. Unluckily, atmospheric nitrogen is almost exclusively dinitrogen (N_2), whose strong triple bonds render it unreactive and thus inaccessible to plants. Worse, nature offers frustratingly few ways to turn dinitrogen into a usable reactive compound. Lightning will do it, as will the bacteria that inhabit the nodules of the roots of some legumes, but that's it.

It took chemists until the nineteenth century to piece all that together. But farmers, in their own way, had comprehended it for millennia. All agricultural traditions, in order for them to last long enough to *be* traditions, require methods for managing nitrogen flows. These are intricate ballets between farmer and earth, choreographed by folk wisdom and danced to the rhythm of the seasons. Nitrogen-rich manures are spread, crops rotated, forests burned, fields left fallow, or lentils planted. Each locale offers its own complicated variation on an enduring theme.

These complex systems faltered, however, in the nineteenth century. Industrialization required raw materials to feed the factories and grain to feed the workers. Farms that used to grow a rotating variety of crops for local consumption started focusing on the most profitable crops and grew them for distant markets. Who has time to plant beans when the British are buying cotton at eleven cents a pound and the ships are waiting?

Worse, by delivering the produce of the countryside to distant cities, the new agriculture broke the age-old cycle that had restored waste—human and animal—to the land, returning nitrates to the soil. Nineteenth-century agronomists cringed at the thought of large cities flushing into rivers and oceans the nitrogenous wastes that could have fertilized the fields. The author of a much-used textbook estimated the annual value of "lost" human feces to be $50 million, which approached the size of the federal budget.

These were not idle worries. Single-crop farms yielded diminishing returns. "Soil exhaustion," as it was called, was the bugbear of nineteenth-century agriculture throughout the industrializing world, and it had taken hold of eastern farms. "The fact is notorious," reported an agricultural expert to the New York Senate, "that there are thousands, if not millions, of acres in this State which once bore 20 bushels of good wheat per acre, that now yield not more than ten."

Farmers scoured their areas for organic material that could be spread on their fields to replenish them. The sheer variety of possibilities discussed in Sir Humphry Davy's authoritative *Elements of Agricultural Chemistry* (1813) gives some sense of how desperate they'd become. Davy considered rapeseed cake, linseed cake, malt dust, seaweed ("as fresh as can be procured"), straw, spoiled hay, oats, "mere woody fiber," "inert peaty matter," wood ash, "the entire parts of the muscles of land animals," putrefied animal remains (horses, dogs, sheep, deer, and "other quadrupeds"), fish, blubber, bone dust, horn shavings, hair, woolen rags, "the offals of the tan-yard," blood, "scum taken from the boilers of the sugar bakers," coral reef, sea sponges, fresh urine, "putrid urine," pigeon dung, chicken dung, rabbit dung, cattle dung, sheep dung, deer dung, and soot.

"Poudrette," a polite name for human feces sold commercially, was of special interest. Even Victor Hugo couldn't run his harried hero Jean Valjean through the sewers of Paris in *Les Misérables* (1862) without pausing—pausing, indeed, for a whole chapter—to remark that it really would be better if some use could be found for Paris's waste. In a section regrettably cut from the musical, Hugo outlined his plan for "a double tubular apparatus, provided with valves and sluices," to carry it back to the fields.

Large-scale fecal repatriation remained the stuff of fiction, though. City feces were too dispersed and heavy to collect and transport, and few of the other "soil amendments" lived up to their reputations.

What *did* work was guano. That term can refer to any bird or bat feces used as fertilizer, but the guano on everyone's minds was the nitrogen-rich droppings of cormorants, boobies, and pelicans on the Chincha Islands off the coast of Peru. Islands make attractive rookeries for seabirds in general. The Chinchas had the additional virtue that they hardly ever saw rain. The guano piled hundreds of feet high and baked in the sun, so that the very rock of the islands was centuries' worth of calcified bird droppings.

Guano was noxious, "a beastly smelling-bottle sort of mess, looking like bad snuff mixed with rotten kittens," as a Vermont paper put it. Virginia's senator deemed it "the most odious and disagreeable material that can be imagined." Its sharp, ammoniacal smell was notorious, perceptible from miles off. Sailors hauling guano could spend no more than fifteen minutes belowdecks with it. They would emerge gasping for breath, sometimes suffering nosebleeds or temporary blindness.

And yet, sprinkled in small quantities over the nitrogen-parched farms of North America, the stuff worked miracles. The first ships carrying Peruvian guano arrived in the 1840s and quickly sparked a mania. It was, crowed the *Cleveland Herald*, the "cheapest, most powerful, enduring, and portable fertilizer" of all. Tall tales spread, about the father who locked his ten-year-old son in a barn with a pile of guano and

Late nineteenth-century sheet music celebrating the Age of Guano

unlocked it hours later to discover a full-grown man in his place, or the farmer whose guanoed cucumber plants shot out of the dirt and seized him with their vines.

★

Peruvian guano may have been miraculous, but it wasn't free. Rabid demand drove up the cost. So did the tight control of the supply by British firms that monopolized guano exports from the Chinchas and kept prices high.

This was, to put it lightly, a problem. The "guano question" came up again and again in Congress. ("This subject is of much less importance than the Pacific railroad," protested a weary California senator. "The Senator has not paid attention to the use of guano, or he would not make that remark" came the curt reply from Virginia.) Guano prices also appeared in four presidential annual messages, most notably in Millard Fillmore's first. "Peruvian guano has become so desirable an article," Fillmore said, that he regarded it as the "duty of the Government" to secure it at a "reasonable price." "Nothing will be omitted on my part," he promised the nation, in the quest for cheap guano.

Those were not empty words. In 1852 Fillmore's secretary of state, Daniel Webster, gave speculators carte blanche to sail to the guano-laden Lobos Islands off the coast of northern Peru and scrape them clean, promising naval protection and dispatching a warship for that purpose. It was a bold yet dangerous plan, as Peru claimed sovereignty over the islands. In response to Webster's move, Peru prepared for war. One Peruvian paper called on its readers to rise up and "exterminate the hated race," to seize U.S. property and "kill before Peruvians should be killed."

Cooler heads soon prevailed, and the United States backed down ("The Peruvian penguin has fairly beaten the American eagle," chortled *The London Times*). But what was clear is that guano had nearly triggered an inter-American war. Nothing guaranteed it wouldn't do so in the future. Just a single Peruvian island, one of Delaware's senators intimated, would be worth more than the Gadsden Purchase, Cuba, and all the rest of the Caribbean combined.

Luckily, there were other ways around the British monopoly. A few years after he finally finished his Leatherstocking saga, which had done so much to cement the mythology of Daniel Boone, James Fenimore Cooper wrote a new novel, *The Crater* (1847), about a guano island in the South Pacific. In the novel, a "vast deposit of very ancient guano" washes down onto the island's plain, which obligingly erupts forth in "verdant glades." Discovering this, a band of travelers from the United States form a colony there. A small, volcanic rock halfway to Fiji was perhaps an unexpected place for Cooper to stage the sequel to his tales of westward expansion, but guano had magnetic lure.

And not just on Cooper. Speculators, too, suspected that unclaimed Pacific islands contained untold guano riches. Two such islands, Howland and Jarvis, in the Central Pacific, more than a thousand miles from the nearest large landmass, had been known for decades to whalers and seemed particularly promising. Guano entrepreneurs hastily formed the American Guano Company, with a capitalization of $10 million (a number that grows more impressive once you realize that all federal expenditures in 1850 totaled less than $45 million). They begged President Franklin Pierce to send the navy to Howland and Jarvis to protect their diggings from foreign interlopers.

Pierce not only obliged, he went one better by backing the Guano Islands Act in 1856. Under its terms, whenever a U.S. citizen discovered guano on an unclaimed, uninhabited island, that island would, "at the discretion of the President, be considered as appertaining to the United States." It was an obscure word, *appertaining,* as if the law's writers were mumbling their way through the important bit. But the point was this: those islands would, in some way, belong to the country.

Perhaps the lawmakers were right to mumble, as this was a significant departure from the past. At every other stage in U.S. history, territorial expansion had been contentious, debated in newspapers and fought over in Congress. Now, if the law passed, any random adventurer would be "at liberty to tramp about the Pacific, or any other ocean, and annex islands to the United States," as one paper put it.

Members of Congress hesitated: this was a "new kind of legislation" with "consequences beyond the mere supply of guano." Senator William Henry Seward, who had sponsored the law, sought to assuage his colleagues' doubts. If the bill had allowed the "prospect of dominion," he acknowledged, they might be right to question it. "But the bill is framed so as to embrace only these more ragged rocks . . . which are fit for no dominion." James Fenimore Cooper's fantasies aside, Seward promised that there would be no "establishment of colonies" on the islands.

That was all Congress needed to hear. The bill passed, and speculators scrambled to stake their claims. It was another land rush, this time in the Pacific and the Caribbean. The first batch of islands were added to

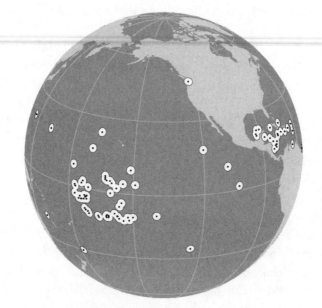

U.S. guano island claims, 1857–1902

the United States in 1857. By 1863, the government had annexed fifty-nine islands. By the time the last claim was filed, in 1902, the United States' oceanic empire encompassed ninety-four guano islands. "The Pacific will be ours, and the Atlantic mainly ours," crowed Walt Whitman. "What an age! What a land!"

★

James Fenimore Cooper, knowing of guano's unparalleled fertilizing powers, imagined his fictional island to be a "little paradise." He could not have been more wrong. What Cooper had failed to grasp is that guano accumulated only in extremely dry climates, oceanic deserts where the lack of rainfall allowed bird droppings to collect for centuries. Such islands were barren rocks, not fertile plains—unpromising sites for human habitation.

Still, the guano didn't hop onto the ships by itself. Guano mining—tunneling, picking, and blasting the stuff loose and hauling it to waiting ships—was arguably the single worst job you could have in the nineteenth century. It offered all the backbreaking labor and lung damage of coal mining, but to do the job, you had to be marooned on a hot, dry, pestilential, and foul-smelling island for months. Respiratory diseases, causing workers to pass out or cough up blood, were common. So were gastrointestinal ailments—the unsurprising consequence of crowded conditions, rotten food, and a dearth of fresh water. Clouds of shrieking seabirds darkened the skies overhead, unleashing the occasional fecal rainstorm ("We were completely encased in a thick film of bird manure," one visitor remembered). On Howland Island, an out-of-control rat population scurried underfoot, adding yet another vile ingredient to the epidemiological stew.

Finding workers wasn't easy. Peruvian guano lords, unable to recruit their compatriots, relied mainly on Chinese laborers, whom they lured onto eastbound ships with false promises or sometimes simply kidnapped—between 1847 and 1874, at least sixty-eight of these ships mutinied. U.S. guano speculators gathered their workforce principally from Hawai'i, where, it was felt, the workers (called "Kanakas") would have some affinity for the landscape. "These patient, hardy, dark-skinned Kanakas who dig and handle the guano, and play the toilsome oar through boiling surf from sunrise to sunset, under the glare of an equatorial sun . . . are a remarkable race of people," wrote one appreciative employer, though he seemed most impressed by their ability to endure hardship, survive disease, and brave the perilous waters to procure fish. "The shark and the Kanaka are on the friendliest terms imaginable," he noted.

The worst of it was on the other side of the globe, on the tiny Caribbean island of Navassa, near Haiti. Rather ominously, it was called Devil's Island.

Although Navassa didn't have much actual guano, its coral reef was packed with deposits of tricalcium phosphate, the fossilized legacy of centuries' worth of marine life—also a rich nutrient for exhausted soil. Under the control of the Navassa Phosphate Company, this would prove to be the most reliable source of fertilizer in the United States' budding island empire.

For workers, the Navassa Phosphate Company used African Americans from Baltimore. Promising a tropical life of picking fruit and romancing beautiful women, the company induced the often-illiterate workers to sign long contracts and step on board.

Yet once the workers disembarked, they found conditions considerably less idyllic. The scorched, jagged, sea-battered island had neither fruit nor women. Instead, it offered a scurvy-inducing diet of hardtack and salted pork, along with the company of abusive white overseers. Such necessities as shirts, shoes, mattresses, and pillows could be got only from the company store at wildly inflated prices. Workers who fell ill were fined. Those who made trouble were "triced": tied up for hours in the hot sun with their arms in the air and their feet barely touching the ground.

In 1889 an argument between an overseer and a worker exploded into violence. White officers fired at their workers, who fought back with axes, razors, clubs, stones, discarded pistols, and dynamite. Five white officers died in the melee. A nearby British steamer picked up the remaining whites and took them to Kingston ("We have been treated like princes from the very moment of our rescue," read the satisfied report). The workers were hauled back to Baltimore and marched through the cold streets, cuffed and in some cases shoeless, to the city jail.

With five white corpses to account for and lurid testimony from the surviving officers filling the papers (THE BLACK BUTCHERS ran one semi-hysterical headline), the defendants' prospects did not look good. Black activists in Baltimore raised funds and hired a formidable legal team, including E. J. Waring, the first black lawyer to pass the Maryland bar.

Waring and his colleagues pointed to the obvious: the wretched con-

EDWARD SMITH alias "Devil"

*CHARLES H. SMITH.

JAMES PHILIPS.

CHARLES H. DAVIS.

*EDWARD WOODFORK.

*JAMES H. ROBINSON.

Navassa rioters: Six of the Navassa Island defendants

ditions and tricing of disobedient workers. But the case ultimately hung on a Hail Mary legal defense. The rioters could not be convicted, their lawyers argued, because the United States lacked jurisdiction. They pointed out that Haiti, too, claimed Navassa. They noted the absence of any U.S. official stationed there. And they probed the curious language of the Guano Islands Act, by which the islands were said to "appertain" to the United States. Appertain? What, exactly, did that mean? As the defense saw it, Navassa was foreign soil.

This was more than an attempt to win freedom for the rioters. It was a challenge to the legality of U.S. empire, and it made its way quickly to the Supreme Court. The court sided with the prosecution, affirming that U.S. law "unequivocally" extended to Navassa. Still, the defense had a point. If this was U.S. territory, where was the government?

President Benjamin Harrison wondered the same thing. He had little doubt that the rioters were "American citizens" who had been working "within American territory." Yet he worried that the Navassa Phosphate Company had turned part of the United States into its own corporate fiefdom, governed not by law, but by corporate regulations.

In a remarkable turn, Harrison sent a warship, the USS *Kearsage*, to investigate—not the typical Gilded Age response to a workers' uprising. When the *Kearsage*'s officers reported that Navassa was being run as "a convict establishment," though without a prison's "comforts and cleanliness," Harrison's sympathies tipped toward the rioters. He commuted the death sentences of the leaders and raised the issue in his annual message. "It is inexcusable that American laborers should be left within our own jurisdiction without access to any Government officer or tribunal for their protection," he said.

It was a thundering presidential endorsement of a principle that had until then remained nebulous. No matter how remote those shit-spattered rocks and islands were, they were, in the end, part of the United States.

★

The story of the guano islands may seem trivial. After all, how important could a few dozen uninhabited islands be? Yet the guano craze of the nineteenth century left three legacies, all of which would shape the fate of the Greater United States.

The first was legal. The Guano Islands Act, the Supreme Court's ruling, and President Harrison's backing of that ruling collectively established that the borders of the United States needn't be confined to the continent. In 1889–90, when the Navassa controversy was in the news, this was a minor concern. But in the decades to come, it would be the foundation for the United States' entire overseas empire.

The second legacy was strategic. The same features that made the islands attractive rookeries for seabirds made them, decades later, desirable sites for airfields. The pointillist empire that the United States built after the Second World War would rely in part on those nineteenth-century guano claims.

The third and most immediate legacy was agricultural. In all, speculators scraped some four hundred thousand tons of rock guano off of U.S. appurtenances. That fell short of speculators' wildest hopes, but it was nevertheless a significant haul.

Guano didn't solve the soil exhaustion crisis, but combined with Chilean sodium nitrates, which companies started selling later in the century, it held it at bay. Mined fertilizers kept industrial agriculture sustainable long enough for scientists to devise a more permanent solution: manufacturing fertilizer from the unreactive N_2 in the atmosphere.

The breakthrough came in 1909, when Fritz Haber, a German-Jewish chemist, developed a technique for synthesizing ammonia, a nitrogen compound. By 1914, the experimental technique had become industrially viable, and in that year Haber's method, called the Haber–Bosch process, yielded as much reactive nitrogen as the entire Peruvian guano trade. The difference was that Haber–Bosch, unlike guano mining, was infinitely expandable. It also didn't require scouring the seas for uninhabited islands.

In a single stroke, Haber had opened the floodgates for the virtually unlimited growth of human life. The Malthusian logic was repealed. Soil exhaustion ceased to be an existential threat; you could just add more chemicals. Without Haber–Bosch, the earth could sustain, at present rates of consumption, only about 2.4 billion people. That is well under half of today's population.

By inventing ammonia synthesis, Fritz Haber became arguably the single most consequential organism on the planet. The toll on his personal life, however, was heavy. His wife, Clara, was herself a promising German-Jewish chemist, indeed the first woman ever to receive a doctorate from the University of Breslau. Local women had crowded there to see her get her degree—"seldom has the awarding of a doctorate been attended by so many," reported the newspaper. But after her marriage, Clara had abandoned her research and become a hausfrau, dedicating her life to supporting Fritz.

It was a *Picture of Dorian Gray* marriage: the more Fritz flourished, the more Clara withered. Just as her husband was honing his invention, Clara wrote an anguished letter to her former scientific mentor: "What Fritz has gained in these last eight years, that—and even more—I have lost, and what is left of me fills with the deepest dissatisfaction."

Fritz had gained quite a lot. His invention won him the directorship of a new institute in Berlin and a central place within the German scientific establishment (a position he used to promote the career of a gifted young Jewish physicist named Albert Einstein). When World War I erupted, Haber volunteered his services. He suggested that the ammonia now pouring out of German fertilizer plants could be repurposed as explosives to bolster Germany's dwindling munitions supplies. Since the war had cut Germany off from imported nitrates, this was an essential contribution. The president of the American Chemical Society calculated that Germany would have lost the war by early 1916 had Haber not replenished its stocks of nitrate explosives.

Nor did Haber stop there. He assembled a supergroup of German scientists, four of whom, like he, would go on to win Nobel Prizes. Overseeing their efforts, he introduced his second great invention: poison gas.

Not only did Haber invent it, he personally supervised its debut in 1915, releasing four hundred thousand tons of chlorine gas upwind of some Algerian troops at the Battle of Ypres. In a delicious historical irony, the man who saved the world from starvation was also the father of weapons of mass destruction.

For this, Haber won still more honors: a military commission, the Iron Cross, and an audience with the emperor. The only one who didn't appear to be celebrating was Clara. Right after gassing the Algerians at Ypres, Fritz returned home for a quick visit. What transpired between husband and wife during that visit is lost to history, but after Fritz went to sleep, Clara went into the garden with his service revolver and shot herself in the heart. The next day, Fritz returned to the front.

There is great interest in Clara today, especially in Germany, where she is celebrated as a martyr to science. No note from Clara survives, and Fritz refused to speak about the subject, so it is impossible to say with certainty why she killed herself. Surely, she had many reasons. But the timing of her suicide and some of the testimony from those who knew her have led many to interpret it as a protest of her husband's invention.

If it was, it was a prescient act. After the war, Fritz continued his work, and his institute developed a promising insecticide called Zyklon A. In slightly modified form, under the name Zyklon B, it would be deployed on Fritz and Clara's fellow Jews, though this time not on the battlefield, but in gas chambers. Clara's relatives were among those who died in the camps.

Luckily, not all of them perished. Although Clara's married name was Haber, she is today known by her maiden name, the name under which she defended her dissertation: Clara Immerwahr.

Her cousin Max was my great-grandfather.

4

TEDDY ROOSEVELT'S VERY GOOD DAY

If there was one symbol that defined the presidency in the age of the settlement boom, it was the log cabin. Voters delighted in imagining their leaders as cider-swilling men of the people, dwelling in rude houses, swinging axes, and fighting bears on the frontier. Candidates were only too happy to oblige, hyping their backcountry roots in their stump speeches.

It was largely show, though. Powerful men usually come from powerful places. There has never been a president born in a U.S. territory, and though a few spent time in the territories, they were rarely there for long. Young Abraham Lincoln and Zachary Taylor moved with their families to western territories, but only just before those territories became states (within months, in Lincoln's case). Andrew Jackson, Zachary Taylor, and William Henry Harrison worked in the territories later in life but in the service of the federally appointed territorial governments, not as settlers. Harrison, for whom the myth of the "log cabin" was invented, spent his childhood on a lavish Virginia plantation and lived in the Northwest Territory not in a cabin, but in the governor's residence.

Few leading politicians, in other words, actually participated in the settlement boom. Few, that is, except for Theodore Roosevelt.

As his five-dollar name suggests, Roosevelt was the scion of the Atlantic elite. He was born into the New York aristocracy—his father helped found the Metropolitan Museum of Art and the American Museum of

Natural History. Educated at Harvard and a rising star in the world of re-form politics, "Thee," as he signed his letters, was as pedigreed an eastern thoroughbred as the country could produce.

Yet there was something of the western mustang in him, too. In 1883 Roosevelt left New York for Dakota Territory, where he established a ranch on the border of the Badlands. There, he threw himself into frontier life with a convert's zeal. Unlike Harrison, he lived in a log cabin. For four years, punctuated by trips back east, Roosevelt felled trees, rounded up bandits, hunted, and braved the elements. His friends included the Wild West showman Buffalo Bill Cody; Pat Garrett, the man who shot Billy the Kid; and Seth Bullock, the famous sheriff of Deadwood.

These were glory days, which Roosevelt was only too happy to chronicle at length in a series of books: *Hunting Trips of a Ranchman* (1885), *Ranch Life and the Hunting Trail* (1888), *The Wilderness Hunter* (1893), and so on. They are tedious, repetitive volumes, largely concerned with his confrontations with wolves, deer, bobcats, and bears (in one retrospectively unsettling episode, Roosevelt shoots an eagle). Light on plot, the books contain mainly rustic wisdom from the trail: "The best way to kill whitetail is to still-hunt carefully through their haunts at dusk," or, "Antelope are very tough, and will carry off a great deal of lead unless struck in exactly the right place."

For the novice, the future president had words of encouragement. "A bear's brain is about the size of a pint bottle," he wrote. "Any one can hit a pint bottle offhand at thirty or forty feet."

Admittedly, there was something buffoonish about Thee's mountain-man routine—an overgrown boy playing cowboys and Indians. The make-believe element reached its peak in his Boone and Crockett Club, a national organization that championed "manliness, self-reliance, and a capacity for self-help" by promoting hunting. It principally drew eastern men of affairs—the banker J. P. Morgan, the politicians Elihu Root and Henry Stimson, and the Philadelphia-born, Paris- and Harvard-educated author Owen Wister, whose cowboy novel *The Virginian* (dedicated to Roosevelt) established the genre of the "Western."

Usually, the club met in Manhattan or Washington, D.C. In a gesture toward the strenuous life, though, Roosevelt arranged for a log cabin to be constructed for it amid the grand classical architecture at the World's Columbian Exposition in Chicago in 1893. There, surrounded by guns,

Go west, young Theodore:
Posing in his Dakota garb in a
New York studio, 1885

knives, playing cards, and lariats, he and his fellow Boone and Crockett-
eers dined and drank champagne on the dirt floor.

For Roosevelt, this went far beyond playacting. He really believed the
stuff. Like no president before or after, Roosevelt identified, viscerally, with
the historical forces that had extended the borders of the country west and
filled it with white settlers.

★

Roosevelt's frontier-centered view of the United States found expression
in *The Winning of the West*, his scholarly exploration of the "great deeds
of the border people" in four volumes. It was history red in tooth and claw.
Roosevelt showed little patience for the "statesmen of the Atlantic sea-
board" who were congenitally "unable to fully appreciate the magnitude
of the interests at stake in the west." In his telling, not George Washington and Thomas Jefferson, but Daniel Boone and Davy Crockett—fighting
Indians, hacking their way through the woods—were the true authors of
the nation's history.

The frontier skirmishes such men started were rough business, Roosevelt conceded, "peculiarly revolting and barbarous." But they were necessary. "The most ultimately righteous of all wars is a war with savages, though it is apt to be also the most terrible and inhuman," he wrote. "The rude, fierce settler who drives the savage from the land lays all civilized mankind under a debt to him."

Roosevelt styled himself as one of those rude, fierce settlers. Yet he didn't drive any savages from the land. He couldn't—he had come west too late. The "bloody fighting and protracted campaigns" were over, he noted with barely concealed regret. The closest he got was when he encountered a party of four or five armed Sioux on the hunting trail. They assured him that they were peaceful, he aimed his rifle at them, and they fled, swearing at him.

"The frontier proper has come to an end," mused a dejected Roosevelt in 1892.

He wasn't the only one to have that thought. A year later, the young historian Frederick Jackson Turner offered a similar reflection, stating it as a hypothesis, known today as the massively influential "frontier thesis." The frontier, Turner argued, had been the great regenerating force in U.S. life—the source of democracy, individualism, practicality, and freedom. And yet, Turner noted, according to the census, the frontier had disappeared as of 1890. The obvious danger was that the national character would die with it.

"I think you have struck some first class ideas," Roosevelt told Turner.

What Roosevelt and Turner had noticed was a fact not just about the United States, but about the world. For industrializing societies, the nineteenth century had been one of relatively easy expansion. The United States spread west, Russia spread east, and the European powers turned south, toward colonies in Asia and Africa.

Yet by the century's end, it looked finished. Indian Country had been ground down to a small nub, Africa was carved up, and even the Pacific islands, save some in the far south, were under the flag of distant governments. Add into the accounting such areas as Latin America, the Middle East, and China, which had been partitioned into spheres of influence and commercial control, and it was hard to see where future expansion might take place.

"The world is nearly all parcelled out, and what there is left of it is being divided up, conquered, and colonised," lamented the British arch-imperialist Cecil Rhodes. The global frontiers had been closed.

★

Roosevelt might have taken this as cause for despair. Yet just as he was reading Frederick Jackson Turner's warnings about the end of the frontier, he was also studying the work of another historian, Captain Alfred Thayer Mahan, of the Naval War College. Mahan's lengthy 1890 treatise, *The Influence of Sea Power upon History*, was hardly a page-turner, but it contained a powerful suggestion. If, according to Turner, the land was closed, Mahan noted that the seas were open.

Mahan didn't care about democracy or individualism, as Turner did. His concern was trade. The wealth of nations, he argued, came from maritime commerce. Yet ships could not simply cast off for distant lands. They needed ports, coaling stations, warehouses, and other way stations along their paths. They also needed naval protection, which required still more overseas bases.

Technically, a country needn't have its own bases. It could borrow them from friendly powers, as indeed the United States had done. But this worked only in peacetime—and in an age of closing frontiers, the peace among great powers had grown fragile. Mahan warned that war might close the seas to the United States. Its ships would then be "like land birds, unable to fly far from their own shores."

That was a serious matter. The more that countries industrialized, the more they depended on the produce of distant locales. They found themselves needing rubber from Southeast Asia, jute from India (for packaging), palm oil from West Africa (an industrial lubricant), tungsten from Korea (for lightbulb filaments), and copper from South America. At times, the Industrial Revolution could look like a worldwide scavenger hunt for obscure tropical products.

The United States got its first taste of this in the 1840s, when it realized that it couldn't run its farms without guano, which was available nowhere within its borders. One option would have been to buy it from abroad. But the machinations of the British-Peruvian guano monopoly inspired another solution: the United States could adjust its borders. That would give the country a measure of security. Even in war, the guano would keep flowing.

The point was general, applying far beyond guano. Annexing territory was a way to secure both sea routes and the vital tropical materials that one could reach by them.

As a naval theorist, Mahan was more concerned with the routes than with their destinations. He envisioned the ocean as a "great highway" and was determined to keep the United States on it. Technically, protecting and provisioning sea-lanes required only a series of points—safe harbors— along the way. But as Mahan recognized, to hold even a point in the face of hostile onslaught, you had to hold the territory around it. Hence the tendency of bases to bloom into full-fledged colonies.

Despite having written a long and dry historical work, Mahan found his ideas received with wild enthusiasm. *The Influence of Sea Power* was speedily translated into the major languages. Mahan dined with Queen Victoria and accepted honorary degrees from Oxford and Cambridge. Kaiser Wilhelm II, with whom Mahan also dined, wrote Mahan to say he was "devouring" the book; he ordered copies for every ship in the German fleet. Japan's naval academy adopted *The Influence of Sea Power* as a textbook.

In the United States, Mahan had an eager reader in Theodore Roosevelt. "During the last two days I have spent half my time, busy as I am, in reading your book," he wrote to Mahan. "I am greatly in error if it does not become a naval classic."

It was, in Roosevelt's eyes, more than a naval classic. It was a playbook for a dynamic country that had just encountered the limits to its growth. The United States must seize an empire. And if it had to carve it out of existing empires, so be it.

"I should welcome almost any war," Roosevelt declared in 1897, "for I think this country needs one."

★

It wasn't hard to guess where. In a world of rising empires, one was conspicuously faltering: Spain's. Once a vast imperium extending from California to Buenos Aires, it had been reduced, in the Western Hemisphere, to Cuba and Puerto Rico and, in the Pacific, to the Philippines and a set of Micronesian islands.

Even these, Spain could barely hold. The late nineteenth century had brought waves of rebellion to Cuba, the Philippines, and, to a lesser extent, Puerto Rico. Spain's grip was slipping most visibly in Cuba, which had seen the Ten Years' War (1868–78), the "Guerra Chiquita" (1879–1880), and smaller insurrections in 1883, 1885, 1892, and 1893 (two that year). In 1895, exiled Cuban rebels returned for yet another major war. The Philippines had its own series of uprisings, culminating in an all-out war in 1896.

There are two ways to respond to rebellion: with reforms or force. Madrid tried both. Cuba and Puerto Rico received new measures of political autonomy. But at the same time, Spain made war on Cuba's rebels—forcing the bulk of the rural population into fortified towns and turning the countryside into a free-fire zone. The predictable result was mass illness, starvation, and death. Hundreds of thousands of Cubans died.

In the Philippines, Spain's confusion about whether to conciliate or conquer found expression in its treatment of nationalist leaders. Spain executed the reformer Jose Rizal, a highly educated novelist and doctor whose modest goals fell short of full independence. The young revolutionary Emilio Aguinaldo, who called for guerrilla warfare, was paid off and sent to a cushy, voluntary exile in Hong Kong.

None of it worked. The rebellions continued, and as the body count in Cuba mounted, the whole thing became an international scandal. This was not "civilized warfare," scolded President William McKinley as he watched Spain massacre its Cuban subjects. "It was extermination."

The newspapers played it up, portraying Cuba as a damsel in distress, her dusky virtue besmirched by the rapacious Catholics of Spain. Should the United States enter the fray? Should it, perhaps, take over? The debate was long and loud. Roosevelt, then serving as assistant secretary of the navy, volunteered to personally invade Cuba. But opinions were decidedly mixed, and McKinley settled on a half measure. At Roosevelt's urging, he agreed to station a warship, the USS *Maine*, off the coast of Havana as a show of resolve. Beyond that, he would continue to wait.

Not for long, as it turned out. On February 15, 1898, the *Maine* mysteriously exploded, killing 262 men. It was, depending on the explanation, possibly an act of war.

"I don't propose to be swept off my feet by the catastrophe," wrote McKinley the next day. "The country can afford to withhold its judgment and not strike an avenging blow until the truth is known."

Roosevelt displayed none of McKinley's caution. "Dirty treachery on the part of the Spaniards" was his diagnosis, and the newspapers concurred.

"Remember the *Maine!*" replaced "Remember the Alamo!" as the battle cry of a wounded nation.

In retrospect, McKinley was right to hesitate. As far as we can tell, the *Maine's* explosion was probably the result of spontaneous combustion in its coal bunkers, a surprisingly common hazard at the time (barely a month later, the USS *Oregon's* coal stores spontaneously burst into flame). Whatever the cause, McKinley was loath to ramp up the conflict with Spain. "I have been through one war," he said, thinking of his service in the Civil War. "I have seen the dead piled up. I do not want to see another."

Roosevelt rolled his eyes. "McKinley is bent on peace, I fear."

★

Normally, when the president of the United States wants one thing and the assistant secretary of the navy wants another, both custom and Constitution dictate that the president prevails. But Roosevelt had an uncanny knack for orchestrating events in his favor.

It helped that he reported to John D. Long, the secretary of the navy, a mild-mannered, grandfatherly figure ("a perfect dear," cooed Roosevelt) given to prolonged absences. Roosevelt had little patience for bureaucratic details, but there was one he comprehended with the utmost clarity: whenever Long was gone, Roosevelt was, technically, the acting secretary of the navy.

On February 25, 1898, Long took the afternoon off to visit an osteopath, and Roosevelt sprang into action. He ordered all squadron commanders to keep their ships full of coal, requisitioned supplies of reserve ammunition, alerted station commanders to the possibility of war, and sent demands to both houses of Congress for the unlimited recruitment of seamen. Most fateful were the orders he sent to Commodore George Dewey of the Asiatic Squadron.

A casual observer might have wondered why a revolution in Cuba required the attentions of the Asiatic Squadron. But Roosevelt, emboldened by Mahan, envisioned an all-out attack on the Spanish Empire. He hoped that if war came, "Dewey could be slipped like a wolfhound from a leash." He thus ordered the commodore to amass his ships in Hong Kong and, in the event of war, attack the Philippines.

Secretary Long had instructed Roosevelt to "look after the routine of the office while I get a quiet day off." When he returned, he was astounded to find that his subordinate had instead laid the groundwork for a transoceanic war. Nevertheless, probably fearful of taking any action that the newspapers might interpret as weakness, Long allowed Roosevelt's orders to stand.

Predictably, McKinley succumbed to popular sentiment and agreed to war. Anti-imperialists in Congress, determined to prevent the affair from spiraling out of control, passed an amendment to the war declaration: the United States could fight Spain, but it couldn't annex Cuba.

That amendment said nothing, however, about the Philippines, to which Commodore Dewey sailed with all due haste.

★

The Battle of Manila Bay, as the resulting conflict was known, made an auspicious start to the war. "Nineteenth century civilization and fifteenth century medievalism lay confronting each other" is how Dewey's aide described the scene. In just over six hours on May 1, 1898, Dewey sank or captured every Spanish ship. The captain of Spain's flagship was killed. The commander of Spain's shoreside batteries committed suicide.

The only U.S. fatality was due to a heart attack.

"That night the scene was awful but grand," reported the crew members of Dewey's flagship as they watched Spain's fleet burn. "Occasionally a magazine would burst, like the eruption of volcano, throwing its flaming debris high into the air."

McKinley, meanwhile, called for 125,000 volunteers to carry the war to the Caribbean. The army was swamped with applicants. And bouncing up and down enthusiastically at the head of the line was one Theodore Roosevelt, assistant secretary of the navy.

Roosevelt's eagerness to leave his post and join the army baffled his friends. "Is his wife dead? Has he quarreled with everybody? Is he quite mad?" asked the historian Henry Adams.

Congress had authorized the formation of three volunteer cavalry regiments, and Roosevelt was offered command of one. In a rare act of self-effacement, he declined, instead arranging to have his friend Leonard Wood take the job, at the rank of colonel. Roosevelt accepted the lower rank of lieutenant colonel and began to gather his men.

The First Volunteer Cavalry recruited from all over the country, and Roosevelt was proud to draw to his ranks not only Harvard men but Yale and Princeton graduates as well. Yet the Ivy Leaguers made up only a small portion of the regiment. To Roosevelt's delight, most of its recruits came from the territories, from "the lands that have been most recently won over to white civilization, and in which the conditions of life are nearest to those that obtained on the frontier when there still was a frontier": Arizona, New Mexico, Oklahoma, and Indian Country. The First Volunteer Cavalry, better known as the Rough Riders, included numerous men who boasted Indian-fighting on their résumés.

Curiously, the regiment also had a few Native Americans. Roosevelt took pride in this, too, though he believed that those lacking white ancestry were of a "wilder type," requiring "rough discipline" from him. "And they got it, too," he wrote.

His unit complete, Roosevelt set out for Cuba. He traveled with two horses, his black manservant ("the most faithful and loyal of men"), a revolver that had been pulled from the wreck of the *Maine,* and his copy of Edmond Demolins's book *Anglo-Saxon Superiority.* The regiment landed easily at Daiquirí and made its way west to Santiago de Cuba, the center of Spain's forces.

★

What happened next has been recounted so many times that it's hard to register how bizarre it was. That the man who played such an important part in starting and expanding the war—a political appointee with no combat experience—should also become the hero of its decisive battle seems more fictional than factual. But an aura of "Wait, that really happened?" engulfed much of Theodore Roosevelt's life.

After all, this was a man who was in turn a Harvard student, cowboy, policeman, war hero, and president, as well as an African explorer—virtually the entire list of boyhood fantasies, minus astronaut. Later in life, as he was about to speak at a campaign event, Roosevelt got shot in the chest at close range and then *proceeded to give his intended speech for an hour* as the blood ran from his body.

So, the battle for the San Juan Heights. It began simply enough. Spain held the hills outside Santiago; the United States wanted them. The Rough Riders stood fifth in line, behind four other regiments, to take Kettle Hill. Meanwhile, another division was charged with capturing the more important San Juan Hill, half a mile away.

Roosevelt bristled at his placement at the back and requested repeatedly to enter the fray. He finally got permission to "support the regulars in the assault." That was all he needed. "The instant I received the order I sprang on my horse and then my 'crowded hour' began."

The horse was important. A transportation logjam en route to Cuba had forced the enlisted Rough Riders to leave their mounts back home, so Roosevelt, as an officer, was one of the few with a horse. That made him faster, but also a target. Undaunted, he rode to the front of the line, ordering his men to follow on foot.

The novelist Stephen Crane, watching from a distance, saw only "a thin line of black figures moving across a field." From Roosevelt's perspective, the dash up Kettle Hill was more dramatic. He lustily galloped up and down the line, "passing the shouting, cheering, firing men." A bullet grazed his elbow as the Rough Riders took the hill.

He could have stopped there, with a wound and a story to tell, but he looked over to San Juan Hill, where a U.S. division had engaged the Spanish, and judged he could take that, too. He let his horse go, jumped a fence, and with a handful of men ("bullets were ripping the grass all around us") charged on foot. Looking back to see no one following, Roosevelt ran *back* to Kettle Hill (still under fire), hopped back over the fence, and berated his troops. Now, with his men finally behind him, he crossed the fence a third time, crested the hill, and killed a Spaniard with his *Maine*-salvaged revolver.

Right after that, with the Spaniards subdued, Roosevelt and the Rough Riders repeated their charge for the benefit of a film crew—the first documentary battle footage ever shot.

★

After San Juan Heights, things fell swiftly into place. U.S. troops laid siege to Santiago de Cuba, and U.S. ships defeated the Spanish fleet outside the city. The Spanish surrendered the city within the month. In Puerto Rico, too, Spanish resistance collapsed quickly; the ground campaign lasted seventeen days and cost only seven U.S. lives. In Manila, the Spanish fought an honor-preserving mock battle, in which they put up a token fight before surrendering.

It was a complete rout. The empire that had once dominated the Americas had been defeated entirely in less than four months—a "splendid little war," the ambassador to Britain remarked to Roosevelt. Back home, writers crowed about the vigor of the United States and the decrepitude of Spain. The Spanish empire was a "house of cards," wrote Woodrow Wilson. "When the American power touched it it fell to pieces." The president of Stanford offered a similar explanation: "We succeeded because we were bigger, richer, and far more capable than our enemy."

Well, maybe.

It's easy to regard Spain as an obsolete feudal power—the Sick Man of the Caribbean. But Spain had a sizable and seasoned imperial army. Its 200,000 troops in Cuba, 30,000 in the Philippines, and 8,000 in Puerto Rico easily outnumbered the 25,000 officers and men that the United States had on hand on the eve of the war. McKinley hastily inflated the army to some 275,000 troops, but it reached that size only at the end of the war, well after the major battles had been won.

How did the United States, outmatched on paper, win so decisively?

Part of the answer, mentioned frequently, is that the U.S. Navy was in better shape than the Spanish one (the consequence of Mahan's influence). But another part, too often ignored, is that the United States was not the only adversary Spain was fighting. The war is usually called the Spanish-American War and is said to have started in 1898. Yet a more accurate name would be the Spanish–Cuban–Puerto Rican–Philippine–American War. Cubans call it the War of 1895, Filipinos date its start at 1896—and neither of those counts the many earlier uprisings and wars.

The United States was, in other words, a latecomer, supplying a burst of force at the end of a long, bloody conflict that had already nearly destroyed the Spanish Empire.

By January 1898, four months before the United States entered the fray, Máximo Gómez, the leader of the Cuban army, described the conflict as a "dead war." Gómez had fought Spain for three decades, but, for the first time, he saw victory clearly in view. "This war cannot last more than a year," he predicted, accurately.

The United States relied on men like Gómez. Roosevelt himself remarked on how easily his regiment had landed at Daiquirí. As few as five hundred Spanish troops could have presented "very great difficulties" to the Rough Riders had they been there to defend the coast, he noted. But the Spanish *weren't* there, and the reason they weren't is that the Cuban army had just run them off. Similarly, the thirty thousand Spanish troops in Oriente Province had not been able to relieve the besieged eight thousand Spanish soldiers in Santiago because Cuban forces had them pinned down.

The pattern held in the Philippines. TELL AGUINALDO COME SOON AS POSSIBLE was Commodore Dewey's cable in the days before he sailed to Manila. Dewey demolished the Spanish fleet and blockaded Manila Bay, but his whole force consisted of 1,743 officers and men. Even with reinforcements, he lacked the power to defeat Spain on land. There, he deferred to Emilio Aguinaldo, the exiled revolutionary, whose forces took city after city in the coming months.

Aguinaldo's operations were carried out with "the greatest vigor and with unvaried success," reported one U.S. writer. "By day we could see their attacks," remembered Dewey, "and by night we heard their firing."

★

Cubans, Filipinos, and (to a much lesser degree) Puerto Ricans had fought Spain for decades, draining its resources and exhausting its morale. Yet little of this registered in the United States. Right after landing in Cuba—the landing enabled by the Cuban defeat of Spanish troops at Daiquirí—Roosevelt eyed his Cuban allies and judged them to be "utter tatterdemalions" of "no use in serious fighting."

"We should have been better off if there had not been a single Cuban with the army," he wrote. "They accomplished literally nothing."

That judgment, which was shared widely, mattered. Feeling that Cubans had contributed little to the war, U.S. commanders felt no compunctions about sidelining them from the peace. Thus did they negotiate first the surrender of Santiago and then of Cuba directly with Spain, excluding the Cubans. Leonard Wood, Roosevelt's friend and the Rough Riders' commanding officer, took charge of Santiago.

The Cuban general Calixto García resigned in protest. "I will never accept that our country be considered as conquered territory," he said. But what could García do? The Cubans, just like the Spanish, were exhausted by decades of harrowing war. Taking on a fresh adversary was hard to contemplate.

It wasn't much different in the Philippines. There, Aguinaldo's forces had liberated most major cities and were laying siege to Manila. Aguinaldo understood all this to be part of the independence war of the Philippines, and in fact had already issued a declaration of independence, raised a flag, and played the Philippine national anthem. Yet, as in Cuba, Spain surrendered to the United States, not the local rebels. When the U.S. and Spanish forces brokered their secret agreement to stage a mock battle over Manila, it was on the condition that the Spaniards relinquish the city to U.S. troops only and that Filipinos not be allowed to enter.

As the Spanish governor-general explained, he was "willing to surrender to white people but never to Niggers."

Filipinos who had besieged Manila for two and a half months, at the cost of thousands of lives, thus watched in astonishment as their allies entered the city unopposed, locked Filipino soldiers out, and fraternized with the enemy.

One minute after the Spanish flag came down over Manila, an enormous U.S. flag climbed the flagpole in its place. The band struck up "The Star-Spangled Banner."

★

The war may have begun as an empire-wide revolt by Spain's colonial subjects, but it ended as the "Spanish-American War." The peace treaty, negotiated in Paris, was between Spain and the United States alone. Spain sold the Philippines to the United States for $20 million. Puerto Rico and Guam (a Micronesian island, valuable as a Mahan-style base) came free. Because of the amendment anti-imperialists had passed, the United States couldn't annex Cuba. But it could *occupy* it, placing the country under military control until a suitable government could be installed—a government suitable to Washington, that is.

No representative from Cuba, Puerto Rico, the Philippines, or Guam had a say in any of this. It's doubtful that they would have agreed to it. "This is not the Republic we fought for, this is not the absolute independence we dreamed about," said a bitter Máximo Gómez.

But it was pretty close to what Teddy Roosevelt had fought for and dreamed about.

5

EMPIRE STATE OF MIND

It had all happened very fast for William McKinley. Imperial affairs were far outside his ken. Speaking of the Philippines, he supposedly confided to a friend that before the war with Spain, he "could not have told where those darned islands were within two thousand miles."

The geography section, moreover, was the easiest part of the exam. The real head-scratcher was the final essay question, worth most of the grade: *Having seized Spain's empire, what should the United States do with it? Explain your answer with reference to economics, geostrategy, and the prevailing racial ideologies of the late nineteenth century.*

The question was particularly vexing with respect to the distant and populous Philippine Islands. They were near China, and thus potential stepping-stones in a trade empire of the sort that Alfred Thayer Mahan had proposed. Yet the United States had no existing business in the Philippines—by one count, there were fewer than ten U.S. citizens there when the war broke out. Commodore Dewey doubted that Washington would take more than a coaling station.

But that was before Dewey dispatched the Spanish fleet to the bottom of Manila Bay, before Teddy Roosevelt crested San Juan Heights. The collapse of Spain's beleaguered empire placed the whole Philippine archipelago in McKinley's surprised hands. What to do? Return the islands to Spain? Sell them? Leave them be? "I walked the floor of the White House night after night until midnight," McKinley explained to an audience of churchmen, "and I am not ashamed to tell you, gentlemen, that I went down on my knees and prayed Almighty God for light and guidance more than one night."

To McKinley, none of the choices was particularly appetizing. Returning the colony to Spain would be "cowardly," handing it over to anyone else would be "bad business." He doubted that Filipinos could govern themselves. He thus saw only one option: take the Philippines, "educate the Filipinos, and uplift and civilize and Christianize them, and by God's grace do the very best we could for them, as our fellow-men for whom Christ also died."

Resolute, he sent for the War Department's cartographer. "I told him to put the Philippines on the map of the United States," he remembered, pointing to the map in question, "and there they are."

★

Indeed, there they were. The war with Spain gave rise to the only moment in U.S. history when cartographers aggressively rejected the logo map. In its place they offered maps of the empire. Publishers, cashing in on empire fever, rushed to put out atlases showcasing the country's new dimensions.

"It does look a little bit odd to see Porto Rico, Hawaii, and the distant Philippine islands on the United States map," reflected one writer. "But there they are and printed as carefully and described as carefully as if they had been for a whole generation in their present honored company."

By 1900, such maps were common. They appeared as a matter of course in atlases, on classroom walls, in textbooks, and at the front of the census report. Some showed the North American mainland surrounded by insets. Others showed the United States stretching out over the world map, from the Caribbean to the edge of China. Either way, the message was clear: the country had undergone a metamorphosis. The caterpillar had unfurled its butterfly wings.

Writers, too, sensed the change and searched for a new name for the transformed country. They offered suggestions in the titles of books: *Imperial America* (1898), *The Greater Republic* (1899), *The Greater United States* (1904), and seven books published in the decade after 1898 whose titles involved the phrase *Greater America*.

"The term 'United States of America' has ceased to be an accurate description of the countries over which the Stars and Stripes float," the au-

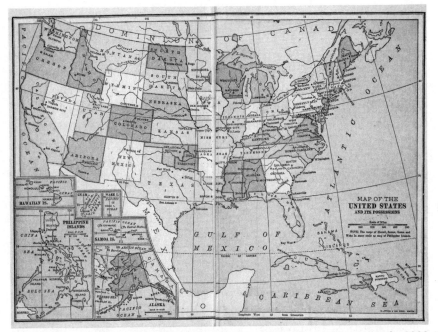

The Greater United States: Maps like this, taken from the inside cover of a 1900 history textbook, appeared frequently starting in 1899, often as the principal maps of the United States. Shown, along with the states, are a much-diminished Indian Country, as well as Hawai'i, Guam, Wake, American Samoa, the Philippines, Alaska, Cuba, and Puerto Rico.

thor of one argued. "Like 'United Kingdom,' it applies merely to the central and dominating body, the seat of empire; and Greater America comprises almost as wide a range of governments as Greater Britain itself."

★

The term "United States of America" has ceased to be an accurate description. It was a remarkable observation. And it gave rise not only to a transient bout of verbal creativity but to a much more enduring nomenclatural shift.

Although the country's official name has always been the United States of America, in the nineteenth century it was common to call it the United States, or perhaps refer to it by its political structure: the Republic or the Union. Though inhabitants of the country were often called Americans, it is striking how infrequently *America* was used. Walt Whitman was fond of the term, as in "I Hear America Singing" (1860) or the Young America movement of which he was a member (Herman Melville, another member, also used *America* at times). But one can search through all the messages and public papers of the presidents—including annual messages, inaugural addresses, proclamations, special messages to Congress, and much more—from the founding to 1898 and encounter only eleven unambiguous references to the country as America, about one per decade.

Nor was the word *America* included in the patriotic songs that got sung before 1898. You won't find it in the lyrics to "Yankee Doodle," "Hail to the Chief," "My Country 'Tis of Thee," "Dixie," "The Battle Cry of Freedom," "The Battle Hymn of the Republic," or "The Stars and Stripes Forever." It isn't even in "The Star-Spangled Banner," the 1814 composition later adopted as the national anthem. The word that does appear in nineteenth-century lyrics is *Columbia*, as in the District of Columbia, an earlier literary name for the country. Though they have fallen from favor today, "Columbia," "Hail, Columbia," and "Columbia, the Gem of the Ocean" were among the most sung anthems of the nineteenth century.

Somewhere around the turn of the century, though, all that changed. One sharp-eared British writer heard the switch. "For some thirty years prior to 1898, while the adjective 'American' has been in general use, the noun 'America' has been extremely rare," he wrote. "One might, up to that *annus mirabilis*, have travelled five thousand miles and read a hundred books and newspapers without ever having once come across it; 'United States' being almost invariably the term employed by the American for his own country." After 1898, though, he noted that "the best speakers and writers," feeling that *the United States* no longer captured the nature of their country, switched to *America*.

If the "best speakers and writers" could be stretched to include presidents, that was true. Though McKinley, like most of his predecessors, declined to use *America* in his public addresses, the reluctance ended there. His successor, Theodore Roosevelt, spoke of America in his first annual message and never looked back. In one two-week period, Roosevelt used the name more than all his predecessors combined had. Every president since has used *America* freely and frequently.

The anthems changed, too: no longer "Columbia, the Gem of the Ocean," but "America the Beautiful" and "God Bless America."

★

Eighteen ninety-eight was a momentous break from the past, requiring new maps and names. But, one might ask, why? Hadn't the country contained both states and territories from the start? Hadn't the borders been in motion since the Louisiana Purchase? Why were new names needed only now?

It's true that the United States had been annexing territory for nearly a century. But there was something different about the post-1898 acquisitions. It wasn't the land. It was the people who lived on it.

Looking back on the years before 1898, one sees a pattern. Though the United States had rapidly annexed new territory, it had rarely incorporated large nonwhite populations. Louisiana, Florida, Oregon, Texas, and the Mexican cessions—these added a lot of area to the country but only relatively small "foreign" populations (Native Americans mainly, but also Mexicans, Spaniards, French, and, in the case of Louisiana, free blacks).

Before 1898, the largest population bump from annexation came from the lands wrested from Mexico (including Texas) between 1845 and 1853. Yet, as bumps go, it wasn't much. While those accessions enlarged the country's area by 69 percent, the accompanying Indians and Mexicans increased its population by less than 1.5 percent over eight years. In the demographically explosive United States, where the population was already growing at more than 3 percent a year, that small influx was easily diluted: a sprinkler in a rainstorm.

This was no accident. The Mexican War of 1846–48 had ended with U.S. forces occupying Mexico City. Some in Congress proposed taking all of Mexico. From a military perspective, that was entirely feasible. But South Carolina senator John C. Calhoun, one of the nation's prime defenders of slavery, objected. "We have never dreamt of incorporating into the Union any but the Caucasian race—the free white race," he insisted on the Senate floor. "Are we to associate with ourselves, as equals, companions, and fellow-citizens, the Indians and mixed races of Mexico?"

Apparently not. The United States annexed the thinly populated northern part of Mexico (including present-day California, Utah, New Mexico, and Arizona) but let the populous southern part go. This carefully drawn border gave the United States, as one newspaper put it, "all the territory of value that we can get without taking the people."

A few wished to go farther. Some proslavery advocates, worried that the booming white settler population might crowd out slavery, sought room for their way of life farther south. They staged a series of "filibusters," private invasions of Latin American republics that, they hoped, would lead to annexations. The most dramatic was William Walker's invasion of Nicaragua in 1855, which improbably propelled Walker briefly to the Nicaraguan presidency.

But Walker was disappointed (and, in 1860, executed). Washington didn't back him, nor did it support the other filibusters. The problem wasn't that men like Walker wanted to expand slavery. The problem was that they wanted to do so by bringing more Latin Americans into the union.

Combine a republican commitment to equality with an accompanying commitment to white supremacy, and this is what you got: a rapidly expanding empire of settlers that fed on land but avoided incorporating people. Uninhabited guano islands—those were fine. But all of Mexico or Nicaragua? No.

In the late 1860s the president of the Dominican Republic signaled that he would welcome the U.S. purchase of his country. President Ulysses S. Grant was eager for the deal—the Dominican Republic was, after all, prime sugar and coffee real estate. Yet even with a rich country served up on a plate, even at the urging of a popular war-hero president whose party controlled Congress, legislators wouldn't swallow the bait. The Dominican Republic was "situated in tropical waters, and occupied by another race, of another color," explained the Massachusetts senator Charles Sumner, and "never can become a permanent possession of the United States."

Alaska, which Andrew Johnson's administration sought to purchase from Russia in 1867, encountered the same resistance. "We do not want . . . Exquimaux fellow citizens," griped *The Nation*. The deal went through only because, in the end, there weren't that many "Exquimaux," and there was quite a lot of Alaska.

Exactly how many Alaska Natives there were is hard to say. The U.S. census did not count them. This was the flip side to the careful annexations, another way to control who was part of the country and who wasn't. From the start, the census had declined to count most indigenous people. Thus, for more than a century, a government that had reliable decennial tallies of its toymakers and chimney sweeps, of its cows and its horses, could not say how many Indians lived within its borders.

When the census did begin to count Alaska Natives, in 1880, and mainland Indians, in 1890, it separated them from the rest of the population lest they contaminate statistics about "the United States." This was the start of the segregated census, the practice of taking some of the enumerated inhabitants to be part of the country and consigning others to a sort of statistical purgatory. In the 1890 census report, you have to turn to page 963 and look in the middle of a paragraph to learn—reported as minor trivia— that the full population of the country, including Natives, was 62,979,766.

★

Excluding Natives from the census was symbolically significant, sustaining the fantasy that settlers were taming an uninhabited wilderness. But statistically, it was less important. In 1890 those page-963 Indians and Alaskans made up only 0.57 percent of the population, the consequence of the dwindling of Native populations and the explosion of Anglo ones.

By 1898, things were different. Spain's colonies were not sparsely settled. In fact, they were more densely populated than the United States was. Their populations were large, too: experts estimated nearly 8 million in the Philippines, Puerto Rico, and Guam. That was more than 10 percent of the U.S. population and nearly equal to the size of the African American population (8.8 million). Further, given the serious doubts at the time as to whether Anglo-Saxons could live in the tropics, it seemed unlikely that the inhabitants of Spain's island colonies would ever be displaced by whites in the way that the Native Americans had.

This was, in other words, a different kind of expansion, reminiscent of the failed vision for Indian Country. Not taking land and flooding it with settlers, but conquering subject populations and ruling them. "It is one thing to admit scattered communities of white, or nearly white, men into the rights of citizenship," one writer put it, "but quite a different matter to act in the same way with a closely packed and numerous brown people." Or as the skeptical Speaker of the House put it, less politely, "I s'posed we had niggers enough in this country without buyin' any more of 'em."

Yet opponents of empire, such as the Speaker, could do little about the heady rush that gripped the country in 1898. The economic tumult at home, the scramble for colonies abroad, the collapse of Spain, and Commodore Dewey's stunning naval triumph—it all came quickly, and it all pointed in the same direction. Anti-imperialists who had successfully blocked expansion into the tropics for decades found the ground crumbling underfoot. Before the war, they had won unanimous passage for a law preventing the United States from annexing Cuba. But now, with war fever high and with the military actually *in* Spain's colonies, they could only watch in mute astonishment as the machine rolled past Cuba, on to nearby Puerto Rico, far-off Guam, and the enormous Philippines.

And it kept rolling. With the logjam broken, expansionists seized the moment to push through long-stalled legislation to acquire Hawai'i, an island kingdom whose economy U.S. planters had gradually taken control of. The usual reluctance to incorporate nonwhite peoples (it would be a "pigmy State of the Union," scoffed the *Chicago Herald*) could no longer hold in the face of the argument that Dewey required Hawai'i to control the Pacific. "We ought to take Hawaii, in the interests of the White race," Roosevelt pressed. And so, over the protests of Native Hawaiians, more than thirty-eight thousand of whom had signed anti-annexation petitions, the United States seized the islands.

The next two years, 1899–1900, saw the United States annexing half of Samoa, another Pacific stronghold that had long been of interest, along with the uninhabited Wake Island.

By the time the shooting stopped and the treaties were ratified, the United States had gained more than seven thousand islands holding 8.5 million people. Counting Alaska, the overseas empire encompassed an area nearly as large as the entire United States had been in 1784 and held a population of more than twice the size.

★

This was, not surprisingly, a controversial matter. During the war, during the congressional debates over the treaty with Spain, and during the heated election of 1900, the question of empire was argued at high volume.

In essence, it was an argument about a trilemma. Republicanism, white supremacy, and overseas expansion—the country could have at most two. In the past, republicanism and white supremacy had been jointly maintained by carefully shaping the country's borders. But absorbing populous nonwhite colonies would wreck all that.

The opponents of empire gathered behind William Jennings Bryan, who had run against McKinley in 1896 and did so again in 1900. Bryan delighted in exposing the contradictions between republicanism and empire. The inalienable rights of man and the injustice of taxation without representation—these were bedrock political values. But imagine, Bryan warned, what would happen if the United States took colonies. Anyone setting forth to speak about republican virtues—say, at a Fourth of July celebration—would be urged to keep silent "lest his utterances excite rebellion among distant subjects."

It was a compelling argument, and Bryan commanded a large and motley coalition of anti-imperialists. It included such African Americans as W.E.B. Du Bois and hard-line white supremacists such as Senator "Pitchfork" Ben Tillman of South Carolina. Businessmen (Andrew Carnegie, who offered to buy the Philippines for $20 million so he could set it free) and labor leaders (Samuel Gompers, president of the AFL) joined the cause. So did the presidents of Harvard, Cornell, Stanford, Michigan, and Northwestern.

But empire, once seized, was hard to drop. Roosevelt wanted it, and behind him stood the bulk of the Republican political establishment. For many, it was a matter of more than just the economic benefits that Alfred Thayer Mahan had promised. As they saw it, overseas colonization was the next phase of Manifest Destiny, the next outlet for the Daniel Boones of the country. "God has given us this Pacific empire for civilization," said Senator Albert Beveridge. "A hundred wildernesses are to be subdued. Unpenetrated regions must be explored. Unviolated valleys must be tilled. Unmastered forests must be felled."

The imperialists offered a different solution to the trilemma. They were willing to sacrifice republicanism, at least as applied to so-called backward races. Roosevelt scorned those "who cant about 'liberty' and the 'consent of the governed,' in order to excuse themselves for their unwillingness to play the part of men." He continued: "Their doctrines, if carried out, would make it incumbent upon us to leave the Apaches of Arizona to work out their own salvation, and to decline to interfere in a single Indian reservation. Their doctrines condemn your forefathers and mine for ever having settled in these United States."

There was, of course, a third option: jettison white supremacy. The overseas territories could be treated as embryonic states and their inhabitants as full citizens. This solution commanded a great deal of enthusiasm within the territories themselves, where political parties in Puerto Rico and the Philippines inserted demands for statehood into their platforms. With the western continental territories in mind, they imagined their countries, in time, entering the union as equals.

Yet mainland support for this was scant. When the prospect of state-hood came up, it did so mainly as a scare tactic—a way for anti-imperialists to underscore the horrors resulting from annexing these places.

At any rate, colonized subjects had little chance to press their case. What is remarkable, in fact, about the mainland debates over empire is how utterly absent Filipinos, Puerto Ricans, Hawaiians, and other inhabitants of the territories were from them. Most mainlanders had never even *seen* a Filipino, a Puerto Rican, or a Hawaiian.

★

It was precisely to address the yawning chasm of ignorance around the colonies that a group of Omaha businessmen staged the First Greater America Colonial Exposition. The late nineteenth century was a great time for fairs, and this one pulled out all the usual stops: mock battles, speeches, parades, and a "World's Congress of Beauties." The main attraction, though, was colonized people. The organizers promised "over a thousand natives of Uncle Sam's insular possessions"—Filipinos, Cubans, Puerto Ricans, and Hawaiians. The Filipino contingent would include not only "civilized Tagals" but "half-wild, monkey-like dwarfs of the interior of Luzon."

Ostensibly, this was a way for the public to meet the people at the center of the empire controversy. But it's telling to note *how* the public would meet them: not giving lectures or speaking with fairgoers, but living on display in model villages, as if they were animals in a zoo.

A "large encampment of Indians from all the various tribes of the great West" would be there, too, just to round out the picture.

Fulfilling these promises meant recruiting colonized subjects and hauling them to the mainland. This wasn't easy. Even with the support of the army and the personal backing of President McKinley, the fair's organizers could induce only thirty-five Filipinos to board the USS *Indiana* for San Francisco. And getting them onto the ship turned out to be the easy part. When the *Indiana* arrived, immigration authorities wouldn't let them disembark.

The Filipinos, languishing for days on board, protested. They were, they maintained, U.S. citizens, fully entitled to move from one part of their new country to another. But the port officers refused to budge. In their eyes, the Filipinos were foreigners and, worse, Asian foreigners, subject to

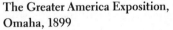

The Greater America Exposition, Omaha, 1899

the same racial exclusion laws that prevented Chinese workers from entering.

The Greater America Exposition had intended to explore the questions of empire. Yet here its organizers had inadvertently raised the knottiest one of all. The territories were on the maps, yes. But were the people who lived in them "Americans"?

★

The Filipinos made it to Omaha (though the secretary of war had to personally promise that they would return home after the fair). There, they made an impression. "They are stylish dressers," wrote the *Omaha Bee*, resembling less a "race of savages" than "a lot of dudes" with their canes, derby hats, and white trousers. Fairgoers expecting the Filipino band to offer exotic folk music were surprised when it struck up a lively rendition of "There'll Be a Hot Time in the Old Town Tonight," the theme song for Roosevelt's Rough Riders. Culturally, the fair's Filipinos seemed to embrace their new nationality.

Legally, however, things remained unresolved. The Fourteenth

Amendment granted citizenship to anyone born in the United States. Did that include the territories?

The 1898–1900 annexations had already raised the question of what the United States *was*, in language and on maps. Now it was coming up in law. And it made its way to the Supreme Court, via a series of connected cases, in 1901.

Weighty legal questions often turn around trivial disputes. Certainly the cases that carried this question up to the Supreme Court seemed piddling: whether an importer shipping oranges from Puerto Rico to New York had to pay a tariff, or whether a soldier returning from the Philippines owed taxes on the diamond rings he'd acquired there. But under them lay a deeper question. The Constitution prohibits taxing commerce between parts of the United States. Did that rule cover the overseas territories, too? In other words, were they part of the country?

The government, which had collected the tariffs, sought to defend its actions. It argued that the term *the United States* was ambiguous. The name could refer to all the area under U.S. jurisdiction, but it could also refer, in a narrower sense, to the union of states. The Constitution's references to "the United States," the argument continued, were meant in that narrow sense, to refer to the states alone. Territories thus had no right to constitutional protections, for the simple reason that the Constitution didn't apply to them. As one justice summarized the logic, the Constitution was "the supreme law of the land," but the territories were "not part of the 'land.'"

This might have come as a surprise to residents of the western territories, who had assumed that they had the same constitutional protections as their compatriots in the states. But, the attorney general maintained, that was a polite fiction with little basis in law. Mincing few words, he reminded the justices that Congress could impose laws on the territories "without asking the consent of the inhabitants, even against their consent and against their protest, as it has frequently done." He brought up Congress's dismantling of Indian Country, and he noted that Alaskans had "no right to elect a single officer, or to form a city, or to establish a political system or anything whatever for their own protection." The overseas territories—which he referred to openly as "colonies"—were no different. The Filipinos in San Francisco Bay had it wrong; they were subjects, not citizens.

This was precisely the sort of talk that raised anti-imperialists' hackles, but the attorney general plowed on. "To be called an American subject is no disgrace," he consoled. Moreover, he continued, the government *needed* the ability to rule its possessions as colonies. This was the age of empire. What if the United States were to annex Egypt, Sudan, part of Central Africa, or "a section of the Chinese Empire"? Would it be forced to apply the Constitution to those places, too? "A great world power, extending its domain from the frozen seas on the North to where the encircling palm trees grow in the Pacific islands, must not be bound by rules too strict or too confining."

The argument prevailed. The court affirmed that "the Constitution deals with states" and that territorial rights were at Congress's discretion. Congress could, if it wished, "incorporate" territories into the union and bring them under the protection of the Constitution, as the court judged that it had in the case of the western territories. Some years later, the court also concluded that Alaska and Hawai'i, the territories beyond the mainland that seemed the most conducive to white settlement, had also been "incorporated." But the point was that incorporation was not automatic, and the court repeatedly denied that Congress had ever incorporated the former Spanish colonies.

Invoking the notion that there were different "senses" of "the United States," a concurring justice articulated the reasoning in a notoriously convoluted phrase. Puerto Rico was "foreign to the United States in a domestic sense," he explained, "because the island had not been incorporated into the United States, but was merely appurtenant thereto as a possession."

Lawyers with long memories would have recognized in that unusual word, *appurtenant*, a reference to the Navassa Island case of more than a decade before. There, the defense had argued that although the guano islands were "appertaining to the United States," they weren't *part* of it, and thus weren't subject to U.S. law. The Supreme Court had disagreed. But whereas the Navassa case had affirmed the government's power to apply federal laws in its territories, the new rulings denied territorial inhabitants the right to federal protections.

★

The 1901 rulings are collectively known as the Insular Cases (the term can also encompass some later cases). But they are not the cases for which the turn-of-the-century court is best known. Eight of the nine justices who de-cided the 1901 Insular Cases also decided *Plessy v. Ferguson* (1896), the notorious case that upheld the constitutionality of "separate but equal" Jim Crow institutions.

On the face of it, the two rulings have much in common. *Plessy* per-mitted segregation, the division of the country into separate spaces, some reserved for whites, others for nonwhites. The Insular Cases split the coun-try into what one justice called "practically two national governments," one bound by the Bill of Rights, the other not.

And, like *Plessy*, the Insular Cases were about race. The main majority decision contained warnings about including "savages" and "alien races" within the constitutional fold. Doing so, one of the justices concurred, would "wreck our institutions," perhaps leading the "whole structure of the government" to be "overthrown."

Yet there is one critical difference between *Plessy* and the Insular Cases. In 1954, in *Brown v. Board of Education*, the Supreme Court over-turned *Plessy*, declaring "separate but equal" facilities to be incapable of securing equality under the law. Today we regard *Plessy* as one of the court's greatest mistakes, an infamously racist ruling that warped the Con-stitution to deprive millions of citizens of their rights.

The Insular Cases are far less well-known. Until very recently, it was not unusual for constitutional scholars to have never heard of them. But they are nevertheless still on the books, and they are still cited as good law. The court has repeatedly upheld the principle that the Constitution applies to some parts of the country but not others. That's why a citizen on the mainland has a constitutional right to trial by jury, but when that citizen travels to Puerto Rico, the right vanishes.

Similarly, the Fourteenth Amendment's citizenship guarantee to anyone born in the United States doesn't apply to the unincorporated territories. In them, citizenship came late and only after struggle. What is more, it arrived as "statutory citizenship," meaning that it was secured by legisla-tion rather than by the Constitution and could therefore be rescinded.

Puerto Ricans became citizens in 1917, U.S. Virgin Islanders in 1927, and Guamanians in 1950, though in all cases, because their citizenship is statutory, it can be revoked. Filipinos were never made citizens in their forty-seven years under U.S. rule. American Samoans, despite having been "American" since 1900, are still legally only "U.S. nationals." They are allowed to fight in the armed forces, which they do in extraordinary numbers—theirs is ranked top of all 885 U.S. Army recruiting stations. But they are not citizens, as the Fourteenth Amendment does not apply to them.

The significance of the Insular Cases goes beyond the law. In distinguishing between "incorporated" and "unincorporated" parts of the United States, these cases enshrined the notion that some places in the country weren't truly *part* of the country. Some territories—namely, the ones filling up with white settlers—could hope for statehood. Others would hang, as the chief justice put it, like a "disembodied shade, in an intermediate state of ambiguous existence for an indefinite period."

That "indefinite period" continues to this day. All the territories that the court deemed "incorporated" have become states. All the territories that it ruled "unincorporated" remain territories. Today, around four million people live in those unincorporated territories—people who have no representation in Congress, who cannot vote for president, and whose rights and citizenship remain a gift from Washington. They could seek statehood, as indeed a large number in Puerto Rico would like to do. But statehood is, like so many other things, at the sole discretion of Congress—a legislative body in which neither Puerto Ricans nor other colonial subjects have a vote.

6

SHOUTING
THE BATTLE CRY
OF FREEDOM

The Greater America Exposition opened on July 1, 1899, with boisterous celebration. Thousands flocked to Omaha to take it all in: the World's Congress of Beauties, a Moorish palace, a rainbow-colored electric fountain, the Filipino band, and a reenactment of Dewey's triumph at Manila Bay. Veterans of the war with Spain, including a troop of Rough Riders, marched through the grounds to loud cheers.

The last in line, though, the First Nebraska Volunteers, raised a few eyebrows. *The Denver Evening Post* couldn't help but notice that "there was something pathetic about their appearance." Their uniforms were tattered, they bore injuries, and they looked harrowed.

They had come from the Philippines.

★

It wasn't supposed to be like this. The war had begun with a promising alliance: the United States and the Philippines against Spain. With Commodore Dewey controlling the sea and Emilio Aguinaldo racking up victories on land, it moved quickly. Dewey ran a naval blockade and supplied Aguinaldo with arms; Aguinaldo used those arms to dislodge the Spaniards.

For Aguinaldo, who had led a failed revolt against Spain in 1896, Dewey's arrival was a deus ex machina. "The Americans, not from mercenary motives, but for the sake of humanity and the lamentations of so many persecuted people, have considered it opportune to extend their protecting mantle to our beloved country," read a message from his junta. "Where you see the American flag flying, assemble in numbers; they are our redeemers!"

Aguinaldo's faith in the United States was buoyed by repeated assurances from Dewey and other U.S. officials that once the war was over, Filipinos would have their independence. Aguinaldo noted with consternation that none of these promises ever appeared in writing, but he pressed on. In June 1898 he established a government (making himself its "dictator") and issued its declaration of independence: "Under the protection of the Powerful and Humanitarian Nation, the United States of America, we do hereby proclaim and declare solemnly in the name by authority of the people of the Philippine Islands, that they are and have the right to be free and independent."

The new government quickly went about the business of state-building. Within months, it had drafted a constitution, established a capital, started a newspaper, opened schools, established a university, issued currency, appointed diplomats, and levied taxes. It had a flag, too. The Philippine Declaration of Independence set the flag's colors as red, white, and blue, "commemorating the flag of the United States of North America, as a manifestation of our profound gratitude towards this Great Nation for its disinterested protection."

The trouble started in August. The siege of Manila—undertaken jointly by the U.S. Army and the Philippine Army of Liberation—ended when Spain surrendered the city to the United States alone. After U.S. troops entered the city, locking out their comrades in arms, McKinley issued *his* declaration. There would be "no joint occupation with the insurgents," and the Filipinos "must recognize the military occupation and authority of the United States."

Thus began a standoff. The United States held Manila and ruled the waves. Aguinaldo's government claimed the rest of the country, although that claim was notional in the less populated and culturally distinct south.

The Philippine troops that had besieged Manila held their positions in the suburbs ringing the city, waiting. U.S. soldiers waited inside the city, biding their time as soldiers often do. Bars opened along the main strip, which the men referred to affectionately as the "Yankee Beer

Chute." Prostitutes raced to Manila from Russia, Romania, Austria, Hong Kong, Singapore, India, and Japan. It was the sex-work equivalent of a gold rush.

As time passed, troops on both sides became restless, shouting insults at each other. Hopes for a diplomatic solution were dashed in December, when McKinley's government signed its treaty with Spain to buy the Philippines for $20 million. That news was "received in the Revolutionary camp like a thunderbolt out of a clear blue sky," wrote Aguinaldo.

McKinley issued a proclamation that the military government of Manila was "to be extended with all possible dispatch to the whole of the ceded territory." Aguinaldo issued a counter-proclamation, denouncing this "violent and aggressive seizure" of the Philippines. He established a new government, this time a republic, and took the oath of office as the Philippines' first president. His inaugural banquet was a sumptuous affair, with a European-style menu written in French.

The more McKinley and Aguinaldo doubled down on their claims to sovereignty, the more skittish Manilans became. In the first week of January 1899, some thirty thousand of them fled the city. Two weeks later, a Chinese man tried to kick a Spaniard's dog, but his wooden shoe flew off his foot and struck a Filipino in the face. Anywhere else, this would have been a nonevent, leading to a fistfight at best. But in Manila, a city on the edge, it was a spark on dry tinder. Doors banged shut, locks slid into place, guns came out, and city dwellers raced for refuge. "Within an area of twenty-five square miles, there was not a man, woman, or child who was not aware that his neighbor was fleeing from some dreadful, unknown monsters," reported the paper. "All were simultaneously affected by the startling awe inspiring stampede."

The International Dog-Shoe-Face Incident subsided with minimal bloodshed. The only casualty was the dog (somebody shot it). But two weeks later, the thing touched off in earnest. Private William W. Grayson and Private Orville H. Miller of the First Nebraska Volunteers (the regiment that would later limp through the parade grounds of the Greater America Exposition) encountered three or four Filipino soldiers while on a nighttime patrol of the Manila suburbs. Grayson ordered them to halt. But who was he to give orders? They ordered *him* to halt.

"I thought the best thing to do was shoot," remembered Grayson, and he did. He and Miller shot three Filipinos and then ran back for reinforcements. "Line up, fellows," Grayson called. "The niggers are in here all through these yards."

"The British are coming!" this was not. But as a call to arms, it sufficed. Within hours, the United States had mounted an offensive. The war had begun.

★

Someone following the war from afar might have judged the two armies to be well matched. The U.S. Army had about twenty thousand soldiers in or around Manila. The Army of Liberation's numbers are harder to know, but estimates ranged from fifteen thousand to forty thousand. The United States Army had better weapons, but the Philippine Army knew the terrain.

Yet the first full day of fighting revealed just how unbalanced things were. On February 5, the bloodiest battle of the war resulted in 238 U.S. casualties and thousands of Filipino casualties. The U.S. Army's official report put the number at four thousand, though that was sheer guesswork.

Weapons were part of the reason. Aguinaldo's men had a few usable guns but little ammunition. A third of the troops surrounding Manila lacked rifles. One unit was armed with spears; another—facing off against the Utah Battery—had bows and arrows. And then there was the "battalion" composed of children instructed to throw stones at the enemy.

A galling gun shortage would cripple the Philippine forces throughout the war. Aguinaldo's men made do with whatever weapons they could smuggle from Asia (not many, given the U.S. blockade) or capture. They gathered tin cans that the U.S. Army had discarded and tried to convert them into cartridges. They melted church bells down for bullets, scraped the heads off matches for fulminate, and used tree resins for gunpowder. Later in the war, independence fighters sent pearl divers to scour the ocean floor for ammunition that the retreating Spaniards might have dropped.

But it was more than just arms. Warfare is, if not a science, then at least an art, requiring practice. U.S. soldiers were trained, and many were seasoned. Many of the generals who led them had fought in the Civil War or against Indians. In 1898, most were in their fifties or sixties.

Not so on the Philippine side. As the colonized subjects of Spain, Filipinos had never had their own army. Many of those who had gained military experience in the 1896 revolt or the 1898 war had died, leaving what

Aguinaldo called a "residual army," a "motley crowd of crude recruits and volunteers." Most were untrained even in basic firearms technique.

And their leaders were astonishingly young. The "Father of the Philippine Army," General Artemio Ricarte, was 32 in 1898. General Emilio Jacinto, regarded as the brains of the revolution, was 24. The other principal commanders were General Antonio Luna (32), General Mariano Noriel (34), General Miguel Malvar (33), General Gregorio del Pilar (23), and—the youngest—General Manuel Tinio (21). Tinio had dropped out of high school to join the revolution in 1896, and two years later he was a general. His aide-de-camp was 15.

Aguinaldo himself was 29 in 1898. He lived until 1964.

This hatchling army fared poorly against the armed forces of the United States. The war had begun in February 1899. In March, the United States seized the capital of the Philippine Republic, Malolos, at the cost of only a single fatality. Aguinaldo escaped and moved his government to San Isidro. When that fell, he moved it to Cabanatuan. Then to Tarlac, his fourth capital. Tarlac fell in November, ten months into the war. Aguinaldo fled to the mountains, refusing to tell even his field commanders his location.

General Arthur MacArthur (father of the better-known Douglas MacArthur), who was commanding the U.S. forces, concluded that the war was over. There was simply "no organized insurgent force left to strike at."

MacArthur was wrong, though. The following months saw engagements between the two sides double, then triple. What MacArthur had taken for the end of the war was instead the debut of a new strategy. Recognizing how badly he was outmatched, Aguinaldo had given up establishing capitals and fighting conventional battles. Instead, he'd ordered his followers to become guerrillas.

It wasn't a bad idea. If set-piece battles had exposed Aguinaldo's weaknesses, guerrilla warfare played to his strengths: knowledge of the land and the popularity of his cause. "Insurrectos," as they were called, could ambush U.S. patrols, hide their weapons, and then melt into the populace. They could draw on towns for food, shelter, and information, even when those towns were officially under U.S. control.

One boy at the time remembered how women haggling in the marketplace would encode observations about U.S. troop size and movement into the mango and guava prices they demanded, which the fruit vendors would then convey to the guerrillas. He remembered how children seeing U.S. sentries approaching would send warnings by "accidentally" throwing balls into the guerrillas' homes.

All this required the support of the populace, which Aguinaldo was not above using force to ensure. But he didn't need much compulsion in 1899. "I have been reluctantly compelled to believe," MacArthur confessed, "that the Filipino masses are loyal to Aguinaldo."

★

Filipinos weren't the constituency that Aguinaldo worried about, at least not at first. He worried about U.S. voters. As he saw it, the point of guerrilla warfare was not to defeat the U.S. Army—nobody thought he could do that—but to wear it down. If Aguinaldo could keep the fight alive through November, he hoped he might influence the 1900 presidential election.

Filipinos couldn't vote in that election, of course. But perhaps they could sway its outcome in other ways. McKinley was running again, this time with Roosevelt as his vice president, so there was little help to be got from the Republicans. Aguinaldo was more interested in McKinley's Democratic opponent, William Jennings Bryan, who had run in 1896 and was also running again. Bryan sought to set the Philippines free.

This was, from Aguinaldo's perspective, a war for hearts and minds. He gambled that mainland voters were uneasy about being colonizers and that the sight of Filipinos dying for independence might make enough of an impression on them that the 1900 election would turn out differently from the one in 1896.

Was there some deep-seated aversion to empire woven into the U.S. national character? Some lingering anti-imperialism held over from the Revolutionary War? Historians have debated that question for decades. But if one were arguing the affirmative side, one could do no better than to introduce into evidence, as Exhibit A, the case of Samuel Clemens, a.k.a. Mark Twain.

Twain was an unusual sort. He defied the buttoned-up conventions of the Victorian age, delighting instead in rude talk and taboo subjects. In his day, this made Twain a court jester, outclassed by such authors as William Dean Howells and Henry Wadsworth Longfellow. But today they are hard to remember, whereas Twain is impossible to forget. He seems more "American" than they do, than nearly anyone does.

The best comparison is not Howells or Longfellow, but Twain's British counterpart, Rudyard Kipling. Both are cherished to this day as authors who wrote in everyday language about life in the backcountry. Twain is best remembered for a novel, *Adventures of Huckleberry Finn* (1885), about a young white boy and an older black man making an odyssey on the Mississippi River. Kipling, who regarded Twain as "the largest man of his time," read *Huck Finn* with admiration. Then he wrote his own major novel, *Kim* (1901), about a young white boy and an older Asian man on an odyssey through colonial India. Twain reread *Kim* every year.

Yet there was a difference between the two authors, one that perhaps reflected a larger divergence between the cultures of Britain and the United States. Kipling was the age's great champion of empire. He befriended Roosevelt and observed the brewing Philippine conflict with interest. He offered his advice in the form of a wildly popular poem. An advance copy went to Roosevelt, but the poem was first published, by an extraordinary stroke of coincidence, on the very day the war broke out. It was called "The White Man's Burden: An Address to the United States," and it began this way:

> Take up the White Man's burden—
>   Send forth the best ye breed—
> Go, bind your sons to exile
>   To serve your captives' need;
> To wait, in heavy harness,
>   On fluttered folk and wild—
> Your new-caught, sullen peoples,
>   Half-devil and half-child.

Today, with imperialism everywhere in disrepute, Kipling's poem stands as a sort of intellectual ruins from a bygone time. It's the single best-remembered paean to empire in the English language.

At the time the poem was published, Twain would probably have endorsed its sentiment. He was a "red-hot imperialist," he recalled. "I wanted the American eagle to go screaming into the Pacific." But as he watched the Philippine conflict unfold, Twain could no longer toe the line. In 1900 he declared himself to be "an anti-imperialist."

Twain was not just *an* anti-imperialist, he was the most famous anti-imperialist in the country. He became the vice president of the Anti-Imperialist League of New York and chronicled the expanding war with withering sarcasm. "There must be two Americas," he mused. "One that sets the captive free, and one that takes a once-captive's new freedom away from him, and picks a quarrel with him with nothing to found it on; then kills him to get his land."

For that second America, Twain proposed adding a few words to the Declaration of Independence: "Governments derive their just powers from the consent of the governed *white men.*" He suggested a modified flag: red, black, and blue, with the stars replaced by a skull and crossbones.

This was strong speech, but remarkably, it wasn't even that far out. As Aguinaldo had hoped, the Philippine War tapped a rich vein of anti-imperialism. Even the Democratic Party—hardly a radical organization in the age of Jim Crow—could go a little spittle-flecked on this issue. The war was "criminal aggression," the Democratic platform charged in 1900, born of "greedy commercialism" and sure to ruin the country. "No nation can long endure half republic and half empire," it warned. "Imperialism abroad will lead quickly and inevitably to despotism at home."

Empire dominated the 1900 election. Kipling, who lived in England, couldn't vote. Twain declined to (though he allowed that any candidate running on an "Anti-Doughnut" platform could have had his support). But for the rest of the country, this was the first time overseas empire was put to a vote. And since the candidates hadn't changed since the last election, it wasn't a bad gauge of the national mood concerning empire.

If it was a test, though, the anti-imperialists flunked it. In 1896 McKinley had won 51 percent of the popular vote. In 1900 he won 52 percent, meanwhile increasing his share of the electoral college from 61 percent to 65 percent. The imperial policy was affirmed, and it would never arise as a serious electoral issue again.

Twain felt the ground shift beneath his feet. Though he continued to criticize imperialism, he kept his most incisive writings private, as he could find no way to publish them. After Twain died, in 1910, his literary estate suppressed them. It wasn't until the 1960s, when those writings were released and taken up by opponents of the Vietnam War, that the reading public grasped the full depth of Twain's hatred for empire.

★

Back in the Philippines, the gloves came off. The election had shone a spotlight on the war, and General MacArthur had obliged McKinley by steering clear of anything that the Democrats might paint as an atrocity. Now, with that spotlight switched off, MacArthur just wanted it over. He issued a new set of orders. Captured insurgents could be killed. Towns supporting them could be destroyed. The preferred method was burning, and since nearly every town in the north of the Philippines was aiding the rebels in some way, every one was potentially kindling.

The men needed little encouragement to carry out these orders. As MacArthur well knew, his soldiers regarded Filipinos not as fellow Americans, but as irksome "natives." When William Howard Taft, then the colony's chief lawmaker, called Filipinos "our little brown brothers," the soldiers scoffed. A song they sang, frequently and loudly, captured their view:

> I'm only a common Soldier-man in the blasted Philippines;
> They say I've got Brown Brothers here, but I dunno what it
>   means.
> I like the word Fraternity, but still I draw the line;
> He may be a brother of William H. Taft, but he ain't no friend
>   of mine.

Brother, indeed, was a word rarely used. The soldiers preferred *gugu*, a word that historians think was the etymological precursor of the epithet *gook*, which featured so prominently in the Korean and Vietnam wars. White soldiers also made use of a tried-and-true favorite from back home: *nigger*. They sang it proudly, as in the extremely-hard-to-misinterpret ballad "I Don't Like a Nigger Nohow."

The black soldiers in the Philippines heard this and winced. They connected the racism that pervaded the war to the racism they had just left at home—the 1890s were the high noon of lynching. Aguinaldo's men made the connection, too, and issued propaganda suggesting that black soldiers might be better off switching sides.

Remarkably, one did. David Fagen of the 24th Infantry accepted a commission in Aguinaldo's army. The U.S. Army, eager to nip this sort of thing in the bud, placed a $600 reward on Fagen's head, equivalent to three years of a private's pay. And that's what it got: Fagen's head—or, at least, a head purported to be Fagen's—dropped off in a cloth sack by a Filipino hunter.

But Fagen was the exception. In general, soldiers closed ranks. To win Filipinos over, they inaugurated an extensive campaign of sanitation, road-building, and education in the areas they controlled. In those they didn't, they staged raids, shooting insurgents and torching villages.

Soldiers used both the carrot and the stick, but it was stick-wielding that shaped their identities. If troops in the Second World War understood themselves as "G.I. Joes"—general-issue cogs in a vast bureaucracy—those who fought in the Philippines understood themselves to be "hikers," humping through hostile territory in search of guerrillas. Today you can find statues named *The Hiker* in dozens of towns. They are the most visible mainland monuments to the war.

The "hikes" did great damage, but they couldn't themselves extirpate the rebellion. The guerrillas remained at large, and the towns kept feeding them. Perhaps Filipinos helped the rebels out of enthusiasm for Aguinaldo's cause; perhaps they simply realized that the nationalists were a lot better at identifying and punishing traitors than the U.S. Army was. Whatever the reason, it was clear that the U.S. inability to distinguish friend from foe was a serious disadvantage. A colonel described the U.S. Army as a "blind giant"—"powerful enough to destroy the enemy, but unable to find him."

Too clumsy to excise the rebellion with a scalpel, the army reached for a bone saw. Adopting a practice called "reconcentration," it herded rural populations into fortified towns or camps where they could be more closely monitored. From the army's perspective, this contributed a satisfying clarity to an otherwise murky situation. Those inside the reconcentration zones were "pacified." Those outside were not, and could be treated accordingly: cutting off their food supplies, burning their homes, or simply shooting them.

Somewhat awkwardly, though, reconcentration was the very tactic that Spain had used against the Cubans, the one that had provoked the United States to "liberate" Cuba in the first place. It "sounds awful," confessed one U.S. official to his diary. "It works, however, admirably."

It *did* seem that the war was winding down. The disappointment of the 1900 election and sheer exhaustion wore the insurrection thin. Rich, educated Filipinos, meanwhile, started to accommodate themselves to U.S.

rule. A month after the 1900 election, more than one hundred members of the colony's elite formed the Federalist Party, which, as its name suggests, sought inclusion within the United States and eventual statehood. And the less likely Philippine independence seemed, the less inclined Filipinos were to support the rebels, an action for which they could be harshly punished by the U.S. Army.

Another blow came in March 1901: the capture of Aguinaldo. Not only did he surrender, he took an oath of allegiance to the United States. "Let the stream of blood cease to flow," he wrote in a proclamation. "Let there be an end to tears and desolation." A spate of surrenders of other high-ranking officers followed. Satisfied that the war was over, McKinley handed most of the Philippines over from the military to the civil government under Taft on the Fourth of July, 1901.

George Frisbie Hoar, the leading anti-imperialist in Congress, shook his head. "We crushed the only republic in Asia."

★

The fantasy of conquest is always the same: defeat the leader and the country is yours. The United States had learned the folly of this when it won the Philippines from Spain, only to find itself fighting the Philippine Army. It was about to learn the lesson again.

The Philippine archipelago contains more than seven thousand islands. The war against Aguinaldo took place mainly on the largest, Luzon, the northern island that contained Manila and half the population. Spain had ruled from Luzon, Aguinaldo had ruled from Luzon, and the United States now sought to do the same.

Defeat the leader, the country is yours.

Yet the farther south you went in the Philippines, the less relevant events in Luzon seemed to be. Particularly Aguinaldo's surrender: in theory, it should have meant the end of the Philippine Republic. But as the United States sought to extend its control south over Samar, the third-largest island in the archipelago, it found a land still beholden to the nationalist cause. In May 1901 MacArthur ordered "drastic measures" to "clean up" Samar "as soon as possible."

Those drastic measures were by now standard fare: interrupting trade, burning crops, resettling civilians, and conducting "hikes" against guerrillas. Yet here, the civilians resisted. A group of five hundred townspeople in Balangiga—who had seen their food supplies destroyed, their agricultural tools confiscated, and their neighbors incarcerated—launched a surprise attack on a U.S. camp. They killed forty-five soldiers in a single day.

The Balangiga Massacre, as it became known, struck terror into the hearts of the colonizers. "Half the people one met could talk of nothing else but their conviction that the whole archipelago was a smouldering volcano and that we were all liable to be murdered in our beds," remembered Taft's wife, Nellie.

The army kicked back into high gear. "They have sown the wind," one captain said. "They shall reap the whirlwind."

The whirlwind came in the form of Major Edwin F. Glenn, who ordered a sweeping investigation. Glenn was a violent interrogator, fond of a technique that had become popular in the army and is uncomfortably familiar today. If the men he was questioning—and these included town officials and priests—failed to answer to his satisfaction, Glenn administered the "water cure." Here is how a soldier explained it: "Lay them on their backs, a man standing on each hand and each foot, then put a round

The site of the Balangiga Massacre is today marked by a large statue group celebrating the heroism of the Balangigans, here shown bursting into an army tent.

stick in the mouth and pour a pail of water in the mouth and nose, and if they don't give up pour in another pail. They swell up like toads."

The whirlwind also took the form of General Jacob Smith. He had fought the Lakota at Wounded Knee and adopted a similarly unyielding approach to Filipinos. "I want no prisoners," Smith allegedly told his subordinate. "I wish you to kill and burn, the more you kill and burn the better you will please me." All rice was to be seized, Smith insisted, and any male over the age of ten who did not turn himself over to the U.S. government should be killed. "The interior of Samar," he ordered, "must be made a howling wilderness."

Smith fell far short of that heinous goal, but the Samar campaign showed the war at its worst. Samar also revealed that whatever they thought in Washington, the war wasn't over. In fact, it wasn't even over in Luzon. There, too, the embers of rebellion glowed hot, with the Province of Batangas in open rebellion and insurgents continuing their attacks throughout the island.

The longer the war wore on, the dirtier it got. Nationalists, finding it increasingly hard to win support and much-needed supplies from the towns, used terror tactics: kidnapping, torturing, and executing "collaborators," sometimes in extravagant ways. The U.S. Army, for its part, expanded its policy of reconcentration. And, though this was prohibited, the men continued to torture their captives. Yet again, like the cast of some hellish musical, the soldiers expressed their feelings in song. One of the men wrote this rousing number, titled "The Water Cure in the P.I.":

Get the good old syringe boys and fill it to the brim
We've caught another nigger and we'll operate on him
Let someone take the handle who can work it with a vim
Shouting the battle cry of freedom

Hurrah. Hurrah. We bring the Jubilee.
Hurrah. Hurrah. The flag that makes him free.
Shove the nozzle deep and let him taste of liberty,
Shouting the battle cry of freedom.

News of these atrocities aroused scandals when they reached the mainland. Major Glenn was tried for torture. General Smith, having ordered a massacre, also faced trial, though not for crimes against Filipinos, but for "conduct to the prejudice of good order and military discipline."

Smith's actions were unrepresentative and clearly embarrassing to the administration. But it was hard to see them as entirely out of step with the higher purposes of the war. Roosevelt himself, who ascended to the presidency after McKinley's assassination, had long understood the fight against "savages" to be a form of warfare "where no pity is shown to non-combatants, where the weak are harried without ruth, and the vanquished maltreated with merciless ferocity." And yet it was, in his judgment, "the most ultimately righteous of all wars."

Glenn was fined and suspended for a month ("nobody was seriously damaged" by the water cure, Roosevelt insisted). Smith was reprimanded and retired from active duty. "Taken in the full, his work has been such as to reflect credit upon the American Army and therefore upon the nation," Roosevelt said. "It is deeply to be regretted that he should have so acted in this instance as to interfere with his further usefulness."

★

However deeply harsh tactics were "regretted" once they came to light, they had a grim efficacy. While U.S. public works campaigns undermined support for the rebels, tortures, torching, and food deprivations punished the holdouts harshly. Insurgents surrendered, or they simply died. A Republican congressman who toured Luzon in 1902 reported what he saw to a newspaper. "The country was marched over and cleaned in a most resolute manner," he said. "Our soldiers took no prisoners, they kept no records; they simply swept the country, and wherever or whenever they could get hold of a Filipino they killed him."

From accounts like this, it can sound as if most Filipinos who perished died at the hands of the zealous "hikers," as if the whole war were Samar. Doubtless, the guns and torches *did* kill tens of thousands. But the full story of Philippine mortality is considerably more complicated. As was often the case in the nineteenth century, most victims of the war died from disease.

Muddying the waters further, the diseases started under Spanish rule. The late nineteenth century had brought tumult to the Philippines, moving people around the archipelago and disrupting long-standing economic arrangements. Both motion and instability carried lethal epidemiological consequences, most notably during the cholera epidemic in 1882–83, which killed hundreds of thousands, and the rinderpest outbreak in 1887, wiping out nine in ten cattle and carabao. Before Dewey ever set eyes on the lights of Manila Bay, the horsemen of the apocalypse were already stalking the Philippines.

When the war with the United States came, those horsemen charged forth, now all at once and galloping: cholera, malaria, dysentery, beriberi, rinderpest, tuberculosis, smallpox, and bubonic plague. "Everything that could possibly happen to a country had happened or was happening," Nellie Taft remembered.

The armies—both sides—carried disease with them on the march. So did the prostitutes who flocked to Manila and the countless refugees the war produced. People moved, as they never had before, in and out of malaria zones, carrying the infection in their bloodstreams. Aguinaldo contracted malaria, and it gutted the troops who fled with him to the mountains.

If movement spread disease, so did confinement. Reconcentration was, from an epidemiological perspective, a particularly horrifying tactic. It forced populations with different immunities and diseases together into close quarters in unsanitary conditions. At the same time, it cut Filipinos off from their fields, leaving them reliant on imported food, often nutritionally poor rice from Saigon, if they got food at all. Malnutrition increased susceptibility to many diseases, and it led directly to beriberi.

Beriberi, it should be noted, is an extremely hard disease to contract. To get it as an adult, you have to eat a profoundly restricted diet, such as milled rice and virtually nothing else, *for months*. But Filipinos, separated from their farms and able to purchase only the cheapest food, suffered from it in large numbers, probably in the tens of thousands. It struck babies the hardest. Although infantile beriberi was unknown to doctors at the time (thus unrecorded as a diagnosis), it is doubtless the reason why Manila during the war had the world's highest recorded infant mortality rate.

Reconcentration took its toll on the countryside, too. Fields went untilled as farmers were forced into garrison towns. In a biblical turn, those untended fields attracted swarms of locusts, which further eroded the food supply. The U.S. Army exacerbated the situation by making war on food: burning grain stores, confiscating or killing animals, and installing blockades to stop trade. Guerrillas starved, but so did everyone else.

Everyone, that is, but the U.S. soldiers. They sucked much of the rice, eggs, chickens, fruit, fish, and meat from the Philippine economy with their purchase orders. And after there was no longer enough meat left in the Philippine economy, the army bought refrigerated beef from Australia. With vaccines, fresh water, sanitation, and ample food, U.S. forces were only grazed by the diseases that decimated the colony.

Up to mid-1902, the U.S. military lost 4,196 men, more than three-quarters of whom died of disease. It counted around 16,000 combat fatalities on the opposite side. But that number represents only recorded war deaths and is a tiny fraction of total mortality. General J. Franklin Bell, the architect of the reconcentration strategy, estimated that on Luzon alone the war had killed one-sixth of the population, roughly 600,000. Textbooks usually offer an estimate of 250,000 for the whole archipelago, though there is no hard evidence behind that figure. The most careful study, made by the historian Ken De Bevoise, found that in the years 1899–1903, about 775,000 Filipinos died because of the war.

"Of course, we do want military glory," wrote Twain, noting the death toll, "but this is getting it by avalanche."

On July 4, 1902, Roosevelt proclaimed the Philippine War over. If De Bevoise's calculations are right, it had claimed more lives than the Civil War.

★

Roosevelt's announcement wasn't the first time the authorities had declared an end to the war. It wasn't even the second time. *The Washington Post* reminded readers that Taft had announced the "fourth and final termination of hostilities" two years earlier and that "the war has been brought to an end on six different occasions since."

"A bad thing cannot be killed too often," the paper concluded.

Having pronounced the war over only to see it rise from the grave time and again, colonial officials shouldn't have been surprised when it turned out that Roosevelt's proclamation was, like the others, too hasty. As before, the trouble lay outside of Luzon, though this time even farther south.

"Moroland"—the islands of Mindanao, Palawan, and Basilan plus the Sulu Archipelago—comprised the less-populated bottom third of the Philippines. It was like a different country. Inhabited mainly by Muslims (called "Moros") rather than Catholics and governed by a system of sultans and datus, it adhered to Islamic law and practiced both polygamy and slavery. With every free Moro man carrying a blade at all times, Moroland was also armed to the teeth.

Spain had never managed to control the area and had settled for something akin to a nonaggression pact with the sultan of Sulu. The United States followed suit, signing an agreement with the sultan that left his legal authority intact. *Did this mean that slavery was once again legal in the United States?* anti-imperialists wondered. "Slaves are a part of our property," the sultan insisted. "To have this property taken away from us would mean a great loss." Washington decided to turn a blind eye, which was all the easier to do once the Insular Cases established that the Thirteenth Amendment didn't apply to the Philippines.

Still, it was hard to imagine that this tenuous peace would last forever, especially as the U.S. Army presence in the south grew. Hostilities erupted in the Battle of Bayan in May 1902, two months before Roosevelt declared the Philippine War over. And those reading Roosevelt's proclamation closely would have realized that even with the war "over," civilian authorities controlled only the Christian areas. In Moroland, and in the Luzon highlands, the military still ruled.

What the military would do with Moroland, however, was an open question. This was the first time the United States was governing Muslims, and attitudes among officials varied enormously.

One approach was championed by Captain John Pershing, who held a post on the shore of Lake Lanao, a large body of water in Mindanao, around which nearly half the Muslim population of Moroland lived. Pershing made the news during the 2016 presidential campaign when Donald Trump described, with relish, how Pershing ("rough guy, rough guy") had captured fifty "terrorists," dipped fifty bullets in pig's blood, lined up his captives, and then shot forty-nine of them, letting the last go to report what happened. "And for twenty-five years there wasn't a problem, okay?" Trump concluded.

Actually, not okay. Setting the ethics of extrajudicial killing aside, Trump's history was wildly off base. In fact, Pershing proved to be extraordinarily sympathetic toward the Moros. He made diplomatic visits to them, unarmed. He studied their language and customs, ate their food ("I have never tasted more delicious chicken"), and counted some as "strong personal friends." By 1903 he was taking low-level meetings without an interpreter.

The friendly overtures worked: Pershing was elected a datu—the only datu within U.S. officialdom—and became honorary father to the wife of the sultan of Bayan. Pershing undertook a seventy-two-mile expedition around the lake, firming up alliances where he could and making war where he couldn't. It was the first time any U.S. or Spanish official had made it all the way around.

For all this, Pershing made headlines. Young, handsome, and peace-seeking, he was the opposite of General Jacob "Howling Wilderness" Smith. Roosevelt made him a brigadier general, jumping him over 909 more senior officers.

But of course, Pershing's desire to conciliate meant tolerating Moro customs, including slavery. Not everyone was willing to do that. Particularly hostile to Pershing's approach was General Leonard Wood, Roosevelt's old comrade in arms from the Rough Riders, who became governor of Moro Province in 1903. Wood was an uncompromising man—"intolerant, arrogantly superior, and cocksure of his rightness" is how a colleague described him—and he had little patience for Moro self-government. At a meeting with the datus of Jolo, Wood announced that "a new order of things has come about. A new and very strong country now owns all these islands; that is the United States."

Wood withdrew from the noninterference agreement, abolished slavery, and established a head tax, knowing full well that these actions would provoke a fight. "One clean-cut lesson will be quite sufficient for them," he wrote to Roosevelt, "but it should be of such character as not to need a dozen frittering repetitions."

In what was by now something of a custom, Wood established reconcentration zones and launched a series of raids.

Wood hoped for "one clean-cut lesson." Instead, he got what he feared: a dozen frittering ones. His raids killed thousands of Moros but never managed to end the war. In 1905, hundreds of resisters—entire families—fled up to the crater of a dormant volcano, Bud Dajo. Objecting to Wood's abolition of slavery and above all to his tax, they had essentially seceded, creating a micro-Confederacy on a hilltop.

It was the fight Wood had been spoiling for. In March 1906 he sent up an expeditionary force. The "battle," lasting four days, was profoundly one-sided—a soldier described the Moros as falling "like dominoes" under machine-gun fire. Wood lost twenty-one men and estimated that six hundred Moros had died, although the Filipino interpreters working with the army put the figure at nearly one thousand. "All the defenders were killed," Wood reported.

Massacres like this weren't unknown in the United States. Wounded Knee, Sand Creek, Bloody Island—the Indian wars had painted the West red. Yet Bud Dajo dwarfed them all. "We abolished them utterly, leaving not even a baby alive to cry for its dead mother," wrote a bitter Mark Twain, privately. *This is incomparably the greatest victory that was ever achieved by the Christian soldiers of the United States.*

"I would not want to have that on my conscience for the fame of Napoleon," Pershing wrote to his wife. Yet Pershing got his own chance to burden his conscience when he became Moro Province's governor in 1909. Despite Wood's hope that "one clean-cut lesson" would end things, the war continued: raids, counterraids, armed bands, and military rule. In 1911 an exasperated Pershing issued an executive order to completely disarm the province, requiring that Moros turn in not just their guns but their bladed weapons, too.

Had a federal official given an order like that on the mainland, it would

Soldiers stand over a trench filled with men's and women's corpses after the Bud Dajo Massacre, 1906. W.E.B. Du Bois declared this photograph to be "the most illuminating thing I have ever seen" and proposed displaying it in his classroom "to impress upon the students what wars and especially Wars of Conquest really mean."

have violated the Second Amendment. Here, it merely incensed and alarmed the populace. Six to ten thousand fled their homes and moved up another volcanic mountain, Bud Bagsak, taking with them some three hundred rifles.

Pershing was more patient than Wood. He waited for months, and eventually, once the food started running out, most of the rebels came back down. But Pershing's patience stretched only so far, and in June 1913 he launched a surprise attack. "The fighting was the fiercest I have ever seen," he wrote, and the Moros were "given a thrashing which I think they will not soon forget." In the end, Pershing lost fifteen men and guessed he had killed some two hundred to three hundred Moros, including women and children. Historians' estimates range from two hundred to more than five hundred.

★

Bud Bagsak did not end the fighting. It went on, with further battles taking place later that month. Violence would rack the region for years. Nevertheless, Moro Province was brought under civilian rule in 1913, ending fourteen years of martial law.

Since 1903, the highest position in the U.S. Army has been chief of staff. J. Franklin Bell, architect of the reconcentration policy, held that post after his time in the Philippines. So did Leonard Wood, four years after the Bud Dajo Massacre. After leaving Moro Province, Pershing commanded the American Expeditionary Forces in Europe, becoming a hero of the First World War. Then he, too, became chief of staff.

Every one of the army's first twelve chiefs of staff, in fact, served in the Philippine War. Stretching from the outbreak of hostilities in 1899 to the end of military rule in Moroland in 1913, it is, after the war in Afghanistan, the longest war the United States has ever fought.

7

OUTSIDE THE
CHARMED CIRCLE

The McKinley administration had hoped that, by overthrowing Spanish tyranny, it would win the allegiance of Spain's former subjects. In the Philippines, this looked like hubris. Instead of cheering crowds, U.S. forces met Emilio Aguinaldo's Army of Liberation, and the war lasted years.

But it wasn't an unreasonable hope. When U.S. troops landed in Puerto Rico, crowds *did* gather to cheer them on. Puerto Ricans shouted *"¡Viva los Americanos!"* and presented the soldiers with cigars, fruit, and flowers. Locals referred to themselves as "Porto Rican, American," and municipal officials renamed streets after Washington and Lincoln.

Many Puerto Ricans believed that they stood to gain by replacing Spain with the United States. Their island was far more reliant on trade than the Philippines was. Economically, U.S. rule would grant access to better markets. Politically, Puerto Ricans expected to gain autonomy. They understood the United States to be a grand federation—a "republic of republics"—and hoped to join it on equal terms, as the western territories had. Politicians formed parties, the Partido Republicano and the Partido Federal, both of which sought statehood. As the Federalist platform put it, Puerto Rico was to be "a prosperous and happy country in the shadow of the American flag."

To Pedro Albizu Campos, a young boy at the time, all this must have made an impression. He grew up in Ponce, the center of the U.S. occupation. The locals there were "the most friendly souls in the world," wrote a U.S. journalist—they were "delirious" with enthusiasm for the United States.

Albizu's father had gone down to the port to welcome the arriving troops and soon found work as a customs official for the new government. Though Albizu had little contact with his father, the boy also seemed eager. He "appeared to be a lover of everything American," recalled his school's superintendent. A teacher remembered how Albizu would stay after class to talk with his mainland teachers, and that he would visit their homes. Eventually the superintendent arranged for a scholarship to send him to the mainland, to the University of Vermont.

From Vermont, Albizu transferred to Harvard, where he earned a bachelor's degree and, later, a law degree. He flourished there. "Pete," as he was known to his English-speaking friends, was a popular student, with a reputation as a gifted speaker. He joined clubs, most notably the Cosmopolitan Club, an organization for Harvard's foreign and international-minded students.

The Cosmopolitan Club was many rungs below such tony clubs as the Porcellian and the Hasty Pudding—Teddy Roosevelt's haunts. Yet it was, in the judgment of Harvard's president, the most interesting club on campus. Its members came from all over the map: China, Germany, Korea, France, Liberia, Japan, South Africa, British Guiana, and beyond.

Misfits in WASP-y Cambridge, such men were nevertheless the hyperelite of their home countries. When Albizu was elected as one of the club's two vice presidents in 1914, the other vice president was T. V. Soong, later reputed to be the world's richest man. One of Soong's sisters was about to marry Sun Yat-sen, the leader of the Chinese revolution. Another would marry Chiang Kai-shek, head of the Republic of China (first on the mainland, then Taiwan) from 1928 to 1975.

Albizu served as president of the Cosmopolitan Club in his senior year. It was an honor, but it came at exactly the wrong time, for midway through Albizu's term, the United States entered the First World War.

It couldn't have been easy for the Cosmopolitan Club's members—pacifists and foreigners in an era of increasingly belligerent nationalism. Around them, every taint of foreign loyalty was being aggressively purged. At the nearby Boston Symphony Orchestra, the German-born conductor was deported, dozens of German musicians were interned, and even Germanic compositions were shunned.

The Cosmopolitan Club was full of Germans. Worse, one of its most devoted faculty allies had been the psychologist Hugo Münsterberg, a German citizen whose over-the-top defenses of his homeland had turned him into a national villain and campus embarrassment. It was doubtless a relief to the Harvard administration when Münsterberg died suddenly in late 1916 of a cerebral hemorrhage.

Not only was Albizu president of the Cosmopolitan Club, he had publicly identified himself with pacifism. He'd spoken out against Harvard students' participation in summer military-preparedness camps. And he'd served on the council of the International Polity Club, a peace organization that had invited Münsterberg to give a political speech at a time when the professor was a pariah.

All that, though, had been back when the United States was a mere onlooker. Once it entered the war, Albizu faced a stark choice. He could stick with his pacifism or stand with his country, but not both.

He collected his thoughts in a letter to *The Harvard Crimson.* "When the Spanish-American war broke out, Porto Ricans looked to this country as their liberator, and a wave of Americanism swept across the country," he wrote. "We welcomed the American flag in 1898 because we believed it, and still believe it, to be a symbol of democracy and justice."

His course, then, was clear. "Gentlemen, let me assure you and the American people of our loyalty to the United States," he continued. "We detest German tyranny and arrogance, and we will give good account of ourselves in actual voluntary military co-operation with the United States."

Three weeks later, Albizu joined the army.

★

Pedro Albizu Campos's faith in the United States was striking, but he had reason for it. Whatever empire fever had gripped the country in 1898 seemed to be subsiding. The scandals and sheer length of the Philippine War had wearied even the most ardent imperialists. In 1907 Theodore Roosevelt himself called the Philippines a "heel of Achilles" and suggested to Taft that the colony be prepared for independence. Even Emilio Aguinaldo allowed that by this time, the United States had begun to "sober up."

Indeed, empire could seem, from the mainland, to be a regrettable drunken binge, best never spoken of. In 1898 the colonies were headline news, but by the 1910s, even with the fighting still ongoing in Moroland,

First Lieutenant Pedro Albizu
Campos

empire was back-page stuff at best. In 1913 the reliably imperialist journal *The Outlook* (Theodore Roosevelt was an editor), while reporting on the Bud Bagsak battle, felt a need to acknowledge that its readers may be surprised to learn that the war was still happening.

The contrast with Britain is telling. After Queen Victoria's death, in 1901, celebrations of "Empire Day" began on Victoria's birthday throughout the British Empire. It became an official holiday in 1916. In the colonies and in the British Isles there were parades, hymns, and speeches. "We were constantly reminded by our teachers that May 24th was Empire Day," one woman from Derby remembered. "The red parts of the globe were proudly pointed out to us." Children dressed in costumes from the different colonies.

The United States had its own patriotic holiday. It started in the schools and, like Empire Day, became an official holiday in 1916. But Flag Day, as it was called, was not about empire. It was, President Woodrow Wilson explained, an opportunity for people "to gather together in united demonstration of their feeling as a Nation" and show that "America is indivisible." Whereas British children were made to examine the world map, U.S.

children venerated the national flag, which had a star for each state but no symbol for territories.

If U.S. teachers *had* pulled out their maps, as many surely did, it's not clear what they would have found on them. The "Greater United States" maps in vogue a decade earlier were no doubt still hanging on some classroom walls, but by 1916 few such maps were being newly commissioned. Cartographers had returned to the logo maps, showing only the states.

Nationalism was seizing the country, all the more so as the First World War approached. And as the idea of the nation—a union of states sharing a culture, language, and history—grew in prominence, the colonies seemed more distant and nebulous, literally vanishing from maps and atlases. For the guano islands, the disappearance was more than cartographic. The State Department stopped insisting on its claims to those uninhabited islands and allowed many to slip unnoticed into foreign hands. Other territories simply received less attention, from Washington and from everywhere else on the mainland.

They lay, as Wilson put it, "outside the charmed circle of our own national life."

★

Helping to brush empire under the rug was the fact that the annexations had largely stopped. One reason why both imperialists and anti-imperialists had been so impassioned is that they imagined the country's pre-1898 borders to be a dam: once it burst, an unending flood of conquests would follow. It was precisely to prevent that from happening that anti-imperialists in Congress had passed their law strictly limiting what the United States could do with Cuba. It prohibited the exercise of "sovereignty, jurisdiction or control" over the island, "except for pacification."

But if expansionists had been stymied in Cuba, they weren't entirely defeated. The law prohibited the U.S. jurisdiction over Cuba except for the purpose of "pacification." And who was to say when Cuba was pacified?

As it turned out, that question had an answer. The man who decided when Cuba was pacified was its military governor, none other than Leonard Wood, Roosevelt's fellow Rough Rider and (later) the orchestrator of the Bud Dajo Massacre in the Philippines. As Wood saw it, Cuba wouldn't be pacified until it had a stable government. And what was a stable government? One in which "money can be borrowed at a reasonable rate of interest" and "capital is willing to invest" was Wood's definition. He wrote to McKinley: "When people ask me what I mean by stable government, I tell them 'Money at six percent.'"

In fact, the McKinley administration wanted more than that. It wanted to ensure that U.S. property claims were protected (a serious concern, given that the Cuban revolutionaries had torched sugar plantations), and it wanted the right to intervene if Cuban politics started looking wobbly. Using the threat of continued military occupation as leverage, Wood got the Cuban legislature to agree to both demands—not only agree to them but write them into law. For more than thirty years the Cuban constitution contained an astonishing clause granting the United States the right to invade Cuba (which it did, four times).

Cuba also agreed, as part of the price of getting Wood to leave, to lease a forty-five-square-mile port to the United States for military use. Guantánamo Bay, as the leased land was called, would technically remain Cuban territory, but the United States would have "complete jurisdiction and control" over it.

This was, to put it mildly, an extraordinary deal. It gave the United States many of the benefits of colonization without the responsibility. Nobody had sought this arrangement—it was a work-around designed to circumvent the restrictions anti-imperialists had enacted. But it opened a fork in history: the Philippines, Hawai'i, Puerto Rico, American Samoa, and Guam went one way; Cuba went another.

The longer the Philippine War groaned on, the better the Cuban path looked to would-be imperialists. Though nominally independent, Cuba was easily absorbed into the U.S. sphere of influence. North Americans owned its sugar fields, its mines, its tobacco industry, its banks, and much of its land. Young Cubans learned English and played baseball.

Even better, Cuba avoided the industrial-grade violence that scarred the Philippines. Or, at least, it avoided such violence at the hands of the United States. In 1912, the year before John Pershing's troops slaughtered hundreds of Moros on the slopes of Bud Bagsak, Cuba encountered its own diffident subjects. Afro-Cubans, who had been excluded from national politics, took up arms, disrupting production in one province.

At the behest of U.S. investors, who feared for their property, President Taft dispatched marines to Guantánamo Bay and assembled a large naval force in the area. But those ships and marines saw no combat. It was the Cuban army that attacked the Afro-Cubans, killing thousands in a war that lasted months.

The Cuban model resonated. When the Roosevelt administration sought a transoceanic canal to connect its Atlantic trade to its Pacific trade (larger now that the United States had Pacific territories), it eyed the Panama isthmus in Colombia. But it neither bought nor conquered it. Instead, Roosevelt's government encouraged Panamanian nationalists to secede from Colombia, and then he negotiated for a small zone in which to build the canal. The U.S. lease was perpetual, and within the zone, the treaty gave the United States "all the rights, power, and authority" it would possess "if it were the sovereign of the territory." But, as in Guantánamo Bay, the United States wasn't the sovereign—technically.

Roosevelt was just getting started. In 1903 the Dominican Republic's finances collapsed. Its president, Carlos Morales, intimated that he would welcome annexation by the United States—the second time that country had offered itself up. A decade earlier, Roosevelt would have jumped at Morales's offer. But now, exhausted by the Philippine War, he wasn't interested. "I have about the same desire to annex it as a gorged boa constrictor might have to swallow a porcupine wrong-end to," he said.

Instead, Roosevelt made a Cuba-style deal. His government would gain temporary control of Dominican finances (thus ensuring repayment of the debt to U.S. banks) in exchange for defending the Morales government from rebels and external enemies. U.S. interests would be protected, and the Dominican Republic would remain independent.

The ploy was used repeatedly, in country after country around the Caribbean. The United States seized the levers of finance and trade but left sovereignty formally intact. "Dollar diplomacy" was the polite name for this, though "gunboat diplomacy" was the more accurate euphemism. To ensure political and financial "stability," U.S. troops entered Cuba (four times), Nicaragua (three times), Honduras (seven times), the Dominican Republic (four times), Guatemala, Panama (six times), Costa Rica, Mexico (three times), and Haiti (twice) between 1903 and 1934. The United States helped to put down revolts, replaced governments when necessary, and offered battleships-in-the-harbor "advice" to others. But the only territory it annexed in that period was the U.S. Virgin Islands, peacefully purchased from Denmark in 1917.

In his letter to *The Harvard Crimson*, Albizu expressed the hope that Puerto Rico might gain independence and become like Cuba.

★

Albizu's hope hinged, above all, on one figure, Woodrow Wilson, elected president in 1912. A Southern Democrat, Wilson was a far cry from the three Republican imperialists who had preceded him: William McKinley, Teddy Roosevelt, and William Howard Taft.

The contrast was clearest with Roosevelt. As a boy, Teddy Roosevelt had cheered for the Union soldiers as they passed through New York on their way to subdue the seceding South—and he grew up to be the single most bellicose and imperialistic president in U.S. history. By contrast, Wilson's earliest memories were of the soon-to-be-defeated Confederate Army, whose wounded and dying members came as patients to his father's church, which served as a Confederate hospital. As an adult, Wilson shared none of Roosevelt's lust for violent conquest. For his secretary of state he chose William Jennings Bryan, the great anti-imperialist.

Upon Wilson's election, some twenty thousand Filipinos gathered in Manila to celebrate—the paper called him "a modern Moses." They had reason for optimism. The 1912 Democratic Party platform condemned imperialism as "an inexcusable blunder, which has involved us in enormous expense, brought us weakness instead of strength, and laid our nation open to the charge of abandonment of the fundamental doctrine of self-government." Wilson himself talked of his desire to see the Philippines let go. Speaking more generally, he told Congress that the colonies were "no longer to be selfishly exploited" and that "the familiar rights and privileges" of citizens should be extended to territorial inhabitants.

This was not empty speech. In the Philippines, he ended military rule and replaced many mainland officials with Filipinos. In 1916 he hesitantly agreed to support a bill to set the colony free in four years. It passed in the Senate by a single vote but died in the House. In its place, Congress passed a weaker and vaguer bill, promising the Philippines liberty whenever it achieved that all-important but conspicuously undefined condition of "stable government."

In 1917, under the pressures of incipient war, Wilson backed another important bill, this one concerning Puerto Rico. It made Puerto Ricans citizens and allowed them to elect legislators (though the Washington-appointed governor could still veto all legislation). This wasn't independence, but it was, Albizu noted with satisfaction, "a form of home rule." The bill passed.

Speaking for Puerto Rico, Albizu wrote, "There is faith in the United States and in the spirit of fairness prevailing here."

★

That Woodrow Wilson, a Southerner, would seek to roll back empires made sense. His sympathy for the colonized was no doubt fueled by his anger at how the North had treated what Wilson called its "conquered possessions"—the former Confederate states—after the Civil War.

But there was another, darker side to Wilson's Southern identity. He was not just a son of the South in general, but the son of a Southern pastor who had defended slavery by writing a pamphlet titled *Mutual Relation of Masters and Slaves as Taught in the Bible*. It was a worldview that Wilson never entirely shook off. As president of Princeton, he stood against admitting black students. As president of the United States, he looked on with approval as his cabinet members segregated large parts of the federal government.

Wilson didn't think of nonwhites as subhuman, as some around him did. But he regarded many of them as "children," requiring "training" before they could rule themselves. The nightmare scenario, in his mind, was that the children might gain power they weren't ready to wield. He thought of the former slaves who had risen to political office immediately after the Civil War. It was a time, Wilson wrote, when the "white men of the South" lay "under the negroes' heels." This was a catastrophe, a "veritable overthrow of civilization." As he saw it, the brief participation of African Americans in politics had left a wound "incomparably deeper, incomparably more difficult to undo" than the war itself had.

These were not casual opinions. They formed a large part of the fifth volume of his *History of the American People* (1902). With its publication Wilson became, as Frederick Jackson Turner saw it, "the first southern scholar of adequate training and power who has dealt with American history as a whole." Other reviewers shared Turner's admiration for Wilson's history, yet they couldn't help but notice the author's fondness for the Ku Klux Klan, an organization whose mission, in Wilson's words, was "to protect the southern country from some of the ugliest hazards of a time of revolution." Wilson scolded Klan members for being hotheaded, yet he defended their motives. They were acting, he wrote, out of "the mere instinct of self-preservation."

That was how Thomas Dixon Jr., Wilson's close friend and former class-mate, saw the Klan, too. Dixon wrote his own work on this theme, a novel entitled *The Clansman*, which was quickly adapted into a stage play. In 1915 Dixon and the director D. W. Griffith used the novel as the basis for a film, *The Birth of a Nation*. It was an epic history about the South's re-demption by the Ku Klux Klan. And it quoted Wilson's historical writings in its title cards.

Black activists, understandably fearing what *The Birth of a Nation* might do to their cause, pressed eastern cities to prohibit the film's opening. Dixon appealed to Wilson for help, and Wilson staged a special screening in the White House. "It teaches history by lightning" was his judgment of the film, according to Griffith, though Wilson declined to issue a public statement. Still, Dixon and Griffith used Wilson's implicit endorsement to persuade municipal officials to allow the film to open.

The Birth of a Nation became the country's most popular film. The Klan, which by 1915 had become defunct, was relaunched. Its recruiters used the film to draw in millions of members.

Five months later, Wilson virtually reenacted the plot of *The Birth of a Nation* by sending the marines to the black republic of Haiti to wrest control from the "unstable" government. The occupation lasted through the rest of Wilson's presidency—and didn't end until 1934.

★

For the inhabitants of the world's colonies, there were two Wilsons: Wil-son the liberator, Wilson the racist. And it wasn't clear which one they would get.

As the First World War approached, Wilson was eager to stress his anti-imperialist side, to present the United States as a beacon of liberty. When the Bolsheviks seized Russia, and their leader, V. I. Lenin, called for the "liberation of all colonies," Wilson did not object. "The day of conquest and aggrandizement is gone by," he told Congress in a speech outlining his war aims. Those aims—Wilson's "Fourteen Points"—included "a free, open-minded, and absolutely impartial adjustment of all colonial claims."

The U.S. government broadcast the Fourteen Points throughout the world. In China, the speech was used for English-language instruction. Many students there could recite the Fourteen Points by heart.

Those Chinese students probably noted a studied vagueness in Wilson's language. Certainly it fell short of Lenin's stark demand for an immediate end to empire. But since Lenin was only the head of a pariah state, whereas Wilson governed the richest country on earth, Wilson's words were the ones that resounded. Hundreds of nationalists from all over the world petitioned him for support. They hoped that with his help, the war consuming Europe might also loosen the hold of European empires.

Albizu had something like that in mind, too. Wilson had "conveyed the impression to the Puerto Ricans that Puerto Rico's independence would be recognized," Albizu wrote. He joined the army in the hopes of ensuring that recognition. Participating in the war, Albizu believed, would "be of great benefit for the Puerto Rican people." He imagined what effect "thirty or forty thousand lame, blinded, or otherwise mutilated Puerto Ricans" returning from heroic combat in Europe would have had on Puerto Rico's bid for self-government. This wasn't an unusual line of reasoning. In India, even the pacifist Mohandas Gandhi urged his fellow Indians to join the war as a way of earning autonomy from the British.

The payoff for all this sacrifice was going to come, nationalists hoped, in the postwar settlement hammered out at the Paris Peace Conference in 1919, where the Treaty of Versailles was composed. That was where the rules of the new international order would be written. The question at hand was what would happen to the colonies of the defeated powers—Germany and the Ottoman Empire. But the larger question was the fate of empire in general.

Getting to Paris, and getting to Wilson, became the chief goal of nationalists everywhere. The Indian National Congress voted to send Gandhi to present its demands. Egyptian nationalists sought to send Sa'd Zaghlul, a leading reformer. Zaghlul began taking English lessons in the hope of meeting Wilson. "No people more than the Egyptian people," he wrote to Wilson, "has felt strongly the joyous emotion of the birth of a new era which, thanks to your virile action, is soon going to impose itself upon the universe." Zaghlul's supporters organized a new political party around the goal of getting him to Paris. They called it the Wafd, which means "delegation" in Arabic.

Less well-known nationalists sought Wilson, too. A twenty-eight-year-old kitchen assistant named Nguyen Tat Thanh, from French Indochina but living in Paris, prepared a document outlining his colony's demands. He signed it "Nguyen the Patriot" (Nguyen Ai Quoc) and walked the peace conference corridors, passing out copies. He gave one to Wilson's aide, who promised to show it to the president.

Albizu also had his eyes on Paris. But to his chagrin, the War Department held him back in Puerto Rico, where he trained troops. Before his unit could ship out, the war ended.

Albizu got another shot. A welcome cable arrived from Cambridge, from the new president of Harvard's Cosmopolitan Club. There would be a delegation from the Cosmopolitan Clubs of the United States to the peace conference. Harvard had chosen Albizu as its nominee. It's unclear whether this meant that Albizu's inclusion was assured, but his classmates seemed to have thought so. In February 1919 they threw a dance to raise $200 to send him to Paris.

★

The leaders of the colonized world raced to Woodrow Wilson in the hopes of winning his support. They were to be profoundly disappointed. The British, who controlled travel within their empire, refused to let Gandhi travel to Paris. They arrested Sa'd Zaghlul and exiled him to Malta (he eventually made it to Paris, but only after Wilson had left).

Pedro Albizu Campos faced his own ordeal. Like many Puerto Ricans, he identified as white. Yet he had Native and black heritage, too (his wife mistook him for South Asian upon meeting him). The army had placed him in a segregated black regiment. Albizu objected, protesting that he was white. In what must have been a humiliating episode, a board of physicians examined him and concluded that he wasn't.

After learning of his chance to go to Paris, Albizu rushed to the mainland to make his journey. This time, though, he couldn't sail straight to the North from Puerto Rico, but had to make his way up through the South from Galveston, Texas. No written evidence survives from Albizu's journey, but his experience traveling through the Jim Crow South as a "black" man appears to have been searing; for the rest of his life he would speak out against Southern-style racism. Whatever happened in the South, it had slowed Albizu considerably. He arrived in Boston too late to get to the peace conference.

Like Gandhi and Zaghlul, Albizu never got to meet Wilson. Even if he had, it's not clear what he could have done. Wilson spoke eloquently on behalf of smaller nations and their right to self-determination, yet he had southeastern European nations in mind: Yugoslavia, Czechoslovakia, Poland, Hungary, and the like. Puerto Rico wasn't even on the agenda.

Not only did Wilson do nothing to liberate Puerto Rico, he took the war as an occasion to *expand* the U.S. Empire. In 1917 his government purchased the Danish West Indies, a small cluster of Caribbean islands next to Puerto Rico that offered a population of some twenty-six thousand and, more important, promising naval bases. This colony, the U.S. Virgin Islands, became the first populated territory annexed since 1900.

When it came to the nationalists of the colonized world, there is no evidence that Wilson even read their many petitions. Nguyen the Patriot got no response from Wilson. The only nationalist leader from outside Europe who won Wilson's ear in Paris was Jan Smuts, soon to be the South African prime minister, who sought an international system that would bolster the white control of southern Africa.

Smuts got what he wanted. Empire survived, and all the victors' colonies were left intact. The defeated powers' colonies, instead of being liberated, were redistributed among the victors. The only novelty was that they were now classified as "mandates" under the League of Nations (this was Smuts's proposal). The mandates were arranged in a transparently racial hierarchy, with Middle Eastern territories on top ("Class A," en route to independence) and African and Pacific Island territories below ("Classes B and C").

The Japanese delegation asked to at least insert language about racial equality into the League of Nations covenant. This proposal had a majority of votes behind it—the French delegation deemed the cause "indisputable." But Wilson blocked it, refusing to let even the principle of racial equality stand.

★

It would be hard to overstate the consequences of these dashed hopes on the colonized world. The year 1919 was, for the colonies, when the switch was thrown, when nationalist movements abandoned polite petitioning. It was the year when Gandhi gave up his hope that India might be an equal partner within the British confederation and set his sights on independence. It was the year when everything seemed to spin out of control for the British in India: Gandhi's nonviolence campaigns, government repression (the "Amritsar Massacre"), an invasion by Afghanistan, and an uprising of Indian Muslims that acquired all-India proportions.

In Egypt, Zaghlul's arrest, along with that of other nationalists, sparked a wave of protests known as the 1919 Revolution. A twelve-year-old boy swept up in it remembers having "exploded with enthusiasm" and going to mosques and meeting halls to deliver impassioned speeches and read poems. Koreans declared independence from Japan in 1919, and they took to the streets in the March First Movement. China had a similar uprising, called the May Fourth Movement, emerging in reaction to the peace conference's handing over of Germany's territory in China to Japan. One disgusted Chinese protester called Allied leaders in Paris "a bunch of robbers bent on securing territories and indemnities."

Such animosity meant little to U.S. leaders at the time—they didn't have much business in places like Egypt and Korea. But later it would come to mean a great deal. The Chinese protester complaining of "robbers" in Paris—that was a young Mao Zedong. Nguyen the Patriot also gained renown, although by another name: Ho Chi Minh. That Egyptian boy reciting poems and making speeches was Sayyid Qutb, a leading Islamist thinker who would become the key inspiration for Osama bin Laden.

And Albizu? Pedro Albizu Campos would become the most dangerous domestic anti-imperialist the United States would ever face.

8

WHITE CITY

From Washington at the turn of the twentieth century, prospects looked good. The United States had gutted Spain's empire. Its industries were growing swiftly, giving it the world's biggest economy. Its two richest inhabitants, John D. Rockefeller and Andrew Carnegie, possessed arguably the largest private fortunes in recorded history.

Yet what struck observers, repeatedly, was how much poverty remained amid the plenty. Gravity-defying skyscrapers spoke to new accumulations of capital, but the shadows of those tall buildings fell over large, polluted slums that were crowded with the unfortunates sucked in by industrialism's undertow.

That the world's richest country should at the same time be so squalid was hard to countenance. The press rumbled with proposals to tame the chaos, clean the cities, and fix whatever was broken. One of the blockbusters of the age was a work of science fiction, *Looking Backward* (1888) by Edward Bellamy. It imagined a man falling asleep in Boston in 1887 and awakening in the year 2000 to a luminously bright future, a future where everything *worked*.

Bellamy's prophecies were exhilarating. Consumers, he predicted, would no longer buy goods in stores. They'd place orders into pneumatic tubes, using what he called "credit cards," and their purchases would come whooshing back via the same tubes. For a small fee, they could even have music piped into their homes as if it were water.

"It appears to me," Bellamy's time traveler marveled in a retrospectively hilarious passage, "that if we could have devised an arrangement for providing everybody with music in their homes, perfect in quality, unlimited in quantity, suited to every mood, and beginning and ceasing at will, we should have considered the limits of human felicity already attained, and ceased to strive for further improvements."

The real showstopper was the city itself. Bellamy's sleeper could barely recognize Boston in 2000. He gaped at its "miles of broad streets," its "large open squares filled with trees," and its "public buildings of a colossal size and architectural grandeur unparalleled in my day." Clean, spacious, and carefully planned—it was the very opposite of the Gilded Age city.

Nobody had ever seen a modern city like that. But five years later they caught a glimpse. Eighteen ninety-three was the occasion of the World's Columbian Exposition in Chicago, staged (a year late) to celebrate the four hundredth anniversary of Columbus's first voyage. To erect the massive ensemble of buildings that would house the exposition, the fair's organizers hired Daniel Burnham, known as one of the first builders of skyscrapers.

Working big appealed to Burnham. He was enchanted by size, seized by what his fellow architect Louis Sullivan diagnosed as a "megalomania concerning the largest, the tallest, the most costly and sensational." With 686 acres of marshy parkland on Chicago's South Side to play with, Burnham wouldn't have to limit himself to individual buildings. He could found his own city.

It was, to be sure, a temporary city, made not of stone, but of spray-painted plaster. And he had to rely on other architects to build it. Still, Burnham placed his indelible stamp on it. The city's structures were enormous, they were neoclassical, and they were, per his instructions, all white.

It struck a resounding chord. Fairgoers bought more than twenty-one million tickets—at a time when the national population was still fewer than seventy million. The crowds were "astonished," Louis Sullivan remembered. "They beheld what was for them an amazing revelation of the architectural art, of which previously they in comparison had known nothing. To them it was a veritable Apocalypse, a message inspired from on high."

★

Burnham's White City *was* astonishing. But the impressive thing wasn't any single building. Rather, it was all the buildings together—more than two hundred of them—designed in a single style, rendered in a single color, and laid out according to a master plan.

It was astonishing because builders at the time couldn't *do* that. They wanted to, certainly. Realizing Bellamy's dream of efficiency, rationality, and hygiene was a chief desire of the leading men and women of the day. It's just that such large-scale social interventions inevitably encountered resistance. It was one thing to build "broad streets" and "large open squares"—of the sort *Looking Backward* described—in an unused park, as Burnham had done. But in a real city, such features would have to be ripped out of an already tightly woven urban fabric. Monied interests would have to be convinced, machine politicians mollified, stubborn city dwellers displaced.

This was how it went in the Progressive Era. In one corner stood reformers, intent on imposing order. In the other, a discordant multitude of crosscutting interests and publics. It wasn't just architecture. From battleground to battleground—politics, public health, the factory floor—the war raged on.

Yet there was one arena where the fight was markedly less fair, where social engineers indisputably held the upper hand: the empire. Although the overseas territories had dropped off the maps, they were, for a certain type of professional, extremely interesting places. They functioned as laboratories, spaces for bold experimentation where ideas could be tried with practically no resistance, oversight, or consequences. And so, as one reformer put it, "ablaze with pity and with righteous wrath, our people flew at the Islands like a White-Wing brigade in a sort of Holy War upon ignorance, superstition, disease and dirt."

In 1904 Burnham enlisted in this holy war himself. He accepted an invitation to draw up plans for Manila and for a new "summer capital" the government sought to establish in the mountains at Baguio.

The White City was going to the Philippines.

★

Burnham's invitation came from Cameron Forbes, Ralph Waldo Emerson's grandson. Forbes had come to the Philippines as commissioner of commerce and police, a wide-ranging job giving him authority over building roads and quashing revolts. In 1909 he became the governor-general. "Who but a mad dreamer could have planned such a career for me?" he asked his diary on his fortieth birthday. "Taken from a counting house in Boston to go to the South Seas, and here, at forty, ruling over such a conglomeration of races, languages, customs, and divergencies as are to be found among the eight millions who live in the Philippine Islands."

Unlike Britain and France, the United States had few colonial careerists. Its officials tended to come and go quickly, seeing the territories as hardship posts that might lead to higher office back home—as quickly as possible, they hoped.

Still, once in a while, someone slipped into the role of sahib and played it to pith-hatted perfection. In the Philippines, that someone was Cameron Forbes. He delighted in life in the tropics: the exotic Orient, the attentive servants, the languid lifestyle. He loved Filipinos, too, though he loved them, as the nationalist leader Manuel Quezon observed, "in the same way the former slave owners loved their Negro slaves."

Forbes filled his diary with tales of polo, baseball, and golf, though usually with a racial twist. One of his favorite polo horses was called Nigger. His baseball team, named after the costume of the Igorot people of the Luzon mountains, was the Gee Strings. "I remember one day playing golf, with a breechless Igorot caddy," Forbes wrote. "I said to myself, 'Now how many am I?' and the boy replied, 'Playing five.' I was as much astonished as though a tree had spoken."

Forbes didn't expect Filipinos to speak, or at least he didn't expect them to say much worth hearing. He knew that many sought independence, but he wrote that "they want it very much as a baby wants a candle because it is bright and because it is held out for him to seize at." He doubted that Filipinos "knew exactly what it meant." At any rate, Forbes didn't "believe in it for them" and felt that their interests were best served by benevolent men from the mainland.

Men, that is, like Daniel Burnham.

Burnham could start with Manila. If Bellamy's twenty-first-century Boston was the dream, Manila was the nightmare. The "ancient pest-hole" (as one reformer called it) was crowded, disease-ridden, and poor. "It has the crookedest streets of any city in the world," the guidebook exclaimed.

Mainlanders blamed all this on Filipinos, but the Manila that Burnham encountered in 1904 had been badly mauled by the forces of history. Its timeline read like a book of the Old Testament: 1899, war; 1901, bubonic plague; 1902, cholera and rinderpest; 1903, the "Great Fire." Nellie Taft, the wife of Governor-General William Howard Taft, recalled the "constant terror," the feeling that "we were living always in the lowering shadow of some dreadful catastrophe."

Yet what was from a human perspective a disaster was, from an urban planner's perspective, an invitation. Large swaths of the city had been cleared by war, by diseases, and by the destructive public health campaigns that accompanied them (involving, in one case, U.S. troops torching an entire district in the name of fighting cholera). Real estate was cheap, and the best land was already in governmental hands, seized by the military at the start of the war.

"Manila has before it an opportunity unique in the history of modern times," pronounced Burnham, "the opportunity to create a unified city equal to the greatest of the Western World."

With Forbes's backing, Burnham dove in. He was willing to defer to the reigning Spanish mission style of architecture, but the city's urban footprint would be radically reconfigured. Under Spain, the center of power, called Intramuros, had been a cloistered, church-studded city within a city, packed within imposing walls and surrounded by a moat. Burnham would fill the moat (unsanitary), punch holes in the walls for traffic, and give the city a new center.

He fixed on the Luneta, a cleared area near the water, where musicians played in the evenings. This, moved a thousand feet to the west and surrounded by governmental buildings, could serve as Manila's command center. Broad avenues would radiate outward from it, cutting diagonally through the street grid. Why? "Because every section of the Capitol City should look with deference toward the symbol of the Nation's power," Burnham explained.

Burnham sought to impress on Filipinos the authority of the colonial government. Yet he was ultimately less concerned with Philippine opinion than with the needs of mainlanders. So, though he had little to say about the many neighborhoods that had been torched or shot up in the previous years (other than to imagine carving boulevards through them), he fretted at length about Manila's lack of a world-class hotel. He proposed placing one (a "world famous resort") adjoining the Luneta. He also left room among the Luneta's governmental buildings for a country club, boat clubs, and a casino. These weren't built for Filipinos, and indeed some clubs would refuse to admit them. They were for foreigners—a promise,

Burnham wrote, of "continuous good times" made in the hopes that "those who make fortunes will stay and others will come."

Forbes loved it. The plan "seems to meet with approval all round," he said, beaming.

★

"If one has capital and a well-considered plan, the thing does itself," Burnham announced confidently the year he erected his White City in Chicago. But subsequent experience had taught him the folly of that statement, if he ever believed it. Plans didn't "do themselves." They needed careful stewardship.

It was a lesson Burnham learned to take seriously. At roughly the same time as he was drawing up his plans for Manila, he started on another large urban plan, for Chicago. Chicago and Manila—they were his most ambitious projects. Today they're the two cities that most clearly bear his mark.

Cities are fiendishly complex, and planning them takes care. In Chicago, where Burnham had lived and worked for decades, he was painstaking. He fired off queries to experts throughout the city. He asked the nine leading shipping firms about the dimensions of their ships. He asked a doctor in a Chicago hospital where his patients came from. He inquired about the backgrounds of the students at Northwestern and the University of Chicago. In its acknowledgments, his *Plan of Chicago*, which took two years and a staff of dozens to produce, thanked 312 people for their help.

Burnham needed that help. The Chicago plan was by necessity a group effort in both conception and implementation. Carrying it out would take decades. A commission of four hundred prominent citizens took charge of executing the plan. They sponsored lectures and made a film with the hope of drumming up support. The commission arranged to have a book about the plan, *Wacker's Manual of the Plan of Chicago*, introduced into the eighth-grade curriculum of the city's public schools, presumably on the theory that the children would preach the Gospel of Burnham to their parents.

Mostly, it worked. Not entirely—large parts of the plan were never realized, such as a Luneta-style core of civic buildings at Congress and Halsted Streets. But between 1912 and 1931, Chicago voters approved some eighty-six plan-related bond issues, for a combined cost of $234 million.

In the Philippines, however, it was different. There weren't any voters to persuade. Burnham spent six weeks in the colony, a place he knew little about before arriving. He toured Manila with Forbes and spoke with some officials, but his contact with Filipinos other than servants was limited. No living Filipino warranted mention in his letters, in his diary, or in the plan itself. In all, Burnham worked on his plan for six months, and that left time for travel, tourism, and his simultaneous work in Baguio.

Burnham could never have gotten away with such haste in Chicago. In Manila, however, it was fine. Three days after the government approved his plan (with no changes), construction began.

Things could move quickly because power over the built environment lay in the hands of a single man, the consulting architect (initially called the insular architect). There was no such position on the mainland. But in the Philippines, Forbes explained, "we so fixed it that the Insular Architect prepared plans for all public buildings, whether insular, municipal, or provincial." Small towns couldn't even modify their walls or parks without the consulting architect's approval. And, by law, the consulting architect was "charged with the interpretation of the Burnham Plan."

Not only did Burnham get an architectural dictator to execute his plan, he got to choose his man. On his recommendation, the government appointed William E. Parsons, an architect trained at Yale and the École des Beaux-Arts, who served from 1905 to 1914. Parsons saw the job as an "architect's dream." He had sole control over all public building in the colony. He also operated, with Forbes's encouragement, a private firm, so he could erect commercial buildings to match the public ones.

Parsons went on a spree, building many of the landmarks of Manila: the Army-Navy Club (whites only), the Elks Club (ditto), the Manila Hotel (de facto whites only), the YMCA (separate entrance for whites), the Central School on Taft Avenue, the University Hall of the University of the Philippines, the railway station, and the Philippine General Hospital. He also issued his own city plans, for Cebu and Zamboanga, along Burnham-style lines.

It didn't take long before Parsons began worrying about the "large and rapidly increasing number of buildings" under his supervision. One solution would have been to delegate. Instead, he standardized. Schoolhouses, markets, hospitals, and even provincial capitols could simply be duplicated.

His office circulated blank forms to collect basic information about building sites and then returned the appropriate blueprints.

It made a certain sense. After all, did a market in Davao really need to be different from one in Balanga? Yet when an efficiency-minded Congress proposed standardizing architecture on the mainland, howls of protest were heard. Each place was unique, critics argued—you couldn't just put the same building everywhere.

Maybe not on the mainland. But in the Philippines, Parsons could do what he liked. It was a fact his mainland colleagues noted with interest and more than a little envy. "I doubt if this method would bear fruit in our own city improvement plans, in which everything depends on slow-moving legislative bodies," observed a correspondent for the *Architectural Record*. "The iron hand of power, when wielded for the public good, is a mighty weapon."

★

Cameron Forbes kept Daniel Burnham apprised of the progress on Manila, reassuring him that "the Burnham plan is sacred and is being strictly adhered to." Burnham was no doubt pleased to hear it. But Manila was not his chief concern. He was, he declared upon arriving in the Philippines, "more deeply interested in the summer capital project," the city he planned at Baguio. Manila offered him a relatively free hand, but Baguio was to be built, like the White City, entirely from scratch. Burnham saw it as his chance "to formulate my plans untrammeled by any but natural conditions."

The idea of a summer capital was not new. European colonizers had built a series of hill stations, most famously Shimla in India, where Rudyard Kipling summered and from which the British ruled during the hot months. U.S. officials, fearing the effect of the Philippine climate on their constitutions, sought a hill station of their own. They chose Baguio, 150 miles north of Manila and five thousand feet above sea level. In 1903 the government declared Baguio the summer capital of the Philippines, and in 1904 Forbes charged Burnham with planning the still-unbuilt town.

Before construction could start, though, there had to be a road. Baguio was accessible only via a long trail zigzagging up a crumbling canyon wall. Getting there was a feat. When the portly William Howard Taft made the trek, he reported proudly to Washington, "Stood trip well. Rode horseback twenty-five miles to five-thousand-foot altitude. Hope amoebic dysentery cured. Great province this."

"How is the horse?" was the secretary of war's cruel reply.

Building a road to Baguio became an obsession of the colonial state. The steep slopes and regular landslides turned it into an all-consuming, Werner Herzog–style man vs. nature affair. At peak, construction employed some four thousand men from dozens of nations. "The Filipinos so far are the worst," complained Forbes. "They are afraid of heights and rolling rocks."

They had good reason to be. Workers fell off cliffs; died from dysentery, malaria, and cholera; and were crushed by bridges that came skidding down the slopes. One part of the trail earned the name the Devil's Slide for the many men it had killed. "Few days pass without casualty," Forbes noted in his diary.

Still, for Forbes, the prize was worth it. Baguio was paradise: perpetual springtime, a cool mist, rolling hills, pine trees galore. It "gives the red corpuscles," he wrote.

Burnham, for his part, could barely contain himself. This was a once-in-a-lifetime chance to build a city—a real city, not a plaster one—from the ground up. The land wasn't empty, as much of it lay in the hands of Igorots, Philippine uplanders. But the mainlander-dominated Philippine Supreme Court held that Igorots, being savages, could not own land. At any rate, the government claimed fourteen thousand acres of it—more than twenty times the area that Burnham had for his White City. If built properly, he salivated, it "could be made equal to anything that has ever been."

Burnham pulled out all the stops: large governmental buildings, commanding views, a grand axis cutting through the Baguio meadow. He placed the most important structures on the slopes that ringed the meadow. Doing so was costly, Burnham acknowledged, but to build them in the valley would ruin what he called the "unusual monumental possibilities" of the area. As Burnham saw it, the governmental buildings should be placed so as to "frankly dominate everything in sight."

Forbes, getting into the spirit, selected a property for himself: a twelve-acre uphill plot overlooking all of Baguio. He made plans to open the Baguio Country Club, featuring an eighteen-hole golf course "equal to the finest in Scotland, where, owing to the clear briskness of the air, no drives will be foozled or balls get dormy."

Upland empire: The governmental center of Baguio, overlooking the valley in accordance with Burnham's plan to erect "monumental buildings where they command a view"

The architecture of power, plus golf: that summed it up well. Though technically Baguio was a command center—the part-time capital of the United States' great Asian colony—it was also a retreat. Forbes saw it as "a blessed relief from Manila," where "the swarm of people who rush in is fearful. Here, people only come if sent for, or if their business is urgent enough to bring them up to the hills."

It doesn't appear that much business made that uphill trek. The Philippine Commission, the colony's appointed body of lawmakers, convened only "every three days," Forbes recorded in his diary, "and we crash through our business in about an hour or less." The real center of life was the Baguio Country Club, where frank conversations could be had over rounds of golf. But of the 161 original members of the club, only 6 were Filipino.

Free from the heat, free from business, and largely free from Filipinos, Governor-General Forbes found time for other pursuits. "I get up leisurely when I feel like it, write in my journal sparingly so as not to run into the error of being too voluminous, and play a few hands of cards to iron the crinkles out of my mind." In the afternoons, Forbes would spend "an hour or so" reading newspaper clippings, but he would stop at four to "take a ride, or play polo, according to the day."

"I have let the great world sweep by," he purred.

★

None of this was cheap. The road alone cost $2 million by the time it opened in 1905—a tenth of what the United States had paid Spain to buy the Philippines. And that didn't count the expensive repairs required every time a monsoon washed parts of the road away, or the many lives lost building it. Then there was the city itself, constructed to Burnham's plan under Parsons's guidance. It was a triumph of modern engineering straight out of Bellamy, boasting wide streets, an excellent sewer system, an ice plant, and, by 1921, hydroelectric power. Added to this municipal investment, which far outstripped investments made in any lowland Philippine city, was the cost of hauling the entire top layer of the government up to the mountains for four months a year.

Even a British reporter, presumably accustomed to this sort of thing, couldn't help but "admire the audacity" of the men who, with disease rampant and a war still raging in the south, had built Shangri-La.

Filipinos were less admiring as they watched money that had been earmarked for postwar reconstruction flow uphill, funding a months-long spa for an unelected government. "Stingy towards the people and lavish toward itself, it has no scruples nor remorse about wasting money which is not its own," one paper complained. In 1913, the year Forbes left, the Philippine Commission finally relented and agreed to conduct its summer business in Manila, though Baguio continued to serve as the government's unofficial nerve center.

The restoration of Manila as the all-seasons capital marked a turning point in colonial politics. It corresponded with Woodrow Wilson's election and his policy of handing over local power to Filipinos. In 1914 more than one in four governmental positions were held by mainlanders. By 1921, it was fewer than one in twenty.

William E. Parsons, Burnham's protégé, found Wilson's Filipinization campaign intolerable. The top men on his staff were mainlanders, and he was unwilling to see that change. "It is impossible to understand how any man, having at heart the welfare of the Filipino people, can conform to the present policy," he wrote in his letter of resignation.

But Parsons left feeling that his work was done. He reported with pride that the main contours of Burnham's Manila were "nailed down, as it were, with permanent public and semi-public buildings." The foundation had been laid. It just remained for his successors to build atop it.

As it happened, Parsons's greatest successor arrived the very year Parsons left. But he wasn't visiting the city for the first time. Juan Arellano had been born there.

★

Juan Arellano was from one of the most extraordinary families in the Philippines. One brother, Arcadio, was the first Filipino architectural adviser hired by the United States. Another, Manuel, would become one of the colony's most noted photographers. Juan's cousin Jose Palma wrote the national anthem used by Aguinaldo's Philippine Republic (which is also the anthem today). His cousin Rafael Palma was one of the six original Filipino members of the Baguio Country Club and the future president of the University of the Philippines.

Juan's métier was painting, and he was among the first Filipino impressionists. He submitted an early work, *Woman Descending Stairway*, to the St. Louis World's Fair in 1904, one of the many mainland fairs that showcased the empire. To his disappointment, it didn't win a prize.

Three years later, Arellano applied to another fair, the Jamestown Exposition. This time he succeeded—not as an artist, but as one of the native "living exhibits" these fairs fed on. For seven months he wore a pineapple-fiber shirt and allowed himself to be ogled. Fairgoers were taken aback, though, when he answered their questions in fluent English.

But Arellano had come to the mainland to study, not to be studied. Once he made enough money working at Jamestown, he moved to Philadelphia to enroll at the Pennsylvania Academy of Fine Arts. He won the academy's annual award for best painting, a prize that automatically placed him in the next year's competition for the Prix de Rome. He was disqualified at the last minute, though, when someone noted that as a Filipino, he wasn't a U.S. citizen.

Arellano then turned to architecture, winning more prizes, securing a diploma from the Drexel Institute and studying the Beaux Arts style in New York. He got a job in New York and eventually found work with

Frederick Law Olmsted Jr., one of Daniel Burnham's close collaborators. Olmsted sparked Arellano's interest in city planning.

Arellano was, in other words, a Renaissance man: painter, builder, and planner. His first major architectural commission upon returning to Manila was the Legislative Building, part of the civic core Burnham had planned around the Luneta. The foundation had been laid by Ralph Harrington Doane, the final mainland consulting architect, in his last year in the Philippines. It was Arellano who expanded the building, gave it a classical façade, and raised it into one of the largest edifices in the colony.

This was a massive undertaking, costing as much as the road to Baguio. Yet here the symbolism was reversed. The Legislative Building was in Manila, not up some mountain, and it was designed to house the Philippine Legislature, the only elected part of the colonial government. More to the point, it had been built by a Filipino.

The press loved it. It was "the most magnificent and impressive structure ever erected in the Philippines," a Manila magazine raved. "Here is a stronger and more enduring argument as to the capacities of the Filipino race than any that the most enthusiastic of the American friends of the Filipinos can formulate," a newspaper wrote. "The pessimists who said that Filipinos were not capable of doing anything have not a leg to stand on."

The Legislative Building was indeed a rebuke to imperialists like Forbes, who doubted Filipinos' abilities. Yet in beating imperialists at their own game, Arellano was also playing their game. Though he later regretted this, he conspicuously built the Legislative Building in the style of the White City rather than the Spanish style that Burnham and even Parsons had gamely accommodated. One of Manila's best-known historians, Nick Joaquin, has identified the Legislative Building as "architecturally, the landmark dividing the American from the Spanish era." That is, it was Arellano's building, not one of Parsons's creations, that marked the full shift to the neoclassical style that, Joaquin writes, "has ever since dominated our public works."

Arellano kept going. He became *the* architect in the colonial Philippines, eventually taking Parsons's former position, consulting architect. He designed the massive post office in Manila. He designed capitol buildings for three provinces. The office of the high commissioner in Manila was another Arellano project—today it serves as the U.S. embassy. In the

Juan Arellano's Legislative Building, completed 1926

1930s the government contemplated moving the capital north from Manila to Quezon City, a planned metropolis of Burnham-style plazas and radial boulevards. Arellano served on the planning commission.

★

Had Daniel Burnham lived through the 1930s and returned to the Philippines, he would have been thrilled by what he saw. In Chicago, he'd struggled mightily for years to realize his vision (and his allies had worked for decades to do so after his death). In the Philippines, however, just half a year's hasty work, only six weeks of it in-country, sufficed to remake one city and build another from the ground up.

Such were the joys of empire. The colonies were, for men like Burnham, playgrounds, places to carry out ideas without worrying about the counterforces that encumbered action at home. Mainlanders could confiscate land, redirect taxes, and waste workers' lives to build paradises in the mountains.

Filipinos, for their part, were relegated to the sidelines. The segregated spaces at the center of Burnham's plans were not for them, though their taxes paid the cost. The best they could hope for was to win some measure of respect by showing themselves worthy in their colonizers' eyes. In the realm of architecture, that looked like Juan Arellano carrying out Burnham's plans with even greater devotion than William Parsons had.

And so, from Burnham to Parsons to Arellano, the torch passed. Looking back on it all, Burnham's biographer concluded that Burnham's vision achieved its "greatest architectural success" not on the mainland, but in the Philippines.

9

DOCTORS
WITHOUT BORDERS

The U.S. conquest of Puerto Rico was relatively painless—"a picnic," as one journalist put it. But if Puerto Ricans had avoided the horrors of war, they met something similar the following year, when a category-4 hurricane slammed into the island. Whole coffee plantations washed down the mountains. Thousands of people were killed, more left homeless.

From the perspective of Assistant Surgeon Bailey K. Ashford, it was Dantesque. Ashford was stationed in Ponce, the hometown of Pedro Albizu Campos. He saw the hurricane wreck the city, demolishing houses, denuding trees, flinging metal roofs through the air. He watched as "hordes of pallid refugees" fled the mountains seeking food, shelter, and medical treatment.

They could have done much worse for a doctor than Ashford. He was a gifted physician whose talents had drawn him to Leonard Wood's attention. Wood had befriended Ashford and encouraged him, which is how Ashford ended up in Puerto Rico in the first place. But unlike Wood, Ashford didn't hold himself aloof from the colonized. He learned Spanish, fell in love with a Puerto Rican woman, María, and had three children with her: Mahlon, Margarita, and Gloria María. He collaborated closely with local physicians, particularly his colleague Dr. Pedro Gutiérrez Igaravídez. Indeed, as Ashford would live on the island for most of his life, he came to see *himself* as Puerto Rican, not as a mainlander.

But that would come later. Now Ashford had a more immediate concern: the refugees. He eyed their "flabby flesh and ghastly pallor" with alarm. His wife, María, explained that what he was seeing was not just the work of the hurricane, but the work of centuries. This was just what peasants looked like, she explained. They are weak and anemic. They die.

Thinking the problem was their poor diets, Ashford fed them meat, beans, and fish. Yet their complexions stayed pale, and they kept dying. He examined their blood and confirmed María's diagnosis: they were severely anemic. But this made no sense. An epidemic of anemia afflicting an entire class? "It was unthinkable."

He inspected one of his patients' feces under a microscope. There he saw something interesting: an "oval thing with four fluffy gray balls inside." An egg. Probably a worm egg. He checked his manual of tropical diseases. It looked like hookworm.

Hookworm—the force of the revelation struck him. It was, he felt, "like a veil had been lifted." Peasants *didn't* just look like that. They weren't simply malnourished because they were oppressed. Nearly all—Ashford would later estimate nine in ten rural Puerto Ricans—were suffering badly from an intestinal parasite.

★

Like most parasites, hookworms are both fascinating and deeply gross. The larvae grow in shaded, moist, warm soil and seek human feet. They bore through the skin, usually the skin between the toes, and worm their way into the bloodstream, then to the lungs, and then, after a cough and a swallow, into the upper part of the small intestine. There, they take up residence and live out their six- or seven-year lives, subsisting on blood. People with enough worms in them—it can be more than two thousand—grow listless, become pale, and lose muscle. They also, through their feces, pass out hundreds of thousands of worm eggs, which, if deposited in the right environment, will hatch, find more human feet, and complete the revolting cycle.

Hookworms have stowed away in humanity's small intestines for some twelve thousand years, a side effect of domesticating dogs. But since the parasites typically weaken rather than kill, and since the African populations most likely to carry them have some immunity, hookworms went unnoticed until the nineteenth century. Western doctors first realized how dangerous they could be in 1880, when a professor at the University of Turin found a lethal form of hookworm disease among workers digging a long tunnel under the Alps between Italy and Switzerland. The tunnel was hot, wet, crowded, and full of feces—hookworm heaven. Rather than carrying just a few worms, the men were overloaded, expelling eggs and reinfecting themselves daily.

It's hard to imagine a habitat as congenial to hookworms as a trans-Alp tunnel, but Puerto Rico came surprisingly close. Not only was the island densely populated, but nearly two-thirds of Puerto Ricans lived in the highlands, where coffee was king. The coffee plantations lacked privies, the workers toiled barefoot, and the harvest was during the rainy season— providing a pretty good approximation of the hot, moist, shaded, and well-trafficked soil of the tunnel.

Hookworms flourished so abundantly on the island's coffee estates that they didn't only enfeeble workers, they killed them. By the turn of the century, anemia was the leading cause of death in the colony, accounting for some 20 to 30 percent of mortality.

But the worms in Puerto Rico were unusual, as Ashford discovered. Unlike the ones in his book, they had no teeth. He returned to Washington "carrying a bottle of my precious worms with me" and presented them to his former professor at Georgetown, Charles Wardell Stiles. Stiles concluded that this was a previously unknown species. He gave it a dramatic name: *Necator americanus*. American murderer.

Luckily for Ashford, *Necator americanus* was easily dealt with. A cheap (though nausea-inducing) pill was all it took to dislodge the worms, and visible recovery took just days. Ashford returned to Puerto Rico and, with his colleague Pedro Gutiérrez Igaravídez, established a clinic at Utuado. Patients came slowly at first, then quickly, until Ashford, Gutiérrez, and their colleagues were treating hundreds a day. The physicians supplied medicine and spoke to their patients about hygiene, explaining the importance of shoes and latrines.

In 1905 the Puerto Rican legislature funded a national program, again under the supervision of Ashford and Gutiérrez. By 1910, they estimated that nearly 30 percent of the population had been treated, for less than a dollar per patient.

★

As Bailey Ashford fought hookworm in Puerto Rico, his professor, Charles Wardell Stiles, continued to contemplate the disease. In 1908 Stiles took a train through North Carolina with Walter Hines Page, the great Southern journalist, and Henry C. Wallace, the Iowa agricultural expert (and father of the future vice president Henry A. Wallace). Wallace pointed to a pale and hunched man by the station. "What on earth is that?" he asked— he hadn't seen anyone like that in Iowa. Page explained that this was a poor white, an all-too-familiar type in the South. Such men were called "dirt eaters."

Stiles piped up. No, that man was suffering from a severe hookworm infestation. His pallor and posture were the result of anemia. Severely anemic people eat dirt or clay; they are hungry for iron. And the man could be cured "at a cost of about fifty cents."

"Good God! Stiles, are you in earnest?" Page exclaimed.

Again, the veil lifted. Is *that* where the "lazy white Southerner" stereotype came from? Is that why Southern whites looked funny—lanky, pale, and slack? Page introduced Stiles to John D. Rockefeller's aide, who arranged for the oil baron to give a million dollars to deworm the South. This was an early venture by Rockefeller into philanthropy, which would culminate in the establishment of the Rockefeller Foundation.

The head of the Rockefeller campaign traveled to Puerto Rico to consult with Ashford. The idea was to start something similar in the South, with Stiles as part of it. Thus, while Ashford battled hookworms on the island, his former teacher would fight them on the mainland.

Even with cheap deworming pills, though, a hookworm campaign was not an easy sell. Stiles, born in New York, found white Southerners prickly to the point of violence when he brought up the delicate subject of their toilet habits. After one address to a school, the local sheriff insisted on guarding Stiles until he made it safely out of town. The editor of a Tampa newspaper threatened to lynch him. The Civil War was over, but it wasn't so far past that Southerners would stand for a Northern doctor diagnosing their entire region as pathologically lazy and unhygienic.

Mark Twain, watching from the sidelines, hooted with delight at the indignity of it all. He wrote a lilting satire in which he imagined biblical figures suffering from the timeless scourge ("Six thousand years ago Shem was full of hookworms").

Few, however, shared Twain's sense of humor. And it seems that elite

Puerto Ricans were as prideful about this matter as Southern whites were. Some mocked the doctors, questioned the diagnosis, and put up active opposition. Yet the manner in which the two campaigns were carried out was a study in contrast, one that says much about how things worked in the colonies.

In the Southern campaign, the Rockefeller men took great care to avoid offending public sensibilities. Instead of sending their own doctors, they worked with state boards of health and employed local doctors—all white. They courted newspaper editors. And they adopted a familiar cultural form for their campaign: the Southern tent revival. Like itinerant preachers, hookworm fighters quietly approached local power holders, secured their blessing, and then brought the show to town with great fanfare. There were picnic lunches, gospel songs, and dramatic conversion testimonies (once I was blind, now I can see; once I was wormy . . .). The dispensaries doled out the medicine—to more than 440,000 patients in five years—and downplayed the stern lectures.

Ashford and Gutiérrez would have loved to run a campaign that way. They envisioned a network of clinics and an army of local Puerto Ricans, men who enjoyed the confidence of the peasants, to "preach the gospel."

But that required funding, which meant squeezing resources from the colonial government. Whereas the Southern campaign began with a million-dollar grant from John D. Rockefeller, the Puerto Rican one started with $5,000 from the colonial treasury. After Ashford and Gutiérrez demonstrated that deworming worked, they begged for funds to permanently eradicate hookworm disease. But the money that arrived was, in their judgment, "utterly inadequate": half what was needed in the best year, then down to a third. In 1908 the government didn't appropriate any funds, so all dispensaries were officially closed (though some persisted, using stockpiles and volunteered labor) for more than three months.

Unable to afford persuasion, Ashford and Gutiérrez tried compulsion. They implored plantation owners to force workers to wear shoes. They advocated a "sanitary ordinance" to be "energetically enforced" throughout the colony. In order to work, peasants should have to carry papers certifying that they were hookworm-free. Such measures would infringe on the "liberty of the citizen," Gutiérrez admitted, but the cause was worth it.

Yet these laws never passed, and it's unclear how well the colonial government would have enforced them. In the end, it didn't matter. Oversight was taken from Gutiérrez (Ashford had already resigned) and placed under a single authority, the Washington-appointed commissioner of health. The campaign fizzled.

The result? Hookworm disease in the South was reduced substantially, with enduring economic effects, mainly due to children staying in school longer. So encouraging were the results that the Rockefeller Foundation took on a more ambitious project: combating hookworm throughout the tropics—history's first global health campaign.

Meanwhile, in Puerto Rico, Ashford, Gutiérrez, and their colleagues treated hundreds of thousands and headed off the direst cases, of which there were many. Hookworm treatment, plus parallel campaigns that the military ran against yellow fever and smallpox, brought the Puerto Rican death rate down dramatically. Yet Ashford and Gutiérrez watched in frustration as their patients succumbed to reinfection again and again. Treatment could forestall death, but all the worm pills in all the dispensaries couldn't change the larger facts: most Puerto Ricans were poor, they worked outdoors without shoes or privies, and their government lacked the resources, and possibly the will, to do much about that.

Medicine reduced hookworm disease's morbidity in Puerto Rico, but not its spread. In 1930 it stood pretty close to where it had been when Ashford first arrived more than thirty years earlier. It was now chronic rather than acute, but it still afflicted eight or nine in ten rural Puerto Ricans.

★

By 1930, hookworm was just one of Puerto Rico's many problems. Two years before, another hurricane—the worst the region had seen in modern times—had sliced across the island. It killed hundreds, inflicted tens of millions of dollars of damage, and nearly destroyed the coffee industry. The next year, 1929, brought the Great Depression, which sent sugar prices and wages tumbling. Incomes in Puerto Rico fell by nearly 30 percent between 1930 and 1933. Meanwhile, prices rose, trade plummeted, unemployment engulfed more than half the workforce, and strikes lit up the ports, needlework factories, tobacco fields, and cane fields.

The causes of Puerto Rico's woes were multiple and complex. Many involved arcane aspects of sugar tariffs and the lax enforcement of landholding laws. Mainlanders, however, tended to focus on a different explanation: overpopulation. It was the very thing that had troubled them about

Puerto Rico back in 1898, when they worried that Spain's colonies had too many nonwhites to be safely annexed.

Puerto Rico *was* densely populated—that's one reason why hookworm spread so easily. But it wasn't any more so in 1930 than New Jersey was. Still, the fingers pointed and heads shook. The governor believed that restricting births "among the lower and more ignorant elements of the population" was "the only salvation for the Island." President Franklin Delano Roosevelt joked grimly to an adviser—at least, I think and fervently hope he was joking—that "the only solution is to use the methods which Hitler used effectively."

"It is all very simple and painless," he continued. "You have people pass through a narrow passage and then there is a brrrrr of an electrical apparatus. They stay there for twenty seconds and from then on they are sterile."

Depression, disease, accusations of overpopulation—this was the state of affairs when another mainland doctor arrived: Cornelius Packard Rhoads, "Dusty" to his friends. Rhoads had trained at Harvard (he overlapped briefly with Albizu) and then went to work for the Rockefeller Institute in San Juan as part of its global fight against hookworm. It was a bitter irony that Puerto Rico, a pioneer of deworming, was now a target in that hookworm campaign. But the island still suffered badly from anemia, and the Rockefeller Foundation's International Health Division hoped that experimental treatments might be tried.

Cornelius P. Rhoads was a far cry from Bailey K. Ashford. Whereas Ashford collaborated easily, including with Puerto Ricans, Rhoads was testier. He was an "outspoken, frequently blunt" man, wrote *The New York Times*, with "hawk-like eyes that burn bright blue through round steel-framed spectacles." "A man of brusque manners and few words" is how one Puerto Rican colleague described him.

His methods differed from Ashford's, too. Ashford had always been cautious about medical experiments. The first time he administered a deworming pill, he stayed up all night making "nervous half-hour visits" until he saw that his patient was unharmed. Rhoads, by contrast, appeared to regard Puerto Rico as an island-size laboratory. He saw the empire much as Daniel Burnham had: a place to try out ideas while facing few consequences.

Rhoads made the most of his carte blanche. He refused treatment to some of his anemia patients so he could compare their progress with treated patients. He tried to induce anemia in others (he referred to them as "experimental 'animals'") by restricting their diets. "If they don't develop something they certainly have the constitutions of oxen," he remarked.

Even with this extraordinary freedom, Rhoads wearied of Puerto Rico. Five months into his stay, he took his car to a party and, when he came out to get it, found it had been stripped. Days later, he wrote a letter to a colleague in Boston. It started off chattily enough, though with an air of petulance:

> Dear Ferdie:
> The more I think about the Larry Smith appointment the more disgusted I get. Have you heard any reason advanced for it? It certainly is odd that a man out with the entire Boston group, fired by Wallach and as far as I know, absolutely devoid of any scientific reputation, should be given the place.

Then it took a turn:

> I can get a damn fine job here and am tempted to take it. It would be ideal except for the Porto Ricans—they are beyond doubt the dirtiest, laziest, most degenerate and thievish race of men ever inhabiting this sphere. It makes you sick to inhabit the same island with them. They are even lower than Italians. What the island needs is not public health work, but a tidal wave or something to totally exterminate the population. It might then be livable. I have done my best to further the process of extermination by killing off 8 and transplanting cancer into several more. The latter has not resulted in any fatalities so far. The matter of consideration for the patients' welfare plays no role here—in fact, all physicians take delight in the abuse and torture of the unfortunate subjects.
> Do let me know if you hear any more news.
> Sincerely, Dusty

Clandestine villainy, an incriminating letter—it was straight out of a nineteenth-century novel. In another novelistic twist, Rhoads composed his letter at the desk of a hospital stenographer and then *accidentally left it there*. It circulated swiftly among the Puerto Rican staff. A lab assistant,

Luis Baldoni, sent the purloined letter to his home in Utuado, a four-hour drive away.

Rhoads blanched. He drove out to Utuado in an unsuccessful attempt to intercept Baldoni. Back at the hospital, he apologized emotionally to the staff, claiming that the letter was written "in a moment of anger" and pointing out that he hadn't actually sent it. "I have a high notion of Puerto Ricans," he explained. He pressed a "loan" on Baldoni. And then he left for New York, never to return.

Rhoads surely hoped that his apology and hasty exit would mark the end of things—what happens in San Juan stays in San Juan. It very well might have ended there, too. Except that Baldoni still had the letter, and he gave it to a man who knew what to do with it.

He gave it to Pedro Albizu Campos.

★

Albizu had changed since the First World War. After failing to get to the Paris Peace Conference, he'd finished his law degree at Harvard. But his enthusiasm for the United States had flagged. The dream of Puerto Ricans in 1898 had been that the island could become a prosperous state, on an equal footing with those of the mainland. By 1930, that dream had revealed itself to be a fantasy. Wilsonianism had yielded no change in status, poverty hadn't budged, and mainlanders seemed plainly hostile to their fellow citizens from Puerto Rico.

When Albizu returned to the island, he joined a small political party, the Nationalists. As he saw, for Puerto Rico to flourish, it must be free.

In poverty-racked Puerto Rico, that wasn't a hard sell. The Liberal Party sought independence, too, and it did well at the polls. The only question was pace. The Liberals, of whom the newspaper editor and rising political star Luis Muñoz Marín was the most able spokesman, sought a managed transition. Albizu and the Nationalists, by contrast, demanded a clean and immediate break.

The disagreement turned, in part, on whether the United States could be trusted. Albizu didn't think it could, and with Rhoads's letter in hand, he had his proof. He sent copies everywhere: to all the papers, the League of Nations, the Vatican, the American Civil Liberties Union. A cover letter by one of his colleagues explained that the United States was seeking to exterminate Puerto Ricans just as it had the North American Indians.

Did Cornelius Rhoads actually kill eight of his patients? The question lives on to this day. Rhoads and his defenders offered multiple and contradictory excuses: he was angry, he was joking, he was drunk. The colonial governor took the matter more seriously. He deemed the letter a "confession of murder" and ordered an investigation.

That investigation uncovered another letter, which the governor viewed as "even worse than the first." But the government suppressed it, and it has never been found. Thirteen patients did die in the Rockefeller Commission's study group (it was a hospital, after all), but they weren't exclusively Rhoads's patients and a review of their records showed nothing amiss. The most damning evidence presented in the investigation was a claim by Baldoni that Rhoads failed to sterilize his needles, though that was contested. In the end, the prosecutor concluded that Rhoads was "a mental case or unscrupulous person," but not a murderer.

A 2003 investigation by an esteemed bioethicist at Yale, Jay Katz, reached a similar conclusion: Rhoads's behavior was reprehensible, but there was no evidence that he'd killed anyone.

Still, an investigation by a government that destroys incriminating evidence and doesn't even require the accused to participate can hardly be called fair or thorough. The 2003 inquiry was based, by necessity, on what documents remained. To this day, many Puerto Ricans are convinced that Rhoads was guilty and that the government covered up his crimes.

Many in the 1930s thought so, too. Puerto Ricans had felt the condescension and scorn of mainlanders. They'd heard the talk about "overpopulation." And now there was this letter—a killer's clear confession—and yet no trial. The whole thing seemed to confirm the worst fears about U.S. imperialism. That a doctor would murder his patients out of racial hatred—to many, it seemed plausible.

The Rhoads affair was a turning point in Puerto Rican politics. Before the letter, the Nationalists were an obscure group. After it, they were a force. For centuries Puerto Rico had endured colonial rule with little direct resistance. But now, with disease and poverty ravaging the island, and with what looked like proof of an official desire to exterminate Puerto Ricans, things were different. Albizu's insistence that independence must be seized, immediately and forcibly, was not so easily dismissed.

★

Waving the Rhoads letter, Albizu led the Nationalist Party in the 1932 elections. He fared poorly, although the pro-independence Liberals did very well. It was Albizu's first and only attempt at electoral politics. Later that year, he drafted a constitution for the Republic of Puerto Rico and created a Liberation Army. The "army" didn't appear to have any weapons—its cadets drilled with wooden replica guns. But they drilled nonetheless.

"Where tyranny is law, revolution is order," Albizu declared.

A bomb went off at the governor's country estate, though nobody was hurt. Then the chief of insular police, Francis Riggs, found four sticks of dynamite in the garden of the governor's mansion—only a defective fuse had prevented them from exploding.

This was just the start. A 1934 sugar workers' strike nearly paralyzed what remained of the economy. Tellingly, the strikers chose Pedro Albizu Campos as their spokesman. With the strikes, the bombs, the poverty, and Albizu's men marching in the streets, mainlanders felt the colony slipping from their grasp. "The sit. is getting worse daily," Riggs wrote to Senator Millard Tydings. "Can't go on much longer!" "*Help* me!!!!!!" he added at the bottom of the letter. (Five days later: "The situation is getting worse . . . Chaos and anarchy!!!!").

"Public order," warned Luis Muñoz Marín, "hangs by a thread."

Nineteen thirty-five was the year of the bomb: at National City Bank (today known as Citigroup), at post offices, at police stations. They exploded on holidays—New Year's Day, the Fourth of July—or directly after Albizu's speeches. Nobody was killed and nobody was convicted, but it wasn't hard to guess who was responsible.

"Some night, here, we will rise," Albizu promised in a radio speech. "There must be placed into the hand of each Puerto Rican a dagger, an arm in order that he may make valid the rights of his country."

In the same speech, Albizu berated students at the University of Puerto Rico for adopting mainland ways. He called the men effeminate and the women prostitutes. When a group of students organized a protest against Albizu, five nationalists drove to the university. What they intended to do is unclear—the police who intercepted them said they were planning to bomb the campus. Someone started shooting, and the police killed four of them, plus a bystander.

Francis Riggs, the chief of police, hinted at more to come. He promised "non-stop war" against "criminals."

"There will be war," Albizu agreed. But it would be "war against the Yankees."

As Riggs made his way home from Mass one Sunday morning, two nationalists shot and killed him. The police captured the assassins, took them back to the station, and killed them there. The official story is that they were "trying to escape."

The insurgency continued, with police and nationalists trading fire in the streets. More bombs went off. Luis Baldoni, the lab technician, got into a shoot-out with the police. A U.S. congressman requested a contingent of marines to accompany him to Puerto Rico; he promised to "clean up" the "Puerto Rican situation" in a week. No troops were forthcoming, but J. Edgar Hoover sent FBI agents to the island to follow Albizu—the start of three decades of continuous surveillance.

To no one's surprise, Albizu was arrested. He was charged with conspiring to overthrow the government—a charge that guaranteed a federal trial. The U.S. attorney in Puerto Rico, A. Cecil Snyder, described it to Roosevelt as "the most important criminal case ever tried in Puerto Rico." When the jury, which included seven Puerto Ricans, failed to convict, Snyder arranged a second trial the next week, this one with a hand-picked jury containing only two Puerto Ricans. It worked. The judge chided Albizu for wasting his Harvard education and sentenced him to ten years in the federal penitentiary at Atlanta.

On Palm Sunday 1937, while Albizu languished in prison, the Liberation Army marched in the streets of Ponce. The marchers carried no weapons, but their opponents did: Ponce's small police force swelled to five times its usual size as more than a hundred officers arrived carrying rifles, gas bombs, revolvers, clubs, and Thompson submachine guns ("tommy guns"). They surrounded the nationalists on all sides. As the marchers began to move, gunfire erupted, and the police let loose a minutes-long fusillade from all directions. Eighteen demonstrators and onlookers died, and two policemen were killed in the cross fire. Probably more than 150 people were wounded.

The governor insisted that the Nationalists had fired first. But an FBI agent reported privately to J. Edgar Hoover that it was a "common fact" that the police were "almost 100 percent to blame." Indeed, an independent investigation, headed by the general counsel of the American Civil Liberties Union, pointed out glaring holes in the government's story. It

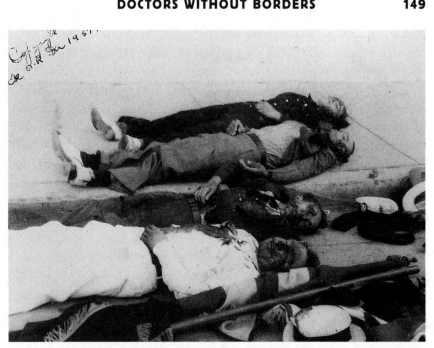

Corpses of bystanders lie in the street after the shooting in Ponce.

concluded that the affair was not an unfortunate mishap, but rather a "massacre."

Albizu's birthplace, once known for being "delirious" with enthusiasm for the United States, was now etched in memory as the site of the Ponce Massacre. To this day, it remains the bloodiest shooting by police in U.S. history.

★

Puerto Rico in the 1930s continued to simmer: an attempt to assassinate the judge who sentenced Albizu, an attempt on the governor's life, more bombs, strikes. But it happened without Albizu, who was sent to Atlanta and would spend most of the rest of his life behind bars.

Things turned out differently for Cornelius Rhoads. News of the scandal had followed him back to the mainland, though in a muted way. *The Washington Post* reported that Rhoads had written a "jocular letter," which Puerto Rican nationalists had blown out of proportion. *Time* printed the letter but, at the urging of the Rockefellers' public relations firm, omitted the more disturbing sentences and described the letter as a parody. Touting

Rhoads's research, the magazine predicted that the doctor's six months on the island would come to be seen as "one of the best things that ever happened to the populace there."

The coverage surely embarrassed Rhoads, but it didn't impede him. Not only was he never tried, he wasn't even fired: he continued to work for the Rockefeller Institute. In 1940 he was made director of Memorial Hospital in New York. In 1942 he was elected vice president of the New York Academy of Medicine. Then, with the United States at war, Rhoads was commissioned as a colonel in the army.

The military was an interesting place for a man of his expertise. Ever since Fritz Haber released chlorine gas at Ypres in 1915, the threat of chemical warfare had hung in the air. Roosevelt pledged that the United States wouldn't be the first to use gas in the Second World War, but the military prepared for a chemical war nonetheless. That meant not only manufacturing poison gas but testing it, too. And the chief of the Chemical Warfare Service's medical division was Cornelius P. Rhoads.

It was an important post. Though the Chemical Warfare Service ran tests on animals—goats were a favorite—it insisted that all gases and equipment be ultimately tested on humans. Those humans were soldiers, recruited with modest inducements such as extra leave time or appeals to patriotism.

They participated in three types of tests. In the drop test, liquid was applied to their skin. In the field test, planes sprayed them from overhead. In the chamber test, sometimes called the "man-break test," participants were locked in gas chambers and gassed until they faltered. Those inhaling gas usually had protective gear, but the tests often pushed past the point where that gear functioned. In some cases, that meant days in gas chambers or in the jungle with gas bombs dropping overhead. Participants seeking to leave midway through were threatened with court-martial.

During the war, the military tested its gases and gear on more than sixty thousand of its own men.

These tests were secret. They rarely appeared on service records, and participants were firmly instructed never to speak of them. By and large, the men complied. Although many suffered debilitating aftereffects—cancer, lung disease, eye problems, skin abnormalities, psychological damage, scarred genitals—the extent of the program remained unknown until the 1990s. Some participants told their families only on their deathbeds.

After the revelation of the tests themselves came another revelation: some of the experiments were race based. African Americans, Japanese Americans, and Puerto Ricans were tested to see if they would fare differently than whites against mustard agents.

Beyond the experimental use of Puerto Ricans in racial tests, the Chemical Warfare Service relied on them for field tests at its "jungle" testing site: San José Island off Panama, an entire island for testing chemical weapons. The Puerto Ricans weren't brought there because of their race per se. They were brought because they were easy to get. The Military Personnel Division refused to send enough men "from the Continental Limits" for the tests but was happy to send Puerto Ricans. One GI who participated in the tests on San José Island (and later developed stomach and throat cancer) observed that more than two-thirds of his fellow soldiers had Spanish surnames and couldn't understand the instructions in English.

Jay Katz, the Yale bioethicist who made the 2003 study of the Rhoads affair, also took part in a review of the chemical warfare tests. Those experiments, he concluded, ran on the principle of the "cheap availability of human beings," with little thought given to how to minimize harm. The soldiers were "manipulated, exploited, and betrayed." What happened, in his judgment, was "unconscionable."

★

Where was Cornelius Rhoads in all this? Right in the middle. As chief of the medical division, he was the highest-ranking doctor involved, charged with approving tests on human subjects. Decisions about safety and, ultimately, ethics were his to make. Yet in my review of the records of the Chemical Warfare Service, I found no evidence of his hesitation regarding any test. Rather, it seems that he participated enthusiastically. He established medical testing stations, including on San José Island. He arranged to transport men to be gassed. He recommended which gases to use and how to use them. He offered comments on the tests, including one of how people of different skin colors responded to chemical burns.

At the war's end, Rhoads won a Legion of Merit award for "combating poison gas and other advances in chemical warfare."

For Rhoads, this was just the beginning. Scientists had known from the start of the war that mustard agents—the main chemicals with which Rhoads was working—targeted lymphoid tissue and bone marrow. Perhaps they could be used to treat lymphoma? Wartime findings were suggestive, but other research had priority.

Scientists planned to return to the issue once the fighting was done, using what they had learned during the war. The military had leftover chemical agents available for research, and Rhoads chaired the committee that decided what to do with them. He divided the stock among three hospitals, one of them his own.

Rhoads also recruited nearly the whole program staff of the Chemical Warfare Service to work for him researching those mustard agents, this time for drug development. He did this at a new center that was started with a $4 million grant from Alfred P. Sloan, the president of General Motors. As the director of both Manhattan's Memorial Hospital and the Sloan Kettering Institute (as it was called) next door, Rhoads was perfectly positioned. He had a massive lab. He had money. And he had a hospital full of terminally ill patients who would eagerly consent to experimental treatments.

Rhoads launched what he called a "frontal attack with all our forces" on cancer, trying chemical after chemical. Given Rhoads's great force of will, his considerable resources, and his intolerance for alternative approaches, his research agenda dominated the scene. The journal *Science* heralded him as "one of the most prominent American medical researchers" of his day. He made the cover of *Time* in 1949.

Today, Cornelius Rhoads lives in Puerto Rican memory as a villain. On the mainland, however, he's been remembered differently: as a pioneer of chemotherapy.

Indeed, more than remembered, he has been honored. Starting in 1980, with money from an anonymous donor, the American Association for Cancer Research (AACR) gave the prestigious Cornelius P. Rhoads Memorial Award annually to the young investigator who showed the most promise in cancer research. Rhoads recipients have gone on to be field leaders; one was a Nobel laureate. But so complete was the informational segregation between Puerto Rico and the mainland that the prize was given for twenty-three years before anyone objected. When a biologist from the University of Puerto Rico lodged a complaint, the AACR was taken aback. "It was just totally shocking to us to receive this barrage of communications from people in Puerto Rico out of the blue," said the CEO. Even the donor who'd funded the award hadn't known of Rhoads's Puerto Rican legacy.

And *that*'s how you hide an empire.

10

FORTRESS AMERICA

For the inhabitants of U.S. territories, empire was an inescapable daily presence. They saluted the U.S. flag. They studied the English language and U.S. history in school. Their money had George Washington's face on it. They observed U.S. holidays—Lincoln's Birthday, the Fourth of July—as well as the anniversary of the U.S. occupation (an occasion that Puerto Rican nationalists celebrated in 1938 by trying to shoot the governor).

Yet on the mainland, empire slipped easily from view. Consider the coverage in *The New York Times* in a representative year, 1930. Its readers were nearly twice as likely to encounter articles about Poland or Brazil as they were about the Philippines. The 13 articles the paper ran about Albania (PLOT AGAINST KING ZOG FOILED, etc.) far outstripped the 6 it printed about Alaska. Hawai'i appeared seven times that year, Guam not once. In contrast, the *Times* ran 639 articles about India, Britain's largest colony. That was nearly three times as many as it ran about all U.S. territories combined, territories in which more than 10 percent of the U.S. population lived.

It wasn't much different in the realm of books. Scanning the library shelves, it's easy to find high-profile books from the interwar period depicting Native Americans and the western frontier (*Little House on the Prairie* is one), but prominent treatments of overseas territories are rare. The only one with a truly large audience was *Coming of Age in Samoa* (1928) by the anthropologist Margaret Mead, a wildly popular ethnography that featured frank discussions of Samoan sexuality and launched Mead's career as one of the most famous scholars in the country. Yet Mead wrote of "Samoa," not "American Samoa" (the colony's legal name), and avoided mention of colonies, territories, and empires altogether. It is entirely possible to read *Coming of Age* without realizing that the "brown Polynesian people" she describes encountering on "a South Sea island" are U.S. nationals.

The indifference toward the colonies in the culture was met with an equal indifference in the government. Whereas Britain governed its possessions from large, prominent, and imposing edifices, the United States had *no* colonial building in its capital. Nor did it have a school to train colonial officials. Its territories were ruled by a haphazard and improvised set of bureaucratic arrangements under the army, navy, and Department of the Interior.

It showed. The men sent to run the territories, unlike the trained administrators who oversaw European colonies, simply didn't know much about the places to which they'd been assigned, and they cycled rapidly through their posts. Between Guam's annexation in 1899 and World War II, it had nearly forty governors. FDR's first governor of Puerto Rico, who served for six months, spoke no Spanish and left reporters with the distinct impression that he didn't know where the island was. There was a period of several months when the territory of Alaska, which is half the physical size of India, didn't have a single federal official in it.

Colonial subjects complained, of course, but few mainlanders listened. As one Filipino Harvard graduate noted in 1926, "It has been impossible to induce the American people to take more than a passing interest in the conduct of Philippine affairs."

Even the people who should have been interested weren't. The Anti-Imperialist League, which in 1899 had claimed more than half a million contributors, atrophied badly after the 1900 election. In 1924, progressives associated with *The Nation* magazine revived the league, but in its new incarnation it had a different focus. Ernest Gruening, who had been *The Nation*'s managing editor, suggested giving the organization a new name, the Pan-American Freedom League. That suggestion accurately captured the organization's interests: not advocating on behalf of the formal territories (only some of which were in the Americas), but resisting U.S. interference with the sovereign states of the Americas. It was an organization, in other words, concerned not with Puerto Rico, Hawai'i, or the Philippines, but with Cuba, Haiti, and Mexico.

Mainland inattentiveness had always been a strain on the territories, but by the 1930s it became an outright danger. That was a decade of economic desperation and military peril, ·when "Fortress America" built protective barriers against a hostile world. Yet the colonies received little protection. Instead, they watched from the outside as the walls around the mainland grew tall.

★

The blurry haze that enshrouded colonial policy was a constant source of complaint. To firm things up, Franklin Delano Roosevelt established a central office in 1934: the Division of Territories and Island Possessions within the Interior Department. For the first time, Puerto Rico, Alaska, Hawai'i, and the U.S. Virgin Islands were under a single authority, and within five years it would cover the Philippines and the major guano islands, too. The only inhabited territories remaining separate were Guam and American Samoa, kept as fiefdoms of the navy.

To head the new office, Roosevelt tapped Ernest Gruening of the revived Anti-Imperialist League. Gruening's colleagues at *The Nation* were ecstatic. "Not in all the years that I have been writing for the press can I recall an appointment which has given me more satisfaction," the magazine's editor wrote. "His whole career would seem to have led right up to this post."

Gruening *had* enjoyed quite a career. Though trained in medicine at Harvard (no overlap with Albizu or Rhoads, unfortunately), he had made his living in journalism and politics. As a (white) member of the Boston branch of the National Association for the Advancement of Colored People, he'd led the campaign to prevent *The Birth of a Nation* from opening in that city. He was also a founding member of the American Birth Control League, the organization that would become Planned Parenthood. He had edited a Spanish-language daily in New York, supervised *The Nation's* critical coverage of the Haitian occupation, and written an important book about the Mexican Revolution.

Few outsiders had mastered Caribbean affairs as thoroughly as Ernest Gruening had. Yet, typical for his generation of anti-imperialists, Gruening knew little of the United States' actual colonies. "Imperialism" was for him a more diffuse notion, one that referred not to formal territorial conquest, but to the informal bullying of weaker states, particularly those in Latin America. In fact, for all his travels, Gruening had spent only a single day in a U.S. colony—a brief stopover in Puerto Rico.

And now he was in charge of the whole empire.

Gruening sought guidance from the president. Roosevelt rattled off his assessments of the territories. Hawai'i was in "pretty good shape." The Virgin Islands needed work. Alaska should be used as a settlement outlet for Dust Bowl refugees—*The Grapes of Wrath on Ice*. "As for Puerto Rico," he continued, "that place is hopeless, *hopeless.*"

"This new division is really the equivalent of the British colonial office, isn't it, Mr. President?" Gruening asked.

"I suppose it is."

"Well," Gruening hesitantly probed, "a democracy shouldn't have any colonies."

Roosevelt smiled. He held his arms out, palms up. "I think you're right. Let's see what you can develop."

★

Let's see what you can develop? This was hardly the faith of the fathers. It was even a new tack for Roosevelt. Early in his career, he had followed in the footsteps of his distant cousin Teddy, serving as assistant secretary of the navy and fantasizing about annexing the Caribbean.

Yet the times had changed. The chief impetus for rethinking the value of colonies was the global Depression. It had triggered a desperate scramble among the world's powers to prop up their flagging economies with protective tariffs. This was an individual solution with excruciating collective consequences. As those trade barriers rose, global trade collapsed, falling by two-thirds between 1929 and 1932.

This was exactly the nightmare Alfred Thayer Mahan had predicted back in the 1890s. As international trade doors slammed shut, large economies were forced to subsist largely on their own domestic produce. *Domestic,* in this context, included colonies, though, since one of empire's chief benefits was the unrestricted economic access it brought to faraway lands. It mattered to major imperial powers—the Dutch, the French, the British—that they could still get tropical products such as rubber from their colonies in Asia. And it mattered to the industrial countries *without* large empires—Germany, Italy, Japan—that they couldn't.

The United States was in a peculiar position. It had colonies, but they weren't its lifeline. Oil, cotton, iron, coal, and many of the important minerals that other industrial economies found hard to secure—the United States had these in abundance on its enormous mainland. Rubber and tin it could still purchase from Malaya via its ally Britain. It did take a few useful goods from its tropical colonies, such as coconut oil from the Philippines and Guam and "Manila hemp" from the Philippines (used to make rope and sturdy paper, hence "manila envelopes" and "manila folders"). Yet the United States didn't depend on its colonies in the same way that other empires did. It was, an expert in the 1930s declared, "infinitely more self-contained" than its rivals.

Most of what the United States got from its colonies was sugar, grown on plantations in Hawai'i, Puerto Rico, the U.S. Virgin Islands, and the Philippines. Yet even in sugar, the United States wasn't dependent. Sugarcane grew in the subtropical South, in Louisiana and Florida. It could also be made from beets, and in the interwar years the United States bought more sugar from mainland beet farmers than it did from any of its territories.

What the Depression drove home was that, three decades after the war with Spain, the United States still hadn't done much with its empire. The colonies had their uses: as naval bases and zones of experimentation for men such as Daniel Burnham and Cornelius Rhoads. But colonial products weren't integral to the U.S. economy.

In fact, they were potentially a threat. Since colonial sugar competed with mainland cane and beet sugar, mainland farmers demanded protection from it. Ernest Gruening objected to the farmers' lobbying. Discriminating against colonial sugar, he testified to Congress, would perpetuate the notion that there were "two kinds of territory" in the country, "a continental and offshore America." But Congress enacted sugar production quotas anyway. The territorial quotas were restrictive; those for continental cane and beet sugar were obliging. Through these and other legal mechanisms, the mainland secured economic relief while the colonies paid the cost.

Beet growers in Colorado weren't the only ones worried about the colonies. West Coast labor unions nervously eyed the tens of thousands of Filipinos who competed with whites for agricultural jobs—since Filipinos were U.S. nationals, no law stopped them from moving to the mainland. Then there was the military situation to consider. Japan had invaded Manchuria in 1931 and seemed poised to advance on Southeast Asia in pursuit of colonies. The Philippines and Guam stood right in its path. Would the United States really go to war over these faraway, barely known, and not-very-profitable possessions?

Maybe it wouldn't have to. Two years into the Depression, Calvin Coolidge noted a "reversal of opinion" about Philippine independence. A number of politicians, FDR included, were coming around on the issue. Rather than absorbing the Philippines' trade and migrants and defending it against Japan, the new thinking went, why not just get rid of it?

The 1930s are known as a decade of protectionism, when the United States put up hefty tariffs to barricade itself against the world. Now it seemed that this spirit was going to change the very borders of the country. The Philippines was going to be dumped over the castle walls.

★

The sentiment behind the campaign in Washington for Philippine independence was hardly noble. "It would be a mortifying spectacle to see the United States readjust its Philippine policy to fit the balance sheets of a select group of industrial and agricultural interests," chided *The Christian Science Monitor.* A comprehensive survey in 1931–32 of nearly three hundred major mainland newspapers found 92 percent against it, including *The New York Times, The Wall Street Journal, The Chicago Daily Tribune,* and the *San Francisco Chronicle.*

Still, for Filipinos, it was an opportunity, and even more so after Roosevelt's 1932 election brought the first Democrat to the White House since Woodrow Wilson. The fortunate alignment of Democrats and depression would "surely never happen again within any reasonable human foresight," noted the president of the University of the Philippines.

There was a third necessary element, though: Manuel Quezon, the president of the Philippine Senate and the indispensable power broker in the colony. Quezon was a master politician, adept at playing all sides at once. He had served on Aguinaldo's staff (at age twenty) during the war, but after Aguinaldo's surrender, he'd spied for the colonial government and helped bring the holdouts to heel. He led the Nationalist Party, but he was also one of the Baguio Country Club's six Filipino founding members.

Cameron Forbes likened Quezon to a "wonderfully trained hunting dog run wild." Handled correctly, he would bring in the sheep. "But alone or in bad company, he goes wrong and ends up killing lambs and devastating hen yards."

A fairer way to put it would be to say that Manuel Quezon embodied the contradictions of colonialism. The desire for the colonizer's approval, the demand for autonomy, conciliation, violence—Quezon contained multitudes. One journalist compared talking with him to trying to pick up mercury with a fork.

Quezon proved especially fluid when it came to independence. Most Filipinos wanted it badly, Quezon knew, and he won votes by demanding it. "I would rather have a government run like hell by Filipinos than a government run like heaven by Americans" was his famous slogan. Yet he also saw, better than anyone, the dangers involved. The mainland may not have depended on the Philippines, but after decades of U.S. rule, the Philippines depended on the mainland very much. By the 1930s, about four-fifths of its trade was going there. And although the colonial government had built a small native army to quash local rebellions, the Philippines had been prevented from developing an outward-facing military able to repel a foreign invader. A sudden, simultaneous loss of U.S. military protection and tariff-free access to mainland markets spelled catastrophe.

In the past, Quezon had squared the circle by publicly demanding independence while privately assuring his contacts in the federal government that this was just empty talk. As long as Washington remained resolute in hanging on to its colony, that strategy worked. But now, in the 1930s, Quezon found himself leaning against an open door. A bill granting the Philippines independence in eight years sailed through the House in forty minutes, with Democrats for it voting unanimously. Panicked, Quezon arranged to have it blocked by the Philippine Legislature. But this was not ultimately a tenable position for the head of the Nationalist Party, so he supported a nearly identical bill that Congress passed the next year. Again acting on Quezon's direction, the Philippine Legislature ratified this version unanimously on May 1, 1934, the thirty-sixth anniversary of the U.S. occupation.

A powerful country setting its largest colony free without threat of violence—it was unheard-of. The nearby Dutch East Indies (now Indonesia) had been under Dutch control for three hundred years, and in the 1930s its governor-general predicted that it would be another three hundred before the colony would see independence. But the Philippines, held by the United States for about one-tenth that time, was about to go free.

To be fair, the Philippine Independence Act did not grant independence immediately. It permitted Filipinos to establish a new government, a "commonwealth," akin to Australia or Canada within the British Empire. If Congress approved the commonwealth constitution and if the commonwealth met certain benchmarks over a ten-year period, *then* the Philippines would be independent.

Meanwhile, the Philippines, though still part of the United States, would be "considered to be a foreign country" for the purposes of immigration. It would also eventually start paying tariffs, low at first but steadily increasing with the years. In principle, the transitional decade would give the Philippines enough time to restructure its economy and build an army.

Manuel Quezon ran for president of this new commonwealth. He beat out Emilio Aguinaldo, who ran on a protest platform of immediate independence. To celebrate his inauguration, Quezon arranged a ceremony outside Juan Arellano's Legislative Building. The Philippine flag, which for years had been prohibited, would ascend the flagpole and rise to the same height as the U.S. flag. Quezon wanted a twenty-one-gun salute, too, but Roosevelt forbade it—that honor was reserved for heads of sovereign states, and the Philippines was still a colony. After hinting at war and briefly threatening to boycott his own inauguration, Quezon acquiesced to nineteen guns.

Not enough guns. That would be a recurring theme in the years to come.

★

The Philippines was the largest U.S. colony. A similar story played out in the second-largest, Puerto Rico. The Depression had wreaked havoc on the island: unemployment, strikes, and—egged on by Pedro Albizu Campos—violence. It was the assassination by nationalists of Police Chief E. Francis Riggs that truly rattled the colonial authorities. He was one of them—the protégé, as it turned out, of Senator Millard Tydings, the chief congressional sponsor of the Philippine Independence Act.

Ernest Gruening was furious. He demanded that Luis Muñoz Marín, Puerto Rico's leading liberal politician, condemn Riggs's assassination. But Muñoz Marín refused—he understood why the nationalists had lashed out, and he was unwilling to confront them. "By his silence he was condoning murder, and indeed the whole Nationalist campaign of violence," Gruening fumed.

Gruening and Tydings joined forces and drafted another piece of independence legislation, based on the Philippine Independence Act but intended for Puerto Rico. On the surface, it was anti-imperialist. But Muñoz Marín could see its vindictive intent—"revenge disguised as political freedom," he called it. Whereas the Philippine Independence Act began imposing the U.S. tariff only in the sixth year of transitional government and increased it slowly thereafter, the bill for Puerto Rico dropped the tariff's full weight in four years. Given that, in 1930, more than 95 percent of Puerto Rico's off-island sales were to the mainland, a sudden tariff would be catastrophic. Among Puerto Rican leaders, only Albizu, monomaniacally focused on independence, was enthusiastic.

Tydings withdrew the bill in a few weeks—just long enough for Muñoz Marín and his colleagues to grasp the threat. If Puerto Ricans kept pushing for independence, they just might get it.

Back in the Philippines, meanwhile, Manuel Quezon contemplated the arrival of independence, and he, too, began to sweat. Would the United States aid in Philippine defense once the colony was independent? "As a matter of cold actuality," a former governor-general told him, "the American people will not jeopardize their interests in the future for an independent Philippines any more than they will for any other nation."

A movement to reverse Philippine independence grew in the late 1930s, especially among Filipino businessmen and mainland officials. The high commissioner of the Philippines, then the colony's top-ranking official, called for a "realistic reexamination" of the independence act. "If our flag comes down, the Philippines will become a bloody ground," he warned in a radio broadcast. Quezon sent him a congratulatory note on the speech, pronouncing its "presentation of the facts" to be "unassailable."

Filipinos were shocked. Had Quezon, the leader of the Nationalist Party, really just endorsed a call to reverse the independence process? Quezon realized this was a bridge too far, and he backed down the next day, claiming to have misunderstood the high commissioner's message.

But privately Quezon was desperate and clawing in every direction. He made secret overtures to Japan. He declared June 19 to be Loyalty Day—an over-the-top demonstration of the "wholehearted and unswerving loy-

A 1936 one-peso commemorative coin showing Franklin Delano Roosevelt and Manuel Quezon gazing ahead, presumably toward independence. The highly unusual design, featuring two leaders rather than one and showing the U.S. eagle over the Philippine seal, expresses the complex sovereignty of the Philippine commonwealth. "Commonwealth of the Philippines" is printed on the obverse, "United States of America" on the reverse.

alty of all the elements of our population to the United States"—in the hopes of wringing more defense funding from Congress. He quietly approached the British embassy about the possibility of *Britain* annexing the Philippines if the United States abandoned it.

At the same time, Quezon began a mad dash to create his own national defense force, funded from the commonwealth's meager budget. To build it, he recruited one of the only men in U.S. officialdom who actually felt a strong connection to the Philippines: the army chief of staff, General Douglas MacArthur.

★

Douglas MacArthur is one of those blips in history, an idiosyncratic figure who, for reasons hard to satisfactorily explain, acquired far more power than he had any reason to. In the United States in the mid-twentieth century, there were three such men, each operating on a different scale. On the level of the city, there was Robert Moses, who somehow managed to trade up authority over New York's parks—a position that traditionally entailed little more than serving the needs of the city's bird-watchers—into a decades-long stranglehold over municipal politics. On the national level, there was J. Edgar Hoover, the spymaster who held presidents under his thumb. And in foreign relations, exercising more effective authority than perhaps anyone else in U.S. history, it was Douglas MacArthur.

A psychoanalyst could have a field day with any member of that trio, though perhaps with MacArthur most of all. He was carefree under enemy fire but lived much of his adult life under the reign of his controlling mother. He was an impeccable dresser who carried himself "as if he had a flagpole for a spine," yet in the telling of his first wife he was an embarrassing sexual failure. Though he was regarded by many as a military genius, his career was punctuated by eye-popping blunders. And he spoke about himself in the third person.

MacArthur was a distant cousin to both Franklin Delano Roosevelt and Winston Churchill, and he had served briefly as an aide to Theodore Roosevelt. But MacArthur never fell in easily with those men. Where the Roosevelts and Churchills orbited the Atlantic, MacArthur arced out on a different path, as if obeying his own gravity. At the height of his fame, from 1937 to 1951, he lived entirely on the Asian side of the Pacific. Although he was frequently discussed as a candidate for president, he didn't return to the mainland once in those fourteen years.

If MacArthur had a home, it was the Philippines. His father, Arthur MacArthur, had been the governor during the Philippine War. It was there that Douglas did his first tour of duty, in 1903. It was where he first saw combat and first drew blood, killing a pair of what he called "desperadoes" (probably rebels, though possibly just criminals) on the still-unpacified island of Guimaras.

MacArthur's first wife, the loudly disappointed one, had originally been General John Pershing's companion. Immediately after she switched from Pershing's arm to MacArthur's, Pershing ordered MacArthur back to the Philippines, presumably as punishment. But MacArthur flourished there. He worked for Leonard Wood, spent a summer in Baguio, and acquired a Filipina mistress—a stage and film actress whom he took back to Washington with him, stashing her in a Georgetown apartment, away from the watchful eye of his mother.

MacArthur's intimate ties to the Philippines put him at odds with the Europe-facing military establishment. Since the early twentieth century, war planners had contemplated the possibility of war with Japan. They generated a plan for this, Plan Orange, adopted first in 1924 and revised multiple times thereafter. But as officials in Washington played out the Japan scenario, they saw immediately how hard it would be to defend the United States' Pacific outposts, particularly Guam and the Philippines. Mounting sufficient defenses would require far more money than an indifferent federal government was willing to pay—it was "not within the wildest possibility," reported the commander of the army's Philippine Department. Instead, the successive Plans Orange envisioned amassing a fleet in Hawai'i or on the West Coast and leaving only small forces in the westernmost territories. If Japan attacked, it would get the western Pacific colonies, but then (the thinking went) the United States could stage a counterattack and eventually win them back.

For MacArthur, the thought that the United States was planning to sacrifice the Philippines was unconscionable. As chief of staff of the army, a post he assumed in 1930, he pressed the issue. He envisioned creating a large Philippine army to hold off the enemy at the shoreline and organizing an immediate, massive relief of that army from Hawai'i. But this was wild optimism, especially in an era marked by severe budgetary constraints and widespread antimilitarism. The director of the War Plans Division regarded MacArthur's proposal as "literally an act of madness."

Part of the problem was the apathy toward the colonies. Even Brigadier General Hugh Drum, one of MacArthur's few allies in the cause of territorial defense, openly conceded that "both the Philippines and Hawaii might be lost to us without materially affecting the safety of the continental United States." Public opinion polls suggested that few mainlanders supported a military defense of anything west of Hawai'i. And when *Fortune* in 1940 asked its readers which "countries" the United States should use its military to protect, only a slight majority (55 percent) favored defending Hawai'i itself, far fewer than the number who would defend Canada (74 percent).

Officials in Hawai'i protested vigorously to *Fortune* that Hawai'i was not a "country." It was "an integral part of the United States."

Another part of the problem was that the government simply didn't trust its own subjects. A full defense of the Pacific would require arming the populations of Hawai'i, American Samoa, Guam, the Philippines, and Alaska. Yet war planners hesitated to do that; they seemed as concerned with defending the United States *against* those colonized peoples as defending it with them. The early plans for Hawaiʻi envisioned deporting or interning the large ethnic Japanese population—a group that had climbed to well over a third of the territory's population by the 1920s. In the Philippines, the army's planners spun out scenarios in which U.S. forces would have to fight Filipino uprisings.

Perhaps they were right to fear colonized peoples. The 1930s, which had unleashed a violent Puerto Rican independence movement, also stirred up turmoil in the Pacific colonies. The late thirties saw a string of militant and racially charged strikes in Hawaiʻi, spreading from the ports to the fields. In the Philippines, a low rumble of rural insurgency erupted in the "Sakdal rebellion" in 1935. Thousands of partially armed peasants and workers, impatient with Quezon's temporizing, seized municipal buildings and demanded immediate independence. Their leader wanted them to kidnap the governor-general, raid armories, and storm the capital.

Filipino police and soldiers suppressed the Sakdal rebellion, killing fifty-nine rebels and dispersing the rest before it got that far. But the army's planners eyed with suspicion even those Filipinos in uniform. And again, they had reason. In 1924, hundreds of Filipino soldiers in the U.S. Army had staged a mutiny over their unequal pay compared with white soldiers. MacArthur himself had overseen the court-martial, in which more than two hundred mutineers received sentences of five to twenty years.

Colonial defense, in other words, was a dicey business. But MacArthur's faith did not waver. On Quezon's invitation, MacArthur—still the army chief of staff—left Washington for the Philippines to undertake what he regarded as "an eleventh-hour struggle to build up enough force to repel an enemy."

★

Douglas MacArthur dragged along his favorite aide, Dwight Eisenhower. Whereas MacArthur regarded Philippine work as a calling, Eisenhower saw it as "just another job." He also believed it to be a "hopeless venture," given Manila's lack of resources and Washington's lack of interest.

One of Eisenhower's ideas was to secure leftover rifles from the U.S. Army at a nominal cost. These weren't rifles the army needed. They were obsolete World War I–era Enfield models, and they didn't work well. Still, Washington hesitated. The chief of the War Plans Division stood against the proposal: he worried that armed Filipinos might rise up against the

United States. And would Japan regard the militarization of the Philippines as provocation? Eisenhower complained in his diary about the lack of "basic appreciation in the War Department of the local defense problem." Eventually the army sold the rifles in cautious batches, some first, then more later if it went well. And it charged more than twice what Eisenhower had expected.

While Eisenhower wrestled with the bookkeeping, MacArthur settled in. He'd met his second wife, Jean, on the trip over. His only son, Arthur MacArthur IV, was born in Manila, with Manuel Quezon as the godfather. MacArthur took up residence in the penthouse of the Parsons-designed Manila Hotel. He became a fixture of Manila society, even receiving a birthday card from his father's old nemesis, Emilio Aguinaldo.

By all appearances, MacArthur intended to stay the course. When the War Department, nervous that his buildup of Philippine defenses might antagonize Japan, recalled MacArthur to the mainland in 1937, he took the extraordinary step of resigning from the army. It was an enormous sacrifice, given his long service (and his father's) to the army, but it allowed him to remain Quezon's military adviser. If MacArthur couldn't be a U.S. general in the Philippines, he would be the field marshal (a grandiose title of his own choosing) of the army of the Philippine Commonwealth.

Eisenhower was apoplectic. "General, you have been a four-star general . . . This is a *proud* thing. There's only been a few who had it. Why in the *hell* do you want a *banana* country giving you a field-marshalship?"

MacArthur was undeterred. He'd had a special uniform designed: a white sharkskin suit, black trousers, four stars on his shoulder, red ribbon at his lapel, and a gold-braided cap. He carried a gold baton.

Ostensibly, the pomp was meant to buck up Philippine morale. But perhaps it was to boost MacArthur's spirits, too. As the years went on, his hope of raising a Philippine reserve army looked increasingly delusional. The gun shortage was only the start of the problems. What little ammunition got shipped to the islands often arrived badly deteriorated, and the recruits didn't have enough of it to train with.

MacArthur asked Washington for help: $50 per Filipino trainee. It wasn't an absurd request, given that the National Guard received a $220-per-traineee subsidy. Yet this one, too, was turned down.

MacArthur understood the Philippines to be "an integral part of the

United States," as deserving of defense as New York. But he had to admit by 1940 that the military forces stationed there were "entirely inadequate for purposes of foreign defense and are little more than token symbols of the sovereignty of the United States."

In May 1941, a very frustrated field marshal cabled Washington to say he was coming home.

★

Ernest Gruening, meanwhile, faced his own ordeal. Despite the large ambit of his job—the supervisor of all the colonies—he didn't have much power. His office was small and could do little more than lobby on behalf of the colonies. Gruening spent most of his time on Puerto Rico, where he held a separate appointment as head of the New Deal administration there.

Though he lacked power, Gruening still managed to acquire a rival, Secretary of the Interior Harold Ickes. Their politics didn't differ much, but the pair nevertheless clashed with all the passion and pointlessness of two apparatchiks in the Soviet bureaucracy. Like any good Kremlin rivalry, it ended with exile in Siberia. Or, in this case, with Ernest Gruening being removed from Washington and sent to Alaska in 1939, where he was to be the colonial governor.

From his new perch in Anchorage, Gruening saw the peril that the Pacific territories faced. Alaska's western Aleutian Islands stretched out toward Japan, reducing the Pacific Ocean "to the width of a ferry boat channel," as one journalist put it. When Alaska had been annexed, in 1867, this had been a promising feature: the islands were stepping-stones to Asia. Now, however, it seemed more likely that the foot traffic would go in the other direction, that Alaska would be the point of entry for a Japanese invasion of North America.

Like MacArthur in the Philippines, Gruening begged for help. He needed it badly. Though Alaska shared a continent with the mainland, no road connected them (the secretary of war had judged the value of such a road to be "negligible"). Alaska had an air force, but only six obsolescent medium bombers and twelve obsolete pursuit planes were able to fly—and there wasn't much gasoline. The assistant secretary of war described the army in Alaska as existing "in little more than name only." There was no navy.

Gruening petitioned Congress for funding, as Alaskans had been doing for years, but with little luck. The New Deal's massive infrastructural investments had passed Alaska by. It wasn't a state, so it had no congressmen to lobby for it. And pleading military peril did nothing to change that. "'We're not going to waste any money on Alaska,' was the consensus," Gruening remembered.

It took the Japanese movement into French Indochina in mid-1941 to break the congressional stonewalling. With Japan on the march, Congress finally saw the wisdom of fortifying its Pacific-facing territory. The Japanese movement terrified the British even more. They feared losing Singapore and pleaded with Roosevelt to mount an Asian defense.

Roosevelt agreed. MacArthur, who had threatened to quit the Philippines, was ordered to stay. He would be welcomed back into the U.S. Army, this time as the commander of all the U.S. forces in Asia, and his Philippine army would be absorbed into the U.S. Army. Although Washington held the line on modern rifles, it began shipping massive B-17 bombers ("flying fortresses," they were called) to the colony. The idea was that, with 128 bombers by February 1942, MacArthur should be able to defend not only the Philippines but the whole theater, including the British possessions. Army Chief of Staff George Marshall saw the B-17s as "the decisive element in deterring Japan."

But the B-17s didn't begin arriving until September 1941. There were other priorities that interfered: hauling as much rubber as feasible from Southeast Asia before a Pacific war closed the markets, shunting destroyers across the Atlantic to aid the British. The matériel intended for Pacific outposts piled up at the ports. "More speed! Congress!" the exasperated editors of a Hawaiian magazine demanded. "More and more speed!"

★

If you had made a flight around the Pacific in late 1941, here's what you'd have seen. Hawai'i's defenses were substantial but incomplete, lacking especially long-range bombers (it had only twelve B-17s in commission). Guam had practically nothing: its one rudimentary base was too small for a bomber to land. Guam's governor despaired that the colony was "absolutely indefensible," and in the military it was common to refer to it in the past tense. Alaska, despite the last-minute reversal of congressional opinion, wasn't much better off. "By no stretch of the imagination" concluded its air force chief, could Alaska's planes "defend the territory against any attack in force."

MacArthur's Philippines was mixed. There was a small regular U.S. Army contingent of 31,095 troops, more than a third of whom were Filipino, plus MacArthur's half-finished reserve army of about 120,000 Filipinos. The reservists were barely trained and badly equipped: canvas shoes, coconut-bark helmets, outmoded rifles, artillery that dated from 1898, and little by way of ammunition. Many had never even fired their rifles. More promising was the growing air force, which, with its fighters and long-range bombers, represented the largest concentration of U.S. warplanes outside the mainland. Still, the planes trickled in slowly, and by the end of 1941 only 35 of the planned 128 flying fortresses had arrived.

MacArthur remained sanguine, insisting loudly to all within earshot that "the Philippines could be defended, and by God, they would be defended." But a confidential report by the high commissioner warned of "glaring deficiencies" in Philippine defenses. It also noted Quezon's private admission that war would find the populace "unprepared and unprotected."

That report was sent on November 30, 1941. A week later, Filipinos noticed some unfamiliar planes in the sky.

11

WARFARE STATE

"War," the comedian Jon Stewart has observed, is "God's way of teaching Americans geography." Certainly the Japanese attacks on December 7/8, 1941, were an education. For those used to the Mercator projection maps that placed Japan on the right side (in the "Far East") and Hawai'i on the left, Pearl Harbor offered a textbook lesson in the perils of representing a round world on a flat surface. Even territories that weren't struck, such as Alaska, popped out with unsettling clarity once Japan had shown the extent of its ambitions.

War planners could finally see what Ernest Gruening had been trying to tell them for years: Alaska extended precipitously into the Pacific, its Aleutian Islands forming a bridge to northern Asia. A colony of some seventy-five thousand people, half Native, with an economy dedicated mainly to fishing, was suddenly at the forefront of military defense. But if Alaska now appeared close to Japan, it also looked remote from the mainland, since no overland route connected it.

Nervous about a Japanese invasion and eager to put its massive Pacific territory to use, the Roosevelt administration set out to build a road. This would not only connect Alaska to the mainland, it would help the government ferry supplies to the allied Soviet Union.

The road was a mind-bogglingly difficult undertaking. Its route, with the ambivalent acquiescence of Canada's government, cut through

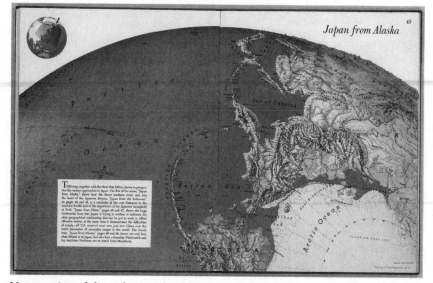

New wartime globe-style map, by the popular cartographer Richard Edes Harrison, highlighting the island bridge connecting Alaska (at bottom) to Japan, 1944

Canada's northern provinces, spanning a distance greater than that between New York and Dallas. The land it crossed was a virtual wilderness, with only a few small towns along the route, so workers would have to haul all their food, supplies, and shelter with them. The shelter was especially important, for temperatures were extremely cold (once during the first winter it dipped below −70°F). And everything would have to be done at top speed.

The United States sent 11,150 troops up north. A third were African Americans—the first black units to serve beyond the mainland in the war. With the 11,150 men came 11,107 pieces of heavy equipment: tractors, bulldozers, dump trucks, crushers, scrapers, steam shovels, boilers, compressors, and generators.

In the stretch between Dawson Creek, British Columbia, and Fairbanks, Alaska, it was as if the entire twentieth century had slammed down all at once. Men and women used to traveling by dogsled watched in astonishment as bulldozers crashed through the thick, trackless forest. Permafrost, buried under vegetation for centuries, saw sunlight for the first time and melted, turning hard ground swampy. People who'd had only limited contact with outsiders were suddenly making unheard-of amounts of money servicing the troops. But they also fell prone to disease. An anthropologist working among the First Nations of Canada in the Northwest Territories decades later found that any discussion of family histories inevitably gave rise to talk of relatives who had "died in '42."

The road was finished in November 1942 at a cost of $19.7 million. It was, Canada's high commissioner judged, the "greatest piece of roadmaking yet undertaken by man."

In all, it stretched 1,650 miles. That was hundreds of miles longer than it needed to be. But the army's engineers, bent on speed above all else, had looped the road around difficult spots—a costly time-saving measure. They were the same way about equipment. When bulldozers broke down, the men abandoned them on the roadside rather than fixing them—it was quicker that way, and there was no shortage of bulldozers.

Because, for the first time in Alaska's history, money was no object.

★

Across the empire, backwaters became battle stations. And with the military came federal money, washing indiscriminately over lands long parched by neglect. In Puerto Rico, workers moved from faltering sugar plantations to jobs building and operating military bases. By 1950, the federal government had spent $1.2 billion there.

The same thing happened to Hawai'i, the hub of the Pacific war. After Pearl Harbor, the military arrived en masse, bringing with it an insatiable demand. Unemployment vanished, the number of restaurants in Honolulu tripled, and bank deposits throughout the territory quintupled. The newly arrived men, their wallets bulging, turned the tourist drag of Hotel Street into a gold mine. Eight parlors supplied some four hundred to five hundred tattoos a day ("Remember Pearl Harbor" was a favorite). The overcrowded brothels, doling out services in three-minute increments, cleared $10 million a year—half the cost of the Alaska Highway, right there.

This transformation wasn't limited to the territories. On the mainland, too, the war brought jobs. It also brought new governmental intrusions into daily life—price restrictions, wage controls, rationing, income tax, war bonds, and conscription. But the difference is that in the territories, all that happened with the volume turned up. These were the parts of the Greater United States that faced foreign lands. So if you want to see governmental growth during World War II, forget Detroit and San Francisco. It was in the territories, particularly Alaska and Hawai'i, where militarization truly took command.

★

The first bombs fell on Pearl Harbor at 7:55 a.m. Eight hours later—before the United States had even declared war—Hawai'i governor Joseph Poindexter suspended the writ of habeas corpus and turned over all effective power in the territory to the army.

The people of Hawai'i watched as a colony best known for its beaches, flowers, and guitars became an armed camp. Parks and schoolyards were gutted by trenches, barbed wire littered the beaches, guards took up posts at major intersections, and thousands of concrete machine-gun nests appeared, suggesting the discomfiting possibility of bullets whizzing through downtown Honolulu. The army and navy claimed hundreds of thousands of acres of land—sometimes bought, often simply taken. At its peak during the war, the army held a third of O'ahu.

Tanks on Beretania Street in Honolulu during Hawai'i's nearly three years of martial law

Life in a war zone was a life shaped by precaution. It meant carrying around a gas mask when out (the University of Hawaii graduates processed in cap and gown and gas mask). It meant obeying strict curfews. It meant "blackouts": extinguishing all light by which Japanese planes might navigate at night.

But the safeguards weren't only against invaders. The military also insisted on extraordinary precautions against the people of Hawai'i themselves. Hawai'i was "enemy country," as the secretary of the navy saw it, with a suspect population, more than one-third of which was of Japanese ancestry. Thus were the territory's residents registered, fingerprinted, and vaccinated—the first mass fingerprinting and the largest compulsory vaccination campaign the United States had ever undertaken. They were required to carry identification cards at all times on pain of arrest. This led to an uncomfortable moment when Governor Poindexter himself was stopped and realized that he had left his ID card in the pocket of another suit.

The regulations emanated, without any legislative check or presidential oversight, from the Office of the Military Governor (OMG or, as some put it, "One Mighty God"). Like any deity, the military governor issued commandments that were onerous: the replacement of U.S. dollars with a Hawai'i-only currency, travel restrictions, press censorship, mail censorship, wage freezes, and prohibitions on quitting jobs in key industries. He could also be a jealous god, as when he set a punishment of up to ten years' hard labor for contempt toward the flag or when he forbade expressions of "hostility or disrespect" (in word, image, or "gesture") toward himself or any member of the armed forces at places of amusement. In other respects, the General Orders read like the Talmud, going well beyond matters of obvious military significance and ruling on the painting of fenders, the preservation of meat, the hours kept by bowling alleys, the transportation of pigeons, and the slaughter of hogs (up to a month in prison for butchering an underweight pig).

"My authority was substantially unlimited," the military governor boasted in his diary.

Behind his many orders stood the strength of the armed forces. The manager of one of Hawai'i's radio stations recalled his first live broadcast under martial law. A naval officer came into the studio, drew his service weapon, and announced, "I've got a .45 in my hand and I'll shoot you if you deviate from the script." The officer was laughing, the manager remembered, but he wasn't joking.

The military police were "known to be overzealous," one Japanese Honolulan recorded in his diary. "They shoot first and ask questions later."

Beyond guns in the street, the army established a system of provost courts to enforce its laws. The justice they dispensed was hasty and harsh. Trials were often held on the day of arrest and lasted minutes. In the first four months in Honolulu, a single judge dispatched about a hundred cases per day. There were no juries, no journalists, no subpoenaing of witnesses, and, for the most part, no lawyers. Armed military officials, who rarely had legal training, interpreted the facts and the law with maximum discretion—defendants could be and were convicted of violating the "spirit of martial law." Not surprisingly, convictions were the rule. Of the more than twenty thousand trials conducted in one of Honolulu's provost courts in 1942, 98.4 percent resulted in guilty verdicts.

The tens of thousands of defendants who passed through Hawai'i's provost courts were not charged with the usual: robbery, assault, fraud, etc. They were tried for failing to show up to work, for breaking curfew, and for committing traffic violations, mainly. Perhaps a few, I like to imagine, were charged with making the aforementioned disrespectful gesture to a member of the armed forces at a place of amusement.

Once tried and, in all likelihood, convicted, defendants in these juryless trials could be fined thousands of dollars or incarcerated for up to five years (more serious crimes meriting longer sentences were handled in a different class of military court). The General Orders specified punishments of up to thirty days' imprisonment for leaving keys in the ignition of a parked car, and of up to a year at hard labor and a $1,000 fine for buying marked playing cards.

Living under this regime could be exasperating. One motorist was fined $50, on the charge of assault and battery, for kicking his own car. One of the most disturbing cases involved a black man who, running away from a bar where he'd been threatened by a bouncer, collided with two military policemen. He was arrested, charged with assaulting a police officer, and sentenced to five years in prison.

As records were not uniformly kept and trials were closed to the public, it's hard to know how common that sort of egregious miscarriage of justice was. But sentences of more than a year's incarceration were rare, and

For blackout and traffic violations
We payed in bonds and blood donations.

A Honolulu children's book from the martial law period showing a defendant trembling before a provost court judge

there's little reason to think that many languished in Hawai'i's prisons. Often, defendants were directed to donate blood in lieu of jail time or purchase war bonds instead of paying fines. In that way, the army compelled the people of Hawai'i to engage in patriotic acts that, for mainlanders, were done by choice.

Martial law in Hawai'i lasted nearly three years, which was two and a half years longer than Japan posed any plausible threat to the islands. Yet Hawai'i's military commanders repeatedly refused to relinquish control. The secretary of the interior started calling it the "American 'conquered territory' of Hawaii."

What ended martial law, ultimately, was a series of legal challenges that brought the issue to public view—a rare occasion when mainlanders paid attention to the territories. The military's lawyers argued before the Supreme Court that Hawai'i's territorial status permitted martial law. Plus, they added, Hawai'i had a "heterogeneous population, with all sorts of affinities and loyalties which are alien in many cases to the philosophy of life of the American Government."

The court, to its great credit, disagreed. Martial law in Hawai'i was illegal, it concluded, and civilians there deserved the same protections as mainland civilians. "Racism has no place whatever in our civilization," one justice scolded. That ruling came, however, only in 1946—by which time not only martial law but the war itself had ended.

★

Not long after Japan seized the Philippines, it moved on Alaska. In June 1942 Japan bombed Dutch Harbor and conquered the Aleutian islands of Agattu, Attu, and Kiska ("Somebody ought to be impeached," grumbled Manuel Quezon when he heard the news of yet another bit of barely defended territory falling into Japanese hands). The Japanese occupied the islands for more than a year and transported Attu's tiny population (42) to Japan as prisoners of war. Half of them died there.

Conquering part of Alaska was a significant achievement, and propagandists brought relics from the Aleutians to the Japanese home islands for proud display. U.S mainlanders were far less aware of the event, and that is because of official censorship. Although Ernest Gruening, as governor, staved off martial law in Alaska, he did so by reluctantly agreeing to cooperate with the military in all governmental matters. Alaska became its own sort of military garrison, with blackouts, travel restrictions, and the rest.

Most striking was the near-total lockdown on information. On the mainland, censorship was handled with a surprisingly light touch. The government merely requested that editors not publish details about sensitive matters. In Alaska, by contrast, censorship was mandatory and vigorous. Printed materials going into the territory were heavily censored, so that even Gruening—the governor—had his mail opened and articles scissored out of his copies of *The Washington Post* and *Newsweek*. Outgoing news was even more strictly controlled. After the Japanese attack, non-Alaskan journalists were expelled (a few eventually came back). Remaining journalists were prohibited from writing about strategic matters, which, in the military's broad interpretation, meant nearly every aspect of Alaskan life.

"Are we foreigners out here?" an Alaskan asked. "Aren't we Americans, too?"

An incensed Ernest Gruening traveled to Washington to complain of the "introduction of Gestapo methods to the United States." But he found, in a perfect catch-22, that the censorship was so complete that even congressmen didn't know of it.

Alaska was thus the "quietest war theater," or the "hidden front," as journalists called it. Today it is the forgotten war. Many people are surprised to learn that the Japanese even came near Alaska.

They are also surprised to learn of the Aleut internment.

★

Japanese internment during World War II is one of the most regretted episodes in U.S. history. In May 1942 some 112,000 residents of western states, some Japanese nationals and some U.S. citizens of Japanese ancestry, were forcibly removed from their homes and held in camps for years. In 1988 Congress apologized for the "fundamental injustice" of this and awarded each internee $20,000—a rare instance of the government paying reparations.

Yet internment is one of those episodes that appear different once you look beyond the logo map. It was in the territories that the government's willingness to violate the civil liberties of its own subjects was on the fullest display. Hawai'i offers one example—a quasi-internment that, instead of targeting a racial group, turned an entire territory into a barbed-wire-encased armed camp, with the military monitoring the movement, communications, and political activity of every inhabitant.

Less familiar is what happened in the Aleutians, the chain of Alaskan islands that stretches toward Asia. Before the war started, Gruening and his colleagues had discussed the possibility of a Japanese attack. Should the islands be evacuated, just in case? Gruening was against it: to remove the Aleuts from their homes, he believed, would be disastrous.

The Japanese invasion forced the issue. The Alaska Command ordered that all Natives living on the Aleutians west of Unimak and on the nearby Pribilof Islands be removed and sent farther inland. This wasn't from fear of disloyalty. It was, rather, a "for your own good" internment, a way to keep civilians out of a war zone (though Aleuts noticed that the *white* residents of Unalaska Island were allowed to stay).

Because Gruening and his colleagues had resisted the notion of Aleut internment, there were no plans in place. Nearly nine hundred Aleuts were shoved hastily onto ships ("while eating breakfast," an officer on Atka recalled—"the eggs were still on the table") and dropped off in unfamiliar Southeast Alaska.

They found this new environment unsettling. By all accounts, the large stands of trees unnerved them. "Feels funny," the chief of the Atka tribe noted with alarm. "No room to walk."

The trees, though, were the least of the Aleuts' problems. Their new "homes" were whatever spaces the navy could find on short notice: abandoned mining camps, fish canneries, and labor camps. Many lacked running water. And despite the millions the military was pouring into the Alaska Highway, it never found the money to fix the internment camps.

So what were the camps like? "I have no language at my command which can adequately describe what I saw," wrote Alaska's attorney general to Gruening after he toured one. "If I had I am confident you would not believe my statements."

A desperate internee tried to draw a picture for officials. The camp was "no place for a living creature," she explained in a letter. "We drink impure water and then get sick the children's get skin disease even the grown ups are sick from the cold. We ate from the mess house and it is near the toilet only a few yards away. We eat the filth that is flying around. We got no place to take a bath and no place to wash our clothes or dry them when it rains."

Gruening visited, accompanied by a doctor. The complaints were accurate. "As we entered the first bunkhouse the odor of human excreta and waste was so pungent that I could hardly make the grade," the doctor recorded. The buildings had no lights, nonfunctioning sewage, and water that was "discolored, contaminated and unattractive."

Despite being loyal citizens who had surrendered their homes at the navy's request, the Aleuts languished in these camps. Though no barbed wire surrounded them, leaving was impossible: the Aleuts needed military permission and (in most camps) a boat to leave, neither of which was forthcoming.

So they stayed, for years. After Japan had been rousted from the Aleutians and the tides of war had turned, there was little likelihood that the islands would face continued peril. At least, the government was comfortable taking the men of the Pribilof Islands back to their homes to work the 1943 seal harvest (the Fish and Wildlife Service had a lucrative deal with a fur company). But once the Pribilovians turned over the furs, they were sent straight back to the camps.

The long internment wasn't born of any animosity toward the Aleuts. They weren't the "enemy." It just seems that officials found it easier to keep the Aleuts where they were—far away—than to bring them home. Plus, the military had taken over many of their homes. And because censorship was watertight, there was no public pressure. Nobody knew.

The delay mattered, though. Sickness in the camps—the predictable result of a near-total lack of infrastructure—turned to death. In the West Coast camps, the death rate of internees was no greater than that of normal civilians. But in Alaskan camps, by the war's end, 10 percent had died.

★

The story of internment in the Greater United States does not end with Hawaiian martial law or the Aleuts' relocation. Though the episode is barely known, the United States interned Japanese in the Philippines, too.

Roosevelt signed the infamous Executive Order 9906, calling for the internment of Japanese in the U.S. West, in February 1942, after much deliberation. The internment of the Japanese-ancestry population (numbering about thirty thousand) in the Philippines required less talk. Months before Pearl Harbor, the Philippine Assembly had passed a bill requiring foreign nationals to register with the government and have their fingerprints taken. Then, on the day of the attack, MacArthur ordered police to round up the Japanese population, including naturalized Philippine citizens and people of Japanese ancestry born in the Philippines. Only career consular officials were excluded.

This was not a polite affair. Soldiers raided Japanese homes, stores, and offices and dragged the Japanese out if necessary. One Filipina described a truckload of families being hauled through the streets:

> People hooted. My houseboy was delirious. "Hang them, the traitors!" he shouted over the fence. He stooped to pick up a stone but I stopped him. "You are not to meddle," I told him sharply. "You must leave it to the Americans, whatever must be done."

With encouragement from the authorities, civilians hunted for any Japanese who remained hidden. Filipinos who helped hide them were arrested. Japanese women were raped, by both civilians and soldiers, and Japanese homes and businesses were ransacked. In Manila, the police parked trucks containing more than a hundred internees in the middle of the street during an air raid, a tempting target for Japan's bombers and a terrifying ordeal for those trapped inside. In Davao, guards repeatedly vented their rage against Japan by arbitrarily shooting prisoners—one internee estimated that they killed fifty in all.

Kiyoshi Osawa, an internee who had lived in the Philippines for sixteen years, since he was a teenager, remembered "the indescribable wave of uncertainty and humiliation" as he "languished in prison."

Osawa and his fellow internees are never mentioned in U.S. accounts of Japanese internment. That's partly because of the general tendency to exclude the colonies from U.S. history, though it surely also has to do with the short-lived nature of the affair. Whereas West Coast internment, Hawaiian martial law, and Aleut internment lasted years, the Philippine internment was ended in weeks by the Japanese invasion in late 1941.

That invasion put internees like Osawa in an interesting position. On the West Coast, official fears that Japanese-ancestry residents would collaborate with Japan turned out to be baseless. There are only a handful of known cases in which mainlanders materially aided Japan. Yet in the Philippines the question of loyalty was posed in a much more acute way, as Japan had actually conquered the territory. Would the Japanese in the Philippines side with Japan or the United States?

Nearly unanimously, they chose Japan. The former internees, bearing guns provided by the Japanese army, took swift and brutal revenge on those who had locked them up. They then served the Japanese occupation as intermediaries and interpreters. Filipinos got used to seeing familiar faces—the gardener, the ice-cream peddler, the house servant—parading in Japanese military uniforms.

"Words cannot describe the seriousness of the dilemma faced by the Japanese residents as we found ourselves caught between the brutality of the Japanese military and the misery of our Filipino friends," Osawa remembered. Nevertheless, he joined the occupation government and served it throughout the war. Despite his "assimilation into Philippine society," he still felt a "fierce pride of being Japanese."

No doubt Osawa's feelings were helped along by the fact that he had just been incarcerated by his Filipino neighbors.

★

Kiyoshi Osawa's predicament wasn't uncommon. Colonized subjects had cause for complaint against the United States—internees especially so. It wasn't unreasonable to suppose that some might side with Japan during the war, as Osawa did. Certainly that fear pervaded the minds of colonial officials throughout the Pacific empire.

Yet that fear was not realized in the Pacific territories beyond Japan's direct reach. Instead, the inhabitants of Hawai'i and Alaska broke the other way and stood behind the United States as few others did. Much in the way that many African Americans fought abroad to vindicate their demands for equality at home, the inhabitants of the Pacific territory joined the war effort with a clear determination, as if they had something to prove. Hawai'i's war bond sales were the highest in the country, consistently between two and nearly four times the national average. Alaska's, as of at least the middle of the war, ranked second. Even as they faced more extreme governmental intrusions than mainlanders, the people of the Pacific territories bankrolled the war.

But the government asked more of them than bond purchases. In Alaska, Gruening, concerned about a Japanese invasion (this was a month before Japan attacked the Aleutians), set out to organize the Alaska Territorial Guard. It was to be a militia, armed citizens prepared to fend off invaders. As Gruening needed the guard to extend up the whole coast, this meant enrolling indigenous people.

"Up until then," Gruening remembers, "I had had very little contact with the Eskimos." He wondered how they might react to the prospect of joining the military. Alaska Natives endured a harsh Jim Crow system: separate seating in theaters, segregated schools, and NO NATIVES ALLOWED signs on hotels and restaurants. Gruening confessed that he "did not know what resentment might lurk behind their smiling faces." Nor did the mainland soldiers, who worried that Alaska Natives, if armed, might turn their guns against the army.

Gruening wagered that they wouldn't, and he toured the territory with Major Marvin Marston to start recruiting. It was the first time a governor had ever visited the Natives of the north. Gruening spoke first, addressing them as "fellow citizens of the United States." Marston then explained the request. They wouldn't be paid or have uniforms, but they'd be soldiers— the "eyes and ears of the Army"—with shoulder badges to signify their membership.

"We will give you guns and ammunition," Marston continued. "If Jap comes here and lands his boat, will you shoot him quick?"

They would. "Everywhere I found only the heartiest response to my pleas for organization in self-defense," Gruening remembered. "In every Eskimo village, I would call a meeting. Everyone came: men, women, children, infants." Counting auxiliaries, some twenty thousand Alaska Natives joined "Gruening's Guerrillas."

They had no funding and little contact with their commanders. And

Major Marston presenting an
Alaska Territorial Guard
member with his rifle. Painting
by Rusty Heurlin, who also
trained ATG members

what contact they did have with the military could be exasperating. "I had a heck of a time," Simeon Pletnikoff remembered, recounting how mainland soldiers captured him, threatened to kill him, and sought to bring him before the provost marshal on the charge of impersonating a soldier.

"What's the matter with you guys?" Pletnikoff asked. "I'm an Aleut."

Despite the humiliations, Territorial Guard members set about fortifying Alaska's north. They built trails, constructed armories and shelters, enforced blackouts, put out tundra fires, and kept watch. When the Japanese floated flaming balloons across the Pacific in a futile attempt to firebomb North America, the Territorial Guard located and retrieved them. Their rifles were the same obsolete World War I–era models that the Filipinos got, but that didn't stop the Alaska Natives from drilling weekly with them.

And, once activated, the Native units continued to serve under the auspices of the National Guard of Alaska, enlisting at rates far outstripping those of mainlanders. They carried out their duties quietly but with remarkable fidelity, well into the Cold War. A general who landed on Little

Diomede Island unannounced in 1969 was shocked to see armed men in uniform meet his plane. Had there been an alert? he asked.

No, they explained, they were just prepared.

★

Alaska Natives toiled in obscurity. The same could not be said of the Japanese Americans from Hawai'i who enlisted in the army. In May 1942 the 100th Infantry Battalion (Separate) was formed from more than fourteen hundred men of Japanese descent, all U.S. citizens. Journalists took a great interest in this outfit, known as the "guinea pigs from Pearl Harbor." "We knew that we had to be as good as any other Caucasian outfit," recalled one member. "And we knew that we had to shed blood."

Japanese from Hawai'i could feel the spotlight's heat. And so they performed. When, the next year, the army called for troops of Japanese ancestry to form the 442nd Infantry Regiment, the slots reserved for mainland Japanese went unfilled (many were still in camps). But nearly ten thousand Japanese from Hawai'i flooded the recruitment office. More than three-quarters of the original recruits in the 442nd were from the islands.

Both the all-Hawai'i 100th and the mainly Hawai'i 442nd, which absorbed the 100th, were sent to Europe. The men fought there with conspicuous valor—"valor" in this case being a euphemism for an extreme disregard for personal safety in the enthusiastic service of killing Nazis.

One soldier, Daniel Inouye, exhibited near-inconceivable levels of valor in Tuscany at the war's end. When three German machine guns pinned his men down, he stood up to charge. He was immediately shot in the stomach, but he ran *toward* the first machine-gun nest and blew it up with a grenade. He then, in his words, "lurched up the hill" toward the second emplacement, dispatching it with two grenades. On his way toward the third nest, his last grenade in hand, a German rifle grenade hit his right elbow and "all but tore my arm off." But his right fist, hanging now from "a few bloody shreds of tissue," still clenched an armed grenade. He pried the grenade free with his left hand and hurled it into the third machine-gun nest. As the few surviving Germans ran out, Inouye unslung his tommy gun and, left-handed, sprayed them with machine-gun fire. It was only after getting shot again, in the leg, that he finally collapsed.

"Get back up that hill!" he berated his comrades as they rushed to help him. "Nobody called off the war!"

Inouye lost the arm but won a Medal of Honor, the highest military decoration the United States bestows. In the Second World War, only four army divisions earned more than ten. The 100th/442nd, though a regiment—one-third the size of a division—earned twenty-one (twenty-two if you count Mr. Miyagi in *The Karate Kid*). It won thousands of other awards, too. Pound for pound, the 100th/442nd was one of the most decorated units in U.S. history.

12

THERE ARE TIMES WHEN MEN HAVE TO DIE

Hawai'i and Alaska were militarized to prepare for an invasion that never came. Both territories were attacked, but except for Alaska's Aleutian Islands, both remained intact. In this, they were lucky. Elsewhere in the Pacific, the war saw Western colonies invaded and conquered.

It started with Pearl Harbor. The event is remembered by mainlanders as an attack on a Hawaiian base, but of course that was only part of it. On that day, the Japanese launched a near-simultaneous strike on the Allies' colonies throughout the Pacific. Because surprise bombings work best at the break of day, the idea was to attack the major targets—Hawai'i, the Philippines, Guam, and Hong Kong—shortly after dawn.

Dawn, however, is a relative concept. The unavoidable flaw in the Japanese plan was that territories that had been hit could warn those farther west, where it was still night. This was particularly a concern with regard to MacArthur's B-17s, his "ace unit" in the Philippines that served as the pillar of Allied defense in the Pacific. With warning from Hawai'i, those flying fortresses could be aloft and ready.

Worse, the Japanese planes at Taiwan that were supposed to strike the Philippines didn't take off on time. Thick fog grounded them for six hours, dramatically expanding the window in which MacArthur could react to the Hawai'i news. Japan's pilots had every reason to fear that by the time they reached the Philippines, MacArthur would be waiting. Perhaps his B-17s would bomb Taiwan before their planes could even take off.

But that's not what happened—not even close. "The sight which met us was unbelievable" is how a Japanese pilot remembered his arrival over the Philippines. "Instead of encountering a swarm of American fighters diving at us in attack, we looked down and saw some sixty enemy bombers and fighters neatly parked along the airfield runways." MacArthur's planes were not in the air, and they were certainly not on their way to Taiwan. They were on the ground, lined up in rows.

The astonished Japanese pilots dropped their bombs.

★

MacArthur *had* gotten the Hawai'i news. The phone rang in his penthouse atop the Manila Hotel at 3:40 a.m., Philippine time. He dressed and rushed to headquarters.

But what happened next is impossible to say. For hours, it appears, MacArthur did practically nothing. His air commander visited MacArthur's headquarters twice in desperate bids for a meeting but saw only MacArthur's closed office door. Repeated warnings from Washington went unacknowledged; direct orders were ignored.

Had MacArthur gone catatonic? Was he playing some devious (yet ineffectual) game? MacArthur's biographer found his behavior "bewildering." It's a "riddle," the biographer wrote, "and we shall never solve it."

Whatever the cause, the effect was catastrophe. The Japanese struck sometime after noon, nine hours after MacArthur's phone had rung. "We could see our beautiful silver Flying Fortresses burning and exploding right before our eyes as we stood powerless to do anything about it," one B-17 navigator wrote. In hours, MacArthur lost eighteen of his thirty-five B-17s and some ninety other aircraft. Many of his remaining planes were badly damaged. His air commander regarded it as "one of the blackest days in U.S. military history."

Before the attack, MacArthur's air force had been incomplete. Now it was inoperable. The Japanese returned again and again, and MacArthur could do nothing. They, not he, had command of the air.

It was 1898 and the Battle of Manila Bay all over again. Except now the United States was in Spain's place: the distant empire losing its fleet in a single day.

★

With the best hope for an Allied defense of the Pacific knocked out in one quick blow, the Japanese made brisk work of the rest. Guam fell on December 10, Thailand on the twenty-first, Wake Island on the twenty-third, and Hong Kong on Christmas Day. New Year's Day saw Manila succumb. Then came the other great colonial capitals of Asia: Singapore on February 15 (the "worst disaster and largest capitulation in British history," Winston Churchill moaned), Batavia on March 5, and Rangoon on the eighth. In three breathtaking months Japan had brought the Dutch, British, and U.S. empires in the Pacific to heel.

MacArthur may have lost his B-17s, but he still had his army, which, counting reservists, was 150,000 strong. Yet those barely armed and undertrained reservists were wholly unprepared to face seasoned Japanese troops. Many simply vanished; in two weeks, the North Luzon Force shrank from 28,000 to 16,000. The troops that remained still outnumbered the first wave of Japanese invaders on Luzon, but that didn't matter. MacArthur's army fought Japan with all the efficacy (as a journalist put it) of a slab of oak fighting a buzz saw.

MacArthur abandoned the fight and concentrated on maneuvering his men on Luzon to the relative safety of the Bataan peninsula. It was a back-pedaling waltz: engage, fall back, dynamite the bridge, repeat. The difficulty was that it was to be danced over long distances (184 bridges destroyed in all) by two of MacArthur's deteriorating forces at once, and all to the accompaniment of enemy fire. Oddly, it was here, in retreat, that MacArthur proved his worth as a commander. The maneuver was by all accounts beautifully executed. General Pershing called it "a masterpiece, one of the greatest moves in all military history."

With his crumbling army converging on Bataan, MacArthur declared Manila an "open city." As of January 1, he would leave it entirely undefended, meaning the Japanese could enter in peace. But before the Japanese took the city, U.S. forces salted the earth. They set oil depots aflame and destroyed the city's main bridges—bridges that the government had built with great pride (and with Filipinos' taxes).

"It was hard to believe that our military situation had become this desperate," one Manilan remarked as he watched the large pillars of black smoke rise over the city.

Once again, as in the days of Cameron Forbes, the whole top layer of government abandoned Manila. But this time it didn't go to Baguio, which had also been attacked (five bomb craters dotted the Baguio Country Club's golf course). Instead, it fled to Corregidor, an island fortress in Manila Bay a little smaller than Lower Manhattan.

If Baguio was an open-air spa, Corregidor was a claustrophobic bunker. More than ten thousand service members and leading politicians crammed into deep tunnels carved from the island's rock. The money was there, too, since Roosevelt had ordered the high commissioner to empty the banks. In all, it was a strange scene: Japanese bombs pounding the earth overhead, MacArthur's three-year-old son marching up and down the tunnels singing "The Battle Hymn of the Republic," and a dragon's hoard—some 5.5 tons of gold, 150 tons of silver pesos, and millions in U.S. bills—just sitting there, glimmering.

Bataan was a more sober sight. From a military perspective, the peninsula was a promising place for siege defense. But to survive a siege, you need food, and there was nowhere near enough to feed eighty thousand troops and twenty-six thousand civilian refugees. The men ate half rations in January; by March, they were lucky to get quarter rations. They foraged desperately, picking clean the area around them. They ate horses, dogs, pack mules, iguanas, snakes, and monkeys ("it looked like roast baby," a nauseated soldier remarked). One sergeant tried eating cigarettes. Unsurprisingly, disease flourished: dysentery, malaria, hookworm, and, that reliable indicator of prolonged nutritional deficiency, beriberi.

"There are no atheists in fox holes" is a familiar wartime proverb, conveying the desperation of frontline combat. It was coined, as it turns out, on Bataan.

★

Had the siege of Bataan pitted Japan against the United States, it would have been dramatic enough. But three-quarters of MacArthur's men there were Filipino. The siege thus layered political questions atop military ones. Would the Filipinos fight for their empire? And would their empire fight for them?

Franklin Delano Roosevelt stated his position clearly enough. "I give to the people of the Philippines my solemn pledge that their freedom will be redeemed and their independence established and protected," he said in a message to the colony. "The entire resources, in men and in material, of the United States stand behind that pledge."

Those were strong words. Yet they were also, when examined closely, vague ones. Philippine freedom would be "redeemed," yes, but didn't that imply it would first be lost? Also, the president had said nothing about *when* this would happen. Immediately after making the statement, Roosevelt sent his press secretary, Steve Early, to clarify its timeline. Early scolded journalists for reading "too much of the immediate rather than the ultimate" into the president's pledge. "You must consider distances," he pleaded.

But Filipinos took the promise seriously. Rumors circulated of a massive convoy, miles in length, brimming with food and equipment, on its way. "In our mind's eyes we saw the vast fleet of steel gray ships steaming toward us, their bows cutting the waves sending up a multi-colored spray," a Filipino officer on Bataan recalled. Even MacArthur believed that Washington was preparing a relief effort.

Yet only a trickle arrived, and as the weeks dragged on, hope turned to rage. It was a feeling that Japanese propagandists seized upon. They dropped leaflets on the starving troops, targeting the Filipinos. "Our fight is not with you but with America," one said. "Surrender, and we will treat you like brothers." The Japanese promised the Philippines independence. They dropped menus from the Manila Hotel, which had the compound effect of redoubling Filipinos' hunger pangs and reminding them of the whites-only high life that mainlanders had enjoyed.

Emilio Aguinaldo took to the airwaves, urging his compatriots to lay down their weapons and cooperate with Japan. When interrogated about this after the war, he was unrepentant. Japan had always supported his cause, he pointed out. "It was only the Americans who betrayed me."

It didn't help MacArthur that Filipinos could hear *all* of Roosevelt's speeches, not just the ones aimed at them. They heard him stress the German enemy over the Japanese one. They heard his firm resolve to defend England.

Barely a week after pledging all the United States' resources to Philippine defense, Roosevelt delivered his State of the Union address. "It was bitter for us not to be able to land a million men in a thousand ships in the Philippine Islands," he said. (*Wait, why is he using the past tense?* Filipinos surely asked.) But, he explained, "we have been faced with hard choices." An attack on Japan would come "in proper time."

Manuel Quezon vibrated with anger. "I cannot stand this constant reference to England, to Europe. I am here and my people are here under the heels of a conqueror," he exclaimed. "How typically American to writhe in anguish at the fate of a distant cousin while a daughter is being raped in the back room."

MacArthur, too, was incensed. The Philippines—the site of his father's glory, his adopted home—was being treated as a sacrifice zone.

MacArthur enlisted the Manila newspaperman Carlos Romulo to put a better spin on things. Romulo was one of the most influential writers in the colony—he would go on to win a Pulitzer Prize and become president of the United Nations General Assembly. From Corregidor, Romulo operated a radio station, the Voice of Freedom. Its goal was not just to counter Japanese propaganda but also, as one of MacArthur's top aides put it, "to erase the unfortunate effect of the Europe-centered voices that came drifting through the air from America." Help was coming, Romulo promised. Whatever it sounded like, help was coming.

But Quezon didn't believe that, and as he stewed, he came to appreciate the logic of Aguinaldo's position. "This war is not of our making," he pointed out in a cable to Washington. What right did the United States have to drag the Philippines into a war and then abandon it? Why was Washington defending an imperialist power, Britain, while letting its own people perish? "While enjoying security itself," Quezon told Roosevelt, "the United States has in effect condemned the sixteen millions of Filipinos to practical destruction."

Quezon demanded immediate independence. That way, he reasoned, he could declare neutrality and negotiate to have both Japan and the United States withdraw their forces. MacArthur endorsed the plan, warning Roosevelt that "the temper of the Filipinos is one of almost violent resentment against the United States."

Now it was Roosevelt's turn to be irate. "You have no authority to communicate with the Japanese government," he scolded Quezon. "So long as the flag of the United States flies on Filipino soil," he promised, "it will be defended by our own men to the death."

"To the death" was not just stirring rhetoric; it was the likely outcome. The Roosevelt administration had already agreed with Britain on a "Germany first" strategy for the war, which meant prioritizing Europe. The acknowledged price of that strategy was letting Japan take the Philippines. Was the United States truly willing to see that happen? Churchill asked.

The secretary of war, a former governor-general of the Philippines, re-assured him: "There are times when men have to die."

In March, Roosevelt ordered MacArthur, Quezon, and other top-ranking officials out of the Philippines. The colony was being abandoned.

First, though, the Corregidor headquarters would have to be scut-tled. The gold was sneaked out, at night, to a waiting submarine, which took it to San Francisco. The paper currency was incinerated to keep it out of Japanese hands. ("Guess what I learned after burning ten million dollars?" one officer said. "That Jackson twenties burn faster than Lincoln fives.") The 150 tons of silver pesos, too bulky to move, were dumped into a secret spot in Manila Bay—a tantalizing challenge for future trea-sure hunters.

Quezon gave Douglas MacArthur half a million dollars from the Phil-ippine treasury—a reward for services rendered. MacArthur, as an officer in the U.S. military, was forbidden to accept it, but he did anyway. Que-zon and MacArthur set off for Australia, with Romulo trailing after them.

"I shall return," MacArthur promised.

The troops on Bataan, though, went nowhere. The song they sang cap-tured their plight vividly:

We're the battling bastards of Bataan:
No mama, no papa, no Uncle Sam,
No aunts, no uncles, no nephews, no nieces,
No rifles, no guns or artillery pieces,
And nobody gives a damn.

★

Inevitably, the Bataan defenses collapsed, though more from starvation than from combat. The Japanese marched the captured troops, Filipino and mainlander alike, great distances to internment camps—the infamous Bataan Death March. Thousands of Filipinos and hundreds of mainland-ers died en route, some executed by the Japanese, others simply keeling over.

It was as if the "world was standing on its head," wrote a Filipina who watched this. "The Americans, rulers and idols for as long as we could re-member, were turned overnight into unshaven, shambling wretches."

Yet in mainlanders' eyes, the whites who had faced Japan were heroes,

MacArthur most of all. While the generals in charge of Hawai'i on December 7 were relieved of their commands and subjected to repeated investigations, MacArthur got a Medal of Honor for his "gallantry and intrepidity." Congress declared June 13, 1942, to be Douglas MacArthur Day, and button makers sold MACARTHUR FOR PRESIDENT pins.

"All the people I know think God comes first and then MacArthur," a shop owner in San Antonio told a reporter. A housewife in Hollywood felt the same: "I've never wanted to sin in my life, but I would with that man."

A book about MacArthur's defeat, W. L. White's *They Were Expendable* (1942), became a hit—the first time a book about the Philippines had ever landed on the bestseller list. The director John Ford, for what was then the highest directorial salary in Hollywood history, made it into a movie starring John Wayne and Robert Montgomery.

It wasn't the only movie. The "Bataan film" became its own genre. There was *Bataan, Texas to Bataan, Corregidor, Manila Calling, So Proudly We Hail, Salute to the Marines, Cry "Havoc," Air Force,* and *Somewhere I'll Find You.* Finally, after years of ignoring the Philippines, mainlanders were paying attention.

Carlos Romulo saw an opportunity not to be missed. He frantically toured the mainland, speaking in an astonishing 466 towns and cities in two and a half years. Everywhere his message was the same: Filipinos weren't foreigners, they were family—and they needed help. The titles of two books he published during the war highlighted that kinship: *Mother America* and *My Brother Americans.*

Romulo's favorite topic was Bataan. He noted that the soldiers there referred to themselves not as Americans or Filipinos, but as "Filamericans." This put him in mind of Rudyard Kipling and of Kipling's famous verse "East is East, and West is West, and never the twain shall meet."

"How I wished he had been with us on Bataan!" Romulo mused. "I should have liked showing him miles of fox holes piled with American and Filipino bodies and asked him to repeat over that mingled flesh 'never the twain shall meet.'"

For Romulo, Bataan was the story of Filipinos sacrificing themselves for the United States. Yet that's not how Hollywood saw it. Although the title of the film *They Were Expendable* accurately captured the Filipinos' plight, the titular "they" referred to the whites in the Philippines—the John Wayne and Robert Montgomery types. In his soliloquy, Wayne's character mourns Bataan and the "thirty-six thousand United States soldiers" stranded there, "trapped like rats but dying like men." Actually, there were easily more than twice that many U.S. soldiers trapped on Bataan. It's just that the other ones were Filipinos.

The films were incorrigible on this score. The stars were white, the writers were white, and the tragedies they acted out befell white people: soldiers, sailors, doctors, and nurses. Even the stereotype-shattering *Bataan*, a heroic tale of a racially mixed patrol (a young Desi Arnaz played a Mexican American), had only one speaking Filipino character, a Moro who used broken English and walked around shirtless. In other films, Filipinos served largely as scenery.

Romulo, seeing this, tried to get cast in a Bataan movie. His idea was to play not some half-mute native helpmeet, but himself: an English-speaking, Ivy League–educated, decorated colonel in the U.S. Army. He didn't get the part, though. There *was* no such part.

In a despondent moment, Romulo confessed to being "shocked and horrified" by mainland indifference to the Philippines. Washington seemed to him to be "crowded with little Neros, each fiddling away blithely" while the empire burned.

★

While Carlos Romulo implored mainlanders to remember that Filipinos were "Americans," too, the Philippines was turning into a different kind of place. The all-white clubs now catered to Asians. The bartender at the Baguio Country Club stopped making mint juleps and started pouring sake—it was a Japanese officers' club. MacArthur's penthouse in the Parsons-built Manila Hotel was preserved as a tourist attraction. The Leonard Wood Hotel, though, became a brothel.

Taft Avenue, Dewey Boulevard, Fort McKinley, and Burnham Green all got Japanese names. This happened throughout the empire, as Western names were replaced. Batavia became Jakarta, Singapore became Syonan, Manchuria became Manchukuo, Guam became Omiya Jima, and Wake became Odori. There was talk of renaming the Philippines, too. One idea was to name it after the nineteenth-century nationalist Jose Rizal, though nothing came of that.

In short, U.S. empire was being uprooted and Japanese empire laid down in its place. Filipinos no longer celebrated the Fourth of July or

Occupation Day; they now observed the Emperor's Birthday and December 8 (National Heroes Day). Rizal's birthday, which Manuel Quezon had celebrated as Loyalty Day to the United States, now commemorated the expulsion of "Western imperialism" from Asia.

Filipinos like Aguinaldo were pleased to see the United States finally ousted, and it wasn't hard to understand why. Even those on the U.S. stronghold of Corregidor had ample cause for resentment. As a young man, Manuel Quezon had languished for four months in a U.S. prison without ever facing charges. Carlos Romulo remembered how U.S. soldiers had sought to kill his father, how they had tortured his grandfather with the "water cure," and how they had hanged his neighbor from a tree, Southern style. "I made up my mind to hate them as long as I lived," a young Romulo had concluded.

Quezon and Romulo eventually made peace with Western empire, but did others? In the late 1930s Romulo had toured Asia. Everywhere he went, he found "a sense of betrayal at white hands." In British-owned Burma, the people he met seemed positively eager for a Japanese invasion. Weren't they worried about how the Japanese would treat them? Romulo asked. "No change could be for the worse," they replied.

Japan latched on to the bitterness of the colonized. Japanese propagandists reminded Filipinos of the United States' long history of empire, starting with the dispossession of North American Indians and moving through the Mexican War, the annexation of Spain's colonies, and the Philippine War, right up to the scorched-earth policy adopted in the face of the Japanese invasion. "America has wasted your funds in the creation of grand boulevards and exclusive mountain resorts," one Japanese writer added, gleefully rubbing salt into the wounds inflicted in the era of Daniel Burnham.

Japan had something different to offer: "Asia for the Asiatics." That slogan may sound banal today, but for a region long colonized, it was a powerful, revolutionary idea. Even Romulo conceded that it was "morally unassailable."

Yet white powers would never allow Asian independence, the Japanese insisted. It had to be seized. Emperor Hirohito claimed that the war's origins lay "in the past, in the peace treaty after World War I," when Woodrow Wilson had blocked Japan's attempt to introduce racial equality into the League of Nations covenant. With the most idealistic of the Allies unwilling to concede even the *principle* that all races deserved the same consideration, what were the chances that Asians would ever be accepted as equals?

★

A more pressing question was whether the Japanese could accept Filipinos as equals. The onset of Japanese rule did not bode well on that score. Japan's first official proclamation after taking Manila was a threat: any hostility or resistance from Filipinos and their "whole native land" would be turned to "ashes."

In the second week, the military government specified seventeen acts punishable by death. They included rebelling, giving false information, damaging anything of military value (including clothing), concealing food, speaking ill of Japanese currency, disobeying orders, obstructing traffic, or acting in any way "against the interests" of the military. Even suggesting these acts was grounds for execution.

"It was as if the Philippines had become one vast military prison," one writer remembered. A diarist described Manila in the second month of Japanese rule: "Every day on my way to the office, I run across dozens of Filipinos who have been tied to posts as punishment for some trivial offense which they have committed. Usually the victims are black and blue or bleeding from the terrific lashings they have received." Public beheadings, carried out on the spot and without a trial, were not uncommon.

Filipinos quickly saw that Japan had come not to liberate the Philippines, but to ransack it. Just as Germany was caged in by neighboring countries, Japan was hemmed in by empires: the British Empire (Malaya, Burma, Singapore, Hong Kong), the Dutch Empire (the Dutch East Indies, now known as Indonesia), the U.S. Empire (the Philippines, Alaska, Hawai'i, Guam), and China, in which every imperialist had a hand. The Japanese called this "ABCD encirclement" (American-British-Chinese-Dutch), and it meant that Japan's access to oil, rubber, tin, and even food depended on foreign markets. The turbulent 1930s, which had shut down international trade, illustrated the danger in this. If Japan wanted its industrial economy to keep growing, it would need to take those colonies itself.

The Philippines was a particularly plump target in this Japanese quest for *Lebensraum.* It stood right between Japan and the resource-rich colonies of Malaya and the Dutch East Indies. Moreover, its own large economy could be fed into the Japanese war machine.

And it was. "The Japanese swarmed all over the Philippines like clouds of termites," a Manila journalist recorded. Purchasing agents scoured the city for war matériel: iron, steel, copper, canvas, corrugated sheets, and machinery. Some factories were placed in Japanese hands; others were strip-mined, with their machines carted away—sometimes the entire factories were removed. Cars were confiscated in the cities, tractors in the country. By 1944, the Japanese were tearing down empty gas stations—the fuel had long since run dry—to get the iron rods embedded in their concrete walls.

The food was the most worrisome thing, though. Japan instituted a command economy, forcing farmers to sell their produce to the government, which would distribute it as rations. But the Japanese ate first, leaving little for Filipinos. And because the government paid farmers in near-worthless occupation currency, many simply abandoned their fields and fled to the cities. Others hid their crops from the government and sold to the black market. Either way, the consequence was hunger.

To those with long memories, it must have felt a lot like 1899. Once again, an imperial power was interfering with the colony's food supply. Once again, cholera struck Manila—a result of the social breakdown and the movement of people. And, once again, Filipinos fought back. Remnants of MacArthur's surrendered forces and newly formed guerrilla armies harried the Japanese.

As in 1899, guerrillas gathered in the places where governmental control was weakest. This meant the mountains and the island of Negros, where rebels established their own shadow government. They transferred Silliman University to the hills and ran it as a "jungle university" (after the war, Philippine universities accepted transfer credits from Jungle University). They established a currency board and printed their own money.

The Japanese military, for its part, fell back on a painfully familiar set of repressive techniques. It blocked movement in and out of towns. It tortured suspects, using among its techniques the infamous "water cure." And it established reconcentration zones.

Yet there was one trick Japan tried that the United States hadn't. It decided to grant the Philippines independence. Not to *promise* independence—the United States had done that, eventually—but to actually grant it.

On October 14, 1943, that's what Japan did.

About half a million people attended the celebration that day on the Luneta. Emilio Aguinaldo was there, carrying the tattered flag that he had once flown against the Spanish in 1898. So was his old comrade Artemio Ricarte, the Father of the Philippine Army, famous for having chosen exile over surrender. Together they raised a new flag, modeled on Aguinaldo's original, in front of Juan Arellano's Legislative Building. It was the first time the Philippine flag had been permitted to fly on its own.

"The applause was deafening," wrote Antonio Molina, who was in the crowd. Molina doubted that much would change. The Japanese army was staying on in the Philippines, though now technically as an "ally." Everybody knew that the new government would follow Tokyo's orders. Still, Molina could not deny an "irrepressible satisfaction upon seeing our national flag flutter alone, at long last." As it climbed the pole, he wept.

A new president was sworn in: Jose Laurel, a Yale-educated justice of the Philippine Supreme Court. His father had died in a U.S. reconcentration camp. Laurel received a twenty-one-gun salute.

★

Douglas MacArthur watched this unfold with grave concern. Japan's military economy was nothing compared with that of the United States. In 1941, a year when the United States was at *peace*, it had produced more than five times as many aircraft and ten times as many ships as Japan had. But those aircraft and ships were mainly going to Europe.

The reason was partly priority—the Roosevelt administration held fast to its "Germany first" strategy. But it was also geography. The distance from San Francisco to MacArthur's headquarters in Australia was more than twice as far as from New York to England. And, whereas the Atlantic supply lines connected large, long-established ports such as New York and Liverpool, the Pacific lines had to rely on hastily developed ports, some built from scratch, including on far-flung Pacific locales such as Guadalcanal, Tutuila, Kwajalein, and Manus.

Until all that was built, MacArthur had to make do with what he called "shoestring equipment." He bellowed at Washington for its stinginess, to little effect. His air commander, who arrived in mid-1942, was shocked to discover a "pitifully small" air force awaiting him, with only six B-17s in operation.

Allied plans called for a limited offensive against Japan, chipping away at it until Germany had been defeated. Even this was a daunting prospect at first. Japanese forces had not only taken the Philippines, they were expanding southward over the Dutch East Indies, New Guinea, and the Solomon Islands. Australia's military planners, expecting invasion, prepared to sacrifice the north of the continent. MacArthur lacked the resources to roll back the Japanese and retake all the territory the Allies had lost.

Instead, he became a genius of economy. He stopped playing Risk and started playing Go, leaping his units over Japanese positions. What MacArthur (along with Admiral Chester Nimitz in the Central Pacific) had grasped was that, in an age of aviation and on a battlefield of islands, you didn't have to maintain a continuous, football-scrimmage front. MacArthur could bypass Japanese strongholds, snip their supply lines, and leave them "pocketed and cut off from outside aid."

He called it his "hit 'em where they ain't—let 'em die on the vine" philosophy.

It worked. MacArthur grumbled that it would work a hell of a lot better if Washington would give him a battleship, but his progress on the map was nevertheless steady—Guadalcanal (August 1942), Buna (November 1942), Cape Gloucester (December 1943), Los Negros and Manus (February 1944), Hollandia (April 1944)—as he bounded from victory to victory up New Guinea and the islands of the South Pacific. Nimitz, driving across the Pacific from Hawai'i, did the same.

The twin Pacific campaigns were long and brutal, and it's telling that many veterans of the war who went on to political greatness earned their spurs in them. John F. Kennedy got shipwrecked in the Solomons (an island there is named after him). Lyndon Baines Johnson won a Silver Star, personally given by MacArthur, for "gallantry" as an observer in New Guinea. Richard Nixon served in air logistics in MacArthur's theater. Gerald Ford gamely puttered around nearly every island group in the ocean on a light aircraft carrier. The twenty-year-old Lieutenant George H. W. Bush was shot down over Chichi Jima in the Bonins. Bush—the plane's sole survivor—got rescued by a submarine. He was extremely lucky. Four other airmen shot down later in the same area were captured and became the unfortunate victims in the highest-profile documented instance of Japanese wartime cannibalism.

The point of this two-pronged offensive, however, was not to build presidential résumés. The point was to end the Pacific War by attacking Japan. Yet the island-hopping strategy had raised a vital question. The Allies could reach Japan without conquering every piece of land en route. So, which islands should they take and which should they leap over?

More important, did they need to bother with the Philippines, where the Japanese had dug in? Why not take the southern Philippines and leave Luzon to the Japanese? Or skip the entire archipelago and take Taiwan, which was, after all, closer to Japan? By mid-1944, the highest-ranking men in the military inclined toward the Taiwan plan: Ernest King, chief of naval operations; Hap Arnold, chief of the Army Air Forces; and, with some vacillation, George Marshall, chief of staff of the army.

To say that MacArthur disagreed would be putting it lightly. He was outraged. For him, the decision about which route to take was not merely military; it was moral. The Philippines was "American territory," he fumed, where seventeen million people were "undergoing the greatest privations and sufferings because we have not been able to support or succor them." So impassioned was MacArthur on this subject that Marshall felt compelled to warn him against allowing "personal feelings" to interfere with strategic decisions.

The issue got thrashed out at a conference with Roosevelt in Honolulu in July 1944. MacArthur gave his all. Bypassing the Philippines, he insisted at great length, would be militarily wrong, psychologically wrong, politically wrong, and ethically wrong. He reminded Roosevelt of the Bataan soldiers languishing in enemy camps. He reminded him that Asians were watching how the United States treated its largest colony. And he reminded him of his pledge to pour the "entire resources" of the United States into rescuing the Philippines. "Promises must be kept," he told the president.

"Douglas, you win," Roosevelt said. The question was not entirely put to rest at Honolulu—war planners would argue Taiwan versus the Philippines for another two months—but MacArthur had gotten through. He would, as promised, return to the Philippines.

★

What might that return look like? When Japan invaded the U.S. Pacific empire in 1941–42, the surrenders had come quickly—Guam gave up within hours, the westernmost Aleutians were taken without a fight. But there were two reasons to think that things might not be so easy going the other direction. First, Japan, unlike the United States, had fortified its front-line colonies. Second, Japanese military culture did not exactly encourage surrendering in the face of superior force.

A hint of what awaited MacArthur could be had in the smaller Pacific territories the United States reconquered before reaching the Philippines. Under U.S. rule, Attu and Kiska in the Aleutians had been barely populated, treeless outposts, far from war planners' machinations. Japan, by contrast, had turned them into battle stations. Hundreds of buildings—bases, workshops, bunkhouses, factories, a hospital, a bakery—supported thousands of troops. They were dug in and ready to fight.

On Attu they did. When Allied forces moved to reclaim the island in 1943, the ensuing battle killed hundreds of U.S. soldiers and wiped out nearly the whole Attu garrison of more than two thousand Japanese soldiers, who fought to the death. It was a high price to pay, on both sides, for an island whose prewar population had been less than fifty.

U.S. commanders expected Kiska, which housed thousands of Japanese troops in its elaborate tunnel system, to be even worse. It turned out not to be. The night before the invasion, Japan's forces had quietly abandoned the island and escaped. The only casualties were Allied soldiers who tripped mines or accidentally shot one another in the fog.

No such escape was feasible from Guam, which the U.S. Marines attacked in the summer of 1944. The invasion was prefaced by thirteen days of aerial and naval attacks, a bombardment that reached "a scale and length of time never before seen in World War II," as the Marine Corps' official history put it. The alternating naval assaults and air raids struck Guamanians and Japanese alike.

Fearing imminent death and worried that Guamanians might aid the enemy, the Japanese troops turned on the populace. Beheadings, rapes, and indiscriminate shooting were common. Japan's soldiers marched the whole local population of some eighteen thousand to the south of the island, massacring many there. In the aftermath, a marine recalled encountering a pile of decapitated corpses: "The heads lay like bowling balls all over the place."

Some fifteen thousand Japanese soldiers and hundreds of Guamanians died. In retaking Guam, the U.S. military laid waste to Guam's capital, bombing and shelling every major structure in the town: the museum, the hospital, the governor's residence, the courthouse. The war destroyed some four-fifths of the island's homes.

The United States then interned thousands of "liberated" Guamanians, over their objections, in camps while the navy tore down what remained of the capital to build a military base. It was yet another occasion when the United States interned its own people during the war.

★

The bloody fighting on Attu and Guam offered a worrying foretaste of what MacArthur might expect in the Philippines, the United States' great abandoned colony. Things there were already rapidly falling apart. Nineteen forty-four was the year when the Japanese army stopped paying for food with its depreciated scrip and started seizing it outright. President Laurel declared a food crisis and ordered every adult under sixty to work eight hours a week increasing food production. By September, a diarist recorded "a noticeable decrease in the cat population" of Manila. By December, starved city dwellers were dropping dead in the streets.

As Japan's imperial forces scraped the bottom of the barrel, the violence worsened. Claro Recto, the Philippines' minister of culture, wrote a daringly frank letter to a Japanese general about it. He noted the routine military practices of "slapping Filipinos in the face, of tying them to posts or making them kneel in public, at times in the heat of the sun, or beating them—this upon the slightest fault, mistake or provocation." Beyond these daily torments, there were "thousands of cases" of people "being either burned alive, killed at the point of bayonet, beheaded, beaten without mercy, or otherwise subjected to various methods of physical torture, without distinction as to age or sex." Recto mentioned a massacre of one hundred in his hometown—part of Japan's ongoing quest to extirpate guerrillas. But there were many other such events he could have mentioned, including a punitive expedition in the Sara district on Panay that killed twenty times that number.

That was the Philippines at peace. In October 1944 more than two hundred thousand of MacArthur's troops began their assault on the Philippines, shutting down sea-lanes and storming the beaches. MacArthur himself waded ashore on the island of Leyte, south of Luzon, on October 20, 1944.

"I have returned," he announced to the Filipino people by radio. "Rally to me."

"I have returned": Douglas MacArthur, in front, stepping back on Philippine soil. Carlos Romulo, wearing a helmet, is behind him.

MacArthur's goal was Manila. And, finally, he had the planes to take it. One Manilan remembered them screaming through the city like the flying monkeys in *The Wizard of Oz*, "winging very low but fast, skimming the top of buildings." They aimed for anything of military value: highways, railroad tracks, trucks, and (yet again) bridges.

Japanese commanders faced a momentous decision. Should they abandon the city, as on Kiska? Or stay and fight, as on Attu? General Yamashita Tomoyuki, commander of Japan's 14th Area Army, saw the writing on the wall. Supplies of all sorts were running low, and with sea and land approaches to Manila cut off, it was hard to see how they could be replenished. Yamashita's army had already reduced its food rations from three pounds a day to nine-tenths of a pound. What is more, Manila was impossible to hold. A large city, inhabited by more than a million hostile civilians, full of flammable buildings, on flat ground—to defend it would be suicide. Just as MacArthur had done in 1941, Yamashita ordered the army out.

But the army was not the only Japanese force in the area. As Yamashita moved his troops out, Rear Admiral Iwabuchi Sanji, commander of the

Manila Naval Defense Force, moved sixteen thousand men *into* the city. He regarded himself duty-bound to protect Manila's military installations.

Iwabuchi must have known that, in the end, MacArthur's forces were going to take Manila. But he could force them to do it the hard way. His men set explosive mines throughout the city. They erected pillboxes at critical intersections and made fortresses of the larger concrete structures in the city. They stockpiled their ammunition.

Yamashita, once he realized what had happened, angrily ordered Iwabuchi to leave Manila. Iwabuchi replied, accurately, that he couldn't. By then, MacArthur's forces had the city surrounded.

"We slammed the back door shut before we began to fight" is how the official history of MacArthur's leading division put it. A group of military historians judged this enclosure of the city to be "*the* strategic blunder of the Philippine campaign." Having cut off Iwabuchi's escape route, MacArthur practically guaranteed that the admiral would make his final stand in a densely populated city.

The battle for Manila would be a fight to the death.

★

When Allied troops arrived in Manila, whatever tenuous truce existed between the Japanese forces and the city's inhabitants broke down entirely. Iwabuchi's command ordered that all non-Japanese on the battlefield be killed. Japanese troops set about destroying the city. They took out the power and water systems. They dynamited factories and warehouses, and the flames predictably spread toward residential areas. As Filipinos fled into the streets (or, as the soldiers no doubt thought of it, the "battlefield"), they were shot down.

Technically, Iwabuchi's men were fighting only "guerrillas." But in the hungry, vengeful, and chaotic days of the U.S. invasion, the line between guerrilla and civilian blurred badly. Excerpts from a captured diary of a Japanese soldier in Manila give a sense of the scale of violence:

> Feb. 7: 150 guerrillas were disposed of tonight. I personally stabbed and killed 10.
> Feb. 10: Guarded approximately 1,000 guerrillas.
> Feb. 13: I am now on guard duty at Guerrilla Internment Camp.
> When I was on duty, approximately 10 guerrillas tried to escape.

They were stabbed to death. At 1600, all guerrillas were burned to death.

The pretense that all victims of the Japanese were guerrillas was easily dispensed with, as when troops rounded up hundreds of young women for sexual predation. Large hotels, including MacArthur's Manila Hotel, became the site of organized mass rapes. Diaries kept during the Battle of Manila are replete with other stomach-churning atrocities: pregnant women disemboweled, babies bayoneted, whole families slaughtered. Prepared to die, Iwabuchi's men felt few moral restraints.

This was the first and, as it happened, the only time that U.S. and Japanese forces would fight in a major city. MacArthur's men entered the bloodbath with caution. Dislodging Iwabuchi's forces while protecting Filipino lives was a delicate operation. When assessing the area of Intramuros, where the Japanese were particularly well entrenched, MacArthur's air commander suggested using napalm to "bomb the place until it was completely destroyed." But MacArthur refused. Intramuros was inhabited by a "friendly" population, he reminded the commander. Aerial bombing was "unthinkable."

Maybe to MacArthur. But within the first days of the battle it grew more thinkable to those under him. The Japanese were holed up in buildings throughout the city. Storming those emplacements one by one using small arms was treacherous. It would be easier to simply bomb or shell entire buildings.

In the approach to the Philippines, when MacArthur's men were fighting the Japanese on isolated islands or in jungle clearings, bombs and artillery fire had worked wonders. They had minimized U.S. casualties and let the United States put its overwhelming industrial capability to use. And it finally *had* that capability. If, in 1941, MacArthur's forces had been poorly equipped, by 1945—with the European war winding down and the U.S. economy in overdrive—they had all they needed. There were lots of explosives on hand.

The 37th Infantry Division, in particular, believed in the "use of heavy firepower to the maximum," as its commander, General Robert S. Beightler, put it. The 37th was known as the most wasteful division in the theater for its use of artillery ammunition. "This reputation has certainly never bothered us," Beightler explained, "for we only point to the fact that

Manila, 1945

we fought for more than two years and lost fewer men than other divisions with comparable fighting."

The 37th handled most of the combat in Manila. On February 9, six days into the battle, it saw nineteen of its men killed and more than two hundred wounded. That was nothing compared with the thousands of Filipinos who were being daily slaughtered, but to Beightler it was "alarming." The division reverted to its tried-and-true tactic. Rather than engage Iwabuchi's men in direct combat, it would simply destroy any buildings in which they might be hiding. "Putting it crudely, we really went to town," Beightler reported. "To me, the loss of a single American life to save a building was unthinkable."

That's a sentence worth reading twice. In Beightler's mind, he was facing a trade-off—and not a particularly difficult one—between lives and architecture. But, as he well knew, those buildings were inhabited. Some by enemy soldiers, of course, but many by civilians. Those civilians were "Americans," too, even if no one treated them that way.

The other divisions attacking Manila also turned up the heat. Though Intramuros was spared aerial napalming, it was nevertheless, with

MacArthur's approval, comprehensively destroyed. During one manic hour on February 23, the closely packed (and still inhabited) section of the city had three tons of explosives hurled at it *per minute*. Shells struck, more than one per second, "hurtling like lightning bolts from the hands of an angry god," as one observer wrote.

"We made a churned-up pile of dust and scrap out of the imposing, classic government buildings," Beightler boasted.

Within a week of fighting, U.S. shelling of the whole area in front of advancing troops became, as one report put it, "the rule rather than the exception." Any structure suspected of containing Japanese troops was a target. "Block after bloody block was slowly mashed into an unrecognizable pulp," recorded the 37th's official history.

That included refugee centers, such as the Philippine General Hospital (a Parsons-built landmark), where a few Japanese soldiers were holed up—and more than seven thousand civilians. The 37th fired at the hospital for two days and nights. These were "days of terror," remembered a Filipino trapped inside. "I can still hear the screams of the wounded clearly to this day." Other refugee shelters—the Remedios Hospital, the Concordia Convent—met similar fates.

★

U.S. shelling and Japanese slaughter combined in a concoction of ghastly lethality. The politician Elpidio Quirino got his own taste of it. Quirino had been one of the delegates who wrote the commonwealth constitution. He'd been a member of Manuel Quezon's cabinet, and later, after the war, he would become president of the country. He lived in the affluent enclave of Ermita (506 Colorado Street) with his wife, Alicia, his sons Tommy and Dody, and his daughters Norma, Vicky, and Fe Angela (who was two).

Quirino's "darkest hour" began with the fires Japan had set. Ermita was particularly in peril, all the more so because the Japanese had taken up fortified positions at the main intersections and were shooting anyone who walked into the street. On the morning of February 9, a U.S. shell crashed into the Quirino home. The family decided to brave Japanese bullets and flee to the home of Alicia's mother, Doña Concepcion Jimenez de Syquia, who lived down the street. Alicia led four of her children out, while Elpidio and Dody stayed behind to gather food. But when Alicia reached the corner where her mother's house stood, a Japanese machine-gun nest opened fire, killing Alicia and Norma. A Japanese marine hurled the infant Fe Angela into the air and impaled her on his bayonet. Only Tommy and Vicky made it to their grandmother's house.

Elpidio left Dody at home and tried to carry food to Doña Concepcion's house. But he was held down by Japanese fire and U.S. shelling and didn't make it until the next day. When he arrived, he discovered that his wife and two daughters were dead. Dody, who had sought to retrieve the bodies of his mother and sisters, was also killed—a shrapnel wound to the temple.

The shelling continued. The Quirinos and the Syquias, fourteen in all, ran back out into the street, darting amid the shells and gunfire from one insecure shelter to another. At night, a U.S. shell struck the house where they had taken refuge, cutting the body of Elpidio's sister-in-law nearly in two. Doña Concepcion had a fatal heart attack during the barrage.

The family fled again. It had to. The house was on fire.

Sanctuary was hard to find. "If you escaped the shells of the Americans, you could not escape the machine guns or bayonets of the Japanese," Elpidio remembered. After stashing his dwindling family in yet another

The Quirinos' neighbors in South Manila flee to U.S. troops for protection.

temporary shelter, he went out again in search of safer ground. Soon after he stepped out, a U.S. shell hit the building, striking five members of his clan and Doña Concepcion's cook. Three died, and three were injured, including his son Tommy. Once again, the Quirinos fled. This time they reached safety.

In four days, Elpidio Quirino had lost eight members of his family, including his wife, his mother-in-law, and three of his five children. A woman who saw him at the end of this remembered Quirino staggering around Manila in his undershirt, smeared with mud, a vacant stare in his eyes—a latter-day Lear.

★

Admiral Iwabuchi took his stand on the Luneta, in the cluster of governmental buildings Daniel Burnham had planned. The very architectural qualities Burnham prized—large, solid concrete structures, commanding views of the city—made them ideal fortresses.

Juan Arellano's Legislative Building served as the headquarters of Iwabuchi's Central Force. Some 250 Japanese troops waited inside. With all approaches to the building on open ground, dislodging them would be difficult. A U.S. battalion tried but was driven back. An attempt to smoke the Japanese out failed, too. So the 37th Infantry Division did what it did best: fired its howitzers and tank guns point-blank into the building for two unrelenting hours, bringing the massive edifice crashing to the ground.

The pride of the colonial state, built by a Filipino to a mainlander's plan, lay in ruins. The symbolism was hard to miss.

Manila wasn't short on symbols. The sixth-largest city in the United States—substantially larger than Boston or Washington, D.C.—had for a month of fighting been converted into an abattoir. South Manila, where Quirino lived, had been leveled. Bodies decomposed everywhere, many bearing the marks of torture or execution. The stench was unbearable.

"The largest buildings had been transformed into mere piles of rubble and debris. Over areas, miles square, hardly one stone was left on top of another. It was as if all the forces of destruction had operated together, and that even this had been exceeded," wrote a local journalist. "This seemed demonic work."

Demonic, maybe, but not indiscriminate. The "better to lose a building than an American life" logic succeeded in protecting mainland sol-

Juan Arellano's Legislative Building after two hours of point-blank shelling by the 37th Infantry Division

diers. In the month of fighting, 1,010 of them died. Compare that with the 16,665 Japanese troops who perished. And compare *that* with the 100,000 Manilans killed. For every "American life" lost, 100 Manilans died.

Or so we think. As usual, mainland lives lost were counted with to-the-last-digit precision, while Filipino fatality numbers were at best informed guesses. The 100,000 estimate, accepted by the U.S. Army, was extrapolated from figures submitted by undertakers after the war.

At any rate, Manila wasn't the only place hit. Smaller towns and cities were bombarded as well. "The whole city of Baguio was razed to the ground," lamented Jose Laurel, the Philippine president. Laurel himself had barely survived the attack there. U.S. planes repeatedly bombed his residence, destroying it entirely. Those planes dropped 466 tons of bombs and nearly five thousand gallons of napalm during the Baguio campaign.

"We levelled entire cities with our bombs and shell fire," admitted the high commissioner. "We destroyed roads, public buildings, and bridges. We razed sugar mills and factories." In the end, he concluded, "there was nothing left."

Senator Millard Tydings surveyed the colony after the war. He estimated that 10 to 15 percent of its buildings had been destroyed, and another 10 percent damaged. After the war, Filipinos submitted claims to the government on behalf of 1,111,938 war deaths. Add Japanese (518,000) and mainlander fatalities (the army counted slightly more than 10,000) and the total climbs to more than 1.6 million.

The Second World War in the Philippines rarely appears in history textbooks. But it should. It was by far the most destructive event ever to take place on U.S. soil.

★

Oscar Villadolid, a boy at the time, remembers a familiar scene from the aftermath of Manila's "liberation." A GI came down his street handing out cigarettes and Hershey bars. Speaking slowly, he asked Villadolid's name. When Villadolid replied easily in English, the soldier was startled. "How'd ya learn American?" he asked.

Villadolid explained that when the United States colonized the Philippines, it had instituted English in the schools. This only compounded the GI's confusion. "He did not even know that America had a colony here in the Philippines!" Villadolid marveled.

Take a moment to let that sink in. This was a soldier who had taken a long journey across the Pacific. He'd been briefed on his mission, shown maps, told where to go and whom to shoot. Yet at no point had it dawned on him that he was preparing to save a U.S. colony and that the people he would encounter there were, just like him, U.S. nationals.

He thought he was invading a foreign country.

PART II

THE POINTILLIST EMPIRE

13

KILROY WAS HERE

"War is hell," the saying goes. The more scientifically inclined might put it differently: War is entropy. Atoms split, buildings tumble, people die, and things fall apart. As wars go, the Second World War was the big one—a giant, planetwide entropic pulse that converted whole cities to rubble and some fifty-five million living humans into corpses. No war has ever killed more or even come close.

From Dresden, Warsaw, Manila, Tokyo, and Hiroshima, that's what the war looked like: a vortex of carnage. Yet, ironically, producing destruction on that scale took a lot of organization. Factories had to work overtime to make trucks, tanks, planes, ships, bombs, uniforms, rations, guns, and spare parts. All that stuff, plus the men to go with it, had to be hauled to distant battlefields. And when the men arrived, they needed bases outfitted with barracks and bakeries, water plants and warehouses, mechanics shops, mess halls, runways, and laundries.

The counter-entropic side of the war was the less glamorous side. Think of a GI, and you're more likely to imagine a soldier on the front lines than a construction worker. But in the case of the United States, the construction worker is the better mental image. During the war, fewer than one in ten U.S. service members ever saw a shot fired in anger. For most who served, the war wasn't about combat. It was about logistics.

The novelist Neal Stephenson got it right when he described the U.S. military in World War II as "first and foremost an unfathomable network of typists and file clerks, secondarily a stupendous mechanism for moving stuff from one part of the world to another, and last and least a fighting organization."

Operating this vast mechanism drew the United States abruptly into world affairs, giving it business in places it had formerly cared little about. Yet it also left the United States less interested in formal empire. Together with innovations in chemistry and industrial engineering, the U.S. mastery of logistics would diminish the value of colonies and inaugurate a new pattern of global power, based less on claiming large swaths of land and more on controlling small points.

★

It made a certain sense that the United States would fight the war by managing the back end of things, for it had the world's largest industrial economy and its factories were far from the fighting. By 1940, nearly every independent nation outside Axis orbits had sought to acquire munitions from the United States.

The Roosevelt administration was only too happy to oblige, via an evolving set of schemes designed to circumvent neutrality laws and conserve the Allies' dwindling dollar reserves. First, there were direct purchases. Then "cash and carry," "destroyers for bases," and finally "lend-lease." Well before the United States declared war, it was sending planes, engines, tanks, and other war goods to the fronts.

That stream of stuff mattered. By early 1941, Britain's Asian empire hung by a thread. Axis forces had largely captured the Mediterranean, and Erwin Rommel's Afrika Korps had knocked the British back on their heels in Egypt. If Britain lost the Middle East, it would lose everything: Iraq's oil fields, stockpiles of war matériel in Egypt, and the Suez Canal, which connected the British Isles to India, Australia, New Zealand, Malaya, Burma, and Singapore. British officials warned Washington of the complete "disintegration of the British commonwealth."

It was easy enough for the United States to supply tanks and planes. The hard part was getting them to the front lines—Detroit to Cairo was a long haul. The tanks could be disassembled and shipped by sea around the southern tip of Africa, but that meant unloading them at Cairo's primitive ports, which had no warehouses, no assembly plants, few railways, light roads, and a dire shortage of mechanics.

"The condition of Egyptian ports" isn't a subject that would have interested many in Washington in 1935. But now it did. The United States launched a massive Middle Eastern infrastructure campaign. Up went new piers with cranes to unload tanks, assembly plants to put them together, railways and hard roads to carry them to the front, and repair shops to keep them running. By June 1942, the depot near Cairo had a large airport, housing for nearly ten thousand men, a thousand-bed hospital, warehouses, and enough spare parts, tools, and skilled mechanics to keep the whole operation functioning.

That's what it took to get tanks to the Middle East. To bring planes and smaller goods, the United States blazed a different trail: an aerial highway of bases dipping down from Miami to Brazil, cutting over to West Africa, and hopping across the Sahara to Cairo. This, too, required serious infrastructural investment. Swamps had to be drained, jungles cleared, rock blasted, and sandstorms fought.

And they were. Buoyed by much-needed U.S. supplies, the British Eighth Army struck back at the Battle of El Alamein in October 1942, pouring fire into Rommel's position. "I have seen many enemy barrages," recorded one terrified driver behind German lines, "but the intensity of this one is beyond our experience." Just as the British pushed Rommel out of Egypt into Tunisia, three mighty fleets collectively containing seven hundred ships landed on African shores with the necessaries to expel the Axis from Africa entirely within six months.

Britain's lifeline to its empire was saved. "It marked in fact the turning of the 'Hinge of Fate,'" Churchill wrote. "It may almost be said, 'Before Alamein we never had a victory. After Alamein, we never had a defeat.'"

The campaign also transformed the Middle East, converting it into what the secretary of state called a "tremendous supply base" for the Allies. Factories in Palestine made batteries, those in Iran made antifreeze, and canning plants in Egypt produced rations for the troops. The northern half of Africa, which had been a virtual terra incognita for the United States, hummed with U.S. bases, ports, assembly plants, barracks, and warehouses.

★

What happened in North Africa and the Middle East happened all over the world. You can think of the U.S. mainland during the Second World

War as a giant heart pumping out rich streams of matériel. Strings of bases functioned as arteries, carrying it to the battlefronts. The bases were where planes landed and ships docked, where spare parts, fuel, and food were stored, where wounded men and damaged things were repaired.

Bases weren't new to U.S. strategy. Captain Mahan, back in the 1890s, had championed acquiring bases so that U.S. ships could venture far into the world. But the basing system Mahan's generation built was modest, limited to a few key points, such as Pearl Harbor and Guantánamo Bay, in the Pacific and the Caribbean.

Now, however, the system grew explosively. This started in 1940, when the Roosevelt administration traded fifty destroyers to Britain for base sites in British territories in the Western Hemisphere—including in Newfoundland, the Bahamas, Bermuda, Jamaica, and Trinidad. The United States didn't own these sites outright; it got them on ninety-nine-year leases. But its jurisdictional powers were startling, "probably more far-reaching than any the British Government has ever given anyone over British territory before," the ambassador to Britain boasted. The United States could raise its flag, confiscate property, and build anything it wanted. Its workers were immune from British taxes and, when they were on base or on duty, from British laws.

In the 1890s Mahan had supposed that bases would lead to colonization. Were the ninety-nine-year base leases a prelude to annexing Britain's colonies in the Western Hemisphere? "Nothing is more certain than they could have become American possessions for the asking," noted a high-ranking U.S. official. Many inhabitants of the British Caribbean—and some pundits in Washington—expected that they'd fall under the U.S. flag soon enough.

The longer the war went on, the more bases the United States took. For some, as in Latin America, it negotiated deals: building roads and extending aid in exchange for leases. Others it claimed from its allies as a matter of wartime exigency. The Soviet Union, alone among the major allies, locked the United States out. Joseph Stalin accepted billions in U.S. aid but refused the entry of U.S. troops. Soviet pilots picked up lend-lease planes in Fairbanks and flew them to the battlefront themselves.

The U.S. basing system girdled the globe with four great highways: northern and southern routes across the Atlantic, and northern and southern routes across the Pacific. The transatlantic routes could make use of existing infrastructure—English roads, African rails, and Latin American

Solomon Islanders unloading crates of beer for U.S. servicemen on Guadalcanal, 1944

ports. Leaping over the enormous Pacific, however, meant landing on small islands. The Seabees (CB: construction battalion) in the navy swelled to nearly two hundred thousand men and built hundreds of Pacific bases, from Aitape to Zamboanga. Construction workers from places like Boston and San Francisco found themselves hauling dirt on Nukufetau, Kwajalein, Sasavele, and Mios Woendi.

In 1919, at the end of the First World War, the chair of the Senate Foreign Relations Committee had doubted that the country's safety hung on "what happens in Africa or in New Guinea and in the Marshall Islands and the Caroline Islands." It's hard to imagine a major politician saying anything like that at the end of the Second World War. By then, U.S. troops were in every one of those places.

During the war, the United States possessed an astonishing thirty thousand installations on two thousand overseas base sites. The men marked their presence with a ubiquitous graffiti tag: a cartoon face peering over a wall, accompanied by the words KILROY WAS HERE.

Kilroy, in fact, was everywhere.

★

It was as if the oceans had been turned into puddles. Men who'd never left their home states zipped busily around the planet, with two thousand "little Americas" rolling out like a red carpet underfoot. "Almost anywhere in the United States you are likely to run into uniformed young men who speak matter-of-factly of Cairo or Chungking or Reykjavik as though any point on the map of the world were just 'up the road a piece,'" one writer noted. "And why not? Yesterday or the day before yesterday they were there."

Presidents, too, began to move as never before. Teddy Roosevelt had been the first sitting president to leave the continental United States—a seventeen-day trip to Panama and Puerto Rico. His successors also journeyed outward while in office but, like him, generally confined themselves to single trips within the Western Hemisphere. William Howard Taft spent a day in Mexico. Warren G. Harding visited Alaska and Vancouver in July 1923, but he became violently ill during the trip and died immediately upon returning. Calvin Coolidge, who succeeded him, went to Cuba for three days, and Herbert Hoover spent three days in Puerto Rico and the U.S. Virgin Islands. Only Woodrow Wilson, who visited Europe twice for the Paris Peace Conference, went abroad more than once or journeyed beyond the Americas.

The stationary presidency ended abruptly with Franklin Delano Roosevelt. As president he left the continental United States twenty-one times, and all but one of those times he journeyed beyond the borders of the Greater United States. He visited Canada, Hawai'i, Puerto Rico, the U.S. Virgin Islands, the Bahamas, Haiti, Colombia, Panama, Trinidad, Brazil, Argentina, Uruguay, Newfoundland, Morocco, Gambia, Liberia, Mexico, Egypt, Algeria, Tunisia, Iran, Malta, Italy, Senegal, and the Soviet Union—some of them multiple times. He was the first president to set foot in South America, Africa, or Asia while in office.

He wasn't the last, though. Every sitting president since has traveled widely. Every one has left the Western Hemisphere.

Simply put, World War II made the United States a planetary presence. State Department officials furiously churned out wartime memos establishing U.S. policy—often for the first time—regarding every nation, colony, region, and sub-duchy on the map. One can almost see the cartoon sweat-bullets popping out from their faces as they wrestled with what position to take vis-à-vis Outer Mongolia, Northern Bukovina, Chinese Turke-

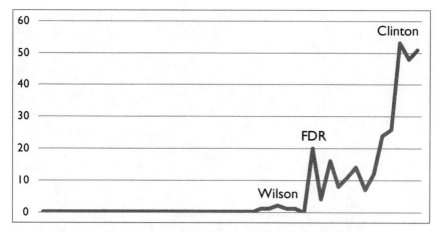

Going global: Number of in-office trips taken abroad, by president, from Washington to Obama

stan, British Borneo, French Somaliland, Jubaland, or Subcarpathian Ruthenia—all places that appeared on their agendas. "Because of the ethnic distribution in Transylvania," they sternly advised, "it would not be possible to fix a boundary that would not give rise to Hungarian or Rumanian irredentism." A lesson well worth heeding.

In 1898 imperial expansion had inspired new maps. The 1940s wartime expansion yielded a similar burst of cartographic innovation. Writers tapped surprisingly deep reservoirs of feeling as they touched on the subject of map projections. The long-familiar Mercator map, which showed North America protected on both sides by enormous oceans, became an object of scorn. It had worked well enough in an age of east-and-west sail, but the editors of *Life* deemed it "a mental hazard" in an age of aviation, when planes could reach Eurasia from North America by flying north over the Arctic Sea.

There were other options, and the public was oddly willing to learn about them. *Life* devoted a fifteen-page spread to the "Dymaxion map" by the inventor Buckminster Fuller: fourteen detachable segments that could be folded into a tetradecahedron or assembled into various flat maps, as the user chose.

More popular was the "polar azimuthal projection" perfected by the dean of wartime cartography, Richard Edes Harrison. It showed the continents huddled around the North Pole, a jarring angle of view that

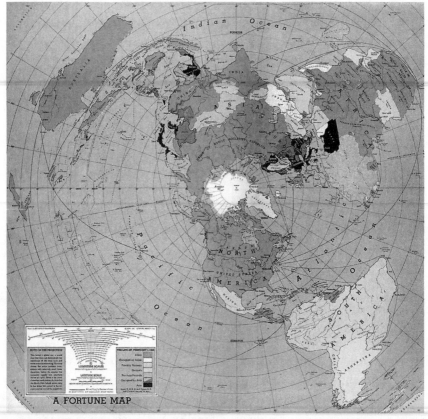

Richard Edes Harrison's polar azimuthal projection, first published by *Fortune* in July 1941 and copied widely thereafter (this is a 1942 version). The original accompanying text explained how "the entire conflict pivots around the U.S." Arrows extending out from New York and San Francisco show the global flow of lend-lease aid.

highlighted aviation routes and showed how dangerously close North America was to Germany's European empire.

The map was an enormous hit, reprinted and copied frequently. Joseph Goebbels waved it in reporters' faces as proof of the United States' world-conquering ambitions. The U.S. Army ordered eighteen thousand copies, and the map became the basis for the United Nations logo, designed in 1945.

"Never before have persons been so interested in the entire world," gushed *Popular Mechanics*. Certainly the technicalities of representing a spherical planet on a map's flat surface had never commanded such fascination. As public consciousness expanded, the details of cartographic pro-

The original UN emblem, designed by Donal McLaughlin, a member of the Office of Strategic Service (the precursor to today's Central Intelligence Agency). McLaughlin modified the emblem a year later, adding the bottom of South America and tilting the map in order to make North America less obviously the center of the world.

jection mattered. The world must be seen anew, the poet Archibald MacLeish wrote, as a "round earth in which all the directions eventually meet." "If we win this war," he continued, "the image of the age which now is opening will be this image of a global earth, a completed sphere."

That word MacLeish chose, *global*, was new. There are scattered instances of its use to refer to the world starting in the nineteenth century, but not many before the 1940s. It took the war to make it popular. With it came entirely new words: *globalist*, *globalism*, and the pejorative *globaloney*, coined by the writer Clare Boothe Luce in reference to the ideas of Vice President Henry Wallace.

If the last war was a world war, this one was, as Franklin Delano Roosevelt put it in September 1942, "a global war." That was the first time a sitting president had publicly uttered the word *global*, though every president since has used it incessantly.

For Christmas that year, George Marshall presented FDR with a five-hundred-pound globe for the Oval Office. Placed next to Roosevelt's desk, it was comically large. It resembled the globe with which Charlie Chaplin had performed an amorous dance two years earlier in *The Great Dictator*, only bigger. Yet photographs show Roosevelt gazing at it with sobriety, curiosity, and respect—a new presence, though not an unwelcome one.

★

In the United States, the war opened horizons. It felt different for other countries. "Just as truly as Europe once invaded us, with wave after wave of immigrants, now we are invading Europe, with wave after wave of sons of immigrants," wrote the journalist John Hersey in 1944. Except it wasn't only Europe. The "invasion" landed in force on every continent save Antarctica.

For the most part, it was friendly. The men arrived in Allied countries not as conquerors, but as builders of the vast logistical network that kept the war running. Still, there were an awful lot of them. "There is not a single square inch of London on which an American is not standing," wrote one U.S. official in 1944.

The 1.65 million U.S. servicemen swarming around Britain, building bases and running jeeps down English country roads, were preparing for the invasion of Normandy of 1944. Yet the British could be forgiven if the sight of so many foreign troops parking their heels on English soil called to mind the Norman invasion of 1066. There were only three things wrong with the GIs, the British quip went. They were "overpaid, over-sexed, and over here."

That was the complaint of an ally. In Axis lands, the U.S. invasion was not metaphorical, but actual. In Europe, U.S. troops briefly occupied parts of Italy and then, at the war's end, gained jurisdiction over sectors of Germany and Austria. The United States also took over the southern half of Korea (the Soviet Union held the northern half).

Most dramatically, the war placed the whole of Japan under occupation. Technically, the occupation was run jointly by the Allies, but in effect it was a U.S. operation (though a contingent of British troops was on hand). Japan was not divided into zones run by different authorities. There was a single supreme commander for the Allied Powers, appointed by President Harry Truman.

Truman picked Douglas MacArthur.

Finally, MacArthur had a task that matched his sense of self. Simultaneously, he led the Japanese occupation, the U.S. military's Far East Command, and the U.S. Army in the Far East. Later, while still holding all those positions, he would also take command of the United Nations forces in the Korean War. Though officially he answered to Washington and to the Allies' Far Eastern Commission, in actuality MacArthur had, as he put it, "absolute control over almost 80-million people."

The U.S. ambassador to Japan gasped. "Never before in the history of the United States had such enormous and absolute power been placed in the hands of a single individual."

MacArthur looked for inspiration to his father's work as governor of the Philippines. Of course Japan wasn't a U.S. territory like the Philippines. But MacArthur nevertheless ran it as if it were. The Japanese flag was prohibited, and the Stars and Stripes rose in its place. Streets and places got new names: Washington Heights, Roosevelt Recreation Area, Doolittle Park (named, awkwardly, after the first man to bomb Tokyo). "Parts of Tokyo look as Oriental as Peoria, Illinois," a journalist observed.

The occupation radically remade Japan, turning it into "the world's greatest laboratory for an experiment in the liberation of people from totalitarian military rule," in MacArthur's telling. The emperor was demoted from an infallible deity to an affable public figure who attended baseball games. A massive land reform campaign dispossessed many absentee landlords. Hundreds of millions of new textbooks were printed to train Japanese students in democratic ways. Public health authorities vaccinated the whole Japanese population—all eighty million—twice for smallpox (the largest vaccination campaign in history to that point) and dusted some fifty million with DDT.

When Japanese politicians failed to write a constitution to MacArthur's satisfaction, he had one drafted, in English, in nine days. "We the Japanese people," it starts, and it goes on to affirm individuals' rights to "life, liberty, and the pursuit of happiness."

But though it borrowed from the U.S. Constitution and Declaration of Independence, the Japanese constitution was far more liberal, the result of a sort of unchecked New Deal that occupation authorities imposed on the country. The new constitution banned war, prohibited racial discrimination, guaranteed academic freedom, forbade torture, and granted all citizens the right to the "minimum standards of wholesome and cultured living."

Somehow, in the anything-goes atmosphere of the occupation, a twenty-two-year-old Jewish woman named Beate Sirota had made it onto the constitutional drafting committee (she had spent part of her childhood in Tokyo and was one of the few whites who spoke Japanese fluently). It was largely owing to her influence that the constitution mandated equal rights within marriage and prohibited sex discrimination—things that the U.S. constitution conspicuously does not do.

That is still Japan's constitution today. In more than sixty years, it hasn't been amended once.

★

The war brought the United States, as Winston Churchill put it, to the "summit of the world." It made more goods, had more oil, held more gold, and possessed more planes than all other countries combined. It was, Truman marveled, "the most powerful nation, perhaps, in all history."

But what is less often appreciated is how much territory the United States had won, too. In 1940 its colonized population had made up about 13 percent of the Greater United States. Now, adding it all up—the colonies and occupations—yielded a much larger total. The overseas area under U.S. jurisdiction contained some 135 million people. That was, remarkably, more than the 132 million who inhabited the mainland.

In other words, if you looked up at the end of 1945 and saw a U.S. flag overhead, odds are that you weren't seeing it because you lived in a state. You were more likely colonized or living in occupied territory. Probably somewhere in the Pacific.

14

DECOLONIZING THE UNITED STATES

World War II ended with the Stars and Stripes flying proudly over thousands of overseas bases and tens of millions of people in colonies and occupied lands. It was the familiar forty-eight-star flag that ran up those countless far-flung poles, with one star for every state.

Yet soon after the war, mainlanders wondered if those forty-eight stars sufficed. The United States is the only country whose flag, by law, must change when the shape of the country does. And so enthusiastic hobbyists bombarded the government with unsolicited proposals for new designs. Forty-nine stars, fifty, fifty-one, more. Some rendered their ideas in crayon or colored pencil. Others went full Betsy Ross and sewed.

There are many ways to arrange stars on a flag, it turns out. The proposals placed them in grids, in circles, and in shapes (an eagle, a larger star, the letters USA). In one, the stars escaped the confines of the blue square and leaped onto the stripes, like inmates on a jailbreak. The schoolchildren of Beaver Creek, Montana, preferred a familiar stars-in-rows configuration but advised clearing room at the bottom for a forty-ninth star, with "plenty of space remaining" should other states be added.

When these amateur vexillologists specified which new states they had in mind, they often pointed to Alaska, Hawai'i, and Puerto Rico. Ernest Gruening and his wife, Dorothy, designed a fifty-star flag, which they flew proudly from the governor's mansion in Anchorage, in support of Alaska and Hawai'i.

Forty-nine-star flag designed
by E. H. Clehouse of Terre
Haute, Indiana

But it's telling that flag designers often left things open. They sensed, correctly, that many futures were possible. There were excited murmurs in Douglas MacArthur's Japan about statehood, and Congress received a petition to make it the forty-ninth state. Mainland papers—including the *Chicago Tribune*, the Washington *Times-Herald*, the New York *Daily News*, *The Atlanta Constitution*, and the influential African American *Amsterdam News*—came out for Philippine statehood, which the chairman of the U.S. House Committee on Military Affairs also supported. ("If the offer is seriously made we are only too willing to consider it," the Philippine delegation to the UN General Assembly replied.) A congressman from California, meanwhile, proposed adding Iceland, then under military control, to the union ("the strategic soundness" of this, noted the *New York Journal-American*, was "manifest"). And in 1945 the House Committee on Naval Affairs raised the possibility of annexing Japan's outlying and mandated islands as the "State of the American Pacific."

Talk of new states could be pie-eyed and fanciful, but the possibility that the United States might undergo *some* form of territorial expansion after the war was completely realistic. In 1940 Assistant Secretary of State

Adolf Berle predicted that the war would make the United States into "an imperial power greater than the world has ever seen." Certainly, with its millions-strong army, it could enforce any territorial arrangement it wished.

"From the point of view of material resources, an imperial career is entirely possible for the United States," the political scientist Albert Viton wrote. "The question is being asked all over the world: How will America use its overwhelming power?"

It was a good question, though it takes a little mental contortion to see how good. Today, the idea that the United States might have annexed France or claimed Europe's Asian colonies in 1945 seems like an absurd counterfactual. But it wasn't unthinkable. That was, in fact, precisely what Germany and Japan *had just done.* And it wasn't too different from what the United States had itself done, repeatedly, to formerly Spanish lands throughout the preceding century.

Indeed, 1945 bore a striking resemblance to 1898, just on a larger scale. As in 1898, the United States had decisively beaten a lesser empire (or, in this case, two) and had troops stationed in the defeated enemy's provinces. Why not annex them? And why not, as it had in 1898 with Hawai'i and American Samoa, take still more territory, beyond the spoils of war? Japan and Germany were wrecked, and it's doubtful that Britain or the Soviet Union could beat back an aggressively expansive United States. At the war's end, the United States possessed the world's fourth-largest empire, accounted for more than half the world's manufacturing production, and had atom bombs. Why not conquer the globe?

But of course, that's not what happened. Not even close. Instead, the United States and its allies did something highly unusual: they won a war and *gave up* territory. The United States led the charge, setting free its largest colony (the Philippines), folding up its occupations, nudging its European counterparts to abandon their empires, and demobilizing its army. It didn't annex any land in the war's aftermath; the closest it came was taking control of the islands of Micronesia in 1947, but technically they remained under the United Nations as the Trust Territory of the Pacific Islands (in 1986 a subset, the Northern Marianas, became a U.S. territory).

In late 1945, counting the occupations, 51 percent of the population of the Greater United States lived outside the states. But by 1960, after Hawai'i and Alaska entered the union, that number had fallen to around 2 percent, which is roughly where it has been ever since. Today, all U.S. overseas territory, including base sites, comprises an area smaller than Connecticut.

How did this happen?

★

There are two answers to that question, both having to do with how empire changed as a result of the Second World War. First, that war fueled a global anti-imperial resistance movement that put up major impediments to colonial empire. Second, it introduced other ways of projecting power across the planet, ways that didn't depend on large colonies.

Both changes were essential. But focus for the moment on the first, which was more conspicuous. World War II spurred a worldwide rebellion against empire. The revolt started in Asia but spread quickly to Africa, the Caribbean, and the Middle East. In a shockingly short period of time, colonized peoples dismantled the world's great empires.

In 1940 nearly one out of every three individuals on the planet was colonized. By 1965, it was down to one in fifty.

It wasn't hard to see this coming. As Douglas MacArthur stood on the deck of the USS *Missouri* in Tokyo Bay, where he accepted Japan's surrender on September 2, 1945, he could smell liberation in the air. The surrender meant not only the defeat of Japan's home islands but also the fall of its empire, a great arc of territory that covered nearly all Southeast Asia, plus Korea, Manchuria, a large hunk of northern China, and thousands of Pacific islands. "Today, freedom is on the offensive," MacArthur said. "Unshackled peoples" were finally "tasting the full sweetness of liberty."

That wasn't the half of it. Asians weren't just free from Japan, they were increasingly envisioning themselves as free from *all* foreign rule. On August 15 the nationalist leader Sukarno declared Indonesia's independence. On September 2, the same day MacArthur was giving his speech, Ho Chi Minh did the same for Vietnam. Four days later, the People's Republic of Korea announced the formation of *its* independent government.

This was what the Second World War had done. Colonized peoples had seen their white overlords defeated by an Asian power—it was the sort of sight that was hard to unsee. They'd heard Japan's message of "Asia for the Asiatics" blaring from radio speakers for years. In Burma and the Philippines, they'd tasted liberty itself when Japan granted those colonies nominal independence in 1943.

Watching from afar, the Harlem poet Langston Hughes offered a prediction. Europe and the United States would take their former possessions back, he wrote. "But when they do, those great cities of the East will never be the same again. The brownskin natives will look at those tall European-style buildings and say, 'Colored people lived there once!' And in their minds they will think, 'We have a right to live there again.'"

Hughes might have gone further. It wasn't just what Asians thought, it was what they could *do*. The tight arms controls that had been a persistent feature of colonial life broke down entirely as the war spread weapons all around Asia. "The bearing of arms was thrilling," remembered Luis Taruc, the leader of the Philippines' largest guerrilla army, the Hukbalahap. Before the war, his men had encountered guns only in the hands of the police, who menaced their picket lines and quashed their insurrections. "Now, standing in an armed group, running their hands down rifle barrels they felt more powerful than any picket line," Taruc wrote.

So they formed armies, armies beyond the control of any outside power. There was Mao Zedong's Red Army in China, the Burma National Army, the Indian National Army, the Viet Minh, the Lao Issara (Free Laos), the Malayan People's Anti-Japanese Army, and the Hukbalahap in the Philippines. Some had grown under Japan's protection, others were born of the anti-Japanese resistance, still others were hastily assembled in the heady days after the war. "From one end of the vast continent to the other," wrote a journalist in Asia, "it has seldom been possible since Japan's collapse to escape the sound of continuing gunfire."

It was the Asian Spring. The whole continent had become, in the words of one of MacArthur's generals, "an enormous pot, seething and boiling."

★

The prospect of Asia boiling over wasn't a happy one for Washington. Yes, the end of the Japanese Empire was a fine thing. But the United States still had business in the region. What of the raw materials, such as the rich Southeast Asian rubber plantations, that Japan had started a global war to seize? Was President Truman really content to see those fall to the Malayan People's Anti-Japanese Army? Or to Ho Chi Minh?

Even in the Philippines, where MacArthur had been allied with the guerrilla armies, there was cause for concern. In the areas the guerrillas controlled, they'd begun a social revolution by dispossessing landlords and redistributing property. In September 1945, more than twenty thousand peasants, organized into the Filipino Democratic Alliance, marched on Manila, demanding immediate independence and the imprisonment or execution of collaborators. Many of those collaborating politicians were part of the Philippine government MacArthur was hastily rebuilding.

After the First World War, the United States had returned virtually its whole army to civilian status within a year. But in the face of the postwar tumult, the Truman administration worried about relinquishing the army. "We are now concerned with the peace of the entire world," explained George Marshall, the army chief of staff. "And the peace can only be maintained by the strong."

In August 1945 the War Department announced that it would need 2.5 million men for the coming year. Planes and ships could be used to command the seas and the air. But to run occupations and put down rebellions? You needed an army for that.

The problem was, the army had to agree. Marshall's plan to keep men overseas provoked a furious reaction. Families of servicemen blasted their representatives with letters and buried congressional offices in baby shoes, all bearing tags reading BRING DADDY HOME. On a single day in December, Truman's office estimated that it had received sixty thousand postcards demanding the troops' return.

Politicians, fearing electoral consequences, pulled strings. As they did, the army emptied out. "At the rate we are demobilizing troops," warned Truman, "in a very short time we will have no means with which to enforce our demands." Worried about the "disintegration of our armed forces" being carried out at "dangerous speed," Truman ordered a slowdown in January 1946. Troops would stay overseas, even if there were ships ready to take them back.

This was, for many, the last straw. Days after Truman's announcement, twenty thousand GIs marched in Manila and gathered at the ruins of the Legislative Building. They wanted to go home, of course—that was the main thing, and for some the only thing. Yet others, including the leaders, had seen the Asian Spring firsthand and objected strenuously to being kept around to suppress it. "Let us leave the Chinese and Filipinos to take care of their own internal affairs," one speaker urged. "The Filipinos are our allies. We ain't gonna fight them!" cried another. The demonstrators read a letter of support from the Filipino Democratic Alliance. The

Yankee, go home!: GIs in Manila protesting their *own* presence overseas

organizers, meanwhile, passed a resolution declaring solidarity with the Filipino guerrillas.

Lieutenant General W. D. Styler, commanding general of the army forces in the West Pacific, addressed the men by radio. He pointed to the "vast new tasks" that the United States must undertake in Asia. But the men didn't listen. They booed and catcalled, drowning out whole paragraphs of Styler's speech.

The Manila protest set off a string of others. Twenty thousand soldiers protested in Honolulu, three thousand in Korea, five thousand in Calcutta. On Guam, the men burned the secretary of war in effigy, and more than three thousand sailors staged a hunger strike. Protests erupted in China, Burma, Japan, France, Germany, Britain, and Austria, too, with supporting demonstrations in Washington, Chicago, and New York.

"What kind of government is this?" asked one of the soldiers. "What are we that scream piously, 'the world must be free,' then keep it to ourselves?"

That sentiment animated the most dogged of the protesters. Another GI complained that "in the Oriental surge toward freedom we cling to imperialism." All the members of the 823rd Engineer Aviation Battalion in Burma, an African American unit, sent Truman a letter saying that they were "disgusted with undemocratic American foreign policy." They did not "want to be associated" with the "shooting and bombing to death the freedom urge of the peoples of the Southeast Asiatic countries. We do not want to 'unify' China with bayonets and bombing planes."

There is a word for it when tens of thousands of uniformed men march in the streets, heckle their commanders, declare solidarity with guerrilla forces, and burn the secretary of war in effigy. It was, as Truman privately put it, "plain mutiny." And under the Articles of War, any officer or soldier who mutinied or even witnessed a mutiny without using "his utmost endeavor" to stop it could be punished by death.

"You men forget you're not working for General Motors," the troops' commander in Manila huffed. "You're still in the Army."

But was the army really going to court-martial tens of thousands of its men? Was it actually going to execute anyone? The uprising had grown so large that this was hard to imagine.

Instead, army leaders meted out minor punishments to nine ringleaders. They accepted MacArthur's charitable judgment that the men were merely suffering from "acute homesickness" and were "not inherently challenging discipline or authority." Boys, that is, will be boys.

Yet even as leaders sought to brush the uprising under the rug, they capitulated to its demands. The men went home, shrinking the army from more than 8 million troops in May 1945 to fewer than 1 million by the end of June 1947—far short of the 2.5 million men the War Department had called for. The army had become, as one official wrote, "a clock running down, losing time, a mechanism without power."

Enough men stayed abroad to occupy Japan and parts of Germany and Austria. But the Korean occupation, which Roosevelt had predicted would last forty years, lasted only three. Truman lamented that "our influence throughout the world, as well as China, waned as the millions of American soldiers were processed through the discharge centers."

That was an exaggeration. The United States still had more ships, planes, and bases than anyone else. But its peacetime army was only the sixth largest in the world. It was in no position to colonize the planet.

★

Could the United States even hold on to the colonies it still had? The big question was the Philippines. In 1934, Congress, eager to relieve itself of the economic and military burdens of empire, had provisionally slated the colony for independence. But independence was firmly predicated on the commonwealth government protecting life and property and assuming the bonded debt held by the colonial government. If it did those things, it would gain its liberty on the Fourth of July, 1946.

But of course, the war had made a shambles of all that. Could the commonwealth government protect life and property? Clearly not, since it had been forced into exile, where it watched from afar as more than a million lives and more than 10 percent of the country's buildings were lost. Could it take over the bonds? Absolutely not. The government, banks, and insurance companies were insolvent, inflation ran rampant, and the high commissioner, Paul McNutt, warned of a looming "food crisis." Furthermore, most of the leading politicians had collaborated with Japan, and there were thousands of armed peasants calling for their heads. Prospects for smooth regime change were inauspicious, to say the very least.

In fact, top officials seriously contemplated retaining the Philippines. The U.S. National Archives contains three sets of orders—all awaiting only the president's signature—to dissolve the commonwealth government. Had any been signed, it's hard to imagine that independence would have gone through, as the chief requirement for independence was that the Philippines show itself capable of self-government.

The first order, drafted with the approval of the Departments of State, War, Navy, and Interior, would have declared martial law and placed the Philippines under the U.S. Army for failing to "provide adequately for its own preservation or maintenance." The second, prepared by the Department of the Interior, dealt with a more obscure problem, "the death or capture of the President of the Philippines." President Quezon had died in 1944 while in exile, when there was no way to run new elections. What if something happened to his vice president and successor, Sergio Osmeña? The order proposed to resolve the constitutional crisis by dissolving the government.

The most intriguing order, drafted right before the sack of Manila, came from the high commissioner's office. It would have liquidated the government for its failure to find any "acceptable or legitimate" successor in the postwar Philippines. In the mind of the official who drafted the order, this was not a hypothetical scenario. The easy collaboration of the Philippine elite with the Japanese regime had already shown the Philippines unable to establish a legitimate postcolonial government. "There is little doubt," he warned, "that the United States will be asked on or before July 4, 1946, to grant independence to a Philippine republic which will be in the control of those who served the enemy."

Two weeks after the army mutiny had set off in Manila in January 1946, High Commissioner McNutt sent Truman a desperate cable. "This situation here is critical," he pleaded. The Philippines had been ravaged by war, it was split between "loyalist and enemy collaborators," and "several sizeable well-armed dissident groups" were "still at large." McNutt asked if it was "humanly possible" for Filipinos to cope with independence amid all this.

This was a serious question, posed by the highest-ranking Philippine official. And yet the White House didn't waver: independence was not up for debate.

Why not? Certainly the reasons that had motivated the mainland drive for independence in the thirties had lost their relevance. The Depression was over, and there was little chance that the war-mangled colony would swamp the mainland market with its produce. And with Japan subdued, the Philippines was no longer a military liability. Just the opposite. If anything, military planners were adamant about *holding* their position in the Philippines, which would allow them to project force into Asia.

Yet if old reasons no longer held sway, new ones had arisen. Policymakers in the 1930s hadn't cared what the Indonesians, Indians, or Indochinese thought about Philippine politics. But now Asia was off the leash, and Washington was searching for its grip. Now it mattered. Dropping the badly bruised Philippines in exchange for goodwill within the tumultuous decolonizing world wasn't a hard choice.

Even High Commissioner McNutt could see this. "All Asia, the billion-peopled Orient, will be watching us in the Philippines," he remarked. The promise of independence had "attracted the wonder and respect of the colonial peoples of the Far East." To renege on that promise, McNutt conceded, would be "to betray Americanism as a byword in this great part of the world."

And so, rather than trying to forcibly retain its colony, as its European counterparts had done, the United States rushed it out the door. "This is the first instance in history where a colony of a sovereign nation has been voluntarily given complete independence," Truman bragged (somewhat stretching the facts). "Its significance will have world-wide effect."

That left the question of the collaborators. FDR, before he died, had insisted that those who served the Japanese during the war be removed from authority. But who had "served" and who hadn't could be a murky question. The mists of uncertainty swirled with a special thickness around Manuel Roxas, a former aide to MacArthur (it was Roxas who had signed over the $500,000 check that MacArthur illegally accepted from the Philippine government before leaving Corregidor). During the war, Roxas had served in the cabinet of the Japanese-backed government. He was "undoubtedly seriously involved" with the Japanese, reported the U.S. consul general, but he had "played safe by helping both sides."

That was enough for MacArthur. "Roxas is no collaborationist," he declared, insisting (though providing no evidence) that Roxas had been "one of the prime factors in the guerrilla movement."

Acting swiftly, MacArthur exonerated Roxas, restored him to his former rank in the U.S. Army, and gave him full back pay for the time he was "captured" by the Japanese. MacArthur also reconvened the Philippine Assembly, even though many of its members had served the enemy. Predictably, they voted Roxas in as president of the senate, understanding that he would seek amnesty for collaborators. Which he did.

"Not a single senator can be justly accused of collaboration!" Roxas declared in the senate, to great applause.

Roxas's government turned immediately on the guerrillas. Hukbalahap leaders were arrested for crimes ostensibly committed during the war. On one occasion, 109 guerrillas were surrounded by governmental forces, disarmed, forced to dig a mass grave, and shot.

The next year, with the support of some of the most powerful men in Philippine society, Roxas was elected president of the independent Philippines. His vice president was Elpidio Quirino, the politician whose family had been killed during the U.S. reconquest.

"We are a troubled people," Roxas admitted in his speech on July 4, 1946. With the cities in ruins and violence brewing in the countryside, that was impossible to deny. But there was joy, too. A specially sewn U.S. flag, with one star stitched in each of the Philippines' forty-eight provinces, was ceremoniously lowered. Up the same cord rose the Philippine flag, to deafening applause.

MacArthur turned to Carlos Romulo. "Carlos," he said, "America has buried imperialism here today."

★

It *was* a moment worth marking. When Filipinos had declared independence in 1898, the United States had fought a bitter, fourteen-year war against them. Generations of politicians had insisted, with some wavering during the Wilson years, that Filipinos were unfit for self-governance. Yet now, with no law or army forcing it to do so, the United States was letting its largest colony go. And it was doing this, remarkably, so as not to look bad in the eyes of Asians.

What is more, it didn't stop. The U.S. Virgin Islands received its first black governor in 1946 and its first native governor in 1950. Guamanians won citizenship and a civil government in 1950, after decades of advocacy. American Samoans remained "nationals" rather than citizens, but they, too, saw naval rule replaced with government by civilians, in 1951.

Larger changes were afoot in Hawai'i and Alaska. As "incorporated" territories, they had been slated—in a nonbinding way—for statehood. But that projected future had been based on the expectation of white settlement, and the white settlers had never arrived in the expected numbers. By the end of World War II, Alaska remained about half Native and half white. In Hawai'i, whites were an outright minority. Many of the territory's inhabitants, because they had come from Japan, weren't even eligible for naturalized citizenship.

Countenancing Philippine independence had required U.S. leaders to let go of the racist fear that Filipinos couldn't govern themselves. Ending the colonial status of Hawai'i and Alaska required overcoming racism of a different sort. To accept Hawaiian and Alaskan statehood, mainland politicians would have to reconcile themselves to the prospect of states not firmly under white control. In 1898 the fear of nonwhite states had motivated the resistance to empire. Decades later, in a country governed by Jim Crow, it was still present. The former president of Columbia University and Nobel laureate Nicholas Murray Butler warned that admitting Hawai'i and Alaska to the union would "mark the beginning of the end of the United States as we have known it."

Hawai'i, well-known for its mixing of Native, Asian, and European strains, seemed particularly threatening. "We do not want those people to help govern the country," a Massachusetts newspaper put it baldly. "When future issues arise in the United States Senate, we do not want a situation where vital decisions may depend upon two half-breed senators."

Such racism had long held Hawaiian and Alaskan statehood at bay, but global decolonization changed things. "Can America lead the world—effectively—toward its principle of government by consent of the governed, when it retains its own obsolete colonialism in Alaska and Hawaii?" Ernest Gruening asked. Or, as he asked privately, "How can we fervently plead for self-determination etc. for Indonesia and every other G-string people when we deny the most elementary expression of self government to our own?"

As the former director of the Division of Territories and Island Possessions, Gruening knew what a sore point this was, and he pressed on it hard. He urged Alaskans to "shout about 'colonialism' at the top of their lungs" and recommended "Boston tea party tactics" for Hawai'i. He drafted a book with the distinctly unsubtle title *Alaska Is a Colony*. He threatened frequently to air colonial matters before the United Nations. That wasn't a toothless threat. To their bottomless embarrassment, U.S. officials were obliged to submit regular reports to the United Nations on the "non-self-governing territories" of Alaska and Hawai'i.

Truman, having already agreed to Philippine independence and the hollowing out of the army, saw which way the winds were blowing. "These are troubled times," he wrote. "I know of few better ways in which we can demonstrate to the world our deep faith in democracy and the principles of self-government than by admitting Alaska and Hawaii to the Union."

From 1948 on, Truman actively pursued that end, conscious of the "tremendous psychological influence" that converting those territories to states would have on "the hearts and minds of the people of Asia and the Pacific islands."

The problem was that statehood, unlike other concessions to decolonization, required Congress's assent. And here Truman came up against a hard fact. In party politics, the two territories were balanced, it being widely assumed that Hawai'i would be a Republican state and Alaska a Democratic one (exactly wrong, it turned out). But their admission would quite obviously unbalance national politics on another axis. Whatever the party allegiances of these new states, their racial composition would put them firmly in the civil rights camp. Southern Democrats in the Senate, nervous about what these states would do to Jim Crow, threatened to filibuster.

Thus opened a front in the war for civil rights that rarely gets mentioned. Racial liberals supported statehood, pointing to Hawai'i especially as proof that integration worked. The champions of Jim Crow, meanwhile, replayed the greatest hits of 1900, rallying the old imperialist rhetoric in defense of their precarious position. Arch-segregationist Strom Thurmond, one of the longest-serving congressmen in the country's history, lectured his colleagues on the "impassible difference" between Western civilization and Eastern ways. "East is East, and West is West, and never the twain shall meet," he admonished, quoting Kipling.

Southern opposition stymied Hawaiian and Alaskan statehood through the forties and fifties, but it could not hold out forever. Well-known among the civil rights movement's triumphs are the desegregation of schools won in *Brown v. Board of Education* in 1954 and the prohibition of racial

Martin Luther King Jr. wearing a Hawaiian lei on his historic march from Selma to Montgomery, 1965. King had visited Hawai'i, which he regarded as a paragon of racial harmony.

discrimination at the polls secured by the Voting Rights Act of 1965. Less touted in the textbooks are the admission of Alaska and Hawai'i as the forty-ninth and fiftieth states in 1959. But those, too, were serious blows against racism. For the first time, the logic of white supremacy had not dictated which parts of the Greater United States were eligible for statehood.

For racists, this spelled catastrophe—"the beginning of the end of the United States as we have known it," as Nicholas Murray Butler had put it. In a way, Butler's prediction turned out to be right. Alaska sent to the Senate Ernest Gruening, who had made a decades-long career of opposing racism and imperialism. In 1964 Gruening achieved national fame as one of only two congressmen—out of 506 voting—to oppose the Gulf of Tonkin Resolution that led to the direct U.S. entry into the Vietnam War.

Hawai'i, for its part, immediately elected nonwhite congressmen: Hiram Fong to the Senate and Daniel Inouye, veteran of the fabled 442nd Infantry Regiment, to the House. Fong was the first Chinese American to serve in the Senate, Inouye the first Japanese American to serve in Congress. Inouye held congressional office in an unbroken stretch from Hawaiian statehood in 1959 until his death in 2012, surpassing even Strom Thurmond's forty-seven-year record of longevity. By the time he died, Inouye was president pro tempore of the Senate, which put him third in the line of succession to the presidency.

Fong and Inouye proved to be, just as white supremacists feared, champions of civil rights. And had the segregationists gazed farther into the future, they would have been still more troubled by something else taking place in Hawai'i at the time.

Nineteen fifty-nine was the year of statehood. The next year, 1960, a Kenyan student met a Kansan one in the Russian class at the University of Hawaii. The two married—an interracial marriage illegal in two dozen states at the time—and had a son, who would grow up partly in Hawai'i, partly in Indonesia. In typical Hawaiian fashion, his profoundly multiracial extended family would grow by marriage to incorporate African American, British, Lithuanian, Indonesian, Malaysian, and Chinese elements. And in 2009 that son, Barack Obama, would become the first black president of the United States.

15

NOBODY KNOWS
IN AMERICA,
PUERTO RICO'S
IN AMERICA

In 1936 a twenty-four-year-old Wenzell Brown made his way from New York to Ponce, Puerto Rico. Brown would later make a name for himself as an author of pulp fiction, writing such ageless classics as *Teen-Age Mafia*, *Prison Girl*, and *The Murder Kick*. But for the moment he was just a young schoolteacher in a strange, new place.

Brown didn't speak a word of Spanish, nor did he know anything about the island. In fact, he couldn't remember Puerto Rico being mentioned once during his years in high school and college. When he'd applied for his teaching post, he had confused Puerto Rico for Costa Rica and so believed that he was going abroad.

It was a quick education. Ponce was Pedro Albizu Campos's hometown, and Brown saw Albizu's Liberation Army march regularly through its streets. He was there for the Ponce Massacre, when, as he put it, "complete madness descended upon the place" and the police went "berserk," shooting more than 150 civilians. He saw poverty, too. "One cannot look at the slums of any Puerto Rican town without feeling that there has been grievous neglect and an obligation unfulfilled," Brown wrote.

Yet what struck him most was the bitterness. Brown recorded with alarm his students' anger as he sought to teach them English. He noted how, years after the publication of Dr. Cornelius Rhoads's letter (which had described physicians delighting in the "abuse and torture" of their patients), many Puerto Ricans still refused to enter governmental hospitals. They feared that mainland doctors were plotting to kill them.

Brown left the island in 1939 but returned in 1945 and found things no better. The war had brought military investment to Puerto Rico, but it had also brought soldiers, censorship, the threat of martial law, shipping shortages, and frequent unrest. Brown perceived an "intense, fanatical nationalism" in the air. The island was, he warned his fellow mainlanders, "dynamite on our doorstep."

★

Wenzell Brown wasn't the only one to recognize Puerto Rico's incendiary potential. The celebrated journalist John Gunther gasped when he saw the island's crowded slums. The sight offered a "paralyzing jolt to anyone who believes in American standards of progress and civilization," he wrote. *Life* magazine ran an exposé of the "cesspool of Puerto Rico" in 1943 and concluded that the colony was an "unsolvable problem."

"El Fanguito," a notorious slum in San Juan, 1941. Such slums, wrote the governor at the time, "would have revolted a Hottentot."

Technically, it was Washington's unsolvable problem. Puerto Rican affairs were the remit of the colonial office Ernest Gruening had established, the Division of Territories and Island Possessions. But that agency was—as was typical of U.S. imperial endeavors—laughably small. Though responsible for virtually all the United States' empire, it had a skeleton crew for a staff. In 1949 it had only ten employees above the level of secretary.

With Washington offering little direction, responsibility fell to the appointed governor in San Juan. Yet, though governors held a great deal of formal power—they could, for example, veto laws—they struggled to use it effectively. Most knew too little and left too quickly to master Puerto Rican politics. FDR's administration alone saw seven governors come and go, not counting three interim appointments.

Under the appointed mainland officials served elected Puerto Rican ones, less powerful but much cannier about local affairs. Chief among these was Luis Muñoz Marín, the leader of the island's dominant party, who towered over the political scene from the 1940s through the 1960s. John Gunther deemed him "the most important living Puerto Rican."

Born just three days after the USS *Maine* exploded in Havana Bay in 1898, Muñoz Marín grew up in the shadow of U.S. rule. His father had been Puerto Rico's nonvoting representative in Congress, so he'd been shuttled back and forth between the mainland and the island. As a young man, Muñoz Marín joined the bohemian demimonde of Greenwich Village and worked as a journalist, writing occasionally for *The Nation* under Ernest Gruening's editorship. He spoke, one governor remembered, a "full, flexible, meaty English without indication of origin, except, perhaps, a trace of New Yorkese in expression"—Muñoz Marín joked that his English was better than his Spanish.

Yet for all his cultural ties to the mainland, Luis Muñoz Marín was a sharp critic of colonial rule. As a young man he had concluded, just as Pedro Albizu Campos had, that Puerto Rico needed independence. It was the only way the island could escape poverty.

One evening in the late 1920s, while dining at the Hotel Palace in San Juan, Muñoz Marín noticed Albizu sitting alone. Muñoz Marín invited Albizu to join him. The two had much in common. They were young, charismatic leaders who spoke English fluently and held law degrees from prestigious mainland universities (Georgetown for Muñoz Marín, Harvard for Albizu). As they talked, they found that their political visions matched.

Still, Muñoz Marín noticed a difference in their motives. Whereas Albizu was obsessed with "getting rid of the Americans," Muñoz Marín's chief concern was "getting rid of hunger."

Were those two goals the same? Given the hardships Puerto Rico faced because Washington controlled its trade, it was easy to suppose they were. Muñoz Marín met with Albizu often and told a newspaper in 1931 that he would vote for Albizu. But as the turbulent decade wore on, Muñoz Marín started to wonder if the relationship between colonialism and poverty wasn't more complicated.

He had cause to rethink his commitment to independence in 1936, when two of Albizu's followers assassinated the chief of police and Ernest Gruening drafted an independence bill in retaliation. The bill was a "weapon of imperial vengeance," wrote Muñoz Marín, one that would subject Puerto Rico to a steep and immediate tariff. He saw, to his horror, that the island had become so dependent on sales to the mainland that any interruption of trade would trigger an economic collapse, destroying "all hope of life and civilization." He felt "emotional confusion" at "wanting independence but not wanting economic upheaval."

In 1938 he launched the Partido Popular Democrático, the party he would lead until the end of his career. It campaigned on a slogan of "Bread, Land, and Liberty," though that last term, *liberty*, was kept ambiguous. It resonated with the widespread resentment of colonial rule in Puerto Rico, yet it was vague enough to encompass many possibilities. Muñoz Marín instructed PPD leaders to studiously avoid the status question. It was, he believed, a political trap.

That wasn't a bad call. In 1940 Muñoz Marín's party received 38 percent of the vote. In 1944 it won 65 percent, establishing itself as the island's dominant party.

In 1946, the year the Philippines gained its liberty, Muñoz Marín came out publicly against independence and purged his party of members who favored it. The PPD would instead champion a middle solution—not independence, not statehood, but something in between. The hope was to gain autonomy for Puerto Rico without losing access to the U.S. market ("the biggest and most prosperous in the world," Muñoz Marín noted).

It was the right time to push. In an age of rapid decolonization, when the Philippines got its independence, Guamanians got citizenship, and Alaska and Hawai'i were on the road to statehood, Washington was ready to resolve the Puerto Rican conundrum. "Two million people cannot permanently be kept in the twilight zone of colonialism," insisted the New Dealer Rexford Tugwell, then serving as this island's governor.

Tugwell agreed with Muñoz Marín's autonomy-plus-development vision, expecting that it would ease the palpable unrest among Puerto Ricans. State Department officials supported the plan, too, hoping that it would relieve the United States of the embarrassment of having to submit a yearly report to the United Nations on the "non-self-governing territory" of Puerto Rico—a report that gave Soviet diplomats an annual opportunity to mock the United States for its hypocrisy.

In 1946 the Truman administration appointed a Puerto Rican as governor, Muñoz Marín's colleague Jesús T. Piñero. In 1948, Congress allowed Puerto Ricans to elect their own governor. Muñoz Marín won easily, and he would keep the position until 1964. Now, holding the highest political office in the colony, he could move Puerto Rico down the new political path. He could also address the island's social issues.

He'd have to, in fact. In gaining local power, Muñoz Marín had also gained responsibility for local affairs. Poverty, resentment, political violence—these were his problems now.

★

Puerto Rico suffered from many maladies, but, in the near-unanimous view of mainlanders, they all stemmed from a single root. The island's women, as one official put it, "kept shooting children like cannon balls at the rigid walls of their economy." Mainlanders lamented the overcrowding on the small island, which by 1950 had nearly 650 inhabitants per square mile. Today, that's not impressive—Bangladesh has nearly 3,000 inhabitants per square mile and the city-state of Singapore has close to 20,000. Yet at the time it was one of the highest population densities on the planet.

"If the United States were as crowded as Puerto Rico," wrote the sociologist C. Wright Mills, "it would contain almost all the people of the world."

Muñoz Marín shared this concern. He'd been talking publicly about overpopulation since the 1920s. As he'd put it then, the problem of hunger in Puerto Rico could be solved in two ways: more food or fewer mouths. Getting more food was a lifelong obsession of his, and he would superintend

Puerto Rico's gradual rise from poverty by promoting economic development. Yet he was also drawn to the second solution. Of the two approaches, he wrote, "I believe that reducing the population is the most important, the most practical, and the cheapest." He identified as a "Malthusian," meaning that he supported birth control.

Muñoz Marín wasn't alone in this. Although the men who controlled Puerto Rico held a variety of opinions on the matter, a good many—including Presidents Herbert Hoover and Franklin Delano Roosevelt—were troubled enough by the island's growing population to deem birth control a necessity. The practice remained deeply controversial on the mainland, but it was, in Ernest Gruening's judgment, Puerto Rico's "only hope."

Still, as Gruening well knew, in an overwhelmingly Catholic society this was a delicate matter. The church attacked Muñoz Marín frequently for his position—at one point, the local bishops declared voting for him to be a sin.

Birth control also stoked the ire of the nationalists, who had learned from the Rhoads affair to view doctors and diagnoses of "overpopulation" with deep suspicion. Albizu regarded Puerto Rico as *under*populated and saw birth control as an insidious attempt to "invade the very insides of nationality," to carry the war against Puerto Rican freedom to the womb.

To avoid controversy, officials—both Puerto Rican and mainlander—soft-pedaled their support for family planning. Government-run clinics provided contraceptives but didn't aggressively foist them onto their patients. Instead, officials fostered birth control quietly through a series of philanthropic initiatives, corporate partnerships, and university pilot projects, starting in the late thirties and gaining speed under Muñoz Marín's governorship. Publicly, the government was agnostic about birth control. Privately, it encouraged doctors, researchers, and pharmaceutical companies to try their best.

That was all it took. The island was, in many ways, the perfect site to test new medical techniques. It was close to the mainland, with doctors and nurses who spoke English and were trained in U.S. methods. Whereas most states had laws outlawing contraception as well as aggressive "bluenose brigades" to enforce them, Puerto Rico had legal birth control and an obliging government. And, of course, Puerto Ricans had a history of serving as subjects for experimental medical research, from anemia to mustard gas. Their poverty and marginal position in U.S. society made them all-too-convenient fodder.

It is perhaps not a surprise, then, that Puerto Rico became the proving ground for one of the twentieth century's most transformative inventions: the birth control pill.

★

Like many key figures in Puerto Rico's history, Gregory Pincus, known as the father of the pill, was a Harvard man. In fact, while there he'd shared a mentor with Cornelius Rhoads: the geneticist William Castle. Castle had directed the Rockefeller Anemia Commission in Puerto Rico and had brought Rhoads to the island. He had also trained Pincus.

But Pincus, a Jew, had struggled to gain the official support Rhoads had always been able to count on. After some sensational research involving the in vitro fertilization of rabbits (headline: RABBIT WITHOUT PARENTS AMAZES MEN OF SCIENCE), Pincus found himself portrayed in the press as a Frankenstein. His bid for tenure at Harvard failed.

Pincus left Harvard and founded his own research center, in Worcester, Massachusetts. His concern about the world "population explosion" led him to propose a study of contraception. Might there be a pill or a shot that could reliably suppress ovulation? It was a fine question, but Pincus couldn't get funding to answer it, either from pharmaceutical companies or from Planned Parenthood.

Pincus's research would quite likely have gone nowhere had the activist Margaret Sanger (who founded Planned Parenthood and popularized the phrase *birth control*) and the heiress Katharine Dexter McCormick not intervened. Recognizing the value of his work, they gave him virtually limitless funding—privately—to research synthetic hormones.

Pincus first tested nearly two hundred compounds on animals. His colleague John Rock meanwhile administered hormone injections to "eighty frustrated, but valiantly adventuresome" infertile women in Massachusetts who were hoping to conceive (the hormones that inhibit ovulation could also, Rock believed, be used to strengthen the reproductive system). But Rock's tests were burdensome, the side effects were serious, and the whole thing depended on the desperation of childless women.

McCormick was impatient for large-scale field trials. "How can we get a 'cage' of ovulating women to experiment with?" she asked Sanger.

The team considered tests in Jamaica, Japan, India, Mexico, and Hawai'i. In 1954 Pincus visited Puerto Rico and was suitably impressed. Here was a place where they could undertake, as Pincus expressed it to McCormick, "certain experiments which would be very difficult in this country."

The first experiment used medical students at the University of Puerto Rico. Despite having their grades held hostage to their participation in the study, nearly half dropped out—they left the university, were wary of the experiment, or found it too onerous. The researchers then tried female prisoners, but that plan fizzled too. In 1956 they began a large-scale clinical trial in a public housing project in Río Piedras.

The pill that Pincus's team administered had a far higher dosage than the pill does today. Many women complained of dizziness, nausea, headaches, and stomach pains. The lead local researcher concluded that the pill caused "too many side reactions to be acceptable generally." Pincus, however, was undaunted. He blamed the complaints on the "emotional super-activity of Puerto Rican women" and tried giving some the pill without warning them of its side effects—a clear violation of the principle of informed consent.

The next year, a team of researchers allied with Pincus began another large-scale trial of the pill in Puerto Rico. Yet again, the side effects were hard to ignore. One researcher noted that the women appeared to be suffering from cervical erosion ("whatever you call it, the cervix looks 'angry'"), but the tests continued. Stopping them would mean delaying approval from the Food and Drug Administration, which the researchers were eager to get.

They got it. In 1960, basing its decision largely on the Puerto Rican trials, the FDA approved the birth control pill for commercial sale.

Nor was it just the pill. With a supportive government and a network of clinics, Puerto Rico became a laboratory for all sorts of experimental contraceptives: diaphragms, spermicidal jellies, spirals, loops, intrauterine devices, hormone shots, and an "aerosol vaginal foam" known as "Emko" distributed to tens of thousands of women. Searle, Youngs Rubber, Johnson & Johnson, Hoffman-La Roche, Eaton Labs, Lanteen Medical Laboratories, and Durex all sponsored research there in the forties and fifties.

★

Puerto Rico is central to the history of contraceptives. Yet contraceptives are not central to the history of Puerto Rico. By the late 1950s, the island had "one of the most extensive systems of birth control clinics in the world," a study found. That same study, however, noted that Puerto Ricans had "a fairly low tolerance for modern contraceptive methods" and used them so irregularly, infrequently, and incorrectly that the effect on population growth was "minimal."

Why did contraceptives fare so poorly in Puerto Rico despite the boundless zeal of birth control advocates? Surely, social stigma was part of the story. But another part was the aggressive promotion of a different form of birth control: female sterilization.

The practice began in Puerto Rican hospitals in the early 1940s, just as Luis Muñoz Marín was rising to power. It quietly spread, typically administered after the birth of a child. By 1949, a survey revealed that 18 percent of all hospital deliveries were followed by "*la operación.*"

No governmental program championed sterilization. The advocates were doctors themselves, both mainlanders and locals. Worried that Puerto Ricans lacked the education to use other methods of birth control, they steered their patients toward the surgical procedure. Sometimes, hospitals offered it free.

Did doctors go beyond mere steering? At times, yes. One hospital refused to admit women for their fourth delivery unless they agreed to be sterilized after. And most sterilizations were performed within hours of childbirth—hardly ideal conditions for informed consent.

Still, documented cases of outright compulsion are hard to find. And given Puerto Rico's strict laws against abortion, taboos against contraception, and patriarchal culture, women had their own reasons to want the operation. "The only way to avoid having children was getting sterilized—free," one remembered. "I just got my husband's signature, went in and got operated on."

Whether because doctors pushed or women pulled, female sterilization in Puerto Rico grew to staggering proportions. In 1965 a governmental survey found that more than a third of Puerto Rican mothers between the ages of twenty and forty-nine had been sterilized, at the median age of twenty-six. Of the mothers born in the latter part of the 1920s, nearly *half* had been sterilized.

Such numbers, stunning on their own, become even more so in comparative context. This was a time when India's rate—one of the world's highest—was six sterilizations for every hundred married women. Puerto Rico had more women sterilized, by far, than anywhere else in the world.

★

Puerto Rico's adventures in reproductive health happened out of view of the mainland. *Life* reported in depth on the field trials for the pill ("a brilliantly successful example of scientific insight and collaboration") but mentioned their colonial location only glancingly.

Yet mainlanders were all too aware of another maneuver in the demography game. Cheap and regular aviation had made it possible for Puerto Ricans—who were, after all, U.S. citizens—to simply leave the island. A trip between San Juan and New York, which took days in the thirties, was by the fifties a matter of hours. And so, just as African Americans made their way in the mid-twentieth century out of the impoverished rural South toward Northern cities—the "Great Migration"—Puerto Ricans made a similar trip. Most landed in New York City.

The difference was that Puerto Ricans had a government prodding them along. In 1947 Muñoz Marín's party created a migration bureau, a rare case of a state agency dedicated to getting people to *leave* an area. The government distributed millions of pamphlets to help people adjust to life on the mainland. Muñoz Marín's colleagues set up a three-month training program for women seeking to enter mainland domestic service. They practiced talking in English, washing dishes, polishing silver, answering the phone, and doing laundry.

When economic forces carry sojourners from a poorer area to a richer one, the fortune seekers are usually men. But the Puerto Rican Great Migration was strikingly female—in the half decade after World War II it was 59 percent so. That was partly because foreign women had a harder time crossing U.S. borders, which left an opening for Puerto Rican women, often in domestic service. But it also owed to the encouragement of the island government, which was eager to see the departure of women of childbearing age.

Many did leave. In 1950 about one in seven Puerto Ricans lived not on the island, but on the mainland. By 1955, it was closer to one in four.

★

For Luis Muñoz Marín, this all hung together. Turning Puerto Rico from an "unsolvable problem" into a viable economy meant doing a lot of things at once: tamping down birthrates, ushering the surplus population off the island, and channeling profits from tariff-free trade into economic development. More food, fewer mouths.

It was a Faustian bargain, though. To secure Puerto Rico a comfortable berth within the U.S. economy, Muñoz Marín had to make peace with the United States. Whereas Albizu insisted on independence, Muñoz Marín sought a less overbearing form of colonialism. Whereas Albizu had used the Cornelius Rhoads affair to whip up nationalist sentiment, Muñoz Marín collaborated eagerly (though quietly) with mainland doctors in their field trials. His debate with Albizu in the thirties—"getting rid of the Americans" versus "getting rid of hunger"—had turned from a friendly dinner disagreement into a profound divergence in worldview.

Albizu and Muñoz Marín had gone their separate ways after that dinner. Muñoz Marín joined the government; Albizu, after the violence of the thirties and his conviction for conspiracy, spent more than a decade on the mainland in federal custody. For Muñoz Marín, Albizu's long absence from Puerto Rico was a relief. Negotiating with Washington was a lot easier when the Liberation Army wasn't drilling in the street.

Yet Albizu returned to the island in December 1947, and several thousand people greeted him at the dock. Forty cadets from the Liberation Army formed an honor guard around him.

Prison had done nothing to dull Albizu's zeal. He regarded Muñoz Marín as a "puppet," the "high priest of slavery," for pulling Puerto Rico closer into the orbit of the mainland. He called for independence. If that couldn't be won peacefully, he wanted "revolution."

"We have to revert to the attitude of those people in the hills who have a machete handy to kill anyone who does not respect his wife or his son," he told his followers.

Violent protection of the family loomed particularly large in Albizu's thinking after his return. He saw contraceptives as an insidious imperial plot ("The United States tells us that we shouldn't have been born"). Sterilization, in his view, was an assault on Puerto Rican women. "The surgeon who sterilizes our women should have his scalpel thrust into his throat," he advised.

Luis Muñoz Marín was aghast. This sort of talk was "ten years behind the time," he scolded, and quite likely to derail the anticipated political settlement. He urged the legislature to make it a felony to oppose the government by force, or even to suggest it. The bill, known as the Gag Law, provided for juryless trials and punishments of up to ten years in prison.

Newspaper editors protested. The American Civil Liberties Union complained that this went "far beyond" any legislation on the mainland and would "threaten the civil liberties of all Puerto Rican citizens." But the law passed and went into effect six months after Albizu's return and six months before Muñoz Marín took office as the colony's first elected governor.

Thus began a delicate waiting game between the two leaders. The police held nationalists under obsessive surveillance, transcribing their speeches and following their movements. Yet Muñoz Marín, hoping to avoid incident, held off making arrests. Time was on his side. The more the economy developed and the more power devolved from mainlanders to locals, the less compelling revolutionary nationalism would seem. The growing migratory stream to New York undercut the cause of independence still further. Each Puerto Rican living there tied the island more tightly to the United States.

Albizu needed time, too. Revolutions don't happen overnight. Winning popular support and rebuilding his organization would take months, if not years. Albizu started secretly stockpiling weapons. If he was going to war, he'd need an arsenal.

In 1950 Albizu concluded that the moment for action had come. His preparations were far from complete, but in July, at Muñoz Marín's urging, Truman signed a law calling for a Puerto Rican constitutional convention to frame a new government. Voter registration for a referendum was scheduled for November. The portcullis was descending and, if Albizu wanted independence, he'd have to grab it soon, before Muñoz Marín won support for his proposal at the polls.

It was the "hour of immortality," Albizu declared.

★

That hour struck on October 30, 1950, just days before voter registration. More than a hundred nationalists declared independence and staged attacks on seven towns and cities at once. They struck governmental buildings, hoisted flags, cut telephone lines, and destroyed records. In

Jayuya, they set the police station and post office on fire. It took three days before police rousted them from the area.

At the same time, six nationalists drove up to the governor's mansion in San Juan and started shooting. Machine-gun fire sprayed the front of the building, sending a bullet through the window of Muñoz Marín's office, where he was taking a meeting. He hit the floor; his daughters cowered behind a bureau. The shoot-out lasted an hour before the police killed five of the would-be assassins and wounded the last.

It was an uprising. Under Muñoz Marín's orders, the Puerto Rican National Guard and the insular police fought back with machine guns, bazookas, and tanks. The 295th Infantry of the National Guard flew planes over Jayuya and the rebel-held town of Utuado, strafing them from the air.

Nor, incredibly, was that the end. The next day, two nationalists in New York, Oscar Collazo and Griselio Torresola, made their way down to Washington, D.C. They were seeking Harry Truman, who was living not at the White House (it was being renovated), but at the nearby Blair House. They wore suits, and they carried guns.

Their idea was simple: shoot their way into Blair House, find Truman, and kill him. All in all, it wasn't a terrible plan, especially in those days of laxer presidential protection. Collazo and Torresola came impressively close to carrying it out.

On the afternoon of November 1, the pair walked up to the Blair House entrance. Collazo was supposed to fire first, but his gun jammed at the crucial moment, which cost them the element of surprise. Still, they held their own, shooting a police officer and two Secret Service agents. Truman, napping inside, inadvisably poked his head out the window, only thirty-one feet above where Torresola was standing. It's unclear if Torresola saw the president, but as two journalists who sorted through the ballistic details have noted, it was a close brush:

> What is known, indisputably, is that a trained, determined assassin with extraordinary combat shooting skills and a known predilection for the highly accurate two-handed shooting stance stood with a gun he was loading, looking in the proper direction at the proper moment and unimpeded by any law enforcement agents. He had a clear shot at the window, and the president was either there or within seconds of getting there.

Albizu's aborted revolution: The failed assassin Oscar Collazo outside Blair House, where Truman had been napping

Before Torresola could sight his target, though, a dying police officer, who himself had been shot multiple times, returned fire and struck Torresola in the head, killing him.

The very near assassination rattled the Secret Service, which drastically increased its security measures. It rattled Truman, too, who brought it up when explaining why he chose not to run for reelection in 1952. That "shooting scrape," as he put it, "has caused us all so much worry and anguish."

Yet the mainland public made surprisingly little of the "scrape." A seven-city revolt in the United States' largest colony that included an assassination attempt on its governor, that required suppression by airpower, and that nearly killed the U.S. president made brief headlines, but rarely were the dots connected. *The New York Times* shrugged it off as "one of those mad adventures that make no sense to outsiders." It was, as one journalist put it, the "news of a day and quickly over, to be forgotten by the average American."

Oscar Collazo, the surviving assassin, insisted to whoever would listen that this wasn't a "mad adventure," but a determined attempt to draw attention to Puerto Rico's plight. He told how his family had lost its farm due to the restrictive sugar quota Washington had slapped on the island in the 1930s. He spoke at his trial of how Cornelius Rhoads had "tried to bring about a campaign of killing the Puerto Rican people." Collazo was astounded that Rhoads had never been punished. It stuck in his mind for decades as a sign of the contempt in which Puerto Ricans were held.

"How little the American people know of Puerto Rico!" Collazo exclaimed in frustration during his trial. He doubted if one in a hundred could place it on a map. "They don't know Puerto Rico is a possession of the United States, even though it has been so for the last fifty-two years."

★

Oscar Collazo received a death sentence (later commuted to life in prison). Back on the island, Luis Muñoz Marín assured the FBI's J. Edgar Hoover that he'd do everything in his power to eradicate the "lawless lunatics." His police rounded up more than a thousand purported nationalists and tried them on various charges for violating the Gag Law. They arrested people for flying the Puerto Rican flag. They arrested lawyers who represented the nationalists. If a town mayor identified a rival as a nationalist, the police arrested him or her, too.

One arrest was important above all others, though: that of Pedro Albizu Campos. Police besieged his apartment, which also served as the Nationalist headquarters, and a two-hour gunfight commenced. One officer testified to seeing Albizu personally throw three bombs off the balcony. Doris Torresola, the sister of Griselio, the failed Blair House assassin, got shot in the throat, the bullet lodging in her left lung. The inside of the apartment "looked like a cheese grater" from all the bullet holes, one nationalist observed. Finally, police used tear gas to clear it and arrest Albizu.

None of this was pretty. Yet the 1950 uprising was, for Muñoz Marín, an unexpected boon. Free to arrest virtually anyone he wanted, he cleared the island of nationalist leaders during the all-important voter registration period. The violence allowed him to promulgate a clear story, which the mainland press reinforced. Reformers pursuing prosperity, like him, were rational. Nationalists, by contrast, were lunatics.

During the two-day registration period, more than 150,000 new voters registered—the largest registration bump in Puerto Rico's history. The referendum that followed didn't ask Puerto Ricans if they wanted statehood

or independence. It just asked them if, within the confines of their existing colonial relationship to the mainland, they'd prefer a new constitution. By four to one, they voted that they would.

The new government was called, in English, a "commonwealth" and
in Spanish a "free associated state." The actual lines of authority didn't
change. Puerto Ricans still fell under the discretionary power of a government for which they could not vote (and Congress used that power
immediately to strike a bill of economic rights from the proposed constitution). The difference, Muñoz Marín argued, was that now the relationship had been approved by the Puerto Rican electorate and was therefore
consensual rather than coerced. This was enough to round Puerto Rico
up to "self-governing" for the purposes of the United Nations.

On July 25, 1952—the anniversary of the U.S. invasion in 1898—Luis
Muñoz Marín was sworn in as the first governor of the Commonwealth
of Puerto Rico. He raised the Puerto Rican flag slowly up the pole until it
reached the height of the Stars and Stripes.

It was hard to know what that flag meant. Was this liberation, or was it
empire by another name? Despite having "free" and "state" in its Spanish-
language name, Estado Libre Asociado de Puerto Rico, the commonwealth was neither. Muñoz Marín, waxing entomological, boasted that it
was a "butterfly of a new species." The writer Irene Vilar called it a "no-
nation," a "somewhat shapeless" polity suspended uncomfortably between
inclusion and independence. The arrangement "defies duplication and
often even description," exclaimed a baffled diplomat.

If the politics of Puerto Rico's new status was ambiguous, the economics was clear. A loophole in the tax code exempted corporations from federal taxes if they were based primarily in the territories. It was one of the
many legal anomalies resulting from the Insular Cases, which had denied
the automatic extension of federal law to the unincorporated territories.
Latching onto it, Muñoz Marín's government turned Puerto Rico into a
tax haven. Mainland corporations were enticed to move to the island with
tax holidays, subsidies from the insular treasury, low-interest loans, and
other aid. The island's economy became more tightly linked than ever to
that of the mainland.

By Muñoz Marín's reckoning, it was worth it. Operation Bootstrap, as
the campaign was called, drew hundreds of mainland firms to Puerto Rico.
By the fifties, its economy was visibly shifting from agriculture to industry.

Its gross national product shot up by more than two-thirds in that decade. At the same time, incomes rose, death rates fell, literacy increased, and manufacturing wages more than doubled.

Puerto Rico was still poorer than any state in the union and poorer than Mexico—hence the stream of migrants to the mainland—but it was doing better than nearly all its Caribbean neighbors. In 1954, *Life*, which had labeled the island an "unsolvable problem" just eleven years earlier, described it as "one of the few spots on the globe that all Americans can feel happy and hopeful about these days."

★

For Luis Muñoz Marín, the problem had been solved. The new constitution had erased "all traces of colonialism," he insisted, and the economy was improving. Yet not everyone agreed. Muñoz Marín's chief legal adviser, who had drafted that constitution, maintained that Puerto Rico was still a colony, subject to the "almost unrestricted whim of Congress." Nationalists, too, believed that all Muñoz Marín had done was brush empire under the rug. The UN's reclassification of Puerto Rico as self-governing, in their eyes, only further perpetuated the lie that Puerto Rico was now free.

On March 1, 1954, shortly after the UN's decision, four nationalists entered the House of Representatives in Washington. They made their way to the upstairs gallery, unfurled a Puerto Rican flag, and shouted "*¡Viva Puerto Rico Libre!*" Then they pulled out pistols and fired twenty-nine rounds into the body politic below. It was, the Speaker of the House remembered, "the wildest scene in the entire history of Congress." Splinters flew as the bullets sprayed over the chamber.

In all, five congressmen were shot. One, Alvin Bentley from Michigan, took a bullet in the chest and went gray. His doctor gave him a fifty-fifty chance of living. He did survive, as did the other four, but a colleague judged that he was never really the same.

To this day, the drawer in the mahogany table used by the Republican leadership has a jagged bullet hole in it.

Had Albizu ordered this? Lolita Lebrón, the chief shooter, took full responsibility. Albizu declared the shooting an act of "sublime heroism" and said no more. Yet Muñoz Marín had little doubt Albizu was behind it. Though he'd previously pardoned Albizu for political reasons, he revoked the pardon and sent police once more to the Nationalist headquarters in San Juan. As before, Albizu and his comrades fired on the police before tear gas filled the apartment. Albizu was carried out, gasping, "I am choked."

It was his third arrest, and it would put him in custody till the last months of his life. For Albizu, this was more than just incarceration. Starting with his second imprisonment, he and his supporters had become convinced that—in a horrifying recapitulation of all the medical experiments run on Puerto Ricans—the government was using cutting-edge technology to kill him. He complained to the warden of a "poisonous wave of electronic emanations" entering through his windows. He perceived "black rays," "white emanations," and "pestilent gases" being pumped into his cell, and he started wearing wet towels on his head to block out radiation.

"We live in the era of the scientific savage," he reflected, "where all the wisdom of science, mathematics and physics are used for the purposes of assassination."

★

Yet again, the mainland press treated the political violence as a freak event. Nationalism in Puerto Rico was "about as lunatic a movement as could exist in the world," wrote *The New York Times*. Albizu and his followers were "fanatics" or "terrorists" in the press's telling—kooks, easily dismissed and quickly forgotten.

They have largely stayed forgotten. Despite his extraordinary career, Pedro Albizu Campos is hard to find in surveys of U.S. history. He's not in comprehensive scholarly series such as the *Oxford History of the United States* or *The New Cambridge History of American Foreign Relations*, and I haven't found a single textbook used in mainland schools that mentions him. Even books designed to uncover suppressed histories, such as Howard Zinn's *A People's History of the United States* and James Loewen's *Lies My Teacher Told Me*, ignore Albizu. The most important academic venue in U.S. history, *The Journal of American History*, has never printed his name.

Of course, Puerto Ricans themselves—on and off the island—are fully aware of Albizu. In my home city of Chicago, there's a public high school named after him (with an adjoining family learning center for teen parents named after Lolita Lebrón, the leader in the 1954 House shootings). There's a K–8 school named for Albizu in Harlem: P.S. 161. Then there's the Dr. Pedro Albizu Campos High School in the mass-produced suburb of Levittown, Puerto Rico (by the same builders as the more famous New York and Pennsylvania Levittowns).

In 2000, the massive Puerto Rican Day Parade in New York was dedicated to Albizu. Hundreds of thousands marched in it, including Hillary Clinton and Rudy Giuliani.

★

Clinton and Giuliani marched in a parade for Albizu, but did they know who he was? Very likely not. The epic battle between Muñoz Marín and Albizu in the fifties transformed Puerto Rican society, but it barely registered elsewhere. If mainlanders think about Puerto Rican history in that period at all, the image that comes to their mind is an entirely different one: juvenile delinquency.

Young Puerto Ricans didn't actually commit many crimes in the postwar period. The evidence suggests that they misbehaved less than other New Yorkers. But as Puerto Ricans poured in from the island, the tabloid press trumpeted sensational tales of their malfeasance. Journalists who had had conspicuously little to say about the anticolonial uprising of 1950 were only too happy to sound off about Puerto Rican gangs, dope fiends, and switchblade artists.

The inflammatory reportage quickly made its way into the culture at large. Wenzell Brown, who by the 1950s had become a major pulp fiction writer, introduced his readers to the Puerto Rican underworld with such lurid novels as *Monkey on My Back*, *The Big Rumble*, and *Run, Chico, Run*. Puerto Rican teens featured in the films *The Young Savages* and *Blackboard Jungle*. The mute youth accused of murder in *12 Angry Men* appeared Puerto Rican. And of course, a Puerto Rican gang—the Sharks—was at the center of one of the most successful musicals ever staged: *West Side Story*.

That musical, written by Arthur Laurents with music by Leonard Bernstein and lyrics by Stephen Sondheim, premiered in 1957, three years after the House shooting. It was first conceived as a Romeo-and-Juliet story about a Jewish woman and a Catholic man (flying initially under the unappetizing title *Gang Bang*). But the creative team, seeking relevance, swapped out the Jews for Puerto Ricans.

Sondheim was nervous. "I can't do this show," he protested at first. "I've never even *known* a Puerto Rican."

His lyrics bore that out. In one draft, the characters fantasize, like the farmers and cowmen of Rodgers and Hammerstein's *Oklahoma!*, about statehood. "When we're a state in America, then we migrate to America!" they sing excitedly in broken English. Of course, Puerto Ricans were already citizens with the right to move anywhere in the country they chose. And, the commonwealth constitution having just passed, statehood was a dim prospect.

Sondheim cut those verses but left in a portrait of island life, offered in the song "America," that managed to capture nearly every stereotype about Puerto Rico. Puerto Rico was, in the song, an "ugly island" of "tropic diseases," with "hurricanes blowing" and its "population growing."

Before *West Side Story* premiered, the editors of *La Prensa*, a Puerto Rican paper in New York, called the show's producers to object to the portrayal of Puerto Rico as disease-ridden. They threatened to picket if the song wasn't altered. Sondheim conceded, later, that their complaint was justified. But he changed nothing.

"I wasn't about to sacrifice a line that sets the tone for the whole lyric," he sniffed.

West Side Story was phenomenally popular; it's had some forty thousand productions since 1957. In 1961 the producers turned it into an equally popular film (with the controversial verse modified), which won ten Academy Awards, including for best picture. It quickly became, as it remains today, the first point of reference for mainlanders thinking about Puerto Rico. And yet, however sympathetically it portrayed young Puerto Ricans in New York, it offered little hint of the island's place within the U.S. Empire or of the political tumult of the 1950s. Whatever ailed the Sharks, it wasn't colonialism.

Oddly, this wasn't the only time Stephen Sondheim would dodge Puerto Rican politics. His 1990 musical, *Assassins*, told the story of nine assassins or would-be assassins of U.S. presidents, from John Wilkes Booth to John Hinckley. But it didn't include Oscar Collazo or Griselio Torresola. Because their motives were political, Sondheim explained, they were "less complex psychologically" than the other assassins. And so Sondheim ended up writing one Broadway musical about New York Puerto Ricans in the fifties and another about presidential assassins—without ever mentioning the New York Puerto Ricans in the fifties who tried to assassinate the president.

Still, he got one thing right. As Sondheim put it, indelibly, in *West Side Story*: "Nobody knows in America, Puerto Rico's in America."

16

SYNTHETICA

By 1960, the U.S. Empire had visibly diminished. The Philippines was independent, Hawai'i and Alaska were states, and Puerto Rico had the nebulous status of "commonwealth." The remaining colonies were small: Guam, the U.S. Virgin Islands, American Samoa—total population 123,151—plus another 70,724 living in the United Nations' "strategic trust territory" in Micronesia under U.S. supervision.

Yet the United States is a restless country, and it didn't take long for new prospects to present themselves. In 1962 President John F. Kennedy called for a mission to the moon. It was, he said, a "new frontier."

Talk of frontiers was a throwback to the nineteenth century, but it made a certain sense. The prospect of claiming the moon—huge, uninhabited, strategically useful, and rich in minerals—is precisely the sort of thing that would have made the world conquerors of old salivate. "I would annex the planets if I could," the British arch-imperialist Cecil Rhodes once mused. "I often think of that."

Lunar colonization was a distant dream in Rhodes's day and even seems far-fetched now, but at the time, it appeared graspable. One has to keep in mind the wrenching technological innovations that the leaders of the United States had already witnessed in their lifetime. Dwight Eisenhower was born into a world containing only a countable handful of cars, a world where lightbulbs were still a novelty. Yet he lived to see computers, nuclear bombs, supersonic jets, and manned spacecraft. Who was to say that the science-fiction tales of settling distant planets were fantasies? A few years after the moon landing, NASA convened a study group on space colonization, which judged it to be both "technically feasible" and "desirable."

And yet the United States didn't annex the moon. It didn't even try. Instead, it went to extraordinary lengths to assure the world that the Apollo program was *not* about expansion or empire. President Lyndon Johnson signed the Outer Space Treaty in 1967, agreeing that no nation could claim sovereignty in space. Then, once it seemed likely that the Apollo missions would succeed, NASA appointed a Committee on Symbolic Activities for the First Lunar Landing and tasked it with ensuring that no one would confuse the moon landing for a landgrab. The committee seriously considered planting the United Nations flag instead of the U.S. one, or perhaps small flags for every country.

In the end, Congress insisted on the U.S. flag. But it issued a declaration explaining that this was simply "a symbolic gesture of national pride" and "not to be construed as a declaration of national appropriation."

The plaque the astronauts left captured that internationalist spirit. "Here men from the planet Earth first set foot upon the moon July 1969, A.D." read the text, under pictures of the hemispheres of the globe. "We came in peace for all mankind."

★

What had happened? How could a country that had once launched wars for foreign lands be so blasé about the largest clump of territory ever to become available? Where had its imperialist spirit gone?

Part of the answer, of course, is the fierce resistance put up by the colonized peoples of the world. They had turned empire into an exhausting and occasionally bloody affair. Whereas colonizers in the nineteenth century had annexed territory with pride, by the 1960s they understood that forthright imperialism risked infuriating the increasingly powerful Third World. By then, even taking the uninhabited moon seemed as if it might kick up trouble.

But the exhaustion of colonialism can't be explained solely by the new balance of forces. Yes, opponents of empire grew stronger after World War II, but so did would-be imperialists. The United States ended that war with a formidable air force, atomic weaponry, and a globe-spanning network of military bases. Its defeat of Japan showed what this firepower could do. Had it truly wished, the United States could have visited the same fate upon its Cold War adversaries in Vietnam and Korea. But it didn't, nor did it even *try* to annex those countries. The newfound power of the Third World peoples cannot alone account for that.

It may help to look at the decline of colonialism from a different angle, focusing not just on supply but on demand as well. The worldwide anti-imperialist revolt drove the cost of colonies up. Yet at the same time, new technologies gave powerful countries ways to enjoy the benefits of empire without claiming populated territories. In doing so, they drove the demand for colonies down.

The "empire-killing technologies" ranged from skywave radio to screw threads, and they worked in different ways. But, collectively, they weaned the United States off colonies. In so doing, they also helped to create the world we know today, where powerful countries project their influence through globalization rather than colonization.

★

In the nineteenth century, there were many reasons why major powers took colonies. Ideologies of "civilization," the international competition for prestige, dark psychosexual urges—these were all present in the tangled business of empire. But by the mid-twentieth century, talk of uplifting savages or carrying Christ to heathen lands had subsided, and starker motives shone through more clearly. Colonies were useful for their produce, and they were useful strategically.

Often, those two motives blended together. Complex industrial societies depended on goods that they couldn't mine or grow at home. But it wasn't just that they needed those goods, they needed *secure* access to them, the kind that couldn't be denied even if war broke out. And if they couldn't get it? Germany had crashed headfirst into that problem during World War I, when its enemies locked it out of South American markets. South America was where the all-important nitrates came from, used to make fertilizer and explosives. Germany found itself in the extremely uncomfortable position of fighting a two-front war without access to either Peru's guano or Chile's sodium nitrates. It was only Fritz Haber's timely invention of ammonia synthesis that kept Germany fighting for four years.

Haber had solved the nitrate problem, but there were many other raw materials that advanced economies required, including petroleum, iron, coal, indigo, tin, copper, sisal, cotton, kapok, silk, quinine, tungsten, bauxite, and palm oil. The United States, with its massive mainland stretching across multiple climatic zones, was blessed with an abundant crop of internal raw materials. But it, too, was dependent. It relied most visibly on rubber, which grew only five to ten degrees from the equator, and which it got mainly by dint of its friendly relations with European empires.

Rubber was a colonial product par excellence. In the late nineteenth century, King Leopold II of Belgium had claimed a vast colony in the Congo and established a brutal regime bent on rubber extraction, one that brought the population down by some ten million. The French, British, and Dutch, for their parts, had set up rubber plantations in their Southeast Asian colonies.

These were profitable ventures, especially as rubber insinuated itself into every nook and cranny of the industrial economy. Tires, tubes, hoses, insulation for electrical wires, raincoats, life rafts, gas masks, and a thousand little parts and bits were made from it. Between 1860 and 1920, world rubber consumption grew nearly two-hundred-fold.

In the auto-mad United States, rubber thirst was unslakable. By the eve of the Second World War, the country consumed some 70 percent of the world's supply, bought mostly from Europe's Asian colonies. If war came, the United States would need still more. A Sherman tank used half a ton of rubber, a heavy bomber used a full ton, and a battleship used more than twenty thousand rubber parts, totaling eighty tons. As the president of the tire manufacturer B. F. Goodrich warned, without rubber the United States "could offer only 1860 defenses against 1942 attacks."

Without rubber—it wasn't a hypothetical scenario. On December 7/8, 1941, Japan, worried about its own access to rubber and other critical raw materials, expanded its war beyond China and moved on to the resource-rich lands of Southeast Asia. Within months, it conquered the European colonies that accounted for 97 percent of the U.S. rubber supply. The United States and its allies were virtually cut off.

It is hard to convey how dire a threat this was. "If a survey were made to determine the most frequently asked question in America today, it would probably turn out to be: 'When are we going to get rubber—and how much?'" wrote the secretary of the interior in mid-1942. "We *must* get rubber—lots of it—and get it rather quickly, or our whole manner of living will be sadly awry."

A high-profile governmental report found the situation "so dangerous that unless corrective measures are taken immediately this country will face both a military and civilian collapse." A military and civilian *collapse*? Franklin Delano Roosevelt agreed, adding that in the short time since the report had been issued, "the situation has become more acute."

The government scrambled to plug the gap. FDR begged citizens to turn over to the government "every bit of rubber you can possibly spare": old tires, raincoats, garden hoses, shoes, bathing caps, gloves. The president's Scottish Terrier, Fala, donated his rubber bones. Eventually nearly seven pounds of scrap rubber were collected for every man, woman, and child in the country.

It wasn't nearly enough. The government pressed engineers to explore substitutes. Could cars roll on wooden wheels? Steel wheels? No, they couldn't.

Foreign markets might yield some rubber, and the State Department negotiated agreements with some twenty countries, mostly in Latin America. Yet the wild rubber secured from these was scant, and newly planted rubber trees would take at least six years to start producing.

Could rubber be extracted from some other plant? Thousands of scientists and technicians were hastily recruited to try—it was like the Manhattan Project for botany—but without success.

To conserve what little rubber remained, the government forbade its use in many forms of manufacturing. A national speed limit of thirty-five miles per hour was imposed to reduce the wear on the mainland's tires. In June 1942 Roosevelt warned that confiscating civilian tires was a real possibility, perhaps an inevitability. A high-ranking official confided to a journalist that soon there might not be enough rubber for baby bottles. Another proposed reducing the length of condoms by half. It took his colleagues a moment to realize he was joking.

There was another way out, a Fritz Haber–style solution. Perhaps the United States could find a way to manufacture rubber, to synthesize it from oil or grain alcohol. Yet this, too, seemed unpromising. On the eve of the war, an economist for the Council on Foreign Relations judged that replacing critical raw materials—rubber and others—with synthetic substitutes was simply "not in sight."

Synthetic rubber was possible in theory, but it was more of a laboratory curiosity than a viable commodity. No U.S. author had ever published a book on rubber synthesis, and the small trickle of man-made rubber that chemists had produced before the war was useful only in highly specialized functions. The idea of conjuring up an entire industry, reliant on as yet unachieved technical breakthroughs, able to supply enough usable rubber to equip the United States *and* its allies in a global war—that remained far-fetched.

As the director the War Production Board's Civilian Supply Division told the Senate, producing the requisite six hundred thousand tons by 1944 would "require a miracle."

★

The United States wasn't the only country facing a rubber drought. Germany had the same problem. As a major industrial power whose colonies had been confiscated after the First World War, Germany depended profoundly on foreign markets for crucial raw materials. It held coal and wood in relative abundance, but when it came to rubber, oil, iron, and many other necessaries, it was, like Japan, a "have-not" nation.

Adolf Hitler was obsessed with this. He'd lived through the First World War, when the British blockade cut Germany off and pushed it to near starvation. Germans had been reduced to using ineffective tires made of metal springs. This must never happen again. "The definitive solution," Hitler believed, lay in "an extension of our living space, that is, an extension of the raw materials and food basis of our nation." It was this quest for "living space," *Lebensraum*, that impelled Hitler to invade neighboring lands and incorporate them into Greater Germany.

War was a dangerous gamble. Yet Hitler had one important weapon in his arsenal: the most advanced chemical industry in the world. Germany's perpetual dearth of raw materials had spurred its chemists to great heights over the years. It wasn't an accident that Fritz Haber had been a German. In the late nineteenth century, Germans had devised synthetic dyes to replace natural plants such as indigo. In World War I they had invented synthetic nitrates and poison gases. In the Weimar period they'd come out with rayon, an artificial silk made from wood pulp that alleviated dependence on trade with Asia (Marlene Dietrich proclaimed proudly that she wore only rayon stockings). By the time Hitler came to power, the

German chemical manufacturer IG Farben was Europe's largest private corporation.

Hitler saw in IG Farben a way to bridge the resource gap just long enough to allow Germany to claim new territories. Not only could the firm make nitrates from air, it could turn coal into fuel and, Hitler hoped, rubber. The Reich's Four Year Plan, inaugurated in 1936, plowed a substantial fraction of the economy into IG Farben and its development of synthetics. Hitler ordered that German tires be made exclusively of artificial rubber by 1939. At a rally at Nuremberg that year, he announced triumphantly that Germany had "definitely solved the rubber problem!" Soon after, he invaded Poland.

But Hitler had not solved the rubber problem. When the war started, Germany's production and stockpiles sufficed for only two months of fighting. Throughout the war, the Wehrmacht was perpetually short of fuel and rubber. Hitler relied on risky blitzkrieg tactics—sudden all-or-nothing attacks—in part because he simply couldn't confront his enemies in sustained combat. His troops moved largely using horses.

Desperate for more rubber, the Reich ordered IG Farben to build a new plant in the east, where it would be safe from Allied bombardment. Ultimately, this would be the single largest expenditure in the Four Year Plan. The company chose a promising site in Upper Silesia, a railway hub close to supplies of coal, lime, and water, just outside the town of Auschwitz. To build the plant, the Reich expanded a transit camp, previously used to hold Polish prisoners pending their deportation farther east, into a massive, lethal *Arbeitslager*.

The Jewish chemist Primo Levi, who would go on to write one of the most haunting survivor's accounts of the Holocaust, was an inmate at Auschwitz. He remembered the "brightly illuminated" sign outside the plant: ARBEIT MACHT FREI, "work makes one free" (it "still strikes me in my dreams," he wrote). Levi toiled in the unforgiving Polish mud to build IG Farben's plant. As it started to produce methanol and other supplies, he was moved to the laboratory.

The new work assignment saved Levi's life by protecting him from the worst of the bitter winter of 1944–45. Others weren't so lucky. In all, at least thirty thousand inmates died building the plant. Yet this forced march did nothing to improve Hitler's rubber prospects. By the end of the war, the plant still hadn't squeezed out a single pound of synthetic rubber.

★

Things went quite differently in the United States. The director of the U.S. rubber program was instructed to "be a son-of-a-bitch," but that meant standing up to oil executives, not driving tens of thousands of enslaved laborers to their deaths.

Difference two: the U.S. program worked. There was no "eureka" moment when the secret to rubber synthesis was revealed. It was the result of a thousand little discoveries made by a small army of well-funded industrial chemists. Those scientists remembered it as a golden age, when men who had formerly labored as rivals in different companies could collaborate with a shared sense of purpose. "I don't think I have ever seen as congenial a group of people work together," said one.

The industrial achievements were as impressive as the scientific ones. By the end of the war, the government had built fifty-one synthetic rubber plants (compared with Germany's three), operating at the collective cost of $2 million a day. Just one such plant, which might employ 1,250 workers, made enough rubber to replace a rubber plantation that had twenty-four million trees and a workforce of at least 90,000. In mid-1944 the supply of rubber met the government's requirements. By 1945, it overshot them. At that point, the plants, not even operating at capacity, were pumping out eight hundred thousand tons a year. That was one-third more than the amount that in 1942 had seemed as if it would require "a miracle."

Jeeps rode on synthetic rubber tires. Tanks rolled on synthetic rubber treads, and they rolled much farther than German panzers, whose inferior treads grew brittle and cracked in the cold. ("The Germans apparently had not controlled the distribution of styrene," one U.S. chemist clucked.) By the war's end, nearly nine in ten pounds of U.S. rubber were factory-made, mostly from oil. This was, wrote an awed observer, "one of the most remarkable industrial achievements of all time."

It was also a political achievement. After the war, the United States resumed buying natural rubber, which it used alongside man-made rubber, but never again would it depend on plantations. When the Korean War broke out in 1950, once again interfering with supply lines, rubber prices shot up, creating a minor shortage. Manufacturers simply opened their taps and flooded the market with synthetic rubber.

A worker at B. F. Goodrich showing that sheets of synthetic rubber (left) and natural rubber (right) are nearly identical except for their color

Rubber—once the cause of war, colonization, and mass death—became a commodity that Washington could be cavalier about. In 1952 a blue-ribbon commission convened to assess U.S. raw material needs concluded that rubber shortages could no longer pose a serious threat to national security.

Natural rubber, coming mainly from Indonesia, Thailand, and Malaysia, still makes up about 30 percent of the market. Yet it's no longer a vital necessity, the sort worth conquering territory to secure. When the supply drops, synthetic rubber plants make up the difference with ease. One such factory is the one outside Auschwitz, which survived the war and is today the third-largest European source of synthetic rubber. That single plant in Poland has the capacity to satisfy 5 percent of the world demand for rubber.

★

The replacement of colonial rubber with synthetic rubber was a sort of magic. Yet it wasn't the only rabbit that chemists yanked from their hats. What's extraordinary is how many raw materials the United States weaned itself off during the war. Silk, hemp, jute, camphor, cotton, wool, pyrethrum, gutta-percha, tin, copper, tung oil—for one after another, the United States found synthetic substitutes. Throughout its economy, it replaced colonies with chemistry.

No synthetic illustrates this better than plastic. Today it has become so ubiquitous that it's hard to imagine a world without it. A few years ago, the writer Susan Freinkel resolved to go a day without touching anything plastic. Yet, upon waking, she realized that her task was impossible. Her mattress, alarm clock, glasses, toilet seat, light switch, toothbrush, underwear, clothes, shoes, and refrigerator were all made with plastic. The composition book and pencil she'd planned to use to record her experiment were part plastic. She declared defeat and decided instead to write down every object she touched during the day.

Nearly two-thirds were plastic.

Plastic is a chemical cousin of synthetic rubber—the ontological line between them can get blurry. Their histories are similar, too, though unlike synthetic rubber, plastic had notable successes well before the Second World War. The first plastic, celluloid, was devised to replace ivory in billiard balls and then made its way into other household goods: combs, knife handles, dentures, and so on. Another, Bakelite, was proudly billed during the interwar period as the "material of a thousand uses." DuPont caused a sensation with its debut of nylon stockings in 1939 ("Better Things for Better Living . . . Through Chemistry"). In 1940 Henry Ford unveiled a plastic car, made principally of soybean-based resin.

Ford's car failed to stir the passions nylon stockings had, but it illustrated the boundless possibilities that entrepreneurs saw in plastic. In 1940, *Fortune* magazine hinted at the plastic future to come when it published a map of "Synthetica," a "new continent of plastics," with such countries as "Vinyl," "Acrylic Styrene," and "Nylon Island." It was a further frontier, though chemical rather than colonial.

Much of this still lay in the realm of fantasy when that map was published. It took the war to make the plastic economy real. The calculus was the same as for rubber. The Axis powers, Japan in particular, had cut the United States off from vital supplies. So the military sought to use plastic, made mostly from oil, as a substitute for any "strategic" material that could no longer be easily got. As much as it could, the war effort should run on plastic.

As they had with rubber, chemists started sprinting. They pooled

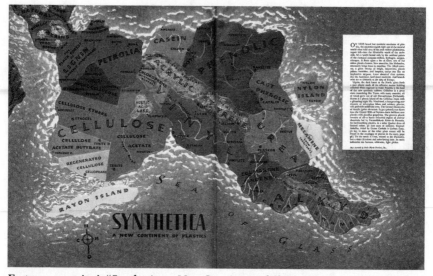

Fortune magazine's "Synthetica, a New Continent of Plastics" imagines the development of plastics as the colonization of a new world, an "illimitable world of the molecule."

information, honed techniques, and experimented wildly. Synthetic rubber had substituted for one big thing. For plastic, they found countless little applications. As plexiglass, it could be the cockpit window of a plane. As cellophane, it could replace a tin can in food storage. Mixed with wood fiber as plywood, plastic could substitute for timber and steel in small boats, making them lighter, faster, and cheaper. Mixed with glass as fiberglass, it could be used to make planes.

In a large battleship like the USS *Missouri*, plastics played more than a thousand roles.

By 1945, a GI could expect his canteen, his knife handle, and parts of his pistol belt to be plastic. His buttons would be olive drab plastic—a substitution that saved the army more than sixty thousand tons of brass a year. If he received a decoration ribbon, it would be of nylon, not silk. So would his parachute, his tent, and, if he had to do any climbing, his rope (formerly made of Manila hemp, but the Japanese had taken the Philippines). His razor handle, bugle, comb, toothbrush, gas mask, goggles, helmet liner, boot insoles, rifle cover, whistle, shoelaces, mosquito netting, breakfast tray, and—if he was a betting man—poker chips were all plastic.

A soldier wounded in battle might receive nylon surgical sutures covered with nylon or rayon gauze (and recuperate on a hospital bed with sheets made not of rubber but of plastic-impregnated rayon). One who lost an eye would get a new plastic one rather than one made of cryolite glass, which could no longer be imported from Germany.

In a vividly metaphorical development, toy soldiers, formerly made of lead or tin, started selling after the war as "little green men" made entirely of molded plastic.

Those little green men were just the start—shock troops in a full-scale economic invasion. At the war's end, one plastics executive remarked, "virtually nothing" in the civilian economy was made of plastic, yet it was clear that "anything could be." And so the military technologies flooded into society at large. Swords were beaten into plowshares but, as an ad in *Modern Plastics* noted, the new plows had plastic handles.

It is striking, in fact, how many of the icons of the postwar consumer culture were wrought of plastic: Tupperware, Velcro, hula hoops, Frisbees, Barbie dolls, GI Joes, Bic pens, credit cards, pink flamingo lawn ornaments, Styrofoam, Formica counters, Naugahyde chairs, Saran wrap, vinyl records, hi-fis, linoleum floors, Silly Putty, Lycra bras, and Wiffle balls.

"The whole world can be plasticized," observed the French philosopher Roland Barthes with evident alarm.

Plastic seeped into the economy in less visible ways, too. Natural fibers such as cotton, wool, and silk were increasingly replaced by nylon or polyester. Midway through the Korean War, the military switched to synthetic blends for its uniforms. Around the same time, the government ordered that all flags flying over public buildings be made of nylon.

It went even deeper. Contact lenses, hearing aids, prosthetics, artificial joints, and intrauterine devices turned postwar consumers into part-plastic cyborgs. In 1952, surgeons started installing artificial aortic valves in patients, so their hearts beat with the help of plastic.

Between 1930 and 1950, the volume of plastics produced annually in the world grew fortyfold. By 2000, it had grown to nearly three thousand times its 1930 size.

★

This was the legacy of the Second World War. Take the world's most advanced economy, cut it off from most tropical trade, and send it into overdrive—it was the perfect recipe for a synthetic revolution.

The replacements came regularly and rapidly. A writer in 1943 giddily described "a regiment of new man-made materials" that was "turning old industries topsy-turvy." The antimalarial drug quinine could be replaced by a synthetic called chloroquine, the opium-derived painkiller morphine by one called methadone. Camphor, a key ingredient in medicines, photographic film, and explosives, came only from Japanese-controlled Taiwan. That is, it did until chemists figured out how to synthesize it from turpentine at one-eighth the cost. When the rubber shortage prevented making liquid incendiaries from rubber and gasoline, a chemist invented napalm.

Whatever the military wanted, remarked an employee of Union Carbide, it got "as simply as turning on the faucet to draw water."

This was the start, the chemist Jacob Rosin predicted, of the "synthetic age." It would bring "freedom from the plant" and "freedom from the mine." In other words, as the laboratory replaced the land as the source of materials, the United States would liberate itself from natural resource constraints. In 1959 the physicist Richard Feynman bragged that the time was soon coming when scientists would know "how to synthesize absolutely anything."

Synthesizing *anything*—that was a lot to ask for. But it wasn't absurd. Two years before Feynman's prediction, in 1957, the chemical company Monsanto had installed the "House of the Future," made entirely from synthetics, at Tomorrowland in Disneyland. By that year, in the United States, synthetic rubber outsold natural rubber, plastic had displaced leather, and margarine was more common than butter. And Gregory Pincus had just begun his birth control experiments with synthetic hormones in Puerto Rico.

★

Synthetics visibly remade everyday life. They also, less visibly, remade geopolitics.

There was little sense, before the Second World War, that they might do this. Geopolitical treatises from the 1930s didn't say much about synthetics. Instead, they moaned about shortages and predicted bloody wars for territory.

By that 1930s logic, the United States should have consolidated its victory in the Second World War by locking down resource-rich territories. In fact, there was some talk of this during the war. War planners recognized that the quest for resources had both triggered the war and deprived the United States of vital raw materials. As a result, they sought ways to prevent that from happening again.

The most popular plan within the State Department in the early years of the war was to place the world's colonies under international management. This was a touch more enlightened than old-school conquest, but the end-state was much the same. Powerful countries would, through some international body, ensure their access to the tropics. It was colonization by committee.

But that vision was never realized. The United States neither claimed new colonies nor organized the joint colonization of the tropics. Instead, synthetics dulled its hunger pangs.

One can see the realization dawning in successive U.S. official reports. An important survey in 1952 warned that scarcities may loom in the future but noted that synthetics had thus far kept them at bay ("We can produce gasoline from coal, cattle feed from sawdust, and commercial power from atomic fission"). The reports that followed spoke even less of scarcity and more of synthetics. By the 1970s, a large survey concluded that resource exhaustion was simply "not a serious possibility." Yes, there might be temporary shortages and the occasional uncomfortable price fluctuation, but the idea that the United States would actually run out of something it needed no longer seemed plausible.

U Thant, the Burmese politician who served as secretary-general of the United Nations in the 1960s, was stunned. "The truth, the central stupendous truth, about developed economies is that they can have—in anything but the shortest run—the kind and scale of resources they *decide* to have," he marveled. "It is no longer resources that limit decisions. It is the decisions that make the resources. This is the fundamental, revolutionary change—perhaps the most revolutionary mankind has ever known."

Thant was exactly right. The synthetic revolution that began in the 1940s had rewritten the rules of geopolitics. Secure access to raw materials—one of the chief benefits of colonization—no longer *mattered* that much. One could procure the necessary goods through trade, and if, as in the thirties and forties, the markets closed down, well, that wasn't the end of the world. It was just time to fire up the synthetic rubber plants.

Industrial economies got so good at inventing substitutes that the suppliers of raw materials panicked. Places that had once been the objects of imperial lust now scrambled to find buyers. Such was the effect of synthetic rubber on the economies of Malaya and Borneo, synthetic antimalarials on the quinine-producing plantations of Latin America, synthetic cordage on the Philippines, Mylar film on the Indian mica industry, synthetic quartz on Brazil, and synthetic diamond bort on the diamond mines of the Congo, Brazil, and South Africa. After World War II, the United States government adopted a policy of buying more natural rubber than it needed, to prop up the imperiled plantations of Southeast Asia. Still, the relative cost of extractive goods fell year by year.

None of this is to say that raw materials became irrelevant. Minerals were harder to synthesize than plants, and military planners kept a wary eye on the global stocks of bauxite, uranium, and cobalt (essential now to smartphone batteries). But the sense of urgency had diminished enough for those commodities to be safely sourced through international trade rather than colonial extraction. That's because national security no longer hung on raw materials. In fact, when Richard Nixon formed a commission to develop a "national materials policy" for the 1970s, the resulting report didn't even *mention* security as a goal.

There was, of course, one exception: oil. Many of the chemistry-for-colonies exchanges the United States made, including synthetic rubber and plastic, involved substituting petroleum for other materials. In 1945, when 59 percent of the world's proven oil reserves lay within U.S. borders, this gave the United States an extraordinary measure of self-sufficiency. But as those reserves got used and large ones opened in other countries, oil became increasingly foreign in provenance.

It is fitting, then, that oil is the one raw material that has most reliably tempted politicians back into the old logic of empire. When faced with an Arab oil embargo, Henry Kissinger suggested that the United States "may have to take some oil fields." "I'm not saying we have to take over Saudi Arabia," the secretary of state continued. "How about Abu Dhabi, or Libya?" It is hard to imagine Kissinger embarking on such unbounded flights of imperialist reverie on behalf of rubber, tin, or any other former colonial commodity.

Still, even when it comes to oil, flare-ups of naked imperialism have been rare and haven't ultimately led to annexations. Kissinger's idea of a U.S. overseas territory of Abu Dhabi was a daydream, not a plan (though it does appear that the Nixon administration was serious about seizing Middle Eastern oil fields if necessary). And, however painful the 1970s oil shock was for the U.S. economy, its danger was a matter of rising prices rather than of absolute, "we can't fight a war" shortages. At no point in the twentieth century was there a serious possibility that oil would actually run out. Today, with new technologies enabling the exploitation of Canadian tar sands and the partial substitution of natural gas for oil, that danger seems as remote as ever.

★

In 1969 the United States achieved what was probably its most technically difficult goal since the Second World War: the moon landing. The most powerful rocket engines in history had to blast the spacecraft into the sky, where the whole thing would progressively dismantle itself mid-flight, shooting a smaller module safely into the lunar gravity well. There is a reason that "rocket science" became the proverbial way to refer to the hardest intellectual challenges out there.

Yet it wasn't all jets and orbits. The moon landing was a triumph of chemical engineering, too. NASA needed light materials that could endure extreme temperatures and micrometeoroid strikes, yet keep pressurized air in. This meant synthetics. The moon suits that Neil Armstrong and Buzz Aldrin wore had twenty-one layers, and twenty either contained or were made entirely of materials manufactured by DuPont. There were familiar inventions—nylon, neoprene, Mylar, and Teflon—and new ones such as Kapton and Nomex. What was harder to find up in space was anything that might once have grown in a colony.

Raw materials just weren't as important as they'd once been. The fifty-star flag that the astronauts planted, marking humankind's highest ambition, was sewn of DuPont nylon.

17

THIS IS WHAT
GOD HATH WROUGHT

In August 1941 the army and navy set out on their first-ever large-scale joint exercise. With war very likely coming, they anticipated having to take foreign beaches under fire. And so, the thought was, they'd practice by invading North Carolina. The men would make an amphibious landing, leaping from ship to shore and carrying their gear and supplies with them.

It seemed straightforward, yet it proved to be anything but. The disembarking troops got tangled up with one another. Men with heavy packs struggled to stand in the water. Tanks hit the soft ground and sank. The ammunition got soaked, as did cardboard boxes of rations, which promptly disintegrated. Cans of vegetable hash and meat stew piled up chaotically on the beach, their boxes broken, their contents no longer identifiable. The equipment that made it ashore then began to rust, as the lubricant—stored deep in the holds of the ships—could not easily be found.

The army's official history allowed that the exercise was "a depressing experience." The men came up with their own way to refer to this sort of logistical face-plant, an acronym they would use frequently during the war: *snafu*. As in, Situation Normal: All Fucked Up.

And that was at midday, under no enemy fire, in calm waters not too far from Myrtle Beach.

★

What those waterlogged troops discovered that afternoon was an age-old truth, one that had governed history up to that point: moving things is *hard*.

It's a point easily forgotten today, when people, objects, and ideas glide easily across the planet's surface. Now markets scamper across borders, planes land anywhere, and communications satellites connect the most seemingly distant places.

But all that is relatively new, an artifact of post–World War II globalization. That globalization, in turn, depended on key technologies devised or perfected by the U.S. military during the Second World War. These were, like synthetics, empire-killing technologies, in that they helped render colonies unnecessary. They did so by making movement easier without direct territorial control.

To appreciate how transformative these technologies were, it's necessary to go back a bit, to fifty years before the Second World War—a time marked not by effortless motion, but by abrasive friction. When Commodore Dewey attacked the Spanish at Manila Bay in 1898, he cut a crucial telegraph cable, and it took a full week for the mainland to learn of his triumph in battle (MANILA PROBABLY OURS was the uncertain headline of one paper). Regular cable contact didn't resume for three months.

After Dewey's victory, Teddy Roosevelt eagerly assembled the Rough Riders to storm Cuba. But they got stuck in Tampa, a port clogged with what Roosevelt called a "swarming ant-heap of humanity," as they waited for transport. The logjam was so great that the enlisted men had to leave their horses behind and take Cuba on foot.

The USS *Oregon* could have helped, and indeed it was dispatched from Seattle. But Seattle to Florida was a two-month journey, requiring the ship to go down the Pacific coast of South America, around Tierra del Fuego, and back up through the Gulf of Mexico.

Had they known what awaited them, Roosevelt's troops might have been happy to wait. Once in Cuba, they suffered mightily from yellow fever, malaria, and diarrhea. Roosevelt wrote a frantic letter to his commander, warning that the fearless Rough Riders were "ripe for dying like rotten sheep" and must be sent home quickly to avoid an "appalling disaster" that might kill "over half the army."

It was a known bug: humans didn't travel well. Take them from one part of the planet to another and their typical response was to get sick and fall down.

Things didn't travel well, either. In 1901, with Manila firmly under white control, General Arthur MacArthur staged a lavish reception in the Philippines for the upper crust of colonial society. The men decided to wear their best frock coats and silk hats. But clothing designed for temperate climates, they discovered, fares poorly in the tropics. The hats had warped, lost their sheen, become sticky, and started to emit a strange odor. Pests had chewed holes in the hat of the secretary of finance and justice. He wore it anyway, though, as he had no means of getting another.

And why not wear it? Many of the early U.S. colonial buildings, made with Oregon pine and California redwood, were also riddled with holes and falling apart. "Decay" was basically the house style.

★

What this rotting empire needed was faster transportation. And that required seizing land. Captain Mahan had suggested opening a canal through the Central American isthmus, which divided the Atlantic and Pacific Oceans, and Roosevelt agreed. He tried to buy territory from Colombia, without luck. He tried threatening and got no further. Finally, concluding that bargaining with Colombia's leaders was liking trying to "nail currant jelly to a wall," Roosevelt threw his support behind rebels, who declared Panama's independence from Colombia. The newly established republic then leased to the United States a ten-mile-wide strip of land slicing through the middle of the country: the Panama Canal Zone.

Still, more territory, more problems—problems of precisely the moving-things-and-people variety. The hot and rainy neck of land throbbed with disease-bearing mosquitoes. Panamanians who had lived with those mosquitoes their whole lives had acquired immunity to yellow fever and resistance to malaria. Outsiders, however, were fresh bait. Of the first batch of U.S. mainlanders to arrive in the Panama Canal Zone, nearly all were immediately laid low by malaria. Later officials came bringing their caskets with them.

They weren't being paranoid. Yellow fever, malaria, chronic diarrhea, dysentery, pneumonia, and bubonic plague tore through the zone. "I shall never forget the train loads of dead men being carted away daily as if they were just so much lumber," remembered a carpenter. "There were days that we could only work a few hours because of the high fever racking our bodies—it was a living hell. Finally, typhoid fever got me."

If not typhoid, malaria, or—Jesus—the plague, then perhaps a venereal disease? It was too much to hope that a construction project involving tens of thousands of workers wouldn't also engender prostitution. The Panamanian cities bordering the zone were a "whirlpool of vice," a New York editor declared. Still, canal workers seemed all too happy to visit them, passing syphilis and gonorrhea to one another in the process.

Those fit to work faced other challenges. The area to be dug out was a "dark and gloomy jungle," one early arrival noted, "an apparently hopeless tangle of tropical vegetation, swamps whose bottoms the engineers had not discovered, black muddy soil, quicksands." The ruins of a previous French effort to dig a canal—abandoned equipment rusted, sunken into the earth, and covered in vines—served as an ominous warning.

The canal's managers understandably sought to escape from this morass by staying in Washington. But communication between Washington and Panama was limited to an expensive telegraphic trickle, making management from afar extremely difficult. Delays, pileups, and breakdowns ultimately provoked Roosevelt to fire the canal commission and install a new one willing to work from Panama.

The point here is that, to open a canal, the United States had to exert colonial control. In fact, it transformed the Panama Canal Zone into one of the most intensively governed spots on the planet. Brigades marched forth to cut brush, drain swamps, and put up screens. They fumigated buildings with pyrethrum, an insecticide made from the petals of chrysanthemums—at peak they imported more than 120 tons a month. To combat mosquitoes, which laid eggs in still water, the authorities made war on puddles. They filled or covered any indentation where water might accumulate. They even ordered the holy water in the font of the cathedral changed daily after finding mosquito larvae in it.

Venereal disease required a different treatment. Canal officials subsidized the arrival of mainland wives and, at great expense, established a smothering social milieu of clubhouses, associations, and organized leisure. Throw enough Bibles at the zone's residents, the theory went, and they'd stay out of Panamanian brothels. But just in case, zone authorities also pressed Panama's government to impose mandatory medical exams and, when necessary, forcibly hospitalize sex workers.

With disease at bay, canal workers turned to the canal with a fury. They blasted their way through mountain. They brought in powerful steam shovels able to haul out eight tons of earth in one scoop. Still, it was Sisyphean work, with the earth slipping regularly back into the cut (about one cubic yard slid back for every five dug). "Today you dig and tomorrow it slides" is how one worker put it. Indeed, a single landslide could reverse months of work, burying the expensive steam shovels in the process.

Altogether, opening the canal took ten years and cost nearly a third of a billion dollars—more if you count the cost of the landslides that perpetually closed the canal in its first years. As usual, records kept on the deaths of nonwhites were shoddy, but we think some fifteen thousand workers, mainly West Indian, died from accident or disease while on the job.

And all to tame a strip of land ten miles wide and not even fifty miles long.

★

The Panama Canal was a significant achievement. But next to the challenges posed by the Second World War, digging it was a gentle warm-up exercise. War planners faced what one dazed general called "ordnance requirements of a size beyond the bounds of imagination." For every soldier overseas, the United States would ship sixty-seven pounds of matériel abroad *per day*. And unlike in the First World War, where the United States shipped to fourteen ports in one theater, now it serviced more than a hundred ports in eleven theaters.

It's telling that before the war started, *logistics* had been a specialist's term, not much heard in general speech. The military academies exalted courage, leadership, and tactical acuity, not procurement and transportation. Yet, fairly soon into the Second World War, commanders grew accustomed to speaking of tonnage, inventory levels, and supply lines with the knowing reverence previously reserved for accounts of battlefield heroics.

What is more, they got good at it. During the war, the military devised a suite of logistical innovations, all designed to move people, things, and information cleanly and quickly around the planet. Planes were the most obvious—the United States came to dominate aviation—but others were no less important. Radio, cryptography, dehydrated food, penicillin, and DDT: these technologies laid the foundations of today's globalization.

The logistical innovations did more than speed everything up. They also enabled the United States to move through places without carefully preparing the ground first, as it had in Panama. No longer would seizing large areas or zones be necessary to run a long-distance transportation network. Mere dots on the map, sometimes little more than airfields in jungle clearings, would suffice. And so, just like plastic and other synthetics, these new technologies helped to make colonies obsolete.

★

For the United States, the war started quickly, with Japan's strikes on December 7/8 and its three-month spree of conquest. Then things slowed. With the Japanese Empire draped plumply across Southeast Asia and Micronesia, the Pacific, once a universe of boundless possibilities, had become a giant oceanic blockade.

The closure of the Pacific alarmed Douglas MacArthur, who had to defend Australia with only the dribble of supplies he could get through the southern part of the ocean. China, fighting Japan on the other side, faced even greater danger. The Chinese were painfully short on the weapons of modern war and, with the Pacific closed, they couldn't import what they needed.

For a while, some matériel could get to China from the other side, via the Burma Road, a twisting, 726-mile path through the mountains. It was largely unpaved and built almost wholly by hand (by half a million laborers), but FDR saw that modest road as a lifeline. He regarded it as "obviously of the utmost urgency" that "the pathway to China be kept open." Soon enough, however, the Japanese seized Burma, closing the road.

It was a classic geopolitical move—the enclosure of an adversary's territory. Japan was guarding China's front and back doors, preventing the Allies from aiding it by land or sea. Yet this timeworn strategy didn't account for aviation. The doors were locked, yes, but the Allies could still come in through the roof.

Planes weren't new. They'd been around in the First World War, and the daring of aviators then was the stuff of legend. But planes hadn't drastically affected that war's outcome. They were small, and there hadn't been that many of them.

The Second World War, it was clear from the start, would be different. When Hitler invaded Poland, his Luftwaffe had four thousand aircraft—a formidable threat that nearly broke Britain's defenses. The United States, in response, began to build its own air fleet, putting its full industrial muscle behind the effort. At peak, U.S. plants churned out more than one plane every four minutes—a Luftwaffe every eleven days.

Abundance in aircraft meant that the Allies could use them for more than combat. They could use them for nearly everything. Even long-distance supply lines, they realized, could be maintained by air.

A decade or two earlier, this would have been unthinkable. The planes, for one, had been too small. The biggest planes in operation in World War I had been the German *Riesenflugzeug* ("giant aircraft"), most notably the Siemens-Schuckert planes, the largest of which could hold two and a half tons—the Germans had built six during the war. But by the end of the Second World War, the United States had produced nearly four thousand B-29 Superfortresses, each of which could carry twenty tons.

As the planes got larger, their cargo shrank. Dehydration reduced eggs, milk, and even vegetables to small fractions of their weight and size. Engineers found ways to shrink vehicles, too. Bulky trucks were hard to haul by air. Truck *parts* were much easier, but that required having a factory at the destination to put the trucks together. The military developed the IKEA solution, "knocked-down shipping," which broke the vehicle down enough so it took up only a third of the space but could still be assembled at the other end by inexperienced men with simple tools. Such innovations—and there were a lot of them—crammed more and more stuff into the waiting aircraft.

The planes to aid China, with their shrunken cargo and enlarged holds, started south from Miami, flying a route called the "Fireball Express." They landed on the eastern edge of Puerto Rico, which, along with the Puerto Rican island of Vieques, had been turned into a giant military base. Then south to more bases on the eastern lobe of Brazil, from which they sped east toward Africa.

There is a small volcanic island called Ascension, situated in the mid-Atlantic between South America and West Africa. It is one of the most unappetizing landing spots on the map: jagged with rocks, waterless, and far from everything. "A crow would break his leg trying to land there," joked one visitor. Yet in early 1942 the U.S. Army engineers had arrived, and within three months they had blasted off the island's top and built a long landing strip, followed soon by barracks, a mess hall, and machine shops—everything needed to refresh the planes and send them onward.

From Ascension, the planes touched down on Africa's west coast and sped across the Sahara. Yet again, bases were needed, and yet again they appeared. Jenifer Van Vleck, a curator at the National Air and Space

Museum, has compiled a list of the types of buildings that went up on eighteen African air bases, which conveys the magnitude of the undertaking:

> Acetylene generator buildings, administration buildings, barber shops, battery shops, butcher shops, carpenter shops, cafeteria buildings, chemical laboratories, churches, classrooms, commissary storehouses, dining halls, dormitories, engine overhaul buildings, electric shops, fire equipment buildings, garages, guard houses, hospital, kitchens, lumber storage, link trainer, laundries, mechanical shops, medical inspection buildings, native barracks (with kitchens, laundries, toilets, and showers), oil storage, office buildings, paint shops, pump houses, power houses, pantries, police post, plumbing shops, radio shops and transmission receiving buildings, stockrooms, slaughter houses, shower buildings, staff buildings and quarters, toilet and locker rooms, warehouses, water towers and tanks, wells.

Some of these bases were deep inland, far from rivers or railroads—this was possible now with aviation. Maintaining them meant hauling tons of supplies for miles along desert trails. To provision one of the more remote bases with fuel, its commander hired out what one of his subordinates estimated to be "probably all the camels in North Africa" to carry gasoline in tins—a four-legged pipeline.

The Fireball Express pushed on to Cairo. It crossed India. Then came the final and most formidable challenge: the 550-mile jump across the Himalayan mountain range. The Himalayas had some of the worst weather in the world, including monsoons, thunderstorms, ice, severe turbulence, and violent downdrafts capable of sucking planes suddenly into the mountainside. Maps were vague, and pilots had to maintain radio silence while flying over enemy territory. They could navigate somewhat by the "aluminum trail," the hundreds of crashed planes that marked the route to China.

Regular flights over "the Hump," as the pilots called it, began in December 1942, landing in Kunming, China. This started as a cowboy operation—high-flying daredevils tempting fate. But as the traffic increased, it fell under the stern direction of General William H. Tunner.

Tunner's nickname, "Tonnage," bespoke his coolly logistical inclinations. He made charts and graphs showing the status of each plane. Under

A C-47 approaches Cairo.

his supervision the corridor between India and China turned into an aerial conveyor belt. The aircraft hauled tanks, trucks, and other heavy machinery along with food, fuel, and arms.

By the end of 1943, planes were touching down in Kunming once every eleven minutes. In a twenty-four-hour period in 1945, Tunner landed one every minute and twelve seconds.

"Roads, it would seem, are no longer essential to military operations" is how a writer summed up the lesson of the Hump. Certainly Japan's control of Burma had been inconvenient, but Tunner had proved that it wasn't fatal. After the Hump, he wrote, he "knew that we could fly anything anywhere anytime."

★

Anything anywhere anytime—this was a far cry from the world of just half a century earlier, when getting to Cuba from Florida was an ordeal. Planes not only added speed, they changed the laws of geopolitics. The surface of the earth, with its strongholds, impassable barriers, and fortified borders, looked different from a cockpit. Contiguous access no longer mattered so much. The old imperialist logic—men with white mustaches coloring in countries on the map—lost a great deal of its force.

In Europe, the Axis was defeated in a familiar war of fronts and flanks. The Soviets overran Germany from the east, the Anglophone powers came from the west, and they collectively wore Greater Germany down to a thin sliver. In the island-strewn Pacific, however, this new territory-defying logic was on vivid display.

It could be seen in the "island-hopping" strategy MacArthur and Nimitz used to storm the Pacific. Instead of fighting for contiguous areas, they overleapt Japanese strongholds and pressed onward. Aviation allowed this.

It also allowed the Allies to do something extraordinary: defeat Japan without setting foot on its main islands. Instead, using bases at Guam, Tinian, Saipan, Okinawa, and Iwo Jima, they laid waste to nearly seventy Japanese cities by air.

The planes delivered death rather than trucks, but otherwise it wasn't too different from the Hump. From a small collection of islands, the United States beat Japan into submission without invading.

The conquest of the Japanese main islands, accomplished entirely by aerial bombing

★

The transcendence of surface-hugging technologies in transportation had a direct analogue in communication. Since 1844, when Samuel Morse had tapped out the question WHAT HATH GOD WROUGHT in the world's first telegram, wires had been a vital instrument of politics. Cables crossed the seas, acting as the nervous systems of large empires. The British, champions of the cable game, had by the early twentieth century gained control of more than half the world's cables. They also, through Malaya, possessed the world's sole supply of the natural latex gutta-percha—the only material until plastic that could effectively insulate deep-sea submarine cables.

Yet mere preponderance wasn't enough. The British obsessed over acquiring an "all red" network, red being the color of the British Empire on the map. Such a network, passing only through British territory, would offer protection from foreign powers that might cut or tap Britain's cables.

Britain achieved its all-red network and, with it, invulnerability. Everyone else, meanwhile, learned the cost of *not* having a secure network. In the opening days of the First World War, Britain cut Germany's transatlantic cables—something it could easily do, as Germany did not control

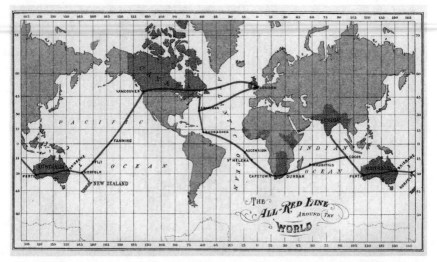

"The All-Red Line Around the World": The main routes of Britain's cable system, connecting its colonies and passing only through British territory (minus a short jaunt through northern Maine), completed in 1902

the territory around them. The Germans were then forced to use unreliable intermediaries to carry their messages, which opened them up to espionage. In 1917 the German foreign secretary Arthur Zimmermann sent a proposal to Mexico promising to help Mexico "reconquer the lost territory in Texas, New Mexico, and Arizona" in exchange for an alliance. But the British intercepted the message and shared it with Washington. The "Zimmermann Telegram," as it is now known, was crucial in drawing the United States into the war.

The United States had the fortune of fighting on the British side—i.e., the side with the cables. But it suffered the indignity of having to rely on its ally's network, which meant both waiting in queue while the British privileged their own messages and leaving itself open to British espionage. In 1917 the only U.S. telegraphic connection between the mainland and the Philippines overloaded and then broke, so that for months Washington had no direct link to its largest colony, or to Asia in general.

Such a feeble, incomplete network wouldn't suffice in World War II, which was, among other things, an information war. Billions of words would eventually flow overseas from the U.S. mainland—somewhere on the order of eight words transmitted for every Allied bullet fired. By D-Day, U.S. teleprinter traffic would reach eight million words a week.

The United States could have tried to handle this verbal barrage by building its own all-red network, but a truly secure planetary cable system required, as the British had shown, a globe-spanning colonial empire. Instead, the United States came to rely on another technology: radio.

Radio, like aviation, was a space-hopping technology. Two transceivers were all that was required—there was no need to control the land in between. Radio not only put far-off locales in contact with one another, it allowed for communication with ships, planes, trucks, tanks, submarines, and men in the field (via the new gee-whiz technology of the "walkie-talkie"). The thousands of disconnected bases the United States built all over the world couldn't have operated without it.

Of course, beaming messages through the air meant that anyone could hear. So the United States also invested heavily in encryption. Sixteen thousand cipher clerks worked encoding and decoding its communications during the war.

With encrypted radio, the United States could run a vast network with a small footprint. All it needed were a few spots, ideally in the equatorial zone, where high-frequency radio waves traveled most easily. Major stations at such places as Asmara, Karachi, New Delhi, Manila, and Honolulu sufficed to handle the greatest informational flood humanity had yet experienced.

"We have got our net in," boasted the chief of the Army Communications Service, "and it is the finest network in the world."

It *was* impressive. Though FDR traveled farther and more frequently than any of his predecessors, the Signal Corps kept him in unbroken contact with his Joint Chiefs of Staff and all field commanders, essentially running a mobile situation room at the president's elbow. At the Yalta Conference in Crimea, he consulted instantaneously with China, France, and Washington. On his return, the stunned president told Congress of the "modern miracle of communications."

Before the invasion of Normandy, George Marshall in Washington used a similar system to confer for more than an hour with Dwight Eisenhower in Europe, Douglas MacArthur in the Southwest Pacific, and John Deane in Moscow. The generals communicated by sending short typed messages, which appeared on a screen. In other words, they texted.

Half a year into the war, the United States figured out how to fax images wirelessly, a technology it used for maps, weather charts, and news photos. The famous Iwo Jima flag-raising photograph traveled by fax. Soon enough, the military was faxing images in color. A color photograph of Truman, Stalin, and Clement Attlee meeting at Potsdam traveled directly to Washington from Berlin.

On the centennial of Samuel Morse's 1844 WHAT HATH GOD WROUGHT message, which had traveled between Washington and Baltimore, the Signal Corps sent the same message around the world in three and a half minutes. Less than a year later, it sent another message around the globe in nine and a half *seconds*. It used only five wireless stations, each able to transmit for thousands of miles by reflecting radio waves off the ionosphere.

The message? THIS IS WHAT GOD HATH WROUGHT. It was signed ARMY COMMUNICATIONS SERVICE.

Half a year later, the Signal Corps started bouncing radio waves off the moon. It was the first use of outer space for communications—a portent of the satellite age to come.

★

Planes and radio meant that cargo and information could move swiftly from spot to spot, leaping over enemy territory if necessary. Yet could the cargo survive the haul? Human cargo was notoriously tricky in this regard, given humans' tendency to contract diseases whenever they moved long distances or en masse. Walt Whitman's characterization of war as "nine hundred and ninety parts diarrhoea to one part glory" was apt well into the twentieth century. World War I had killed about eight million in the various belligerents' militaries. But that was nothing compared with the pandemic of Spanish flu that the war unleashed, which killed somewhere between fifty million and one hundred million.

World War II looked as if it might be even worse. Its global expanse and surfeit of airplanes threatened to carry diseases rapidly around the planet, touching off pandemic after pandemic.

MacArthur's troops in the South Pacific were in this respect the proverbial canaries in the coal mine. Technically they were fighting the Japanese, but their far more serious enemy was malaria, which initially caused eight to ten times as many casualties as combat did. The lucky ones who dodged malaria had tropical sores, dengue fever, dysentery, and typhus to look forward to. One observer judged MacArthur's emaciated, sunken-eyed men in New Guinea to be "perhaps the most wretched-looking soldiers ever to wear the American uniform . . . There was hardly a soldier, among the thousands who went into the jungle, who did not come down with some kind of fever."

Malaria was especially nettlesome because the customary remedies were no longer available. More than 95 percent of the supply of quinine, the most effective antimalarial, had come from the cinchona plantations of the Dutch East Indies—now in Japanese hands. And the insecticide used to fumigate the Panama Canal Zone, pyrethrum, had come principally from Japan.

It was the rubber problem all over again, and scientists raced to solve it. Dozens of university laboratories screened more than fourteen thousand compounds in search of a synthetic antimalarial. Prisoners and conscientious objectors were brought in as guinea pigs.

Two compounds worked well: atabrine and chloroquine. Atabrine turned the skin an alarming shade of yellow and disturbed the gastrointestinal tract, but it brought down malaria rates considerably. Chloroquine, which debuted at the end of the war, worked even better. Together, the synthetic drugs not only replaced quinine, they surpassed it.

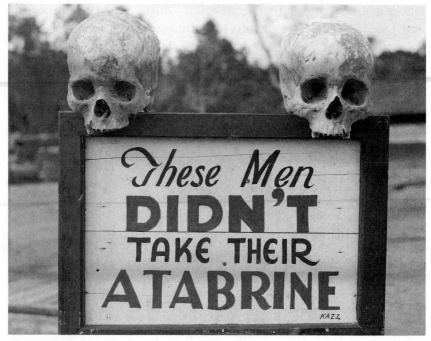

Sign at army hospital in Port Moresby, Papua New Guinea

The most impressive synthetic countermeasure wasn't a drug, but an insecticide. Dichlorodiphenyltrichloroethane, known by the mercifully short acronym DDT, had been developed shortly before the war in a Swiss lab, but it was the U.S. military that started mass-producing it. It seemed miraculous: cheap, easy to apply, easy to ship, and astonishingly persistent—a single application lasted months. Better still, it worked against all sorts of bugs, not only mosquitoes but lice, crop-munching beetles, and other pests.

Insect control in the days of the Panama Canal had been an arduous, artisanal process, requiring workers to fumigate every house and interrogate every puddle. DDT, by contrast, could be sprayed by planes—Skeeter Beaters, they were called. Whole Pacific islands were blanketed by DDT in advance of landings, destroying the main vectors of disease before the first men hit the beaches.

A naval medical officer who watched the Skeeter Beaters work their magic in the Pacific theater described the scene, noting with awe the "complete destruction of plant and animal life" DDT could cause. On Saipan, he wrote, "scarcely a living thing" remained after the planes had made their passes. "No birds, no mammals, no insects, except a few flies, and the plant life was decreasing." It's likely that some of the devastation he saw was caused by the solvent used with DDT rather than the insecticide itself, but the lesson was nonetheless clear.

Combined, the antimalarials and DDT were transformative. By 1944, the malaria rate in MacArthur's disease-ridden command had dropped 95 percent. Serving under MacArthur, by then, was only slightly more dangerous than serving on the mainland, from a disease perspective. After the war, the officer in charge of the antimalarial campaign proudly reported that "man has developed a mastery of malaria."

And not only malaria. A group of new sulfonamide-based drugs could treat dozens of bacterial diseases and infections: gonorrhea, pneumonia, strep throat, burns, scarlet fever, dysentery, and so on. Penicillin, the most powerful bacteria killer, was honed during the war, too, turning battlefield injuries from likely killers to recoverable setbacks. The death rate for all disease in the army in World War II was just 4 percent of what it had been in the First World War.

The new drugs and sprays not only made war safer, they made movement safer. No longer were areas like Panama graveyards for mainlanders, the sorts of places to which they'd bring their coffins in their luggage. In fact, during the war the United States established 134 bases in Panama *outside* the carefully policed Canal Zone. Those bases were partly to protect the canal, but they also served as places to practice maneuvers and experiment with chemical weapons, such as the jungle tests Cornelius Rhoads oversaw.

Using the Panamanian jungle for tests or training would have been insane a few decades earlier. But with Skeeter Beaters (which could kill 95 percent of the adult mosquitoes), insect repellents, antimalarials, mosquito netting, and ground spraying, a forbidding environment became hospitable. The soldiers plunged into the thick brush. And they were fine.

★

What of the other cargo the planes carried, the objects? How would they fare when transported across the world? We rarely contemplate this, but for most of history, objects hadn't been built to travel. The predicament of the attendees of Arthur MacArthur's 1901 party in the Philippines—their buildings rotting, their hats dripping down their faces—had been a perpetual hazard.

The troubles with transport continued into the Second World War, which exposed vital matériel to rough handling, sandstorms, high altitudes, subzero temperatures, seawater, and sweltering jungles. An observer visiting New Caledonia in MacArthur's command was shocked by what the climate had done to storage depots. Cans were "completely covered by rust." Wooden crates, which worked perfectly well on the mainland, had rotted so badly that "the wood could be mashed between one's fingers." The center of large stacks of stored food "looked like a big mold culture."

Specialized equipment proved especially vulnerable. Gas masks and electrical equipment grew fungus in the tropics. Batteries were particularly finicky, giving perpetual trouble. In New Guinea, ants chewed through the insulation on telephone wires and radio equipment. An inspection on major Pacific bases found that 20 to 40 percent of the matériel in depots was unusable.

Yet again, the engineers went to work. Their task was a remarkable one: to world-proof the inventory of the military. To make sure that objects didn't stop working whenever they moved.

The quartermaster's office devised what it called "amphibious" packaging, made from newly developed materials that could withstand long voyages and exposure to the elements. Plasticized paper, silica gel, sisal, and asphalt featured in these multilayer packages, which portended today's foil-plastic-paper shelf-stable milk cartons. Burlap sacks were similarly replaced by multiwall sacks of paper, plastic, and asphalt. Tin cans, for their part, could be coated in lacquer or enamel to withstand rust.

It went beyond the packaging. The military also learned to world-proof its equipment, rendering objects themselves suitable for any climate. Matériel was coated, sprayed, and sheathed in plastic to render it impervious to the elements. One of the most impressive achievements, because it was so complex, was the rugged, portable high-frequency radio unit developed for use in the field.

In area after area, the military confronted the challenges of world shipping. It is in no small part due to its accomplishments that our world today is the way it is—a place where objects are not confined to climatic zones, but can move without malfunctioning.

Medical breakthroughs enabled men to parachute into difficult environments and survive. Engineering innovations meant that the things they carried could, too.

★

Aviation, knocked-down shipping, wireless communication, cryptography, chloroquine, DDT, and world-proofing. These were disparate technologies, but what united them was their effect on movement. They allowed the United States to move easily through foreign lands it didn't control, substituting technology for territory.

The substitution was never complete. It's not as if, even today, all transit is by plane or all information is sent wirelessly (underwater cables play a surprisingly large role in our internet-connected world). But the important thing was that objects, people, and messages *could* be moved this way. That possibility diminished the importance of strategically valuable areas.

The Panama Canal Zone is a telling example. At the start of the Second World War, the United States had been so nervous about losing access to the canal that it established 134 bases in Panama. But at the end of that war, the military had gotten so comfortable moving around the planet without colonies that Harry Truman relinquished all those bases and proposed turning the canal over to the United Nations. Every president after Truman sought to extricate the United States from the increasingly irrelevant Canal Zone in various ways, though it wasn't until Jimmy Carter's presidency in the 1970s that a treaty ending U.S. jurisdiction over the zone was finally signed.

It wasn't the canal that was obsolete—traffic through it continued to grow steadily in the postwar years. It was the Canal *Zone*, which guaranteed access to the canal and granted control over it. That was the part that no longer seemed essential to national security.

Space-annihilating technologies helped set the terms of the burgeoning Cold War, a war that featured very little annexation by its principals. In 1945 the Allies had divided Germany into zones of occupation, and they did the same to the city of Berlin, lodged within the Soviet zone. Yet in their haste, the occupiers had failed to sign any agreement granting the Western powers *access* to their zones in Berlin. Since all the ground approaches passed through Soviet-occupied Germany, this meant that Joseph Stalin could entirely blockade the Western sectors of Berlin. Which, in 1948, he did.

It was a bold move. Berlin was importing fifteen thousand tons of goods per day. Stalin apparently hoped that by sealing it off, he could force the West to abandon it and perhaps retreat from Germany altogether.

That probably would have worked in the past. Indeed, after the First World War cut Belgium off from its markets, Herbert Hoover, tasked with relieving the Belgians, had been compelled to negotiate the right of free passage from Britain, France, and Germany to get supplies in. If he hadn't gotten ground access, he wouldn't have been able to aid Belgium.

Berlin was Belgium without the permission slips. Yet the experience of the Second World War raised a question. Was permission even necessary?

"I may be the craziest man in the world," said the U.S. military governor of occupied Germany, Lucius Clay, to the mayor-elect of Berlin, "but I am going to try the experiment of feeding this city by air."

General William "Tonnage" Tunner, hero of the Hump, was placed in charge of the operation. It was a fitting hire, "like appointing John Ringling to get the circus on the road," noted the commander of the air force in Europe. Tunner brought his familiar bureaucratic style. "The real excitement from running a successful airlift comes from seeing a dozen lines climbing steadily on a dozen charts," he wrote.

The lines did climb. Tunner set the planes in a brisk three-takeoffs-per-minute cadence. Flights were synchronized to the second and kept on an exact path by ground-to-air radio. To celebrate Easter, Tunner tapped the accelerator and landed a plane in Berlin every 61.8 seconds.

The aircraft, departing from bases in western Germany, flew necessities: coal, oil, flour, dehydrated food, and salt. But they also flew grand pianos and, in one case, a power plant. Berlin's economy ran by air. Stalin, ultimately, could not hold out—the blockade hurt him more than it hurt his adversaries. In the eleventh month, after more than a quarter of a million flights, he lifted the barriers.

The lesson was clear: Stalin had territorial control, but that didn't mean what it used to.

It was a lesson Moscow would be taught repeatedly. Starting in the late forties, the United States started beaming radio broadcasts into the USSR and its satellites—the communications equivalent of the Berlin Airlift. A few high-powered broadcasting stations in Western Europe were all it took to shred the informational sovereignty of the Eastern Bloc. The Voice of America and two CIA-backed operations, Radio Free Europe and Radio Liberation (later renamed Radio Liberty), egged on dissenters, incited uprisings, and aired governmental secrets.

The Soviets tried to jam the broadcasts; by 1958, they were spending more on jamming than on their own transmissions. But they never managed to shut off the stream of information. Multiple times it appears that the Soviets assassinated or tried to assassinate Western journalists. In 1981 the headquarters of Radio Free Europe and Radio Liberty in Munich was bombed. Yet not even that stopped the broadcasts.

"When it came to radio waves, the iron curtain was helpless," remembered Lech Walesa, the leader of Poland's dissident Solidarity movement. Solidarity had relied heavily on Western radio, which Walesa credited with the collapse of communism in Europe.

"The frontiers could be closed," he wrote. "Words could not."

18

THE EMPIRE OF
THE RED OCTAGON

The Second World War left the United States in an extraordinary position. It was rich, it was powerful, and, thanks to its chemists and engineers, it had the means to deal with foreign lands without colonizing them. But the war also conferred another advantage, harder to see and operating on a deeper level. It had to do with standards.

Standards—the protocols by which objects and processes are coordinated—are admittedly one of the most stultifying topics known to humankind. A sample of headlines from the journal *Industrial Standardization* gives a sense of the exquisite heights to which boredom can be taken:

Industry Approves Recommended List of Paper Sizes
New Law Requires Labels for Wool
Brochure Tells About Building Coordination
Revision of List of Recommended Paper Sizes
How Durable Is Rapid-Hardening Concrete?
American Standards for Wood Poles!
National Unification Settles Questions of Number of Flutes for
    Reamers and Reamer Tolerances
Tolerances for Cylindrical Fits (a four-part series)
Sheet Labels Now Furnish Much Useful Information

Glass Jars of Recommended Sizes Used for Mayonnaise Products
Agriculture Department Defines "Lard"

And I'll confess a special fondness for this one:

ASA Approval of Pipe Standards Important Event in Pipe History

It's easy to chuckle. But were it not for agreements on cylindrical fits and reamer tolerances, it's hard to know how our world could operate. The more we fill our lives with complex manufactured objects and the more those objects move around, the more important it is that they play well with one another.

In 1904 a massive fire ravaged Baltimore. Engine companies sped from New York, Philadelphia, Annapolis, Wilmington, and Harrisburg to help. Yet there was little they could do, for when they arrived, they found that their hoses couldn't connect to Baltimore's hydrants (or, indeed, to one another's hoses). For thirty helpless hours they watched as 1,562 buildings burned.

Through the early twentieth century, compatibility failures like that were chronic, and they made any attempt to move between jurisdictions exasperating. A "bushel" of greens weighed ten pounds in North Carolina, thirty in neighboring Tennessee. The standard berry box in Oregon was illegal in California. Every time truckers crossed state lines, they had to pull over to demonstrate that their vehicles conformed to local standards. And they didn't always. Height, length, and weight allowances varied wildly from state to state, so that the longest permissible truck in Vermont, a 50-footer, was 24.5 feet too long to enter Kentucky.

College football was a popular sport in the 1920s, yet it wasn't until 1940 that colleges agreed on what a "football" was. Home teams would just supply whatever vaguely football-shaped objects they wanted. Teams that liked to pass used slim balls, teams that emphasized kicking (which early football rules encouraged) proffered short and fat ones.

It wasn't until 1927 that *traffic lights* were standardized. Before that, drivers in Manhattan stopped on green, started on yellow, and understood red to mean "caution." A different system prevailed in Cleveland, a different one in Chicago, a different one in Buffalo, and so on.

It's easy to ignore standards. But once you start thinking about them, you see them everywhere. You realize how much relies on the silent coordination of extremely complex processes. And you start to earnestly wonder how society can go a day without bridges collapsing, planes dropping from the sky, appliances spontaneously exploding, and everything good burning up in a swelling ball of flame.

★

In 1900, after the war with Spain, the secretary of the Treasury put the issue of standards before Congress. It was a new world, he argued. Science and technology had made "exceedingly rapid progress," and the country had just claimed new and far-flung territories. For this growing society to hold together, it would need standards.

Congress agreed and established the National Bureau of Standards. There was a lot of work to do. A few months after the devastating Baltimore conflagration, a fire broke out on the bureau's grounds. The night watchman rushed to grab hoses—stored in different buildings—to extinguish it. But he encountered the Baltimore problem: the hoses couldn't connect. He had to stamp out the fire with his feet.

The next day, a bureau employee remembered, "there was quite a discussion." Even at the *Bureau of Standards*, hoses from two different buildings couldn't be coupled.

It's not hard to appreciate the bureau's plight. Everybody wanted standards—it's not as if manufacturers took pride in making incompatible hoses. It's just that each firm desperately wanted *its* way of doing things to be the standard way, and for good reason. Losing a standards war meant having to retool, which might require purchasing expensive new machines. It meant seeing one's existing stock become obsolete. And it meant paying those costs while a competitor—the one whose standard was adopted—got to race ahead unimpeded. With stakes that high, it was easy for firms to get locked into standards battles, leaving hapless firefighters cursing their incompatible hoses.

Resolving these paralyzing disputes was potentially a job for government. It helped that the bureau had, in the 1920s, one of the most trusted public officials at its helm: Secretary of Commerce Herbert Hoover. Today Hoover is remembered as the president unfortunate enough to have been in office during the 1929 stock market crash. Yet the popular image of him as a bumbler misses a lot. He may have been a maladroit politician and a poor steward of the economy, but Hoover was an astonishingly capable bureaucrat. And there was little he cared about as much as standardization.

Herbert Hoover, as a man, can best be understood as the opposite of Teddy Roosevelt. Whereas Roosevelt lusted for combat and styled himself as a cowboy, Hoover was a Quaker who had lived for a year among Osages in Indian Country (he later had Charles Curtis, a Native American with Osage heritage, as his vice president). Roosevelt chafed at rules; Hoover once refused to let former president Benjamin Harrison into a college baseball game without a ticket. Roosevelt gave his horse the dramatic name Rain-in-the-Face; Hoover's animal companion was a cat, whom he addressed as Mr. Cat. And whereas Roosevelt had a lifelong obsession with big game hunting, Hoover's love was fishing, an activity he revered for its "quieting of hate," "hushing to ambition," and promotion of "meekness."

Perhaps the only thing you need to know about Herbert Hoover is that he wore a jacket and tie to fish.

Hoover made his fortune as an engineer and his fame organizing the relief of Belgium during World War I, an enormous logistical operation that required orchestrating the movement of more than five million tons

The Great Standardizer:
Herbert Hoover, fishing in a
starched collar and a suit

of food by rail, ship, and canal boat. Though contemplated by both parties as a presidential candidate in 1920, Hoover instead became secretary of commerce. He'd been told by a predecessor that the job required merely turning the lighthouses out at night and putting the fish to bed, but for Hoover it was more than that. It was a calling.

As he saw it, the true problem with the economy was neither the injustice of capitalists nor the impatience of workers, but the inefficiency of objects. So much time and money were wasted on things that just didn't work. Solve *that* problem, Hoover thought, and there'd be more than enough to go around. Standardizing and simplifying were, in his mind, the keys to prosperity. When he took his position as secretary, he rearranged the Commerce Department to ensure that he'd supervise the Bureau of Standards personally.

Under Hoover, the bureau developed a system. It would call a small group of industrial representatives to Washington, draft a standard based on their conversations, and then call a larger convention, again in Washington, to adopt or, in rare cases, amend the standard. Hoover insisted that the process be voluntary, as he doubted that imposed standards would gain adherents. But the mere act of the government calling an all-industry convention was often enough to secure agreement.

It started with a conference of brickmakers who, after a few hours with Hoover, agreed to reduce sixty-six varieties of paving brick to eleven (and eventually to five). Then came new standards for lumber, cement, doors, wood, steel, bedsprings, mattresses, hospital linen, ball bearings, and brake linings. Glass tumblers, it was decided, had to be able to withstand six hours in boiling water. Tires must have at least 70 percent new rubber on their treads. Red ink had to be a certain proportion of scarlet dye to water.

Hoover's greatest challenge was one of the least visible: the humble screw thread. Screws, nuts, and bolts are universal fasteners. They function in industrial societies, as one writer put it, like salt and pepper "sprinkled on practically every conceivable kind of apparatus." Yet every such society encounters, early on, the vexing problem of incompatible screw threads. Different screws have different measurements, including the thread angles. If those don't line up between the males and the females, you are, so to speak, screwed.

"The screw thread is a simple device," one senator put it, "but it ties together the whole mechanical skeleton of our civilization."

Or it doesn't. For the entire nineteenth century and well into the twentieth, screw threads were at the manufacturer's discretion. The result was an anarchic profusion of standards and a civilization very much *not* tied together. A worker, Hoover complained, "had to find a bolt of the same make before he could screw a nut on it and had to search among a hundred different diameters." And if the manufacturer who made your screws went out of business, good luck.

Screw thread incompatibilities grew even more worrisome with the advent of cars and planes—complex vibrating objects whose failure could mean death. The problem had hobbled the armed forces in the First World War, which led Congress to appoint a National Screw Thread Commission. Still, it took years, until 1924, before the first national screw thread standard was finally published. It wasn't a big-splash innovation like the Model T or the airplane, but that hard-won screw thread standard quietly accelerated the economy nonetheless.

"Now the half-inch nuts screw onto all the half-inch bolts," announced a satisfied Herbert Hoover.

★

Setting standards on the mainland was hard work. It went easier in the territories. There, industrial interest groups were weaker (when they existed at all) and the unelected government felt free to act with greater force. The exhausting business of cajoling manufacturers, calling conferences, and consulting with interested parties could be dispensed with. Authorities just declared standards and enforced them.

The ability of empires to promulgate standards was a major benefit of colonial conquest. Imperial standardization meant that even in faraway lands, the colonizers' practices would be adhered to. Empires imprinted colonies with new laws, ideas, languages, sports, military conventions, fashions, weights and measures, rules of etiquette, money, and industrial practices. In fact, that's what colonial officials spent much of their time doing.

There's a reason, in other words, that the British measurement system (feet, yards, gallons, pounds, tons) is called the *imperial* system. Those weights and measures were promulgated to secure commensurability throughout Britain's realm, far beyond the British Isles. Even where local measures were used, they were defined in British terms, such as the

Indian measure of mass called the *maund*, standardized in the nineteenth century to equal a hundred pounds.

Empires standardized people, too. Take nursing in the Philippines. Mainlanders venturing out to the colony needed the attention of nurses, particularly given the diseases that the war had unleashed. And yet, since few mainland nurses were willing to move to the Philippines, that meant relying on Filipinos. Soon after annexation the government began training them.

Nursing wasn't new to the Philippines. There'd been hospitals in the country for centuries, and nurses had played an important part in the Philippine Revolution (Emilio Aguinaldo's wife, Doña Hilaria, established a Filipino Red Cross to treat rebel soldiers). But the training the U.S. government offered was designed to aggressively overwrite previous Filipino and Spanish codes. Nursing students were hived off from the general population and placed in special dormitories where they studied English, cooked and ate mainland food, and learned mainland etiquette. They were drilled in mainland notions of hygiene. Sandals were replaced by shoes, long dresses by crisp gingham worn over stockings.

The Philippine schools were essentially satellites of mainland universities. The Philippine Medical School, for instance, copied its curriculum from Johns Hopkins. Promising Filipino nurses were brought to the mainland to study. The result was hospitals staffed not just by trained nurses but by *mainland*-trained nurses. This allowed freshly arrived mainlanders to fit easily into roles as teachers and supervisors, with little adjustment.

Aligning nursing practices in the Philippines with those of the mainland made the empire run smoother. But it has also had a profound unintended consequence. Once standards are firmly established, they are hard to dislodge, and the Philippines has remained, even after independence, extraordinarily U.S.-centric in its nursing practices. So, as the U.S. population has aged, requiring more health care, and as the Philippine economy has faltered, more and more nurses from the Philippines have left to work in the United States. Today, a massive pipeline carries tens of thousands of Filipino nurses to jobs in U.S. health centers.

At this point, not only are Filipino nurses training in preparation for emigration, but Filipino *doctors* are retraining as nurses so that they too can find work abroad.

Medical expertise flows out of the country, money flows in. It's had a mixed effect. But the point here is that the easy flow, which has made the Philippines the United States' top supplier of foreign nurses since the 1960s, is not the consequence of markets alone. The Philippines has a competitive advantage because of the generations of nurses who learned their craft precisely to U.S. standards.

The half-inch nuts screw onto the half-inch bolts.

★

Men like Herbert Hoover standardized the mainland. Colonial rulers then imposed those standards on the territories. But both processes stopped at the border. Within the Greater United States, one way of doing things prevailed. Foreign countries had their own nursing practices and screw thread angles.

In Hoover's day, it was hard to imagine changing that. Getting brick manufacturers in one country to agree had been difficult enough. Who was going to get French brickmakers into agreement with Japanese ones? The difficulty of standardizing across jurisdictions explains why countries through the first half of the twentieth century had largely distinct material cultures.

The First World War drove this point home. The United States sent its troops to Europe. They found, on arriving, that Europeans used different weapons, had a different sizing system for uniforms, and measured distance differently.

They also found that there wasn't much they could do about it. The U.S. Army was fighting an away game, so it made uncomfortable adjustments. It switched over to the metric system for the war's duration, manufacturing metric provisions, issuing metric maps, and giving its orders in metric units. Fighting in kilometers and kilograms wasn't easy for men who'd grown up with miles and pounds, but that was the price of coordinating with their French allies.

Standards clashed again in the Second World War. This time the problem was even worse. This time the United States wasn't sending only men and money to Europe. It was supplying a relentless torrent of stuff to theaters all over the world.

It was doing this even before it formally entered the war, a practice that Roosevelt strove to justify to a hesitant public. "Suppose my neighbor's home catches fire, and I have a length of garden hose," he argued in a famous analogy. "If he can take my garden hose and connect it up with his hydrant, I may help him to put out his fire."

It was a metaphor, obviously. But it isn't hard to picture Herbert Hoover in the back of the room, raising his hand. *What if your hose doesn't fit his hydrant?*

That would have been a good question to ask. The United States made guns with 0.30-inch cartridges; the British Empire used 0.303-inch cartridges. Similarly, British bombs didn't fit the racks on U.S. planes. A Canadian naval officer deemed it a "frightful commentary" on the state of international cooperation that at the start of the war, "there was not a single gun or a single round of ammunition" that could be shared among the Allies.

It was even worse than that. The British had adopted a 55-degree thread angle for their screws, whereas the U.S. standard, in which Hoover took so much pride, was 60 degrees. It was as if the things themselves spoke different languages. "We can't borrow parts from the British," one U.S. mechanic complained. "We can't even steal them. *They don't fit.*"

In the First World War, which was still fought with horses, industrial

Wartime poster illustrating the problem with noncompliant parts

incompatibilities among allies had been inconvenient. Now, in a war of jeeps and bombers, they were crippling. When the U.S. manufacturer Packard contracted to make engines for British planes, its engineers spent ten months redrawing some two thousand British blueprints to translate them into the U.S. screw system. Throughout the war, the United States spent $600 million sending spare screws, nuts, and bolts overseas to compensate for the incompatibility.

Could manufacturers not just adopt European standards, as they had in the last war? Perhaps. The British and French spent $84 million to establish and expand factories in the United States that were capable of making European-style aircraft engines, essentially planting European industrial outposts on U.S. soil. The U.S. Army also adopted some items of the British arsenal as its own and built racks for British bombs.

Yet deferring to European standards only made sense if Europe was the heart of the Allied war economy, and Europe soon lost its centrality. The fall of France and bombing of Britain took European factories offline. At the same time, U.S. manufacturing kicked into high gear. By the war's end, the United States had produced 84,000 tanks, 2.2 million trucks, 6.2 million rifles, and 41 *billion* rounds of small ammunition. The war against Hitler may have been a European fight, but it was very much made in the U.S.A.

The more U.S. factories made, the more fine-grained their standardization became. The goal, as two prominent experts put it, was "the integration of the entire process into a smooth flow like a great river system." That meant not just making parts from the same factory interchangeable, but also making them interchangeable across factories, indeed across industries—all of which required mind-boggling levels of precision.

Consider the Fenn Manufacturing company, which produced specialized machinery. Before the war, its vice president explained, no one had ever *heard* of making parts with tolerances of plus-or-minus 0.0002 inches. Anyone suggesting such precision would have been deemed "absolutely insane." But that's what the vast military economy demanded, and Fenn was forced to retool virtually its whole plant. It had to install a constant-temperature room to check fixtures and gauges for minuscule variations.

In Washington, engineers turned out "war standards" with ferocity. It was the same ballet between governmental officials and industrial leaders that Herbert Hoover had choreographed, danced at twice the tempo.

Standardizers gamely wrote specifications for new materials, new equipment, and new designs. At its wartime peak in 1944, the budget of the National Bureau of Standards was 7.5 times larger than it had been a decade earlier.

All this turned the United States into the undisputed standard-setter for the Allies. The war had united their economies, but Washington set the terms of the union.

You could see this in Australia. As a British dominion, Australia had adhered to British standards before the war, with some local variations. Yet it didn't take long for it to tip into the gravity well of the United States' war economy.

The key period was from 1942 to 1944, after Douglas MacArthur abandoned the Philippines but before the United States could fully provision his troops via the mainland. MacArthur still relied on the United States for ships and weapons, but for high-volume, low-value items such as food and clothing, Australia became the source. At peak, some 15 percent of Australia's national income came from meeting MacArthur's procurement orders.

Meeting those orders was a challenge, especially when it came to food. Australian farmers often worked small plots, weeding by hand and selling to local markets. Machines played a small role in crop cultivation, and safety measures such as milk pasteurization were costly luxuries, ill suiting the farmer's-market milieu of Australian agriculture.

All that would have to change. The United States sent over experts, agricultural missionaries bearing machines, herbicides, and fungicides. Their charge? Transform a continent.

They bombarded farmers with lectures, radio broadcasts, educational films, leaflets, and field demonstrations, all to teach the U.S. way of farming. Australian manufacturers were given models of U.S. tractors, mowers, harvesters, and dusters and taught how to make them. Australian canners learned to can the army way. Dairy farmers were ordered to pasteurize their milk and test their cows for tuberculin. Given the sheer size of MacArthur's purchase orders, to resist would have been economic suicide.

"Almost every phase of Australia's food industry has been profoundly affected by the activities of the remarkable team of specialists brought out here for the US to guide and advise us," wrote one witness to the transformation.

Tastes changed, too. Australian troops used to mutton watched as their U.S. allies consumed much larger rations built around beef, pork, and ham and supplemented with spaghetti, coffee, and eggs. It was decided that serving different rations to different troops would be too dispiriting to the Australians. So they, too, started eating U.S. rations. Australian meatpackers, for their part, got the hang of making new foods: chili con carne, corned beef hash, ham and eggs, luncheon meat, Vienna sausage.

The entire Australian shoe industry was similarly overturned as shoemakers retooled to make shoes in U.S. sizes rather than British ones. With sixty thousand pairs of shoes ordered a month for army use, they couldn't afford not to.

"Without any inhibitions of any kind," announced Australia's prime minister early in the war, "I make it quite clear that Australia looks to America, free of any pangs as to our traditional links or kinship with the United Kingdom." In the realm of standards, that was an unavoidable truth. Politically, Australia remained British. But materially, it looked a lot like a U.S. colony.

★

Australia was just the start. During the war, the Allies formed a standards coordinating committee with headquarters in New York and London. It oversaw agreements on repair parts for aircraft, the width of rail lines, and radio broadcasting frequencies. Generally, these agreements specified that U.S. standards would be adopted, since the United States' planes, trains, and radios were essential to the war. In 1943 the British signaled that they were willing to talk screw threads.

A British mission traveled to New York that year. For nearly two weeks, some thirty experts debated screws, pipe threads, gas cylinder threads, hose couplings, and cylindrical fits. Everyone agreed that "unification" of the Anglophone countries was essential. But unification on whose terms? The U.S. representatives suggested that the British Empire retool. The British agreed to think about it.

A longer summit followed in London. Bombs dropped overhead in an "unending stream," reported the president of the American Society of Mechanical Engineers. Perhaps the bombardment softened the British up. The U.S. delegates had planned to spring the subject of unification on the British at the last moment, but to their surprise the British brought it up

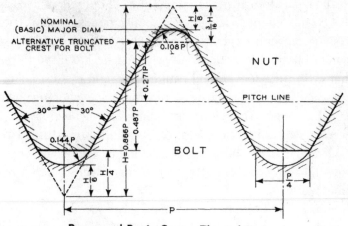

Proposed Basic Screw Thread Form

The proposed new unified basic form of thread has an angle of 60 degrees and a rounded crest and root. The radius of the root of the screw is larger than the radius of its crest. Truncation of the crest of the screw is permissible.

One thread to rule them all: The 1945 standard

immediately. Abandoning 55-degree screws for 60-degree ones would devastate British manufacturers. But given the exigencies of war, they were willing to try it temporarily.

A third conference in Ottawa in 1945 clinched the deal. This time the battered British delegates simply surrendered. Britain would wholeheartedly accept a new standard, with a screw thread angle of 60 degrees. British manufacturers would retool. U.S. manufacturers, by contrast, would barely notice the shift, since screws made under the new Anglophone standard were practically interchangeable with screws made under the old national agreement that Herbert Hoover had secured.

It was, as they say, an important event in pipe history.

★

The same month the Anglophone powers agreed on a screw thread, they established the International Organization for Standardization (better known by its short-form name, ISO). It was to be a United Nations for things. It had an administrative committee modeled after the UN's Security Council: permanent seats for the five great powers (United States,

Britain, France, China, and the Soviet Union) and rotating seats for other countries. The first president was from the United States.

One of the first topics ISO discussed was, of course, screw threads. Peace and prosperity called for global unification. But the British refused to revamp again, noting that they had already endured considerable hardship in adopting the 60-degree standard. Nor was the United States open to change. The other powers grumbled that the United States and Britain had "beaten the gun" in international standardization. Still, faced with the combined bulk of the British and U.S. empires, there was little they could do. Bowing to inevitability, they voted overwhelmingly to adopt the Anglophone thread angle as the international one (the Soviet Union was the only member to vote no). Countries could still use their national standards, but if they wanted international compatibility, their screw thread angles would need to be 60 degrees.

Quite a lot of things, in fact, would have to be remade to a metaphorical 60-degree angle. The war had stripped economies down, and now they sought to rebuild themselves by tapping into a world market. Yet that market was dominated by the United States, which accounted for an astonishing 60 percent of the industrialized world's economic production in 1946. "America is our largest buyer, our largest seller," noted French standardizers. And so agreement after agreement affirmed the centrality of the United States.

The United States wasn't just an economic superpower, it was a military one, too. Its vast armed forces had been agents of standardization during the Second World War, and they continued to be so afterward, during the Cold War. Washington flooded the world with its arms and equipment. In accepting them, foreign militaries had to adopt U.S. standards as well.

The North Atlantic Treaty Organization (NATO) pushed standardization even further. It established a permanent military alliance of twelve countries, the first of its kind. This alliance turned military standardization from an acute wartime problem into a chronic peacetime one, which NATO administrators solved by going through the supply catalog and, one by one, standardizing items in it. They started with rifles, which were put on the U.S. system of 0.30-inch cartridges. By 1953, the U.S. representative to NATO's Defense Production Board bragged, fighter planes featuring Belgian engines perfectly fit Dutch frames. A medical standardization program had just begun, too, and he expected that within two or three years "a British stretcher will fit the trolleys of an American ambulance, and a Turkish needle will fit on a French syringe."

In 1953 the leading British standards journal filled an issue with articles reprinted from its counterpart journal in New York. It was a remarkable capitulation—in standards, the British were now just taking dictation.

The Third World was taking notes, too. Poorer countries found it hard to set standards themselves—laboratories, conferences, and journals cost money—and they had strong incentives to use the standards of their richer trading partners. And so, just as European powers flocked to U.S. standards, their former colonies did the same. U.S. engineers helped by advising foreign governments and staffing overseas field offices for standards associations.

It was a worthwhile investment. By exporting its standards, Harry Truman noted, the United States was "smoothing the flow of international trade" and "enabling buyers and sellers in different nations to speak the same language." He didn't need to specify *whose* language was spoken.

★

In industry after industry, the world tuned itself to the United States. This happened literally in music, where countries bickered over the pitch of a concert A. The United States had been tuning its instruments to an A of 440 hertz since 1917. But continental Europe was officially tuned to the "French pitch," a slightly flatter A of 435 hertz, closer to the classical pitches of the eighteenth and nineteenth centuries. Austrian delegates pushed for A435 at the United Nations. Yet with U.S. recordings flooding the market and the U.S. government broadcasting a pure A440 tone around the world from powerful radio stations in Maryland and Hawai'i as a "service" to musicians, the Austrians stood little chance. Today, except for those playing period instruments such as baroque flutes or older church organs, A440 is the law of the land.

Something similar happened in the skies. International aviation relies on standards. Air traffic controllers and pilots must speak the same language, plane parts must be similar enough that repairs can be made in any country, and the world's radio frequencies must be arranged so that the navigational channels in one country are the same as in the next. Representatives of the U.S. aviation industry worked aggressively to secure all these objectives and to make sure that the language of the air was English. By 1950, they had largely succeeded.

It's not shocking that aviation is strictly standardized, given its frequently international character. More impressive is what the United States did to ground travel. For the first half of the twentieth century, traffic engineers in the United States had been concerned with securing nationwide standards—traffic light colors, signs, and so forth. Yet in 1953 the deputy commissioner of the Bureau of Public Roads explained that "we now think in terms of world-wide uniformity."

Worldwide uniformity. Had this been the ambition of a transportation official from, say, Thailand, it would have been laughable. Yet from the United States it was wholly feasible. That year, the international Convention on a Uniform System of Road Signs and Signals reproduced the U.S. practices with remarkable fidelity. Traffic light colors, pavement striping rules, and even to a large degree road signs followed the U.S. system, including the well-known yellow octagon with the word STOP printed on it.

Wait—yellow? Yes. The octagonal stop sign came from Michigan, born when a Detroit police sergeant clipped the corners off a square sign to give it a more distinctive shape. But the early signs were yellow, not red. The first national agreement of U.S. state highway professionals rejected the use of red on any sign, since it was hard to see at night. So the U.S. stop sign, adopted as an international standard in 1953, was yellow.

Yet just a year later, in 1954, the United States changed its mind about the yellow. Experts thought that red better signified danger, and new developments in industrial chemistry allowed for durable, reflective red finishes. So, to what I can only imagine was the apoplectic fury of traffic engineers worldwide, the United States abandoned the global standard— its own standard, designed in Michigan and foisted on the world—and began to replace its yellow signs with red ones.

This, more than anything, showed the stupefying privilege the United States enjoyed in the realm of standards. It could force other countries to adopt its screw thread angle in the name of international cooperation. But it was never bound by those imperatives itself.

This unique exemption from international standards is not a secret. You see it every day in the realm of weights and measures. While other countries have reconciled themselves to the metric system, designed by the French in the late eighteenth century, the United States has held out. As late as 1971, an extraordinary 56 percent of mainlanders claimed to not even be *aware* of the metric system.

The ongoing U.S. rejection of metric measures leads to frequent annoyance and occasional catastrophe—a Boeing 767 plane carrying dozens that lost power midair because its fuel load had been mistakenly calculated in pounds, a Mars probe that disintegrated because of U.S. software that used pounds rather than kilograms. Although the United States secured worldwide adoption of its screw thread angle, it has squandered part of that advantage by sticking (in some contexts) to screws measured in inches, which aren't compatible with those measured metrically. Still, the United States has refused to relinquish its inches, pounds, and gallons. It stands with Myanmar, Liberia, the Independent State of Samoa, Palau, the Federated States of Micronesia, and the Republic of the Marshall Islands as the sole holdouts against the metric system.

If it is the privilege of the United States to depart from international standards, it has been the burden of the rest of the world to indulge it. Two years after the United States finished switching its stop signs from yellow to red, the United Nations convened a grand meeting of 134 nations to revisit the issue of traffic signs. The yellow octagon was dropped for a red one (an inverted red triangle in a red circle was also given official imprimatur, though few nations chose it). The United States didn't even sign the new agreement, yet its standard prevailed.

Today, the empire of the red octagon is global. There are minor variations: in Japan it's a red triangle, in Papua New Guinea it's a red shield, and in Cuba it's a red triangle in a red circle. But by my count, at least 91 percent of the world's population stops at red octagons. Even the North Koreans do.

★

The stop sign can be added to the list of empire-killing technologies. Taken together, they have had a formidable effect. Synthetics diminished the great powers' need for strategic raw materials by offering substitutes. Aviation, cryptography, radio, and satellites, meanwhile, enabled those powers to run secure transportation and communication networks without worrying about contiguous territorial access. Innovations in medicine and engineering—such as DDT, antimalarials, plastic-based packaging, and "world-proofed" electronic equipment—further reduced the need for territorial control. They allowed objects and humans to safely travel to hostile terrains, meaning that colonizers didn't have to soften the ground beforehand.

Standardization, similarly, made foreign places more accessible. Standards had been facilitating long-distance trade for centuries before World War II, of course, but mainly *within* political jurisdictions. You had to colonize to standardize, roughly speaking (and with important exceptions). What changed in the Second World War was scale. The United States took advantage of its position—as the undisputed economic and political superpower, with its wartime logistical network installed in more than a hundred countries—to push its standards beyond its borders. The wave of U.S.-centered standardization that followed transcended the scale of the nation or the empire. This was standardization at the scale of the planet.

Together with the other empire-killing technologies, global standards changed the rules of the game. Powerful countries had long secured their ability to both claim resources and move around the planet by controlling land. Those were the rules the United States had played by when it expanded westward and overseas. Those were the rules Germany and Japan had played by in the Second World War. By those rules, the end of the war had brought the United States to the dizzying heights of imperial possibility. It had new ambitions and every chance to back those ambitions by seizing territory. Had it done so, it could have locked down a resource base and a strategic position unrivaled in history.

That the United States declined to follow victory with annexations— that instead it *decolonized*—cannot be explained by a sudden onset of altruism. It was due in part to the revolt of colonized peoples worldwide. It was also due to the lessons learned in the war. Fighting and winning that war had taught Washington the art of projecting power without claiming colonies. New technologies helped it achieve, as a writer in the forties put it, "domination without annexation."

Those technologies laid the foundation for our world today. It's a far cry from the world Teddy Roosevelt envisioned, in which the strong violently subdue the weak and take their land. It is much closer to the one Herbert Hoover imagined, held together not by empires, but by the market. It's a world where the great coordinating process isn't colonial rule, which operates within borders, but globalization, which crosses them.

The replacement of colonialism with globalization, it should be said, hasn't exactly leveled the playing field. A previously bumpy world may have become "flat," as the pundit Thomas L. Friedman has put it. But who flattened it? For the most part, it was the U.S. military, seeking to project power around the planet. Given that, it shouldn't come as a surprise to learn that globalization, at least at first, favored the United States. U.S. planes filled the skies, U.S. broadcasts flooded the airwaves, U.S.-made synthetic goods replaced colonial ones, and U.S. standards held it all together.

Not all those advantages have endured. Today, China makes more plastic than the United States does. Yet even if it has not won every match, the United States has consistently enjoyed a sizable home-court advantage. It has had the luxury of sticking to its ways while forcing other countries to retool their factories and retune their instruments. The benefits of this are many. Yet one sticks out and is worth special examination. That is the global adoption of a single language: English.

19

LANGUAGE IS A VIRUS

In 1620 a group of English settlers, known today as the Pilgrims, arrived on the shores of North America. They'd been at sea for more than two months—an arduous voyage that killed two of their number.

That was, it turned out, the easy part. The settlers landed in an unfamiliar place where they had no friends. They tried to grow food but failed badly. In the first winter, more than half died from disease and starvation. A group of Indians, the Pauquunaukit Wampanoag, watched them flail from afar. Finally, in the spring, after many of the colonists had perished, the Pauquunaukit sent over an emissary, a man named Samoset.

He greeted them in English.

Samoset, it turned out, had learned some "broken English" (as one colonist described it) from fishermen plying the Maine coast. A few days later, Samoset returned with a Patuxet man who spoke the language even better: Tisquantum, better known as Squanto. Not only did Squanto speak English, he'd *lived in London*. Seven years before meeting the Plymouth colonists, he had been kidnapped by an English captain and taken to Europe. He'd sailed across the Atlantic four times—once after being captured, once back and forth on a journey to Newfoundland, and back again with another expedition to his homeland of Patuxet—i.e., southern New England.

For the colonists, who had crossed the Atlantic only once, this was a near-inconceivable stroke of luck. A small, nomadic band of Europeans far out of their element had somehow managed to run into one of the few individuals from the vast North American continent who had actually spent time in their home country. Squanto was, in the eyes of the colonists, a "special instrument sent of God." He translated for them, brokered key diplomatic alliances with Native polities, and taught them the tricks of local agriculture. Quite likely he was the difference between their survival and their death.

Today, four centuries later, the society those Pilgrims founded enjoys a similar good fortune. Its inhabitants can travel to nearly any spot on the map, confident that someone within hailing distance will speak their language. Yet unlike the Pilgrims, they don't need luck. English has spread like an invasive weed, implanting itself in nearly every habitat. It has created a world full of people ready and able to assist English speakers, wherever they may roam. A world almost *designed* for the convenience of the United States.

A world of Squantos.

★

Languages are standards, just like stop signs and screw threads, but they run much deeper. Languages shape thought, making some ideas more readily thinkable and others less so. At the same time, they shape societies. Which languages you speak affects which communities you join, which books you read, which places you feel at home. That a single language has become the dominant tongue on the planet, spoken to a degree by nearly all educated and powerful people, is thus an occurrence of profound consequence.

It is particularly astonishing because there is no historical precedent for it. Scholars had used Latin widely in Western Europe, but it never achieved the universality sometimes attributed to it. Other languages from Spanish to Swahili have also knit regions together, but none has done more than that. The norm in history has been linguistic difference, not sameness.

That was certainly true of the United States at its start: a polyglot crazy quilt of Native American, African, and European tongues. Even Ben Franklin, restricting himself to the European languages, felt it necessary to master French, German, Italian, Spanish, and Latin along with his native English. He published a newspaper in German, *Die Philadelphische Zeitung*, and suspected that German might displace English in Pennsylvania.

Franklin was right to wonder. There were serious questions about whether English would hold throughout the new United States. There'd never been a native language that stretched over such a large distance as the expanding United States without splitting apart. That it worked—that Virginians spoke the same language as Californians—can be credited to the settlement boom, which swiftly propelled a fairly homogeneous population over a vast expanse. The same wagons and trains that carried the settlers carried the language, too, which survived the long journey with only minor mutations.

Outside of the settler population, though, enforcing English as a national language proved to be a more violent undertaking. Slave owners made a point of separating African slaves who spoke the same language. Those caught speaking their home languages could face serious punishment; there are reports of some having their tongues cut out. The result was total linguistic annihilation. Although traces of African idioms can be found in today's black speech, not a single African language made it over on the slave ships and survived.

Indigenous languages were sites of conflict, too. Starting in the late nineteenth century, reformers pushed tens of thousands of Native American children into white-run boarding schools. There, cut off from their families and communities, the students studied English. "We shall break up all the Indian there is in them in a very short time," promised the founder of one such school. Students caught speaking indigenous languages were routinely beaten or had their mouths washed with soap and lye. Not surprisingly, Indian parents were rarely enthusiastic about this, but governmental officials and school administrators used bribes, threats, the withholding of rations, and outright force—essentially kidnapping the children—to fill the schools.

Authorities tried the same tactics in the overseas territories. "They beat the language out of us in school," remembered one elderly Alaska Native. "Whenever I speak Tlingit, I can still taste the soap," another confirmed (his language now has fewer than a thousand speakers). On Guam, the naval government prohibited the use of Chamoru on school grounds, in courts, and in governmental offices. Children caught speaking it in schools would be beaten or fined. One naval officer collected all the Chamoru dictionaries he could find and burned them.

Yet the empire was vast, and there simply weren't enough colonial officials to wash out every offending mouth. So the government relied on other tools. It passed laws in English, demanded that civil servants use English, and, in the U.S. Virgin Islands, made English proficiency a requirement for voting. Most important, colonial authorities turned to education. Inculcating English was the "cardinal point" of the whole Philippine school system, explained the superintendent of education there. Across the empire, students were expected, at least at the higher grades, to work in English.

Committed anticolonialists, such as Emilio Aguinaldo, resisted—he died in 1964 still unable to speak English. Pedro Albizu Campos spoke the language well, but he came to regard it as an instrument of imperialism. "I am astounded that the Puerto Ricans have tolerated this mutilation of the mentality of their children," he told his followers. "The United States wants not only to destroy our culture and disintegrate our nation, but also to destroy our language" and "force upon us their culture and language, casting out our books and substituting theirs."

Local instructors proved less than steadfast in their dedication to the imperial tongue. A report on Philippine schools found that the students were being taught English "by teachers who themselves cannot speak English," and a former governor complained that their accents were sliding into incomprehensibility. The governor of Puerto Rico accused local teachers of giving English lessons "with a left-handed gesture." Teachers there organized a stubborn resistance to anglicization, even at the cost of being blacklisted and fired.

Overall, English proficiency rose, but slowly. By 1940, roughly a quarter of Puerto Ricans and Filipinos could speak the language. In Hawai'i, a polyglot pidgin was still the language of the streets.

★

The wider world was no better. Among Western countries, English deferred routinely to its rivals. French was the language of diplomacy. In science, French was joined by German and (in chemistry) Russian. As late as 1932, French was allowed as an official language at 98.5 percent of international scientific conferences, whereas English was accepted only at 83.5 percent.

If English speakers wanted to talk with foreigners, they needed to master other languages. That's what Ben Franklin had done in the eighteenth century, and that's what his successors did in the twentieth. Teddy Roosevelt, though obsessed with the "English-speaking peoples," spoke French and German and could follow along in Italian. Woodrow Wilson, the era's other scholar-president, read German scholarship and contemplated moving to Europe to better learn the language. Herbert Hoover ranged even further. He had tried to learn Osage as a boy, his first publication was a translation of a sixteenth-century Latin treatise on mining, and he and his wife, Lou, used Mandarin (learned while living in China) when they wished to speak privately. The polyglot presidency was a reaction to a world teeming with languages, a world where English got you only so far.

The limits of English became painfully clear during the Second World War. "It was then," recalled a prominent philologist, "that many of us realized that foreign languages have actual, objective reality, that there are large areas of the earth where, strange as it may seem, English is neither spoken nor understood." The United States had built for itself a "neat little world in which everyone spoke English," he noted. Yet "suddenly these pesky foreigners rose up before us in their own lands, doggedly refusing to understand our tongue, no matter how slowly and loudly we spoke it. It was little short of outrageous."

The army launched a training program to give soldiers a crash course in the languages they'd need to fight a global war. Eventually it encompassed some forty languages (and it pioneered the "audio-lingual" method used in classrooms today). But training an army of millions to speak the dozens of languages its men might encounter as they hopped from continent to continent was wholly impractical.

It really would be better if the foreigners could learn English.

★

As Allied leaders contemplated how the world might look after the war, they thought about language. "The empires of the future are empires of the mind," Winston Churchill announced in 1943 in a speech at Harvard. The key to that mental colonization, he believed, was linguistic. Churchill invited Harvard students to imagine the "grand convenience" that English speakers would enjoy if their language were used globally. No longer hemmed in by territorial empires, they'd be able to "move freely about the world."

It was a stirring vision. Yet it was also, Churchill recognized, far from reality. English wasn't a global lingua franca in 1943, and it didn't seem likely to become one anytime soon. It had a daunting vocabulary, with its largest dictionaries containing some half a million words. Its spelling was a cruel farce. Even Albert Einstein had been brought to his knees by what he called English's "underhanded orthography."

Churchill took these concerns seriously. In his Harvard speech, he declared his support for Basic, a drastically reduced version of English containing 850 words, only 18 of them verbs (*come, get, give, go, keep, let, make, put, seem, take, be, do, have, see, say, send, may*, and *will*). Basic was English for foreigners. The entire system—grammar and vocabulary—could be printed legibly on one side of a sheet of paper, with space left over for sample sentences.

It may be surprising to hear that Churchill, an undisputed virtuoso of the English language, would so readily trade his Steinway grand for a toy piano. But he wasn't the only one. Basic's champions, besides Churchill, included Ezra Pound, Lawrence Durrell, and George Orwell. "In Basic you cannot make a meaningless statement without it being apparent," Orwell noted. H. G. Wells predicted that Basic would "spread like wildfire" and that by 2020 there would be "hardly anyone in the world" unable to understand it.

Britain's most esteemed professor of literature, I. A. Richards, made Basic his calling. He had taught in China, which led him to worry about the spread of English. "The majority of Chinese students are *never* going to learn to understand much literary English," he judged. Richards saw Basic as the best way to acquaint them with the "enormous number of ideas, feelings, desires, and attitudes that they can only gain through some form of Western language."

In 1937 Richards managed the extraordinary feat of getting the Chinese government to agree to teach Basic in its schools. This was almost immediately undercut by the Japanese, who launched their full-scale invasion of China that year. Still, Richards pressed on, and the war's end saw him in Miami using Basic to train Chinese seamen at a naval facility.

"It takes only 400 words of Basic to run a battleship," Richards told *Time.* "With 850 words you can run the planet."

Franklin Delano Roosevelt took note. Basic "has tremendous merit in it," he told his secretary of state, and might allow English to dislodge French as the language of diplomacy. Roosevelt's enthusiasm didn't prevent him from mocking Churchill, though. He wrote the prime minister to ask how well Churchill's famous "blood, toil, tears, and sweat" speech would have gone down if it had been delivered in Basic, with Churchill offering his countrymen his "blood, work, eye-water and face-water."

"Seriously, however, we are interested," Roosevelt hastily added.

Still, as Roosevelt had intuited, dehydrated English was surprisingly difficult to use. Native English speakers struggled mightily to restrict themselves to Basic's 850 approved words. Foreigners, for their part, were baffled by Basic's tortuous circumlocutions, particularly around verbs. "The Koreans, Spaniards, and Russians have a right to ask why it is easier to say 'I went in the air by jumping' than 'I jumped,'" one critic aptly wrote.

★

In the end, Basic never truly went in the air by jumping. Speakers didn't take to it, and its advocates lost interest. Yet slimming English down wasn't the only way to win it a global following. By the 1940s, eager reformers had proposed dozens of schemes to tame its irregular orthography. There was Anglic ("Forskor and sevn yeerz agoe our faadherz braut forth on dhis kontinent a nue naeshon"), the Fonetik Crthqgrafi, the Nue Spelling, the Alfabet for the World of Tomorrow, and a curiously vowel-stingy system advertised as "1 Wrld, 1 Langwij."

The boldest scheme came from a former senator, Robert Latham Owen. Part Cherokee (he was known as "Oconostota" among the Cherokees), Owen had been one of the leaders of the failed attempt to establish the largely Indian state of Sequoyah in 1905. After Congress rejected Sequoyah and admitted the larger (and whiter) state of Oklahoma instead, Owen got elected to the Senate. He and Charles Curtis, Herbert Hoover's future vice president, were the only Indians there.

Owen's hoped-for state of Sequoyah was named after the man who had designed a non-roman script for the Cherokee language, a script that Cherokees had learned rapidly and enthusiastically. Could something like that be done for English? Owen had toyed for some time with creating a new phonetic alphabet. On December 7/8, 1941, the day of Japan's attack, he resolved to see it through.

Owen's "global alphabet," as he called it, didn't use roman letters. It looked more like Arabic or shorthand. By eschewing familiar letter forms, Owen could circumvent orthographic questions entirely. Words were

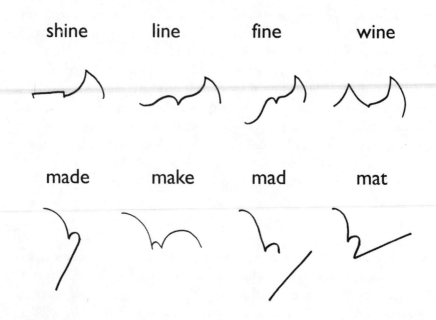

The global alphabet: Robert Latham Owen's system

spelled exactly as they sounded. This was the means, Owen insisted, "by which we can teach the English language to all the world at high speed."

He predicted that with the global alphabet, English could be made "the conversational language of the world within two or three years." And, he added, his system was fully compatible with Basic.

Owen's idea made the rounds. FDR passed the scheme on to his secretary of state for consideration. The Senate Committee on Foreign Relations held hearings on it ("I do not think any person could contribute more to humanity than by evolving a universal method of communication," a senator from New Mexico exclaimed). The writer George Bernard Shaw was taken by it and willed part of his estate to fund the creation and promotion of a non-roman phonetic alphabet. The cautionary note came from Eleanor Roosevelt, who feared it was too hard to learn. Still, Owen was encouraged enough to build a special typewriter for his alphabet.

It was the first such typewriter, and it was the last—the alphabet never caught on. Yet that Owen got even this far is striking. So nervous were leaders in the United States and Britain about the prospects of normal English that they were willing to consider drastic measures to reform it.

Housebroken English—reduced to eighteen verbs, written in squiggles— was a price they seriously entertained paying for Churchill's hoped-for "empires of the mind."

★

The challenges English faced went beyond the technical ones. Colonial rule, which had been one of the chief vehicles for spreading English, was visibly breaking down. Decolonization would ultimately release more than six hundred million people from rule by Britain and the United States. Would they stick with English?

Very likely not. Many complained bitterly of the havoc English had wreaked on their countries. Mohandas Gandhi regarded India's reliance on English as a "sign of slavery." The Kenyan author James Ngugi judged the "psychological violence of the classroom" to have been just as harmful as the "physical violence of the battlefield." He recalled his own childhood in a mission school, when students caught speaking their native Gikuyu were beaten, fined, or made to wear signs reading I AM STUPID or I AM A DONKEY. After decolonization, he changed his name to Ngũgĩ wa Thiong'o and gave up writing novels in English.

Manuel Quezon complained, too. Even though few adult Filipinos spoke English fluently by the time the Philippines became a commonwealth and Quezon became its president, the looming presence of English in the schools and government had blocked local languages from taking root. The result was, after hundreds of years of colonial rule (counting Spain), the Philippines had *no* indigenous language spoken throughout the archipelago.

"When I travel through the provinces and talk to my people, I need an interpreter," Quezon lamented. "Did you ever hear of anything more humiliating, more horrible than that?"

The Philippines needed "a language of her own," he insisted. It must be indigenous to the Philippines and taught nationally. Without such a language, Quezon continued, "a national soul cannot exist."

Having gained some autonomy from Washington with the establishment of the commonwealth in 1935, Quezon founded a national language institute. Its task was to develop a local language—it chose Manila-based Tagalog—into a national one. Turning a vernacular into an official language and promulgating it would take time (the National Council of

Education suggested Basic Tagalog, patterned on Basic English, as a bridge). But Quezon hoped that it would eventually undo the anglicization of the colonial era.

As decolonization proceeded, it became clear that many countries shared that goal. At independence, India took Bharat as an official name and Hindi as its official language, demoting English to subsidiary status and promising to drop it entirely by 1965. The British colony of Singapore set Malay as its official language in 1959, when it gained self-governance. In Sri Lanka, the Sinhala Only Act of 1956 did the same for Sinhalese.

In 1949 the United Nations General Assembly resolved that member states should teach primary and secondary students in their native languages. That year, Mao Zedong took power in China; his Cultural Revolution would prohibit English and make English-language teachers targets of violence. In the Eastern Bloc, the Soviet Union sought to ban English as a "decadent" subject and to promote Russian throughout its realm.

The Organization of African Unity declared that European languages would be "only provisionally tolerated" in independent Africa and set up an Inter-African Bureau of Languages to replace them with indigenous ones.

Perhaps this could be done. In the British mandate of Palestine, Jewish settlers had revived the ancient scriptural language of Hebrew and taught it to their children as a mother tongue. They got far enough with Hebrew that in 1948, when Palestine gained independence as the State of Israel, it dropped English as an official language. A language that, in living memory, had counted no native speakers had nonetheless beaten English into retreat.

I. A. Richards watched all this with alarm. Third World nationalism, he warned, could "wreck all hopes for English."

★

How *did* English prevail? In the forties, FDR and Churchill expected that they'd have to drastically alter English to turn it into a global language. Decolonization, by placing men like Manuel Quezon in power, only worsened English's prospects. Yet English surmounted these obstacles and became a true world language. How?

Part of the story, some linguists have insisted, is the foreign policies of the United States and Britain. Even as Anglophone powers lost political control over much of the world, this explanation goes, they found ways to impose their language on weaker countries.

They did that in large part through education. The hundreds of thousands of foreign students streaming into U.S. universities (120,000 a year by 1969) didn't just study math and sociology. They studied math and sociology *in English*. They then carried English back to their home countries, where they ranked among the most educated and powerful. Add to those students the nearly half a million foreign military trainees who studied at U.S. military academies, schools, bases, and special facilities.

While students rushed in, English oozed out. By the 1960s, at least forty U.S. government agencies sponsored English teaching abroad, most notably the Peace Corps (an instrument of "Western psychological warfare," charged the president of Ghana). The radio stations, too, beamed English into foreign countries. In 1959 the Voice of America adopted a limited-vocabulary "Special English," reminiscent of Basic, for some broadcasts. Textbooks, comics, and movies all poured from the Anglophone countries into the rest of the world, sometimes with governmental subsidies.

But was that enough? It couldn't have been. English had muscle behind it, yes, but non-Anglophone countries had formidable defenses. They set curricula in their schools, granted languages other than English official status, and broadcast their own radio programs. With children learning Swahili or Sinhala in school, what could a hundred Peace Corps volunteers do?

What is more, the Anglophone governments didn't ultimately place much priority on language export. Though agencies like the Voice of America and the Peace Corps promoted English, that wasn't their main mission. It wasn't until 1965 that the U.S. government even set the promulgation of English as a foreign policy objective.

It's helpful to look in the other direction. Global English isn't really, in the end, the product of a few big decisions made in Washington or London. It's the product of a billion or so smaller ones made all around the world. Those billions of decisions have been, to be sure, profoundly influenced by the predominant position of the United States in the world. But ultimately the language wasn't imposed from the top down. It emerged from the bottom up.

★

That's the thing about standards; they work differently from other kinds of power. Governments can tax, enlist, and imprison their subjects. They do those things all the time. But standards are harder to impose, languages especially so. Colonial authorities spent fifty years trying to drum the English language into Puerto Ricans' heads yet managed to get only a quarter of the population even *conversant* in it. They had such a hard time because, in the streets and in the home, Puerto Ricans still spoke Spanish.

Standards reflect power, but the real compulsion rarely comes from the state. It comes, rather, from the community. Take a textbook case of standard setting: the rival formats for videocassette recorders. In 1975 Sony put out the first consumer VCR, which used a tape format called Betamax. The next year, Sony's rival JVC began selling VCRs that used a different format, VHS. Each had virtues—Betamax offered better image and sound quality, VHS tapes played longer. In 1980, consumers might have had good reason for choosing either.

But not in 1990. By then, something had happened. Enough people had chosen VHS for it to acquire a critical mass. Rental stores stopped stocking Betamax; new movies came out only on VHS. Sony itself reluctantly decided to start making VHS-compatible hardware. "Speaking frankly, we didn't want to manufacture VHS," its deputy president confessed. "However, you don't conduct business according to your feelings."

Sony hadn't been *compelled* to give up on Betamax, exactly. It's just that the cost of sticking with it had become prohibitively high. Too many people had already chosen VHS.

Something similar has happened in language. As distant cultures have come into closer contact, the need for common tongues has grown. Yet which language to use hasn't exactly been a free choice for everyone. You pick the language others have chosen, the language you think will get you the furthest. And once a critical mass has been reached, that choice becomes practically mandatory.

Different people have undergone this process at different paces. The international communities on globalization's leading edge were the first to feel the need for a uniform language. They latched on to English early, and as each one adopted it, the language's momentum grew, eventually dragging whole countries along for the ride.

The first group to fully go in for English was the air traffic controllers.

Aviation, being technically complex and profoundly international, is an area where standards are vital. A common language is especially so, given the paramount importance of clear communication in the skies. In the 1950s a Soviet plane carrying the USSR's foreign minister, Andrei Gromyko, to London twice overshot Heathrow Airport and nearly crashed because the pilot struggled to understand the control tower's instructions.

Yet such misunderstandings are happily rare, for when the rules of the international aviation system were agreed upon in 1944, a standard language was chosen for international flights. It was, not surprisingly, English. This wasn't a choice made because of a desire to turn the world Anglophone. It was made from necessity: there had to be one language, and the United States at that point was responsible for nearly 70 percent of the world's passenger miles.

Non-English speakers chafed at this. In the 1970s, Francophones in Quebec sought to use French in the air for local flights when convenient. They weren't demanding that French be the main language of the skies, just that it be an option. Yet pilots and air traffic controllers fought back. They were generally of a global ilk and had adapted themselves to English. They went on strike, crippling aviation in Canada for nine days until the government agreed to prohibit French in the air.

The world community of pilots has grown dramatically more diverse over the subsequent decades, but English has stuck. Korean, German, Brazilian, and Algerian pilots all speak it. In large single-language regions, such as Latin America, they might bend the rules and switch to their native tongues. But they must snap back to English when Anglophones are present.

The next group to go in for English was the scientists. Modern science has always been international, and scientists were accustomed to having to learn one another's languages to read the latest research. In the twentieth century, they seriously considered adopting invented languages to speed their work. They were particularly interested in a postwar bridge language called Interlingua, designed especially for science. The prestigious *Journal of the American Medical Association* printed abstracts in it ("Velocitates de conduction esseva determinate in 126 patientes qui presentava con disordines neurologic"). A journal of molecular spectroscopy appeared entirely in the language.

Such internationalist ambition, though laudable, couldn't overcome the gravitational force of the United States. In the first decade and a half following the Second World War, 55 percent of the Nobel Prizes in science went to scholars at U.S. universities, and 76 percent of laureates were at Anglophone ones. By the 1960s, more than half of publications on natural science in the world were in English.

Again, a tipping point was reached. With half of the publications in English and more than half of the Nobel laureates speaking it, what were the odds that Interlingua or any other language could hold out? Scientists from non-Anglophone countries had to learn English to read cutting-edge scholarship in their field. Increasingly, they had to write in it, too. The proportion of scientific publications in English shot up as more and more non-Anglophone scientists made the switch. Today it is well over 90 percent.

In Israel, scientists joke that God himself couldn't get tenure at the Hebrew University of Jerusalem—he only has one publication, and it's not in English. They're not wrong. Of the 1,921 research publications listed on the websites of the faculty members at Hebrew University's Racah Institute of Physics, *every one* is in English.

Air traffic control and scientific research turned out to be mere preludes. The most powerful force for anglicization has been the internet. It has promoted international communication, but it has set English proficiency as the price. The web was invented in the United States and has been disproportionately Anglophone ever since. In 1997 a survey of language distribution found that 82.3 percent of randomly chosen websites, from all over the world, were in English.

It's not just that English users dominate the internet. The medium itself favors English. Its programming languages are derived from English, so anyone seeking to master Python, C++, or Java—to name three popular coding languages—will have a much easier time if they speak English.

Residing at a deeper level are the encoding schemes that translate bits (ones and zeroes) into characters. The encoding most frequently used in the early days of the internet was ASCII, a scheme designed to support English. ASCII makes no provision for non-roman languages such as Arabic and Hindi. It can't even handle frequently used symbols in European languages, such as ø, ü, ß, or ñ. ASCII nudges everything toward English.

Today there are more accommodating encodings, covering languages from Cherokee to Cuneiform, but they aren't universally supported. That

Roman characters are featured first on the search engine Baidu, the most visited web page in China.

means there's no guarantee that a non-English email or text will display correctly. Web addresses are still nearly all in ASCII, which is why the most popular website in China is accessed by typing baidu.com, not 百度.中文网. And even if it *did* have a Chinese web address, users would still have to use QWERTY keyboards—the global standard, designed in New York around the English alphabet—to type it.

The dominance of English on the internet is, in a way, the result of free choices. No government commanded it, no army enforces it. Yet many who have chosen to work in English have done so reluctantly, in the way a Betamax fan might bow to inevitability and purchase a VHS system. They use English because there is no other viable choice.

"It is the ultimate act of intellectual colonialism," sighed the director of an internet provider in Russia. "The product comes from America so we must either adapt to English or stop using it. That is the right of business. But if you are talking about a technology that is supposed to open the world to hundreds of millions of people you are joking. This just makes the world into new sorts of haves and have nots."

The president of France, Jacques Chirac, deemed the English-dominant internet "a major risk for humanity."

★

Air traffic controllers, then scientists, then internet users. As each increasingly large technical community adopted English, the momentum grew. Whole countries—some containing hundreds of millions of people who have never attended a scientific conference and may not even use the internet often—were dragged into the vortex.

This process now appears inexorable, but it took a while to become so. In 1969 a prominent linguist at Columbia University noted that a world language was probably inevitable. Yet even at that late date he wasn't sure English would be it. Yes, some 60 percent of the world's radio and television broadcasts were in English. But resistance to the language was strong enough that he earnestly considered the possibility that the artificial language of Esperanto, which was easier to learn and had little of English's cultural baggage, might prevail.

Betamax, in other words, was still an option.

Yet the period of choice lasted only so long, and 1969 was pretty near to the end. The following decades saw country after country succumbing to English. Even as they tried to escape from it, they fell into its growing gravity well.

India had, at its independence, temporarily allowed English to remain a "subsidiary official" language, with the understanding that the government would switch entirely to Hindi in 1965. But not only did English persist, it grew. Today, advertisements are in English, higher education is in English, and Bollywood movies feature generous helpings of English. The language remains in official use and is heard in parliamentary debates at roughly the same frequency as Hindi. The "bitter truth," reported *The New York Times* recently, is that "English is the de facto national language of India."

That is the bitter truth of many countries. Sri Lanka, which once passed a Sinhala Only Act, has restored English to its former official status ("Welcome to Official Web Portal of Government of Sri Lanka," its home page awkwardly beams). Singapore, which had replaced English with Malay, launched a Speak Good English movement in 2000. "Investors will not come if their supervisors and managers can only guess what our workers are saying," the prime minister explained. "Poor English reflects badly on us and makes us seem less intelligent."

The Philippines fell, too. Despite Manuel Quezon's quest to establish a national indigenous language to dislodge it, English remains both an official language and a constant presence. The Philippines has more call-center workers than any other country. It's also an international center for teaching English, a place where aspiring speakers can learn the language cheaply, with a clear mainland accent.

English's gravitational pull extends far beyond the domain where Anglophone powers promoted their language. It would be hard to find a place further removed, culturally or politically, from Washington and London than Mongolia. But in 2004 its prime minister, a Harvard graduate, an-

"Conquer English to make China stronger": Li Yang, the media personality who is China's most popular English teacher, claims to have taught millions in his campaign to turn China into a global hegemon through the mastery of English.

nounced that English would replace Russian as the first foreign language in Mongolian schools. He hoped to turn Mongolia's capital, Ulaanbaatar, into a hub for call centers.

The most remarkable conquest by English has been China. In 1978, under the reformist premier Deng Xiaoping, China restored English as a permissible foreign language and encouraged it as part of China's path to prosperity. Chinese television started broadcasting an English-language teaching show, *Follow Me*, starring a British woman and commanding an audience of tens of millions. Today the top Chinese universities offer hundreds of degree programs in subjects ranging from history to nuclear physics taught in English. Some hundred thousand native speakers of English have found work as teachers in China.

"If the Chinese . . . rule the world some day," the linguist John McWhorter has written, "I suspect they will do it in English."

★

English is not the language with the most native speakers today. Mandarin Chinese is, followed by Spanish. There are many people in the United States itself who struggle with English. But what's remarkable about

English is that it's the language with the most *non*native speakers. Estimates vary widely, but it seems that roughly one in four humans on the planet can now speak it. That number appears to be growing.

For those who speak English as a foreign language, the reasons are clear. English is the language of power. Speaking it means going to better schools, getting better jobs, and moving in more elite circles. A study commissioned by the British Council of five poorer countries (Pakistan, Bangladesh, Cameroon, Nigeria, and Rwanda) found that professionals who spoke English earned 20 to 30 percent more than those who didn't.

In South Korea, parents alert to this dynamic have sent their young children, usually under the age of five, to clinics for lingual frenectomies, surgery to cut the thin band of tissue under the tongue. The operation ostensibly gives children nimbler tongues, making it easier for them to pronounce the difficult *l* and *r* sounds. If masters once cut slaves' tongues out to prohibit native languages, today people do the cutting themselves. And they do it to enable English.

Lingual frenectomies, it should be said, aren't common. Nevertheless, their mere existence speaks to a widely felt hunger for English. Even in South Korea, which has never been colonized by an Anglophone power, mastering the language is of overwhelming importance. As a professor at a Seoul university put it, "English is now becoming a means of survival."

★

For the inhabitants of the United States, the anglicization of the world is, just as Churchill predicted, a "grand convenience." It allows them to do business in any part of the world. It also helps their ideas and ambitions to resound. Films, books, shows, music, and advertisements flow easily out of the United States, so that even the remotest foreign countries feel like home.

Perhaps the most extraordinary privilege, though, is that people from the United States don't have to struggle with foreign languages. While everyone else pays the cognitive tax of learning English, English speakers can dispense with language classes entirely. In 2013 the Modern Language Association found that college and university enrollments in foreign languages were half what they had been fifty years earlier. In other words, U.S. students have responded to globalization by learning half as many languages.

And why should they bother? If, in the early twentieth century, internationally inclined and ambitious men such as Theodore Roosevelt, Woodrow Wilson, and Herbert Hoover had to learn foreign languages, their counterparts today do not. Barack Obama, despite his almost comically cosmopolitan background (a Kenyan father who met his mainland mother in a Russian class, a childhood spent in Hawaiʻi and Indonesia), speaks only English.

"It's embarrassing," Obama has admitted. "When Europeans come over here, they all speak English, they speak French, they speak German. And then we go over to Europe and all we can say is *merci beaucoup.*"

20

POWER IS SOVEREIGNTY, MISTER BOND

"Ah, Mr. Powers . . . welcome to my hollowed-out volcano," says Dr. Evil, gesturing to his elaborate underground base on a tropical island. The scenario, from *Austin Powers: The Spy Who Shagged Me*, is instantly recognizable. The deranged supervillain, his island lair, the threat of world destruction—it's so familiar you forget how bizarre it is.

Of all the potentially menacing locales, why do our most ambitious evildoers, the ones bent on world domination, seek out remote specks of land in the middle of seas and oceans? You'd think the qualities of islands that make them desirable vacation spots—their distance from population centers, their relaxed pace of life—would ill suit them as launchpads for global conquest. After all, Napoleon's adversaries sent him to Elba to exile him, not to encourage him to have another go.

It's true that there has long been an association with islands and malfeasance, at least in Western fiction. It's not hard to think of examples of islands as lawless and dangerous spaces, such as *Treasure Island* (1883), H. G. Wells's *The Island of Doctor Moreau* (1896), or Skull Island in *King Kong* (1933).

World domination from an island, though—that's different. As far as I can tell, it's a more recent literary phenomenon. As far as I can tell, it begins with Bond.

★

Ian Fleming, the creator of James Bond, knew about islands and the villainy they engendered. During the Second World War, he served as the assistant to Britain's director of naval intelligence. In 1943 he traveled to Kingston, Jamaica, for a high-level naval intelligence conference with the United States. The Caribbean was then in dire straits, tormented by German submarines that evaded the Allied navies. Rumors floated that the U-boats were finding safe berth at a secret harbor built by Axel Wenner-Gren, a Swedish multimillionaire who had established himself on an island in the Bahamas.

Wenner-Gren was a shadowy figure, moving, as one of his chroniclers put it, "behind the curtains of history, profoundly influencing the course of events." He was a striking physical specimen, with piercing blue eyes, snow-white hair, bronzed skin, and ramrod-straight posture. He'd made his first fortune manufacturing vacuum cleaners, but his sprawling multinational business empire grew to incorporate munitions, matches, wood pulp, planes, monorails, banking, telecommunications, and, ultimately, computers. The Disneyland and Seattle monorails were built by Wenner-Gren's company. Telmex, the Latin American telecommunications company (now the core of the fortune of the world's-richest-man contender Carlos Slim), was founded by Wenner-Gren.

Wenner-Gren had left Sweden for the Bahamas, apparently for tax reasons. There, he'd purchased the bulk of an island, established an estate called Shangri-La, and anchored his yacht, the largest in the world, equipped with state-of-the-art radio communications.

"He is too big for Sweden," a magazine from his home country wrote. "He is an international power."

Wenner-Gren did, it was true, have a foreign policy all his own. He theorized that science and rationality were bringing forth an era of peace. To nudge the new age along, he backed one of the period's many spelling reform schemes, Anglic, in the hopes of turning English into a global language. He also pursued peace by serving as a back-channel emissary between British prime minister Neville Chamberlain and Hermann Göring, the second-in-command in the Nazi leadership. Wenner-Gren was, in fact, one of the last diplomatic links between Britain and Germany before Hitler invaded Poland.

Wenner-Gren's ties to Göring threw a pall of suspicion over him. "I have not a shred of evidence, but I have a very strong feeling that this man acts as a spy for the German government," the U.S. undersecretary of state reported. The FBI put Wenner-Gren under surveillance, the U.S. government froze his accounts, and wild accusations flew. It was said that he was helping Nazis transfer wealth, that Göring had sneaked a mysterious bundle onto Wenner-Gren's yacht, or that every member of the yacht's crew was a spy.

It surely didn't help that the FBI was aggressively investigating a member of Wenner-Gren's coterie, Inga Arvad, a Danish beauty queen sometimes mistaken for his mistress. Arvad was a favorite of the Nazi leadership; Hitler had judged her to be the most "perfect example of Nordic beauty" he'd ever seen, and he had hosted her in his private box during the 1936 Olympics. Whether that meant she was spying was hard to say. The main revelation from the FBI's round-the-clock surveillance was not that Arvad was consorting with Nazis, but that she was conducting a torrid, involved affair—one the FBI recorded on tape—with a young naval ensign named John F. Kennedy. (When Kennedy was elected president, J. Edgar Hoover used the FBI's dossier on Arvad as blackmail to ensure his reappointment as FBI director.)

This was the hotbed of international intrigue Ian Fleming encountered in 1943.

The accusations that Wenner-Gren had built a secret harbor for German U-boats proved false. Still, Fleming found the whole rum-soaked milieu irresistible. "When we have won this blasted war," Fleming told his friend, "I am going to live in Jamaica. Just live in Jamaica and lap it up, and swim in the sea and write books."

He bought an estate there, Goldeneye, named after one of the intelligence operations he'd participated in during the war.

★

Jamaica was, for Fleming, one of those "blessed corners of the British empire," a place where brown-skin natives still served drinks at the club and the fantasies of colonial life could be indulged for just a while longer. In 1956 Britain lost control of the Suez Canal, an incident that foretold the end of the empire. ("In the whole of modern history I can't think of a comparable shambles," wrote Fleming.) It was to Jamaica that prime minister Anthony Eden repaired to recuperate from that defeat. He stayed at Goldeneye.

Fleming spent every winter in Jamaica from 1946 until his death, in

1964. It was where he wrote all the Bond books. Jamaica was also where Fleming conducted an affair with a rich widow named Blanche Black-well, who was in turn having an affair with Fleming's neighbor, Errol Flynn. Scampering underfoot at Goldeneye was Blackwell's young son, Chris, who would later grow up to found Island Records and launch the reggae musicians Bob Marley, Jimmy Cliff, Toots and the Maytals, and Peter Tosh onto the world scene. (After Fleming's death, Bob Marley bought Goldeneye, but he deemed it "too posh" and sold it to Chris Blackwell, who owns it now.)

Fleming set three Bond novels in Jamaica, though none captured the scene as vividly as *Doctor No* (1958). After a group of assassins destroy the British Secret Service's radio station, severing the connection between Jamaica and England, Bond is dispatched. The clues point to a nearby island. A guano island, as it happens.

Fleming's readers probably knew little of guano, but he was eager to remedy their ignorance. When Bond first arrives in Jamaica, the colonial secretary sits him down for a lecture on guano's history ("Bond prepared to be bored"). This, remarkably, lasts an entire chapter. The secretary un-spools the whole story, starting with the British-Peruvian monopoly and working his way up to Fritz Haber's invention of ammonia synthesis.

"Bitten off a bit more than you can chew on guano," he natters on. "Talk to you for hours about it."

The point, as he comes to it, is that there are small, uninhabited is-lands scattered around the Caribbean. And one has been purchased by a mysterious international figure, Doctor Julius No.

It's hard not to see Axel Wenner-Gren in the figure of Julius No. The two are tantalizingly similar: physically striking, obsessed with science, loyal to no country, eager to meddle in world politics, and possessors of vast fortunes. Wenner-Gren even insisted on being called "Dr. Wenner-Gren," by dint of an honorary doctorate from a Peruvian university.

And, of course, both owned Caribbean islands. In the novel, Doctor No tells Bond how he bought his island and developed it into "the most valuable technical intelligence center in the world." From it, he can use radio to monitor, jam, and redirect the United States' missiles ("I can bend the beams on which these rockets fly, Mister Bond"), claiming for himself the arms of a superpower.

The fact that it is an island matters enormously to Doctor No. "Mister

Bond, power is sovereignty," he explains. "Who in the world has the power of life or death over his people? Now that Stalin is dead, can you name any man except myself? And how do I possess that power, that sovereignty? Through privacy. Through the fact that nobody *knows*. Through the fact that I have to account to no one."

If there was one moment in literature when the switch was thrown, this was it. Fictional islands before *Doctor No* were the godforsaken outskirts of civilization. After it, they were centers of global power.

The films took the idea and ran with it. The private island looms large in the film of *Dr. No*, a film for which Chris Blackwell worked as a location scout. Similar locales can be found in other Bond films: *Thunderball* (filmed on Wenner-Gren's island), *You Only Live Twice* (rocket base under a Japanese volcanic island), *Diamonds Are Forever* (offshore oil rig), *Live and Let Die* (small Caribbean island dictatorship), *The Man with the Golden Gun* (private Thai island), *The Spy Who Loved Me* (giant sea base), and *Skyfall* (abandoned island). There is also a sequence in the 2006 *Casino Royale* shot, as was *Thunderball*, on Wenner-Gren's island.

The world of James Bond contains much that is absurd. The exploding pens, shark tanks, and endless procession of round-heeled female helpmeets seem more the fruits of Fleming's seasoned imagination than insights into actual espionage. Yet with the island thing, Fleming was onto something.

Just as he saw, islands *are* instruments of world domination.

★

They hadn't always been that way. Though the United States had begun its overseas expansion by collecting guano islands, its interest waned after they were scraped clean. In 1904 a State Department official announced that the United States claimed "no sovereign or territorial rights over guano islands"—a bizarre statement, even more so because it was apparently unprovoked.

Civil servants cannot single-handedly de-annex parts of the United States. Still, the statement captured the prevailing mood of the time. The United States was actively interested in colonies and was fighting a bloody war to hold on to its largest one, the Philippines. But remote atolls and sandbars meant much less. Washington made no objection and perhaps didn't even notice when other powers set up shop on some of its guano islands.

This blithe attitude may have served in the nineteenth and early twentieth centuries, but new technologies endowed islands with new significance. Aviation meant they could serve as landing strips; radio meant they could host transmitters. In 1935 the State Department announced that it was annexing Baker, Howland, and Jarvis Islands in the central Pacific. Two days later, it hastily rescinded the announcement. The United States didn't need to annex those islands, officials clarified with embarrassment. A consultation of the records had revealed that it already owned them.

It was a telling oversight, one that captured well the shambolic character of U.S. imperial administration. But it changed nothing from a strategic perspective. Franklin Delano Roosevelt called in Ernest Gruening, then the head of the Division of Territories and Island Possessions, for a chat about those islands. "Are we in an acquisitive mood today?" Roosevelt asked.

Gruening assured the president he was.

Roosevelt sent Gruening on a Pacific tour. As Gruening saw it, legal claims dating from the nineteenth century weren't enough. To "maintain the sovereignty of the United States," he believed, the guano islands must be actively colonized. And so, playing the part of one of history's last conquistadors, Gruening set off to plant the flag in the soil and claim the islands in the name of his country.

The plan, undertaken in secret starting in 1935, was to visit the Pacific guano islands, raise a flag, install a plaque, and drop off "colonies" of four or more Hawaiians on each. Why Hawaiians? "Because of their adaptability to prevailing conditions," Gruening explained. Thus the finest products of the Kamehameha Schools in Hawai'i were deposited in small groups on remote islands, with drums of water, crates of canned goods, and instructions to ward off invaders.

It didn't go perfectly. Arriving on Canton Island, Gruening's men found a British radio operator there. "I am instructed to inform you that this is British territory and to protest against your raising the American flag," he said. But they hoisted the flag and dropped off the Hawaiians anyway.

Howland Island was of special interest, as it was to be a stop in the aviator Amelia Earhart's round-the-world journey (she died en route to it). But to tame it, the Hawaiians would have to deal with an out-of-control rat

Ernest Gruening (back row, right) and four Hawaiian colonists on Howland Island

population—the same rats that had tormented the island's guano miners some eighty years earlier. The settlers used red quill powder as a poison. The powder killed the rats but acted slowly enough that the island's few other animals were able to regurgitate it.

The resulting scenario was surreal, half *Heart of Darkness*, half Salvador Dalí. At the very least, it would make a striking diorama: four Hawaiians eating out of crates, waiting for a famous aviator who would never arrive on a tiny, poisoned island that was littered with guano, crab vomit, and dead rats. And the Stars and Stripes flapping crisply in the breeze.

★

There was a comic air to the reconquest of the guano islands. Yet, zooming out, we can see the event as an important inflection point in U.S. history. Tiny islands such as Howland proved to be, just as Roosevelt and

Gruening foresaw, extremely useful. They and other small pockets of land became the mainstays of the United States' territorial empire.

Small specks of land acquired special importance in the twilight of formal empire. The global tide of decolonization washed most imperial arrangements from the map, but it left a few nooks and crannies, nearly all small islands. Large colonies could hope for self-sufficiency and launch nationalist movements to seize it. Small ones could not. For them, as Luis Muñoz Marín had observed, independence might mean economic suicide. And for places as small as Guam on the U.S. Virgin Islands, to stage armed revolutions would be actual suicide.

Similar calculations ran on the other side of the equation. Synthetics, international standardization, and the technologies of movement had alleviated the pressure on rich countries to colonize, since colonial products became both less necessary and easier to get through international (rather than imperial) trade. But geopolitics did not entirely vanish. Great powers still played games on the maps. It's just that with the advent of planes and wireless, they no longer needed to bother with difficult-to-hold populated colonies, as they had in Captain Mahan's day. They could focus instead on small pockets of control.

The United States, in other words, did not abandon empire after the Second World War. Rather, it reshuffled its imperial portfolio, divesting itself of large colonies and investing in military bases, tiny specks of

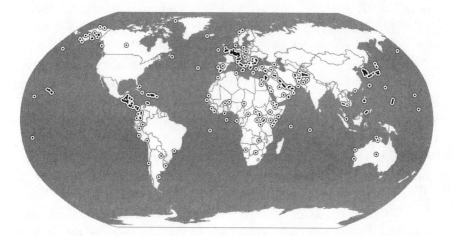

The pointillist empire today: Known U.S. bases beyond the mainland

semi-sovereignty strewn around the globe. Today there are roughly eight hundred such bases, some of the most important of them on islands.

It's telling that the guano islands were recolonized at the same time as the Philippine commonwealth was being established—i.e., just as the largest colony was put on track for independence. It's as if the United States, standing before the world map, put down the imperialist's paint roller and picked up the pointillist's brush.

★

Gruening's Gilbert and Sullivan–style adventures in the Pacific in the 1930s marked the turn toward pointillism. The Second World War locked the trajectory in. That war gave the United States more than two thousand overseas base sites. And it was hard to imagine giving them all back.

Right at the war's end, Harry Truman announced that his country coveted no territory. It was an anodyne statement, nearly identical to those his predecessors had often made. Yet this time it triggered what the State Department called a "storm of comment" from the press, Congress, and military leaders. What about the bases? they asked. Surely Truman wasn't going to let them go, was he?

Truman hastily clarified. The United States would take no colonies, he explained, but it *would* "maintain the military bases necessary for the complete protection of our interests and of world peace." (It was straight out of *Tom Sawyer*, one critic cackled: "We seek no territorial expansion or selfish advantage except maybe a few battered old bases that nobody else wants and that aren't much good anyhow.")

This was the new way. As the United States loosened its grip on large colonies, it grabbed bases and small islands more tightly. In the Philippines, it refused to leave entirely after independence. Instead, it insisted, as the price of reconstruction aid to the Philippines, on receiving ninety-nine-year leases on select base sites.

It was the same in Puerto Rico. Washington allowed gubernatorial elections and commonwealth status, but it clamped down on the eastern island of Vieques, which the navy turned into a sort of Caribbean Pearl Harbor. Around ten thousand of the poorest Puerto Ricans lived there, and many had their homes taken. Pedro Albizu Campos regarded the surrender of Vieques as the "vivisection" of Puerto Rico. As a community leader described Vieques, "We are the lamb that has been sacrificed so that the big island lives comfortably."

On Guam, increased rights and citizenship came at the cost of a massive military buildup—today, more than a quarter of the island is military bases. Hawaiian statehood was accompanied by the military takeover of the smallest of Hawai'i's major islands, Kaho'olawe, for use as a firing range and bombing site. Dwight Eisenhower, as president, had sought something similar in Alaska. His idea was to grant statehood but cleave off the strategically valuable portion of the territory, which would remain in military hands.

The same dynamic prevailed in Japan. The United States occupied the main islands until 1952 but continued to hold strategically useful outer islands for far longer. It kept Iwo Jima until 1968, Okinawa until 1972. Even today, with Okinawa back in Japanese hands, the U.S. military still dominates its landscape. "The military doesn't have bases on Okinawa," a naval officer has explained. "The island itself is the base."

Then there were Japan's mandated islands in Micronesia, which the United States had seized during the war. In the postwar settlement, they were taken from Japan and collectively placed under the authority of the United Nations as a strategic trust territory. Yet because those lightly inhabited islands (with some thirty thousand people living on them) were of great strategic value, Truman insisted that the United States have supervisory power. It got that power, and with little UN oversight.

In 1958, the same year Fleming published *Doctor No*, a naval officer named Stuart Barber rolled all this into a strategic plan. Decolonization, Barber argued, was sweeping the globe, making it harder for Western powers to secure access to foreign lands. So, rather than claim colonies or negotiate with decolonizing nations, Barber suggested that the United States seek out "relatively small, lightly populated islands, separated from major population masses" for its bases.

This was Barber's "strategic island concept," and it gave a name to what the United States was already doing. It underscored the point that in this new pointillist empire, colonialism was a liability, not an asset. The best bases were those that *didn't* enmesh large populations. They were places where, in the words of Doctor No, the United States would have to "account to no one."

Or, as Albizu put it, "The Yankees are interested in the cage but not the birds."

★

What, specifically, could the United States do with an island base? A good example is the Swan Islands, a small cluster of three islands in an isolated patch of the Caribbean, not far from the fictional location of Doctor No's island. The Swans were in the first batch of guano islands the United States had claimed.

The guano ran dry, but after the Second World War, Washington found other uses for the Swans. The USDA used them to quarantine imported livestock suspected of carrying foot-and-mouth disease. In the 1950s the CIA secretly took over Great Swan and built a landing strip and a fifty-thousand-watt radio transmitter. That extremely powerful transmitter could reach South America, allowing the United States to cover with its radio beams territory inaccessible by ground.

Soon after the CIA built its radio station, a mission of armed Honduran students traveled to Great Swan to liberate the islands and claim them for Honduras. They had no idea of the CIA's presence, and the agency was determined to keep them in the dark. GIVE THEM PLENTY OF BEER AND PROTECT THE FAMILY JEWELS was the frantic cable from Washington (i.e., don't let them discover the broadcasting equipment). Marines sped to the island to repel the invasion.

The episode that followed is best appreciated by reading the cable traffic from Swan to Washington:

Swan to HQ: HONDURAN SHIP ON HORIZON. BEER ON ICE. TALKED TO STUDENTS. THEY CONFABING. HAVE ACCEPTED BEER.

Swan to HQ: STUDENTS MIXING CEMENT IN WHICH THEY INTEND TO WRITE "THIS ISLAND BELONGS TO HONDURAS." ONE GROUP MALINGERING, LISTENING TO EARTHA KITT RECORDS AND DRINKING FIFTH BEER.

Swan to HQ: STUDENTS HAVE JUST RAISED HONDURAN FLAG. I SALUTED.

Swan to HQ: BEER SUPPLIES RUNNING LOW. NOW BREAKING OUT THE RUM. THESE KIDS ARE GREAT.

Swan to HQ: STUDENTS HAVE EMBARKED FOR HONDURAS. LIQUOR SUPPLY EXHAUSTED. FAMILY JEWELS INTACT.

In the end, the students were permitted to sing the Honduran national anthem, take a census, and raise their flag (on a CIA-supplied pole). The students left, never realizing who their drinking buddies were. Or that a contingent of marines had been waiting, ready to start shooting if the beer didn't work.

The family jewels were worth protecting. In 1954 the CIA had successfully used radio to spread fake news during a coup it helped stage to overthrow Guatemala's democratically elected but left-leaning government. With its transmitter on Swan Island, it could run an even more secure and sophisticated operation, this time directed at Fidel Castro's socialist regime in Cuba. Through "Radio Swan," which posed as a privately run station, the United States promulgated false news reports and trolled the Cuban government. Castro and his lieutenants were "pigs with beards," Raul Castro was "a queer with effeminate friends." Radio Havana Cuba shot back that Radio Swan was "a cage of hysterical parrots." Hysterical or not, Radio Swan boasted fifty million regular listeners throughout the Caribbean and Central and South America.

In 1961 the United States sent seven ships of paramilitaries to invade Cuba—the failed Bay of Pigs invasion. The day before the invasion, Radio Swan sowed confusion with cryptic messages designed to confound Castro: "Look well at the rainbow." "The fish will rise very soon." "Chico is in the house. Visit him." During the invasion, Radio Swan issued orders to nonexistent battalions to give courage to the rebels and spread fear among the authorities.

When this became public, journalists snickered over the resemblance between the operation and the plot of *Doctor No*. But the similarities may have been more than coincidence. The director of the CIA, Allen Dulles, gushed about the Bond novels and owned a complete set—a gift from the author. Moreover, Dulles had solicited Ian Fleming's advice on how to dislodge Castro. To his colleagues' surprise, Dulles had given every sign of taking that advice seriously.

The Bay of Pigs debacle forced Dulles into retirement and blew Radio

Swan's cover, but the CIA still found uses for the islands. In the 1980s the agency outfitted Great Swan with a port to off-load cargo intended for its favored political allies. Munitions, uniforms, parachutes, and other matériel flowed from the island to the rebels in Nicaragua who sought to bring down the leftist government. Great Swan was where right-wing paramilitaries trained, where Rhodesian mercenary pilots took off for their airdrops over Nicaragua.

The CIA island was in fact a central node in the vast and distinctly not-legal plot to overthrow the Nicaraguan government. That plot in its fullness incorporated arms dealers, drug traffickers, Middle Eastern governments, religious organizations, Cuban exiles, retired generals, and Rambo-style soldiers of fortune. Had such a multifarious scheme appeared in one of Fleming's novels, it might have strained his readers' patience. It is a victory for the forces of concision that today we know it simply by two words, albeit incongruous ones: the Iran-Contra affair.

★

In the 1958 novel *Doctor No*, guano is ubiquitous. Bond observes the thickly flocking birds, watches the miners, and smells the stink of the stuff. His love interest, Honeychile Rider, gets covered in it (she is "powdered white . . . except where the tears had marked her cheeks"). At the end of the novel, Bond defeats Doctor No by burying him in a guano pit, the villain's "screaming lungs stuffing with the filthy dust" until he dies.

In the 1962 film version, however, there is no trace of guano. Instead, Honeychile gets covered in "radioactive contamination." Doctor No's base is powered by a nuclear reactor, and Bond triumphs in the end by triggering a meltdown, drowning Doctor No in the pool containing the overheating reactor and wrecking the island. (That Bond's action would quite likely have turned Jamaica and its environs into a Chernobyl-style fallout zone goes narratively unexplored.)

The film's introduction of the nuclear theme was not a random choice. There is a special connection between nuclear weapons and islands, one that has placed the world's greatest instruments of destruction on some of its most remote locales. The very distance of small islands from large populations has made them ideal sites to test and store nuclear devices.

When the United States tested its first atomic bomb, scientists used the New Mexican desert. But for subsequent tests the Atomic Energy Commission sought places far from the mainland. "We just took out dozens of maps and started looking for remote sites," recalled one of the naval officers tasked with the hunt for islands. He lit on the Bikini Atoll in the Marshall Islands. Conveniently, it belonged to the Micronesian islands that the United States had seized at the end of the war (which would soon become the U.S.-supervised strategic trust territory).

Less conveniently, the atoll was populated; it had 167 inhabitants. What would become of them? The navy made a great show of asking them to leave. It filmed a meeting between the military governor of the Marshalls and King Juda of the Bikini Marshallese. In the film, which was shown widely, the Marshallese solemnly consider the request. "We will gladly go," Juda answers. "Everything in God's hands."

The reality wasn't so clean. "We didn't know what was going on," remembered Kilon Bauno, one of the Marshallese who was there. "We were very confused . . . Back then I had no idea what an atomic bomb was. None of us had." The navy's film, it turned out, showed not the actual discussion, but an awkwardly staged reenactment. After a few tense retakes, Juda stormed off.

Nevertheless, the Marshallese were ushered off the atoll, and the military detonated two atomic bombs there on July 1, 1946, each more powerful than those dropped on Japan. The test made the once-obscure atoll a household name. Four days after it, the French fashion designer Louis Réard debuted a two-piece bathing suit. He dubbed it the "bikini," on the grounds that the sight of a woman's mostly unclothed body was as sensational as the bomb.

Réard unveiled the bikini on July 5, 1946. The day before, the Fourth of July, was another historic day: the independence of the Philippines. The high commissioner, in his speech, couldn't resist spelling out the connection between decolonization and the atomic tests of a few days before. The Philippines was finally independent, he proudly announced. Nevertheless, he reminded, "all nations have yielded some of their independence, of their absolute independence, to the airplane, the radio, and the atom bomb."

★

The Bikini Marshallese, removed from their home, were placed on the atoll of Rongerik. Within two months, their food and water started running out. They asked to return home to Bikini.

Of course, they couldn't. Not only was their homeland radioactive, but the military had no intention of abandoning its valuable testing site.

Between 1946 and 1958, the United States detonated sixty-six more nuclear weapons on or near Bikini and the next-door atoll of Enewetak. To the proverbial Martian looking on from space, it must have appeared that humanity was for some indiscernible reason waging furious, unrelenting war on a string of sandbars in the middle of the Pacific.

One such test at Bikini was of a hydrogen bomb, the "Bravo shot" in 1954. Its fifteen-megaton yield was twice as large as expected, and unusually strong winds carried the fallout well beyond the cordoned-off blast zone. Had it detonated over Washington, D.C., it could have killed 90 percent of the populations of Washington, Baltimore, Philadelphia, and New York within three days.

On Rongelap, more than a hundred miles from ground zero, islanders watched radioactive white ash fall from the sky like snow. (Eighty suffered from radiation poisoning, and the island had to be evacuated for three years.) A Japanese tuna fishing boat, the *Lucky Dragon*, also outside the blast zone, was engulfed in the fallout. All twenty-three of its crew members got radiation poisoning, and one died.

The Democratic presidential candidate Adlai Stevenson proposed halting open-air bomb testing for fear of the cancer risks (a later study by the National Cancer Institute confirmed that nearby Marshall Islanders had endured cancer-causing levels of radiation exposure). Richard Nixon dismissed this as "catastrophic nonsense." Cornelius Rhoads, who by then had moved on from experimenting on Puerto Ricans to become the most prominent cancer researcher in the country, agreed with Nixon. "We have no prudent course except to continue the development and testing of the most modern weapons of defense," Rhoads wrote in a letter cosigned by eleven leading scientists.

Henry Kissinger, the country's most esteemed civilian nuclear expert, voiced the prevailing attitude in blunter fashion. "There are only 90,000 people out there," he said, referring to Micronesia. "Who gives a damn?"

★

Kissinger was right; few on the U.S. mainland cared about Micronesia. But had he visited Japan, he would have seen a nation that very much gave a damn.

When the radiation-sick crew of the *Lucky Dragon* limped back to port carrying a catch of radioactive tuna, it ignited a media frenzy. Japan was a country with firsthand experience of radioactive fallout. Rumors flew that the irradiated fish had made their way onto the market. The tuna industry briefly collapsed.

The Japanese government conducted tests of the fallout (something the U.S. government declined to do). It found alarming levels of radioactivity in seawater as far as two thousand miles away from Bikini and strong radioactivity in the rain that fell on Japan.

The emperor himself began traveling with a Geiger counter.

Fishmongers and sushi shopkeepers protested the United States' nuclear testing. Women in the Suginami ward in Tokyo circulated a petition to ban atomic and hydrogen bombs entirely. In a month, they collected more than 260,000 signatures, nearly two-thirds of the population of the ward. In a year and a half, 20 million signed it.

Among those swept up by the antinuclear movement was a young film producer, Tomoyuki Tanaka. He would later go on to produce such high-end classics of Japanese cinema as Akira Kurosawa's *Yojimbo*, but in the year of the Bravo shot Tanaka had something else in mind. He hired the director Ishirō Honda, who had traveled through Hiroshima in 1945 and seen the devastation firsthand.

Gojira, the phenomenally popular film Tanaka and Honda made, was about an ancient dinosaur awakened by U.S. hydrogen bomb testing. Gojira first destroys a Japanese fishing boat—a thinly veiled *Lucky Dragon*—before attacking and irradiating a Bikini-like island called Odo. Gojira, who is said to be "emitting high levels of H-bomb radiation," then turns on Tokyo, breathing fire and laying waste to the city.

As films go, *Gojira* isn't subtle. It's full of talk of bombs and radiation. "If nuclear testing continues, then someday, somewhere in the world, another Gojira may appear" are its somber final words.

That message, however, got lost in translation. *Gojira* was remixed for the United States, using much of the original footage but splicing in a white, English-speaking protagonist played by Raymond Burr. What got cut out was the antinuclear politics. The Hollywood version contains only two muted references to radiation. And it ends on a much happier note: "The menace was gone," the narrator concludes. "The world could wake up and live again."

The Japanese *Gojira* was a protest film, hammering away at the dangers of the U.S. testing in the Pacific. The English-language *Godzilla*, by contrast, was just another monster flick.

★

The Japanese were right to be nervous. Despite all the duck-and-cover warnings about Soviet strikes on Cincinnati and Dubuque, the real front lines of nuclear confrontation were the overseas bases and territories. Hundreds of nuclear weapons, we now know, were placed in South Korea, the Philippines, Guam, and Puerto Rico. Throughout most of the sixties, there were more than a thousand on Okinawa. Johnston Island, one of the guano islands Ernest Gruening had recolonized, bristled with nuclear-armed Thor missiles. An unknown number of nuclear weapons were stored in Hawai'i, Alaska (including on the Aleutian Islands), and Midway.

Arming the bases brought the United States' nuclear arsenal closer to potential war zones, making its threats more credible. It also distributed risk. With the U.S. stockpile spread widely, Moscow couldn't target the mainland alone. If it wanted to eliminate the United States' retaliatory capability, it would have to strike the bases, too, making the operation vastly more difficult.

Yet while nukes on bases protected the mainland, they imperiled the territories and host nations. Flying nuclear weapons around the bases—something the military did routinely—risked catastrophic accident. Even when the weapons stayed put, their presence turned the bases into tempting targets, especially since overseas bases were easier for Moscow to hit than the mainland was. Arming the bases was essentially painting bright red bull's-eyes on them.

A sense of the risk can be gained by considering the Arctic base at Thule in Greenland. Greenland was a colony of Denmark, having roughly the same place in the Danish Kingdom as Puerto Rico had in the United States. This made it an attractive locale for bases, as Greenlanders' protests counted less with the Danish government than those of Copenhageners. When Washington's gaze fell on the village of Thule as a base site, the Danish government obliged by removing the indigenous Inughuit community there. The Inughuits were dropped off unceremoniously with blankets, tents, and the very best of wishes in "New Thule," some sixty-five miles north.

The virtue of Thule was that it was close enough to the Soviet Union that from there, the United States could lob missiles over the North Pole at Moscow. The drawback was that the Soviets could fire missiles back. The Soviet premier warned Denmark that to allow the United States to house its arsenal at Thule—or anywhere on Danish soil—would be "tantamount to suicide." Nervous Danish politicians incorporated a "nonuclear" principle into the platform of their governing coalition: the United States could have its base, but no nukes.

Despite this, Washington pressed the issue. When the Danish prime minister didn't explicitly object, U.S. officials took his silence for winking consent and secretly moved nuclear weapons to Thule. Soon the air force began covertly flying nuclear-armed B-52s over Greenland daily. This was part of an airborne alert program to keep armed planes aloft and ready to strike the Soviet Union at all times—the subject of Stanley Kubrick's *Doctor Strangelove*, filmed partly over Greenland.

The general responsible for the program readily conceded how much danger this placed Greenland in. Thule, he told Congress, would be "one of the first ones to go" if war came. Even without war, it faced peril. In 1967, three planes carrying hydrogen bombs made emergency landings on Greenland. The next year, a B-52 flying near Thule with four Mark 28 hydrogen bombs crashed, hard.

The plane plowed into the ice at more than five hundred miles an hour, leaving a trail of debris five miles long. Nearly a quarter million pounds of jet fuel ignited, setting off the conventional explosives in all four bombs. Those bombs were supposedly "one-point safe," meaning that the explosives around the core could go off without detonating the bomb, so long as they didn't go off simultaneously (which would violently compress the core and trigger nuclear fission). Yet some bombs in the arsenal had proved *not* to be one-point safe, and a lot could go wrong in a crash, especially with weapons that fell below today's safety standards, such as those at Thule.

The accident at Thule didn't set off a nuclear explosion. It did, however, spew plutonium all over the crash site. The air force scrambled to clean up the mess before the ice thawed and carried radioactive debris into the ocean. The recovered waste filled seventy-five tankers. Had an accident of that scale happened over a city, it would have been mayhem.

Could that have happened? Yes. The Thule plane crashed on Greenland, one of the world's most sparsely populated landmasses. But the same

airborne alert system carried planes over one of the most densely populated landmasses, Western Europe. Two years before the Thule accident,
a B-52 crashed over the Spanish village of Palomares while carrying four
hydrogen bombs, each seventy-five times as powerful as the Hiroshima
bomb. Part of the plane landed 80 yards from an elementary school, another chunk hit the earth 150 yards from a chapel. The conventional explosives went off in two of the bombs, sowing plutonium dust into the
tomato fields for miles.

The third bomb landed intact. But the fourth? It was nowhere to be
found. Officials searched desperately for nearly three months. The hunt
had "all the makings of a James Bond thriller," *The Boston Globe* reported.
In fact, it bore an unnerving resemblance to *Thunderball*, the Bond film
about missing nuclear weapons that was dominating the box office at the
time. When the military finally found the bomb resting on the seabed, it
proudly showed it off for the cameras—the first time the public had seen
a hydrogen bomb.

It looked, *Time* noted approvingly, "just the way it looked in *Thunderball*."

21

BASELANDIA

In 1949 George Orwell conjured up a dark future for Britain. Atomic warfare had ravaged the industrial world. A dictator had taken command. Seeking to "narrow the range of thought," the government was gradually replacing the English language with a nightmare version of Basic, called Newspeak. And Britain had been absorbed into the United States. Its name had even been changed, from Britain to "Airstrip One."

Orwell's novel *1984* was mainly a warning about totalitarianism. But in imagining Britain as a forward base for a U.S.-centered empire, Orwell noted another important trend. The Second World War had seen millions of U.S. servicemen touch foot on British soil. In theory, their presence had been temporary. But as the "cold war" (a term of Orwell's coinage) began, it became clear that the United States would be staying for some time.

During World War II, one of the most important British bases for the United States had been Burtonwood, which hosted more than eighteen thousand personnel at peak. In 1948, the year before Orwell published *1984*, the U.S. Air Force returned there. Burtonwood was repurposed to support the Berlin Airlift. It became the largest air force base in all Europe. Thousands of servicemen stayed there, and they didn't leave until the 1990s.

This was an important feature of the United States' pointillist empire. Some of its "points" were on islands or remote spots, such as Thule, the

Bikini Atoll, or the Swan Islands. But others were in heavily populated areas. Troops spilled out from the bases, drinking, frequenting clubs, trading on the black market, and organizing trysts. And people who lived nearby found work on the bases or in selling to servicemen. The bases and their environs, in other words, were bustling borderlands where people from the United States came into frequent contact with foreigners.

The bases were there by agreement—Washington offered protection and usually funds in exchange for the right to plant its outposts. But for the people who lived next to them, it could feel like colonialism. French leftists complained of U.S. "occupiers" and grumbled about "coca-colonization." In base-riddled postwar Panama, thousands marched carrying signs reading DOWN WITH YANKEE IMPERIALISM and NOT ONE MORE INCH OF PANAMANIAN TERRITORY.

For the British, the main issue was the nuclear weapons. The United States had been storing its weapons at British bases, and it flew B-47s over England. Were they carrying nuclear bombs? "Well, we did not build these bombers to carry crushed rose petals," the U.S. general in charge told the press in 1958. He was bluffing, slightly—those bombs were unarmed. But the terrified British public had no way of knowing that.

Within months, more than five thousand well-dressed protesters gathered in the rain at Trafalgar Square. From there, they marched for four days to a nuclear weapons facility in Aldermaston. By the time they reached it, the crowd had grown to around ten thousand.

These numbers weren't enormous. But the fact that people had turned out at all, in the 1950s, in the heart of NATO country, to protest the logic of the Cold War was impressive. NUCLEAR DISARMAMENT and NO MISSILE BASES HERE, their banners read in sober black and white.

An artist named Gerald Holtom designed a symbol for the Aldermaston march. "I was in despair," he remembered. He sketched himself "with hands palm out stretched outwards and downwards in the manner of Goya's peasant before the firing squad. I formalized the drawing into a line and put a circle around it."

The lone individual standing helpless in the face of world-annihilating military might—it was "such a puny thing," thought Holtom. But his creation, the peace symbol, resonated and quickly traveled around the world.

★

In Holtom's eyes, the bases sowed fear. Yet seen in another light, they had a certain glamour. The men posted to them were flush with money and consumer goods. So even as the bases provoked protests, they also stirred other passions.

Take Liverpool, a port city in the north of England. Before the war, it had been a dreary factory town without much by way of entertainment beyond the music-hall scene that typified much of provincial England. Then suddenly, in the 1950s, it lit up like a Christmas tree. It turned out far more chart-topping acts in the following decades than it had any right to. Some, like the Searchers or Gerry and the Pacemakers, have faded with time. Others, like the Beatles, have not.

A classmate of John Lennon's estimated that between 1958 and 1964, five hundred bands were playing Merseyside, the area around Liverpool.

Why? "There has to be some reason," wrote the Beatles' producer George Martin, "that Liverpool, of all British cities, actually had a vibrant teenage culture centred around pop music in the 1950s, when the rest of Britain was snoozing gently away in the pullovered arms of croon." That Liverpool had a port surely helped. Yet for Martin, the answer was to be found elsewhere. Liverpool was a base city. It was, in fact, fifteen miles west of Burtonwood, the largest U.S. Air Force base in Europe.

Burtonwood was, it must be emphasized, enormous. It was the "Gateway to Europe," where transatlantic military flights landed. Its 1,636 buildings included the largest warehouse in Europe and the military's only European electronics calibration laboratory, which technicians used to set their instruments and test standards. It had a baseball team, a soccer team, a radio station, and a constant influx of entertainers from the United States (Bob Hope, Nat King Cole, Bing Crosby).

Burtonwood's significance would be hard to overstate. Whole neighborhoods of Liverpool had been bombed during the war, especially around the Penny Lane area, and its economy was still in shambles. The thousands of U.S. servicemen who came through were like millionaires. Teenage girls charged at them at the train station (*The Daily Mirror*, suspecting prostitution, judged this "shoddy, shameful, and shocking").

In its official contracts alone, Burtonwood plowed more than $75,000 into the local economy per day. And that doesn't count the money for entertainment. Musicians did especially well. They could get gigs on the base, or they could catch the troops who, pockets bulging with dollars, made their way to the Merseyside clubs at night.

In George Martin's eyes, this was transformative. The troops, he recalled, "brought their culture—and their favourite records—plugging both directly into the mainstream of Liverpool life." The men dispensed nylon stockings, chocolate, money, and records like an army of boisterous nocturnal Santa Clauses. The base became "an absolute magnet for any woman between the ages of fifteen and thirty."

Young men got caught in its magnetic field, too—John Lennon, Paul McCartney, George Harrison, and Ringo Starr especially. Ringo's stepfather worked on the base and fed Ringo a steady diet of comic books and records from the United States. John's mother, Julia, was known as a "good-time girl," an avocation that, whatever else it entailed, left her with an admirably large and up-to-date record collection, which John and Paul eagerly raided. George got his records by stealing them from Brian Epstein's shop, which, thanks to the troops, was brimming with the latest music from across the Atlantic (Epstein later became the Beatles' manager).

At a time when Britain's cultural institutions were locked in the vaudeville age and the BBC was trying to stamp out rock, Liverpudlians found themselves in a special position. They had records, particularly those featuring African American artists, that no one else had access to. And they had strong financial incentives to master the songs emanating from the United States.

Their music scene exploded. Tellingly, the Liverpool groups were essentially cover bands. They one-upped one another not by composing new songs, but by replicating faithfully the sounds they heard on records and the radio.

The first side that John, Paul, and George recorded was "That'll Be the Day," a Buddy Holly number performed with remarkable fidelity to the original. They weren't trying to dislodge Holly, just to establish themselves as recording artists in his style. There was only one copy pressed, which the bandmates passed around—today it's the most valuable record in existence.

They cut it in 1958, the same year the antinuclear marchers moved on Aldermaston. The Beatles and the peace symbol, in other words, debuted within four months and a day's train ride of each other. And both were side effects of the U.S. basing system.

★

Eventually the Beatles themselves would join the movement that began with the march on Aldermaston. Paul McCartney appeared on television in 1964 calling for a ban on nuclear weapons. Three years later, John Lennon offered his own protest of the United States' basing system. "Look what they do here," he complained. "They're spending billions on nuclear armaments and the place is full of U.S. bases that no one knows about."

Such opinions may sound strange coming from a band that owed its very existence to the U.S. military, but that's often how it went. Those who lived in the shadow of the bases both resented them and built their lives around them, vacillating between protest and participation.

The same ambivalence could be seen on the other side of the world, in postwar Japan. Rarely had a country endured such wrenching transformations at such high speed. In just two years the Japanese saw dozens of their largest cities firebombed, two cities destroyed by nuclear weapons, the collapse of their empire, their mainland conquered, their emperor humbled, and Douglas MacArthur's men fanning out across their country. To Edwin Reischauer, who had grown up in Japan, the entire country seemed "confused" and "dazed."

Humiliated would have been an apt word, too. The Japanese had gone from being the masters of Asia to subjects in an occupied country. MacArthur ruled Japan unabashedly as a dictator. He refused to socialize with the Japanese or even to travel within the country that he was ruling. Instead, he hunkered down in "Little Tokyo," an unbombed section of central Tokyo that the occupation authorities turned into a command center. From it, MacArthur censored the press, ran the economy, and set the curriculum of the schools.

The Japanese quickly adapted to the new reality. The first postwar bestseller was a thirty-two-page English-language phrase book, which sold millions of copies. Children mastered key phrases such as "give me chocolate" and attached themselves to the legs of wandering GIs. Tens of thousands of women found work as prostitutes. Sex work was, in the early days, one of the most dynamic sectors of the economy.

The occupation lasted six years and eight months. Yet even after it ended, in 1952, nearly two hundred thousand troops remained on more than two thousand base facilities on the Japanese main islands. This kept Japan "bound hand and foot" to the United States, a leading politician charged. Only 18 percent of those polled after the occupation's end felt unreservedly that Japan was truly independent. There were too many foreign troops still milling around.

And Japan *wasn't* entirely independent, as the United States continued to occupy parts of Japan outside the main islands, including Okinawa. The U.S. ambassador referred to Okinawa openly as "a colony of one million Japanese." Almost 5 percent of its population consisted at that point of U.S. military personnel and their dependents. Okinawa wouldn't be returned to Japanese rule for another two decades.

The Japanese bases were run as "America Towns," sealed-off enclaves of the United States within foreign territory. They had their own offices, housing, shopping centers, schools, and fire stations. But the bases were never perfectly self-contained. Sometimes they expanded physically, gobbling up land to make room for enlarged facilities. Other times, base activities seeped out into the surrounding areas. In 1951 a fighter plane's fuel tank fell from the sky onto a house, killing six. In 1959 a jet crashed into an elementary school, killing seventeen and wounding more than a hundred. Such "incidents and accidents" were frequent and, to those who lived near the bases, terrifying (1965: trailer from an airplane falls and crushes a girl to death; 1966: tanker airplane crashes and kills a local; 1967: high schooler is killed by a military vehicle in a hit-and-run and a four-year-old is crushed by a military trailer; etc.).

There were crimes, too. In 1957 the Japanese public was outraged when a U.S. sergeant shot an empty shell case from his grenade launcher at a forty-six-year-old woman, killing her (he was irritated that she was collecting scrap from an army shooting range). Killings, rapes, and assaults by the men on the bases were not uncommon. The year after the occupation ended, more than a hundred Japanese died at the hands of U.S. service members. Technically, crimes committed by uniformed perpetrators were subject to trial in Japanese courts. But the Japanese government relinquished jurisdiction in 97 percent of cases in the early years, turning thousands of alleged criminals over to their superior officers for punishment.

Yet, as the Japanese were well aware, hosting bases didn't mean just enduring bar brawls, plane crashes, and jeeps driven drunkenly down crowded streets. It also meant that Japan had a special place within the sprawling U.S. military complex. During the Cold War, that was one of the largest and steadiest streams of cash on the planet.

The U.S. military was, in fact, a major employer in Japan. On the base, Japanese found jobs as interpreters, stenographers, drivers, maids, and construction workers. Off the base, the bars and brothels did a steady business. And then there were the servicemen stationed around Asia who converged on Japan for their furloughs. Officially the program was called R&R, for rest and recuperation, but informally the men spoke of I&I: intercourse and intoxication. Whatever the letters, it meant money flying around hotels, shops, bars, and brothels.

More transformative still were the large military procurement orders, which began in 1950 with the Korean War. Goods from the U.S. mainland heading for Asia might take weeks to arrive. Those from Japan could be made cheaply and arrive in hours. And so the U.S. military began a shopping spree. From the start of the Korean War to the end of the Vietnam War, Japanese firms took in at least $300 million a year from U.S. purchase orders. At the peak of the Korean War, 1952, it was nearly $800 million.

This was *huge*. The president of the Bank of Japan called the procurement orders "divine aid." Japan's prime minister called them a "gift of the gods." On the eve of the Korean War, the auto firm Toyota had laid off workers, cut wages, and reduced pensions by half. It was the military contracts that reversed its fortunes. They were, the firm's president recalled, "Toyota's salvation." Toyota's output swelled between three and four times its size in the six years between 1948 and 1954.

Not only did the contracts provide profits, they offered Japanese firms a chance to master U.S. standards—i.e., the standards that were rapidly spreading out all over the world. The U.S. military was the largest and one of the most exacting standard-setting agencies on the planet. Producing for it was like having a well-paid internship: lucrative in the moment but also conferring skills that would prove extremely valuable later.

It is telling that one of the visitors from the United States whom the Japanese held in the highest regard was a statistician named W. Edwards Deming. He'd worked in logistics during the Second World War, and his specialty was quality control—techniques for ensuring that industrial products were built to specification (the Total Quality Management movement derived in part from his ideas). None of this earned him much renown in the United States, but he was, as they say, big in Japan. Engineers there flocked to his lectures, read his works, and signed up for courses from him. "I never felt so important," Deming remembered. He received a medal from the emperor.

Was this because Deming was a genius? Probably not. It didn't take

Japanese engineers long to absorb what he knew and surpass it. Deming was famous, rather, for what he stood for. As one of Sony's founders put it, he was the "patron saint" of quality control in Japan. In a dependent economy, where so much hung on winning military contracts and adhering to standards, that was the saint who was prayed to the most.

Deming's beatification spoke to the centrality of the U.S. military in Japan's economic growth. The more that military fought, the more Japanese firms profited. The Korean War had been a godsend. The Vietnam War helped, too. The men who fought it drank Kirin beer, carried Nikon cameras, rode Honda motorbikes, and dropped bombs with Sony parts. The polyethylene body bags they came home in? Made in Japan.

Not every corner of Baselandia made out as well as Japan did. The Philippines, for example, hosted large contingents of U.S. service members, yet no one was driving Philippine trucks to the battlefronts. It mattered that Japan had other factors spurring its growth, including a high rate of savings, market protections, an entrepreneurial culture, and a government that ably promoted industrial development. Still, the patronage of the United States was essential to the recipe.

Whatever the proportion of ingredients, their combined effect was staggering. Between the end of the Second World War and the end of the Vietnam War, the Japanese economy grew fifty-five-fold. It was, by that point, common to speak of Japan's growth as a "miracle."

★

Yet even for Japan, the most prosperous site in Baselandia, success came at a cost. In exchange for its privileged position within the world economy, Japan surrendered a great deal of autonomy. It had to stand aside as the United States used Japanese land to launch Asian wars, spy on the Soviet Union, and store nuclear weapons, with all the dangers that entailed.

Public sentiment was profoundly complicated. Japanese people protested base expansions, but they also protested plans by the United States to *remove* its servicemen, since the bases were vital sources of employment. In polls from 1958 to 1966, most respondents registered disapproval of the bases. Yet their responses grew more ambivalent over time, with increasing numbers confessing that they weren't sure how they felt. Even a leader in the campaign to end the occupation of Okinawa acknowledged the "contradiction": Okinawans had little interest in helping the United States fight in Vietnam, but they desperately needed the money.

On occasion, Japanese antipathy toward the bases erupted into serious protests. The antinuclear movement after the Bikini tests in 1954 was one example—it gave the world Godzilla. There was another eruption in 1959–60, during the run-up to the renewal of the basing agreement between the United States and Japan. Demonstrators took to the streets of Tokyo roughly every other day—the largest protest drew nearly a third of a million people. Eisenhower had planned to come to Japan to celebrate the renewal of the agreement, but when his press secretary arrived to prepare for the visit, some eight to ten thousand protesters blocked his path from the airport. They surrounded his limousine, breaking its windows, rocking it back and forth, and jumping on the roof—it took a U.S. Marine helicopter to rescue him. Eisenhower had to cancel his visit because the Japanese prime minister couldn't guarantee his safety.

Japan renewed its basing agreement, yet the toll this took on its government was evident. The day the treaty was signed in 1960, the prime minister announced his resignation. The next month, a protester stabbed him six times in the leg.

Ten years later, the treaty came up again for renewal, and Japanese protesters once more took to the streets. They called for an end to the Vietnam War, the return of Okinawa, and closure of the bases. In the Okinawan city of Koza, things turned violent. Koza was the Okinawan Liverpool, a base city with a vibrant rock scene pulsating to the music of Jimi Hendrix, Deep Purple, Cream, and Led Zeppelin. When a GI-driven vehicle hit an Okinawan man and then the police released the driver, a riot broke out. Protesters threw Molotov cocktails, burned dozens of cars, and broke into the base itself, where they smashed windows and attacked schools. Even the rockers, many of whom spoke English and had GI fathers, rioted.

Yukio Kyan, the bassist in Okinawa's first rock band, the Whispers, told a historian why. He had strong connections to the United States: his sister's father was from there, so was his wife's. And, of course, he owed his career to the free-spending men from the base. Yet, at the same time, Kyan felt that the occupiers had "screwed up" his family. His home had been destroyed by bombers during the war. His aunt was killed after a U.S. jeep hit her—the driver rushed back to the base and was never punished.

Marine Corps Air Station Futenma: An outpost of the United States lodged in the heart of a tightly packed Okinawan city

Kyan confessed that, even as he played U.S. music, a hatred for the United States had built up. His feelings had been "pent up" until finally, in the 1970 riot, they "exploded."

In the face of the protests, the United States returned Okinawa to Japan in 1972. But it kept the bases. Today, 20 percent of the island is used by the U.S. military.

★

The protests that gripped Japan weren't a surprise. Officials in Washington knew that bases caused unrest—that's why they sought out islands and remote locales when feasible. Or they sited bases in places where dissent counted for less: Okinawa rather than the Japanese main islands, Guam rather than California, Greenland rather than Denmark.

But as prescient as Washington's planners were about the political blowback from bases, they thought little about the economic consequences. They propped up Japan's economy, including allowing it to discriminate against U.S. imports, on the assumption that it would be a regional powerhouse but never a rival to the United States. As John Foster

Dulles, who presided over the treaty ending the occupation, put it, Japanese products had "little future" in the United States. They were just "cheap imitations of our own goods."

Dulles was, to put it gently, wrong about that. What he didn't foresee—what no one foresaw—was that in using Japan to launch its military campaigns in Asia, the United States was sowing the seeds of its own deindustrialization.

To understand how that happened, turn back again to the end of the war, to a Japan on the brink of starvation. That might not have seemed like an auspicious time to start a technology company, but for Masaru Ibuka, a technical officer in the then-defunct Japanese navy, it was probably as good a time as any. Japan was so destroyed that pretty much anything could find a market.

Ibuka set up shop in Tokyo, on the third floor of a burned-out department store. He recruited a friend from the navy, a physicist named Akio Morita. In the usual course of things, Morita would have been the fifteenth-generation heir to one of Japan's oldest sake-brewing firms. But in the aftermath of war, all bets were off. Morita became Ibuka's vice president, and the two established their new company, Tokyo Tsushin Kogyo—the Tokyo Telecommunication Engineering Company. It went by Totsuko, for short.

Ibuka and Morita's company didn't make any one thing in particular. Rather, Totsuko made whatever its workers could piece together from the scraps they found: a rudimentary electric rice cooker, some drastically unsafe electrically heated cushions, vacuum-tube voltmeters. Ibuka and Morita fashioned tools from the junk lying around, such as screwdrivers made from motorcycle springs. They also relied heavily on "Yankee Alley," a black market where GIs fenced items they stole from the bases. That's where Ibuka and Morita got their vacuum tubes.

What really interested them was sound. "The Americans had brought their music with them," Morita remembered, "and people were hungry for it." Ibuka declared that the company would try to make a wire recorder, though early efforts proved challenging.

In the meantime, Totsuko worked other jobs, including taking contracts from the occupation authorities. One was to supply a broadcast mixing unit to the Japanese national radio station, then an arm of MacArthur's occupation. When Masaru Ibuka dropped the unit off, he saw something he'd never seen before: a tape recorder, which the U.S. troops had brought with them. *This is what Totsuko should be making*, he thought. He persuaded an officer to bring it by Totsuko's shop so his entire staff could examine it.

The engineers at Totsuko understood how tape recorders worked. The occupation authorities had stocked a library in central Tokyo with up-to-date Western technical journals, which Japanese scientists copied out by hand and disseminated. Where Totsuko's engineers struggled was in finding the materials. Japan had no plastic for the tape, so they tried to use a stiff paper instead. After endless trial and error, they figured out a way to magnetize it using local materials. They fried up ferrous oxalate in a pan to make ferric oxide and then painted it by hand onto the paper, using the soft bristles from a raccoon's belly. It wasn't how 3M back in the United States did it, but it worked. Totsuko's hundred-pound tape recorder hit the market in 1950.

Could Japanese buyers afford the tape recorder? Did any want it? Akio Morita was the one who worked out how to market it. The occupation authorities were replacing rote memorization in Japanese schools with audiovisual learning. This meant flooding the schools with U.S.-made educational films. Unfortunately—and this was typical of the occupation— the films were in English, which Japanese students didn't speak.

Morita saw a way to attach his firm, like a remora, to the underside of the occupation. Totsuko would make tapes of Japanese translations designed to accompany U.S. filmstrips. The market for the tape recorders would thus be not individuals, but schools. It was Totsuko's first major success.

By this time, Ibuka and Morita had figured out which side their bread was buttered on. The tech came from the United States. The money came, directly or indirectly, from the United States. If their company wanted to grow, it was to the United States that it must look.

Ibuka, despite speaking almost no English, visited for the first time in 1952. While there, he learned of the transistor Bell Labs had developed. Again, as he had with the tape recorder, he made up his mind to invest heavily in a new U.S.-derived technology. He bought a Japanese patent for the transistor, despite warnings from U.S. engineers that the most profitable application for it was probably hearing aids. Ibuka waved them off. He wanted to make radios.

He also wanted to market them beyond Japan. For this, his firm would need a new name. Morita had also visited the United States and discovered that the old name—Tokyo Tsushin Kogyo—while perfectly normal for a Japanese business, tripped up English speakers. Even the short version, Totsuko, got him nowhere.

Ibuka and Morita sought a name that "could be recognized anywhere in the world, one that could be pronounced the same in any language," Morita recalled. He wanted it to be short, like Ford. The two passed possibilities back and forth and ransacked dictionaries. Though neither yet spoke English well, they were drawn to the word *sonus*, the Latin root for the English *sound*. It had an additional resonance in Japan. GIs used an affectionate term for Japanese men: *sonny* or *sonny boy*. To many, that surely sounded condescending. But to strivers like Ibuka and Morita, it sounded like money.

We "thought of ourselves as 'sonny-boys' in those days," Morita noted. "We were little boys in the business of sound."

They knocked off an *n* and trademarked the name: Sony. Noting the spread of English in Japan and elsewhere, they insisted on writing it in roman rather than Japanese characters, even for their advertisements in Japan. They adopted a mascot for the firm: "Sony Boy." He was brown-haired, eager, and, to Western eyes, Caucasian.

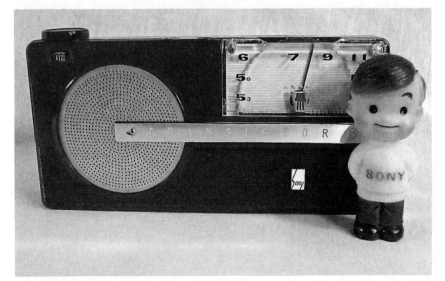

"Little boys in the business of sound": Sony's transistor radio and its brown-haired mascot, Sony Boy

Sony's first transistor radio, introduced in 1955, wasn't the world's first—a U.S. firm had beat it to the market. But Sony's radios were the ones that sold. And starting with the 1957 model, they sold in the United States.

Not only did the radios sell, they effected a momentous shift in consumer culture. Before Sony, radios, tape recorders, and record players were furniture. They were large and expensive, and manufacturers competed to offer the purest sound—"hi-fidelity" was the buzzword. Sony changed that. Transistors allowed for tiny, cheap, battery-powered radios, which meant that music could be consumed by an individual rather than a household. Morita bragged that Sony's radios were better than "portable"; they were "pocketable." To drive the point home, he had his salesmen carry them in their (slightly enlarged) shirt pockets.

Sony wasn't just selling a radio, it was selling a new way to consume media. Young listeners could now tune in without adult supervision (a teenage John Lennon had a transistor radio on display, the Beatles chronicler Bob Spitz has written, "like priceless art in his bedroom"). To the degree that we live in a world of pocket-size personal devices rather than one of large screens and subwoofers, we have Sony to thank. Or blame.

Sony's transistor radio also inaugurated another epochal trend: Japanese technology firms producing superior goods. No longer was Sony the remora on the underside of the U.S. leviathan. It had detached and swum ahead.

Way ahead. Sony was the Apple of its day. In the 1960s it introduced the portable television, high-quality color television, and the first desktop calculator that didn't require vacuum tubes. In the 1970s it was the VCR and the Walkman. In the 1980s Sony debuted compact discs, the Discman, the camcorder, the 3.5-inch floppy computer disk, and—despite its predilection for small sizes—the jumbotron.

Sony's story was similar to that of the Beatles. Enterprising young men living cheek by jowl with the U.S. military get their start by imitating what they see around them. They learn guitar licks from Buddy Holly songs or struggle with stiff paper and raccoon-hair brushes to replicate a tape recorder. But give them time, and soon enough you're listening to *Abbey Road* on your Walkman.

★

Standards work in a funny way. The firms or countries whose standards prevail sprint ahead while their competitors retool or learn the new system. Economists call it a "first-mover advantage." But that advantage subsides with time. Once everyone uses 60-degree screw threads, there's no benefit to having been the *first* one to have used them (though there may be other rewards for having gotten ahead of the learning curve). The longer the race, the less meaningful a head start is.

The United States' ability to promulgate its standards gave it considerable first-mover advantages. But those who adopted U.S. standards early did well, too—call them the second movers. In nursing, the Filipinos were the second movers. In rock, it was the Liverpudlians. In industry, it was Sony and the other Japanese firms that grew up around the U.S. military. Their privileged position within the world economy, close to the source of standards and technology and with easy access to U.S. markets, allowed them to go global.

In other words, the international order that the United States built around itself after 1945 redounded to its benefit, but not permanently. Once other countries mastered U.S. standards, they too could profit and even compete with the United States itself. It is telling that the countries hosting the most U.S. peacetime bases—such as Britain, Japan, West Germany, and South Korea—numbered among the United States' most formidable competitors.

In the sixties, the "British Invasion" reversed the cultural flow of rock music. Starting with the Beatles, British musicians who had mastered rock and blues made their way to the United States: the Rolling Stones, Eric Clapton, the Who, Pink Floyd, Van Morrison, and Led Zeppelin. Whatever first-mover advantage artists such as Elvis Presley and Chuck Berry used to enjoy had clearly expired, as the British bands could dominate the charts just as easily.

Sony started something similar with its transistor radio. And after it came still more Japanese firms. Such names as Nikon, Canon, Mitsubishi, Honda, Toyota, Subaru, Nissan, Mazda, Kawasaki, Toshiba, Sanyo, Panasonic, and Nintendo gained household familiarity in the United States. The trade balance between the two countries flipped in 1965, ten years after the introduction of Sony's transistor radio. Now Japan was selling more to the United States than it was buying. California's governor described this, with great chagrin, as a "colonial" relationship. "We ship her raw materials, she ships us finished goods."

Japan's rise was particularly conspicuous in the auto industry, a linchpin of the U.S. economy. In 1980, hundreds of thousands of U.S. workers lost their jobs as auto companies closed forty assembly plants and some fifteen hundred dealerships. Meanwhile, small, fuel-efficient Japanese cars claimed ever-larger slices of the market.

Desperate business leaders tried to unlock the secret of Japan's success. NBC ran a documentary called *If Japan Can, Why Can't We?* that profiled W. Edwards Deming. Finally, after decades of semi-obscurity, Deming could command the fame in his own country that he'd enjoyed in Japan. "I'm proud to call myself a disciple of Dr. Deming," Ford's CEO declared.

Yet while an urge to emulate Japan seized executive suites, despair reigned on the shop floor. You could hear it in the music. The bubbly tunes of Buddy Holly had given way to gloomier fare. "Born down in a dead man's town" was how Bruce Springsteen, the bard of deindustrialization, began his grim assessment of the national prospects in the song "Born in the U.S.A." Five years later, Sony bought Columbia Records, Springsteen's label. "Born in the U.S.A." was now the property of Japan.

Nor was it just Springsteen. In buying Columbia Records, Sony claimed the catalogs of Bob Dylan, Johnny Cash, Simon and Garfunkel, and many other rock mainstays. Next, Sony bought Columbia Pictures, which owned such film classics as *On the Waterfront, Ghostbusters,* and *The Bridge on the River Kwai.* Mitsubishi bought Rockefeller Center in New York.

"Imagine, a few years from now. It's December and the whole family is going to see the big Christmas tree in Hirohito Center," warned an ad by General Motors. "Go on, keep buying Japanese cars."

Resentment curdled, at least in some quarters. "They come over here, they sell their cars, their VCRs. They knock the hell out of our companies," complained the real estate mogul Donald Trump on television. This issue marked Trump's first foray into politics, and it struck a chord. The show's host, Oprah Winfrey, noted that Trump's message sounded like "presidential talk." Would he ever consider running? "Probably not," Trump replied, "but I do get tired of seeing the country ripped off."

The author Michael Crichton took Japan-bashing further with his 1992 novel *Rising Sun*, a thriller about sinister, sexually perverse Japanese businessmen, one of whom murders a white woman. The film, starring Sean Connery and Wesley Snipes, opened to protests by Asian Americans, who worried that it would incite violence. There had already been some. In Flint and Lansing in Michigan, Japanese cars had had their windows smashed and tires slashed. In Detroit, a Chrysler manager and a laid-off worker literally beat a Chinese American man's brains out with a baseball bat—apparently they mistook him for Japanese. ("It's because of you little motherfuckers that we're out of work," a witness testified hearing one of the killers say.)

Akio Morita of Sony, who lived in New York, was the face of Japan at this tense moment. In the early 1970s, when *Time* started reporting on Japan's economic success in the United States, it ran a story, "How to Cope with Japan's Business Invasion." The cover showed a portable Sony TV, with Morita's face beaming out against a background of yellow light.

Morita had always taken pains to seem unthreatening. He'd written two affable English-language books about his thoughts on business, stressing how much he'd learned from the United States. But in 1989 he began to publish some distinctly undeferential thoughts about his adoptive home. He excoriated the United States for its racism, economic inequality, and lack of business acumen.

Morita may have gotten rich off the U.S. military-industrial complex, but his gratitude, it turned out, was not bottomless. "Let's become a Japan that can say no," he advised his compatriots. He coauthored a book of that name—*The Japan That Can Say No*—written with a right-wing national-ist. He published it in Japanese and refused to have it translated. It was a far cry from his days as a self-styled "sonny boy."

Akio Morita, as it happens, wasn't the only beneficiary of the United States' pointillist empire who would come to say no.

22

THE WAR OF POINTS

Of all the dots on the map that the United States would claim, few were as initially unpromising as Dhahran. The site itself was a blank spot in the desert. The nearest town, Khobar, wasn't much more—a "few mud huts," one observer wrote. And Dhahran was situated in Saudi Arabia, a monarchy not known for welcoming outsiders.

Yet Saudi Arabia had oil, and oil makes the world go round. A U.S. conglomerate called Aramco (it included Standard Oil, Texaco, and later Exxon and Mobil) bought the rights to explore for that oil. It was Aramco that established the initial settlement at Dhahran in the 1930s. And it was Aramco that built it up.

Or, at least, it was Aramco that paid. The construction itself was done by workers from the region. One, a Yemeni bricklayer named Mohamed, seemed particularly capable. He was illiterate and had only one eye, but he was "friendly and energetic," as one of his colleagues put it, and a good builder. His story wasn't all that different from Akio Morita's at Sony or John Lennon's in Liverpool—Mohamed was someone who'd figured out how to prosper in the shadow of a U.S. enclave. Like Morita and Lennon, he learned the ropes and then set off on his own. With Aramco's blessing, he and his brother started their own construction firm: Mohamed and Abdullah, Sons of Awadh bin Laden.

It was the right time to break into the market. Aramco was expanding.

The oil-rich Saudi royal family was building palaces and roads. The United States, which had come to see Saudi Arabia as a node in its world transportation network, also had plans. The country was like "an immense aircraft carrier lying athwart a number of the principal air traffic lanes of the world," a State Department cable put it. And so Washington arranged in 1945 to lease a large air base at Dhahran. That, too, would need building.

But the base was a delicate matter. The Saudi royals worried how it might look to let a U.S. flag fly over the land of Mecca and Medina. So nervous was the king that he forbade the U.S. consulate at Dhahran from physically planting a flag. Instead, the Stars and Stripes was attached to the side of the building to prevent its touching Saudi soil. And the site was to be called an "airfield," never a base.

Still, the deal went through, and Dhahran—half company town, half base—grew larger. Aramco would claim that it was the largest concentration of U.S. citizens abroad. It looked, wrote a visitor in the 1950s, "just like a bit of U.S.A.—modern air-conditioned houses, swimming pool, movie theater etc."

Just as the king feared, many Muslims blanched. The Dhahran complex brought Christians and Jews to the Holy Land, making the House of Saud complicit in the kingdom's desecration. Internally, the royal family could (and did) quash the grumblings of dissent. But it could do little to silence the Voice of the Arabs, an Egyptian radio station critical of the Saudi state, which invoked Dhahran as its prime example of U.S. imperialism. Eventually the Saudi government relented and ended the lease. The U.S. military left the base in 1962.

These were choppy political waters, but Mohamed bin Laden surfed them adroitly. He became the Saudi government's preferred builder. At the same time, he did so much business with the United States that he retained an agent in New York. He built classified projects for the U.S. military, including air bases and garrisons around Saudi Arabia's western coast. He sent his oldest son, Salem, to England for a Western education. Four other sons would go on to study civil engineering in the United States.

Bin Laden died in 1967 in a plane crash (his pilot, like most of the men who flew him around, was a U.S. Air Force veteran). He left his fifty-four children shares in his construction firm, worth hundreds of millions. Some of his sons were happy to simply take the profits. Others got involved in the family business, which continued to win large defense and infrastructure contracts. One son, Osama, took up the work with a special zeal. He seemed to have a knack for the technical details.

Osama bin Laden also took an interest in politics. He'd learned it in school—the brother of the famed Islamist Sayyid Qutb had lectured at Osama's university in Jeddah. As Osama came to see it, there was a great conflict between Islam and Western empires. Muslim lands, he concluded, must be defended against imperialists.

Unfolding events confirmed that view. In 1978, communists in Afghanistan staged a coup, deposing the elected president. Not only was this a revolution led by infidels, it gave the Soviet Union a foothold in the region as it sent troops to support the faltering new regime. Moscow intended this as temporary. "It'll be over in three to four weeks," predicted Leonid Brezhnev, the Soviet leader.

It wasn't. Resistance fighters, known as the mujahidin, made protracted war on the Soviet-backed state. The Saudi government, eager to establish itself as the world defender of Islam, supported them. So did the United States, which enjoyed watching the *other* side expend its energies in a luckless war in Asia. It was time to "finally sow shit in their backyard," as National Security Adviser Zbigniew Brzezinski said. The two governments agreed to bankroll the mujahidin via a matching arrangement: one U.S. dollar for every Saudi one.

Osama bin Laden, keen to take on the godless superpower occupying Muslim lands, joined the mujahidin. He began by traveling back and forth between Saudi Arabia and Peshawar, just on the Pakistani side of the Afghan border, to raise funds and recruit fighters. But eventually he moved to Peshawar. He brought with him what he estimated to be a hundred tons of heavy construction equipment from Saudi Arabia: bulldozers, dump trucks, and trench-digging equipment. He dug tunnels and built roads. He put up air-raid shelters. He built a hospital.

Bin Laden was, in other words, an infrastructure guy. He was essentially running a mujahidin base in Pakistan. In 1988 he formed a small organization to direct the jihad. It was called, fittingly, al-Qaeda al-Askariya ("the Military Base"). Or just al-Qaeda ("the Base"), for short.

Was al-Qaeda a big deal? Not really. It played only a small part in ousting the Soviet Union from Afghanistan. But the experience had taught Bin Laden an important lesson. He'd seen one of the world's great armies beaten back by a ragtag (though well-funded) guerrilla alliance. In 1989 the Red Army retreated to Uzbekistan. By 1991, the whole Jenga tower of European communism had come crashing down.

"The myth of the superpower was destroyed not only in my mind but also in the minds of all Muslims," Bin Laden reflected. And if one superpower could collapse easily, why not another?

★

Bin Laden wasn't the only one thinking along such lines. In 1990 Saddam Hussein, the dictator of Iraq, invaded Kuwait. It was a bold and sudden attack. Within four hours of crossing the border, the Iraqi army had reached Kuwait's capital, attacked the emir's palace, and set it aflame. Days later, Hussein annexed Kuwait. This gave him control of two-fifths of the world's oil supply. And it looked very much as if he might invade Saudi Arabia next.

Bin Laden, who regarded Hussein as unconscionably secular, volunteered to fight. He had driven the infidels from Afghanistan. Surely he could do the same on the Arabian Peninsula.

But the Saudi government balked. "There are no caves in Kuwait," the government's representative, Prince Sultan, reminded Bin Laden. "What will you do when he lobs the missiles at you with chemical and biological weapons?"

"We will fight him with faith," Bin Laden answered.

The House of Saud knew from faith, but it had little confidence in Bin Laden's plan. Instead, King Fahd had agreed to meet with Defense Secretary Dick Cheney, who'd flown to Jeddah a day after the invasion with General Norman Schwarzkopf and the Pentagon's Paul Wolfowitz in tow. Cheney wanted to reopen Dhahran to the U.S. military. "After the danger is over, our forces will go home," he promised.

"I would hope so," Crown Prince Abdullah responded under his breath, in Arabic.

Abdullah was nervous, but King Fahd agreed. "Come with all you can bring," he told Cheney. "Come as fast as you can."

They did. The first planes landed at Dhahran within twenty-four hours, and they kept coming. The Pentagon put "everything aloft that could fly," wrote Colin Powell—nearly all the transport planes the air force could spare plus 158 civilian planes drafted into service. Measured in ton-miles per day, the airlift to Saudi Arabia was ten times the size of the Berlin Airlift.

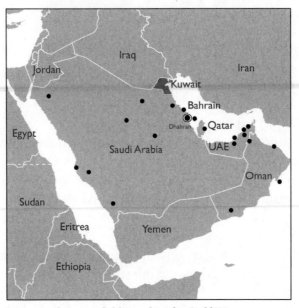

Major coalition airfields used in the Gulf War

"You could have walked across the Mediterranean on the wings of C-5s, C-141s, and commercial aircraft moving across the region," one pilot marveled.

The frenzy of the airlift reflected the severity of the threat. For years Hussein had funneled Iraq's oil revenues and foreign aid (some from the United States) into its military, and it showed. Iraq had seized Kuwait with some three hundred thousand seasoned troops, four thousand tanks, and hundreds of combat aircraft. The Iraqi army was the fourth largest in the world (ranking just below the U.S. Army), the Iraqi air force was the sixth largest. Garrisoned in Saudi Arabia, General Norman Schwarzkopf worried, he recollected, "about getting kicked back into the sea and losing thousands and thousands of lives."

Schwarzkopf's apprehensions weren't just related to the size of Iraq's military. The larger fear, hanging thickly in the air, was that the Gulf War would become "another Vietnam." The generals in 1990 had all lived through that humiliating ordeal. They'd seen a superpower armed with the latest technology locked in an interminable and ultimately unwinnable fight. *Quagmire* was the metaphor they used: the ground that sucks you in.

Military planners in the Vietnam War had hoped to avoid that ground and triumph through airpower, leveraging the United States' considerable technological advantages. They sent B-52s on carpet-bombing runs and equipped helicopters with napalm. When trees interfered with the pilots' views, the crews sprayed them with the defoliant Agent Orange. ("Only we can prevent forests" was their unofficial slogan.)

In all, the United States dropped 5 million tons of bombs, more than 250 pounds for every person in Vietnam. But dropping bombs and achieving goals are two different things. One of the most important targets was the enormous Thanh Hóa Bridge, which carried both a highway and a railroad and served as a crucial link between the north and the south. The United States spent years trying to bomb it, flying more than eight hundred sorties and losing eleven aircraft in the process. Yet it succeeded in knocking the bridge out of commission only in 1972, at the very end of the war.

Bombs and planes were, in the end, not enough. More than 2.5 million U.S. service members cycled through Vietnam during the war. But they fared no better than the planes did. In 1973 the last combat troops left. The greatest military power on earth had fought a peasant army and lost.

So it was with understandable trepidation that Schwarzkopf and his colleagues watched Saddam Hussein ready his forces. Hussein's tanks were "dug in," stashed in sand-covered bunkers that would make them impossible to see until they attacked. He was preparing for a war of attrition, the kind of drawn-out, bloody confrontation that the United States had lost in Vietnam and the Soviet Union had lost in Afghanistan.

It would be, Hussein promised, the "mother of all battles."

★

Operation Desert Storm, the name for the coalition campaign against Iraq, began in Louisiana. Seven B-52G Stratofortresses took off from Barksdale Air Force Base on a bombing run. Their arrival in Baghdad fifteen hours later was timed perfectly to coincide with a virtual explosion of the skies. Bombers from England, Spain, Saudi Arabia, and the remote island of Diego Garcia dropped their payloads. Tomahawk missiles fired from ships in the Gulf tore down Baghdad's streets. Stealth planes entered Iraqi airspace and released precision-guided bombs.

Ten minutes into the attack, much of Iraq's infrastructural network, including the Baghdad power grid, had been disabled. Within hours, Hussein's communications were knocked out.

The barrage continued for forty-three days. Fighting an air war over a desert was much easier than fighting one over a jungle, it turned out. Yet the real key was technology. This was the first major conflict where the global positioning system (GPS) was used. That, plus "smart" bombs—some guided by laser, others with built-in navigation systems—yielded stunning results.

"You pick precisely which target you want," boasted the commander of the 37th Tactical Fighter Wing. "You can want the men's room or you can want the ladies' room."

Of course there was still Iraq's army to worry about, with its thousands of dug-in tanks. But an important fact about those buried metal tanks was that they cooled at a different rate than the sand around them did. This meant that during the enchanted hours between dusk and midnight, fighter pilots could switch on their infrared vision and see the tanks clearly. They dropped five-hundred-pound laser-guided bombs on them. "Tank plinking" is what the pilots called it. *Plink, plink, plink*—there went the tanks.

Ultimately, Schwarzkopf marched across Iraq's border. Yet the promised mother of all battles proved to be anything but. Schwarzkopf led his troops in a GPS-guided charge across the desert and caught the remnants of Iraq's battered army by surprise (the Iraqis, assuming no army could navigate the trackless expanse, had expected the invasion to come via the roads). The ground war lasted one hundred hours, cost the coalition forces 366 lives, and consisted mainly of accepting Iraqi surrenders. Iraq was wrecked: its military hobbled, its troops terrified, and its infrastructure in ruins—a consequence of the war that Iraqis would have to live with for years to come.

Several high-ranking Iraqi prisoners confessed that the ground campaign probably hadn't even been necessary. A couple more weeks of the air war, and Iraq's army—again, the world's fourth largest—would have withdrawn without ever having faced an adversary on the ground.

This was astonishing. It confirmed the thought, batted around by Soviet and U.S. theorists in the seventies and eighties, that technology was changing the face of war. A "revolution in military affairs," they called it. What was the use of armored divisions, heavy artillery, large infantries, and foreign occupations in the age of GPS? Why even field an army when you could just call in air strikes from a nearby base?

The Russian military theorist Vladimir Slipchenko noted that the very spatial categories of war were changing. In the future, he suggested, area-based military concepts such as front, rear, and flank would be irrelevant. There would be only "targets and non-targets." Further, Slipchenko predicted, "there will be no need to occupy enemy territory." Controlling territory wouldn't matter, because war was no longer about area. It was about points.

★

It wasn't only the fighting that had gone pointillist. To launch planes and fire missiles, the United States needed platforms. Bases and ships, not too far from the combat zone, were essential. Hence the buildup of a basing network in Saudi Arabia, especially at Dhahran.

But hosting U.S. forces at Dhahran was no less of a touchy subject in the 1990s than it had been in the 1950s. Saudis near the base were unnerved by seeing female service members driving vehicles and wearing T-shirts. And radio broadcasts from Baghdad charged that U.S. forces were defiling Islam's holiest sites.

Washington had worried about exactly this. After the deal to reopen the base was struck, the U.S. ambassador to Saudi Arabia had confided to Robert Gates his terror about what would happen if a soldier "inadvertently pissed on a mosque." Great efforts were taken to prevent friction. The military banned pornography and alcohol, told Christians to wear their crucifixes under their shirts, and took the extraordinary step of helicoptering Jewish service members out to ships anchored in the Gulf for their religious services, lest Saudi complain of rabbis in the Holy Land.

"We had to avoid giving the impression that western 'colonialists' had unilaterally imposed their will," explained Schwarzkopf. To that end, he convened a regular "Arab reaction seminar" to assess how locals might perceive the military's actions.

Yet no amount of precaution could change the basic fact that one country was stationing its troops in another's land. It's not hard to imagine how the people of the United States would have reacted to a Saudi base in, say, Texas. In fact, it's not even necessary to imagine. In the eighteenth century, the stationing of British soldiers in North America was so repellent to the colonists that it fueled their revolution. Their Declaration of Independence denounced the king for "quartering large bodies of armed troops among us" and exempting those troops from punishment for crimes.

So it was not entirely a surprise when Saudi clerics complained. For Osama bin Laden, the bases weren't only an affront to religion, they were maddening hypocrisy. At the behest of his government, Bin Laden had risked his life to oust infidels from the Muslim country of Afghanistan. And now that same government was *inviting* nonbelievers in? To the land of Mecca and Medina?

"It is unconscionable to let the country become an American colony with American soldiers—their filthy feet roaming everywhere," he fumed. The United States, he charged, was "turning the Arabian Peninsula into the biggest air, land, and sea base in the region."

At the urging of the nervous Saudi government, Bin Laden left the country, making his way eventually to Afghanistan. But he did not drop the issue. That the U.S. troops stayed in Saudi Arabia after the Gulf War, in breach of Cheney's promise, only added fuel to Bin Laden's fire.

In 1995, a car bomb went off in Riyadh in front of a U.S. training facility. It killed seven people, five from the United States, and wounded thirty-four others. The Saudi government arrested four suspects who confessed that they'd been inspired by Bin Laden. Whether or not he was responsible, he took credit.

The next year, another bomb exploded, this one at a housing facility at Dhahran. Nineteen U.S. Air Force personnel died, and 372 people were wounded. Again, Bin Laden claimed responsibility. It's genuinely unclear whether he was involved, but *someone* hated the base enough to bomb it.

In search of security, the air force issued a contract for a $150 million compound in a remote location in the Saudi desert. "You can see something coming for miles," the spokesman explained. It was to be a military oasis, with forty-two hundred beds and eighty-five buildings, including a dining hall, a gym, a swimming pool, and a recreation facility. What was most remarkable, though, was the builder that the Saudi government hired to erect the base: the Bin Laden firm.

If there is one episode that perfectly captures the dual nature of the U.S. basing empire, it's this one. Participation and protest—the Beatles and the peace sign, Sony and the Okinawa riots—braided within a single family. The Bin Ladens built the bases. A Bin Laden would seek to destroy them.

Osama bin Laden issued his "Declaration of War Against the Americans Occupying the Land of the Two Holy Places" in 1996, after the Dhahran bombing. On the face of it, this seemed an absurdly imbalanced war: an exile living in a cave complex in Tora Bora, Afghanistan, taking on the most powerful military in existence. Yet Bin Laden had absorbed the lessons of the revolution in military affairs. From his mountain base, he could, like some sort of Central Asian Doctor No, order pinpoint strikes without *needing* an army.

What he did need was technology, and Bin Laden proved to be an astute consumer of it. The same year he declared jihad, he acquired one of the first commercially available satellite phones. It was the size of a laptop and retailed for about $15,000, but it allowed him to communicate globally. (This happened just as his brothers had become key investors in a different satellite phone company.)

Bin Laden used his phone to coordinate the first attacks that we are certain were his doing: bombings, five minutes apart, of the U.S. embassies in Kenya and Tanzania. More than two hundred people died, and several thousand were wounded. It was as if the first day of the Gulf War had been reflected in a mirror: satellite technology used to coordinate synchronized strikes on key targets, all ordered from another continent.

It was no accident that the bombs went off on August 7, 1998, the eighth anniversary of the arrival of U.S. troops at Dhahran.

Thirteen days later, President Bill Clinton ordered Tomahawk missiles fired simultaneously at al-Qaeda bases in Afghanistan (Bin Laden was believed to be at one) and at a pharmaceutical plant in Sudan that was suspected of having manufactured chemical weapon precursors for al-Qaeda. This was called Operation Infinite Reach.

It was a disaster. Not only was Bin Laden not at the Afghan base, no other al-Qaeda leader was killed. The Sudanese pharmaceutical plant was destroyed, but it is doubtful that it had any role in making chemical weapons. The United States had thus expended nearly three-quarters of a billion dollars' worth of missiles to kill a dozen or two low-level al-Qaeda members and destroy the factory that made more than half of Sudan's medicine, including vital antimalarials. Since sanctions against Sudan made importing medicine difficult, this caused an uncounted number of needless deaths—Germany's ambassador to Sudan guessed "several tens of thousands"—in one of the world's poorest countries.

The botched missile strikes added to Bin Laden's fame and gave him rich material for recruitment—*The Economist* warned that they might create "100,000 new fanatics." The strikes also suggested a target for revenge. In 2000, suicide bombers in a small fiberglass boat approached the USS *Cole,* a billion-dollar, high-tech destroyer anchored off Yemen that had launched missiles in Operation Infinite Reach. The bombers set off hundreds of pounds of explosives, killing seventeen U.S. servicemen and disabling the ship, which had to be towed back home.

The United States wasn't the only one whose reach was infinite, in other words.

The climax came the next year, with what al-Qaeda called its "planes operation." Nineteen hijackers, fifteen from Saudi Arabia, commandeered four commercial aircraft. One hit the Pentagon ("a military base," Bin Laden explained). Two more struck the World Trade Center. ("It wasn't a children's school!") The fourth, en route to the U.S. Capitol, crashed in a field in Pennsylvania. Bin Laden had found a way to make air strikes without an air force.

The attacks baffled many in the United States. "To us, Afghanistan seemed very far away," wrote the members of the 9/11 Commission. So why was a Saudi man there attacking Washington and New York?

The answer is that for Bin Laden, the United States was not "very far away." "Your forces occupy our countries," he wrote in his message to the U.S. populace. "You spread your military bases throughout them." Bin Laden's list of grievances against the United States was long, ranging from its support of Israel to Bill Clinton's affair with Monica Lewinsky. ("Is there a worse kind of event for which your name will go down in history?" he asked.) But his chief objection, voiced consistently throughout his career, was the stationing of troops in Saudi Arabia.

This is worth emphasizing. After the 9/11 attacks, "Why do they hate us?" was the constant question. Yet Bin Laden's motives were neither unknowable nor obscure. September 11 was, in large part, retaliation against the United States for its empire of bases.

★

Al-Qaeda's planes operation seems to have been guided by a larger strategy: provoke the United States, draw it into a war in the Middle East, force infidel governments there into crisis (they would have to either accommodate the unpopular occupiers or fight them), and then defeat the United States on the ground, just as the mujahidin had defeated the Soviet Union. But for this to work, Bin Laden needed Washington to send troops, not just shoot a few Tomahawk missiles. He wagered that the resulting war would be a quagmire.

In a way, Bin Laden got lucky with George W. Bush, who had recently succeeded Bill Clinton. Bush could have treated the 9/11 attacks as a crime, arrested the perpetrators, and brought them to justice. Instead, he declared a "war on terror" of global expanse and promised to "rid the world of evil-doers."

Yet despite his grand ambitions, Bush had little interest in the sort of ground campaign typical of the age of colonialism, the sort Bin Laden was banking on. As a presidential candidate, he'd come out strongly against occupations: "I just don't think it's the role of the United States to walk into a country and say, we do it this way, so should you." Instead, he called for an agile military, able to strike quickly and then leave. It was the revolution in military affairs.

Bush gave the job of remaking the military to his defense secretary, Donald Rumsfeld, who'd served in the same position in the Ford administration. You could see why Bush chose him. Not only was Rumsfeld obsessed with thrift, but since the Ford years he'd served as CEO of two technology companies. The first was Searle Pharmaceuticals, which had patented the first birth control pill and then, under Rumsfeld's direction, brought a synthetic substitute for sugar, aspartame, to the market. The other company was General Instrument, which specialized in satellite television equipment. Now back in government, Rumsfeld was given the job to create a small-footprint, tech-savvy military: fewer tanks, more GPS-guided air strikes.

He succeeded, at first. The initial invasions of Afghanistan, in 2001, and Iraq, in 2003, were, as Bush had hoped, swift and decisive. Air defenses were knocked out, major cities seized, and the Afghan and Iraq militaries left in shambles. Rumsfeld estimated that in the two months it took the coalition to dislodge the Taliban from Afghanistan's main cities, it had killed between eight and twelve thousand Taliban and al-Qaeda fighters, at a cost of 11 U.S. lives. The 122 U.S. service members killed in the first three weeks of the Iraq War largely died from accidents or friendly fire.

But the war on terror wasn't ultimately a fight between countries, as the Gulf War had been. It was a "very new type of conflict," Rumsfeld told the press a week after 9/11. "We'll have to deal with the networks."

This metaphor of the *network*—a set of connected points—became ubiquitous, acquiring the same sort of buzzword cachet that *quagmire* had possessed in the Vietnam War. The connotation pointed in another direction, though. If *quagmire* described a fight on the ground, *network* suggested that the space of the battlefield would be different, or that it might not even make sense to speak of battle as taking place on a field.

Having identified the adversary as a series of points, Rumsfeld happily deployed the precision weaponry that had come to dominate the military's arsenals. In the early weeks of the Afghan war, coalition forces established a pattern. Special forces teams, CIA operatives, and their Afghan allies would scout enemy strongholds on the ground and then call out the coordinates to the planes overhead. The pilots called it "Taliban-plinking."

From the cockpit, it was a video game, but it felt different from the ground. "The planes poured down their fire on us," remembered Osama bin Laden, who was nearly killed. "The American forces barraged us with smart bombs, bombs weighing a thousand pounds, cluster bombs, and bunker busters. Bombers like the B-52 circled above us, one of them for more than two hours, dropping twenty to thirty bombs at a time."

Bombers and smart munitions were one thing. But the United States quickly debuted another, even more remarkable technology: the armed drone. Drones were almost perfectly adapted for the fight against Bin Laden. In fact, the Bush administration had first taken an interest in them when, shortly before September 11, counterterrorism officials had tested an unarmed Predator drone over Kandahar and spotted a tall man in white, flowing robes surrounded by a security detail—quite likely Bin Laden himself. Arming the drones would ensure that the United States could act should it sight him again.

Drones carried pointillist warfare to its logical endpoint. Unlike manned planes, they could hover for hours, gathering information with high-resolution cameras. With information collection handled from the sky, even the small special forces teams on the ground weren't, strictly speaking, necessary. What is more, by patiently stalking their prey, drones could target not just buildings but individuals—they could put "warheads on foreheads," as the military vernacular had it.

The face of battle in a war of points

The enemy in this style of warfare was not a country, but a GPS coordinate.

Thanks to drones, battles could be replaced by the targeted killing of individuals. With this, the lines of war blurred. What was a combat zone and what wasn't could be confusing. The most conspicuous use of armed drones has been, in fact, in "friendly" nations. Drones have killed (by the CIA's estimate) more than two thousand people in Pakistan, including Osama bin Laden's son Saad. Drone warfare has crept into Somalia, Yemen, Libya, and Syria, too.

What the revolution in military affairs promised was immaculate warfare: precise strikes, few civilian casualties, and, above all, no occupying armies. The Vietnam-learned aversion to territorial entanglement was, in fact, a key theme of the Bush administration. "We're not a colonial power," Rumsfeld told reporters. "We don't take our force and go around the world and try to take other people's real estate."

There is every reason to think that Rumsfeld spoke from the heart. One of his greatest blunders in Iraq was banking on what one official called a "*Wizard of Oz* moment," when the wicked witch would be killed (perhaps in an air strike) and the liberated inhabitants of Oz would joyously take over. Expecting a seamless transition, the Pentagon's planning for the postwar occupation was last-minute, haphazard, and badly underfunded. The occupation leadership didn't even arrive in Iraq until weeks after Baghdad's fall, by which point the city had no electricity, was running low on water, and was seeing its ministries and museums stripped of records and valuables.

"We need to create a colonial office—fast," wrote Max Boot, a conservative critic of the administration. The British historian Niall Ferguson agreed. The United States had proved to be "a surprisingly inept empire builder" and should take a page from Britain's history. Zapping targets from above, Boot and Ferguson argued, was no substitute for governing.

This criticism met with little sympathy in the White House. "We're not an imperial power," Bush insisted. "We're a liberating power." Rumsfeld was determined to keep the occupying force small. And so for the first three years of the Iraq War—until Rumsfeld's resignation—troops kept mainly to their bases, most notably the heavily fortified "Green Zone" around the grounds of the former Republican Palace in Baghdad. In the Red Zone, outside, the city was collapsing. Inside, service members enjoyed air-conditioning, pools, gyms, bars, and the sounds of Freedom Radio.

★

"We covet no one's land"—it was a line Rumsfeld and his colleagues repeated over and over. And it was right. However often the Bush administration was accused of imperialism, it exhibited very little interest in colonizing. "If we were a true empire, we would currently preside over a much greater piece of the earth's surface," noted Vice President Dick Cheney, not without warrant.

Yet if the Bush administration had no evident lust for sheer acreage, there were certain small spots that it cared about very much. Even drones needed launchpads, and the war on terror relied on a string of bases running from the U.S. mainland to the hot spots and war zones.

The problem, Rumsfeld confessed, was that often "the presence and activities of our forces grate on local populations." In fact, the military had been kicked out of place after place. In Hawai'i, activists in the 1990s wrested Kaho'olawe, the smallest of the state's main islands, from the hands of the military. Filipino politicians wrote a clause into their 1987 constitution banning the storage of nuclear weapons, and they evicted the United States entirely in 1992. The large naval base in Puerto Rico at Vieques provoked such fierce protest, including from Puerto Ricans in New York, that the military abandoned it in 2003. That was the same year the Saudi government once again closed its bases, including Dhahran, to the United States. Uzbekistan, which had granted the United States bases close to Afghanistan, followed suit two years later. In 2009, politicians in Kyrgyzstan voted to expel the United States, too.

Even Okinawa, a bastion of U.S. power in Asia, looked shaky. When three marines raped a twelve-year-old girl in 1995, it provoked another long wave of protest. The next year, the politician Yukio Hatoyama established a new political party, the Democratic Party of Japan, and set out to remove bases from Japanese soil entirely. In 2009 he became the prime minister and promised that he'd close at least the major marine base at Futenma. Ultimately, Hatoyama failed and, as a consequence, resigned. It was the second time a Japanese prime minister was brought down by the U.S. basing system.

The more other bases faltered, the more military planners turned to Guam. Stationing forces on Guam, unlike stationing them in Saudi Arabia or Okinawa, did not require negotiating with foreign governments. Nor did Guamanians have congressional representation, as residents of Hawai'i did directly or as Puerto Ricans did indirectly through the New York diaspora. When protests imperiled the Okinawa bases, the government proposed transferring some seventeen thousand marines and their dependents to Guam—a decision made without consulting anyone from the island.

Had they been consulted, Guamanians would have voiced mixed opinions. Guam was already a crucial node in the U.S. military network—the "tip of the spear," as many call it. As such, its economy depended utterly on the military; Guam has far more military enlistment than any state. Many on Guam saw in the base expansion the prospect of more jobs. Yet, at the same time, activists put up determined resistance, noting how the base expansion would plow under the ancient village of Pågat and draw Guam even more tightly into the military economy.

"This is old-school colonialism all over again," protested LisaLinda Natividad, a professor at the University of Guam. "It boils down to our political status—we are occupied territory."

Whether Guamanians supported the move was irrelevant, as a graduate student who secured an interview with a surprisingly candid air force analyst discovered. People on Guam were forgetting that "they are a possession, and not an equal partner," the analyst explained. "If California says they want to do this or that, it is like my wife saying that she wants to move here or there: I'll have to respect her wish and at least discuss it with her. If Guam says they want to do this or that, it is as if this cup here," he continued, pointing to his coffee mug, "expresses a wish: the answer will be, you belong to me and I can do with you as best I please."

The planned move from Okinawa to Guam has stalled owing to complications on the Okinawan side. Yet one thing is clear: Guam may be a small island, but it matters tremendously that there is this one spot, far into the Pacific, that the U.S. military can use without asking anyone's permission.

★

Guam wasn't the only point in the U.S. Empire to prove useful. The Sunday after the 9/11 attacks, Dick Cheney went on television and announced that the government would have to work "the dark side."

"It's going to be vital for us to use any means at our disposal," Cheney explained. In practice, this meant indefinitely detaining and forcefully interrogating suspected terrorists. Laws prohibited this—both international treaties outlawing torture and constitutional guarantees of the right of due process. Yet as the Bush administration discovered, those laws didn't hold with the same force everywhere.

The United States by law couldn't torture. But it could transfer suspects to its allies for interrogation, even allies known for their loose adherence to international conventions. Through a process known as "extraordinary rendition," the CIA used a secret air fleet to fly more than a hundred and possibly thousands of detainees to foreign countries, particularly Egypt, Morocco, Syria, Uzbekistan, and Jordan. "They are outsourcing torture because they know it is illegal" is how one victim of the system put it. He'd been held and tortured for months (due to a false confession elicited from another torture victim) before being released without charges.

The government also made use of what it called "black sites." In these, detainees were held in CIA custody, but covertly and on foreign soil, where they could be dealt with more harshly. The program remains swathed in secrecy, but it appears that more than a hundred suspected terrorists were held this way in at least eight countries. In a throwback to the days of 1898, a small handful were waterboarded, a torture reminiscent of the "water cure" used on Filipino rebels.

Extraordinary rendition and black site prisons required foreign partners. Yet the Bush administration figured out that it could use the U.S. Empire to similar effect. After considering erecting a prison on the U.S. islands of Tinian, Wake, and Midway, the administration fastened on Guantánamo Bay, held on indefinite lease from Cuba since 1903—a prize from the 1898 war with Spain.

The lease gave the United States "complete jurisdiction and control" over Guantánamo Bay, though Cuba retained "ultimate sovereignty." Similar legal frameworks had been used for the Panama Canal Zone and Okinawa. The virtue of this, advised lawyers John Yoo and Patrick Philbin of the Office of Legal Counsel, is that it gave the government a spot of land under its exclusive control that was nevertheless "foreign territory, not subject to U.S. sovereignty."

The CIA established a prison at Guantánamo Bay. The officers named it after the Beatles song "Strawberry Fields," on the presumption that detainees would linger there "forever."

Permanent detention was feasible, however, only if Guantánamo Bay was indeed foreign. Was it? Lawyers representing the detainees tested the matter. They filed a writ of habeas corpus, arguing that the base was a "fully American enclave," with a shopping mall, a McDonald's, a Baskin-Robbins, a Boy Scout contingent, and a Star Trek fan club. The idea that Cuba retained sovereignty was, they maintained, a fiction. They noted that Fidel Castro refused to recognize the lease (he made a point of never cashing the annual $4,085 checks that the United States sent) and insisted repeatedly that the navy leave. If the United States wouldn't leave when Castro asked, how could Cuba be the sovereign?

This was one of those "Is it the United States or not?" questions that had dogged the empire for more than a century. The case went to the Supreme Court in 2004. To the White House's surprise, the court ruled that Guantánamo detainees *could* seek justice in federal courts. Guantánamo Bay was held by lease, Justice Anthony Kennedy wrote, but "this lease is no ordinary lease."

In its peculiar legal status, Guantánamo Bay was not far off from Guam. They're a fitting pair: two U.S. outposts, spoils of a not-much-remembered nineteenth-century war, both *in* the United States without being *of* it. Such places may seem like bizarre vestiges of a long-ago imperialist era, but they aren't. Small dots on the map like these are the foundation of the United States' pointillist empire today.

Foreign prisons, walled compounds, hidden bases, island colonies, GPS antenna stations, pinpoint strikes, networks, planes, and drones—these are the locales and instruments of the ongoing war on terror. This is the shape of power today. This is the world the United States made.

CONCLUSION: ENDURING EMPIRE

The island of Saipan is one of the most staggeringly beautiful places on earth. It's got it all: blue skies, clear water, lush vegetation, warm beaches. It also, starting in the 1990s, boasted a huge garment-manufacturing center. The workers came from China, the Philippines, and Bangladesh, lured by promises of high wages. But they found themselves deeply in debt on arrival and forced to work furiously in sweatshops to pay for their travel and housing. At its peak, Saipan's garment industry sent a billion dollars' worth of clothing a year (wholesale) to such large retailers in the United States as the Gap, Anne Taylor, Ralph Lauren, Calvin Klein, Liz Claiborne, Target, Walmart, and J. Crew.

Why? Saipan is a small island near Guam, twice the size of Manhattan. It's about five thousand miles from the U.S. mainland, where those garments were sold. And it's nearly two thousand miles from China, where most of the labor force came from. There are factories in China. Why haul workers from Chinese slums to a small Pacific island just so they can make shirts for Ralph Lauren?

The answer is that Saipan is in the Commonwealth of the Northern Mariana Islands. The Northern Marianas, in turn, were part of Micronesian islands that the United States seized from Japan after the Second World War. This wasn't an annexation, as the islands were a strategic trust territory under the ultimate sovereignty of the United Nations. But the United States was nevertheless the sole administrator.

Quarter from the Northern Marianas

In an elongated process stretching from the 1970s to the 1990s, the Trust Territory of the Pacific Islands was broken up. The Republic of the Marshall Islands, the Federated States of Micronesia, and the Republic of Palau became sovereign states "freely associated" with the United States, receiving economic assistance in exchange for offering base sites. The Northern Marianas, however, became a commonwealth akin to Puerto Rico. In 1986, when the legislation finally went through, its residents—some thirty thousand people—became U.S. citizens.

Like Puerto Rico, the Northern Marianas were subject to some U.S. laws but not others. The federal minimum wage and much of immigration law were waived. The nearest Occupational Safety and Health Administration office was thousands of miles away. At the same time, for the purposes of trade, the Northern Marianas counted as part of the country. The combination was potent: a legal environment where foreign workers could toil for paltry wages with little oversight to stitch garments labeled MADE IN THE USA.

Saipan functioned as a sort of standing loophole. Starting in 1995, as stories of its exploited workers made their way to the mainland, members of Congress sought to close it. Over the next decade or so, they would submit at least twenty-nine bills to change some part of the relevant law. Twice the Senate voted unanimously for wage and immigration reforms, only to have the bills die in the House Committee on Resources. A 1999 House bill had 243 cosponsors, a substantial majority. But it, too, died.

The Northern Marianas government and the garment manufacturers, it turned out, had hired a lobbyist to defend their lucrative arrangement. A really, really good lobbyist. He offered junkets to every Congress member and congressional aide who wanted to visit Saipan—more than 150 went. The visitors enjoyed golfing, luxurious hotels, snorkeling, and, in some cases, the services of prostitutes (some of the guest workers on Saipan were driven by poverty into sex work, others were forced into it outright).

A private firm couldn't have easily offered such all-expenses-paid trips to lawmakers. But, the lobbyist explained, "one of the grand constitutional loopholes we had used to our advantage for years was the provision that when a 'government' pays for travel—or, in fact, confers any gift or gratuity—representatives and staff are not required to report those expenses."

So, for the purposes of labor law, the Northern Marianas wasn't part of the United States. For the purposes of trade, it was. And for the purposes of lobbying regulations, it was a foreign government.

Nearly half the Republican members of the House Committee on Resources went to Saipan or sent staffers there. Tom DeLay, the House majority whip, visited the island with his wife, his daughter, and six aides. "You are a shining light," he told local officials. "You represent everything that is good about what we're trying to do in America, in leading the world in the free-market system."

Later, DeLay told *The Washington Post* that Saipan was "a perfect petri dish of capitalism." "It's like my Galapagos Island," he boasted.

For the lobbyist, this was a triumph. Despite the overwhelming opposition (*two* unanimous Senate votes), he'd arranged enough golf rounds and snorkeling trips to keep the loophole open for more than a decade. It was the first in a string of legally creative maneuvers that would turn him into Washington's highest-paid lobbyist—"The Man Who Bought Washington," *Time* called him—and a household name.

That name? Jack Abramoff.

For the top-earning lobbyist in Washington, Abramoff had an odd portfolio. He didn't represent Fortune 500 companies. Instead, he worked the loopholes. His next victory after the Northern Marianas was for the Mississippi Band of Choctaw Indians, who were fighting off a gaming tax. He used the same strategy as in Saipan, exploiting the fact that an Indian tribal government could give politicians unreported gifts. He took on more Indian tribes and nations as clients. He started representing a Puerto Rican business group. He organized junkets to the Republic of the Marshall Islands, and he got involved in Guam's gubernatorial race.

What Jack Abramoff had discovered in Saipan was the same thing the Bush administration lawyer John Yoo had discovered in Guantánamo Bay: empire is still around, and places with anomalous legal statuses can be extremely useful.

★

In 2005 an international treaty eliminated quotas on textile imports to the United States. Two years later, Congress finally extended federal minimum wage legislation to the Northern Marianas. The garment industry in Saipan collapsed, and manufacturers moved to China, Vietnam, and Cambodia.

By that time, Jack Abramoff had been convicted of conspiracy, fraud, and tax evasion for his numerous shady dealings, most notably defrauding the Native American tribes that had hired him. His malfeasance filled a 373-page report authored by the incensed chairman of the Senate's Indian Affairs Committee, John McCain. Or, as Abramoff called him, "my hangman."

Skewering the country's most notorious lobbyist showed McCain in a flattering light. That, in turn, helped his presidential bid. In 2008, campaigning on his reputation for integrity, he won the Republican nomination.

But McCain had his own empire problems. The son of a naval officer, McCain had been born not on the mainland, but in the Panama Canal Zone. He hadn't lived there long, but his birthplace nevertheless raised questions. There'd never been a president born in a territory. Was McCain even eligible for the office?

The Constitution requires that the president be a "natural born citizen," yet it's not clear what that means. At minimum, everyone agrees, it means the president must be a citizen from birth. But does "natural born" include those born in territories where citizenship is statutory rather than constitutional? The Supreme Court has never weighed in.

The Republican presidential nominee in 1964, Barry Goldwater, had been born in the Territory of Arizona. He'd faced questions, but since he lost the election, the matter was never resolved. McCain's case was more complicated. The Fourteenth Amendment grants citizenship to "all persons born or naturalized in the United States, and subject to the jurisdiction thereof," but the Insular Cases had established that this didn't apply to unincorporated territories. At the time of McCain's birth, there was a law granting citizenship (with exceptions) to children born to citizen parents "out of the limits and jurisdiction of the United States," but McCain was born in the Panama Canal Zone, a Guantánamo-like space under exclusive U.S. jurisdiction.

In the 1930s, Congress addressed this issue. As a House report put it, "the citizenship of persons born in the Canal Zone of American parents, has never been defined either by the Constitution, treaty or congressional enactment." After debate, Congress passed a statute making them citizens. It applied not only to future children but, retroactively, to anyone who'd been born in the Canal Zone to a citizen parent in the past. The law passed in 1937.

John McCain was born in 1936.

Had this been litigated, it would have made for fascinating case law. McCain was, per the 1937 statute, a citizen by virtue of his birth. But he wasn't born a citizen, as no law made him a citizen at the *time* of his birth. Arguably, then, he was not a "natural born citizen" and thus not eligible for the presidency. As Gabriel Chin, the law professor who unearthed this, put it, McCain was born "eleven months and a hundred yards short of citizenship."

★

Gabriel Chin's case against John McCain was never heard. Still, McCain's Senate colleagues were nervous enough to pass a nonbinding resolution declaring him to be a natural born citizen. Yet it's hard to imagine that this would have helped him in court. The Senate can't stipulate an interpretation of the Constitution by resolution.

Oddly, this wasn't the end of McCain's empire woes. For his running mate, he picked the governor of Alaska, Sarah Palin. She was born in Idaho, but her family had moved to Alaska when she was a newborn. There, she met and married Todd Palin, an oil field worker of part Yup'ik ancestry. They had five children, all of whom are, by law, like their father, Alaska Natives.

Palin made no secret of her Native ties. She drafted Todd's grandmother, who used to work as a Yup'ik/English translator, to appear onstage with her at the Alaska Federation of Natives convention during her gubernatorial campaign. Her mixed family, she argued, was an example for the state.

Yet when she entered national politics as McCain's running mate, one aspect of Todd's background proved tricky. Not only was Todd Palin Yup'ik, he'd been, for seven years, a member of the Alaskan Independence Party. And Sarah had attended conventions with him.

The Alaskan Independence Party rejected the legitimacy of the process by which Ernest Gruening had guided the territory to statehood. As the party's chair argued, that process had been tainted because Alaska Natives who didn't speak English couldn't vote and military personnel stationed on Alaskan bases could. "Alaska was no different from other colonies," she explained. "As Algerians did not see themselves as a part of France, or as Libyans did not see themselves as a part of Italy, most Alaskans did not see themselves as part of U.S.A." The party sought a new referendum, possibly leading toward independence.

Sarah Palin was supportive. "Your party plays an important role in our state's politics," she said in a video address to the party's 2008 convention. "Good luck on a successful and inspiring convention. Keep up the good work."

★

In the end, McCain and Palin weren't much impeded by their colonial entanglements. They were white, and they projected an image of being "American"—McCain a war hero from a military family, Palin a fierce defender of what she called "the real America."

The same immunity was not enjoyed by their opponent in the 2008 election, Barack Obama. On paper, Obama had fewer colonial liabilities than his opponents. He'd been born in Hawai'i two years after it became a state, so there was no question as to his eligibility for the presidency—he didn't have the McCain problem. And though Hawai'i, like Alaska, has a formidable sovereignty movement, Obama had never engaged with it— he didn't have the Palin problem, either. He spoke little of Hawai'i while campaigning. Instead, he stressed his Kansan mother and his political education as a community organizer in Chicago.

Still, Obama's rivals smelled blood. His Hawaiian upbringing and time in Indonesia were a "very strong weakness," argued Hillary Clinton's senior strategist, Mark Penn. "His roots to basic American values and cultures are at best limited," Penn wrote in a 2007 memo to Clinton. "I cannot imagine America electing a president during a time of war who is not at his center fundamentally American in his thinking and in his values." Penn suggested that Clinton, who was running against Obama for the Democratic nomination, emphasize her own status as a daughter of the land.

"Every speech should contain the line you were born in the middle of America," Penn advised. "Let's explicitly own 'American' in our programs, the speeches and the values. He doesn't."

Hillary Clinton didn't take Penn's advice. Two sources inside her campaign told a journalist that Penn's memo caused a "near staff revolt" (another source claimed the memo was barely discussed). Nevertheless, Obama's perceived foreignness rankled some in Clinton's base. After Obama clinched the nomination, her supporters began to fantasize that he might be disqualified by the "natural born citizen" clause. They circulated an anonymous email claiming that he was born in Kenya.

Factually, there was nothing to support this. But culturally, it registered. Even when Obama's campaign released his certification of live birth, even when a page from *The Honolulu Advertiser* announcing his birth was published on the web, the suspicions lingered. The documents must be forged, the "birthers" concluded. To them, a mixed-race man named Barack Hussein Obama born on a Pacific island just *seemed* foreign.

Obama was admittedly unusual for the mainland. But he certainly wasn't unusual for Hawai'i, whose current congressional delegation includes a Samoan Hindu and a Japan-born Buddhist, but not a single WASP. Consider the last names of the other children whose births were announced in *The Honolulu Advertiser* on August 13, 1961:

> Arakawa, Asing, Ayau, Brown, Caberto, Chun, Clifford, Durkin, Earnest, Haas, Hatchie, Kamealoha, Kitson, Liu, Mokuani, Nagaishi, Raymond, Simpson, Staley, Takahashi, Waidelich, Walker, Wright, Wong

Maybe a Simpson or Durkin from Hawai'i could have run for president without a problem. But a Kamealoha? A Nagaishi? A Caberto? It's likely that any of these would have stoked the same suspicions Obama did.

Despite its origin among Clinton-supporting Democrats, the birther conspiracy theory hopped party lines in the general election. The Fox News host Sean Hannity picked up the issue, as did the CNN host Lou Dobbs. Seventeen Republicans in Congress either suggested that Obama wasn't born in the United States or voiced a strategic uncertainty. ("I think there are questions. We'll have to see" was a typical evasion, offered by Representative Charles Boustany of Louisiana.) Sarah Palin felt that "the public rightly is still making it an issue." "I think it's a fair question," she added.

In July 2009, half a year into Obama's presidency, a poll found that 58 percent of Republicans either thought Obama wasn't a natural born citizen or weren't sure.

With time, the issue retreated from the headlines to the back rooms of the internet. But it returned in 2011, when the real-estate developer Donald Trump summoned it forth. "Why doesn't he show his birth certificate?" Trump asked on *The View*. "There's something on that birth certificate that he doesn't like."

"There's at least a good chance that Barack Hussein Obama has made mincemeat out of our great and cherished Constitution!" Trump wrote to *The New York Times*. If so, he reasoned, it was "the greatest 'scam' in the history of our country."

Trump had waded into political waters before. This, however, was a cannonball dive. He doggedly pursued the issue, claiming to have hired private investigators. He threatened to write a book about it. It garnered him headlines and served as the first step in his own bid for the presidency. Though suspicion of foreigners of all stripes propelled Trump to the White House, this was where it started. Without the public doubts concerning Obama's "Americanness," Trump would quite likely not have been elected.

★

You might see the intrusions of colonialism into recent politics as a sort of hangover—a price paid for yesterday's excesses. In this view, empire is an affair of the past, even if its effects linger on.

But empire is not yet past. In August 2017, North Korea, eager to demonstrate its destructive power but unable to reliably reach the U.S. mainland with its missiles, threatened to create "an enveloping fire" around Guam, which the United States uses as a launchpad to fly B-1 bombers over the Korean Peninsula. Yet again, it seemed that a territory might become a military sacrifice zone, and yet again the mainland press showed more concern for the fate of the troops stationed there than for the colony itself. "Guam is American soil," its governor nervously reminded. "We are not just a military installation."

The next month, Hurricane Maria slammed into Puerto Rico, taking out the island's power grid, water system, and communications. It also exposed the parlous state of affairs in the United States' largest remaining colony. Although Luis Muñoz Marín's strategy of using tax loopholes to draw mainland corporations to the island had dramatically improved Puerto Rico's economy in the 1950s and for decades after, Congress removed those loopholes in the 1990s, triggering corporate flight, economic collapse, and an exodus of employable Puerto Ricans to the mainland. By the time Maria struck, more than 60 percent of the island's remaining inhabitants were on Medicare or Medicaid. Because the federal government funds those programs less generously in Puerto Rico than on the mainland, the commonwealth found itself accruing unsustainable debt to pay its bills.

The hurricane turned crisis into catastrophe. Puerto Ricans were knocked back a century as they made do without phones or electricity. Doctors were forced to perform surgeries by flashlight, city dwellers to search desperately for clean water. Hurricane Maria struck at nearly the same time as two other storms hit the mainland, Hurricane Harvey in Texas and Hurricane Irma (which also struck the U.S. Virgin Islands) in Florida. The difference in response was palpable. Though Puerto Ricans were far more likely to die from storm damage, they saw fewer federal personnel, markedly less media coverage, and only a fraction of the charitable giving.

"Recognize that we Puerto Ricans are American citizens," the island's governor pleaded. Yet a poll taken after Maria found that only a slight majority of mainlanders (and only 37 percent of those under thirty) knew that fact.

There are about four million people living in the territories today, in Puerto Rico, Guam, American Samoa, the U.S. Virgin Islands, and the Northern Marianas. They're subject to the whims of Congress and the president, but they can't vote for either. More than fifty years after the Voting Rights Act, they remain disenfranchised. As Guamanians and Puerto

Ricans have recently seen, this disenfranchisement carries potentially lethal consequences.

Empire lives on, too, in the overseas bases that dot the globe. It's easy to think of foreign policy as an affair of the negotiating table: sovereign nation-states sit down to threaten, bargain, or cooperate. But U.S. foreign policy, nearly uniquely, has a territorial component. Britain and France have some thirteen overseas bases between them, Russia has nine, and various other countries have one—in all, there are probably thirty overseas bases owned by non-U.S. countries. The United States, by contrast, has roughly eight hundred, plus agreements granting it access to still other foreign sites. Dozens of countries host U.S. bases. Those that refuse are nevertheless surrounded by them. The Greater United States, in other words, is in everyone's backyard.

★

So does all this mean the United States can be classified as an empire? That term is most often used as a pejorative, as an unfavorable character assessment. Empires are the bullies that bat weaker nations around. It's not hard to argue that the United States is imperialist in that sense. Certainly its corporations and armed forces have spread themselves out comfortably all over the world.

Yet *empire* is not only a pejorative. It's also a way of describing a country that, for good or bad, has outposts and colonies. In this sense, *empire* is not about a country's character, but its shape. And by this definition, the United States has indisputably been an empire and remains one today.

Oddly, though the United States is frequently accused of imperialism, its territorial dimensions go largely unnoticed. So much energy has gone into presenting the United States via the logo map that even its critics, the ones most eager to cry *empire*, have little to say about overseas territory.

Still, if there is one thing the history of the Greater United States tells us, it's that such territory *matters*. And not only for the people who live in colonies or near bases. It matters for the whole country. World War II began, for the United States, in the territories. The war on terror started with a military base. The birth control pill, chemotherapy, plastic, Godzilla, the Beatles, *Little House on the Prairie*, Iran-Contra, the transistor radio, the name *America* itself—you can't understand the histories of any of these without understanding territorial empire.

Territory still matters today. Colonialism hovers in the background of politics at the highest level. McCain, Palin, Obama, and Trump have all been touched by it. That may seem like an odd and surprising fact. But we should get over our surprise. The history of the United States is the history of empire.

NOTES

ABBREVIATIONS USED

AHC — American Historical Collection, Rizal Library, Ateneo de Manila University

Albizu FBI File — FBIPR Files, Pedro Albizu Campos, FBI File No. 105–11898, Archives of the Puerto Rican Diaspora, Centro de Estudios Puertorriqueños, Hunter College, City University of New York

APP — Gerhard Peters and John T. Woolley, *The American Presidency Project*, www.presidency.ucsb.edu

Burnham Collection — Daniel H. Burnham Collection, Ryerson and Burnham Archives, Art Institute of Chicago

CHF — Othmer Library of Chemical History, Chemical Heritage Foundation, Philadelphia

CWS — Chemical Warfare Service, Record Group 175, NACP

DH — *Diplomatic History*

FDR Library — Franklin D. Roosevelt Presidential Library and Museum

FO — *Founders Online*, National Archives, founders.archives.gov

Forbes Diary — W. Cameron Forbes Diary, W. Cameron Forbes Papers, Manuscript Division, Library of Congress

FRUS — *Foreign Relations of the United States* (Washington, DC)

Gruening Papers — Ernest Gruening Papers, Alaska and Polar Regions Department, Archives and Manuscripts, University of Alaska, Fairbanks

HC–DC — Office of the High Commissioner of the Philippines, Records of the Washington, DC, Office, 1942–46, ROT

HC–Manila — Office of the High Commissioner of the Philippine Islands, Records of the Manila Office, 1935–46, ROT

HC–Pol/Econ	Office of the High Commissioner of the Philippines, Records Concerning Political and Economic Matters, 1927–1946, ROT
HSA	Hawai'i State Archives, Honolulu
HWRD	Hawai'i War Records Depository, Archives and Manuscripts Department, University of Hawai'i, Mānoa
LTR	*The Letters of Theodore Roosevelt*, ed. Elting E. Morison (Cambridge, MA, 1952)
MPD	Maddison Project Database, January 2013 update, Groningen Growth and Development Centre, www.gddc.net/maddison /maddison-project/home.htm
NACP	United States National Archives, College Park, Maryland
NADC	United States National Archives, Washington, DC
Nicholson Scrapbooks	A. J. Nicholson, Scrapbooks Relating to the Spanish-American War and the Philippine Insurrection, Bancroft Library, University of California, Berkeley
NLP	National Library of the Philippines, Manila
Notter Records	Record Group 59, General Records of the Department of State, Records of Harley A. Notter, 1939–1945, NACP
NYT	*The New York Times*
Padover File	Specialized Functions, Records of the Research Unit on Territorial Policy, Reference File of Saul K. Padover, ROT
Pershing Papers	Papers of John J. Pershing, Manuscript Division, Library of Congress
Rem.	Douglas MacArthur, *Reminiscences* (New York, 1964)
Reynolds Papers	Ruth M. Reynolds Papers, Archives of the Puerto Rican Diaspora, Centro de Estudios Puertorriqueños, Hunter College, City University of New York
ROT	Records of the Office of Territories, Record Group 126, NACP
Stat.	*United States Statutes*
Tydings Papers	Papers of Millard E. Tydings, Special Collections, Hornbake Library, University of Maryland, College Park
WTR	*The Works of Theodore Roosevelt* (New York, 1926)

INTRODUCTION: LOOKING BEYOND THE LOGO MAP

3 *Salanga*: Alfrredo Navarro Salanga, "They Don't Think Much About Us in America," in *Poems 1980–1988: Turtle Voices in Uncertain Weather* (Manila, 1989), 180–81.

4 *The army's official history*: Louis Morton, *The Fall of the Philippines* (Washington, DC, 1953), 88.

4 *"Pearl Harbor" wasn't how people*: The etymology of that term, which debuted in the Portland *Oregonian* two days after the attack, is discussed in Emily S. Rosenberg, *A Date Which Will Live: Pearl Harbor in American Memory* (Durham, NC, 2003), 16.

5 *JAPS BOMB MANILA, HAWAII*, etc.: Beth Bailey and David Farber, "The Attack on Pearl Harbor . . . and Guam, Wake Island, Philippines, Thailand, Malaya, Singapore, and Hong Kong: December 7/8, the Pacific World, American Empire, and the American Political Imaginary," in *Pearl Harbor and the Attacks of December 8, 1941: A Pacific History*, ed. Beth Bailey and David Farber (Lawrence, KS, forthcoming).

5 *Sumner Welles*: Sumner Welles Papers, Speeches and Writings, "Speech Draft, December 8, 1941," 16, FDR Library.

5 *Eleanor Roosevelt*: Speech, December 7, 1941, Eleanor Roosevelt Papers, Speech and Article File, December 1941–January 1942, FDR Library.

6 *"bombing in Oahu,"* etc.: Draft 1, Significant Documents Collection, FDR Library.

6 *Polls taken*: Earl S. Pomeroy, *Pacific Outpost: American Strategy in Guam and Micronesia* (Stanford, CA, 1951), 140. Another factor that probably contributed to Roosevelt's editing of the manuscript was confusion as to whether the Philippines had been struck. It's possible that Roosevelt's inclusion and then deletion of the Philippines was in response to an initial false report that the Philippines had been hit and then a retraction. Yet Roosevelt continued to edit that same draft into the night of December 7, by which time the Philippines *had* been attacked and Roosevelt knew it—he penciled in the Philippines and Guam on the list of targets. If Roosevelt crossed the Philippines out because of the retraction, the question becomes why he didn't, once he had a correct report of the Philippine raid, revert to his original "Hawaii and the Philippines" formulation (or, for that matter, change it to "Hawaii, the Philippines, and Guam"). On these issues, see my chapter and Bailey and Farber's chapter in their edited collection, *Pearl Harbor*.

7 *"very much in passing,"* etc.: John Hersey, *Men on Bataan* (New York, 1942), 365.

7 *called them, colonies*: WTR, 11:250; Woodrow Wilson, *A History of the American People* (New York, 1902), 5:295.

7 *"The word colony"*: Quoted in Rebecca Tinio McKenna, *American Imperial Pastoral: The Architecture of U.S. Colonialism in the Philippines* (Chicago, 2017), 110.

8 *"logo map"*: Benedict Anderson, *Imagined Communities: Reflections on the Origin and Spread of Nationalism*, rev. ed. (New York, 2006), 179. The theoretical foundation for the logo map is Thongchai Winichakul's concept of the "geo-body" from *Siam Mapped: A History of the Geo-Body of a Nation* (Honolulu, 1994).

9 *Greater United States map*: Inspired by Bill Rankin's map, "The Territory of the United States," 2007, radicalcartography.net/us-territory.

9 *"Greater United States"*: Term discussed in Daniel Immerwahr, "The Greater United States: Territory and Empire in U.S. History," *DH* 40 (2016): 378–81.

11 *fifth largest*: Bouda Etemad, *Possessing the World: Taking the Measurements of Colonisation from the Eighteenth to the Twentieth Century*, trans. Andrene Everson (New York, 2007), 131.

11 *12.6 percent*: This includes military personnel.

11 *one in twelve was African American*: Immerwahr, "Greater United States," 376. The count of African Americans includes those in the territories.

12 *seventh-grade girls*: Letters collected in "World's Colonies—General" folder, box 67; 9-0-1, Administrative, World's Colonies; Office of Territories Classified Files, 1907–1951; ROT.

12 *"Although Hawaii"*: Helen Johnson of Rand McNally to Donna Kowalski, circa 1942, in ibid.

12 *"We believe,"* etc.: Barbara Frederick to Harold Ickes, January 14, 1943, in ibid.

12 *official clarified*: Ruth Hampton to Barbara Frederick, January 30, 1943, in ibid.

13 *1910 report*: U.S. Bureau of the Census, *Thirteenth Census of the United States*, vol. 1, *Population: 1910* (Washington, DC, 1913), 17.

13 *"Most people"*: Saul Padover, "The Overseas Expansion Policy of the U.S.," c. 1943, "Reports" folder, box 12, Padover File.

13 *"global American empire"*: Howard Zinn, *A People's History of the United States, 1492–Present*, rev. ed. (New York, 1995), 492.

13 *"traveling the same path"*: Patrick J. Buchanan, *A Republic, Not an Empire: Reclaiming America's Destiny* (1999; Washington, DC, 2002), 6.

14 *case can be made*: A helpful overview is Paul A. Kramer, "Power and Connection: Imperial Histories of the United States in the World," *American Historical Review* (2011): 1348–91.

14 *Du Bois*: See especially his *Dark Princess: A Romance* (New York, 1928) and *Color and Democracy: Colonies and Peace* (New York, 1945).

14 *211 times in 67 countries*: Barbara Salazar Torreon, *Instances of Use of United States Armed Forces Abroad, 1798–2016*, Congressional Research Service Report R42738, 2016. This doesn't count routine stationing of troops, covert operations, or disaster relief.

14 *"worst chapter"*: James A. Field Jr., "American Imperialism: The Worst Chapter in Almost Any Book," *American Historical Review* 83 (1978): 644–68.

15 *assiduously researched*: Key works are listed in Immerwahr, "Greater United States." Two very recent books are also worth mentioning: Brian Russell Roberts and Michelle Anne Stephens, eds., *Archipelagic American Studies* (Durham, NC, 2017), and A. G. Hopkins, *American Empire: A Global History* (Princeton, NJ, 2018).

15 *confusion and shoulder-shrugging*: This can be seen not only in textbooks but higher up the academic food chain, in the flagship research journal in U.S. history, the *Journal of American History*. The Philippines was the United States' largest colony by an order of magnitude, yet in the past fifty years the *JAH* has published only one research article about it (i.e., only one non-review article mentioning the Philippines in its title). That article, Walter L. Williams's "United States Indian Policy and the Debate over Philippine Annexation: Implications for the Origins of American Imperialism," was published in 1980. Inevitably, it covered 1898 and its immediate aftermath.

16 *Philippine bill was the basis*: Alvita Akiboh, "Pocket-Sized Imperialism: U.S. Designs on Colonial Currency," *DH* 41 (2017): 874.

17 *135 million*: Immerwahr, "Greater United States," 388.

18 *eight hundred overseas military bases*: David Vine, *Base Nation: How U.S. Military Bases Abroad Harm America and the World* (New York, 2015), 4.

18 *Rankin*: William Rankin, *After the Map: Cartography, Navigation, and the Transformation of Territory in the Twentieth Century* (Chicago, 2016).

1. THE FALL AND RISE OF DANIEL BOONE

25 *Boone*: In the following account, I've relied on John Mack Faragher, *Daniel Boone: The Life and Legend of an American Pioneer* (New York, 1992); Stephen Aron, *How the West Was Lost: The Transformation of Kentucky from Daniel Boone to Henry Clay* (Baltimore, 1996); and Meredith Mason Brown, *Frontiersman: Daniel Boone and the Making of America* (Baton Rouge, LA, 2008).

25 *"So rich a soil"*: Felix Walker, quoted in Brown, *Frontiersman*, 73.

26 *"first white man"*: Timothy Flint, *The First White Man of the West* (Cincinnati, 1856).

26 *European literature*: On Boone's European reception, see Richard Slotkin, *Regeneration Through Violence: The Mythology of the American Frontier, 1600–1860* (Middletown, CT, 1973), chaps. 10–11.

26 *wasn't much revered*: Louise Phelps Kellogg, "The Fame of Daniel Boone," *Register of the Kentucky State Historical Society* 32 (1934): 187–98.

26 *"Had the horses"*: *New-York American*, reprinted in the *Alexandria Gazette*, July 11, 1826.

27 *nation's "refuse"*: Benjamin Franklin, *The Interest of Great Britain Considered*, 1760, FO. On early scorn of frontier dwellers, see David Andrew Nichols, *Red Gentlemen and White Savages: Indians, Federalists, and the Search for Order on the American Frontier* (Charlottesville, VA, 2008).

27 *"no better"*: J. Hector St. John de Crèvecoeur, *Letters from an American Farmer and Others Essays*, ed. Dennis D. Moore (Cambridge, MA, 2013), 33.

27 *"white savages"*: John Jay to Thomas Jefferson, December 14, 1786, FO. I have modernized eighteenth-century capitalization throughout this chapter.

27 *"settling, or rather"*: Washington to James Duane, September 7, 1783, FO.

28 *"exceedingly familiar and friendly"*: Boone, quoted in Brown, *Frontiersman*, 137.

28 *This was exactly the sort*: My account of Washington and the West draws heavily on Fred Anderson and Andrew Cayton, *The Dominion of War: Empire and Liberty in North America, 1500–2000* (New York, 2005), chap. 4. Another crucial guide is Colin G. Calloway, *The Indian World of George Washington: The First President, the First Americans, and the Birth of a Nation* (New York, 2018).

28 *"murders, and general dissatisfaction"*: September 12, 1784, *The Diaries of George Washington*, ed. Donald Jackson and Dorothy Twohig (Charlottesville, VA, 1978), 4:19.

28 *"labour very little,"* etc.: Ibid., October 4, 1784, 4:66.

28 *"become too open, violent"*: Washington to Jefferson, September 15, 1792, FO.

29 *"first and only"*: Joseph J. Ellis, *His Excellency: George Washington* (New York, 2005), 225.

29 *"compact" manner*: Washington to Duane, September 7, 1793, FO. An excellent overview of the resistance to western settlement is Paul Frymer, *Building an American Empire: The Era of Territorial and Political Expansion* (Princeton, NJ, 2017), chaps. 2–3.

29 *(55 percent) was covered by states*: Calculated from Franklin K. Van Zandt, *Boundaries of the United States and the Several States* (Washington, DC, 1966), 262–64, and Thomas Donaldson, *The Public Domain: Its History, with Statistics* (Washington, DC, 1884), 87–88.

30 *"equal footing"*: Northwest Territory Ordinance of 1787, 1 *Stat.* 51, section 14, article 5.

30 *"In effect"*: Monroe to Jefferson, May 11, 1786, FO.

30 *"despotic oligarchy"*: Jefferson to Henry Innes, January 23, 1800, FO.

30 *"poor devil"*: St. Clair to Alexander Hamilton, August 9, 1793, FO.

30 *"dependent colony"* . . . *"citizens"* . . . *"subjects"*: Arthur St. Clair, quoted in Peter S. Onuf, *Statehood and Union: A History of the Northwest Ordinance* (Bloomington, IN, 1987), 71.

30 *"white Indians"*: Quoted in Andrew R. L. Cayton, *The Frontier Republic: Ideology and Politics in the Ohio Country, 1780–1825* (Kent, OH, 1986), 8.

30 *"ignorant"* . . . *"ill qualified"*: St. Clair, quoted in Onuf, *Statehood and Union*, 70. On the imperial features of territorial government, see (besides above-cited works by Onuf, Cayton, and Frymer) Whitney T. Perkins, *Denial of Empire: The United*

States and Its Dependencies (Leiden, Netherlands, 1962), chap. 1; Jack Ericson Eblen, *The First and Second United States Empires: Governors and Territorial Government, 1784–1912* (Pittsburgh, 1968), chap. 2; and Julian Go, *Patterns of Empire: The British and American Empires, 1688 to the Present* (New York, 2011), chap. 1.

31 *"This Constitution never was"*: Annals of Congress, 11th Cong., 3d sess., 1811, 537.

31 *"incapable of self-government"*: Quoted in Bartholomew H. Sparrow, *The* Insular Cases *and the Emergence of American Empire* (Lawrence, KS, 2006), 22.

31 *largest contingent of the army*: Peter J. Kastor, *The Nation's Crucible: The Louisiana Purchase and the Creation of America* (New Haven, CT, 2004), 90.

31 *"mental darkness"* . . . *"dangerous experiment"*: Quoted in Perkins, *Denial of Empire*, 21.

31 *"Do political axioms"*: Pierre Sauve, Pierre Derbigny, and Jean Noël Destrehan, "Remonstrance of the People of Louisiana Against the Political System Adopted by Congress for Them," 1804, in *American State Papers*, 10, *Miscellaneous*, 1:397.

31 *did nothing*: Kastor, *Nation's Crucible*, 58–60.

31 *"cover the whole"* . . . *"distant times"*: Jefferson to James Monroe, November 24, 1801, FO. On Jeffersonians versus Federalists regarding territorial government, see Cayton, *Frontier Republic*.

31 *"wide and fruitful"*: Jefferson, Inaugural Address, March 4, 1801, APP.

32 *"I told him no"*: Robert R. Livingston to James Madison, April 11, 1803, FO.

32 *"the best use"*: Jefferson to John Breckinridge, August 12, 1803, FO.

32 *"shut up"*: Jefferson to John Dickinson, August 9, 1803, FO.

32 *"advancing compactly"*: Jefferson to Breckinridge, August 12, 1803, FO.

32 *European populations had grown*: MPD.

32 *the best available statistics*: Alfred Owen Aldridge, "Franklin as Demographer," *Journal of Economic History* 9 (1949): 25–26.

32 *Disease took so many*: Jack P. Greene, *Pursuits of Happiness: The Social Development of Early Modern British Colonies and the Formation of American Culture* (Chapel Hill, NC, 1988), 82.

32 *one to two miles a year*: Dale Van Every, *Ark of Empire: The American Frontier, 1784–1803* (New York, 1963), 21.

33 *Franklin was the first*: Benjamin Franklin, *Observations Concerning the Increase of Mankind, Peopling of Countries, &c.* (Boston, 1755), 9. On the foundation for Franklin's calculations, see William F. Von Valtier, "'An Extravagant Assumption': The Demographic Numbers Behind Benjamin Franklin's Twenty-Five-Year Doubling Period," *Proceedings of the American Philosophical Society* 155 (2011): 158–88.

33 *"rapidity of increase"*: Thomas Robert Malthus, *First Essay on Population* (London, 1798), 105.

33 *Malthus, in turn*: Joyce E. Chaplin, *Benjamin Franklin's Political Arithmetic: A Materialist View of Humanity* (Washington, DC, 2009), 45.

33 *1890 census*: Conway Zirkle, "Benjamin Franklin, Thomas Malthus and the United States Census," *Isis* 48 (1957): 62.

33 *surpassed that of Britain*: MPD.

33 *population of France*: U.S. and French figures from MPD. For my understanding of U.S. population growth, I am indebted to D. W. Meinig, *The Shaping of America: A Geographical Perspective on 500 Years of History*, vol. 2 (New Haven, CT, 1993), and James Belich, *Replenishing the Earth: The Settler Revolution and the Rise of the Anglo-World, 1783–1939* (Oxford, UK, 2009).

34 *nearly forty miles a year*: Van Every, *Ark of Empire*, 21.

34 *influxes from Europe and Africa*: Michael R. Haines, "The Population of the United States, 1790–1920," in *The Cambridge Economic History of the United States*, ed. Stanley L. Engerman and Robert E. Gallman (Cambridge, UK, 2000), 2:153.

34 *"Wave after wave"*: Kah-Ge-Ga-Gah-Bouh, *Organization of a New Indian Territory East of the Missouri River* (New York, 1850), 3.

34 *the cities the settlers built*: On Cincinnati and Chicago: Belich, *Replenishing the Earth*, 196, 1.

34 *"homesteads"*: This transformation is helpfully discussed in Frymer, *Building an American Empire*, and Paul W. Gates, *History of Public Land Law Development* (Washington, DC, 1968), chaps. 10 and 15.

35 *"most infamous system"*: Earl S. Pomeroy, *The Territories and the United States, 1861–1890: Studies in Colonial Administration* (Philadelphia, 1947), 104.

35 *Appointed governors . . . new territories*: Eblen, *First and Second U.S. Empires*, 140.

35 *"manifest destiny"*: "Annexation," *United States Magazine and Democratic Review*, July–August 1845, 5. Though the unsigned article has long been attributed to the magazine's editor, John L. O'Sullivan, Linda S. Hudson has used textual analysis to argue that it was "likely written" by Jane Cazneau. *Mistress of Manifest Destiny: A Biography of Jane McManus Storm Cazneau, 1807–1878* (Austin, TX, 2001), 61.

2. INDIAN COUNTRY

36 *Thornton*: Russell Thornton, *American Indian Holocaust and Survival: A Population History Since 1492* (Norman, OK, 1987), 32. Low and high estimates, respectively, from Alfred L. Kroeber and Henry F. Dobyns, are assessed and extrapolated at 25–26.

36 *closer to half a million*: Paul Stuart, *Nations Within a Nation: Historical Statistics of American Indians* (New York, 1987), 52.

37 *the population started rebounding*: Russell Thornton, *The Cherokees: A Population History* (Lincoln, NE, 1990), chap. 3. The following account of the Cherokees draws on Gary E. Moulton, *John Ross: Cherokee Chief* (Athens, GA, 1978); Theda Purdue and Michael D. Green, *The Cherokee Nation and the Trail of Tears* (New York, 2007); and Brian Hicks, *Toward the Setting Sun: John Ross, the Cherokees, and the Trail of Tears* (New York, 2011).

37 *"It's like Baltimore"*: Hicks, *Setting Sun*, 148.

37 *"like the whiteman"*: John Ross, "To the Senate," March 8, 1836, in *The Papers of Chief John Ross*, ed. Gary E. Moulton (Norman, OK, 1978), 1:394.

37 *"would not be countenanced"*: Andrew Jackson, Annual Message, December 8, 1829, APP.

38 *"removal beyond" . . . "protection and peace"*: Quoted in Moulton, *Ross*, 38.

38 *"We can't be a Nation"*: Ibid., 51.

38 *a third or half of what it would have been*: Estimate is for the total population, not just the removed Cherokees. Thornton, *Cherokees*, 76.

39 *"admitted as a state"*: House Committee on Indian Affairs, H. Rep 474, *Regulating the Indian Department*, 23d Cong., 1st sess., 1834, 14.

39 *"not republican" . . . "despotism"*: *Register of Debates*, 23d Cong., 2d sess., February 20, 1835, 1447.

39 *"add to our Union"*: *Register of Debates*, 23d Cong., 1st sess., June 25, 1834, 4776.

39 *"I am not prepared"*: *Register of Debates*, 23d Cong., 2d sess., February 20, 1835, 1454.

39 *"full-blood savage"*: Ibid.

40 *farming equipment*, etc.: D. W. Meinig, *The Shaping of America: A Geographical Perspective on 500 Years of History* (New Haven, CT, 1993), 2:99–100.

40 *"effectual and complete"*: *Register of Debates*, 23d Congress, 1st sess., June 25, 1834, 4764.

41 *"Indian barrier"* . . . *"Where will they go?"*: William E. Unrau, *The Rise and Fall of Indian Country, 1825–1855* (Lawrence, KS, 2007), 125–26. See also Anne F. Hyde, *Empires, Nations, and Families: A New History of the North American West, 1800–1860* (Lincoln, NE, 2011), part II.

41 *"She didn't know"*: Laura Ingalls Wilder, *The Little House Books*, ed. Caroline Fraser (New York, 2012), 287.

41 *"'When white settlers'"*: Ibid., 366.

42 *"I'll not stay"*: Ibid., 401.

42 *Osages*: Dennis McAuliffe Jr., *The Deaths of Sybil Bolton: An American History* (New York, 1994), 110–17. See also Frances W. Kaye, "Little Squatter on the Osage Diminished Reserve: Reading Laura Ingalls Wilder's Kansas Indians," *Great Plains Quarterly* 20 (2000): 123–40.

42 *"The question will suggest"*: McAuliffe, *Sybil Bolton*, 116.

42 *By 1879, it contained*: Roy Gittinger, *The Formation of the State of Oklahoma, 1803–1906* (1917; Norman, OK, 1939), 264–65.

43 *"We are here"*: *Congressional Record*, 48th Cong., 2d sess., 505.

43 *"No matter how little"*: "The Oklahoma Boomers," *Cherokee Advocate*, October 12, 1887.

43 *"most rapid settlement"*: *Statistical Atlas of the United States* (Washington, DC, 1914), 40.

44 *less than one-quarter Indian*: Paul Frymer, *Building an American Empire: The Era of Territorial and Political Expansion* (Princeton, NJ, 2017), 167.

45 *"jist plumb"* . . . *"furrin country"*: Lynn Riggs, *Green Grow the Lilacs* (New York, 1931), 161.

45 *"I kept"*: Phyllis Cole Braunlich, *Haunted by Home: The Life and Letters of Lynn Riggs* (Norman, OK, 1988), 179.

3. EVERYTHING YOU ALWAYS WANTED TO KNOW ABOUT GUANO BUT WERE AFRAID TO ASK

46 *"dagger pointed"*: Lubna Z. Qureshi, *Nixon, Kissinger, and Allende: U.S. Involvement in the 1973 Coup in Chile* (Lanham, MD, 2009), 86. The joke is originally Richard Edes Harrison's.

47 *"power of population"*: Thomas Robert Malthus, *First Essay on Population* (London, 1798), 44.

48 *value of "lost" human feces*: George E. Waring, *The Elements of Agriculture* (New York, 1854), 129, discussed in Richard A. Wines, *Fertilizer in America: From Waste Recycling to Resource Exploitation* (Philadelphia, 1985), 25.

48 *"The fact is notorious"*: "Selections by the Committee: Extracts from Dr. Lee's Report in N.Y. Legislature," *Sentinel and Witness* (Middletown, CT), May 7, 1845.

48 *Davy*: Humphry Davy, *Elements of Agricultural Chemistry* (London, 1813), lecture 6. On fertilizer, I've learned much from Ariel Ron, "Developing the Country:

'Scientific Agriculture' and the Roots of the Republican Party" (Ph.D. diss., University of California, Berkeley, 2012).

49 *"double tubular apparatus"*: Victor Hugo, *Les Misérables*, trans. Isabel F. Hapgood (New York, 1887), 2:85.

49 *What did work*: The best accounts of guano are Wines, *Fertilizer;* Jimmy M. Skaggs, *The Great Guano Rush: Entrepreneurs and American Overseas Expansion* (New York, 1994); Edward D. Melillo, "The First Green Revolution: Debt Peonage and the Making of the Nitrogen Fertilizer Trade, 1840–1930," *American Historical Review* 114 (2012): 1028–60; and Gregory T. Cushman, *Guano and the Opening of the Pacific World: A Global Ecological History* (New York, 2013).

49 *"beastly smelling-bottle"*: "Guano," *Vermont Watchman and State Journal*, December 27, 1844.

49 *"the most odious"*: *Congressional Globe*, 34th Cong., 1st sess., 1856, 1740.

49 *Sailors hauling guano*: "Beauties of Guano Digging," *New York Herald*, May 3, 1845; Skaggs, *Guano Rush*, 160.

49 *"cheapest, most powerful"*: "Guano," *Cleveland Herald*, July 19, 1844.

49 *Tall tales*: "The Effects of Guano—Munchausen Beaten All Hollow!!!" *Weekly Raleigh Register and North Carolina Gazette*, June 27, 1845; "Remarkable Properties of Guano," *The Floridian*, September 4, 1847.

50 *"This subject"* . . . *"The Senator"*: *Congressional Globe*, 34th Cong., 1st sess., 1856, 1741.

50 *"Peruvian guano"*: Millard Fillmore, First Annual Message, December 12, 1850, *APP.*

51 *"exterminate the hated race"*: Dan O'Donnell, "The Lobos Islands: American Imperialism in Peruvian Waters in 1852," *Australian Journal of Politics and History* 39 (2008): 45.

51 *"The Peruvian penguin"*: *London Times*, October 6, 1852.

51 *Just a single Peruvian island*: *Congressional Globe*, 33d Cong., 1st sess., 1854, 1194.

51 *"vast deposit"* . . . *"verdant glades"*: James Fenimore Cooper, *The Crater, or, Vulcan's Peak* (New York, 1847), 1:186, 185.

51 *capitalization of $10 million*: Skaggs, *Guano Rush*, 54; federal expenditures in 1850 were $44.8 million according to U.S. Department of the Treasury, *Annual Report of the Secretary of the Treasury on the State of Finances for the Fiscal Year Ended June 30, 1934, 1935*, 303.

51 *"at the discretion"*: Guano Islands Act, U.S. Code 48 (1856), §1411.

52 *"at liberty"*: Rene Bach, "Our Ocean Empire," *Morning Oregonian*, July 11, 1897.

52 *"new kind"* . . . *"consequences beyond"*: *Congressional Globe*, 34th Cong., 1st sess., 1856, 1699, 1698.

52 *"prospect of dominion,"* etc.: Ibid., 1698.

53 *fifty-nine islands . . . ninety-four guano islands*: Skaggs, *Guano Rush*, 71, 199. These numbers refer to ratified claims. But some claims were vague, and I haven't been able to confirm that every one corresponded to an actual island.

53 *"Pacific will be ours"*: Walt Whitman, *Democratic Vistas and Other Papers* (London, 1888), 66.

53 *"little paradise"*: Cooper, *Crater*, 184.

53 *"completely encased"*: Gregory Rosenthal, "Life and Labor in a Seabird Colony: Hawaiian Guano Workers, 1857–1870," *Environmental History*, 17 (2012): 764.

53 *sixty-eight of these ships mutinied*: Melillo, "First Green Revolution," 1047.

NOTES

54 *"The shark and the Kanaka"*: "Life on a Guano Island," *Weekly Georgia Telegraph*, May 7, 1869.

54 *Navassa*: On Navassa, I've relied on W. M. Alexander, *The Brotherhood of Liberty, or, Our Day in Court* (Baltimore, 1891); John Cashman, "'Slaves Under Our Flag': The Navassa Island Riot of 1889," *Maryland Historian* 24 (1993): 1–21; Skaggs, *Guano Rush*, chap. 10; and Jennifer C. James, "'Buried in Guano': Race, Labor, and Sustainability," *American Literary History* 24 (2012): 115–42.

54 *"We have been treated"*: "Rescued from Death," *Rocky Mountain News*, October 11, 1889.

54 *BLACK BUTCHERS*: "The Black Butchers," *Galveston Daily News*, October 11, 1889.

55 *"appertain"*: "The Navassa Murder Cases," *New York Age*, April 19, 1890; Christina Duffy Burnett, "The Edges of Empire and the Limits of Sovereignty: American Guano Islands," *American Quarterly* 57 (2005): 779–803.

55 *"unequivocally"*: *Jones v. United States*, 137 U.S. 211 (1890).

55 *"American citizens"*: Harrison, quoted in "Sentence Commuted," *Atchison Champion*, May 19, 1891.

56 *"a convict establishment"*: "The Navassa Prisoners," *New York Age*, May 30, 1891.

56 *"It is inexcusable"*: Benjamin Harrison, Third Annual Message, December 9, 1891, APP.

56 *four hundred thousand tons*: Skaggs, *Guano Rush*, 153.

57 *By 1914*: Cushman, *Guano*, 155.

57 *Haber*: I've relied especially on Vaclav Smil, *Enriching the Earth: Fritz Haber, Carl Bosch, and the Transformation of World Food Production* (Cambridge, MA, 2001); Dietrich Stolzenberg, *Fritz Haber: Chemist, Nobel Laureate, German, Jew* (Philadelphia, 2004); and Daniel Charles, *Master Mind: The Rise and Fall of Fritz Haber, the Nobel Laureate Who Launched the Age of Chemical Warfare* (New York, 2005).

57 *2.4 billion*: Smil, *Enriching the Earth*, 160.

57 *"seldom has the awarding"*: Charles, *Master Mind*, 49.

57 *"What Fritz has gained"*: Stolzenberg, *Haber*, 174.

57 *president of the American Chemical Society*: Julius Stieglitz, introduction to Edwin E. Slossen, *Creative Chemistry* (Garden City, NY, 1919), iii.

58 *protest of her husband's invention*: Morris Goran asserts—and the assertion has often been quoted—that Clara regarded poison gas "not only as a perversion of science but also as a sign of barbarism" and "pleaded with her husband" to forsake it (*The Story of Fritz Haber* [Norman, OK, 1967], 71). Yet Goran offers documentation for none of this. A far more cautious account is Bretislav Friedrich and Dieter Hoffman, "Clara Haber, nee Immerwahr (1870–1915): Life, Work and Legacy," *Zeitschrift für Allgemeine und Anorganische Chemie* 642 (2016): 437–88.

4. TEDDY ROOSEVELT'S VERY GOOD DAY

59 *Powerful men*: A helpful examination of presidential origins is Edward Pessen, *The Log Cabin Myth: The Social Backgrounds of the Presidents* (New Haven, CT, 1984).

60 *"whitetail"* . . . *"Antelope"*: WTR, 1:86, 1:403.

60 *"A bear's brain"*: WTR, 1:241.

60 *"manliness, self-reliance"*: Quoted in Richard Slotkin, *Gunfighter Nation: The Myth of the Frontier in Twentieth-Century America* (New York, 1992), 37.

60 *surrounded by guns*: The event is described in Evan Thomas, *The War Lovers: Roosevelt, Lodge, Hearst, and the Rush to Empire, 1898* (New York, 2010), 53–54.

61 *"great deeds"*: WTR, 8:xliv.

61 *"statesmen"* . . . *"unable to fully appreciate"*: WTR, 8:17–18.

62 *"peculiarly revolting"*: WTR, 9:58.

62 *"The rude, fierce settler"*: WTR, 9:57.

62 *"bloody fighting"*: WTR, 1:4.

62 *armed Sioux*: WTR, vol. 1, chap. 7 of *Ranch Life*.

62 *"frontier proper"*: WTR, 12:254.

62 *"frontier thesis"*: Frederick Jackson Turner, "The Significance of the Frontier in American History," 1893, in *The Frontier in American History* (New York, 1920).

62 *"I think you have"*: Edmund Morris, *The Rise of Theodore Roosevelt* (New York, 1979), 466.

62 *"The world is nearly"*: W. T. Stead, ed., *The Last Will and Testament of Cecil John Rhodes* (London, 1902), 190. On the closure of global frontiers, see Neil Smith, *American Empire: Roosevelt's Geographer and the Prelude to Globalization* (Berkeley, CA, 2003), chap. 1.

63 *"like land birds"*: Alfred Thayer Mahan, *The Influence of Sea Power upon History, 1660–1783* (1890; New York, 1957), 72.

64 *"great highway"*: Ibid., 22.

64 *tendency of bases*: Walter LaFeber, in "A Note on the 'Mercantilist Imperialism' of Alfred Thayer Mahan," *Mississippi Valley Historical Review* 48 (1962): 674–85, points out that Mahan's calls for empire were strategic, not economic, and did not require annexing large colonies. Yet Mahan's admiration for the British Empire is clear from *Sea Power*, as is his understanding that, historically, bases "naturally multiplied and grew until they became colonies" (Mahan 24).

64 *Mahan found his ideas received*: David Milne, *Worldmaking: The Art and Science of American Diplomacy* (New York, 2015), 22, 47–48.

64 *"During the last two days"*: Roosevelt to Mahan, May 12, 1890, in Richard W. Turk, *The Ambiguous Relationship: Theodore Roosevelt and Alfred Thayer Mahan* (Westport, CT, 1987), 109. There is a question, as in the case of Turner, as to whether Mahan influenced Roosevelt or merely confirmed his existing beliefs.

64 *"I should welcome"*: Roosevelt to Francis V. Greene, September 23, 1897, quoted in Howard K. Beale, *Theodore Roosevelt and the Rise of America to World Power* (Baltimore, 1956), 37.

65 *Spain's grip was slipping*: Louis A. Pérez Jr., *Cuba: Between Reform and Revolution*, 3d ed. (New York, 2006), 120.

65 *"civilized warfare"* . . . *"extermination"*: William McKinley, Message to Congress, April 11, 1898, APP.

65 *damsel in distress*: An astute analysis of gender's role in the affair is Kristin L. Hoganson, *Fighting for American Manhood: How Gender Politics Provoked the Spanish-American and the Philippine-American Wars* (New Haven, CT, 1998).

65 *"I don't propose"*: G.J.A. O'Toole, *The Spanish War: An American Epic—1898* (New York, 1984), 125.

65 *"Dirty treachery"*: Morris, *Rise of Roosevelt*, 600.

66 *"I have been through"*: Hermann Hagedorn, *Leonard Wood: A Biography* (New York, 1931), 1:141.

66 *"McKinley is bent"*: O'Toole, *Spanish War*, 146.

66 *"a perfect dear"*: Morris, *Rise of Roosevelt*, 566.

66 *"Dewey could be slipped"*: WTR, 20:220.

66 *"look after the routine"*: Joseph Bucklin Bishop, *Theodore Roosevelt and His Time* (New York, 1920), 1:86.

67 *The Battle of Manila Bay*: My account of the war from the perspective of the United States relies on David F. Trask, *The War with Spain in 1898* (New York, 1981); O'Toole, *Spanish War*; and Ivan Musicant, *Empire by Default: The Spanish-American War and the Dawn of the American Century* (New York, 1998).

67 *"Nineteenth century civilization"*: Joseph Stickney, *War in the Philippines: Life and Glorious Deeds of Admiral Dewey* (Chicago, 1899), 37.

67 *"That night"*: "The Battle of Manila Bay," *The Bounding Billow*, June 1898, in Nicholson Scrapbooks.

67 *"Is his wife dead?"*: Morris, *Rise of Roosevelt*, 612.

68 *"the lands that have been"*: WTR, 11:11.

68 *"wilder type,"* etc.: WTR, 11:17.

68 *"most faithful and loyal"*: WTR, 11:40.

68 *Demolins's book*: WTR, 11:32.

68 *battle for the San Juan Heights*: See, in addition to the military histories cited above, Roosevelt's *The Rough Riders* in WTR, vol. 11, and Morris, *Rise of Roosevelt*, chap. 25.

69 *"support the regulars"*: Morris, *Rise of Roosevelt*, 654.

69 *"The instant I received"*: WTR, 11:81.

69 *"a thin line"*: *The Works of Stephen Crane*, ed. Fredson Bowers (Charlottesville, VA, 1971), 9:158.

69 *"passing the shouting"*: WTR, 11:85.

69 *"bullets were ripping"*: WTR, 11:88.

69 *killed a Spaniard*: A more skeptical account is Trask, *War with Spain*, chap. 10.

69 *first documentary battle footage*: Bonnie M. Miller, *From Liberation to Conquest: The Visual and Popular Cultures of the Spanish-American War* (Amherst, MA, 2011), 98.

69 *"splendid little war"*: John Hay to Roosevelt, July 29, 1898, in William Roscoe Thatcher, *The Life and Letters of John Hay* (Boston, 1915), 2:337.

70 *"house of cards"*: Woodrow Wilson, *A History of the American People* (New York, 1902), 5:295.

70 *"We succeeded"*: David Starr Jordan, *Imperial Democracy* (New York, 1899), 91.

70 *Spain had a sizable*: Spanish troops: Sebastian Balfour, *The End of the Spanish Empire, 1898–1923* (Oxford, UK, 1997), 39. U.S. troops: Graham A. Cosmas, *An Army for Empire: The United States Army in the Spanish-American War* (Columbia, MO, 1971), 5, 136.

70 *a latecomer*: This interpretation of the war, as regards Cuba, is advanced brilliantly in Louis A. Pérez Jr., *The War of 1898: The United States and Cuba in History and Historiography* (Chapel Hill, NC, 1998). A nearly identical case can be made for the Philippines, and Renato Constantino, *A History of the Philippines: From the Spanish Colonization to the Second World War* (New York, 1975), chaps. 9–12, supplies the details. On the more limited role Puerto Ricans played in dislodging Spain, see Fernando Picó, *Puerto Rico 1898: The War After the War*, trans. Sylvia Korwek and Psique Arana Guzmán (1987; Princeton, NJ, 2004).

70 *"dead war"* . . . *"This war cannot last"*: Pérez, *Cuba: Between Reform and Revolution*, 135.

70 *"very great difficulties"*: WTR, 11:49.

70 *thirty thousand Spanish troops* . . . *eight thousand Spanish soldiers*: Balfour, *End of the Spanish Empire*, 39.

71 TELL AGUINALDO COME: Felipe Agoncillo, *To the American People* (Paris, 1900), 40.

71 *his whole force*: Joseph L. Schott, *The Ordeal of Samar* (New York, 1964), 151.

71 *"the greatest vigor"*: Trumbull White, *Our New Possessions* (Chicago, 1898), 79.

71 *"By day"*: *Autobiography of George Dewey, Admiral of the Navy* (New York, 1913), 247.

71 *"utter tatterdemalions"*: WTR, 11:49.

71 *"We should have been better off"*: Louis A. Pérez Jr., *Cuba Between Empires: 1878–1902* (Pittsburgh, 1983), 201.

71 *"I will never accept"*: Ibid., 209.

72 *"willing to surrender"*: Quoted in Musicant, *Empire by Default*, 569.

72 *One minute after*: White, *Our New Possessions*, 104.

72 *"This is not the Republic"*: Pérez, *Cuba Between Empires*, xv.

5. EMPIRE STATE OF MIND

73 *"could not have told"*: Stanley Karnow, *In Our Image: America's Empire in the Philippines* (New York, 1989), 104.

73 *fewer than ten U.S. citizens*: Michael Adas, *Dominance by Design: Technological Imperatives and America's Civilizing Mission* (Cambridge, MA, 2006), 131.

73 *Dewey doubted*: *Autobiography of George Dewey, Admiral of the Navy* (New York, 1913), 185.

73 *"I walked the floor"* . . . *"and there they are"*: James F. Rusling, "Interview with President McKinley," *Christian Advocate*, January 22, 1903, 137.

74 *"It does look"*: Quoted in Susan Schulten, *The Geographical Imagination in America, 1880–1950* (Chicago, 2001), 178. For imperial maps in general, see 38–44, 176–80.

74 *They offered suggestions*: Daniel Immerwahr, "The Greater United States: Territory and Empire in U.S. History," *DH* 40 (2016): 378–80.

75 *"The term 'United States of America'"*: Archibald Ross Colquhoun, *Greater America* (New York, 1904), 253.

76 *eleven unambiguous references*: *The Messages and Papers of the Presidents: Washington–Taft (1789–1913)* digitally searched at APP. I counted only instances of *America* that clearly referred to the United States, not the Americas or the British North American colonies. George Washington, Special Message, May 31, 1790; Washington, Inaugural Address, 1793; John Adams, Inaugural Address, 1797 (used twice); Andrew Jackson, "Regarding the Nullifying Laws of South Carolina," 1832; Martin Van Buren, Inaugural Address, 1837; James Polk, First Annual Message, 1845 (though Polk also refers to "the nations of America" in the same speech); Abraham Lincoln, "Remarks at a Fair in the Patent Office," 1864; Chester Arthur, First Annual Message, 1881; Arthur, Third Annual Message, 1883; Grover Cleveland, Third Annual Message, 1895.

76 *patriotic songs*: Samuel F. Smith, who wrote the words of "My Country 'Tis of Thee," called his 1831 composition "America," but it was nevertheless known as "My Country 'Tis of Thee" and its lyrics don't mention *America*. On *Columbia*, see Thomas

J. Schlereth, "Columbia, Columbus, and Columbianism," *Journal of American History* 79 (1992): 937–68.

76 *"For some thirty,"* etc.: Beckles Wilson, *The New America: A Study of the Imperial Republic* (London, 1903), 255, 256. Wilson also noted that the British were far more likely to refer to the United States as *America*, often getting corrected (before 1898) by U.S. interlocutors.

76 *In one two-week period*: The ten above-cited speeches from 1789–1898 contain eleven references to *America*. Roosevelt, in his trip to California, used the name twelve times in ten different speeches (all in *APP*): Remarks at Barstow, May 7, 1903; Address at San Bernardino, May 7, 1903; Address at Pasadena, May 8, 1903; Address at Santa Barbara, May 9, 1903; Address at San Luis Obispo, May 9, 1903 (two mentions); Remarks at Stanford University, May 12, 1903; Address at the Mechanic's Pavilion in San Francisco, May 13, 1903; Address at the Dedication of a Navy Memorial Monument in San Francisco, May 14, 1903; Address at Truckee, May 19, 1903 (two mentions); Remarks at Dunsmuir, May 20, 1903.

76 *The anthems changed*: "America the Beautiful" was originally a poem titled "Pike's Peak," written in 1893 by Katharine Lee Bates. It languished in obscurity, though, until it was republished (1904) and set to music (1910).

77 *lands wrested from Mexico*: Richard L. Nostrand calculates that those cessions incorporated 80,302 Mexicans into the United States, and the 1853 census report estimated the number of Indians in the new areas (including "Indians of the plains or Arkansas River") at 205,000. Nostrand, "Mexican Americans circa 1850," *Annals of the Association of American Geographers* 65 (1975): 378–90; J.D.B. De Bow, *The Seventh Census of the United States: 1850* (Washington, DC, 1853), xciv. Together they make up 1.48 percent of the 1845 population of the United States as given in MPD. The Mexican annexations introduced an absolutely larger new population into the United States than the Louisiana Purchase did, but whether they introduced a *relatively* larger new population is hard to say because of poor counts of Indians.

77 *"We have never dreamt,"* etc.: Speech on the War with Mexico, January 4, 1848, in *Papers of John C. Calhoun*, ed. Clyde Wilson and Shirley Bright Cox (Columbia, SC, 1999), 25:64, 65.

77 *"all the territory"*: *Louisville Democrat*, March 9, 1848, quoted in Frederick Merk, *Manifest Destiny and Mission in American History: A Reinterpretation* (New York, 1963), 151.

78 *"situated in tropical waters"*: Quoted in Eric T. L. Love, *Race over Empire: Racism and U.S. Imperialism, 1865–1900* (Chapel Hill, NC, 2004), 66. Another important account of the conflict between racism and imperialism is Paul Frymer, *Building an American Empire: The Era of Territorial and Political Expansion* (Princeton, NJ, 2017).

78 *"We do not want"*: Love, *Race over Empire*, 32.

78 *could not say how many Indians*: Some Indians were counted, but because, by the Constitution, "Indians not taxed"—Indians living outside the U.S. political community—didn't count toward congressional apportionment, they weren't included in the census.

79 *1890 census report*: Department of the Interior, *Report on the Population of the United States at the Eleventh Census: 1890*, part 1, 1895, 963.

79 *8.8 million*: *Statistical Atlas of the United States, 1900* (Washington, DC, 1903), 25.

79 *"It is one thing"*: Archibald R. Colquhoun, *The Mastery of the Pacific* (New York, 1904), 50–51.

79 *"I s'posed"*: Thomas Brackett Reed's remark, reported in Lemuel Quigg to Theodore Roosevelt, May 16, 1913, *LTR*, 2:921n.

80 *"pigmy State"*: Love, *Race over Empire*, 103.

80 *"We ought to take Hawaii"*: Roosevelt to James Bryce, September 10, 1897, *LTR*, 1:672.

80 *thirty-eight thousand of whom had signed*: Noenoe K. Silva, *Aloha Betrayed: Native Hawaiian Resistance to American Colonialism* (Durham, NC, 2004), 151.

81 *"lest his utterances"*: Bryan, "Annexation," 1899, in Murat Halstead, *Pictorial History of America's New Possessions* (New Haven, CT, 1899), 545.

81 *a compelling argument*: On the imperialism debates, see especially Robert L. Beisner, *Twelve Against Empire: The Anti-Imperialists, 1898–1900* (New York, 1968), and David Healy, *US Expansionism: The Imperialist Urge in the 1890s* (Madison, WI, 1970).

81 *"God has given"*: Albert J. Beveridge, "The Republic's Task," February 1899, in *Patriotic Eloquence*, ed. Robert I. Fulton and Thomas C. Trueblood (New York, 1900), 33.

81 *"who cant about 'liberty,'"* etc.: *WTR*, 13:329–30.

81 *political parties in Puerto Rico and the Philippines*: Julian Go, *American Empire and the Politics of Meaning: Elite Political Cultures and the Philippines and Puerto Rico During U.S. Colonialism* (Durham, NC, 2008).

82 *all the usual stops*: "Omaha's Colonial Exposition," *Weekly Register-Call* (Central City, CO), July 7, 1899.

82 *"over a thousand"*: "Greater America Exposition of 1899," *Daily Mining Record*, 25 February 1899.

82 *"civilized Tagals,"* etc.: "Gossip Gather in Hotel Lobbies," *Daily Picayune* (New Orleans), March 30, 1899.

82 *"large encampment"*: *Greater America Exposition* (Omaha, 1899), 13.

82 *thirty-five Filipinos*: The story is from Michael C. Hawkins, "Undecided Empire: The Travails of Imperial Representation of Filipinos at the Greater America Exposition, 1899," *Philippine Studies* 63 (2015): 341–63.

83 *"They are stylish,"* etc.: Ibid., 356–57.

84 *series of connected cases*: On the Insular Cases, see especially Christina Duffy Burnett and Burke Marshall, eds., *Foreign in a Domestic Sense: Puerto Rico, American Expansion, and the Constitution* (Durham, NC, 2001); Bartholomew H. Sparrow, *The Insular Cases and the Emergence of American Empire* (Lawrence, KS, 2006); and Gerald L. Neuman and Tomiko Brown-Nagin, eds., *Reconsidering the Insular Cases: The Past and Future of American Empire* (Cambridge, MA, 2015).

84 *"the supreme law"*: *Dorr v. United States*, 195 U.S. 138, 155 (1904) (Harlan, J., dissenting).

84 *"without asking"* . . . *"no right to elect"*: John W. Griggs, in *The Insular Cases, Comprising the Records, Briefs, and Arguments of Counsel in the Insular Cases of the October Term, 1900, in the Supreme Court of the United States* (Washington, DC, 1901), 333, 282.

85 *"To be called"* . . . *"section of the Chinese Empire"* . . . *"A great world power"*: Ibid., 314, 367, 338.

85 *"the Constitution deals"*: *Downes v. Bidwell*, 182 U.S. 244, 251 (1901).

85 *"foreign to the United States"*: Downes, 182 U.S. at 341 (White, J., concurring).
86 *"two national governments"*: Downes, 182 U.S. at 380 (Harlan, J., dissenting). For an important caution about the degree to which the Insular Cases carved out a new "extraconstitutional zone" of unincorporated territories, see Christina Duffy Burnett, *"Untied* States: American Expansion and Territorial Deannexation," *University of Chicago Law Review* 72 (2005): 797–879.
86 *"savages"* . . . *"alien races"*: Downes, 182 U.S. at 279 and 287.
86 *"wreck our institutions,"* etc.: Downes, 182 U.S. at 313 (White, J., concurring).
86 *not unusual for constitutional scholars*: Sanford Levinson, "Installing the *Insular Cases* into the Canon of Constitutional Law," in Duffy Burnett and Marshall, *Foreign in a Domestic Sense*, 122–23.
87 *ranked top of all 885*: As of September 9, 2014, according to the U.S. Army Reserve, www.usar.army.mil/Featured/Army-Reserve-At-A-Glance/American-Samoa.
87 *"disembodied shade"*: Downes, 182 U.S. at 372 (Fuller, C. J., dissenting).

6. SHOUTING THE BATTLE CRY OF FREEDOM

88 *Greater America Exposition*: "Omaha's Colonial Exposition," *Weekly Register-Call* (Central City, CO), July 7, 1899.
88 *"there was something pathetic"*: "Back from the Wars," *Denver Evening Post*, July 2, 1899.
88 *"The Americans, not from mercenary motives"*: Congressional Record, 57th Cong., 1st sess., 7708.
89 *"Under the protection"*: Declaration of Philippine Independence, in Sulpicio Guevara, ed., *The Laws of the First Philippine Republic* (Manila, 1972), 204.
89 *the business of state-building*: Paul A. Kramer, *The Blood of Government: Race, Empire, the United States, and the Philippines* (Chapel Hill, NC, 2006), 98–100.
89 *"commemorating the flag"*: Declaration of Philippine Independence, 206.
89 *"no joint occupation"*: Executive Order, August 17, 1898, APP.
89 *"Yankee Beer Chute"*: David Starr Jordan, *Imperial Democracy* (New York, 1899), 96.
90 *Prostitutes*: Ken De Bevoise, *Agents of Apocalypse: Epidemic Disease in the Colonial Philippines* (Princeton, NJ, 1995), 86–87.
90 *"received in the Revolutionary camp"*: Emilio Aguinaldo, *True Version of the Philippine Revolution* (Tarlac, Philippines, 1899), 42.
90 *"to be extended"*: Executive Order, December 21, 1898, APP.
90 *"violent and aggressive"*: John Morgan Gates, *Schoolbooks and Krags: The United States Army in the Philippines, 1898–1902* (Westport, CT, 1973), 38.
90 *inaugural banquet*: Renato Constantino, *A History of the Philippines: From the Spanish Colonization to the Second World War* (New York, 1975), 216.
90 *thirty thousand of them fled*: Leon Wolff, *Little Brown Brother: America's Forgotten Bid for Empire Which Cost 250,000 Lives* (London, 1961), 202.
90 *"Within an area"*: "The Big Scare," unknown paper, January 24, 1899, in Nicholson Scrapbooks.
90 *"I thought the best thing,"* etc.: Interview with Grayson in *Congressional Record*, 57th Cong., 1st sess., 7634.
91 *war had begun*: There are many histories of the Philippine War, especially between 1899 and 1902. I've relied especially on Glenn Anthony May, *Battle for Batangas: A*

Philippine Province at War (New Haven, CT, 1991); De Bevoise, *Agents of the Apocalypse*; Reynaldo C. Ileto, *Knowing America's Colony: A Hundred Years from the Philippine War* (Manoa, 1999); Resil B. Mojares, *The War Against the Americans: Resistance and Collaboration in Cebu: 1899–1906* (Quezon City, 1999); Brian McAllister Linn, *The Philippine War, 1899–1902* (Lawrence, KS, 2000); Angel Velasco Shaw and Luis H. Francia, eds., *Vestiges of War: The Philippine-American War and the Aftermath of an Imperial Dream, 1899–1999* (New York, 2002); Kramer, *Blood of Government*; and David J. Silbey, *A War of Frontier and Empire: The Philippine-American War, 1899–1902* (New York, 2007).

91 *Someone following the war*: On troop sizes, see Linn, *Philippine War*, 42.

91 *238 U.S. casualties*: Ibid., 52.

91 *lacked rifles . . . spears . . . bows and arrows . . . the "battalion"*: Wolff, *Little Brown Brother*, 207, 219.

91 *gathered tin cans*: May, *Batangas*, 173–74.

91 *melted church bells . . . matches . . . tree resins*: Mojares, *War Against the Americans*, 75, 223n22.

91 *pearl divers*: James R. Arnold, *The Moro War: How America Battled a Muslim Insurgency in the Philippine Jungle, 1902–1913* (New York, 2011), 100.

92 *"residual army"*: Emilio Aguinaldo with Vicente Albano Pacis, *A Second Look at America* (New York, 1957), 97.

92 *Tinio*: Orlino A. Ochosa, *The Tinio Brigade: Anti-American Resistance in the Ilocos Provinces, 1899–1901* (Quezon City, 1989), 30.

92 *seized the capital*: What was a "capital" and what simply a headquarters is hard to tell. I'm relying on Aguinaldo's own account from *Second Look at America*, 109.

92 *a single fatality*: "The Capture of Malolos," *Manila Freedom*, April 2, 1899.

92 *"no organized insurgent force"*: MacArthur to Theodore Schwan, November 23, 1899, in *Annual Reports of the War Department for the Fiscal Year Ended June 30, 1900*, 1900, 275.

92 *double, then triple*: Frank Hindman Golay, *Face of Empire: United States–Philippine Relations, 1898–1946* (Madison, WI, 1998), 65.

92 *One boy at the time*: Carlos P. Romulo, *Mother America: A Living Story of Democracy* (Garden City, NY, 1943), 27.

93 *"I have been reluctantly compelled"*: James H. Blount, *The American Occupation of the Philippines, 1898–1912* (New York, 1913), 24.

94 *"largest man" . . . Twain reread Kim*: Leland Krauth, *Mark Twain and Company: Six Literary Reflections* (Athens, GA, 2003), 215. See chap. 6 for the many connections between the two writers.

94 *"Take up"*: Rudyard Kipling, "The White Man's Burden: An Address to the United States," *London Times*, February 4, 1899.

94 *"red-hot imperialist," etc.*: "Mark Twain Home, an Anti-Imperialist," *New York Herald*, October 15, 1900, in *Mark Twain's Weapons of Satire: Anti-Imperialist Writings on the Philippine-American War*, ed. Jim Zwick (Syracuse, NY, 1992), 5.

95 *"two Americas"*: Twain, "To a Person Sitting in Darkness," 1901, in ibid., 33–34.

95 *"Governments derive"*: Ibid., xxx. Emphasis mine.

95 *modified flag*: Ibid., 39.

95 *"criminal aggression"*: Democratic Party Platform of 1900, APP.

95 *"Anti-Doughnut"*: Twain, "Speech on Municipal Corruption," in Zwick, *Twain's Weapons*, 14–15.

95 *his literary estate*: Jim Zwick, "Mark Twain's Anti-Imperialist Writings in the 'American Century,'" in Shaw and Francia, *Vestiges of War*, 38–56.

96 *"little brown brothers"*: Stuart Creighton Miller, *"Benevolent Assimilation": The American Conquest of the Philippines, 1899–1903* (New Haven, CT, 1982), 134, 296–97.

96 *"I'm only a common"*: "The Little Brown Brother," *Life*, October 15, 1903, 372.

96 *soldiers preferred* gugu: On racial insults, see Kramer, *Blood of Government*, 124–30.

96 *"I Don't Like a Nigger Nohow"*: Willard B. Gatewood Jr., *"Smoked Yankees" and the Struggle for Empire: Letters from Negro Soldiers, 1898–1920* (Urbana, IL, 1971), 244.

96 *black soldiers*: George P. Marks III, ed., *The Black Press Views American Imperialism* (New York, 1971); Willard B. Gatewood Jr., *Black Americans and the White Man's Burden, 1898–1913* (Urbana, IL, 1975).

96 *Fagen*: Michael C. Robinson and Frank N. Schubert, "David Fagen: An Afro-American Rebel in the Philippines, 1899–1901," *Pacific Historical Review* 44 (1975): 80.

97 *sanitation, road-building, and education*: Gates, *Schoolbooks and Krags*; Linn, *Philippine War*, 200–206; and Michael Adas, *Dominance by Design: Technological Imperatives and America's Civilizing Mission* (Cambridge, MA, 2006), chap. 3.

97 *"hikers"*: Oscar V. Campomanes, "Casualty Figures of the American Soldier and the Other: Post-1898 Allegories of Imperial Nation-Building as 'Love and War,'" in Shaw and Francia, *Vestiges of War*, 134–62.

97 *Perhaps Filipinos helped*: The complex issue of collaboration is treated skillfully and sensitively in Mojares, *War Against the Americans*, chap. 9.

97 *"blind giant"*: Ileto, *Knowing America's Colony*, 28.

97 *"reconcentration"*: See especially ibid, lecture 1, and May, *Batangas*.

97 *"sounds awful"*: Forbes Diary, 1:1, August 22, 1904.

98 *more than one hundred members*: Julian Go, *American Empire and the Politics of Meaning: Elite Political Cultures and the Philippines and Puerto Rico During U.S. Colonialism* (Durham, NC, 2008).

98 *"Let the stream"*: Constantino, *History of the Philippines*, 229.

98 *"We crushed"*: Robert L. Beisner, *Twelve Against Empire: The Anti-Imperialists, 1898–1900* (New York, 1968), 162.

98 *"drastic measures,"* etc.: MacArthur, quoted in Linn, *Philippine War*, 306.

99 *Balangiga*: Rolando O. Borrinaga, *The Balangiga Conflict Revisited* (Quezon City, 2003).

99 *"Half the people"*: Helen Herron Taft, *Recollections of Full Years* (New York, 1914), 225.

99 *"They have sown"*: Joseph L. Schott, *The Ordeal of Samar* (New York, 1964), 55.

99 *"Lay them on their backs"*: Quoted in Richard Franklin Pettigrew, *The Course of Empire: An Official Record* (New York, 1920), 285.

100 *"I want no prisoners"* . . . *"The interior of Samar"*: Schott, *Ordeal*, 78, 98.

100 *increasingly hard to win support*: On revolutionaries' difficulties in commanding loyalty, see Gates, *Schoolbooks and Krags*, 225–30, and Brian McAllister Linn, *The U.S. Army and Counterinsurgency in the Philippine War, 1899–1902* (Chapel Hill, NC, 1989), 18–19, 167–68.

100 *"Water Cure in the P.I."*: May, *Batangas*, 147, discussed in Kramer, *Blood of Government*, 141.

101 *"savages,"* etc.: WTR, 9:58, 57.

101 *"nobody was"*: Roosevelt to Speck von Sternberg, July 19, 1902, LTR, 3:297–98.

101 *"Taken in the full"*: "Court Martial of General Smith," *The Army and Navy Journal,* July 19, 1902, 1166.

101 *"The country was"*: *Boston Transcript,* 1902, quoted in Moorfield Storey and Marcial P. Lichauco, *The Conquest of the Philippines by the United States* (New York, 1926), 121–22.

101 *died from disease*: The following account of Philippine mortality leans heavily on May, *Batangas,* and De Bevoise, *Agents of the Apocalypse.* On public health during the war, see also Reynaldo C. Ileto, "Cholera and the Origins of the American Sanitary Order in the Philippines," in *Discrepant Histories: Translocal Essays on Philippine Culture,* ed. Vicente L. Rafael (Philadelphia, 1995), 51–82, and Warwick Anderson, *Colonial Pathologies: American Tropical Medicine, Race, and Hygiene in the Philippines* (Durham, NC, 2006).

102 *"Everything that could"*: Taft, *Recollections,* 253.

102 *Aguinaldo contracted malaria*: Aguinaldo, *Second Look at America,* 107; Simeon A. Vilal Diary, Rare Books, NLP.

102 *only the cheapest food . . . infant mortality rate*: De Bevoise, *Agents of the Apocalypse,* 61, 140.

103 *killed one-sixth of the population*: Storey and Lichauco, *Conquest,* 121. The historian Resil Mojares estimates that one-sixth of the population of Cebu died as well—a hundred thousand deaths from war, including disease, between the years 1898 and 1906. *War Against the Americans,* 135.

103 *The most careful study*: De Bevoise, *Agents of the Apocalypse,* 13.

103 *"Of course, we do want"*: Twain, "Review of Edwin Wildman's Biography of Aguinaldo," 1901–1902, in Zwick, *Twain's Weapons,* 103.

103 *claimed more lives than the Civil War*: This is true even when the fatalities of soldiers in the Civil War, around 620,000, are combined with the uncounted death toll of civilians, estimated at 50,000. Drew Gilpin Faust, *This Republic of Suffering: Death and the American Civil War* (New York, 2008), xi–xii.

103 *"fourth and final,"* etc.: "It Must Be Over Now," *Washington Post,* May 6, 1902, discussed in Kramer, *Blood of Government,* 155.

103 *this time even farther south*: Hostilities continued in the north, too, though there is debate about whether to classify them as war or crime. See, for example, Orlino A. Ochosa, *Bandoleros: Outlawed Guerrillas of the Philippine-American War, 1903–1907* (Quezon City, 1995).

103 *"Moroland"*: An extraordinarily useful account of the Moroland war is Peter Gordon Gowing, *Mandate in Moroland: The American Government of Muslim Filipinos, 1899–1920* (Quezon City, 1977). I also rely on Frank E. Vandiver, *Black Jack: The Life and Times of John J. Pershing,* vol. 1 (College Station, TX, 1977); Robert A. Fulton, *Moroland: The History of Uncle Sam and the Moros, 1899–1920* (Bend, OR, 2009); essays by Joshua Gedacht and Patricio N. Abinales in *Colonial Crucible: Empire in the Making of the Modern American State,* ed. Alfred W. McCoy and Francisco A. Scarano (Madison, WI, 2009); and Arnold, *Moro War.*

104 *"Slaves are a part"*: Gowing, *Mandate,* 56. On this issue, see Michael Salman, *The Embarrassment of Slavery: Controversies over Bondage and Nationalism in the American Colonial Philippines* (Berkeley, CA, 2001).

104 *"rough guy,"* etc.: Donald Trump, February 29, 2016, campaign rally, North Charleston, South Carolina.

104 *"I have never tasted"*: John J. Pershing, *My Life Before the World War, 1860–1917*, ed. John T. Greenwood (Lexington, KY, 2013), 152.

104 *"strong personal friends"*: Donald Smythe, *Guerrilla Warrior: The Early Life of John J. Pershing* (New York, 1973), 84.

104 *without an interpreter*: Pershing, *My Life*, 189.

104 *elected a datu . . . honorary father*: Vandiver, *Black Jack*, chap. 9.

105 *909 more senior officers*: The figure of 862 is commonly reported, but see ibid., 390n88.

105 *"intolerant"*: Rexford Guy Tugwell, *The Stricken Land: The Story of Puerto Rico* (Garden City, NY, 1946), 414.

105 *"a new order of things"*: Hermann Hagedorn, *Leonard Wood: A Biography* (New York, 1931), 2:8.

105 *"One clean-cut lesson"*: Wood to Roosevelt, August 3, 1903, in Gowing, *Mandate*, 156.

105 *"like dominoes"*: Brian McAllister Linn, *Guardians of Empire: The U.S. Army and the Pacific, 1902–1940* (Chapel Hill, NC, 1997), 39.

105 *six hundred Moros had died*: For contemporary estimates, which ranged as high as fifteen hundred, see Fulton, *Moroland*, 339. The interpreters' figure comes from the report of Major Omar Bundy, March 12, 1906, 8, Record Group 94, Records of the Adjutant General's Office, Document File 1890–1917, entry 25, NADC. I'm grateful to Joshua Gedacht for supplying this document.

106 *"All the defenders"*: Despite Wood's pronouncement, some Moros survived, maybe up to one hundred. See Fulton, *Moroland*, 339, and Jack McCallum, *Leonard Wood: Rough Rider, Surgeon, Architect of American Imperialism* (New York, 2006), 229.

106 *Bud Dajo dwarfed them all*: There's something both difficult and distasteful in comparing the size of massacres. The difficulty is that perpetrators rarely perform corpse censuses; the distasteful part is that comparing body counts can suggest that the lesser massacre was "less bad," implying an uncomfortably glib moral mathematics wherein killing forty people is exactly half as wrong as killing eighty. Still, for what it's worth, we think that Sand Creek (about 150), Wounded Knee (about 200), and Bloody Island (75–200) killed fewer people *combined* than Bud Dajo. Bloody Island, however, is especially hard to count. Reports from those who were there vary wildly, with 75–200 a rough median, but with the extremes varying from 16 (the report of a Pomo chief) to more than 800 (a U.S. major who arrived on the scene two months after). Sand Creek: *Report of the John Evans Study Committee* (Evanston, IL, 2014), 7; Wounded Knee: Jerome A. Greene, *American Carnage: Wounded Knee, 1890* (Norman, OK, 2014), 288; Bloody Island: Benjamin Madley, *An American Genocide: The United States and the California Indian Catastrophe* (New Haven, CT, 2016), 131–33.

106 *"We abolished them"*: Twain, "Comments on the Moro Massacre," 1906, in Zwick, *Twain's Weapons*, 172.

106 *"I would not want"*: Fulton, *Moroland*, 370.

106 *"most illuminating,"* etc.: Du Bois to Moorfield Storey, in *The Correspondence of W.E.B. Du Bois*, ed. Herbert Aptheker (Amherst, MA, 1973), 1:136.

107 *"The fighting was"* . . . *"given a thrashing"*: Pershing to "Frank," June 19, 1913, folder 1, and Pershing to Leonard Wood, July 9, 1913, folder 3, box 371, Pershing Papers.

107 *guessed he had killed*: Pershing, *My Life*, 302. In his official report, Pershing estimated, based on "Moro sources," that there had been "between three and five hundred" defending Bud Bagsak, though some Moros escaped during the fighting and
it's unclear if the 300–500 estimate includes them. Pershing, Report of Bud Bagsak
Operations, October 15, 1913, folder 4, box 372, Pershing Papers.

107 *Historians' estimates*: Smythe puts the death toll at "over 500" (*Guerrilla Warrior*,
200); Gowing at 300–500 (*Mandate*, 240); Fulton at 200–400 (*Moroland*, 449–50);
Linn at more than 500 (*Guardians*, 41).

107 *further battles*: Arnold, *Moro War*, 240–41.

7. OUTSIDE THE CHARMED CIRCLE

108 *When U.S. troops landed*: Julian Go, *American Empire and the Politics of Meaning:
Elite Political Cultures and the Philippines and Puerto Rico During U.S. Colonialism*
(Durham, NC, 2008), 55. More generally, see Emma Dávila-Cox, "Puerto Rico in
the Hispanic–Cuban–American War: Re-assessing 'the Picnic,'" in *The Crisis of
1898: Colonial Redistribution and Nationalist Mobilization*, ed. Angel Smith and
Emma Dávila-Cox (London, 1999), 96–127.

108 *Many Puerto Ricans believed*: Go, *American Empire*, 81. See also Christina Duffy
Ponsa, "When Statehood Was Autonomy," in *Reconsidering the Insular Cases: The
Past and Future of American Empire*, ed. Gerald L. Neuman and Tomiko Brown-
Nagin (Cambridge, MA, 2015), 1–28.

108 *"a prosperous and happy country"*: Duffy Ponsa, "When Statehood Was Autonomy," 25.

108 *Albizu Campos*: Prominent biographical accounts are Federico Ribes Tovar, *Albizu
Campos: Puerto Rican Revolutionary*, trans. Anthony Rawlings (New York, 1971);
Benjamín Torres, Marisa Rosado, and José Manuel Torres Santiago, eds., *Imagen
de Pedro Albizu Campos* (San Juan, 1973); Luis Angel Ferrao, *Pedro Albizu Campos
y el nacionalismo puertorriqueño* (San Juan, 1990); Marisa Rosado, *Pedro Albizu
Campos: Las llamas de la aurora*, 2d ed. (Santo Domingo, 1998); Laura Meneses de
Albizu Campos, *Albizu Campos y la independencia de Puerto Rico* (San Juan, 2007);
and Nelson A. Denis, *War Against All Puerto Ricans: Revolution and Terror in America's
Colony* (New York, 2015).

109 *"the most friendly" . . . "delirious"*: Richard Harding Davis, *The Cuban and Porto
Rican Campaigns* (New York, 1898), 325, 350.

109 *Albizu's father*: Ferrao, *Albizu*, 122.

109 *"appeared to be"*: Charles Horton Terry, paraphrased in Dante Di Lillo and Edgar K.
Thompson, "Pedro Albizu Campos," Report, February 19, 1936, Albizu FBI File,
sec. 1.

109 *stay after class*: Bill O'Reilly, "The Apotheosis of Hate," *Palabras Neighbors* 5, c. 1951,
in Albizu FBI File, sec. 8.

109 *arranged for a scholarship*: Di Lillo and Thompson, Albizu Report, February 19, 1936,
Albizu FBI File.

109 *"Pete"*: Laura Meneses de Albizu Campos, "Como conoci a Albizu Campos," September 1957, folder 7, box 31, Reynolds Papers. On Albizu's time at Harvard, see Rosado, *Albizu*, and Anthony de Jesús, *"I Have Endeavored to Seize the Beautiful
Opportunity for Learning Offered Here*: Pedro Albizu Campos at Harvard a Century
Ago," *Latino Studies* 9 (2011): 473–85.

109 *most interesting club*: E. D. M., "International Clubs in German Universities," *Unity*, June 13, 1912, 238.

109 *China, Germany*, etc.: Based on consultation of *The Harvard Crimson* in years between the club's establishment in 1908 and the end of Albizu's time in 1921.

109 *Boston Symphony Orchestra*: Barbara Tischler, "One Hundred Percent Americanism and Music in Boston During World War I," *American Music* 4 (1986): 164–76.

110 *Münsterberg*: Jutta Spillman and Lothar Spillman, "The Rise and Fall of Hugo Münsterberg," *Journal of the History of the Behavioral Sciences* 29 (1993): 322–38.

110 *He'd spoken out*: "Forum Upheld Military Camps," *Harvard Crimson*, April 3, 1915.

110 *International Polity Club*: "Polity Club Changes Program," *Harvard Crimson*, October 18, 1916. On Albizu's membership, see "Polity Club Elects New Officers," *Harvard Crimson*, June 2, 1915.

110 *"When the Spanish-American,"* etc.: Pedro Albizu Campos, "Porto Rico and the War," *Harvard Crimson*, April 14, 1917.

110 *"heel of Achilles"*: Roosevelt to William Howard Taft, August 21, 1907, *LTR*, 5:762.

110 *"sober up"*: Emilio Aguinaldo with Vicente Albano Pacis, *A Second Look at America* (New York, 1957), 133.

111 *The Outlook*: "A Battle with Moros," *The Outlook*, June 21, 1913.

111 *"We were constantly reminded"*: Jim English, "Empire Day in Britain, 1904–1958," *The Historical Journal* 49 (2006): 251.

111 *"to gather together"*: Address on Flag Day, June 14, 1916, in *The Foreign Policy of President Wilson: Messages, Addresses and Papers*, ed. James Brown Scott (New York, 1918), 176, 175.

112 *The State Department stopped insisting*: Jimmy M. Skaggs, *The Great Guano Rush: Entrepreneurs and American Overseas Expansion* (New York, 1994), chaps. 7 and 11.

112 *"outside the charmed circle"*: Woodrow Wilson, First Annual Message, December 2, 1913, *APP*.

112 *"sovereignty, jurisdiction"*: Joint Resolution for the Recognition of the Independence of the People of Cuba, 1898, 30 *Stat.* 739.

113 *"money can be borrowed"* . . . *"When people ask"*: Louis A. Pérez Jr., *The War of 1898: The United States and Cuba in History and Historiography* (Chapel Hill, NC, 1998), 32.

113 *"complete jurisdiction"*: Quoted in Jana K. Lipman, *Guantánamo: A Working-Class History Between Empire and Revolution* (Berkeley, CA, 2009), 24.

113 *Cuba was easily absorbed*: Louis A. Pérez Jr., *Cuba and the United States: Ties of Singular Intimacy* (Athens, GA, 1990), chaps. 4–5.

113 *Afro-Cubans*: See Alejandro de la Fuente, *A Nation for All: Race, Inequality, and Politics in Twentieth-Century Cuba* (Chapel Hill, NC, 2001), chap. 2.

114 *"all the rights"*: Hay–Bunau-Varilla Treaty, Convention for the Construction of a Ship Canal, November 18, 1903, 33 *Stat.* 2234.

114 *"I have about the same"*: Roosevelt to Joseph Bucklin Bishop, February 23, 1904, *LTR*, 4:734.

114 *To ensure political*: Barbara Salazar Torreon, *Instances of Use of United States Armed Forces Abroad, 1798–2016*, Congressional Research Service Report R42738, 2016.

115 *In his letter*: Albizu, "Porto Rico and the War."

115 *twenty thousand Filipinos . . . "modern Moses"*: Paul A. Kramer, *The Blood of Government: Race, Empire, the United States, and the Philippines* (Chapel Hill, NC, 2006), 344–45.
115 *"an inexcusable blunder"*: Democratic Party Platform, June 25, 1912, APP.
115 *"no longer to be,"* etc.: Woodrow Wilson, First Annual Message, December 2, 1913, APP.
115 *not empty speech*: Wilson's views and actions are helpfully discussed in Roy Watson Curry, "Woodrow Wilson and Philippine Policy," *Mississippi Valley Historical Review* 41 (1954): 435–52.
116 *"a form of home rule" . . . "There is faith"*: Albizu, "Porto Rico and the War."
116 *"conquered possessions"*: Woodrow Wilson, *A History of the American People* (New York, 1902), 5:3.
116 *"children" . . . "training"*: Woodrow Wilson, "The Ideals of America," *Atlantic Monthly*, December 1902, 731, 733.
116 *"white men of the South,"* etc.: Wilson, *History*, 5:38, 5:49, 5:78.
116 *"the first southern scholar"*: Frederick Jackson Turner, *American Historical Review* 8 (1903): 764.
116 *couldn't help but notice*: See reviews by Francis Wayland Shepardson, George McLean Harper, and C. H. Van Tyne in *The Papers of Woodrow Wilson*, vol. 14, ed. Arthur S. Link (Princeton, NJ, 1972).
116 *"to protect"*: Wilson, *History*, 5:62.
117 *"the mere instinct"*: Ibid., 5:58.
117 *"It teaches history"*: "It's like writing history with lightning. My only regret is that it is all so terribly true" is how the quotation is usually given. But that version appeared in 1937, twenty-two years after the event, and there is not much evidence in favor of it. Griffith's version, by contrast, was printed in the *New York American* on February 28, 1915. For a full and judicious account, see Mark E. Benbow, "Birth of a Quotation: Woodrow Wilson and 'Like Writing History with Lightning,'" *Journal of the Gilded Age and the Progressive Era* 9 (2010): 509–33.
117 *most popular film*: Leon F. Litwack, "The Birth of a Nation," in *Past Imperfect: History According to the Movies*, ed. Ted Mico et al. (New York, 1995), 136.
117 *recruiters used the film*: The connections between Wilson and *Birth* are detailed in Lloyd E. Ambrosius, "Woodrow Wilson and *The Birth of a Nation*: American Democracy and International Relations," *Diplomacy and Statecraft* 18 (2007): 689–718.
117 *"liberation of all colonies"*: Erez Manela, *The Wilsonian Moment: Self-Determination and the International Origins of Anticolonial Nationalism* (New York, 2007), 37.
117 *"The day of conquest,"* etc.: Woodrow Wilson, Address to a Joint Session of Congress on the Conditions of Peace, January 8, 1918, APP.
118 *In China*: Erez Manela, "Global Anti-Imperialism in the Age of Wilson," in *Empire's Twin: U.S. Anti-Imperialism from the Founding Era to the Age of Terrorism*, ed. Ian Tyrrell and Jay Sexton (Ithaca, NY, 2015), 145.
118 *"conveyed the impression"*: [Pedro Albizu Campos], editorial annotations on biographical writing about Albizu, folder 4, box 30, Reynolds Papers. The context and use of the first person in the handwritten version of the annotations establish that their author is Albizu.
118 *"thirty or forty thousand"*: Meneses de Albizu Campos, *Albizu*, 29.
118 *getting to Wilson*: Anti-imperialists' campaign to catch Wilson's attention in 1919 is chronicled in Manela, *Wilsonian Moment*. Manela's extraordinary work supplies the

narrative frame for this section and is one source for my accounts of Gandhi, Zaghlul, Thanh (Ho), and Mao. See also Emily S. Rosenberg, "World War I, Wilsonianism, and Challenges to U.S. Empire," *DH* 38 (2014): 852–63.

118 *"No people"*: Manela, *Wilsonian Moment*, 71.

119 *Nguyen Tat Thanh*: William J. Duiker, *Ho Chi Minh* (New York, 2000), 58–60. See also Sophie Quinn-Judge, *Ho Chi Minh: The Missing Years, 1919–1941* (Berkeley, CA, 2002).

119 *Albizu got another shot*: See Albizu's autobiographical note in Wells Blanchard, *Harvard College Class of 1916: Secretary's Third Report* (n.p., 1922) and the following *Harvard Crimson* articles: "Campos, 2L., for Peace Conference," January 13, 1919; "Cosmopolitan Club Plans for 'International Night,'" Feb. 21," January 25, 1919; "Cosmopolitan Club Will Hold Dance," February 25, 1919.

119 *he identified as white*: Albizu listed his race as "white" on his Selective Service questionnaire in World War II according to John M. Hansell, Report 100–47403, July 5, 1944, Albizu FBI File, sec. 3. Albizu never denied his nonwhite ancestry, he simply rejected the "one-drop" racial classification system.

119 *his wife mistook*: Meneses de Albizu Campos, "Como conoci."

119 *a humiliating episode*: Described in Carl E. Stanford, Report 100–3906, May 26, 1943, Albizu FBI File, sec. 2. Andrea Friedman cautions against making too much of this incident in *Citizenship in Cold War America: National Security State and the Possibilities of Dissent* (Amherst, MA, 2014), 145–46.

119 *He arrived in Boston too late*: Albizu in Blanchard, *Harvard Class of 1916*. Albizu's reactions to his Southern journey are described in Ribes Tovar, *Albizu*, 20–21. An alternative account of Albizu's radicalization, arguing that he was a nationalist from high school, is Juan Antonio Corretjer, *Albizu Campos and the Ponce Massacre* (New York, 1965), 9–12.

120 *Jan Smuts*: See Mark Mazower, *No Enchanted Palace: The End of Empire and the Ideological Origins of the United Nations* (Princeton, NJ, 2009), especially chap. 1.

120 *"indisputable"*: Naoko Shimazu, *Japan, Race and Equality: The Racial Equality Proposal of 1919* (London, 1998), 9.

121 *"exploded with enthusiasm"*: Sayyid Qutb, *A Child from the Village*, trans. John Calvert and William Shepard (1946; Syracuse, NY, 2005), 96.

121 *"a bunch of robbers"*: Manela, *Wilsonian Moment*, 195.

8. WHITE CITY

122 *largest private fortunes*: Calculations of wealth across history are difficult. Consulting with economists, *Business Insider* ranked Rockefeller and Carnegie the two richest humans of all time (Gus Lubin, "The 20 Richest People of All Time," *Business Insider*, September 2, 2010, www.businessinsider.com/richest-people-in-history-2010-8).

123 *"It appears to me"*: Edward Bellamy, *Looking Backward, 2000–1887* (Boston, 1888), 157–58.

123 *"miles of broad streets,"* etc.: Ibid., 52.

123 *Burnham*: The classic biographies are Charles Moore, *Daniel H. Burnham: Architect, Planner of Cities* (Boston, 1921), and Thomas S. Hines, *Burnham of Chicago: Architect and Planner*, rev. ed. (Chicago, 1979). On the connections between Bellamy and Burnham, see Mario Manieri-Elia, "Toward an 'Imperial City': Daniel H. Burnham and the City Beautiful Movement," in *The American City: From the Civil*

War to the New Deal, ed. Giorgio Cuicci et al., trans. Barbara Luigia La Penta (1973; Cambridge, MA, 1979), 1–142.

123 *"megalomania"*: Louis H. Sullivan, *The Autobiography of an Idea* (1924; New York, 1954), 288.

123 *twenty-one million tickets*: Reid Badger, *The Great American Fair: The World's Columbian Exposition and American Culture* (Chicago, 1979), 131.

123 *"They beheld"*: Sullivan, *Autobiography*, 321.

124 *"ablaze with pity"*: Katherine Mayo, *The Isles of Fear: The Truth About the Philippines* (New York, 1925), 83. Mayo's reference is to the Philippines in particular.

124 *"Who but a mad dreamer"*: Forbes Diary, 1:4, May 21, 1910.

125 *"in the same way"*: Manuel Quezon, quoted in *Origins of the Philippine Republic: Extracts from the Diaries and Records of Francis Burton Harrison*, ed. Michael P. Onorato (Ithaca, NY, 1974), 6.

125 *favorite polo horses*: Forbes Diary, 1:5, September 4, 1913.

125 *Gee Strings*: Ibid., 1:4, April 15, 1911.

125 *"I remember"*: Ibid., 1:3, March 27, 1909.

125 *"they want it"*: Ibid., 1:1, February 1, 1904.

125 *"knew exactly"*: Ibid., 1:1, 439n.

125 *"believe in it"*: Ibid., 1:3, July 18, 1910.

125 *"ancient pest-hole"*: Mayo, *Isles of Fear*, 84.

125 *"It has the crookedest streets"*: George A. Miller, *Interesting Manila* (Manila, 1906), 54.

126 *"constant terror"*: Helen Herron Taft, *Recollections of Full Years* (New York, 1914), 254, 256.

126 *torching an entire district*: Reynaldo C. Ileto, "Cholera and the Origins of the American Sanitary Order in the Philippines," in *Discrepant Histories: Translocal Essays on Philippine Culture*, ed. Vicente L. Rafael (Philadelphia, 1995), 51–82.

126 *"Manila has before it"*: D. H. Burnham, assisted by Peirce Anderson, "Report on the Improvement of Manila, P.I.," June 28, 1905, 33, folder 7, box 57, ser. 5, Burnham Collection. On the relationship between Burnham's plans and Manila's decimation, see Estela Duque, "Militarization of the City," *Fabrications* 19 (2009): 48–67.

126 *"Because every section"*: Burnham, "Improvement of Manila," 19.

126 *"world famous resort,"* etc.: Ibid., 25.

127 *"seems to meet"*: Forbes Diary, 1:1, January 5, 1905.

127 *"If one has capital"*: Moore, *Burnham*, 1:73.

127 *his Plan of Chicago*: See William E. Parsons, "Burnham as Pioneer in City Planning," *Architectural Record* 38 (1915): 13–31; Moore, *Burnham*; Hines, *Burnham*; and especially Carl Smith, *The Plan of Chicago: Daniel Burnham and the Remaking of the American City* (Chicago, 2006). Details drawn from Smith's book.

127 *Chicago voters approved*: Smith, *Plan of Chicago*, 133.

128 *In the Philippines*: On Burnham and colonial architecture, see, besides the biographies, Thomas S. Hines, "Daniel H. Burnham and American Architectural Planning in the Philippines," *Pacific History Review* 41 (1972): 33–53; Robert R. Reed, *City of Pines: The Origins of Baguio as a Colonial Hill Station and Regional Capital* (Berkeley, CA, 1976); Winand Klassen, *Architecture in the Philippines: Filipino Building in a Cross-Cultural Context* (Cebu City, 1986), chap. 5; David Brody, "Building Empire: Architecture and American Imperialism in the Philippines," *Journal of Asian American Studies* 4 (2001): 123–45; Gerard Lico, *Arkitekturang Filipino: A History*

of Architecture and Urbanism in the Philippines (Quezon City, 2008), chap. 5; Christopher Vernon, "Daniel Hudson Burnham and the American City Imperial," *Thesis Eleven* 123 (2014): 80–105; and Rebecca Tinio McKenna, *American Imperial Pastoral: The Architecture of U.S. Colonialism in the Philippines* (Chicago, 2017).

128 *No living Filipino*: The one Filipino name that appears in Burnham's Manila plan is that of "Dr. Razal [*sic*]," i.e., the late Jose Rizal, mentioned (once, glancingly) in Burnham's one-paragraph history of Manila from 1571 to the onset of U.S. rule. Thanks to Margaret Garb for pointing out Burnham's isolation from Filipinos.

128 *Three days after*: A. N. Rebori, "The Work of William E. Parsons in the Philippine Islands," *Architectural Record* 40 (1917): 433.

128 *"we so fixed it"*: Forbes Diary, 1:1, 392*n*.

128 *"charged with"*: William E. Parsons, Annual Report of the Consulting Architect, November 17, 1905, to June 30, 1906, 2, folder 9, box 57, ser. 5, Burnham Collection.

128 *Parsons*: See Rebori, "Parsons"; Thomas S. Hines, "American Modernism in the Philippines: The Forgotten Architecture of William E. Parsons," *Journal of the Society of Architectural Historians* 32 (1973), 316–26; Michelangelo E. Dakudao, "The Imperial Consulting Architect: William E. Parsons (1872–1939)," *Bulletin of the American Historical Collection* 12 (1994): 7–43; and Lico, *Arkitekturang Filipino*, chap. 5.

128 *"architect's dream"*: Parsons, quoted in Forbes Diary, 1:1, March 12, 1906.

128 *"large and rapidly increasing"*: Parsons, 1906 Annual Report, 10.

128 *he standardized*: Ibid.; Rebori, "Parsons," 433; and Lico, *Arkitekturang Filipino*, 262–72.

129 *howls of protest*: Ralph Harrington Doane, "The Story of American Architecture in the Philippines," *Architectural Review* 8 (1919): 121.

129 *"I doubt if this method"*: Rebori, "Parsons," 433.

129 *"the Burnham plan is sacred"*: Quoted in Hines, "Burnham in the Philippines," 51.

129 *"more deeply interested"* . . . *"to formulate my plans"*: "Plan Queen City for the Far East," *Chicago Tribune*, September 18, 1904.

129 *"Stood trip well"* . . . *"How is the horse?"*: Pershing, *My Life Before the World War*, 253.

130 *four thousand men*: Reed, *City of Pines*, 109.

130 *"The Filipinos so far"*: Forbes Diary, 1:1, September 17, 1904.

130 *Devil's Slide*: W. Cameron Forbes, *Notes on Early History of Baguio* (Manila, 1933), 32.

130 *"Few days pass"*: Forbes Diary, 1:1, September 17, 1904. On the road, see Greg Bankoff, "'These Brothers of Ours': Poblete's Obreros and the Road to Baguio 1903–1905," *Journal of Social History* 38 (2005): 1047–72, and McKenna, *American Imperial Pastoral*, chap. 2.

130 *"gives the red corpuscles"*: Forbes Diary, 1:1, January 1, 1905.

130 *could not own land*: One land seizure in Baguio was challenged and eventually overturned by the U.S. Supreme Court. Justice Oliver Wendell Holmes chided that colonialism in the Philippines should not proceed "like the settlement of the white race in the United States." Its purpose should be "to do justice to the natives, not to exploit their country for private gain." *Carino v. Insular Government*, 212 U.S. 449, 458 (1909). The story is in McKenna, *American Imperial Pastoral*, chap. 3.

130 *"could be made equal"*: D. H. Burnham, "Preliminary Plan of Baguio Province of Benguet, P.I.," June 27, 1905, 2, folder 3, box 56, ser. 5, Burnham Collection.

130 *"unusual monumental possibilities"*: D. H. Burnham, "Report on the Proposed Plan of the City of Baguio, Province of Benguet, P.I.," October 3, 1905, 2, in folder 4, box 56, ser. 5, Burnham Collection.

130 *"frankly dominate"*: Burnham, "Preliminary Plan of Baguio," 1.

130 *"equal to the finest"*: Forbes's Prospectus of the Baguio Country Club, quoted in Virginia Benitez Licuanan, *Filipinos and Americans: A Love-Hate Relationship* (Baguio, 1982), 71.

131 *"monumental buildings where"*: Burnham, "Proposed Plan of Baguio," 6.

131 *"blessed relief"* . . . *"the swarm"*: Forbes Diary, 1:5, March 9, 1913.

131 *"every three days"*: Ibid., 1:3, May 14, 1908.

131 *6 were Filipino*: Licuanan, *Filipinos and Americans*, 91.

131 *"I get up leisurely,"* etc.: Forbes Diary, 1:5, March 9, 1913.

132 *"I have let"*: Ibid., 1:3, May 14, 1908.

132 *triumph of modern engineering*: S. R. Afable, "Most Progressive City," in J. C. Orendain, *Philippine Wonderland* (Baguio, 1940), 35–40.

132 *"admire the audacity"*: "America in the Philippines, Part VII," *London Times*, December 1, 1910.

132 *"Stingy towards"*: *La Vanguardia*, June 20, 1912, quoted in Reed, *City of Pines*, 108.

132 *one in four . . . one in twenty*: Cristina Evangelista Torres, *The Americanization of Manila, 1898–1921* (Quezon City, 2010), 43.

132 *"It is impossible"*: Hines, "Modernism in the Philippines," 325.

133 *"nailed down"*: Parsons, "Burnham as Pioneer," 24.

133 *Juan Arellano*: Surprisingly few accounts of Arellano's life and career exist. The best are I. V. Mallari, "Architects and Architecture in the Philippines," *Philippine Magazine*, August 1930, 156–57, 186–94; Ernesto T. Bitong, "Portrait of an Architect in Retirement," *Sunday Times Magazine* (Manila), June 16, 1957, 3–6; Dominador Castañeda, *Art in the Philippines* (Quezon City, 1964), 94–95; Klassen, *Architecture in the Philippines*, chap. 5; and Lico, *Arkitekturang Filipino*, chap. 5.

133 *it didn't win*: *Report of the Philippine Exposition Board to the Louisiana Purchase Exposition* (St. Louis, 1904), 87.

133 *Jamestown Exposition*: Bitong, "Portrait of an Architect."

133 *disqualified*: Castañeda, *Art in the Philippines*, 94.

134 *Olmsted*: Mallari, "Architects and Architecture," 190.

134 *"the most magnificent"*: A.V.H. Hartendorp, "The Legislative Building," *Philippine Education Magazine*, October 1926, quoted in Rodrigo D. Perez III, *Arkitektura: An Essay on the American Colonial and Contemporary Traditions in Philippine Architecture* (Manila, 1994), 5.

134 *"Here is a stronger"*: "Designed by Filipino Brains, and Built by Filipino Hands," *The Philippine Republic*, February 1927, 5.

134 *he later regretted*: Arellano's striking repudiation of the "Occidental influence" is articulated in "Fine and Applied Arts in the Philippines: An Interview with Juan M. Arellano," *Philippines Herald Year Book*, September 29, 1934, 53, 58, 62.

134 *"architecturally, the landmark"*: Nick Joaquin, *Almanac for Manileños* (Manila, 1979), 213, 214. Later, Arellano would adopt other styles, notably Art Deco.

136 *"greatest architectural success"*: Hines, "Burnham in the Philippines," 50.

9. DOCTORS WITHOUT BORDERS

137 *"a picnic"*: Richard Harding Davis, *The Cuban and Porto Rican Campaigns* (New York, 1898), 299–300.

137 *"hordes of pallid refugees"*: Bailey K. Ashford, *A Soldier in Science: The Autobiography of Bailey K. Ashford* (New York, 1934), 3. My account of Ashford relies also on Bailey K. Ashford and Pedro Gutiérrez Igaravídez, "Summary of a Ten Years' Campaign Against Hookworm Disease in Porto Rico," *Journal of the American Medical Association* 54 (1910): 1757–61; Bailey K. Ashford and Pedro Gutiérrez Igaravídez, *Uncinariasis (Hookworm Disease) in Porto Rico: A Medical and Economic Problem* (Washington, DC, 1911); Warwick Anderson, "Going Through the Motions: American Public Health and Colonial 'Mimicry,'" *American Literary History* 14 (2002): 686–719; Nicole Trujillo-Pagan, *Modern Colonization by Medical Intervention: U.S. Medicine in Puerto Rico* (Leiden, Netherlands, 2013); and especially José Amador, *Medicine and Nation Building in the Americas, 1890–1940* (Nashville, 2015), chap. 3.

137 *Wood's attention*: Ashford, *Soldier in Science*, 17–18.

137 *came to see* himself: In ibid., Ashford calls Puerto Rico "home" (325), describes himself as a "Puerto Rican" (412), and speaks critically of "our northern brothers" on the mainland (332).

138 *"flabby flesh"*: Ibid., 41.

138 *"It was unthinkable"*: Ibid., 42.

138 *"oval thing"*: Ibid., 4.

138 *"like a veil"*: Ibid., 43.

138 *nine in ten rural*: "Report of the Porto Rico Anemia Commission," 1904, in Ashford and Gutiérrez, *Uncinariasis*, 136.

139 *long tunnel*: Steven Palmer, "Migrant Clinics and Hookworm Science: Peripheral Origins of International Health, 1840–1920," *Bulletin of the History of Medicine* 83 (2009): 688–90.

139 *two-thirds of Puerto Ricans*: José G. Amador, "'Redeeming the Tropics': Public Health and National Identity in Cuba, Puerto Rico, and Brazil, 1890–1940" (Ph.D. diss., University of Michigan, 2008), 119.

139 *leading cause*: "Report of the Porto Rico Anemia Commission," 1904, in Ashford and Gutiérrez, *Uncinariasis*, 127–28.

139 *"carrying a bottle"*: Ashford, *Soldier in Science*, 45.

139 *nearly 30 percent*: Ashford and Gutiérrez, *Uncinariasis*, 35. The two were joined in their work by three other physicians: Walter W. King and, later, Isaac González Martínez and Francisco Sein y Sein.

140 *"What on earth,"* etc.: Story recounted (by Stiles) in Mark Sullivan, *Our Times: The United States, 1900–1925* (New York, 1930), 3:319–20. See also Burton J. Hendrick, *The Training of an American: The Earlier Life and Letters of Walter H. Page, 1855–1913* (Boston, 1928), 370–71.

140 *give a million dollars*: My account of the Rockefeller Sanitary Commission is from John Ettling, *The Germ of Laziness: Rockefeller Philanthropy and Public Health in the New South* (Cambridge, MA, 1981).

140 *local sheriff*: Charles Wardell Stiles, "Early History, in Part Esoteric, of the Hookworm (Uncinariasis) Campaign in Our Southern United States," *Journal of Parasitology* 25 (1939): 298.

140 *Tampa newspaper*: Sullivan, *Our Times*, 328.

140 *"Six thousand years ago"*: Mark Twain, *Letters from the Earth* (New York, 1962), 33.

141 *were as prideful*: Ashford and Gutiérrez, *Uncinariasis*, 30–31.

141 *Southern tent revival*: Discussed with great clarity in Ettling, *Germ of Laziness*, chaps. 6–7.

141 *"preach the gospel"*: "Second Report of the Porto Rico Anemia Commission," 1906, in Ashford and Gutiérrez, *Uncinariasis*, 170.

141 *"utterly inadequate"*: Ashford and Gutiérrez, *Uncinariasis*, 19.

141 *"sanitary ordinance"* . . . *"energetically enforced"* . . . *"liberty"*: "Third Report of the Porto Rico Anemia Commission," 1907, in ibid., 213, 214.

142 *campaign fizzled*: Ashford, *Soldier in Science*, 71–72, 87–88. On the mainland versus colonial hookworm campaigns, see Anderson, "Going Through the Motions," 701–702.

142 *enduring economic effects*: Hoyt Bleakley, "Disease and Development: Evidence from Hookworm Eradication in the American South," *Quarterly Journal of Economics* 122 (2007): 73–117.

142 *first global health campaign*: John Farley, *To Cast Out Disease: A History of the International Health Division of the Rockefeller Foundation, 1913–1951* (New York, 2004); Steven Palmer, *Launching Global Health: The Caribbean Odyssey of the Rockefeller Foundation* (Ann Arbor, MI, 2010).

142 *headed off the direst*: Ashford and Gutiérrez, *Uncinariasis*, 21–22.

142 *afflicted eight or nine in ten*: Arnold Dana, *Porto Rico's Case, Outcome of American Sovereignty* (New Haven, CT, 1928), 39; Lawrence D. Granger, "A Study of the Rural Social Problems in Porto Rico" (M.A. thesis, University of Southern California, 1930), 62–63; and Farley, *Cast Out Disease*, chap. 5.

142 *killed hundreds*, etc.: Thomas Mathews, *Puerto Rican Politics and the New Deal* (Gainesville, FL, 1960), chap. 1.

142 *sugar prices and wages*: Emilio Pantojas-Garcia, "Puerto Rican Populism Revisited: The PPD During the 1940s," *Journal of Latin American Studies* 21 (1989): 523.

142 *Incomes in Puerto Rico*: James L. Dietz, *Economic History of Puerto Rico: Institutional Change and Capitalist Development* (Princeton, NJ, 1986), 139.

143 *"among the lower"*: James R. Beverley, quoted in Annette B. Ramírez de Arellano and Conrad Seipp, *Colonialism, Catholicism, and Contraception* (Chapel Hill, NC, 1983), 186n56.

143 *"only solution,"* etc.: "Top Secret" annex to memorandum by Charles W. Taussig, March 15, 1945, quoted in William Roger Louis, *Imperialism at Bay: The United States and the Decolonization of the British Empire* (New York, 1978), 486–87n.

143 *hoped that experimental treatments*: Farley, *Cast Out Disease*, chap. 5.

143 *"outspoken"* . . . *"hawk-like"*: "Cancer Fighter, Dr. Cornelius Rhoads," *NYT*, October 10, 1956.

143 *"A man of brusque manners"*: Luis Baldoni, Testimony in Cornelius Rhoads Case, 1932, 1, folder 4, box 31, Reynolds Papers.

143 *"nervous half-hour visits"*: Ashford, *Soldier in Science*, 44.

143 *refused treatment*: C. P. Rhoads et al., "Observations on the Etiology and Treatment of Anemia Associated with Hookworm Infection in Puerto Rico," *Medicine* 13 (1934): 353, 361.

144 *"experimental 'animals'"* . . . *"If they don't"*: Susan E. Lederer, "'Porto Ricochet': Joking About Germs, Cancer, and Race Extermination in the 1930s," *American Literary History* 14 (2002): 725.

144 *Dear Ferdie*: Full letter reprinted in Truman R. Clark, *Puerto Rico and the United States, 1917–1933* (Pittsburgh, 1975), 152–53.

144 *Clandestine villainy*: The most thorough accounts are Lederer, "Porto Ricochet," and Pedro Aponte Vázquez, *The Unsolved Case of Dr. Cornelius P. Rhoads: An Indictment* (San Juan, 2004). For the view from the Rockefeller Institute, see Farley, *Cast Out Disease*, chap. 5.

145 *"in a moment" . . . "I have a high notion" . . . "loan"*: Baldoni, Testimony, 5, 8.

145 *gave it to a man*: "Patients Say Rhoads Saved Their Lives," *NYT*, February 2, 1932.

145 *cover letter*: Lederer, "Porto Ricochet," 726.

146 *"confession of murder"*: Douglas Starr, "Revisiting a 1930s Scandal, AACR to Rename a Prize," *Science* 300 (2003): 574.

146 *"even worse"*: James R. Beverley to Wilber A. Sawyer, February 17, 1932, reprinted in Aponte Vázquez, *Unsolved Case*, 35–36.

146 *"a mental case"*: Lederer, "Porto Ricochet," 734.

146 *Katz*: Starr, "Revisiting a Scandal," 573.

147 *"Where tyranny"*: Juan Manuel Carrión et al., eds., *La nación puertorriqueña: Ensayos en torno a Pedro Albizu Campos* (San Juan, 1997), 234.

147 *four sticks of dynamite*: Mathews, *Puerto Rican Politics*, 103.

147 *Riggs wrote to*: E. Francis Riggs to Millard Tydings, January 3, 1934, and January 8, 1934, "Commission on Territories and Insular Affairs, 1933–December 10, 1934" folder, box 1, ser. 4, Tydings Papers.

147 *"Public order"*: A. W. Maldonado, *Luis Muñoz Marín: Puerto Rico's Democratic Revolution* (San Juan, 2006), 132.

147 *exploded on holidays*: Dante Di Lillo and Edgar K. Thompson, "Pedro Albizu Campos," supplementary report, February 26, 1936, 3, Albizu FBI File, sec. 1.

147 *"Some night"*: Dante Di Lillo, "Pedro Albizu Campos," report, April 4, 1936, 32, Albizu FBI File, sec. 1.

147 *"non-stop war"*: *La Democracia*, October 26, 1935, discussed in Luis A. Ferrao, "29 Lies (and More to Come) in the Fictitious War Against All Puerto Ricans," *Diálogo UPR*, September 24, 2015, www.dialogoupr.com.

148 *"There will be war"*: Carl E. Stanford, report 100-3906, "Pedro Albizu Campos," May 26, 1943, 5, Albizu FBI File, sec. 2.

148 *shoot-out with the police*: Juan Manuel Carrión, "The War of the Flags: Conflicting National Loyalties in a Modern Colonial Situation," *CENTRO Journal* 28 (2006): 112.

148 *"clean up"*: "Zioncheck Offers to Clean Up Island," *NYT*, May 14, 1936.

148 *"the most important"*: Ronald Fernandez, *The Disenchanted Island: Puerto Rico and the United States in the Twentieth Century*, 2d ed. (Westport, CT, 1996), 128.

148 *hand-picked jury*: Evidence presented by Rep. Vito Marcantonio in "Five Years of Tyranny in Puerto Rico," *Congressional Record*, 76th Cong., 1st sess., appendix, 4062–69.

148 *gunfire erupted*: Details all from Arthur Garfield Hays, Report of the Commission of Inquiry on Civil Rights in Puerto Rico, May 22, 1937.

148 *"common fact"*: Edgar K. Thompson to Hoover, December 22, 1939, Albizu FBI File, sec. 2.

149 *"massacre"*: Hays, Report of Commission, 28.

149 *"jocular letter"*: "Porto Rico 'Plot' Fails at Hearing," *Washington Post*, February 7, 1932.

149 Time *printed the letter*: "Porto Ricochet," *Time*, February 15, 1932, 38. On public relations, see Lederer, "Porto Ricochet."

150 *didn't impede him*: A good overview of Rhoads's career (though it omits Puerto Rico) is C. Chester Stock, "Cornelius Packard Rhoads, 1898–1959," *Cancer Research* 20 (1960): 409–11.

150 *Chemical Warfare Service ran tests*: See Committee on the Survey of the Health Effects of Mustard Gas and Lewisite, *Veterans at Risk: The Health Effects of Mustard Gas and Lewisite*, ed. Constance M. Pechura and David P. Rall (Washington, DC, 1993), and Susan L. Smith, *Toxic Exposures: Mustard Gas and the Health Consequences of World War II in the United States* (New Brunswick, NJ, 2017).

151 *race based*: Susan L. Smith, "Mustard Gas and American Race-Based Human Experimentation in World War II," *Journal of Law, Medicine and Ethics* 36 (2008): 517–21.

151 *"from the Continental Limits"*: William N. Porter to Commanding General, May 5, 1944; "200, San Jose Project" folder; box 56; Entry 2B, Misc. Series, 1942–45; CWS. This was part of a general War Department strategy of deploying Puerto Rican troops in the Caribbean to free up "continental" troops for combat, on which see Steven High, *Base Colonies in the Western Hemisphere, 1940–1967* (New York, 2009), 39–41.

151 *One GI*: John Lindsay-Poland, *Emperors in the Jungle: The Hidden History of the U.S. in Panama* (Durham, NC, 2003), 59.

151 *"cheap availability,"* etc.: Jay Katz to David Rall, June 16, 1992, in *Veterans at Risk*, 388, 389.

151 *established medical testing stations*: "Col. Rhoads Is Cited for Poison Gas Study," NYT, May 6, 1945.

151 *He arranged to transport*: Rhoads to Jake T. Nolan, August 31, 1944; "200, Bushnell Project" folder; box 56; Entry 2B, Misc. Series, 1942–45; CWS.

151 *recommended which gases*: Cornelius P. Rhoads, "Estimates of the Extent of Ground Contamination Necessary for the Production of Casualties by Mustard Vapor Effects on Masked Troops in the Contaminated Area"; folder 470.6; box 154; Entry 4M, Subject Series, 1942–45; and Cornelius P. Rhoads, "The Assessment of Casualties Produced by WP and PWP," September 19, 1944; folder 704; box 178; Entry 4B, Misc. Series, 1942–45; both in CWS.

151 *offered comments*: See, for example, Rhoads to John R. Wood, August 13, 1943; "400.112 Mustard Liquid" folder; box 151; Entry 4A, Subject Series, 1942–45; CWS.

151 *"combating poison gas"*: "Rhoads Cited for Gas Study."

152 *to treat lymphoma*: On mustard agents and medical uses, see Cornelius P. Rhoads, "The Sword and the Ploughshare," 1946, reprinted in *CA: A Cancer Journal for Clinicians* 28 (1978): 306–12; Alfred Gilman, "The Initial Clinical Trial of Nitrogen Mustard," *American Journal of Surgery* 105 (1963): 574–78; Peggy Dillon, National Cancer Institute, Oral History Interview Project, Interview with Joseph Burchenal, January 26, 2001, history.nih.gov/archives/oral_histories; Vincent T. DeVita Jr. and Edward Chu, "A History of Cancer Chemotherapy," *Cancer Research* 68 (2008): 8643–53; and especially Smith, *Toxic Exposures*, chap. 4.

152 *divided the stock*: Rhoads, "Sword and Ploughshare," 312.

152 *Rhoads also recruited*: DeVita and Chu, "History of Chemotherapy," 8646.

152 *"frontal attack"*: "Frontal Attack," *Time*, June 27, 1949, 66.

152 *intolerance for alternative approaches*: Rhoads especially sidelined approaches championed by women. See Virginia Livingston-Wheeler and Edmond G. Addeo, *The*

Conquest of Cancer: Vaccines and Diet (New York, 1984), 72–79, 84–88; Ralph W. Moss, *The Cancer Industry: Unraveling the Politics* (New York, 1989), 478; and Matthew Tontonoz, "Beyond Magic Bullets: Helen Coley Nauts and the Battle for Immunotherapy," *Cancer Research Institute Blog*, April 1, 2015, www.cancerresearch.org.

152 *"one of the most prominent"*: Starr, "Revisiting a Scandal," 573.

153 *"It was just totally shocking"*: Eric T. Rosenthal, "The Rhoads Not Given: The Tainting of the Cornelius P. Rhoads Memorial Award," *Oncology Times*, September 10, 2003, 20. See also ibid.

10. FORTRESS AMERICA

154 *inescapable daily presence*: On this, I have learned much from Alvita Akiboh and her article "Pocket-Sized Imperialism: U.S. Designs on Colonial Currency," *DH* 41 (2017): 874–902.

154 *coverage in* The New York Times: *New York Times Index: Annual Cumulative Volume Year 1930* (New York, 1931).

155 *"brown Polynesian people,"* etc.: Margaret Mead, *Coming of Age in Samoa* (1928; New York, 2001), 8. Mead's silence on the colonial aspects of her subject is discussed in Derek Freeman, *Margaret Mead and Samoa: The Making and Unmaking of an Anthropological Myth* (Cambridge, MA, 1983). Mead's book contains only three instances of the term *American Samoa* (two of which are parenthetical), one *colony* (a classical reference, though), one *navy*, and no mentions of *territory*, *empire*, or *imperialism*.

155 *didn't know where the island was*: Hubert Herring, "Rebellion in Puerto Rico," *The Nation*, November 29, 1933, 618–19.

155 *didn't have a single federal official*: That episode, in 1878–79, is described in A. P. Swineford, *Alaska: Its History, Climate and Natural Resources* (Chicago, 1898), 66.

155 *"It has been impossible"*: Moorfield Storey and Marcial P. Lichauco, *The Conquest of the Philippines by the United States* (New York, 1926), 203.

155 *Anti-Imperialist League*: Robert L. Beisner, *Twelve Against Empire: The Anti-Imperialists, 1898–1900* (New York, 1968), 225. See also Jim Zwick, "The Anti-Imperialist League and the Origins of Filipino-American Oppositional Solidarity," *Amerasia Journal* 24 (1998): 65–85.

155 *Pan-American Freedom League*: Robert David Johnson, *Ernest Gruening and the American Dissenting Tradition* (Cambridge, MA, 1998), 67.

156 *"Not in all the years"*: Oswald Garrison Villard, "Ernest Gruening's Appointment," *The Nation*, August 29, 1934, 232.

156 *quite a career*: Johnson, *Gruening*, and Robert David Johnson, "Anti-Imperialism and the Good Neighbour Policy: Ernest Gruening and Puerto Rican Affairs, 1934–1939," *Journal of Latin American Studies* 29 (1997): 89–110.

157 *spent only a single day*: Ernest Gruening, *Many Battles: The Autobiography of Ernest Gruening* (New York, 1973), 181.

157 *Roosevelt rattled off his assessments*: Ibid., 181, and Ernest Gruening, *The Battle for Alaska Statehood* (Seattle, 1977), xi.

157 *fantasizing about annexing*: Lowell T. Young, "Franklin D. Roosevelt and America's Islets: Acquisition of Territory in the Caribbean and the Pacific," *The Historian* 35 (1973): 206.

157 *falling by two-thirds*: David M. Kennedy, *Freedom from Fear: The American People in Depression and War, 1929–1945* (New York, 1999), 77.

158 *"infinitely more"*: Brooks Emeny, *The Strategy of Raw Materials: A Study of America in Peace and War* (New York, 1938), 174.

158 *bought more sugar*: A. G. Hopkins, *American Empire: A Global History* (Princeton, NJ, 2018), 517.

158 *"two kinds of territory"*: Gruening, *Many Battles*, 229.

158 *colonies paid the cost*: April Merleaux, *Sugar and Civilization: American Empire and the Cultural Politics of Sweetness* (Chapel Hill, NC, 2015), chap. 7.

159 *"reversal of opinion"*: "Calvin Coolidge Says," *New York Herald-Tribune*, May 25, 1931.

159 *"It would be a mortifying spectacle"*: "The Philippines and Economics," *Christian Science Monitor*, July 20, 1931, 14.

159 *comprehensive survey*: Ten Eyck Associates, *Philippine Independence: A Survey of the Present State of American Public Opinion on the Subject* (New York, 1932), 31.

159 *"surely never happen"*: Quoted in Manuel V. Gallego, *The Price of Philippine Independence Under the Tydings McDuffie Act: An Anti-View of the So-Called Independence Law* (Manila, 1939), 85.

159 *Quezon was a master politician*: On Quezon's career, see Carlos Quirino, *Quezon: Paladin of Philippine Freedom* (Manila, 1971), chaps. 3–5; Alfred W. McCoy, *Policing America's Empire: The United States, the Philippines and the Rise of the Surveillance State* (Madison, WI, 2009), 187–88.

159 *"wonderfully trained"*: McCoy, *Policing America's Empire*, 188.

160 *mercury with a fork*: John Gunther, *Inside Asia*, war ed. (1939; New York, 1942), 316.

160 *about four-fifths*: O. D. Corpuz, *An Economic History of the Philippines* (Quezon City, 1997), 243.

160 *privately assuring his contacts*: Herbert Hoover, *Memoirs* (New York, 1952), 2:361; Theodore Friend, *Between Two Empires: The Ordeal of the Philippines, 1929–1946* (New Haven, CT, 1965), chap. 1; and Michael Paul Onorato, "Quezon and Independence: A Reexamination," *Philippine Studies* 37 (1989): 221–31.

160 *ratified this version*: The best guide to this complicated episode is Friend, *Between Two Empires*, part 3.

160 *governor-general predicted*: Theodore Friend, *The Blue-Eyed Enemy: Japan Against the West in Java and Luzon, 1942–1945* (Princeton, NJ, 1988), 33.

161 *"considered to be"*: Philippine Independence Act, March 24, 1934, 48 *Stat.* 462.

161 *Quezon arranged a ceremony*: Chronicled in Francis Burton Harrison, *Origins of the Philippine Republic: Extracts from the Diaries and Records of Francis Burton Harrison*, ed. Michael P. Onorato (Ithaca, NY, 1974), 17–18.

162 *"By his silence"*: Gruening, *Many Battles*, 197.

162 *"revenge disguised as political freedom"*: Luis Muñoz Marín, *Memorias: Autobiografía pública, 1898–1940* (San Juan, 1982), 1:149.

162 *95 percent of Puerto Rico's off-island sales*: James L. Dietz, *Economic History of Puerto Rico: Institutional Change and Capitalist Development* (Princeton, NJ, 1986), 120.

162 *"As a matter of cold actuality"*: Theodore Roosevelt Jr. to Quezon, quoted in Theodore Roosevelt Jr., *Colonial Policies of the United States* (Garden City, NY, 1937), 187.

162 *reverse Philippine independence*: Gerald E. Wheeler, "The Movement to Reverse Philippine Independence," *Pacific History Review* 33 (1964): 167–81.

162 *"realistic reexamination"* . . . *"If our flag"*: Paul V. McNutt, radio address, March 14, 1938, "Commonwealth (Administration) Philippines" folder, box 2, Padover File.

162 *"presentation of the facts"*: "Quezon Proves to be Irresponsible!" *Philippine-American Advocate*, 1938, clipping in "Independence—Philippines" folder, box 4, Padover File.

162 *"wholehearted and unswerving loyalty"*: Quezon, Loyalty Day Declaration, 1941, in *World War II and the Japanese Occupation*, ed. Ricardo Trota Jose (Quezon City, 2006), 14.

163 one-peso commemorative coin: Thanks to Alvita Akiboh for drawing this to my attention.

163 Britain *annexing the Philippines*: R. John Pritchard, "President Quezon and Incorporation of the Philippines into the British Empire, 1935–1937," *Bulletin of the American Historical Collection* 12 (1984): 42–63.

164 *"as if he had a flagpole"*: John Hersey, *Men on Bataan* (New York, 1942), 279.

164 sexual failure: Michael Schaller, *Douglas MacArthur: The Far Eastern General* (New York, 1989), 11.

164 a military genius: The MacArthur literature is extensive. I've relied mainly on *Rem.*; D. Clayton James, *The Years of MacArthur*, vol. 1 (Boston, 1970); William Manchester, *American Caesar: Douglas MacArthur, 1880–1964* (Boston, 1978); Carol Morris Petillo, *Douglas MacArthur: The Philippine Years* (Bloomington, IN, 1981); Schaller, *MacArthur*; and Richard Connaughton, *MacArthur and Defeat in the Philippines* (Woodstock, NY, 2001).

164 *"desperadoes"*: *Rem.*, 29. MacArthur describes Guimaras as "infested with brigands and guerrillas" but does not say which the men he slew were.

165 Plan Orange: Earl S. Pomeroy, *Pacific Outpost: American Strategy in Guam and Micronesia* (Stanford, CA, 1951); Louis Morton, "Germany First: The Basic Concept of Allied Strategy in World War II," in *Command Decisions*, ed. Kent Roberts Greenfield (Washington, DC, 1960), 11–47; Stetson Conn, Rose C. Engelman, and Byron Fairchild, *Guarding the United States and Its Outposts* (Washington, DC, 1961); Louis Morton, *The War in the Pacific: Strategy and Command: The First Two Years* (Washington, DC, 1962); Timothy P. Maga, "Democracy and Defence: The Case of Guam, U.S.A., 1918–1941," *Journal of Pacific History* 20 (1985): 156–72; Edward S. Miller, *War Plan Orange: The U.S. Strategy to Defeat Japan, 1897–1945* (Annapolis, MD, 1991); John Costello, *Days of Infamy: MacArthur, Roosevelt, Churchill—The Shocking Truth Revealed* (New York, 1994); Brian McAllister Linn, *Guardians of Empire: The U.S. Army and the Pacific, 1902–1940* (Chapel Hill, NC, 1997); and Galen Roger Perras, *Stepping Stones to Nowhere: The Aleutian Islands, Alaska, and American Military Strategy, 1867–1945* (Vancouver, 2003).

165 *"not within the wildest"*: Richard H. Rovere and Arthur Schlesinger Jr., *The MacArthur Controversy and American Foreign Policy* (1951; New York, 1965), 44.

165 *"literally an act of madness"*: Morton, *War in the Pacific*, 34.

165 *"both the Philippines and Hawaii"*: Linn, *Guardians*, 147.

165 Public opinion polls: Pomeroy, *Pacific Outpost*, 140.

165 Fortune *in 1940*: "Fortune Magazine Survey XXVI," "Fortune Magazine Survey" folder, box 1, Hawaii Equal Rights Commission Records, COM16, HSA.

165 protested vigorously: John Snell to *Fortune*, January 27, 1940, along with other letters in ibid.

165 war planners: Linn, *Guardians*, chaps. 4 and 6.

166 *"Sakdal rebellion"*: Motoe Terami-Wada, *Sakdalistas' Struggle for Philippine Independence, 1930–1945* (Quezon City, 2014), 4.

166 *killing fifty-nine rebels*: Ibid.

166 *court-martial*: Linn, *Guardians*, 148.

166 *"an eleventh-hour struggle"*: Rem., 109. MacArthur's appointment as chief of staff ended, to his annoyance, while he was en route to the Pacific.

166 *"just another job"* . . . *"hopeless venture"*: Dwight D. Eisenhower, *At Ease: Stories I Tell to Friends* (Garden City, NY, 1967), 222, 225.

166 *worried that armed Filipinos*: Ricardo Trota Jose, *The Philippine Army, 1935–1942* (Manila, 1992), 64.

167 *"basic appreciation"*: Daniel D. Holt and James W. Leyerzapf, eds., *Eisenhower: The Prewar Diaries and Selected Papers, 1905–1941* (Baltimore, 1998), 307.

167 *birthday card*: James, *Years of MacArthur*, 1:564.

167 *"General, you have been"*: As recounted by Eisenhower to Peter Lyon, reported in Lyon's *Eisenhower: Portrait of the Hero* (Boston, 1974), 78.

167 *special uniform*: Rovere and Schlesinger, *MacArthur Controversy*, 42.

167 *$50 per Filipino trainee*: James, *Years of MacArthur*, 1:608.

167 *"an integral part"* . . . *"entirely inadequate"*: MacArthur to Quezon, October 1940, reprinted in ibid., 1:541–42.

168 *"to the width"*: Joseph Driscoll, *War Discovers Alaska* (Philadelphia, 1943), 20.

168 *"negligible"*: Henry Stimson, quoted in Kenneth S. Coates and William R. Morrison, *The Alaska Highway in World War II: The U.S. Army of Occupation in Canada's Northwest* (Norman, OK, 1992), 26.

168 *Alaska had an air force*: Brian Garfield, *The Thousand-Mile War: World War II in Alaska and the Aleutians* (Garden City, NY, 1969), 64.

168 *"in little more"*: Harry W. Woodring, quoted in Perras, *Stepping Stones*, 21.

169 *"'We're not going to waste'"*: Gruening, *Many Battles*, 295.

169 *B-17 bombers*: Costello, *Days of Infamy*, chap. 2. A good assessment of the War Department's provisioning of MacArthur is Louis Morton, *The Fall of the Philippines* (Washington, DC, 1953), chap. 3.

169 *"the decisive element"*: Quoted in William H. Bartsch, *December 8, 1941: MacArthur's Pearl Harbor* (College Station, TX, 2003), 98.

169 *other priorities*: Linn, *Guardians*, 217.

169 *"More speed!"*: "Speed! Congress! Speed!" *Paradise of the Pacific*, February 1939, 32.

169 *Hawai'i's defenses*: Linn, *Guardians*, 217.

169 *"absolutely indefensible"*: Lewis H. Brereton, *The Brereton Diaries: The War in the Air in the Pacific, Middle East, and Europe, 3 October 1941–8 May 1945* (New York, 1946), 17.

169 *past tense*: Timothy P. Maga, *Defending Paradise: The United States and Guam, 1898–1950* (New York, 1988), 164.

169 *"By no stretch"*: Perras, *Stepping Stones*, 53.

170 *U.S. Army contingent*: On troop sizes, Morton, *Fall of the Philippines*, 49, 27.

170 *canvas shoes*: Glen M. Williford, *Racing the Sunrise: Reinforcing America's Pacific Outposts, 1941–1942* (Annapolis, MD, 2010), 102.

170 *helmets*: Holt and Leyerzapf, *Eisenhower Diaries*, 405.

170 *artillery*: Connaughton, *MacArthur*, 155.

170 *never even fired their rifles*: Rigoberto J. Atienza, *A Time for War: 105 Days in Bataan* ([Philippines], 1985), 10; Morton, *Fall of the Philippines*, 28.

170 *growing air force*: Morton, *Fall of the Philippines*, 39, 42.

170 *"the Philippines could be defended"*: "Destiny's Child," *Time*, December 29, 1941, 16.

170 *"glaring deficiencies"* . . . *"unprepared"*: High Commissioner's Office to FDR, November 30, 1941, "Civilian Defense" folder, box 1, HC–Pol/Econ.

11. WARFARE STATE

171 *"God's way"*: *The Daily Show with Jon Stewart*, Comedy Central, August 12, 2008. The joke is often misattributed to Ambrose Bierce or Mark Twain. Various incarnations can be found dating to the nineteenth century, but not by Bierce or Twain.

171 *build a road*: See Philip Paneth, *Alaskan Backdoor to Japan* (London, 1943); David A. Remley, *Crooked Road: The Story of the Alaska Highway* (New York, 1976); Kenneth S. Coates, ed., *The Alaska Highway: Papers of the 40th Anniversary Symposium* (Vancouver, 1985); Kenneth S. Coates and William R. Morrison, *The Alaska Highway in World War II: The U.S. Army of Occupation in Canada's Northwest* (Norman, OK, 1992); and John Virtue, *The Black Soldiers Who Built the Alaska Highway: A History of Four U.S. Army Regiments in the North, 1942–1943* (Jefferson, NC, 2013).

172 *11,150 troops*: Coates and Morrison, *Alaska Highway in World War II*, 47.

172 *heavy equipment*: Ibid., 41.

173 *An anthropologist*: Julie Cruikshank, "The Gravel Magnet: Some Social Impacts of the Alaska Highway on Yukon Indians," in Coates, ed., *Alaska Highway*, 182.

173 *"greatest piece of roadmaking"*: Malcolm MacDonald, quoted in Virtue, *Black Soldiers*, 160.

173 *the men abandoned them*: Remley, *Crooked Road*, 60.

173 *$1.2 billion*: César J. Ayala and José L. Bolivar, *Battleship Vieques: Puerto Rico from World War II to the Korean War* (Princeton, NJ, 2011), 25.

173 *number of restaurants*: "Honolulu . . . Island Boomtown," *Paradise of the Pacific*, May 1944.

173 *bank deposits*: Gwenfread Allen, *Hawaii's War Years, 1941–1945* (Honolulu, 1950), 284.

173 *Eight parlors . . . The overcrowded brothels*: Beth Bailey and David Farber, *The First Strange Place: Race and Sex in World War II Hawaii* (Baltimore, 1992), 105, 103.

173 *new governmental intrusions*: Discussed cogently in James T. Sparrow, *Warfare State: World War II Americans and the Age of Big Government* (New York, 2011). Sparrow's book, from which this chapter takes its title and inspiration, deals exclusively with the mainland.

174 *turned over all effective power*: On wartime Hawai'i, see Allen, *Hawaii's War Years*; J. Garner Anthony, *Hawaii Under Army Rule* (Palo Alto, CA, 1955); and Bailey and Farber, *First Strange Place*. The definitive account of martial law is Harry N. Scheiber and Jane L. Scheiber, *Bayonets in Paradise: Martial Law in Hawai'i During World War II* (Honolulu, 2016).

174 *third of O'ahu*: Allen, *Hawaii's War Years*, 221.

175 *University of Hawaii graduates*: Louise Stevens, "A Gas Mask Graduation Class," *Paradise of the Pacific*, August 1942.

175 *"enemy country"*: Frank Knox to FDR, quoted in Scheiber and Scheiber, *Bayonets*, 135.

175 *an uncomfortable moment*: Allen, *Hawaii's War Years*, 120.

175 *"One Mighty God"*: Scheiber and Scheiber, *Bayonets*, 86.

175 *"hostility or disrespect"*: Territory of Hawaii, Office of the Military Governor, General Orders 31 and 42, Uncatalogued Subject Files, box 8, HWRD.

175 *General Orders read like*: Territory of Hawaii, OMG, General Orders 129, 164, 167, 84, 88, respectively, in ibid.

175 *"My authority"*: Scheiber and Scheiber, *Bayonets*, 59.

175 *"I've got a .45"*: Jim A. Richstad, *The Press Under Martial Law: The Hawaiian Experience* (Lexington, KY, 1970), 13–14.

176 *"known to be overzealous"*: George Akita, diary excerpted in Hawaii Nikkei History Editorial Board, *Japanese Eyes . . . American Heart: Personal Reflections of Hawaii's World War II Nisei Soldiers* (Honolulu, 1998), 40.

176 *a single judge*: "Taking Stock of Hawaii," *Honolulu Star Bulletin*, April 6, 1942.

176 *98.4 percent resulted*: Anthony, *Hawaii Under Army Rule*, 27, 52.

176 *They were tried for*: Scheiber and Scheiber, *Bayonets*, 109.

176 *keys in the ignition . . . playing cards*: Territory of Hawaii, OMG, General Orders 113 and 134, HWRD.

176 *One motorist*: Drew Pearson, "Demand Cessation of Military Rule in Hawaii," *Washington Post*, December 26, 1942.

176 *One of the most disturbing*: Important complicating factors: The defendant, Fred Spurlock, begged for mercy and got his sentence commuted to probation. But then Spurlock was arrested again, for getting into a fight. The Honolulu Provost Court, noting that Spurlock was on probation, sentenced him to five years' hard labor on the spot. Spurlock wasn't allowed to testify or call witnesses. The trial, according to him, lasted fewer than ten minutes. *Ex Parte Spurlock*, 66 F. Supp. 997 (D. Hawaii 1944).

176 *sentences of more than*: On sentencing, see Scheiber and Scheiber, *Bayonets*, 109–10. By March 1944, O'ahu's prison contained fewer than a hundred convicts, far short of the thousands who had been convicted in Honolulu's provost court. Ernest May, "Hawaii's Work in Wartime," *Honolulu Star Bulletin*, May 18, 1944.

177 *"American 'conquered territory'"*: Harold Ickes, quoted in Scheiber and Scheiber, *Bayonets*, 214.

177 *"heterogeneous population"*: Quoted in *Duncan v. Kahanamoku*, 327 U.S. 304, 333 (1946).

178 *"Racism has no place"*: *Duncan*, 327 U.S. at 334 (Murphy, J., concurring).

178 *"Somebody ought"*: Michael P. Onorato, ed., *Origins of the Philippine Republic: Extracts from the Diaries and Records of Francis Burton Harrison* (Ithaca, NY, 1974), 154.

178 *Half of them died*: The ordeal is detailed in Nick Golodoff, *Attu Boy*, ed. Rachel Mason (Anchorage, 2012).

178 *brought relics from*: Leocadio de Asis, *From Bataan to Tokyo: Diary of a Filipino Student in Wartime Japan, 1943–1944*, ed. Grant K. Goodman (Lawrence, KS, 1979), 65.

178 *surprisingly light touch*: Sam Lebovic, *Free Speech and Unfree News: The Paradox of Press Freedom in America* (Cambridge, MA, 2016), 118–25.

178 *had his mail opened*: Claus-M. Naske, *Ernest Gruening: Alaska's Greatest Governor* (Fairbanks, 2004), 73.

178 *"Are we foreigners"*: Quoted in Joseph Driscoll, *War Discovers Alaska* (Philadelphia, 1943), 27.

178 *"introduction of Gestapo methods"*: Quoted in Robert David Johnson, *Ernest Gruening and the American Dissenting Tradition* (Cambridge, MA, 1998), 160.

178 *catch-22*: Naske, *Gruening*, 77.

179 *"quietest war theater"*: "Alaska Quietest War Theater—In Communiqués," *Chicago Daily Tribune*, July 12, 1942.

179 *"hidden front"*: William Gilman, *Our Hidden Front* (New York, 1944).

179 *Aleut internment*: My account relies primarily on Commission on Wartime Relocation and Internment of Civilians, *Personal Justice Denied* (Washington, DC, 1982); Ryan Madden, "The Forgotten People: The Relocation and Internment of Aleuts During World War II," *American Indian Culture and Research Journal* 16 (1992): 55–76; Dean Kohlhoff, *When the Wind Was a River: Aleut Evacuation in World War II* (Seattle, 1995); and Russell W. Estlak, *The Aleut Internments of World War II: Islanders Removed from Their Homes by Japan and the United States* (Jefferson, NC, 2014).

179 *"fundamental injustice"*: Civil Liberties Act of 1988, 102 *Stat.* 904.

179 white *residents of Unalaska*: Madden, "Forgotten People," 62.

179 *"while eating"*: Kohlhoff, *Wind*, 70.

179 *"Feels funny"*: Driscoll, *War Discovers Alaska*, 48.

180 *"I have no language"*: Kohlhoff, *Wind*, 116.

180 *"no place for,"* etc.: *Personal Justice Denied*, 339.

180 *"As we entered,"* etc.: Ibid., 340.

180 *Pribilovians*: Ryan Madden, "The Government's Industry: Alaska Natives and Pribilof Sealing During World War II," *Pacific Northwest Quarterly* 91 (2000): 202–209.

181 *MacArthur ordered police*: "25,000 Japanese Interned," *Manila Tribune*, December 9, 1941; Richard Connaughton, *MacArthur and Defeat in the Philippines* (Woodstock, NY, 2001), 189.

181 *raided Japanese homes*: John Hersey, *Men on Bataan* (New York, 1942), 35–36.

181 *"People hooted"*: Pacita Pestaño-Jacinto, *Living with the Enemy: A Diary of the Japanese Occupation* (Pasig City, 1999), 3.

181 *civilians hunted*: Eliseo Quirino, *A Day to Remember* (Manila, 1958), 20.

181 *Filipinos who helped*: "Filipino Arrested for Hiding 'Friend,'" *Manila Tribune*, December 12, 1941.

181 *raped . . . ransacked*: Maria Virginia Yap Morales, ed., *Diary of the War: World War II Memoirs of Lt. Col. Anastacio Campo* (Quezon City, 2006), 30, 43–46.

181 *parked trucks*: "Internees Cower as Sirens Sound," *Manila Daily Bulletin*, December 29, 1941.

181 *shooting prisoners*: Hiroyuki Mizuguchi, *Jungle of No Mercy: Memoir of a Japanese Soldier* (Manila, 2010), 33–36. Further abuses are described in P. Scott Corbett, *Quiet Passages: The Exchange of Civilians Between the United States and Japan During the Second World War* (Kent, OH, 1987), 50–52.

182 *"the indescribable wave"*: Kiyoshi Osawa, *The Japanese Community in the Philippines Before, During, and After the War* (Manila, 1994), 222.

182 *swift and brutal revenge*: Described in Marcial P. Lichauco, *"Dear Mother Putnam": A Diary of the War in the Philippines* (Manila, c. 1949), 17. See also Hayase Shinzo, "The Japanese Residents of 'Dabao-Kuo,'" in *The Philippines Under Japan: Occupation Policy and Reaction*, ed. Ikehata Setsuho and Ricardo Trota Jose (Quezon City, 1999), 247–87.

182 *"Words cannot describe,"* etc.: Osawa, *Japanese Community*, 162.

183 *Hawai'i's war bond sales*: William K. Hanifin, "Bond Sales," April 30, 1946, folder 66, box 37, HWRD.

183 *Alaska's, as of*: Naske, *Gruening*, 97.

183 *"Up until then"* . . . *"did not know what resentment"*: Ernest Gruening, *Many Battles: The Autobiography of Ernest Gruening* (New York, 1973), 210. On Alaskan segregation (which Gruening opposed vigorously), see Terrence M. Cole, "Jim Crow in Alaska: The Passage of the Alaska Equal Rights Act of 1945," *Western Historical Quarterly* 23 (1992): 429–49.

183 *might turn their guns*: Muktuk Marston, *Men of the Tundra: Eskimos at War* (New York, 1969), 156.

183 *"fellow citizens"* . . . *"eyes and ears"*: Henry Varnum Poor, *An Artist Sees Alaska* (New York, 1945), 123.

183 *"We will give"*: Marston, *Men of the Tundra*, 58.

183 *"Everywhere I found"*: Gruening, introduction to Marston, *Men of the Tundra*, 4.

183 *twenty thousand Alaska Natives*: Captain Richard Neuberger, "Eskimo Guerrillas," *Saturday Evening Post*, February 17, 1945, 6; Marston, *Men of the Tundra*, 156.

184 *Pletnikoff*: Ray Hudson, "Aleuts in Defense of Their Homeland," in *Alaska at War, 1941–1945: The Forgotten War Remembered*, ed. Fern Chandonnet (Anchorage, 1995), 163.

184 *fortifying Alaska's north*: Charles Hendricks, "The Eskimos and the Defense of Alaska," *Pacific Historical Review* 54 (1985): 281.

184 *enlisting at rates*: Ibid., 292.

185 *shocked to see armed men*: C. F. Necrason, epilogue, Marston, *Men of the Tundra*, 179.

185 *"guinea pigs"*: Masayo Umezawa Duus, *Unlikely Liberators: The Men of the 100th and the 442nd*, trans. Peter Duus (1983; Honolulu, 1987), 113.

185 *"We knew that we had to be"*: Robert Asahina, *Just Americans: How Japanese Americans Won a War at Home and Abroad* (New York, 2006), 35. The history of the 100th/442nd has been told often, with Asahina's book one of the best renditions. A useful global perspective is T. Fujitani, *Race for Empire: Koreans as Japanese and Japanese as Americans During World War II* (Berkeley, CA, 2011), chap. 5.

185 *Daniel Inouye*: Story and quotations from Daniel K. Inouye, *Journey to Washington* (Englewood Cliffs, NJ, 1967), 150–54.

186 *Medal of Honor*: Medals for the 100th/442nd and army divisions counted from list at U.S. Army Center of Military History, history.army.mil/moh.

186 *Pound for pound*: On comparing decorations between units, see James M. McCaffrey, *Going for Broke: Japanese American Soldiers in the War Against Nazi Germany* (Norman, OK, 2013), 346–47.

12. THERE ARE TIMES WHEN MEN HAVE TO DIE

187 *near-simultaneous strike*: On the attack, see especially Louis Morton, *The Fall of the Philippines* (Washington, DC, 1953); D. Clayton James, *The Years of MacArthur*, vol. 2 (Boston, 1975), chap. 1; John Costello, *Days of Infamy: MacArthur, Roosevelt, Churchill—The Shocking Truth Revealed* (New York, 1994); Richard Connaughton, *MacArthur and Defeat in the Philippines* (Woodstock, NY, 2001); and William H. Bartsch, *December 8, 1941: MacArthur's Pearl Harbor* (College Station, TX, 2003).

187 *"ace unit"*: Douglas MacArthur, quoted in Bartsch, *December 8*, 193.

187 *Thick fog*: Costello, *Days of Infamy*, 20–21.

188 *"The sight which,"* etc.: Connaughton, *MacArthur*, 169.

188 *"bewildering"* . . . *"and we shall"*: William Manchester, *American Caesar: Douglas MacArthur, 1880–1964* (Boston, 1978), 206, 205. Manchester hypothesizes that MacArthur may have suffered "input overload." John Costello, using notes from an unpublished 1942 interview with Lewis Brereton, MacArthur's air commander, suggests a more damning possibility: MacArthur *did* meet with Brereton that morning (despite Brereton's and MacArthur's subsequent denials) and ordered Brereton not to strike back; MacArthur hoped to keep the Philippines neutral, and thus intact, in the coming war with Japan. Costello, *Days of Infamy*, 23. A more cautious account is James, *Years of MacArthur*, 2:3–15.

188 *"We could see"*: Costello, *Days of Infamy*, 34.

188 *"one of the blackest"*: Lewis H. Brereton, *The Brereton Diaries: The War in the Air in the Pacific, Middle East, and Europe, 3 October 1941–8 May 1945* (New York, 1946), 44.

188 *Now it was inoperable*: Morton, *Fall of the Philippines*, 95–96.

189 *"worst disaster"*: Winston S. Churchill, *The Second World War* (1950; Boston, 1985), 4:81.

189 *North Luzon Force*: James, *Years of MacArthur*, 2:45.

189 *slab of oak*: John Gunther, *Inside Asia*, war ed. (1939; New York, 1942), 309.

189 *"a masterpiece"*: Manchester, *American Caesar*, 218.

189 *"It was hard to believe"*: Fernando J. Mañalac, *Manila: Memories of World War II* (Quezon City, 1995), 10.

190 *five bomb craters*: "Ethel Herold's Baguio War Memories," *Bulletin of the American Historical Collection* 10 (1982): 12.

190 *MacArthur's three-year-old*: Frances Bowes Sayre, *Glad Adventure* (New York, 1957), 232

190 *dragon's hoard*: Ibid., 235; Steve Mellnik, *Philippine Diary, 1939–1945* (New York, 1969), 116.

190 *eighty thousand . . . twenty-six thousand*: James, *Years of MacArthur*, 2:35.

190 *The men ate half rations*: Morton, *Fall of the Philippines*, 367–68.

190 *horses, dogs, etc.*: Ibid., 369–70.

190 *"it looked like"*: Connaughton, *MacArthur*, 273.

190 *eating cigarettes*: Rigoberto J. Atienza, *A Time for War: 105 Days in Bataan* (Philippines, 1985), 102.

190 *"There are no atheists"*: Carlos P. Romulo, *I Saw the Fall of the Philippines* (Garden City, NY, 1943), 263.

190 *"I give to the people,"* etc.: Roosevelt, Message of Support to the Philippines, December 28, 1941, *APP*.

191 *"too much of the immediate,"* etc.: Quoted in John Hersey, *Men on Bataan* (New York, 1942), 257.

191 *"In our mind's eyes"*: Atienza, *Time for War*, 119.

191 *"Our fight"* . . . *"Surrender"*: Quoted in Romulo, *Fall of the Philippines*, 108.

191 *menus from the Manila Hotel*: Atienza, *Time for War*, 117.

191 *"It was only the Americans"*: William A. Owens, *Eye-Deep in Hell: A Memoir of the Liberation of the Philippines, 1944–45* (Dallas, 1989), 102.

191 *"It was bitter"*: Roosevelt, State of the Union address, January 6, 1942, *APP*.

191 *"I cannot stand,"* etc.: Charles A. Willoughby and John Chamberlain, *MacArthur: 1941–1951* (New York, 1954), 56.

192 *"to erase"*: Ibid.

192 *"This war is not"*: Quezon to Roosevelt, January 28, 1942, in *World War II and the Japanese Occupation*, ed. Ricardo Trota Jose (Quezon City, 2006), 79. Quezon describes the interchange in *The Good Fight* (New York, 1946), 259–74.

192 *"While enjoying security"*: Douglas MacArthur to George Marshall, February 8, 1942, *FRUS 1942*, 1:894.

192 *Quezon demanded immediate independence*: Ibid.

192 *"the temper of the Filipinos"*: Ibid., 1:896.

192 *"You have no authority"*: L. T. Gerow to Douglas MacArthur, February 11, 1942, *FRUS 1942*, 1:900.

192 *"So long as the flag"*: George Marshall to Douglas MacArthur, February 9, 1942, *FRUS 1942*, 1:898.

192 *"Germany first" strategy*: Louis Morton, "Germany First: The Basic Concept of Allied Strategy in World War II," in Kent Greenfield, ed., *Command Decisions* (Washington, DC, 1959), 11–47.

193 *"There are times"*: Manchester, *American Caesar*, 241.

193 *"Guess what I learned"*: Mellnik, *Philippine Diary*, 116.

193 *secret spot*: John G. Hubbell, "The Great Manila Bay Silver Operation," *Reader's Digest*, April 1959, 123–34.

193 *half a million dollars*: Carol Morris Petillo, "Douglas MacArthur and Manuel Quezon: A Note on an Imperial Bond," *Pacific Historical Review* 48 (1979): 110–17.

193 *"We're the battling bastards"*: Jonathan Wainwright, *General Wainwright's Story* (Garden City, NY, 1946), 54.

193 *"The Americans, rulers and idols"*: Carmen Guerrero Nakpil, *A Question of Identity: Selected Essays* (Manila, 1973), 202.

194 *"gallantry and intrepidity"*: James, *Years of MacArthur*, 2:132.

194 *"All the people"* . . . *"I've never wanted"*: Hersey, *Men on Bataan*, 4, 5.

194 *bestseller list*: www.booksofthecentury.com.

194 *highest directorial salary*: Camilla Fojas, *Islands of Empire: Pop Culture and U.S. Power* (Austin, TX, 2014), 39. On Philippine World War II films, see Fojas, *Islands of Empire*, chap. 1, and Charles Affron and Mirella Jona Affron, *Best Years: Going to the Movies, 1945–46* (New Brunswick, NJ, 2009), chap. 4.

194 *466 towns and cities*: Carlos P. Romulo, *My Brother Americans* (Garden City, NY, 1945), 21.

194 *"Filamericans"*: Romulo, *Fall of the Philippines*, 217–18.

194 *"How I wished,"* etc.: Carlos P. Romulo, *Mother America: A Living Story of Democracy* (Garden City, NY, 1943), 1.

195 *"thirty-six thousand"* . . . *"trapped like rats"*: *They Were Expendable*, dir. John Ford (MGM, 1945).

195 *Filipinos served largely*: A notable exception is *Back to Bataan* (1945), written and directed by two leftists later blacklisted for their politics. Though it focuses on a white colonel (John Wayne), it features numerous Filipino characters. However, the film was completed *after* the U.S. reconquest of the Philippines and so did nothing to stir up support for a military rescue.

195 *His idea was to play*: Michael P. Onorato, ed., *Origins of the Philippine Republic: Extracts from the Diaries and Records of Francis Burton Harrison* (Ithaca, NY, 1974), 203.

195 *"shocked and horrified"*: Frank S. Adams, "Visitor from Bataan," *NYT*, June 24, 1945.

195 *"crowded with little Neros"*: Romulo, *My Brother Americans*, 8.

195 *pouring sake*: Virginia Benitez Licuanan, *Filipinos and Americans: A Love-Hate Relationship* (Baguio, 1982), 145.

195 *MacArthur's penthouse*: Richard Connaughton, John Pimlott, and Duncan Anderson, *The Battle for Manila* (London, 1995), 46.

195 *Leonard Wood Hotel*: A.V.H. Hartendorp, *The Japanese Occupation of the Philippines* (Manila, 1967), 1:481.

195 *One idea was to name*: Manuel E. Buenafe, *Wartime Philippines* (Manila, 1950), 172.

196 *now commemorated*: Pronouncement of Jorge Vargas, 1942, in Jose, *World War II and the Japanese Occupation*, 122.

196 *Quezon had languished*: Quezon, *Good Fight*, 83.

196 *Romulo remembered how . . . "I made up"*: Romulo, *Fall of the Philippines*, 48.

196 *"a sense of betrayal" . . . "No change"*: Romulo, *Mother America*, 92, 96.

196 *"America has wasted"*: Propaganda Corps, Imperial Japanese Forces, *Significance of Greater East Asia Co-Prosperity Sphere* (Manila, n.d.), 4. See also *America: A Revelation of Her True Character* (Manila, n.d.). Both in AHC.

196 *"morally unassailable"*: Carlos Romulo, "Asia Must Be Free," *Collier's*, October 20, 1945, 11.

196 *"in the past"*: Gerald Horne, *Race War: White Supremacy and the Japanese Attack on the British Empire* (New York, 2004), 36.

197 *"whole native land"*: First Proclamation, January 3, 1942, *Proclamations of the Commander-in-Chief, Japanese Expeditionary Forces* (Manila, 1942), in AHC.

197 *seventeen acts . . . "against the interests"*: Seventh Proclamation, January 14, 1942, in ibid.

197 *"It was as if"*: Eliseo Quirino, *A Day to Remember* (Manila, 1958), 79.

197 *"Every day on my way"*: Marcial P. Lichauco, *"Dear Mother Putnam": A Diary of the War in the Philippines* ([Manila], 1949), 26.

197 *Japan's access*: A fine overview is Jonathan Marshall, *To Have and Have Not: Southeast Asian Raw Materials and the Origins of the Pacific War* (Berkeley, CA, 1995).

198 *"The Japanese swarmed"*: Hartendorp, *Japanese Occupation*, 1:191.

198 *scoured the city*: Quirino, *Day to Remember*, 138–39.

198 *tearing down empty gas stations*: Lichauco, *Mother Putnam*, 158.

198 *Jungle University . . . currency board*: Earl Jude Paul L. Cleope, *Bandit Zone: A History of the Free Areas of Negros Island During the Japanese Occupation, 1942–1945* (Manila, 2002), 64, 79.

198 *repressive techniques*: Quirino, *Day to Remember*, 67; Lichauco, *Mother Putnam*, 120; and Joan Orendain, "Children of War," in *Under Japanese Rule: Memories and Reflections*, ed. Renato Constantino (Quezon City, 1993), 112, 116.

198 *reconcentration zones*: Described in Cleope, *Bandit Zone*. A more common spatial technique was "zonification," in which the Japanese military would lock down an area until everyone in it was screened by informants and declared loyal or not.

199 *half a million*: Reynaldo C. Ileto, "Wars with the U.S. and Japan, and the Politics of History in the Philippines," in *The Philippines and Japan in America's Shadow*, ed. Kiichi Fujiwara and Yoshiko Nagano (Singapore, 2011), 48.

199 *"The applause" . . . "irrepressible satisfaction"*: Antonio M. Molina, *Dusk and Dawn in the Philippines: Memoirs of a Living Witness of World War II* (Quezon City, 1996), 153.

199 *His father had died*: With Japan's encouragement, wartime Filipinos articulated the suppressed trauma of U.S. colonial violence. On this, see Reynaldo C. Ileto, "World War II: Transient and Enduring Legacies for the Philippines," in *Legacies of World War II in South and East Asia*, ed. David Koh Wee Hock (Singapore, 2007), 74–91, and Ileto, "Wars with the U.S. and Japan."

199 *twenty-one-gun salute*: Hartendorp, *Japanese Occupation*, 1:648.

199 *five times as many aircraft*, etc.: Michael H. Hunt and Steven I. Levine, *Arc of Empire: America's Wars in Asia from the Philippines to Vietnam* (Chapel Hill, NC, 2012), 78.

199 *"shoestring equipment"*: Rem., 168.

199 *to little effect*: Manchester, *American Caesar*, 284–86.

199 *"pitifully small"*: George C. Kenney, *The MacArthur I Know* (New York, 1951), 70, 48.

200 *prepared to sacrifice*: Manchester, *American Caesar*, 296.

200 *"pocketed and cut off"*: Rem., 195.

200 *"hit 'em where"*: Ibid., 169.

200 *George H. W. Bush*: James Bradley, *Flyboys: A True Story of Courage* (Boston, 2003).

201 *inclined toward the Taiwan plan*: Robert Ross Smith, *Triumph in the Philippines* (Washington, DC, 1963), part I.

201 *"American territory"* . . . *"undergoing"*: Willoughby and Chamberlain, *MacArthur*, 235–36.

201 *"personal feelings"*: Marshall, quoted in Max Hastings, *Retribution: The Battle for Japan, 1944–1945* (New York, 2008), 27.

201 *"Promises must be kept"*: Manchester, *American Caesar*, 368.

201 *"Douglas, you win"*: John Gunther, *The Riddle of MacArthur: Japan, Korea and the Far East* (New York, 1951), 10.

202 *Hundreds of buildings*: Brendan Coyle, *Kiska: The Japanese Occupation of an Alaska Island* (Fairbanks, 2014), 76–77.

202 *the ensuing battle*: Ibid., 122–23.

202 *"a scale and length"*: Henry I. Shaw, Bernard C. Nalty, and Edwin T. Turnbladh, *History of U.S. Marine Corps Operations in World War II* (Washington, DC, 1966), 3:448.

202 *"The heads lay like"*: Quoted in Robert F. Rogers, *Destiny's Landfall: A History of Guam* (Honolulu, 1995), 192.

203 *four-fifths of the island's homes*: Ibid., 201.

203 *interned thousands*: On this sort of "friendly" internment, which occurred on many Pacific islands, see Lamont Lindstrom and Geoffrey M. White, *Island Encounters: Black and White Memories of the Pacific War* (Washington, DC, 1990), 61.

203 *Japanese army stopped paying*: Teodoro A. Agoncillo, *The Fateful Years: Japan's Adventure in the Philippines, 1941–1945* (Quezon City, 1965), 2:556.

203 *Laurel declared*: Pacita Pestaño-Jacinto, *Living with the Enemy: A Diary of the Japanese Occupation* (Pasig City, 1999), 205.

203 *"a noticeable decrease"*: Lichauco, *Mother Putnam*, 182.

203 *dropping dead in the streets*: Daniel F. Doeppers, *Feeding Manila in Peace and War, 1850–1945* (Madison, WI, 2016), 324–25.

203 *"slapping Filipinos,"* etc.: Claro M. Recto to T. Wachi, June 20, 1944, in *Documents on the Japanese Occupation of the Philippines*, ed. Mauro Garcia (Manila, 1965), 113–14.

203 *Panay*: William Gemperle statement, in General Headquarters, South West Pacific Area, Military Intelligence Section, General Staff, *Report on the Destruction of Manila and Japanese Atrocities*, February 1945, appendix, 13.

203 *"I have returned"*: Rem., 216.

204 *"winging very low"*: Mañalac, *Manila*, 90.

204 *They aimed for anything*: Smith, *Triumph*, 91.

204 *Yamashita's army had already reduced*: Ibid.

204 *Yamashita ordered the army*: The Yamashita/Iwabuchi conflict is described in ibid., part 4, and Alfonso J. Aluit, *By Sword and Fire: The Destruction of Manila in World War II, 3 February–3 March 1945* (Manila, 1994), 372–79.

205 *"We slammed the back door"*: Stanley A. Frankel, *The 37th Infantry Division in World War II* (Washington, DC, 1948), 73.

205 *"the strategic blunder"*: Connaughton et al., *Battle for Manila*, 142.

205 *When Allied troops arrived*: The Battle of Manila is chronicled in numerous diaries and memoirs (many cited here). Three overviews are indispensable: Smith, *Triumph*; Aluit, *Sword and Fire*; and Connaughton et al., *Battle for Manila*.

205 *a captured diary*: Diary of member of Akatsuki 16709 Force, in *Report on the Destruction of Manila*, 35.

206 *"bomb the place"*: Kenney, *MacArthur I Know*, 98.

206 *"friendly"* . . . *"unthinkable"*: Quoted in Smith, *Triumph*, 294.

206 *"use of heavy firepower"* . . . *"This reputation"*: Robert S. Beightler, *Report on the Activities of the 37th Infantry Division, 1940–1945*, quoted in Connaughton et al., *Battle for Manila*, 175.

207 *"alarming"*: Robert S. Beightler, *Report After Action: Operations of the 37th Infantry Division, Luzon P.I., 1 November 1944 to 30 June 1945 (M-1 Operation)*, September 1945, 51, New York Public Library.

207 *"Putting it crudely"* . . . *"To me"*: Beightler, *Report on Activities*, quoted in Connaughton et al., *Battle for Manila*, 175–76.

208 *more than one per second*: Aluit, *Sword and Fire*, 355.

208 *"like lightning bolts"*: Owens, *Eye-Deep in Hell*, 122.

208 *"We made a churned-up pile"*: Beightler, *Report on Activities*, quoted in Connaughton et al., *Battle for Manila*, 176.

208 *"the rule rather"*: XIV Corps, *Japanese Defense of Cities as Exemplified by the Battle for Manila* (Army Chief of Staff, G-2, Headquarters, Sixth Army, July 1, 1945), 20.

208 *"Block after bloody block"*: Frankel, *37th Infantry*, 283.

208 *Philippine General Hospital*: Aluit, *Sword and Fire*, 389; Frankel, *37th Infantry*, 281–83.

208 *"days of terror"* . . . *"I can"*: Miguel P. Avanceña, quoted in Aluit, *Sword and Fire*, 391.

208 *Elpidio Quirino*: The following is derived, except where noted, from two survivors' accounts: Tommy Quirino's in ibid., 217–301 passim, and Vicky Quirino's in Connaughton et al., *Battle for Manila*, 133–38.

208 *"darkest hour"*: Elpidio Quirino, "Oration on President Quezon," in *The Quirino Way: Collection of Speeches and Addresses of Elpidio Quirino*, ed. Juan Collas ([Philippines], 1955), 23.

209 *Dody, who had sought*: Sol H. Gwekoh, *Elpidio Quirino: The Barrio School Teacher Who Became President*, 2d ed. (Manila, 1950), 85–86.

209 *"If you escaped"*: Elpidio Quirino, "The Sad Plight of the Philippines," November 14, 1945, in *Quirino: Selected Speeches*, ed. Carlos R. Lazo (Manila, 1953), 15.

210 *A woman who saw him*: Kiyoshi Osawa, *A Japanese in the Philippines*, trans. Tsunesuke Kawashima (Tokyo, 1981), 195.

210 *Arellano's Legislative Building*: Smith, *Triumph*, 303–304; Frankel, *37th Infantry*, 293–94.

210 *sixth-largest city*: Manila contained 623,492 people in 1939, according to the census. But by the war's end it had roughly 1 million. Aluit, *Sword and Fire*, 398.

210 *"The largest buildings"* . . . *"This seemed"*: Hartendorp, *Japanese Occupation*, 2:604–605.

211 *In the month of fighting*: Fatality figures from Connaughton et al., *Battle for Manila*, 174.

211 *extrapolated from figures*: Aluit, *Sword and Fire*, 398–99.

211 *"The whole city"*: Jose P. Laurel, *War Memoirs* (Manila, 1962), 35.

211 *Those planes dropped*: Beightler, *Report After Action*, 118.

211 *"We levelled entire cities,"* etc.: Paul V. McNutt, address at Beta Theta Pi Fraternity, November 27, 1946, "McNutt, P. V., Correspondence and Speeches, 1945–46" folder, box 7, HC–DC.

212 *Senator Millard Tydings surveyed*: Millard Tydings, "Report on the Philippine Islands," June 7, 1945, 22, "Philippine Rehabilitation Commission" folder, box 2, ser. 4, Tydings Papers.

212 *1,111,938 war deaths*: Reported in "Our Bid for Survival," 1947, in Collas, *Quirino Way*, 51, and Joaquin M. Elizalde, "The Case for the Prompt Ratification of the Japanese Peace Treaty," 1952, 5, in AHC.

212 *Add Japanese*: Miki Ishikida, *Toward Peace: War Responsibility, Postwar Compensation, and Peace Movements and Education in Japan* (New York, 2005), 12.

212 *mainlander fatalities*: 10,640 dead (not counting the Leyte and Samar campaigns) according to Smith, *Triumph*, 652.

212 *"How'd ya learn,"* etc.: Oscar S. Villadolid, *Born in Freedom: My Life and Times* (Quezon City, 2004), 191. Similar stories discussed in Daniel Immerwahr, "'American Lives': Pearl Harbor and the United States' Empire," in *Pearl Harbor and the Attacks of December 8, 1941: A Pacific History*, ed. Beth Bailey and David Farber (Lawrence, KS, forthcoming).

13. KILROY WAS HERE

215 *fewer than one in ten*: James T. Sparrow, *Warfare State: World War II Americans and the Age of Big Government* (New York, 2011), 202.

215 *"first and foremost"*: Neal Stephenson, *Cryptonomicon* (New York, 1999), 548.

216 *nearly every independent nation*: Richard M. Leighton and Robert W. Coakley, *Global Logistics and Strategy, 1940–1943* (Washington, DC, 1955), 39.

216 *"disintegration of the British commonwealth"*: Quoted in ibid., 48. The mechanics of aid to Britain in Egypt are described in Edward R. Stettinius Jr., *Lend-Lease: Weapon for Victory* (New York, 1944), chaps. 12–13 and 26; Ivan Dmitri, *Flight to Everywhere* (New York, 1944); and Hugh B. Cave, *Wings Across the World: The Story of the Air Transport Command* (New York, 1945), part 3.

217 *"I have seen many"*: Max Hastings, *Inferno: The World at War, 1939–1945* (New York, 2011), 361.

217 *"It marked in fact,"* etc.: Winston S. Churchill, *The Second World War* (1950; Boston, 1985), 4:541.

217 *"tremendous supply base"*: Stettinius, *Lend-Lease*, 288.

217 *Factories in Palestine*, etc.: Ibid., 294.

218 *"probably more far-reaching"*: John G. Winant, quoted in Steven High, *Base Colonies in the Western Hemisphere, 1940–1967* (New York, 2009), 6.

218 *"Nothing is more"*: Rexford Guy Tugwell, *The Stricken Land: The Story of Puerto Rico* (Garden City, NY, 1946), 113.

218 *expected that they'd fall*: Annette Palmer, "Rum and Coca Cola: The United States in the British Caribbean, 1940–1945," *The Americas* 43 (1987): 441–43; John Gunther, *Inside Latin America* (New York, 1941), 420.

218 *The Soviet Union, alone*: Kenneth S. Coates and William R. Morrison, "The American Rampant: Reflections on the Impact of United States Troops in Allied Countries During World War II," *Journal of World History* 2 (1991): 217. Stalin did allow some exceptions: three bases in Ukraine toward the end of the war and two navy-manned weather stations near the Japanese frontier. See Alexandra Richie, *Warsaw 1944: Hitler, Himmler, and the Warsaw Uprising* (New York, 2013), 538–40.

219 *Nukufetau, etc.*: A full list of Seabee locations is in William Bradford Huie, *From Omaha to Okinawa: The Story of the Seabees* (1945; Annapolis, MD, 1999), appendix.

219 *"what happens in Africa"*: Henry Cabot Lodge, quoted in "Colony Plan Stirs Senate," *NYT*, February 1, 1919.

219 *thirty thousand installations on two thousand*: James R. Blaker, *United States Overseas Basing: An Anatomy of the Dilemma* (New York, 1990), 33.

220 *"Almost anywhere,"* etc.: Cave, *Wings*, i.

220 *Presidents, too, began to*: "Travels Abroad of the President," Office of the Historian, U.S. State Department, history.state.gov/departmenthistory/travels/president.

221 *"Because of the ethnic distribution"*: Security Technical Committee Minutes 7, February 3, 1943, Records of the Advisory Committee on Post-War Foreign Policy, 1942–45, Box 79, Notter Records. The sudden onset of U.S. planetary interests is discussed helpfully in Andrew Preston, "Monsters Everywhere: A Genealogy of National Security," *DH* 38 (2014): 477–500; John A. Thompson, *A Sense of Power: The Roots of America's Global Role* (Ithaca, NY, 2014); and Stephen Wertheim, "Tomorrow the World: The Birth of U.S. Global Supremacy in World War II" (Ph.D. diss., Columbia University, 2015).

221 *"a mental hazard"*: "Maps: Global War Teaches Global Cartography," *Life*, August 3, 1942, 57–65.

221 *"Dymaxion map"*: "R. Buckminster Fuller's Dymaxion World," *Life*, March 1, 1943, 41–55.

221 *Richard Edes Harrison*: Alan K. Henrikson, "The Map as an 'Idea': The Role of Cartographic Imagery During the Second World War," *The American Cartographer* 2 (1975): 19–53; Susan Schulten, "Richard Edes Harrison and the Challenge to American Cartography," *Imago Mundi: The International Journal for the History of Cartography* 50 (1998): 174–88; Susan Schulten, *The Geographical Imagination in America, 1880–1950* (Chicago, 2001), chap. 9; and William Rankin, *After the Map: Cartography, Navigation, and the Transformation of Territory in the Twentieth Century* (Chicago, 2016), chap. 2.

222 *Goebbels waved*: Henrikson, "Map as 'Idea,'" 37–38.

222 *United Nations logo*: Donal McLaughlin, *Origin of the Emblem and Other Recollections of the 1945 U.N. Conference* (Garrett Park, MD, 1995).

222 *"Never before have persons"*: Wayne Whittaker, "Maps for the Air Age," *Popular Mechanics*, January 1943, 162.

223 *"round earth,"* etc.: Archibald MacLeish, "The Image of Victory," *Atlantic Monthly*, July 1942, 5.

223 global . . . globalist, globalism, *and the pejorative* globaloney: On initial usages, see *Oxford English Dictionary Online*, Oxford University Press. On frequency, see Google Books Ngrams Viewer, books.google.com/ngrams.

223 *"a global war"*: Franklin Delano Roosevelt, Fireside Chat, September 7, 1942, APP. Past presidential speech searched at *APP*.

224 *"Just as truly"*: John Hersey, *A Bell for Adano* (New York, 1944), vii.

224 *"There is not a single"*: C. D. Jackson, quoted in Lynne Olson, *Citizens of London: The Americans Who Stood with Britain in Its Darkest, Finest Hour* (New York, 2010), 272.

224 *1.65 million U.S. servicemen swarming*: A very good overview is Coates and Morrison, "American Rampant."

225 *"absolute control"*: *Rem.*, 180.

225 *"Never before"*: William J. Sebald, quoted in William Manchester, *American Caesar: Douglas MacArthur, 1880–1964* (Boston, 1978), 470.

225 *looked for inspiration*: *Rem.*, 282.

225 *"Parts of Tokyo"*: John Gunther, *The Riddle of MacArthur: Japan, Korea and the Far East* (New York, 1951), 84.

225 *"the world's greatest"*: *Rem.*, 282.

225 *Public health authorities*: Gunther, *Riddle of MacArthur*, 138–39.

225 *"We the Japanese people,"* etc.: Constitution of Japan, 1946, preamble and article 13.

225 *Sirota*: John W. Dower, *Embracing Defeat: Japan in the Wake of World War II* (New York, 1999), chap. 12.

226 *"summit of the world"*: "Final Review of the War," August 16, 1945, in Winston S. Churchill, *His Complete Speeches, 1897–1963*, ed. Robert Rhodes James (New York, 1974), 7:7211.

226 *"the most powerful"*: Radio Report to the American People on the Potsdam Conference, August 9, 1945, APP.

226 *135 million*: Hajo Holborn put the number "under the control of American military government" at 150 million, but I have been unable to reproduce his calculations (*American Military Government: Its Organizations and Policies* [Washington, DC, 1947], xi). My own accounting, which covers all the colonies plus Japan, Micronesia, and the U.S. sectors of Germany, Austria, and Korea, is in "The Greater United States: Territory and Empire in U.S. History," *DH* 40 (2016): 388. It doesn't include the transitory stationing of U.S. troops under the banner of "liberation," as in France, or the very short occupations, such as that of parts of Czechoslovakia for months in 1945, listed in Susan L. Carruthers, *The Good Occupation: American Soldiers and the Hazards of Peace* (Cambridge, MA, 2016), 6–7.

14. DECOLONIZING THE UNITED STATES

227 *"plenty of space"*: Press release, Interior Department, March 23, 1946; "Mts.—Seals & Flags" folder; box 70; 9-0-2, Office of Territories Classified Files, 1907–1951; ROT. See rest of folder for other flag proposals.

227 *Gruening and his wife*: Ernest Gruening, *Many Battles: The Autobiography of Ernest Gruening* (New York, 1973), 371.

228 *There were excited murmurs*: Michio Kitahara, *Children of the Sun: The Japanese and the Outside World* (New York, 1989), 95; William Manchester, *American Caesar: Douglas MacArthur, 1880–1964* (Boston, 1978), 474.

228 *Philippine statehood*: Hernando J. Abaya, *Betrayal in the Philippines* (New York, 1946), 171–79; "Philippine Statehood" folder, box 17, HC–DC; "Statehood for P.I.," *Manila Evening News*, January 26, 1946; Gladstone Williams, "What to Do Now with the Philippines?" *Atlanta Constitution*, February 28, 1945; and "World Fronts," *Amsterdam News*, March 3, 1945.

228 *proposed adding Iceland*: Proposal by Rep. Bud Gearhardt, discussed in "The Ramparts of the North," *New York Journal-American*, July 21, 1945.

228 *"State of the American Pacific"*: CDA 315, "A Study of Pacific Bases: A Report by the Subcommittee, House of Representatives," August 22, 1945, 21, Notter Records, box 126.

229 *"an imperial power"*: Quoted in Julian Go, *Patterns of Empire: The British and American Empires, 1688 to the Present* (New York, 2011), 103. See also 117–23 for a survey of U.S. territorial ambitions at the end of the Second World War.

229 *"From the point of view"* . . . *"The question"*: Albert Viton, *American Empire in Asia?* (New York, 1943), 286–87. On public expressions of annexationism during the war, see William G. Carleton, "The Dawn of a New Day," *Vital Speeches of the Day*, December 1, 1943, 117–25.

229 *fourth-largest empire*: Dismantling Japan's empire bumped the United States up in the ranks to the world's fourth-largest empire by population.

229 *manufacturing production*: Paul Kennedy, *The Rise and Fall of the Great Powers: Economic Change and Military Conflict from 1500 to 2000* (1987; New York, 1989), 358.

230 *area smaller than Connecticut*: Daniel Immerwahr, "The Greater United States: Territory and Empire in U.S. History," *DH* 40 (2016): 389–90.

230 *one out of every three . . . one in fifty*: 1940: 31.10 percent; 1965: 2.18 percent. Calculated from MPD. This count is of annexed colonies, not satellites (e.g., East Germany under the Soviet Union) or occupied countries (e.g., Japan under MacArthur).

230 *"Today, freedom,"* etc.: Rem., 276.

231 *"But when they do"*: Langston Hughes, "Colored Lived There Once," *Chicago Defender*, January 27, 1945.

231 *"The bearing"* . . . *"Now"*: Luis Taruc, *Born of the People* (New York, 1953), 64–65.

231 *"From one end"*: Harold R. Isaacs, *No Peace for Asia* (New York, 1947), 1.

231 *"an enormous pot"*: Albert C. Wedemeyer, quoted in Ronald H. Spector, *In the Ruins of Empire: The Japanese Surrender and the Battle for Postwar Asia* (New York, 2007), 21. See also Christopher Bayly and Tim Harper, *Forgotten Wars: Freedom and Revolution in Southeast Asia* (Cambridge, MA, 2007). The notion of a "Malayan Spring," from which I have extrapolated a more general "Asian Spring," is discussed in Harper's *The End of Empire and the Making of Malaya* (New York, 1999), chap. 2.

232 *twenty thousand peasants*: Described in Abaya, *Betrayal*, 125–30. A figure of thirty-five thousand is given in "GIs Fear Plan to Use Them Against Filipinos," *Daily Worker*, January 9, 1946.

232 *"We are now,"* etc.: *General Marshall's Report: The Winning of the War in Europe and the Pacific* (New York, 1945), 118.

232 *War Department announced*: John C. Sparrow, *History of Personnel Demobilization in the United States Army* (Washington, DC, 1952), 141.

232 *On a single day*: Steven Kalgaard Ashby, "Shattered Dreams: The American Working Class and the Origins of the Cold War, 1945–1949" (Ph.D. diss., University of Chicago, 1993), 130.

232 *"At the rate"* . . . *"in a very"*: Truman to John Folger, November 16, 1945, quoted in David R. B. Ross, *Preparing for Ulysses: Politics and Veterans During World War II* (New York, 1969), 187.

232 *"disintegration"* . . . *"dangerous speed"*: Harry S. Truman, *Memoirs* (Garden City, NY, 1955), 1:509.

232 *"Let us leave"* . . . *"The Filipinos"*: Abaya, *Betrayal*, 135, 148.

232 *letter of support*: Ashby, "Shattered Dreams," 143.

233 *passed a resolution*: Erwin Marquit, "The Demobilization Movement of January 1946," *Nature, Society, and Thought* 15 (2002): 24–25.

233 *"vast new tasks"*: "Styler Gives Talk on Redeployment," *Daily Pacifican*, January 8, 1946.

233 *booed and catcalled*: "20,000 Attend Orderly Meeting," *Daily Pacifican*, January 8, 1946.

233 *Honolulu . . . Korea . . . Calcutta*: Ashby, "Shattered Dreams," 138.

233 *Guam*: Sparrow, *Personnel Demobilization*, 163; Ashby, "Shattered Dreams," 138.

233 *"What kind,"* etc.: William D. Simpkins, letter, *Daily Pacifican*, November 15, 1945.

233 *"in the Oriental surge"*: Robert B. Pearsall, letter, *Daily Pacifican*, November 30, 1945.

234 *"disgusted with,"* etc.: Daniel Eugene Garcia, "Class and Brass: Demobilization, Working Class Politics, and American Foreign Policy Between World War and Cold War," *DH* 34 (2010): 694–95.

234 *"plain mutiny"*: Ashby, "Shattered Dreams," 170–71.

234 *under the Articles of War*: *The Articles of War, Approved June 4, 1920*, articles 66 and 67.

234 *"You men forget"*: R. Alton Lee, "The Army 'Mutiny' of 1946," *Journal of American History* 53 (1966): 562.

234 *"acute homesickness"* . . . *"not inherently"*: MacArthur, quoted in Sparrow, *Personnel Demobilization*, 322.

234 *"a clock"*: Rexford Guy Tugwell, *The Stricken Land: The Story of Puerto Rico* (Garden City, NY, 1946), v.

234 *"our influence"*: Truman, *Memoirs*, 2:91.

234 *sixth largest*: Terry H. Anderson, *The United States, Great Britain, and the Cold War, 1944–1947* (Columbia, MO, 1981), 152.

235 *take over the bonds*: The history of the Philippine bonded debt to the United States is detailed in Manuel Roxas, address, January 26, 1948, in "Territories Committee, Philippine Islands" folder, box 5, ser. 4, Tydings Papers.

235 *"food crisis"*: Press release, April 22, 1946, "Pub. Relations Press Releases, 1946, Pt. B" folder, box 11, HC–Manila.

235 *"provide adequately"*: "Doc. B.," 1940, enclosed in E. D. Hester to Frank P. Lockhart, November 13, 1944, "Emergency Proclamation" folder, box 1, HC–Pol/Econ.

235 *"the death or capture"*: "Doc. A," November 13, 1944, enclosed in ibid.

235 *"acceptable or legitimate"*: E. D. Hester to Frank P. Lockhart, January 12, 1945, "Emergency Proclamation" folder, box 1, HC–Pol/Econ.

236 *"There is little doubt"*: E. D. Hester to Richard R. Ely, July 3, 1945, "Hester, E. D." folder, box 2, HC–Pol/Econ.

236 *"This situation,"* etc.: "McNutt Raises Question of P.I. Readiness for Freedom July 4th," *Manila Evening News*, January 23, 1946.

236 *"All Asia"*: Paul V. McNutt, Report on the Philippines," 1945, 14, "McNutt, P. V., Correspondence and Speeches, 1945–46" folder, box 7, HC–DC.

236 *"attracted the wonder"* . . . *"to betray"*: Paul V. McNutt, "The Filipinos Are Our Friends," *Manila Evening News,* January 26, 1946.

236 *"This is the first instance,"* etc.: Harry S. Truman to Kenneth McKellar, April 3, 1946, "Independence, Ceremonies, 1946" folder, box 4, HC–DC.

237 *"undoubtedly seriously involved"*: Paul Steintorf to James F. Byrnes, September 19, 1945; "Collaboration" folder, box 1, HC–Pol/Econ.

237 *"Roxas is no,"* etc.: Douglas MacArthur, quoted in press release from the Office of the Commanding General, Army Forces of the Pacific, May 9, 1946; "Pub. Relations Press Releases, 1946, Pt. A" folder, box 11, HC–Manila.

237 *"Not a single senator"*: Abaya, *Betrayal,* 92.

237 *109 guerrillas*: Benedict J. Kerkvliet, *The Huk Rebellion: A Study of Peasant Revolt in the Philippines* (Berkeley, CA, 1977).

237 *"We are a troubled"*: *Manila Evening News,* July 4, 1946.

237 *specially sewn*: Press release, May 31, 1946; "Pub. Relations Press Releases, 1946, Pt. A" folder, box 11, HC–Manila.

238 *"America has buried"*: Quoted in Go, *Patterns of Empire,* 105.

238 *Hawai'i and Alaska*: The most thorough account of Hawai'i/Alaska statehood is John S. Whitehead, *Completing the Union: Alaska, Hawai'i, and the Battle for Statehood* (Albuquerque, NM, 2004). In what follows, I have relied on research connecting statehood to decolonization, namely Robert David Johnson, *Ernest Gruening and the American Dissenting Tradition* (Cambridge, MA, 1998); Gretchen Heefner, "'A Symbol of the New Frontier': Hawaiian Statehood, Anti-Colonialism, and Winning the Cold War," *Pacific Historical Review* 74 (2005): 545–74; Sarah Miller-Davenport, "State of the New: Hawai'i Statehood and Global Decolonization in American Culture, 1945–1978" (Ph.D. diss., University of Chicago, 2014); Robert David Johnson, "Alaska, Hawai'i, and the United States as a Pacific Nation," in his *Asia Pacific in the Age of Globalization* (New York, 2015), 162–71; and A. G. Hopkins, *American Empire: A Global History* (Princeton, NJ, 2018), chap. 14.

238 *"mark the beginning"*: Butler to Julius A. Krug, March 7, 1947, "Citizens' Statehood Committee, 1947–51" folder, Governor's Files, GOV9-3, HSA.

239 *"We do not want,"* etc.: "Hawaii Can Wait," *Worcester Telegram,* March 1947, in "Editors—Opposition to Statehood" folder, box 4, Hawaiian Statehood Commission Records, COM18, HSA.

239 *"Can America lead"*: Ernest Gruening, "Alaska Statehood Delay Invites Red Attack," *San Francisco Examiner,* March 9, 1950.

239 *"How can we fervently"*: Gruening to Sam Wilder King, c. 1952–1954, folder 226, box 59, Gruening Papers.

239 *"shout about 'colonialism'"*: Quoted in Johnson, *Gruening,* 191.

239 *"Boston tea party"*: Gruening to King, c. 1952–1954, folder 226, box 59, Gruening Papers.

239 *Alaska Is a Colony*: Held in folder 316, box 754, Gruening Papers.

239 *"These are troubled,"* etc.: Truman to Joseph C. O'Mahoney, May 5, 1950, APP.

239 *"tremendous psychological,"* etc.: Truman, Letter to the President of the Senate on Statehood for Hawaii and Alaska, November 27, 1950, APP.

240 *"impassible difference,"* etc.: Quoted in Heefner, "Symbol," 546.

15. NOBODY KNOWS IN AMERICA, PUERTO RICO'S IN AMERICA

242 *didn't speak a word . . . Costa Rica*: Wenzell Brown, *Dynamite on Our Doorstep: Puerto Rican Paradox* (New York, 1945), 32, 6.

242 *"complete madness" . . . "berserk" . . . "One cannot"*: Ibid., 71, 90, 193.

243 *feared that mainland doctors*: Ibid., 79.

243 *"intense, fanatical nationalism"*: Ibid., 201.

243 *"paralyzing jolt"*: John Gunther, *Inside Latin America* (New York, 1941), 423.

243 *"cesspool" . . . "unsolvable"*: "Puerto Rico: Senate Investigating Committee Finds It an Unsolvable Problem," *Life*, March 8, 1943.

243 *"would have revolted"*: Rexford Guy Tugwell, *The Stricken Land: The Story of Puerto Rico* (Garden City, NY, 1946), 126.

244 *only ten employees*: James P. Davis, "Statement of the Director of Territories and Island Possessions, Department of the Interior, Before the Senate Committee on Interior and Insular Affairs," January 10, 1949; "Comm. on Interior & Insular Affairs" folder; box 28; Office of Territories Classified Files, 1907–1950; 9-0-1 Administrative, Committees, Interior; ROT.

244 *"the most important"*: Gunther, *Inside Latin America*, 427.

244 *"full, flexible" . . . Muñoz Marín joked*: Tugwell, *Stricken Land*, 10.

244 *Muñoz Marín invited*: Luis Muñoz Marín, *Memorias: Autobiografía pública, 1898– 1940* (San Juan, 1982), 1:63.

245 *vote for Albizu*: Ibid., 76–77.

245 *"weapon of imperial vengeance"*: Ibid., 150.

245 *"all hope of life"*: Luis Muñoz Marín, "Alerta a la conciencia puertorriqueña," *El Mundo*, February 10, 1946.

245 *"emotional confusion" . . . "wanting"*: Luis Muñoz Marín, Speech at Baranquitas, July 17, 1951, in Kal Wagenheim and Olga Jiménez de Wagenheim, *The Puerto Ricans: A Documentary History* (Princeton, NJ, 2013), 219.

245 *Muñoz Marín's party received*: César J. Ayala and Rafael Bernabe, *Puerto Rico in the American Century: A History Since 1898* (Chapel Hill, NC, 2007), 153.

245 *"the biggest and"*: Luis Muñoz Marín, "Nuevos caminos hacia viejos objectivos," *El Mundo*, June 28, 1946.

246 *"Two million people"*: "Tugwell Assails Lack of Policy for Puerto Rico," *New York Herald Tribune*, September 17, 1943.

246 *"kept shooting children"*: Earl Parker Hanson, *Transformation: The Story of Modern Puerto Rico* (New York, 1955), 61.

246 *"If the United States were"*: C. Wright Mills, Clarence Senior, and Rose Kohn Goldsen, *The Puerto Rican Journey: New York's Newest Migrants* (New York, 1950), 3.

247 *"I believe that" . . . "Malthusian"*: "El partido socialista—dice Muñoz Marín—es sencillamente un partido de gente pobre," *El Mundo*, June 27, 1923. Two illuminating accounts of the politics of birth control in Puerto Rico are Annette B. Ramírez de Arellano and Conrad Seipp, *Colonialism, Catholicism, and Contraception* (Chapel Hill, NC, 1983), and Laura Briggs, *Reproducing Empire: Race, Sex, Science, and U.S. Imperialism in Puerto Rico* (Berkeley, CA, 2002). I draw on both heavily in this chapter.

247 *Herbert Hoover*: Herbert Hoover, *Memoirs* (New York, 1952), 2:359.

247 *Franklin Delano Roosevelt*: Tugwell, *Stricken Land*, 35–36.

247 *"only hope"*: Quoted in Ramírez de Arellano and Seipp, *Colonialism, Catholicism, and Contraception*, 46.

247 under*populated*: Muñoz Marín, *Memorias, 1898–1940*, 1:152.
247 *"invade the very insides"*: Irene Vilar, *The Ladies' Gallery: A Memoir of Family Secrets*, trans. Gregory Rabassa (1996; New York, 2009), 45.
247 *Whereas most states*: Ramírez de Arellano and Seipp, *Colonialism, Catholicism, and Contraception*, 108–109.
248 *Pincus*: Detailed accounts of Pincus and the pill are James Reed, *From Private Vice to Public Virtue: The Birth Control Movement and American Society Since 1830* (New York, 1978), part 7, and Margaret Marsh and Wanda Ronner, *The Fertility Doctor: John Rock and the Reproductive Revolution* (Baltimore, 2008), chaps. 6–7.
248 RABBIT WITHOUT: "Rabbit Without Parents Amazes Men of Science," *Chicago Daily Tribune*, November 2, 1939.
248 *"population explosion"*: Gregory Pincus, *The Control of Fertility* (New York, 1965), 6.
248 *"eighty frustrated"*: Rock, quoted in Marsh and Ronner, *Fertility Doctor*, 154. Pincus's team would also try hormonal contraceptives on a small group of psychotic women at the Worcester State Hospital before launching the Río Piedras study.
248 *"How can we get"*: Reed, *From Private Vice*, 358.
249 *team considered tests*: Lara V. Marks, *Sexual Chemistry: A History of the Contraceptive Pill* (New Haven, CT, 2001), 98; Marsh and Ronner, *Fertility Doctor*, 170.
249 *"certain experiments"*: Pincus to McCormick, March 4, 1954, quoted in Bernard Asbell, *The Pill: A Biography of the Drug That Changed the World* (New York, 1995), 116.
249 *The first experiment*: Ramírez de Arellano and Seipp, *Colonialism, Catholicism, and Contraception*, 110.
249 *"too many side"*: Edris Rice-Wray, quoted in Marsh and Ronner, *Fertility Doctor*, 195.
249 *"emotional super-activity"*: Ramírez de Arellano and Seipp, *Colonialism, Catholicism, and Contraception*, 116.
249 *"whatever you call"*: Adaline Satterthwaite, quoted in ibid., 118.
249 *all sorts of experimental contraceptives*: Briggs, *Reproducing Empire*, 124.
250 *"one of the most,"* etc.: Reuben Hill, J. Mayone Stycos, and Kurt W. Back, *The Family and Population Control: A Puerto Rican Experiment in Social Change* (Chapel Hill, NC, 1959), 116, 169, 174.
250 *18 percent of all hospital deliveries*: J. Mayone Stycos, "Female Sterilization in Puerto Rico," *Eugenics Quarterly* 1 (1954): 4.
250 *No governmental program*: Hill et al., *Family and Population Control*, 180.
250 *fourth delivery*: Briggs, *Reproducing Empire*, 157.
250 *informed consent*: A case for the sterilizations as nonconsensual is Bonnie Mass, "Puerto Rico: A Case Study of Population Control," *Latin American Perspectives* 4 (1977): 66–81. A thoughtful and strongly cautionary view, finding "no evidence" of a campaign to coerce women, is Laura Briggs, "Discourses of 'Forced Sterilization' in Puerto Rico: The Problem with the Speaking Subaltern," *Differences* 10 (1998): 30–66.
250 *"The only way"*: Iris Lopez, *Matters of Choice: Puerto Rican Women's Struggle for Reproductive Freedom* (New Brunswick, NJ, 2008), 7–8.
250 *nearly* half: 46.7 percent. Harriet B. Presser, *Sterilization and Fertility Decline in Puerto Rico* (Berkeley, CA, 1973), 61–66. For a review of other studies that corroborate Presser's figures, see Mass, "Case Study," 72.
251 *anywhere else in the world*: Presser, *Sterilization and Fertility*, chap. 10. The India figure counts sterilizations per 100 married women, but many of India's steriliza-

tions were vasectomies, making Puerto Rico's high rate of sterilized *women* still more striking.

251 *"a brilliantly successful"*: Robert Coughlan, "World Birth Control Challenge," *Life*, November 23, 1959, 170.

251 *leave the island*: Especially helpful accounts are Jorge Duany, *The Puerto Rican Nation on the Move: Identities on the Island and in the United States* (Chapel Hill, NC, 2002), and Eileen J. Suárez Findlay, *We Are Left Without a Father Here: Masculinity, Domesticity, and Migration in Postwar Puerto Rico* (Durham, NC, 2014).

251 *training program for women*: Findlay, *Left Without a Father*, 76–77.

251 *59 percent*: Mills et al., *Puerto Rican Journey*, 88.

251 *one in seven*: Findlay, *Left Without a Father*, 93.

251 *one in four*: Clarence Senior's figures, reported in Elena Padilla, *Up from Puerto Rico* (New York, 1958), 21.

252 *several thousand people . . . Forty cadets*: A. C. Schlenker to J. Edgar Hoover, December 23, 1947, in Albizu FBI File, section 5, box 2.

252 *"puppet" . . . "high priest" . . . "revolution"*: Quoted in A. W. Maldonado, *Luis Muñoz Marín: Puerto Rico's Democratic Revolution* (San Juan, 2006), 299.

252 *"We have to revert"*: Albizu's speech reported in Schlenker to Hoover, December 23, 1947, and in Jack West, report on Pedro Albizu Campos, May 4, 1948, 22, both in Albizu FBI File, section 5, box 2.

252 *"The United States tells" . . . "The surgeon"*: Speech at Arecibo, March 15, 1948, in West, report on Albizu, May 4, 1948, 45.

252 *"ten years behind"*: Quoted in Schlenker to Hoover, December 23, 1947.

253 *"far beyond"*: ACLU statement, quoted in Ruth M. Reynolds, *Campus in Bondage: A 1948 Microcosm of Puerto Rico in Bondage* (New York, 1989), 198.

253 *The police*: Ivonne Acosta, *La mordaza: Puerto Rico, 1948–1957* (Río Piedras, 1989), 107.

253 *growing migratory stream*: The tension between migration and independence is explored with great acuity in Duany, *Nation on the Move*.

253 *moment for action*: Calculations behind the timing are discussed in Olga Jiménez de Wagenheim, *Nationalist Heroines: Puerto Rican Women History Forgot, 1930s–1950s* (Princeton, NJ, 2017), 26–27.

253 *"hour of immortality"*: June 11, 1950, speech at Manati, reported in Robert E. Thornton, report on Pedro Albizu Campos, May 22, 1951, Albizu FBI File, section 9, box 2.

253 *That hour struck*: On the 1950 Uprising, I've relied on Miñi Seijo Bruno, *La insurrección nacionalista en Puerto Rico, 1950* (Río Piedras, 1997), and Jiménez de Wagenheim, *Nationalist Heroines*.

254 *bullet through the window . . . hit the floor . . . daughters cowered*: Luis Muñoz Marín, *Memorias: Autobiografía pública, 1940–1952* (San German, PR, 1992), 2:238.

254 *"What is known"*: Stephen Hunter and John Bainbridge Jr., *American Gunfight: The Plot to Kill Harry Truman—and the Shoot-Out That Stopped It* (New York, 2005), 242.

255 *drastically increased its security*: Ibid., 317.

255 *"shooting scrape"*: Drew Pearson, "'Shooting Scrape' Upset Truman," *Washington Post*, April 13, 1952.

255 *"one of those mad"*: "Uprising in Puerto Rico," *NYT*, November 1, 1950.

255 *"news of a day"*: Paul Harbrecht, "Puerto Rico: Operation Bootstrap," *America*, December 9, 1950, 301.

256 *lost its farm*: Robert J. Donovan, *The Assassins* (New York, 1955), 174.

256 *"tried to bring about"*: Quoted in Benjamin Bradlee, "Planned Riot Demonstration, Collazo Says," *Washington Post*, March 6, 1951.

256 *stuck in his mind*: Donovan, *Assassins*, 177.

256 *"How little"* . . . *"They don't know"*: Ibid., 173.

256 *"lawless lunatics"*: Quoted in Jiménez de Wagenheim, *Nationalist Heroines*, 263.

256 *police rounded up*: Acosta, *La mordaza*, 119.

256 *One officer testified*: Officer Melendez, testimony in William B. Holloman, report on Pedro Albizu Campos, January 31, 1955, Albizu FBI File, section 14, box 2. Carmen María Pérez González, one of Albizu's comrades, also claimed that Albizu fired guns (Jiménez de Wagenheim, *Nationalist Heroines*, 109).

256 *"looked like a cheese grater"*: Seijo Bruno, *La insurrección nacionalista*, 170.

256 *cleared the island*: Documented in Acosta, *La mordaza*, 120.

256 *two-day registration*: Maldonado, *Muñoz Marín*, 305.

257 *United Nations*: The UN decision to remove Puerto Rico from the list of colonies was contested at the time, and later, the Decolonization Committee proposed reconsidering the case of Puerto Rico and the General Assembly agreed. Excellent guides to the complex politics of the constitution and of the UN are José Trías Monge, *Puerto Rico: The Trials of the Oldest Colony in the World* (New Haven, CT, 1997), chaps. 10–12, and Ayala and Bernabe, *Puerto Rico*, chap. 8.

257 *"butterfly"*: Muñoz Marín, *Memorias, 1940–1952*, 2:383.

257 *"no-nation"* . . . *"somewhat shapeless"*: Vilar, *Ladies' Gallery*, 72.

257 *"defies duplication"*: Chester Bowles, foreword to Hanson, *Transformation*, x.

257 *Operation Bootstrap*: Overview in James L. Dietz, *Economic History of Puerto Rico: Institutional Change and Capitalist Development* (Princeton, NJ, 1986), chaps. 4–5.

258 *"one of the few"*: "Thank Heaven for Puerto Rico," *Life*, March 15, 1954, 24.

258 *"all traces"*: Muñoz Marín to Truman, April 9, 1952, quoted in Maldonado, *Muñoz Marín*, 317.

258 *"almost unrestricted"*: Trías Monge, *Puerto Rico*, 3.

258 *"the wildest scene"*: Joe Martin, *My First Fifty Years in Politics* (New York, 1960), 217. For a detailed chronicle based on interviews with two shooters, see Manuel Roig-Franzia, "A Terrorist in the House," *Washington Post*, February 22, 2004.

258 *fifty-fifty*: "Fanatics Shoot Five in Congress," *Los Angeles Times*, March 2, 1954.

258 *never really the same*: Paul Kanjorski, views reported in Roig-Franzia, "Terrorist."

258 *jagged bullet hole*: Thanks to Jennifer Blancato at the Architect of the Capitol for confirming this.

258 *"sublime heroism"*: Quoted in Peter Kihss, "San Juan Studies Rebel Chief's Act," *NYT*, March 4, 1954. On who gave the orders, see Jiménez de Wagenheim, *Nationalist Heroines*, 252.

259 *fired on the police*: Discussion of Albizu's role in the violence in Jiménez de Wagenheim, *Nationalist Heroines*, 174.

259 *"I am choked"*: Peter Kihss, "Terrorists' Chief Held in San Juan After Gun Battle," *NYT*, March 7, 1954.

259 *"poisonous wave,"* etc.: Albizu to Nieves Tarrido, June 3, 1951, in Albizu FBI File, section 10, box 2.

259 *"We live"*: Ibid. Albizu's followers reported similar experiences when imprisoned or under government surveillance. They saw colored rays, heard electronic voices, and felt electric shocks and radiation waves. A helpful discussion is Andrea Friedman,

Citizenship in Cold War America: National Security State and the Possibilities of Dissent (Amherst, MA, 2014), chap. 4.

259 *"about as lunatic"*: "Aftermath in Puerto Rico," *NYT*, March 7, 1954.

260 *they misbehaved less*: Clarence Senior, *The Puerto Ricans: Strangers—Then Neighbors* (Chicago, 1965), 51–52.

260 West Side Story: Useful accounts are Frances Negrón-Muntaner, "Feeling Pretty: *West Side Story* and Puerto Rican Identity Discourses," *Social Text* 18 (2000): 83–106, and Elizabeth A. Wells, *West Side Story: Cultural Perspectives on an American Musical* (Lanham, MD, 2011). I've relied here especially on Julia L. Foulkes, *There's a Place for Us: West Side Story and New York* (Chicago, 2016).

260 *"I can't do"*: Quoted in Craig Zadan, *Sondheim and Co.* (New York, 1974), 13.

261 *"When we're a state"*: Foulkes, *Place for Us*, 51.

261 La Prensa . . . *"I wasn't about"*: Stephen Sondheim, *Finishing the Hat* (New York, 2010), 42.

261 *forty thousand productions*: Foulkes, *Place for Us*, 1.

261 *"less complex"*: Stephen Sondheim, *Look, I Made a Hat* (New York, 2011), 112.

16. SYNTHETICA

262 *"new frontier"*: State of the Union, January 11, 1962, *APP*.

262 *"I would annex,"* etc.: W. T. Stead, ed., *The Last Will and Testament of Cecil John Rhodes* (London, 1902), 190.

263 *"technically feasible"* . . . *"desirable"*: 1975 study, results published in Richard D. Johnson and Charles Holbrow, eds., *Space Settlements: A Design Study* (Washington, DC, 1977), 1, 181.

263 NASA *appointed*: Anne M. Platoff, "Where No Flag Has Gone Before: Political and Technical Aspects of Placing a Flag on the Moon," NASA Contractor Report 188251, www.jsc.nasa.gov/history/flag/flag.htm.

263 *"a symbolic"* . . . *"not to be construed"*: Ibid., 6.

263 *internationalist spirit*: On the non-imperial character of the event, see Daniel Immerwahr, "The Moon Landing: Twilight of Empire," *Modern American History* 1 (2018): 129–33.

263 *new balance of forces*: The insufficiency of the "power" explanation for global decolonization is intelligently discussed in Frank Ninkovich, "Culture and Anti-Imperialism," in *Asia Pacific in the Age of Globalization*, ed. Robert David Johnson (New York, 2015), 259–70.

264 *new technologies*: An important overview touching on these issues is Daniel R. Headrick, *Power over Peoples: Technology, Environments, and Western Imperialism, 1400 to the Present* (Princeton, NJ, 2008).

265 *down by some ten million*: Adam Hochschild, *King Leopold's Ghost: A Story of Greed, Terror, and Heroism in Colonial Africa* (New York, 1998), 223.

265 *world rubber consumption*: Harry Barron, *Modern Synthetic Rubbers*, 3d ed. (London, 1949), 8.

265 *70 percent of the world's supply*: Brooks Emeny, *The Strategy of Raw Materials: A Study of America in Peace and War* (New York, 1938), 132.

265 *Sherman tank . . . heavy bomber . . . battleship*: Mark R. Finlay, *Growing American Rubber: Strategic Plants and the Politics of National Security* (New Brunswick, NJ, 2009), 171.

265 *"could offer only"*: Quoted in Charles Morrow Wilson, *Trees and Test Tubes: The Story of Rubber* (New York, 1943), 232.

265 *97 percent of the U.S. rubber*: Reconstruction Finance Corporation, *The Government's Rubber Projects: A History of the U.S. Government's National and Synthetic Rubber Programs, 1941–1955* (Washington, DC, 1955), 2:361.

265 *"If a survey,"* etc.: "Rubber to Stretch," July 1942, in Papers of Harold L. Ickes, Manuscript Division, Library of Congress, box 113.

266 *"so dangerous"*: Bernard Baruch, Report of the Rubber Survey Committee, September 10, 1942, 5.

266 *"the situation"*: Letter to Rubber Director, November 26, 1942, *APP.*

266 *"every bit of rubber"*: Radio Address on the Scrap Rubber Campaign, June 12, 1942, *APP.*

266 *seven pounds of scrap rubber*: Seth Garfield, *In Search of the Amazon: Brazil, the United States, and the Nature of a Region* (Durham, NC, 2013), 83.

266 *wooden wheels? Steel wheels?*: RFC, *Government's Rubber Projects*, 2:500.

266 *Thousands of scientists*: See Finlay, *Growing American Rubber*.

266 *baby bottles*: Wilson, *Trees and Test Tubes*, 132, 206.

266 *condoms*: Stephen Fenichell, *Plastic: The Making of a Synthetic Century* (New York, 1996), 186.

266 *"not in sight"*: Eugene Staley, *Raw Materials in Peace and War* (New York, 1937), 7.

267 *"require a miracle"*: Leon Henderson, quoted in Wilson, *Trees and Test Tubes*, 209.

267 *"The definitive solution"*: Quoted in Alfred E. Eckes Jr., *The United States and the Global Struggle for Minerals* (Austin, TX, 1979), 67.

267 *Dietrich*: Yvette Florio Lane, "'No Fertile Soil for Pathogens': Rayon, Advertising, and Biopolitics in Late Weimar Germany," *Journal of Social History* 44 (2010): 546.

268 *"definitely solved"*: Fenichell, *Plastic*, 183.

268 *Hitler had not solved*: My account depends on Peter Hayes, *Industry and Ideology, IG Farben in the Nazi Era*, new ed. (New York, 2001), and Adam Tooze, *The Wages of Destruction: The Making and Breaking of the Nazi Economy* (New York, 2006).

268 *two months of fighting*: Hayes, *Industry and Ideology*, 191.

268 *largely using horses*: David Edgerton, *The Shock of the Old: Technology and Global History Since 1900* (New York, 2007), 35.

268 *"brightly illuminated"* . . . *"still strikes"*: Primo Levi, *Survival in Auschwitz: The Nazi Assault on Humanity*, trans. Stuart Woolf (1958; New York, 1976), 19.

269 *"be a son-of-a-bitch"*: Bernard Baruch's instructions to Bradley Dewey, quoted in Henry J. Inman, *Rubber Mirror: Reflections of the Rubber Division's First 100 Years* (Akron, OH, 2009), 111.

269 *"I don't think"*: C. S. Marvel, interview by J. E. Mulvaney, n.d., 11, folder 1-5, box 1, Carl S. Marvel Papers, CHF.

269 *Just one such plant*: Norman V. Carlisle and Frank B. Latham, *Miracles Ahead!: Better Living in the Postwar World* (New York, 1944), 151.

269 *In mid-1944*: Wartime production figures from Fenichell, *Plastic*, 194, and Robert A. Solo, *Synthetic Rubber: A Case Study* (Washington, DC, 1959), 87.

269 *"The Germans apparently"*: William O. Baker, interview by Marcy Goldstein and Jeffrey L. Sturchio, May 23 and June 18, 1985, 49, CHF.

269 *nine in ten pounds*: Rubber Reserve Company, *Report on the Rubber Program, 1940–45*, Supplement No. 1, Year 1945 (Washington, DC, 1946), 15.

269 *"one of the most remarkable"*: Melvin A. Brenner, *The Outlook for Synthetic Rubber* (Washington, DC, 1944), 1.

269 *Korean War*: Vernon Herbert and Attilio Bisio, *Synthetic Rubber: A Project That Had to Succeed* (Westport, CT, 1985), 142–44.

270 *blue-ribbon commission*: The President's Materials Policy Commission, *Resources for Freedom* (Washington, DC, 1952), 2:101.

270 *30 percent of the market*: Finlay, *Growing American Rubber*, 12.

270 *5 percent of the world demand*: Tooze, *Wages of Destruction*, 446.

271 *Freinkel*: Susan Freinkel, *Plastic: A Toxic Love Story* (New York, 2011), 2–3. On plastic, I've also relied on Jeffrey L. Meikle, *American Plastic: A Cultural History* (New Brunswick, NJ, 1995), and Fenichell, *Plastic*.

271 *"Synthetica"*: "Plastics in 1940," *Fortune*, October 1940, 92–93.

271 *sought to use plastic*: Fenichell, *Plastic*, 206; Freinkel, *Plastic*, 6.

272 *large battleship*: Barrett L. Crandall, *The Plastics Industry* (Boston, 1946), 11.

272 *a GI could expect*: B. H. Weil and Victor J. Anhorn, *Plastic Horizons* (Lancaster, PA, 1944), 77–82; Erna Risch, *United States Army in World War II: The Technical Services; The Quartermaster Corps: Organization, Supply, and Services* (Washington, DC, 1953), 1:58–74.

273 *"virtually nothing"* . . . *"anything"*: Meikle, *American Plastic*, 146.

273 *plastic handles*: Weil and Anhorn, *Plastic Horizons*, 130.

273 *"The whole world"*: Roland Barthes, *Mythologies*, trans. Annette Lavers (1957; New York, 1972), 99.

273 *all flags*: Jacob Rosin and Max Eastman, *The Road to Abundance* (New York, 1953), 29, 32.

273 *volume of plastics*: Vaclav Smil, *Transforming the Twentieth Century: Technical Innovations and Their Consequences* (New York, 2006), 122.

274 *"a regiment,"* etc.: Williams Haynes, *The Chemical Front* (New York, 1943), 12–13.

274 *Camphor*: Carlisle and Latham, *Miracles Ahead!*, 168.

274 *"as simply as"*: Haynes, *Chemical Front*, 16.

274 *"synthetic age"* . . . *"freedom"*: Rosin and Eastman, *Road to Abundance*. See Edward D. Melillo, "Global Entomologies: Insects, Empires, and the 'Synthetic Age' in World History," *Past and Present* 223 (2014): 233–70.

274 *"how to synthesize"*: Richard P. Feynman, "There's Plenty of Room at the Bottom," *Caltech Engineering and Science* 23 (1960): 36.

274 *rubber . . . plastic . . . margarine*: J. C. Fisher and R. H. Pry, "A Simple Substitution Model of Technological Change," *Technological Forecasting and Social Change* 3 (1971): 87.

274 *Geopolitical treatises*: See, for example, Staley, *Raw Materials*, and Emeny, *Strategy*. The science journalist Edwin E. Slossen saw far more clearly than the strategists how the laboratory might replace the land, but even he recommended that the United States acquire more colonies in pursuit of rubber. *Creative Chemistry* (Garden City, NY, 1919), 156.

275 *international management*: A cogent presentation of the idea is C.W.W. Greenidge, "Tasks for an International Colonial Conference," *The Crown Colonist*, December 1943, 833–35. Enthusiasm within the State Department is registered throughout the Notter Records. See, for example, CDA 159, "Summary Analysis of Certain

Problems Relating to the Development of the Petroleum and Other Resources of Dependent Areas," May 1944 (box 124); PWC 248, "Proposal for an International Trusteeship System," May 1944 (microfilm 1221); and DA 30, "The United States and Trusteeship," December 1945 (box 132).

275 *"We can produce"*: PMPC, *Resources for Freedom*, 131.

275 *reports that followed*: Important surveys are Hans H. Landsberg, Leonard L. Fischman, and Joseph L. Fisher, *Resources in America's Future: Patterns of Requirements and Availabilities, 1960–2000* (Baltimore, 1963); National Commission on Materials Policy, *Material Needs and the Environment Today and Tomorrow* (Washington, DC, 1973); and National Commission on Supplies and Shortages, *Government and the Nation's Resources* (Washington, DC, 1976).

275 *"not a serious"*: NCSS, *Government and the Nation's Resources*, ix.

275 *"The truth,"* etc.: U Thant, "The Decade of Development," 1962, in *Public Papers of the Secretaries-General of the United Nations*, ed. Andrew W. Cordier and Max Harrelson (New York, 1976), 6:118.

276 *Places that had once been*: On synthetic competition, see Eckes, *Struggle for Minerals*, 234. On quinine, see Paul F. Russell, *Man's Mastery of Malaria* (London, 1955), 112.

276 *cost of extractive*: Harold J. Barnett and Chandler Morse, *Scarcity and Growth: The Economics of Natural Resource Scarcity* (Baltimore, 1963), chap. 8.

276 *didn't even* mention *security*: NCMP, *Material Needs and the Environment*. The irrelevance of raw materials to major postwar interventions is explored in Stephen D. Krasner, *Defending the National Interest: Raw Materials Investments and U.S. Foreign Policy* (Princeton, NJ, 1978).

276 *59 percent of the world's proven oil*: Geir Lundestad, "Empire by Invitation?: The United States and Western Europe, 1945–52," *Journal of Peace Research* 23 (1966): 264.

276 *"may have to,"* etc.: Daniel J. Sargent, *A Superpower Transformed: The Remaking of American Foreign Relations in the 1970s* (New York, 2015), 185.

277 *Nixon administration was serious*: Lizette Alvarez, "Britain Says U.S. Planned to Seize Oil in '73 Crisis," NYT, January 2, 2004.

277 *matter of rising prices*: A governmental investigation attributed the 1973–74 oil shock to panicked hoarding rather than inadequate supply. NSCC, *Nation's Resources*, chap. 4. Also see Timothy Mitchell, *Carbon Democracy: Political Power in the Age of Oil* (London, 2011), chap. 7.

277 *The moon suits*: NASA, "Space Suit Evolution: From Custom Tailored to Off-the-Rack," 1994, history.nasa.gov/spacesuits.pdf.

277 *The fifty-star flag that*: DuPont, "DuPont Science: Out of This World and Down to Earth," www2.dupont.com/Media_Center/en_US/assets/downloads/pdf/DuPont _SpaceEarth_FactSheet.pdf.

17. THIS IS WHAT GOD HATH WROUGHT

278 *"a depressing experience"*: Richard M. Leighton and Robert W. Coakley, *Global Logistics and Strategy, 1940–1943* (Washington, DC, 1955), 68.

279 MANILA PROBABLY OURS: *Lowell Evening Mail*, April 30, 1898.

279 *"swarming ant-heap"*: WTR, 11:43.

279 USS Oregon: Julie Greene, *The Canal Builders: Making America's Empire at the Panama Canal* (New York, 2009), 20.

279 *"ripe for dying"*: WTR, 11:143.

280 *MacArthur staged a lavish reception*: Helen Herron Taft, *Recollections of Full Years* (New York, 1914), 144–45.

280 *early U.S. colonial buildings*: Gerard Lico, *Arkitekturang Filipino: A History of Architecture and Urbanism in the Philippines* (Quezon City, 2008), 230.

280 *"nail currant jelly"*: Theodore Roosevelt, "The Panama Canal," in *The Pacific Ocean in History*, ed. H. Morse Stephens and Herbert E. Bolton (New York, 1917), 145.

280 *Panama Canal Zone*: In the following account, I've relied especially on David McCullough, *The Path Between the Seas: The Creation of the Panama Canal, 1870–1914* (New York, 1977); Greene, *Canal Builders*; and Noel Maurer and Carlos Yu, *The Big Ditch: How America Took, Built, Ran, and Ultimately Gave Away the Panama Canal* (Princeton, NJ, 2011).

280 *yellow fever and resistance to malaria*: J. R. McNeill, *Mosquito Empires: Ecology and War in the Greater Caribbean, 1620–1914* (New York, 2010), chap. 2.

280 *caskets*: Marie D. Gorgas and Burton J. Hendrick, *William Crawford Gorgas: His Life and Work* (New York, 1924), 143, 174.

280 *"I shall never forget"*: Alfred Dottin, in *Competition for the Best True Stories of Life and Work on the Isthmus of Panama During the Construction of the Panama Canal* (Balboa, Panama, 1963), 105.

281 *"whirlpool"*: Quoted in Jeffrey W. Parker, "Empire's Angst: The Politics of Race, Migration, and Sex Work in Panama, 1903–1945" (Ph.D. diss., University of Texas, Austin, 2013), 23.

281 *"dark and gloomy," etc.*: Gorgas and Hendrick, *Gorgas*, 141.

281 *Delays, pileups, and breakdowns*: Maurer and Yu, *Big Ditch*, 99–101.

281 *pyrethrum*: McCullough, *Path Between the Seas*, 460.

281 *mainland wives, etc.*: Greene, *Canal Builders*, 116–21; Michael E. Donoghue, *Borderland on the Isthmus: Race, Culture, and the Struggle for the Canal Zone* (Durham, NC, 2014), chap. 2.

281 *medical exams . . . forcibly hospitalize*: Parker, "Empire's Angst," chap. 3.

282 *eight tons of earth*: McCullough, *Path Between the Seas*, 496.

282 *one cubic yard*: Maurer and Yu, *Big Ditch*, 103.

282 *"Today you dig"*: Matthew Parker, *Panama Fever: The Battle to Build the Canal* (London, 2007), 341.

282 *records kept on the deaths*: Michael L. Conniff, *Black Labor on a White Canal: Panama, 1904–1981* (Pittsburgh, 1985), 31.

282 *"ordnance requirements"*: R. H. Somers, "Ordnance Inspection," *Industrial Standardization*, June 1942, 155.

282 *sixty-seven pounds*: Robert W. Coakley and Richard M. Leighton, *Global Logistics and Strategy, 1943–45* (Washington, DC, 1968), 825.

282 *fourteen ports . . . a hundred ports*: Frank T. Hines, "Two Wars," *Army Transportation Journal*, August 1945, 21–22.

282 *logistics had been a specialist's term*: Leighton and Coakley, *Global Logistics and Strategy, 1940–1943*, 9–11.

283 *"obviously" . . . "pathway to China"*: Quoted in Frank H. Heck, "Airline to China," in *The Army Air Forces in World War II*, ed. Wesley Frank Craven and James Lea Cate (Chicago, 1958), 7:114.

283 *four thousand aircraft*: Kevin Conley Ruffner, *Luftwaffe Field Divisions* (Oxford, UK, 1990), 3.

283 *one plane every four minutes*: Jeffrey A. Engel, *Cold War at 30,000 Feet: The Anglo-American Fight for Aviation Supremacy* (Cambridge, MA, 2007), 20.

284 *"knocked-down shipping"*: Leighton and Coakley, *Global Logistics and Strategy, 1940–1943*, 640.

284 *"A crow"*: Ivan Dmitri, *Flight to Everywhere* (New York, 1944), 26.

284 *Van Vleck, a curator*: Jenifer Van Vleck, *Empire of the Air: Aviation and the American Ascendancy* (Cambridge, MA, 2013), 142.

285 *"probably all the camels"*: Hugh B. Cave, *Wings Across the World: The Story of the Air Transport Command* (New York, 1945), 62.

285 *"aluminum trail"*: William H. Tunner, *Over the Hump* (1964; Washington, DC, 1985), 46–47.

286 *once every eleven minutes*: Reginald M. Cleveland, *Air Transport at War* (New York, 1946), 113.

286 *one every minute and twelve seconds*: Tunner, *Over the Hump*, 113.

286 *"Roads, it would seem"*: Cave, *Wings*, 106.

286 *"knew that we could fly"*: Tunner, *Over the Hump*, 59.

288 *Britain cut Germany's transatlantic cables*: An excellent account of this and the Zimmermann telegram is Daniel R. Headrick, *The Invisible Weapon: Telecommunications and International Politics, 1851–1945* (New York, 1991), chap. 9. On cables, I've been guided also by Jonathan Reed Winkler, *Nexus: Strategic Communications and American Security in World War I* (Cambridge, MA, 2008).

289 *U.S. telegraphic connection*: Winkler, *Nexus*, 152–54.

289 *eight words transmitted . . . eight million words*: U.S. Army Forces in the European Theater, *Service: The Story of the Signal Corps* (Paris, 1945), 8.

289 *Sixteen thousand cipher clerks*: Headrick, *Invisible Weapon*, 223.

290 *Major stations*: George Raynor Thompson and Dixie R. Harris, *United States Army in World War II: The Technical Services; The Signal Corps* (Washington, DC, 1966), 3:607.

290 *"We have got our net"*: Ibid., 3:582.

290 *"modern miracle"*: Rebecca Robbins Raines, *Getting the Message Through: A Branch History of the U.S. Army Signal Corps* (Washington, DC, 1996), 262.

290 *Before the invasion of Normandy*: Thompson and Harris, *Signal Corps*, 3:586.

290 *faxing*: Ibid., 3:605.

290 *WHAT HATH GOD WROUGHT . . . THIS IS WHAT*: Ibid., 3:607.

291 *"nine hundred and ninety"*: *With Walt Whitman in Camden* (Boston, 1906), 3:293.

291 *caused eight to ten times*: Edmund Russell, *War and Nature: Fighting Humans and Insects with Chemicals from World War I to Silent Spring* (Cambridge, UK, 2001), 113.

291 *"perhaps the most"*: Emory C. Cushing, *History of Entomology in World War II* (Washington, DC, 1957), 43.

291 *More than 95 percent of the*: James Phinney Baxter III, *Scientists Against Time* (Cambridge, MA, 1946), 307.

291 *fourteen thousand compounds*: Paul F. Russell, *Man's Mastery of Malaria* (London, 1955), 112–13.

291 *Prisoners, etc.*: Baxter, *Scientists Against Time*, 318.

292 *"complete destruction,"* etc.: E. Russell, *War and Nature*, 136. On DDT, see also David Kinkela, *DDT and the American Century: Global Health, Environmental Politics, and the Pesticide That Changed the World* (Chapel Hill, NC, 2011).

293 *dropped 95 percent*: E. Russell, *War and Nature*, 117.

293 *"man has developed"*: P. F. Russell, *Man's Mastery*, 243.

293 *death rate for all disease*: Vannevar Bush, *Science: The Endless Frontier* (Washington, DC, 1945), 1.

293 *95 percent of the adult mosquitoes*: Cushing, *Entomology in World War II*, 34.

294 *"completely covered,"* etc.: Quoted in Harold W. Thatcher, *The Packaging and Packing of Subsistence for the Army* (Washington, DC, 1945), 3.

294 *Specialized equipment*: J. B. Dow, "How the Navy Uses Standards in Its Electronics Program," *Industrial Standardization*, May 1945, 97–99; John C. MacArthur, "Fungus Proofing of CWS Equipment in the Field," May 20, 1945; folder 470.72; box 54; Entry 2B, Misc. Series, 1942–45; CWS; John Perry, *The Story of Standards* (New York, 1955), 179; Raines, *Getting the Message Through*, 263.

294 *20 to 40 percent of the matériel*: Russell Jones, "The Packaging Problem," *Army Transportation Journal*, August 1946, 6.

294 *"amphibious" packaging*: Thatcher, *Packaging and Packing*, chaps. 2–3; Alvin P. Stauffer, *The Quartermaster Corps: Operations in the War Against Japan* (Washington, DC, 1956), chap. 7.

295 *Every president after*: Maurer and Yu, *Big Ditch*, chap. 7.

296 *fifteen thousand tons*: Tunner, *Over the Hump*, 159.

296 *"I may be the craziest"*: Roger G. Miller, *To Save a City: The Berlin Airlift, 1948–1949* (Washington, DC, 1998), 23.

296 *"like appointing John Ringling"*: Curtis LeMay, quoted in ibid., 46.

296 *"The real excitement"*: Tunner, *Over the Hump*, 162.

296 *The lines did climb*: Ibid., 222.

296 *beaming radio broadcasts*: The extraordinary story is told in Michael Nelson, *War of the Black Heavens: The Battles of Western Broadcasting in the Cold War* (Syracuse, NY, 1997).

297 *"When it came to radio,"* etc.: Lech Walesa, foreword to ibid., xi.

18. THE EMPIRE OF THE RED OCTAGON

299 *fire ravaged Baltimore*: John Perry, *The Story of Standards* (New York, 1955), 140–41; Rexmond C. Cochrane, *Measures for Progress: A History of the National Bureau of Standards* (Washington, DC, 1966), 84–86.

299 *compatibility failures*: A. H. Martin Jr., "Diverse Local Standards Bar Free Trade in Many States," *Industrial Standardization*, July 1940, 181–92.

299 *College football*: "Standard Gauge for Standard Football," *Industrial Standardization*, April 1940, 96.

299 traffic lights: P. G. Agnew, "Consumer Standards on the Way," *Industrial Standardization*, February 1940, 45; "How Standards Eliminate Trade Barriers," *Industrial Standardization*, April 1940, 86.

300 *"exceedingly rapid"*: Lyman J. Gage, "National Standardizing Bureau," April 18, 1900, reprinted in *Science* 11 (1900): 698.

300 *"there was quite a discussion"*: Quoted in Cochrane, *Measures*, 84.

300 *Hoover*: I've relied on Richard Norton Smith, *An Uncommon Man: The Triumph of Herbert Hoover* (New York, 1984); Kendrick A. Clements, *The Life of Herbert Hoover: Imperfect Visionary, 1918–1928* (New York, 2010); and Glen Jeansonne, *The Life of Herbert Hoover: Fighting Quaker, 1928–1933* (New York, 2012).

301 *Osages*: Louise Morse Whitham, "Herbert Hoover and the Osages," *Chronicles of Oklahoma* 25 (1947): 2–4.

301 *Harrison into a college baseball game*: Smith, *Uncommon Man*, 16.

301 *Rain-in-the-Face*: WTR, 11:40.

301 *Mr. Cat*: Smith, *Uncommon Man*, 19.

301 *"quieting of hate"* . . . *"hushing to ambition"* . . . *"meekness"*: Herbert Hoover, *Memoirs* (New York, 1952), 2:158.

302 *turning the lighthouses out*: Oscar Straus, quoted in Cochrane, *Measures*, 229.

302 *bureau developed a system*: Described in Clements, *Hoover*, 255.

302 *brickmakers*: Perry, *Story of Standards*, 132; Clements, *Hoover*, 111.

302 *Then came new standards*: On Hoover's other standardizations, see Cochrane, *Measures*, 258.

302 *"sprinkled on practically"*: W. C. Stewart, "Serving All Industries!—Bolts and Nuts," *Industrial Standardization*, July 1941, 165.

302 *"The screw thread is a simple"*: Ralph Flanders, quoted in George S. Case, "What Can Be Done Toward World Unification of Screw Threads?" *Standardization*, November 1949, 290.

303 *"had to find"*: Herbert Hoover, "Crusade for Standards," *Standardization*, December 1951, 381.

303 *"Now the half-inch"*: Ibid., 282.

303 imperial *system*: Aashish Velkar, *Markets and Measurements in Nineteenth-Century Britain* (New York, 2012), 63–66.

304 *nursing in the Philippines*: I'm guided by Catherine Ceniza Choy, *Empire of Care: Nursing and Migration in Filipino American History* (Durham, NC, 2003), chap. 2, and Ma. Mercedes G. Planta, "Prerequisites to a Civilized Life: The American Public Health System in the Philippines, 1901 to 1927" (Ph.D. diss., National University of Singapore, 2008).

304 *Nursing wasn't new*: Anastacia Giron-Tupas, *History of Nursing in the Philippines*, rev. ed. (Manila, 1961), 11–15.

304 *aggressively overwrite*: Details from ibid., chap. 3, and Lavinia L. Dock, *A History of Nursing: From the Earliest Times to the Present Day with Special Reference to the Work of the Past Thirty Years* (New York, 1912), 4:307–20.

304 *more and more nurses from the Philippines*: See Choy, *Empire of Care*; Barbara L. Brush and Julie Sochalski, "International Nurse Migration: Lessons from the Philippines," *Policy, Politics, and Nursing Practice* 8 (2007): 37–46; and Barbara L. Brush, "The Potent Lever of Toil: Nursing Development and Exportation in the Postcolonial Philippines," *American Journal of Public Health* 100 (2010): 1572–81.

305 *switched over to the metric system*: Hector Vera, "The Social Life of Measures: Metrication in the United States and Mexico" (Ph.D. diss., The New School, 2011), 95.

305 *"Suppose my neighbor's,"* etc.: Roosevelt, Press Conference, December 17, 1940, *APP*.

306 *0.30-inch cartridges . . . bombs*: M. F. Schoeffel, "Some Adventures in Military Standardization," *Standardization*, September 1951, 277.

306 *"frightful commentary"*: J. B. Carswell, "Postwar Standardization," *Industrial Standardization*, October 1944, 211.

306 *"We can't borrow parts"*: Benjamin Melnitsky, *Profiting from Industrial Standardization* (New York, 1953), 42.

307 *$600 million sending spare screws*: Ralph E. Flanders, "How Big Is an Inch?" *Atlantic Monthly*, January 1951, 45.

307 *$84 million to establish*: Edward R. Stettinius Jr., *Lend-Lease: Weapon for Victory* (New York, 1944), chap. 5.

307 *U.S. Army also adopted*: Schoeffel, "Adventures," 277.

307 *By the war's end*: Richard M. Leighton and Robert W. Coakley, *Global Logistics and Strategy, 1940–1943* (Washington, DC, 1955), 5.

307 *"the integration"*: Howard Coonley and P. G. Agnew, "The Role of Standards in the System of Free Enterprise," *Industrial Standardization*, April 1941, part 2, 12.

307 *Fenn Manufacturing*: W. L. Fenn, "Standards Smooth the Path of the Subcontractor," *Industrial Standardization*, June 1942, 163.

308 *7.5 times larger*: Cochrane, *Measures*, appendix F.

308 *15 percent of Australia's national income*: Charles A. Willoughby and John Chamberlain, *MacArthur: 1941–1951* (New York, 1954), 71.

308 *Australian agriculture*: My account is from Alvin P. Stauffer, *The Quartermaster Corps: Operations in the War Against Japan* (Washington, DC, 1956), chap. 5.

308 *"Almost every phase"*: K. R. Cramp, 1945, quoted in Michael Symons, *One Continuous Picnic: A Gastronomic History of Australia*, 2d ed. (Melbourne, 2007), 187.

309 *"Without any inhibitions"*: John Curtin, quoted in Winston S. Churchill, *The Second World War* (1950; Boston, 1985), 4:7.

309 *standards coordinating committee*: "United Nations Standards Committee Opens New York Office," *Industrial Standardization*, October 1944, 209–10.

309 *For nearly two weeks*: Meeting described in various articles in *Industrial Standardization*, especially "British Mission and American Groups Confer on Screw Thread Standards," December 1943, 364–65, and John Gaillard, "New War Standard for American Truncated Whitworth Threads," July 1944, 129–31.

309 *longer summit*: See December 1944 issue of *Industrial Standardization*.

309 *"unending stream"*: Robert M. Gates, "How British and American Screw Threads Differ," *Industrial Standardization*, December 1944, 246.

310 *conference in Ottawa*: "'Inch' Screw Thread Practice Unified," February 1946, *Industrial Standardization*, 36–42.

311 *"beaten the gun"*: Case, "Unification of Screw Threads," 304.

311 *60 percent of the industrialized world's economic production*: Daniel J. Sargent, *A Superpower Transformed: The Remaking of American Foreign Relations in the 1970s* (New York, 2015), 15.

311 *"America is our largest"*: Quoted in Roger E. Gay, "World Significance of Standardization," *Industrialization*, September 1952, 305.

311 *fighter planes . . . "a British stretcher"*: William L. Batt, "Europe Discovers America," *Standardization*, January 1953, 8. On NATO, see also Willard L. Thorp, "Standards and International Relations," in *National Standards in a Modern Economy*, ed. Dickson Reck (New York, 1956), 343–51.

312 *leading British standards journal*: "British Consider U.S. Views," *Standardization*, June 1953, 179.

312 *The Third World*: The process by which poorer countries adopted the standards of richer ones is described in Lal C. Verman, *Standardization: A New Discipline* (Hamden, CT, 1973), 166–67, and Lal C. Verman, "India Reports Active Program," *Industrial Standardization*, September 1948, 122–24.

312 *"smoothing the flow,"* etc.: Truman to George F. Hussey, May 21, 1952, reprinted in "Welcome to ISO from the President of the United States," *Standardization*, September 1952, 269.

312 *440 hertz*: Bruce Haynes, *A History of Performing Pitch: The Story of* "A" (Lanham, MD, 2002), 360–61; "What's the Pitch, Boys?" *Standardization*, April 1949, 101–102; and Perry, *Story of Standards*, 120.

313 *"we now think in terms"*: H. E. Hilts, "International Signs for the World's Traffic," *Standardization*, August 1953, 239.

313 *yellow octagon*: Clay McShane, "The Origins and Globalization of Traffic Control Signals," *Journal of Urban History* 25 (1999): 382; H. Gene Hawkins Jr., "Evolution of the MUTCD: Early Standards for Traffic Control Devices," *ITE Journal*, July 1992, 24.

313 *changed its mind*: H. Gene Hawkins Jr., "Evolution of the MUTCD: The MUTCD Since World War II," *ITE Journal*, November 1992, 18.

313 *56 percent of mainlanders*: John Bemelmans Marciano, *Whatever Happened to the Metric System?: How America Kept Its Feet* (New York, 2014), 243. Awareness rose in the 1970s as the federal government moved to convert to metric, but that conversion was never complete.

314 *sole holdouts against*: Vera, "Social Life of Measures," 60–61. Palau, the FSM, and the RMI were formerly part of the United States' strategic trust territory in Micronesia.

314 *convened a grand meeting*: Some background on the 1968 Vienna Convention on Road Signs and Signals is in E. W. Foell, "Traffic Signs Baffling the World Over," *Los Angeles Times*, June 4, 1970.

314 *91 percent of the world's population*: Thanks to the intrepid Callie Leone for help in producing this figure.

315 *"domination without"*: George Marion, *Bases and Empire: A Chart of American Expansion* (New York, 1948), chap. 12.

315 *great coordinating process*: A point developed cogently in Neil Smith, *American Empire: Roosevelt's Geographer and the Prelude to Globalization* (Berkeley, CA, 2003).

315 *"flat"*: Thomas L. Friedman, *The World Is Flat: A Brief History of the Twenty-First Century* (New York, 2005).

19. LANGUAGE IS A VIRUS

317 *"broken English"*: William Bradford, *History of Plymouth Plantation, 1606–1646*, ed. William T. Davis (1651; New York, 1908), 135. On Squanto, I've relied on Neil Salisbury, "Squanto: Last of the Patuxets," in *Struggle and Survival in Colonial America*, ed. David G. Sweet and Gary B. Nash (Berkeley, CA, 1981), 228–46.

318 *"special instrument"*: Bradford, *History*, 111.

318 *polyglot crazy quilt*: On eighteenth-century language, I've used Jill Lepore, *A Is for American: Letters and Others Characters in the Newly United States* (New York, 2002); Marc Shell, ed., *American Babel: Literatures of the United States from Abnaki to Zuni* (Cambridge, MA, 2002); and Vicente L. Rafael, "Translation, American English, and the National Insecurities of Empire," in *Formations of United States Colonialism*, ed. Alyosha Goldstein (Durham, NC, 2014), 335–60.

319 *tongues cut out*: Marc Shell, "Babel in America," in *American Babel*, 4.

319 *traces of African idioms*: African survivals are most discernible in Gullah, spoken to this day on the Sea Islands and the coasts of Georgia and South Carolina. But Gullah is a creole based on English, not an African language.

319 *"We shall break up"*: Richard Henry Pratt, quoted in Margaret D. Jacobs, *White Mother to a Dark Race: Settler Colonialism, Maternalism, and the Removal of Indigenous Children in the American West and Australia, 1880–1940* (Lincoln, NE, 2009), 27.

319 *Students caught speaking*: Brenda J. Child, *Boarding School Seasons: American Indian Families, 1900–1940* (Lincoln, NE, 1988), 28.

319 *bribes, threats*, etc.: Practices described in Jacobs, *White Mother*, chap. 4.

319 *"They beat"*: Nora Marks Dauenhauer and Richard Dauenhauer, "Technical, Emotional, and Ideological Issues in Reversing Language Shift: Examples from Southeast Alaska," in *Endangered Languages: Language Loss and Community Response*, ed. Lenore A. Grenoble and Lindsay J. Whaley (Cambridge, UK, 1998), 65.

319 *Chamoru*: Sharleen J. Q. Santos-Bamba, "The Literate Lives of Chamorro Women in Modern Guam" (Ph.D. diss., Indiana University of Pennsylvania, 2010), chap. 5.

319 *Chamoru dictionaries*: Jack Fahy, special assistant to the secretary, "Preliminary Report of Naval Administration of Island Possessions," April 15, 1945, 8; "Pacific Planning" folder; box 156; R-0-40, Administrative, World War; Office of Territories Classified Files, 1907–1951; ROT.

320 *Virgin Islands*: William W. Boyer, *America's Virgin Islands: A History of Human Rights and Wrongs* (Durham, NC, 1983), 182.

320 *"cardinal point"*: Fred Atkinson, quoted in Funie Hsu, "Colonial Articulations: English Instruction and the 'Benevolence' of U.S. Overseas Expansion in the Philippines, 1898–1916" (Ph.D. diss., University of California, Berkeley, 2013), 20.

320 *"I am astounded,"* etc.: Speech, December 20, 1947, recorded in Jack West, report on Albizu, May 4, 1948, 34–35, Albizu FBI File, section 5, box 2.

320 *"by teachers"*: Ford Report, 1913, quoted in Cristina Evangelista Torres, *The Americanization of Manila, 1898–1921* (Quezon City, 2010), 154. On this, see also Vicente L. Rafael's insightful *Motherless Tongues: The Insurgency of Language Amid Wars of Translation* (Durham, NC, 2016).

320 *former governor*: *Origins of the Philippine Republic: Extracts from the Diaries and Records of Francis Burton Harrison*, ed. Michael P. Onorato (Ithaca, NY, 1974), 117.

320 *"with a left-handed"*: Robert H. Gore, quoted in Thomas Mathews, *Puerto Rican Politics and the New Deal* (Gainesville, FL, 1960), 64.

320 *Teachers there*: Solsiree del Moral, *Negotiating Empire: The Cultural Politics of the Schools in Puerto Rico, 1898–1952* (Madison, WI, 2013), 16.

320 *roughly a quarter*: 27.8 percent in Puerto Rico, 26.6 percent in the Philippines. Amílcar Antonio Barreto, *The Politics of Language in Puerto Rico* (Gainesville, FL, 2001), 21; Andrew B. Gonzalez, *Language and Nationalism: The Philippine Experience Thus Far* (Quezon City, 1980), 26.

320 *polyglot pidgin*: John E. Reinecke, " 'Pidgin English' in Hawaii: A Local Study of the Sociology of Language," *American Journal of Sociology* 5 (1938): 778–89.

320 *scientific conferences*: Michael D. Gordin, *Scientific Babel: How Science Was Done Before and After Global English* (Chicago, 2015), 180.

321 *Woodrow Wilson*: Ronald J. Pestritto, *Woodrow Wilson and the Roots of Modern Liberalism* (Lanham, MD, 2005), 34.

321 *tried to learn Osage*: Louise Morse Whitham, "Herbert Hoover and the Osages," *Chronicles of Oklahoma* 25 (1947): 3.

321 *used Mandarin*: Herbert Hoover, *Memoirs* (New York, 1951), 1:36.

321 *"It was then,"* etc.: Mario Pei, *One Language for the World* (New York, 1958), 31–32.

321 *"The empires of the future,"* etc.: "Anglo-American Unity," September 6, 1943, in Winston S. Churchill, *His Complete Speeches, 1897–1963*, ed. Robert Rhodes James (New York, 1974), 7:6826.

322 *"underhanded orthography"*: Gordin, *Scientific Babel*, 205.

322 *Basic's champions*: W. Terrence Gordon, "C. K. Ogden's Basic English," *ETC: A Review of General Semantics* 45 (1988): 339.

322 *"In Basic"*: Alok Rai, *Orwell and the Politics of Despair: A Critical Study of the Writings of George Orwell* (Cambridge, UK, 1988), 125–26.

322 *"spread like wildfire,"* etc.: H. G. Wells, *The Shape of Things to Come* (New York, 1934), 417.

322 *"The majority of Chinese,"* etc.: I. A. Richards, *Basic in Teaching: East and West* (London, 1935), 45.

322 *Chinese government to agree*: Rodney Koeneke, *Empires of the Mind: I. A. Richards and Basic English in China, 1929–1979* (Stanford, CA, 2004), 5.

322 *"It takes only"*: "Globalingo," *Time*, December 31, 1945, 48.

322 *"has tremendous merit"*: FDR to Cordell Hull, June 5, 1944, FDR Library, docs .fdrlibrary.marist.edu/psf/box37/t335k03.html.

323 *"blood, work"* . . . *"Seriously"*: FDR to Churchill, June 1944, FDR Library, docs .fdrlibrary.marist.edu/psf/box37/a335k01.html.

323 *"The Koreans"*: Chad Walsh, "Basic English: World Language or World Philosophy," *College English* 6 (1945): 456.

323 *dozens of schemes*: Pei, *One Language*, 119; Edmund Vincent Starrett, "Spelling Reform Proposals for the English Language" (Ed.D. diss., Wayne State University, 1981).

323 *Owen*: Narcissa Owen, *A Cherokee Woman's America: Memoirs of Narcissa Owen, 1831–1907* (Gainesville, FL, 2005), 97.

323 *On December 7/8, 1941*: *Global Alphabet: Hearing Before the Committee on Foreign Relations, United States Senate*, 79th Cong., 1st sess., November 7, 1945 (Washington, DC, 1945), 6.

324 *"by which we can"*: "Former Senator Owen Devises Global Alphabet," *New York Herald Tribune*, July 29, 1943.

324 *"the conversational language"* . . . *compatible with Basic*: *Global Alphabet*, 65, 4.

324 *FDR passed the scheme*: Ibid., 48.

324 *"I do not think"*: Carl Hatch, quoted in ibid., 11.

324 *Shaw*: Starrett, "Spelling Reform," 260–61.

324 *Eleanor Roosevelt*: Mario Pei, *The Story of English* (Philadelphia, 1952), 314.

324 *special typewriter*: "Appeal for Global Alphabet Made," *Baltimore Evening Sun*, December 18, 1946.

325 *"sign of slavery"*: M. K. Gandhi, *Hind Swaraj and Other Writings* (New York, 2009), 102.

325 *"psychological violence"* . . . *mission school*: Ngũgĩ wa Thiong'o, *Decolonising the Mind: The Politics of Language in African Literature* (London, 1986), 9, 11.

325 *"When I travel"* . . . *"Did you ever"* . . . *"a language"* . . . *"a national soul"*: Quezon, speech, November 7, 1937, in *The Great Quezon's Dream: A National Language for*

the Filipinos, 4–5, typescript, in AHC. Language in the Philippines is best approached through Rafael, *Motherless Tongues*.

326 *Basic Tagalog*: "Eureka! Basic Tagalog!" *Manila Evening News*, January 17, 1946.

326 *"decadent" subject*: Pei, *Story of English*, 347.

326 *"only provisionally"*: Quoted in Robert Phillipson, *Linguistic Imperialism* (Oxford, UK, 1992), 27.

326 *"wreck all hopes"*: Quoted in ibid., 167.

326 *some linguists have insisted*: The argument is made best in Phillipson's *Linguistic Imperialism* and Diana Lemberg, "'The Universal Language of the Future': Decolonization, Development, and the American Embrace of Global English, 1945–1965," *Modern Intellectual History* 15 (2018): 561–592.

327 *foreign students*: Paul A. Kramer, "Is the World Our Campus?: International Students and U.S. Global Power in the Long Twentieth Century," *DH* 33 (2009): 792.

327 *forty U.S. government agencies*: Phillipson, *Linguistic Imperialism*, 157.

327 *instrument of "Western psychological"*: Kwame Nkrumah, *Neo-Colonialism: The Last Stage of Imperialism* (New York, 1965), 248.

327 *"Special English"*: Arika Okrent, *In the Land of Invented Languages: Esperanto Rock Stars, Klingon Poets, Loglan Lovers, and the Mad Dreamers Who Tried to Build a Perfect Language* (New York, 2009), 141–42.

327 *priority on language export*: Phillipson's interviews with governmental officials clarify this. See *Linguistic Imperialism*, 310.

327 *It wasn't until 1965*: National Security Action Memorandum 332, 1965, discussed in Lemberg, "Universal Language," 587.

327 *from the bottom up*: See especially David Crystal, *English as a Global Language*, 2d ed. (New York, 2003), and David Northrup, *How English Became the Global Language* (New York, 2013).

328 *quarter of the population*: 26.1 percent speaking English by 1950: Barreto, *Politics of Language*, 21.

328 *compulsion rarely comes from*: The case is made cogently in David Singh Grewal, *Network Power: The Social Dynamics of Globalization* (New Haven, CT, 2008).

328 *"Speaking frankly,"* etc.: Masaaki Morita, quoted in *Genryu*, the 50th-anniversary history of Sony, translated and abbreviated at sony.net/SonyInfo/CorporateInfo/History/SonyHistory.

329 *Gromyko*: Pei, *One Language*, 51.

329 *70 percent of the world's passenger miles*: Jenifer Van Vleck, *Empire of the Air: Aviation and the American Ascendancy* (Cambridge, MA, 2013), 170.

329 *Francophones in Quebec*: Sandford F. Borins, *The Language of the Skies: The Bilingual Air Traffic Control Conflict in Canada* (Montreal, 1983). Three years after the strike, the government relented and allowed French to be used in limited circumstances.

329 *scientists*: My account of science—both its pursuit of international languages and its succumbing to English—is derived from Gordin, *Scientific Babel*.

330 *Nobel Prizes*: Counting prizes in physics, chemistry, and physiology or medicine and using laureate biographies from www.nobelprize.org.

330 *half of publications*: Ulrich Ammon, "Linguistic Inequality and Its Effects on Participation in Scientific Discourse and on Global Knowledge Accumulation," *Applied Linguistics Review* 3 (2012): 338.

330 *well over 90 percent*: Ibid.

330 *Hebrew University's*: I counted refereed papers or those intended for peer review on faculty websites linked at www.phys.huji.ac.il/people_faculty, accessed May 30, 2017.

330 *82.3 percent of randomly chosen websites*: David Crystal, *Language and the Internet* (New York, 2001), 217.

330 *ASCII*: Daniel Pargman and Jacob Palme, "ASCII Imperialism," in *Standards and Their Stories: How Quantifying, Classifying, and Formalizing Practices Shape Everyday Life*, ed. Martha Lampland and Susan Leigh Star (Ithaca, NY, 2009), 177–99.

331 *QWERTY*: The long shadow cast by that English-language typewriter over global information processing is discussed brilliantly in Thomas S. Mullaney, *The Chinese Typewriter: A History* (Cambridge, MA, 2017).

331 *"It is the ultimate act,"* etc.: Crystal, *Global Language*, 117.

331 *"a major risk"*: Quoted in "The Coming Global Tongue," *The Economist*, December 21, 1996, 75.

332 *60 percent of the world's radio*: Daniel Nettle and Suzanne Romaine, *Vanishing Voices: The Extinction of the World's Languages* (New York, 2000), 18.

332 *language of Esperanto*: Mario Pei, *Wanted: A World Language* (New York, 1969).

332 *"bitter truth,"* etc.: Manu Joseph, "India Faces a Linguistic Truth: English Spoken Here," NYT, February 16, 2011. On the general trend, see Joshua A. Fishman, Andrew W. Conrad, and Alma Rubal-Lopez, eds., *Post-Imperial English: Status Change in Former British and American Colonies, 1940–1990* (Berlin, 1996).

332 *"Investors will not"*: Goh Chok Tong, quoted in Phyllis Ghim-Lian Chew, *Emergent Lingua Francas and World Orders: The Politics and Place of English as a World Language* (New York, 2009), 141.

332 *call-center workers*: Funie Hsu, "The Coloniality of Neoliberal English: The Enduring Structures of American Colonial English Instruction in the Philippines and Puerto Rico," *L2 Journal* 7 (2015): 124, 139–40.

332 *Mongolia*: Nicholas Ostler, *The Last Lingua Franca: English Until the Return of Babel* (New York, 2010), 15.

333 *hundred thousand native speakers*: Daniel Goodard, "Teaching English Abroad Is an Increasingly Popular Choice for Struggling Undergraduates," *The Independent*, November 19, 2012.

333 *"If the Chinese"*: John McWhorter, "Where Do Languages Go to Die?" *The Atlantic*, September 10, 2015, www.theatlantic.com/international/archive/2015/09/aramaic -middle-east-language/404434/.

333 *language with the most native speakers*: Language rankings from "Summary by Language Size," *Ethnologue*, www.ethnologue.com/statistics/size. For the limits of English, see Barbara Wallraff, "What Global Language?" *Atlantic Monthly*, November 2000, 52–66.

334 *roughly one in four*: Crystal, *Global Language*, 69.

334 *study commissioned by the British Council*: Robert Pinon and John Haydon, *The Benefits of English Language for Individuals and Societies: Quantitative Indicators from Cameroon, Nigeria, Rwanda, Bangladesh, and Pakistan* (London, 2010), 11.

334 *lingual frenectomies . . . "English is now"*: Kathy Marks, "Seoul Tries to Shock Parents out of Linguistic Surgery," *The Independent*, January 3, 2004.

334 *Modern Language Association*: David Goldberg, Dennis Looney, and Natalia Lusin, "Enrollments in Languages Other Than English in United States Institutions of

Higher Education," 26, Modern Language Association, February 2015, apps.mla.org /pdf/2013_enrollment_survey.pdf.

335 *"It's embarrassing"*: Maria Gavrilovic, "Obama: 'I Don't Speak a Foreign Language. It's Embarrassing!'" *CBS News*, July 11, 2008, cbsnews.com.

20. POWER IS SOVEREIGNTY, MISTER BOND

337 *Rumors floated*: Ivar Bryce, *You Only Live Once: Memories of Ian Fleming* (London, 1975), 68. On Fleming, see also Matthew Parker, *Goldeneye, Where Bond Was Born: Ian Fleming's Jamaica* (New York, 2015).

337 *"behind the curtains"*: Stanley Ross, *Axel Wenner-Gren: The Sphinx of Sweden* (New York, 1947), 1. A more sober account is Ilja A. Luciak, "Vision and Reality: Axel Wenner-Gren, Paul Fejos, and the Origins of the Wenner-Gren Foundation for Anthropological Research," *Current Anthropology* 57 (2016): S302–S332.

337 *"He is too big,"* etc.: Quoted in Ross, *Wenner-Gren*, 3.

337 *science and rationality*: Axel Wenner-Gren, *Call to Reason: An Appeal to Common Sense* (New York, 1938).

337 *Anglic*: "Anglic Urged as World Tongue," *Albuquerque Journal*, December 8, 1931.

337 *"I have not a shred"*: Sumner Welles, quoted in Luciak, "Vision and Reality," S314.

338 *"perfect example"*: Scott Farris, *Inga: Kennedy's Great Love, Hitler's Perfect Beauty, and J. Edgar Hoover's Prime Suspect* (Guilford, CT, 2016), 137.

338 *J. Edgar Hoover*: Farris notes that the *recordings* of Kennedy and Arvad having sex were likely lost by the 1960s but that Hoover nevertheless took pains to assure Kennedy that he was keeping the file on the pair "safe." See *Inga*, 240–42.

338 *"When we have won"*: Bryce, *You Only Live Once*, 72.

338 *"blessed corners"*: Quoted in Tao Leigh Goffe, "007 Versus the Darker Races: The Black and Yellow Peril in *Dr. No*," *Anthurium: A Caribbean Studies Journal* 12 (2015): 1.

338 *"In the whole"*: Quoted in Parker, *Goldeneye*, 212.

339 *Blackwell's young son*: Mark Binelli, "Chris Blackwell: The Barefoot Mogul," *Men's Journal*, March 2014, www.mensjournal.com/features/chris-blackwell-the-barefoot -mogul-20140319.

339 *"too posh"*: Edward Helmore, "Chris Blackwell: The Original Trustafarian," *London Telegraph*, May 8, 2012.

339 *"Bond prepared"* . . . *"Bitten off"*: Ian Fleming, *Doctor No* (1958; New York, 2002), 53.

339 *"the most valuable"* . . . *"I can bend"*: Ibid., 175, 178.

340 *"Who in the world"*: Ibid., 161–62.

340 *"no sovereign or territorial"*: Jimmy M. Skaggs, *The Great Guano Rush: Entrepreneurs and American Overseas Expansion* (New York, 1994), 200.

341 *A consultation of the records*: Ibid., 216.

341 *"Are we in an acquisitive"*: Ernest Gruening, *Many Battles: The Autobiography of Ernest Gruening* (New York, 1973), 235. On the 1930s recolonization of the equatorial guano islands, see Roy F. Nichols, *Advance Agents of American Destiny* (Philadelphia, 1956), chap. 9; Lowell T. Young, "Franklin D. Roosevelt and America's Islets: Acquisition of Territory in the Caribbean and the Pacific," *The Historian* 35 (1973): 205–20; Skaggs, *Guano Rush*, chap. 11; and *Under a Jarvis Moon*, dir. Noelle Kahanu and Heather Giugni (Bishop Museum, 2011).

341 *"maintain the sovereignty"*: Ernest Gruening, "General Information, Equatorial Islands," c. 1939; "World's Colonies—General" folder; box 607; 9-0-1, Administrative, World's Colonies; Office of Territories Classified Files, 1907–1951; ROT.

341 *"Because of their adaptability"*: Ibid.

341 *deposited in small groups*: Details in Interior Department press memos, 1938, in "Colonization—Other Islands" folder, box 12, Padover File.

341 *"I am instructed"*: Gruening, *Many Battles*, 236.

341 *Howland Island*: William Atherton DuPuy, "Our New Islands," *Current History*, February 1937, 62–64.

344 *eight hundred such bases*: David Vine offers this reasonable estimate in *Base Nation: How U.S. Military Bases Abroad Harm America and the World* (New York, 2015), 4.

344 *pointillist's brush*: My notion of a pointillist empire derives from William Rankin's discussion of "territorial pointillism" in *After the Map: Cartography, Navigation, and the Transformation of Territory in the Twentieth Century* (Chicago, 2016) and the insights of Ruth Oldenziel in her chapter "Islands: The United States as a Networked Empire," in *Entangled Geographies: Empire and Technopolitics in the Global Cold War*, ed. Gabrielle Hecht (Cambridge, MA, 2011), 13–42. The "bases are the new form of empire" historical literature was sparked by Chalmers Johnson, *Blowback: The Costs and Consequences of American Empire* (New York, 1999). See also the ensuing historical scholarship cited in Daniel Immerwahr, "The Greater United States: Territory and Empire in U.S. History," *DH* 40 (2016): 390n.

344 *"storm of comment"*: CDA 359, "American Opinion of 'Trusteeship' for Pacific Bases," November 1945, 5, Notter Records, box 126.

344 *"maintain the military bases"*: Truman, Radio Report to the American People on the Potsdam Conference, August 9, 1945, APP.

344 *"We seek no territorial"*: George Marion, *Bases and Empire: A Chart of American Expansion* (New York, 1948), 11.

344 *"vivisection"*: Quoted in Amílcar Antonio Barreto, *Vieques, the Navy, and Puerto Rican Politics* (Gainesville, FL, 2002), 24.

345 *"We are the lamb"*: Alba Encarnación, quoted in ibid., 40.

345 *On Guam*: Department of Defense, *Base Structure Report, Fiscal Year 2015 Baseline*, 42.

345 *something similar in Alaska*: John S. Whitehead, *Completing the Union: Alaska, Hawai'i, and the Battle for Statehood* (Albuquerque, NM, 2004), 277–78.

345 *"The military doesn't have"*: Quoted in Vine, *Base Nation*, 75.

345 *"relatively small"*: Quoted in ibid., 65. Stuart Barber and the strategic island concept are also discussed in David Vine, *Island of Shame: The Secret History of the U.S. Military Base on Diego Garcia* (Princeton, NJ, 2009), chaps. 2–3.

346 *"The Yankees"*: Benjamín Torres, ed., *Pedro Albizu Campos: Obras escogidas, 1923–1936* (San Juan, 1975), 271.

346 *cable traffic*: Reprinted in Daniel C. Walsh, *An Air War with Cuba: The United States Radio Campaign Against Castro* (Jefferson, NC, 2012), 17.

347 *"pigs"* ... *"a queer"* ... *"a cage"*: "Swans, Spooks, and Boobies," *Time*, December 6, 1971.

347 *fifty million regular listeners*: James McCartney, "Radio on Swan Island an Outpost of Free Cuba," *Boston Globe*, April 23, 1961.

347 *cryptic messages*: "Swans, Spooks, and Boobies."

347 *journalists snickered*: David Wise and Thomas B. Ross, *Our Invisible Government* (New York, 1964), 329.

347 *Fleming's advice*: Christopher Moran, "Ian Fleming and CIA Director Allen Dulles: The Very Best of Friends," in *James Bond in World and Popular Culture: The Films Are Not Enough*, 2d ed., ed. Robert G. Weiner, B. Lynn Whitfield, and Jack Becker (Newcastle, UK, 2011), 208–15.

348 *CIA still found uses*: Sam Dillon, *Comandos: The CIA and Nicaragua's Contra Rebels* (New York, 1991), 177–82.

348 *"powdered white"* . . . *"screaming lungs"*: Fleming, *Doctor No*, 214, 211.

348 *"We just took out"*: Quoted in Sasha Davis, *The Empires' Edge: Militarization, Resistance, and Transcending Hegemony in the Pacific* (Athens, GA, 2015), 61.

349 *"We will gladly"*: Carey Wilson, dir., *Bikini: The Atom Island* (MGM, 1946).

349 *"We didn't know"*: Interviewed in Robert Stone, dir., *Radio Bikini* (IFC Films, 1988).

349 *staged reenactment*: Peter Bacon Hales, *Outside the Gates of Eden: The Dream of America from Hiroshima to Now* (Chicago, 2014), chap. 1.

349 *"all nations have yielded"*: Paul V. McNutt, Address at the Inauguration of the Philippine Republic, July 4, 1946; "McNutt, P. V., Correspondence and Speeches, 1945–46" folder, box 7, HC–DC.

350 *detonated sixty-six more*: Dick Thornburgh et al., "The Nuclear Claims Tribunal of the Republic of the Marshall Islands: An Independent Examination and Assessment of Its Decision-Making Processes," 2003, www.bikiniatoll.com/ThornburgReport.pdf.

350 *90 percent of the populations*: Davis, *Empires' Edge*, 53.

350 *National Cancer Institute*: Simon L. Steven et al., "Radiation Doses and Cancer Risks in the Marshall Islands Associated with Exposure to Radioactive Fallout from Bikini and Enewetak Nuclear Weapons Tests: Summary," *Health Physics* 99 (2010): 105–24.

350 *"catastrophic nonsense"*: Lawrence S. Wittner, *Resisting the Bomb: A History of the World Nuclear Disarmament Movement, 1954–70* (Stanford, CA, 1997), 14.

350 *"We have no prudent"*: "12 Scientists Ask Bomb Tests Go On," *NYT*, October 21, 1956.

350 *"There are only 90,000"*: Davis, *Empires' Edge*, 86. Kissinger's population estimate was considerably inflated.

350 *a nation that very much gave a damn*: My account draws on two articles: George O. Totten and Tamio Kawakami, "Gensuikyō and the Peace Movement in Japan," *Asia Survey* 4 (1964): 833–41, and Toshihiro Higuchi, "An Environmental Origin of Antinuclear Activism in Japan, 1954–63: The Government, the Grassroots Movement, and the Politics of Risk," *Peace and Change*, 33 (2008): 333–67.

351 *the director Ishirō Honda*: The following discussion derives from Yuki Tanaka, "Godzilla and the Bravo Shot: Who Killed and Created the Monster?" in *Filling the Hole in the Nuclear Future: Art and Popular Culture Respond to the Bomb*, ed. Robert Jacobs (Lanham, MD, 2010), 159–70.

351 *"emitting high levels"* . . . *"If nuclear testing"*: *Gojira*, dir. Ishirō Honda (Toho, 1954).

351 *"The menace was"*: *Godzilla, King of the Monsters!*, dir. Terry Morse (Transworld, 1956).

352 *front lines of nuclear confrontation*: Details on nuclear weapon storage from Office of the Assistant to the Secretary of Defense, *History of the Custody and Deployment of Nuclear Weapons, July 1945 Through September 1977*, 1978, www.dod.mil/pubs

/foi/Reading_Room/NCB/306.pdf. A helpful decoding of this important document is Robert S. Norris and William M. Arkin, "Where They Were," *Bulletin of the Atomic Scientists* 55 (1999): 26–35. Nuclear weapons were also stored in allied countries such as Britain, Canada, and West Germany.

352 *"New Thule"*: Deneen L. Brown, "Trail of Frozen Tears: The Cold War Is Over, but to Native Greenlanders Displaced by It, There's Still No Peace," *Washington Post*, October 22, 2002.

353 *"tantamount to suicide"*: Nikolai Bulganin to H. C. Hansen, March 28, 1957, quoted in Nikolaj Petersen, "The H. C. Hansen Paper and Nuclear Weapons in Greenland," *Scandinavian Journal of History* 23 (1998): 32. See also Danish Institute of International Affairs, *Greenland During the Cold War: Danish and American Security Policy, 1945–68*, trans. Henry Myers (Copenhagen, 1997).

353 *"no-nuclear" principle*: Petersen, "H. C. Hansen Paper," 33.

353 *"one of the first ones"*: Thomas Power, 1950, quoted in Scott D. Sagan, *The Limits of Safety: Organizations, Accidents and Nuclear Weapons* (Princeton, NJ, 1993), 170.

353 *a B-52 flying near Thule*: History and Research Division, Headquarters, Strategic Air Command, *Project Crested Ice: The Thule Nuclear Accident*, vol. 1, SAC Historical Study 113, 1969; Sagan, *Limits of Safety*, chap. 4.

353 *"one-point safe"*: Excellent discussions of these issues are in Sagan, *Limits of Safety*, chap. 4, and Eric Schlosser, *Command and Control: Nuclear Weapons, the Damascus Accident, and the Illusion of Safety* (New York, 2013).

353 *seventy-five tankers*: Calculated from figures for phases 1 and 2 given in *Project Crested Ice*, 24, 56.

354 *village of Palomares*: Details from Tad Szulc, *The Bombs of Palomares* (New York, 1967).

354 *"all the makings"*: "The Missing H-Bomb," *Boston Globe*, March 4, 1966.

354 *"just the way"*: "¡La Bomba Recuperada!" *Time*, April 15, 1966, 35.

21. BASELANDIA

355 *"narrow the range"* . . . *"Airstrip One"*: George Orwell, *1984* (1949; New York, 1984), 53, 186.

355 *"cold war"*: George Orwell, "You and the Atom Bomb," November 19, 1945, in *The Collected Essays, Journalism, and Letters of George Orwell*, ed. Sonia Orwell and Ian Angus (Boston, 2000), 4:9.

355 *Burtonwood*: Details from Aldon P. Ferguson, *Eighth Air Force Base Air Depot Burtonwood* (Reading, UK, 1986). Burtonwood was briefly closed as a U.S. base in the 1960s.

356 *"occupiers"* . . . *"coca-colonization"*: Richard F. Kuisel, *Seducing the French: The Dilemma of Americanization* (Berkeley, CA, 1993).

356 *postwar Panama*: Thomas L. Pearcy, *We Answer Only to God: Politics and the Military in Panama, 1903–1947* (Albuquerque, NM, 1998), 175.

356 *"Well, we did not"*: Thomas S. Power, *Design for Survival* (New York, 1965), 132; Eric Schlosser, *Command and Control: Nuclear Weapons, the Damascus Accident, and the Illusion of Safety* (New York, 2013), 188.

356 *Within months, more than five thousand*: Ken Kolsbun, *Peace: The Biography of a Symbol* (Washington, DC, 2008), 41, 43.

356 *"I was in despair"*: Gerald Holtom, "A Prelude to the Dance of Life," quoted in Andrew Rigby, "A Peace Symbol's Origins," *Peace Review* 10 (1998): 477. Another story is that Holtom's design combined the semaphore signs for *N* and *D*: nuclear disarmament.

356 *"such a puny"*: Ibid.

357 *five hundred bands*: Bill Harry, *Bigger Than the Beatles* (Liverpool, 2009), 9.

357 *"that Liverpool"*: George Martin, *Summer of Love: The Making of Sgt. Pepper* (New York, 1994), 41.

357 *1,636 buildings*: Ferguson, *Burtonwood*, 103, 88, 96.

357 *"shoddy, shameful"*: Ibid., 81.

357 *official contracts*: Ibid., 97. The case for the Beatles as a base band is ably made in Keith Gildart, *Images of England Through Popular Music: Class, Youth and Rock 'n' Roll, 1955–1976* (New York, 2013), chap. 3. On Burtonwood and music, see also Harry, *Bigger Than the Beatles*, 45, and Helen Southall, "'Total War': Effects of World War II on the Live Music Industry in Cheshire and North Wales," in *World War II and the Media*, ed. Christopher Hart, Guy Hodgson, and Simon Gwyn Roberts (Chester, UK, 2014), 137–53.

358 *"brought their culture"* . . . *"an absolute magnet"*: Martin, *Summer of Love*, 42.

358 *Ringo's stepfather*: Brian Roylance, ed., *The Beatles Anthology* (San Francisco, 2000), 35.

358 *John and Paul . . . George got his records*: Bob Spitz, *The Beatles: The Biography* (New York, 2005), 27, 55, 110, 123.

359 *McCartney appeared on*: Lawrence S. Wittner, *Resisting the Bomb: A History of the World Nuclear Disarmament Movement, 1954–70* (Stanford, CA, 1997), 196.

359 *"Look what they do"*: Quoted in Hunter Davies, "The Beatles," *Life*, September 20, 1968, 76.

359 *protest and participation*: An excellent discussion of this dynamic in the domestic context is Gretchen Heefner, *The Missile Next Door: The Minuteman in the American Heartland* (Cambridge, MA, 2012).

359 *"confused"* . . . *"dazed"*: Edwin O. Reischauer, *The United States and Japan* (Cambridge, MA, 1954), 217.

359 *MacArthur ruled*: Details, unless otherwise indicated, from John W. Dower's extraordinary *Embracing Defeat: Japan in the Wake of World War II* (New York, 1999).

359 *two hundred thousand troops remained*: Sarah Kovner, "The Soundproofed Superpower: American Bases and Japanese Communities, 1945–1972," *Journal of Asian Studies* 75 (2016): 90, 96.

359 *"bound hand and foot"*: Suzuki Mosaburo, quoted in George R. Packard, *Protest in Tokyo: The Security Treaty Crisis of 1960* (Princeton, NJ, 1966), 19.

359 *18 percent of those polled*: Justin Jesty, "Tokyo 1960: Days of Rage and Grief: Hamaya Hiroshi's Photos of Anti-Security-Treaty Protests," *Asia-Pacific Journal* 13 (2015): 6.

360 *"a colony"*: Thomas R. H. Havens, *Fire Across the Sea: The Vietnam War and Japan, 1965–1975* (Princeton, NJ, 1987), 193.

360 *5 percent of its population*: Tessa Morris-Suzuki, *Borderline Japan: Foreigners and Frontier Controls in the Postwar Era* (Cambridge, UK, 2010), 137.

360 *"incidents and accidents"*: Masumichi S. Inoue, *Okinawa and the U.S. Military: Identity Making in the Age of Globalization* (New York, 2007), 50–51.

360 *more than a hundred Japanese died*: Kovner, "Soundproofed Superpower," 98.

360 *relinquished jurisdiction*: Walter LaFeber, *The Clash: U.S.-Japanese Relations Through-out History* (New York, 1997), 316.

361 *$800 million*: Richard Stubbs, *Rethinking Asia's Economic Miracle: The Political Economy of War, Prosperity, and Crisis* (New York, 2005), 68.

361 *"divine aid"*: Michael Schaller, *The American Occupation of Japan: The Origins of the Cold War in Asia* (New York, 1985), 289.

361 *"gift of the gods"*: LaFeber, *Clash*, 287.

361 *"Toyota's salvation"*: Schaller, *American Occupation*, 289.

361 *Toyota's output*: Fujita Kuniko, "Corporatism and the Corporate Welfare Program: Impact of the Korean War on the Toyota Motor Corporation," in *The Occupation of Japan: The Impact of the Korean War*, ed. William F. Nimmo (Norfolk, VA, 1990), 124.

361 *well-paid internship*: On the relationship between military contracts, standardization, and Asian growth, I've learned much from Jim Glassman and Young-Jin Choi, "The *Chaebol* and the US Military-Industrial Complex: Cold War Geopolitical Economy and South Korean Industrialization," *Environment and Planning* A 46 (2014): 1160–80, and Patrick Chung, "Building Global Capitalism: Militarization, Standardization, and U.S.–South Korea Relations Since the Korean War" (Ph.D. diss., Brown University, 2017).

361 *Deming*: My understanding of Deming and his place in Japan is from William M. Tsutsui, "W. Edwards Deming and the Origins of Quality Control in Japan," *Journal of Japanese Studies* 22 (1996): 295–325.

361 *"I never felt"*: Andrea Gabor, *The Man Who Discovered Quality* (New York, 1990), 80.

362 *"patron saint"*: Akio Morita, *Made in Japan: Akio Morita and Sony* (New York, 1986), 165.

362 *Vietnam War helped*: Havens, *Fire Across the Sea*, 98.

362 *fifty-five-fold*: Chalmers Johnson, *MITI and the Japanese Miracle: The Growth of Industrial Policy, 1925–1975* (Stanford, CA, 1982), 6.

362 *Japan's growth*: Important perspectives are Johnson, *MITI*, and essays by Bruce Cumings and Laura Hein in *Postwar Japan as History*, ed. Andrew Gordon (Berkeley, CA, 1993).

362 *sentiment was profoundly complicated*: Details on protests and polls from Kovner, "Soundproofed Superpower," 94–95, 100.

363 *"contradiction"*: Havens, *Fire Across the Sea*, 194.

363 *serious protests*: Details from Packard, *Protest in Tokyo*.

363 *Okinawan city of Koza*: Inoue, *Okinawa*, 53–55; Miyume Tanji, *Myth, Protest and Struggle in Okinawa* (London, 2006), 103–104; James E. Roberson, "'Doin' Our Thing': Identity and Colonial Modernity in Okinawan Rock Music," *Popular Music and Society* 34 (2011): 593–620.

363 *Yukio Kyan*: Roberson, "Doin' Our Thing," 606; see also Justin Zaun, "It's Only Rock and Roll," *Okinawa Living*, October 2004, 10–17.

364 *"little future"* . . . *"cheap imitations"*: Michael Schaller, *Altered States: The United States and Japanese Since the Occupation* (New York, 1997), 3.

364 *Ibuka set up shop*: My account of Sony is from Nick Lyons, *The Sony Vision* (New York, 1976); Akio Morita, *From a 500-Dollar Company to a Global Corporation* (Pittsburgh, 1985); Morita, *Made in Japan*; John Nathan, *Sony: The Private Life* (Boston, 1999); and *Genryu*, the 50th-anniversary history of Sony, translated and abbreviated at sony.net/SonyInfo/CorporateInfo/History/SonyHistory.

365 *"Yankee Alley"*: Nathan, *Sony*, 15.

365 *"The Americans had brought"*: Morita, *Made in Japan*, 51.

366 *stocked a library*: Hyungsub Choi, "Manufacturing Knowledge in Transit: Technical Practice, Organizational Change, and the Rise of the Semiconductor Industry in the United States and Japan, 1948–1960" (Ph.D. diss., Johns Hopkins, 2007), 109–10. Morita writes that Sony cooked "oxalic ferrite" to make ferric oxide (*Made in Japan*, 56). This seems to be a slightly garbled translation of ferrous oxalate.

367 *"could be recognized"*: Morita, *Made in Japan*, 70.

367 *"thought of ourselves"*: Ibid.

367 *"We were little boys"*: Morita, *500-Dollar Company*, 223.

367 *"Sony Boy"*: Sony Boy still would have been read in Japan as Japanese.

368 *"like priceless art"*: Spitz, *Beatles*, 35.

369 *The trade balance*: Aaron Forsberg, *America and the Japanese Miracle: The Cold War Context of Japan's Postwar Economic Revival, 1950–60* (Chapel Hill, NC, 2000), 10.

369 *"colonial"* . . . *"We ship her"*: Jerry Brown, quoted in M. J. Heale, "Anatomy of a Scare: Yellow Peril Politics in America, 1980–1993," *Journal of American Studies* 43 (2009): 23. See also Andrew C. McKevitt, *Consuming Japan: Popular Culture and the Globalizing of 1980s America* (Chapel Hill, NC, 2017).

370 *closed forty assembly plants*: Judith Stein, *Pivotal Decade: How the United States Traded Factories for Finance in the Seventies* (New Haven, CT, 2010), 252–59.

370 *"I'm proud"*: Gabor, *Man Who Discovered Quality*, 126.

370 *"Imagine, a few years"*: Quoted in Andrea Chronister, "Japan-Bashing: How Propaganda Shapes Americans' Perceptions of the Japanese" (M.A. thesis, Lehigh University, 1992), 74.

370 *Trump on television*: *The Oprah Winfrey Show*, ABC, April 25, 1988. Trump's complaints extended to the nations of the Persian Gulf, too.

371 *"It's because of you"*: *Who Killed Vincent Chin?*, dir. Christine Choy (Film News Now Foundation, 1987).

371 Time *started reporting*: *Time*, May 10, 1971.

371 *"Let's become a Japan"*: Akio Morita and Shintaro Ishihara, *The Japan That Can Say No: The New U.S.–Japan Relations* (Ann Arbor, MI, 1989), 36. Translation published without Morita's permission.

22. THE WAR OF POINTS

372 *"few mud huts"*: Lloyd Hamilton, 1934, quoted in Robert Vitalis, *America's Kingdom: Mythmaking on the Saudi Oil Frontier* (London, 2009), 54.

372 *"friendly and energetic"*: Lawrence Wright, *The Looming Tower: Al-Qaeda and the Road to 9/11* (New York, 2007), 65.

372 *Awadh bin Laden*: In my account of the Bin Laden family, I've leaned heavily on Steve Coll, *The Bin Ladens: An Arabian Family in the American Century* (New York, 2008). Details from that book unless otherwise cited.

373 *"an immense aircraft"*: Ibid., 42.

373 *consulate at Dhahran*: Parker T. Hart, *Saudi Arabia and the United States: Birth of a Security Partnership* (Bloomington, IN, 1998), 31–32, 85.

373 *largest concentration*: Vitalis, *America's Kingdom*, 34.

373 *"just like a bit of U.S.A."*: Mary Eddy, 1954, quoted in ibid., 80.

373 *Voice of the Arabs*: Hart, *Saudi Arabia and the U.S.*, 82–85.

374 *"It'll be over"*: Thomas Borstelmann, *The 1970s: A New Global History from Civil Rights to Economic Inequality* (Princeton, NJ, 2011), 199.

374 *"finally sow shit"*: Peter L. Bergen, *Holy War, Inc.: Inside the Secret World of Osama bin Laden* (London, 2001), 69.

374 *hundred tons of heavy construction equipment . . . tunnels*, etc.: Bruce Lawrence, ed., *Messages to the World: The Statements of Osama bin Laden*, trans. James Howarth (London, 2005), 48; Wright, *Looming Tower*, 114.

375 *"The myth of the superpower"*: Lawrence, *Messages to the World*, 48.

375 *Within four hours*: Richard P. Hallion, *Storm over Iraq: Air Power and the Gulf War* (Washington, DC, 1992), 134.

375 *"There are no caves,"* etc.: Dialogue reported in Steve Coll, *Ghost Wars: The Secret History of the CIA, Afghanistan, and Bin Laden, from the Soviet Invasion to September 10, 2001* (New York, 2004), 223.

375 *"After the danger"* . . . *"I would hope so"*: Bob Woodward, *The Commanders* (New York, 1991), 270.

375 *"Come with all"* . . . *"Come as fast"*: Wright, *Looming Tower*, 157.

375 *"everything aloft"*: Colin Powell, *My American Journey* (New York, 1995), 468.

375 *ten times the size of the Berlin Airlift*: Hallion, *Storm over Iraq*, 138.

376 *"You could have walked"*: Ibid., 137.

376 *Iraq had seized Kuwait*: Thomas A. Keaney and Eliot A. Cohen, *Revolution in Warfare?: Air Power in the Persian Gulf* (Annapolis, MD, 1995), 7–9.

376 *fourth largest . . . sixth largest*: Hallion, *Storm over Iraq*, 128.

376 *"about getting kicked"*: H. Norman Schwarzkopf, *It Doesn't Take a Hero* (New York, 1992), 332.

377 *triumph through airpower*: On airpower in Vietnam and Desert Storm, I've been guided by Michael Adas, *Dominance by Design: Technological Imperatives and America's Civilizing Mission* (Cambridge, MA, 2006), chaps. 6–7.

377 *5 million tons . . . 250 pounds*: Christian G. Appy, *American Reckoning: The Vietnam War and Our National Identity* (New York, 2015), 229.

377 *Thanh Hóa Bridge*: Walter J. Boyne, "Breaking the Dragon's Jaw," *Air Force Magazine*, August 2011, 60.

377 *Operation Desert Storm*: My account is from Hallion, *Storm over Iraq*; Michael J. Mazarr, Don M. Snider, and James A. Blackwell Jr., *Desert Storm: The Gulf War and What We Learned* (Boulder, CO, 1993); and Benjamin S. Lambeth, "Air Power, Space Power, and Geography," *Journal of Strategic Studies* 22 (1999): 63–82.

378 *"You pick precisely"*: Mazarr et al., *Desert Storm*, 96.

378 *GPS-guided charge*: On the use of GPS, see Michael Russell Rip and James M. Hasik, *The Precision Revolution: GPS and the Future of Aerial Warfare* (Annapolis, MD, 2002), chap. 5.

378 *hadn't even been necessary*: Thomas Mahnken and Barry D. Watts, "What the Gulf War Can (and Cannot) Tell Us About the Future of Warfare," *International Security* 22 (1997): 160–61.

378 *"revolution in military affairs"*: Useful overviews of the RMA are Eliot A. Cohen, "A Revolution in Warfare," *Foreign Affairs* 75 (1996): 37–54, and Michael Ignatieff, *Virtual War: Kosovo and Beyond* (London, 2000).

379 *"targets and non-targets,"* etc.: Quoted in Rip and Hasik, *Precision Revolution*, 131. I've been guided in my understanding of this by William Rankin, *After the Map:*

Cartography, Navigation, and the Transformation of Territory in the Twentieth Century (Chicago, 2016), chap. 6.

379 *a touchy subject*: Powell, *American Journey*, 474; Schwarzkopf, *Doesn't Take a Hero*, 332–35.

379 *"inadvertently pissed"*: Rachel Bronson, *Thicker Than Oil: America's Uneasy Partnership with Saudi Arabia* (New York, 2006), 195.

379 *Great efforts were taken*: Powell, *American Journey*, 474; Schwarzkopf, *Doesn't Take a Hero*, 332.

379 *"We had to avoid"*: Schwarzkopf, *Doesn't Take a Hero*, 355.

380 *For Osama bin Laden*: On Bin Laden, al-Qaeda, and the road to 9/11, I've relied especially on Bergen, *Holy War, Inc.*; Coll, *Ghost Wars*; *The 9/11 Commission Report: Final Report on the National Commission on Terrorist Attacks upon the United States* (Washington, DC, 2004); and Wright, *Looming Tower*.

380 *"It is unconscionable"*: Wright, *Looming Tower*, 209–10.

380 *"turning the Arabian Peninsula"*: Lawrence, *Messages to the World*, 16.

380 *It's genuinely unclear*: The *9/11 Commission Report* judged the bombing to be "principally" the work of Saudi Hezbollah but mentioned "signs that al Qaeda played some role" (60).

380 *"You can see,"* etc.: Rowan Scarborough, "Air Force Barracks Is Built by Bin Laden's Family Firm," *Washington Times*, September 15, 1998.

381 *first commercially available satellite phones*: Coll, *Bin Ladens*, 467.

381 *"several tens of thousands"*: Werner Daum, "Universalism and the West," *Harvard International Review*, Summer 2001, 19. Similar estimates are discussed in Noam Chomsky, *9-11: Was There an Alternative?* (New York, 2011), 79–80.

382 *"100,000 new fanatics"*: "Punish and Be Damned," *The Economist*, August 27, 1998, 16.

382 *"a military base"* . . . *"It wasn't a children's school"*: Lawrence, *Messages to the World*, 119.

382 *"To us, Afghanistan"*: *9/11 Commission Report*, 340.

382 *"Your forces"* . . . *"You spread"* . . . *"Is there a worse"*: Lawrence, *Messages to the World*, 163, 167.

383 *"rid the world"*: "Bush Vows to Rid the World of 'Evil-Doers,'" CNN, September 16, 2001, edition.cnn.com/2001/US/09/16/gen.bush.terrorism.

383 *"I just don't think"*: Presidential Debate in Winston-Salem, North Carolina, October 11, 2001, APP.

383 *Rumsfeld estimated*: Donald Rumsfeld, *Known and Unknown: A Memoir* (New York, 2011), 400.

383 *122 U.S. service members*: Terry H. Anderson, *Bush's Wars* (New York, 2011), 136.

384 *"very new type"* . . . *"We'll have to"*: "Text: Pentagon Briefing on Military Response to Terrorist Attacks," *Washington Post*, September 18, 2001.

384 *metaphor of the* network: A helpful exploration is Stuart Elden, *Terror and Territory: The Spatial Extent of Sovereignty* (Minneapolis, 2009).

384 *"Taliban-plinking"*: Benjamin S. Lambeth, *Air Power Against Terror: America's Conduct of Operation Enduring Freedom* (Santa Monica, CA, 2005), 95–96.

384 *"The planes"* . . . *"The American forces"*: Lawrence, *Messages to the World*, 182.

385 *Drones have killed*: Figures discussed in Chris Woods, "Understanding the Gulf Between Public and U.S. Government Estimates of Civilian Casualties in Covert Drone Strikes," in *Drones and the Future of Armed Conflict: Ethical, Legal, and Strategic Implications*, ed. David Cortright, Rachel Fairhurst, and Kristen Wall (Chicago,

2015), 186. An excellent guide to drones is Peter L. Bergen and Daniel Rothenberg, eds., *Drone Wars: Transforming Conflict, Law, and Policy* (New York, 2015).

385 *"We're not a colonial"*: "Secretary Rumsfeld Interview with Al Jazeera," February 25, 2003, www.digitaljournal.com/article/34851.

385 *"Wizard of Oz moment"*: Quoted in Anderson, *Bush's Wars*, 141.

386 *"We need to create"*: Max Boot, "Washington Needs a Colonial Office," *Financial Times*, July 3, 2003.

386 *"a surprisingly inept"*: Niall Ferguson, *Colossus: The Price of America's Empire* (New York, 2004), 2.

386 *"We're a liberating power"*: "Text of President Bush's Press Conference," *NYT*, April 13, 2004.

386 *"Green Zone"*: Rajiv Chandrasekeran, *Imperial Life in the Emerald City: Inside Iraq's Green Zone* (New York, 2006).

386 *"We covet no one's"*: Rumsfeld, briefing, November 16, 2001, avalon.law.yale.edu /sept11/dod_brief93.asp.

386 *"If we were a true empire"*: Eric Schmitt and Mark Landler, "Cheney Calls for More Unity in Fight Against Terrorism," *NYT*, January 25, 2004.

386 *"the presence and activities"*: Donald H. Rumsfeld, "Positioning Our Military for a Rapidly Changing World," *Seattle Times*, September 24, 2004.

386 *kicked out of place after place*: On U.S. base closures, see Sasha Davis, *The Empires' Edge: Militarization, Resistance, and Transcending Hegemony in the Pacific* (Athens, GA, 2015). On foreign base closures, see Stacie L. Pettyjohn and Jennifer Kavanaugh, *Access Granted: Political Challenges to the U.S. Overseas Military Presence, 1945–2014* (Santa Monica, CA, 2016).

387 *Hatoyama*: Yuko Kawato, *Protests Against U.S. Military Base Policy in Asia: Persuasion and Its Limits* (Stanford, CA, 2015), chap. 2.

387 *Many on Guam saw in the base expansion*: Frank Quimby, "Fortress *Guåhån*: Chamorro Nationalism, Regional Economic Integration and US Defence Interests Shape Guam's Recent History," *Journal of Pacific History* 46 (2011): 373.

387 *activists put up determined resistance*: Tiara Rose Na'puti, "Charting Contemporary Chamoru Activism: Anti-Militarization and Social Movements in Guåhån" (Ph.D. diss., University of Texas, Austin, 2013).

387 *"This is old-school"*: Quimby, "Fortress *Guåhån*," 373.

388 *"they are a possession,"* etc.: Lieutenant Colonel Douglas, quoted in Ronald Stade, *Pacific Passages: World Culture and Local Politics in Guam* (Stockholm, 1998), 192–93.

388 *"the dark side"* . . . *"It's going to be vital"*: *Meet the Press*, NBC, September 16, 2001.

388 *those laws didn't hold*: An important overview: Kal Raustiala, *Does the Constitution Follow the Flag?: The Evolution of Territoriality in American Law* (New York, 2009), chap. 7.

388 *"They are outsourcing"*: Maher Arar, quoted in Jane Mayer, *The Dark Side: The Inside Story of How the War on Terror Turned into a War on American Ideals* (New York, 2008), 133. See 108–109 for estimates of the scope of extraordinary rendition. On the CIA's private fleet, see Stephen Grey, *Ghost Plane: The True Story of the CIA Torture Program* (New York, 2006).

388 *"black sites"*: A key source is Dana Priest, "CIA Holds Terror Suspects in Secret Prisons," *Washington Post*, November 2, 2005.

389 *a small handful*: Despite the prominent controversy, for years only three detainees were known to have been waterboarded. But in 2012 Human Rights Watch interviewed two detainees rendered to Libya who offered credible reports of water torture. In 2014 the Senate Intelligence Committee released a redacted report referring to waterboarding paraphernalia stored at an Afghan detention site that was *not* a location the CIA had used for the three detainees. See *Delivered into Enemy Hands: US-Led Abuse and Rendition of Opponents to Gaddafi's Libya* (Washington, DC, 2012); 51; *Report of the Senate Select Committee on Intelligence Committee Study of the Central Intelligence Agency's Detention and Interrogation Program*, Senate Report 113–288, December 9, 2014, 51*n245*.

389 *Tinian, Wake, and Midway*: Simon Reid-Henry, "Exceptional Sovereignty?: Guantánamo Bay and the Re-Colonial Present," *Antipode* 39 (2007): 629.

389 *"foreign territory, not subject"*: Patrick F. Philbin and John C. Yoo, "Possible Habeas Jurisdiction over Aliens Held in Guantanamo Bay, Cuba," December 28, 2001, in *The Torture Papers: The Road to Abu Ghraib*, ed. Karen J. Greenberg and Joseph L. Dratel (New York, 2005), 37. A useful discussion of Guantánamo Bay as imperial history is Amy Kaplan, "Where Is Guantánamo?," *American Quarterly* 57 (2005): 831–58.

389 *"Strawberry Fields"*: Mark Mazzetti, *The Way of the Knife: The CIA, a Secret Army, and a War at the Ends of the Earth* (New York, 2013), 17.

389 *"fully American enclave,"* etc.: Amended Petition for Writ of Habeas Corpus, *Rasul v. Bush*, February 19, 2002, in *The Enemy Combatant Papers: American Justice, the Courts, and the War on Terror*, ed. Karen J. Greenberg and Joseph L. Dratel (New York, 2008), 21.

389 *"this lease"*: *Rasul v. Bush*, 542 U.S. 466, 487 (2004) (Kennedy, J., concurring).

CONCLUSION: ENDURING EMPIRE

391 *huge garment-manufacturing center*: *Behind the Labels: Garment Workers on U.S. Saipan*, dir. Tessa Lessin (Oxygen, 2001); John Ydstie, "The Abramoff-DeLay-Mariana Islands Connection," *NPR: Weekend Edition*, June 17, 2006; Rebecca Clarren, "Paradise Lost: Greed, Sex Slavery, Forced Abortions and Right-Wing Moralists," *Ms.*, Spring 2006, www.msmagazine.com/spring2006/paradise_full.asp.

392 *Congress sought to close it*: Lessin, *Behind the Labels*; Clarren, "Paradise Lost."

393 *He offered junkets*: Jack Abramoff, *Capitol Punishment: The Hard Truth About Washington Corruption from America's Most Notorious Lobbyist* (Washington, DC, 2011), 77.

393 *The visitors enjoyed*: Clarren, "Paradise Lost"; John Bowe, *Nobodies: Modern American Slave Labor and the Dark Side of the New Global Economy* (New York, 2007), 182; 20/20, ABC News, May 24, 1999.

393 *"one of the grand constitutional"*: Abramoff, *Capitol Punishment*, 125.

393 *"You are a shining light"* . . . *"You represent"*: 20/20, ABC News, May 24, 1999.

393 *"a perfect petri dish"* . . . *"It's like my"*: Juliet Eilperin, "A 'Petri Dish' in the Pacific," *Washington Post*, June 26, 2000.

393 *"The Man Who Bought"*: *Time*, cover, January 8, 2006.

394 *"my hangman"*: Abramoff, *Capitol Punishment*, 175.

395 *"out of the limits"*: Citizenship Act of 1934, 48 Stat. 797.

395 *"the citizenship of persons"*: House Report 75–1303, quoted in Gabriel J. Chin, "Why Senator John McCain Cannot Be President: Eleven Months and a Hundred Yards Short of Citizenship," *Michigan Law Review First Impressions* 107 (2008), 7.

395 *"eleven months and"*: Ibid.

395 *Palin made no secret*: Tom Kizzia, "Yup'ik Ties Give Palins Unique Alaska Connection," *Seattle Times*, October 23, 2008.

396 *member of the Alaskan Independence Party*: Kate Zernike, "A Palin Joined Alaskan Third Party, Just Not Sarah Palin," *NYT*, September 3, 2008.

396 *"Alaska was no different,"* etc.: Lynette Clark, interviewed in Lisa Karpova, "Alaska Independence Movement," *Pravda*, April 20, 2008, www.pravdareport.com/world /americas/20-04-2008/104960-alaskaindep-0.

396 *"Your party plays,"* etc.: Sarah Palin, Address to the Alaskan Independence Party Convention, 2008, youtu.be/ZwvPNXYrIyI.

396 *"very strong weakness,"* etc.: Mark Penn, "Weekly Strategic Review on Hillary Clinton for President Campaign," March 19, 2007, posted at www.theatlantic.com/politics /archive/2008/08/penn-strategy-memo-march-19-2008/37952.

397 *"near staff revolt"*: Kyle Cheney, "No, Clinton Didn't Start the Birther Thing. This Guy Did," *Politico*, September 16, 2016, www.politico.com/story/2016/09/birther -movement-founder-trump-clinton-228304.

397 *They circulated an anonymous email*: John Avlon, *Wingnuts: Extremism in the Age of Obama* (New York, 2014), 204–207.

398 *"I think there are questions"*: Gabriel Winant, "The Birthers in Congress," *Salon*, July 28, 2009, www.salon.com/2009/07/28/birther_enablers.

398 *"the public rightly,"* etc.: Quoted in Jed Lewison, "Palin Goes Birther," *Daily Kos*, December 3, 2009, www.dailykos.com/storyonly/2009/12/3/810660/-Palin-goes -birther.

398 *58 percent of Republicans*: Poll by Research 2000, reported in "Birthers Are Mostly Republican and Southern," *Daily Kos*, July 31, 2009, www.dailykos.com/storyonly /2009/7/31/760087/-Birthers-are-mostly-Republican-and-Southern.

398 *"Why doesn't he,"* etc.: *The View*, ABC, March 23, 2011.

398 *"There's at least,"* etc.: "Donald Trump Responds," *NYT*, April 8, 2011.

398 *threatened to write a book*: *The Situation Room with Wolf Blitzer*, CNN, January 6, 2016.

398 *"an enveloping fire"*: Choe Sang-hun, "North Korea Says It Might Fire Missiles into Waters Near Guam," *NYT*, August 9, 2017.

399 *"Guam is American,"* etc.: Eddie Baza Calvo, August 9, 2017, youtu.be/YgdXG -LPUBw.

399 *60 percent of the island's*: Michael Kranz, "Here's How Puerto Rico Got into So Much Debt," *Business Insider*, October 9, 2017.

399 *more likely to die . . . fewer federal personnel*: A. J. Willingham, "A Look at Four Storms from One Brutal Hurricane Season," *CNN*, November 21, 2017. A full comparison of Maria and Harvey is Danny Vinik, "How Trump Favored Texas over Puerto Rico," March 27, 2018, *Politico*, www.politico.com/story/2018/03/27/donald-trump -fema-hurricane-maria-response-480557.

399 *less media*: Anushka Shah, Allan Ko, and Fernando Peinado, "The Mainstream Media Didn't Care About Puerto Rico Until It Became a Trump Story," *Washington Post*, November 27, 2017.

399 *charitable giving*: Marco delia Cava, "Why Puerto Rico Donations Lag Behind Fundraising for Harvey, Irma Victims," *USA Today*, October 5, 2017.

399 *"Recognize that we"*: "In Battered Puerto Rico, Governor Warns of a 'Humanitarian Crisis,'" *NYT*, September 25, 2017.

399 *a slight majority of mainlanders*: Morning Consult, National Tracking Poll 170916, September 2017, morningconsult.com/wp-content/uploads/2017/10/170916_crosstabs_pr_vl_KD.pdf.

400 *thirty overseas bases*: David Vine, *Base Nation: How U.S. Military Bases Abroad Harm America and the World* (New York, 2015), 5.

400 *U.S. bases*: Department of Defense, *Base Structure Report, Fiscal Year 2015 Baseline*, 6; Vine, *Base Nation*, 4.

ACKNOWLEDGMENTS

This book wouldn't have been remotely possible without the work of previous scholars who have insisted, for decades, that the U.S. Empire is a worthy object of study. My citations convey only a small fraction of my debts to them.

Nor were those the only debts accrued. I began my research in 2011 on a yearlong fellowship at Columbia University's Committee on Global Thought. The National Endowment for the Humanities funded another year's research at the Huntington Library (with support from my employer, Northwestern University). An Andrew Carnegie Fellowship allowed me to finish the thing. The three uncluttered years these fellowships provided were an obscene privilege, the contemplation of which often reduces me to guilty twitching.

Putting me still further in the red are the debts to colleagues who took the time to read chapters and offer their suggestions, corrections, and/or alarmingly accurate disquisitions on my personal and intellectual inadequacies. They were unstinting and, lacking any realistic prospect of repayment, I offer my bare gratitude here. May glory everlasting shine upon Ken Alder, Hannah Appel, Seth Archer, Beth Bailey, Juliana Barr, Kathleen Belew, Daniel Bessner, Megan Black, Brooke Blower, Catherine Carrigan, Oliver Charbonneau, Will Chou, Patrick Chung, Brian DeLay, Kornel Ehmann, José-Antonio Espín-Sánchez, David Farber, Dexter Fergie, Ted Fertik, Caitlin Fitz, Camilla Fojas, Danna Freedman, Andrew Friedman, Paul Frymer, Margaret Garb, Lally Gartel, Adam Goodman, Antara Haldar, Gretchen Heefner, Laura Hein, Mariah Hepworth, Rebecca Herman, Lauren Beth Hirshberg, Hiʻilei Hobart, Alex Hobson, Phil Hoffman, A. G. Hopkins, James Hudspeth, Adam Immerwahr, Julia Irwin, Sheyda Jahanbani, Sylvester Johnson, Tim Johnson, Peter Kastor, Jinah Kim, Sam Kling, Naomi Lamoreaux, Henri Lauzière, Sam Lebovic, Bobby Lee, Niko Letsos, Beth Lew-Williams, Erez Manela, Dan Margolies, Diana Martinez, Rebecca McKenna, Alison McManus, Fred Meiton, Stephen Mihm, Sarah Miller-Davenport, Garrett Dash Nelson, Tore Olsson, Louis Pérez, Margaret Power, Andrew Preston, Bill Rankin, Ben Remsen, Paul Rhode, Ariel Ron, Eric Rutkow, Daniel

Sargent, Nitasha Sharma, Carl Smith, Susan Smith, George Spisak, Helen Tilley, Jonathan Winkler, and Marilyn Young. My fellow Huntingtonians, busy with books of their own, charitably faked interest as I tried my thoughts on guano and hookworm out on them. ("Perhaps you could branch out to other topics?" was the sage though ultimately fruitless advice.) In that group, Danna Agmon, Tom Cogswell, Alice Fahs, Dena Goodman, Steve Hindle, Peter Lunenfeld, Tawny Paul, and Asif Siddiqi are to be particularly commended for keeping their eye-rolling to a minimum.

Other readers, hallowed be their names, risked still higher levels of exposure to this book in its radioactive draft state. Alvita Akiboh, Michael Allen, Kevin Boyle, Gerry Cadava, Doug Kiel, Susan Pearson, and Mike Sherry donned lead aprons and tentatively probed large chunks of the manuscript at a workshop at Northwestern. For his aid with the military-related chapters, Colonel Aaron O'Connell deserves a Purple Heart. Deborah Cohen, David Hollinger, Tanner Howard, John Immerwahr, Tom Meaney, Sam Means, and Stephen Wertheim, placing concerns for personal safety and future reproductive health aside, read the entire manuscript. Their advice mattered enormously.

Special mentions are due to Brooke Blower, for drawing my attention to the empire-concealing aspects of FDR's Pearl Harbor speech, and to Herman Eberhardt, for helping me understand its context. Chris Capozzola introduced me to the term *Greater United States*. Katharina Pistor recruited me to Standardization Studies. A. G. Hopkins generously shared the fruits of his own research in imperial history. Another mention is due to Ken Alder. "Nothing is more boring than the histories of engineering and chemistry," Ken once told me. "And nothing is more interesting." He was right, and it was under Ken's influence that I saw just how interesting boring things could be.

I read Julian Go's lucid *Patterns of Empire* at the start of my research, and it's still ringing in my ears (Julian bravely read a large portion of this book). Bill Rankin's *After the Map* also induces tinnitus. I've adapted "territorial pointillism," a featured concept in that book, for my own purposes.

Talk of *After the Map* brings me to another sinkhole of uncomfortably deep debt. When I began, I knew nothing about making maps. Katie Chiu, Dave Sivertsen, and Ann Aler remedied that. Kelsey Rydland of Northwestern completed the training, which required hours of patient instruction of the "No no, you have to *right* click" variety. Having Bill Rankin on hand to critique the results was like getting Putt-Putt pointers from Tiger Woods. David Vine shared his astonishingly comprehensive data set for the world map of military bases, and Bobby Lee talked me through the complex business of nineteenth-century land cessions for my Indian Country map.

Throughout this project, I've had the luck of working with highly capable research assistants: Callie Leone, Ryan Scales, Eddie Stein, and Adam Voortman.

One always learns from one's students, but rarely has a professor been as thoroughly schooled as I have by Alvita Akiboh and Michael Falcone. They read drafts, did research, and hashed out nearly every aspect of this book with me, from plot to prose. I've been greatly edified, to say the very least, by Akiboh's dissertation on the material culture of the overseas territories and Falcone's on the technologies of U.S. hegemony.

Edward Orloff of McCormick Literary has been far more than an agent. He's been an indispensable collaborator, to be praised for both his perspicacity and his patience. ("Edward, I think this book should be eight hundred pages and solely about infrastructure in the Second World War." "Mmm, I see. And why do you think that?") It was Edward who proposed the scope and structure of this book, Edward who set its tone.

And Edward who dropped me into the deft hands of Alex Star at Farrar, Straus and Giroux. "You're working with *Alex Star?*" was the spit-take reaction this news often elicited. The reputation is entirely deserved. Alex edited with gentle but authoritative discernment, saving me from my worst habits and encouraging my best. FSG's intrepid Dominique Lear kept things moving briskly, Maxine Bartow hunted down textual errors like a hungry eagle terrorizing a rabbit warren, and, over at The Bodley Head, Stuart Williams and Jorg Hensgen offered sage advice from afar. To them all, I raise a full glass.

Finally, life occasionally contains things beyond books. For this, I thank Lucas Alvarez, Erin Barnes, Brianna Benner, Gloria Bruce, Catherine Carrigan, Lally Gartel, Miklos Gosztonyi, Marion Gutwein, James Hudspeth, Adam Immerwahr, John Immerwahr, Stephen Immerwahr, Orion Johnstone, Pam Krayenbuhl, Sam Means, Wendy Seider, Teya Sepinuck, Jonathan Spies, and Charlie Max Ward.

INDEX

Page numbers in *italics* refer to illustrations.

ILLUSTRATION CREDITS

page 5: Draft of the "Infamy" speech: Draft 1, Significant Documents Collection, Franklin D. Roosevelt Presidential Library and Museum

page 16: Philippine ten-peso note: U.S. Bureau of Engraving and Printing

page 40: Indian Country in 1834: Data from U.S. Forest Service, *Tribal Lands Ceded to the United States*

page 43: Map of Indian removals: After Theodore Taylor, *The Bureau of Indian Affairs: Public Policies Toward Indian Citizens* (Boulder, CO, 1984), 13

page 44: A delirious land rush: Studio of William S. Prettyman / Oklahoma Historical Society

page 50: Sheet music: Jay T. Last Collection of Agricultural Prints and Ephemera, Huntington Library

page 52: U.S. guano island claims, 1857–1902: Data from Jimmy M. Skaggs, *The Great Guano Rush: Entrepreneurs and American Overseas Expansion* (New York, 1994), appendix

page 55: Navassa rioters: Thomas I. Hall and Columbus Gordon, *The Navassa Island Riot* (Baltimore, 1889)

page 61: Young Theodore Roosevelt: George Grantham Bain / 2009633164, Library of Congress

page 75: The Greater United States: Allen C. Thomas, *An Elementary History of the United States* (Boston, 1900)

page 83: The Greater America Exposition: *Greater America Exposition* (Omaha, 1899), Huntington Library

page 99: Balangiga Massacre site: Courtesy of Gloria Sommer

page 111: First Lieutenant Pedro Albizu Campos: Folder 1, box 38, Ruth M. Reynolds Papers, Archives of the Puerto Rican Diaspora, Centro de Estudios Puertorriqueños, Hunter College, City University of New York

page 131: The governmental center of Baguio: I1626, American Historical Collection, Rizal Library, Ateneo de Manila University

page 135: Legislative Building: Filipinas Heritage Library

page 149: Corpses in Ponce: Carlos Torres Morales / "Palm Sunday Massacre" folder, box 257, Harold L. Ickes Papers, Library of Congress

page 172: New wartime globe-style map: David Rumsey Map Collection, courtesy of the Richard Edes Harrison estate

page 174: Tanks on Beretania Street: Hawai'i War Records Depository 1054, Archives and Manuscripts Department, University of Hawai'i, Mānoa

page 177: Honolulu children's book: Frances Baker, *We the Blitzed* (Honolulu, 1943), Hawai'i War Records Depository, Archives and Manuscripts Department, University of Hawai'i, Mānoa

page 184: Major Marston and Alaska Territorial Guard member: Rusty Heurlin / 1976-021-00157, box 826, Ernest Gruening Papers, Alaska and Polar Regions Department, Archives and Manuscripts, University of Alaska, Fairbanks

page 204: "I have returned": Gaetano Faillace / U.S. Army

page 207: Manila, 1945: I10836, American Historical Collection, Rizal Library, Ateneo de Manila University

page 209: The Quirinos' neighbors: IIIA2014, American Historical Collection, Rizal Library, Ateneo de Manila University

page 211: Legislative Building after shelling: U.S. Army / 01218902, Getty Images

page 219: Solomon Islanders unloading crates of beer: U.S. Army / 111-SC-339250, United States National Archives

page 221: Presidential in-office trips: Data from State Department, history.state.gov /departmenthistory/travels/president

page 222: Polar azimuthal projection: *Fortune*, March 1942 / Cornell University Library, courtesy of the Richard Edes Harrison estate

page 223: Original UN emblem: *Charter of the United Nations and Statute of the International Court of Justice* (San Francisco, 1945)

page 228: Forty-nine-star flag: "Mts.—Seals & Flags" folder; box 70; 9-0-2, Office of Territories Classified Files, 1907–1951; Records of the Office of Territories, Record Group 126; United States National Archives, College Park, Maryland

page 233: GIs protesting in Manila: Dave Davis, ACME Photos / 2008680591, Library of Congress

page 240: Martin Luther King Jr.: Associated Press File Photo

page 243: "El Fanguito": Jack Delano / 2017798176, Library of Congress

page 255: Oscar Collazo: Harvey Georges / Associated Press

page 270: B. F. Goodrich worker: DC-54, Lot 3464, Prints and Photographs Division, Library of Congress

page 272: "Synthetica, a New Continent of Plastics": Ortho Plastic Novelties / *Fortune*, October 1940

page 287: Conquest of the Japanese main islands: Data from Kenneth Hewitt, "Place Annihilation: Area Bombing and the Fate of Urban Places," *Annals of the Association of American Geographers* 73 (1983), table 3

page 288: "The All-Red Line Around the World": George Johnson, *The All Red Line: Annals and Aims of the Pacific Cable Project* (Ottawa, 1903)

page 292: Sign at army hospital: MAMAS D44-145-1, National Museum of Health and Medicine

page 301: Herbert Hoover: Harris & Ewing / 2016882827, Library of Congress

page 306: Wartime poster: National Aircraft Standards / *Industrial Standardization*, January 1943

page 333: Li Yang: China Photos / 73813303, Getty Images

page 342: Ernest Gruening: *Paradise of the Pacific*, January 1938

page 343: The pointillist empire today: Foreign bases, David Vine, www.basenation.us /maps; domestic/territorial bases, www.data.gov

page 364: Marine Corps Air Station Futenma: Wikimedia Commons

page 367: Sony transistor radio and mascot: Courtesy of Michael Jack

page 376: Major coalition airfields: After Richard P. Hallion, *Storm over Iraq: Air Power and the Gulf War* (Washington, DC, 1992)

page 385: The face of battle in a war of points: Steve Horton / 070807-F-9602H-101, U.S. Air Force